ROYAL HISTORICAL SOCIETY

GUIDES AND HANDBOOKS

No. 3

MEDIEVAL LIBRARIES OF GREAT BRITAIN

MEDIEVAL LIBRARIES
OF GREAT BRITAIN

A LIST OF SURVIVING BOOKS

EDITED BY

N. R. KER

Reader in Palaeography
in the University of Oxford

SECOND EDITION

LONDON

OFFICES OF THE ROYAL HISTORICAL
SOCIETY

96 CHEYNE WALK, S.W.10

1964

Made and Printed in Great Britain by Butler & Tanner Ltd, Frome and London

TABLE OF CONTENTS

REVISED PREFACE TO THE
FIRST EDITION[1]

THE interest of finding out what books people read in monasteries and colleges of the Middle Ages needs no underlining, and various ways are open to the inquirer. By a close study of some single author, one may be able to form an impression—as Professor Laistner does by studying Bede—of the books at the command of that author and his circle. Medieval catalogues, also, show (with less certainty that the books were actually read) what books were available in particular libraries at particular times. But these methods of investigation have their obvious limits. Another way of obtaining a view of the *scriptoria* and libraries of the Middle Ages is to identify exactly the provenance of as many surviving books as possible. For the majority of foundations listed in this volume no medieval catalogue or book-list survives, and so we must often rely entirely on the books themselves for our knowledge of the contents of the libraries. The survivors give some useful indications: suggesting, for instance, the preponderance of vernacular and devotional works in the nunneries and in the Charterhouses. The handwriting and illumination of the manuscripts also acquire new significance when a sufficient number from the same institution are brought together. The characteristic products of the scribes of Durham and Worcester are to be studied in examples now scattered afar as well as in those still at their original homes. Our list will help to make a comparative study of such scripts more complete. The very notes of ownership are instructive. They show how the libraries were accumulated, what class of donor helped monks and friars and universities at different periods, what a large amount of individual ownership there was in the monasteries of the later Middle Ages. We get some indications, too, of the transfer of books. Royal MS. 13 D.iv was written for St Albans in the twelfth century, sold to Richard de Bury, bishop of Durham, and bought back by St Albans from the bishop's executors in 1346. Balliol College acquired six Buildwas books from two sources in the fifteenth century (one of them had been in pawn in Oxford in 1421), the dean and canons of Windsor got two other Buildwas books (Bodl. 371 and 395), almost certainly in the same century, the London Carmelites had another (Bodl. 730). Twelve monastic books, forming a complete glossed Bible, very probably from Osney, belonged to an Oxford master, John Grene, in s.xv, and are now at Magdalen College.

Such details are interesting, but it has been impossible to expound them within the limits of this work. *Medieval Libraries of Great Britain*

---

[1] This preface has been brought up to date, but not fundamentally altered. The principal differences between the first and second editions are noticed in the preface to the second edition.

cannot, in fact, be used properly by itself. It is intended as a guide to medieval books and book-catalogues and to the modern catalogues in which they are described.

Method of compilation. The printed list is derived immediately from a list on cards, compiled by C. R. Cheney, R. W. Hunt, J. R. Liddell, R. A. B. Mynors and myself. We have aimed at recording on the cards the actual words of inscriptions of ownership, some details of the evidence for provenance, if there is no inscription, medieval pressmarks, the dates and positions of inscriptions and pressmarks, names of individual owners and the survival of medieval binding. This information is taken principally from printed catalogues of modern collections, from special studies of particular medieval libraries, and from introductions to modern editions of medieval texts, supplemented often, and especially when the evidence is not clear, by actual inspection of the books themselves and by reports from librarians. The cards have been deposited in the Bodleian Library, by kind permission of Bodley's Librarian, and are accessible there to inquirers.

Scope. The list is of manuscripts and printed books which belonged in the medieval period to religious houses and their members, cathedral and collegiate churches, universities, colleges, and other corporate bodies in England, Scotland, and Wales. Books belonging to the medieval libraries of Cambridge University and of the colleges at Oxford and Cambridge are not included, if they still remain in the modern libraries at these places. Manuscripts belonging to medieval Scotch libraries are included, but not printed books.[2] Books belonging to the secular clergy and to members of colleges are not included. There is an appendix of parish church books.

The limit of date is about 1540 for English and Welsh libraries and a decade or two later for Scotch libraries. Books with inscriptions, etc., dating from the period of the Marian revival are not listed.

Cartularies, rentals, inventories, surveys, statutes of cathedrals and colleges, mortuary rolls, letter-books and all books concerned with the business and administration of particular establishments are excluded.[3] Book-catalogues forming complete volumes by themselves or occurring among other inventories of goods or in a cartulary are noticed in the heading, but not in the list of books under each library, nor in the index. In practice it has been difficult to decide whether to include certain business books or not. We have aimed at including formularies and ordinals, but formulary material is often mixed up in the letter-books, and directions for the order of church services tend to be associated with statutes. Chronicle and chronological material occurs in many cartularies and three texts of Walter of Henley's Husbandry are in books which, except for this, would be excluded. It is hoped that most of the business books which contain any large amount of matter falling within the scope of the list have been included, but it is likely that some with good claims for admission are not here.

Service-books are included, although they belonged to the church

[2] See p. xxvii, below.
[3] See G. R. C. Davis, *Medieval Cartularies of Great Britain* (London, 1958). For a list of letter-books see W. A. Pantin, 'English Monastic Letter-books', *Historical Essays in honour of James Tait* (Manchester, 1933), pp. 213–22.

rather than to the library of an institution; the justification for including them is that they may provide the student with useful evidence of script or illumination, and with names of donors and *ex libris* inscriptions which will help to identify the provenance of yet more books from the same places. Moreover, in these books there is often much extraneous matter of historical or literary interest which makes it inadvisable to exclude them from the list by any rigid classification. No attempt has been made, however, to enter either with a query or as rejects all those service-books for which a particular home has been suggested, more or less doubtfully, for liturgical reasons. Pontificals have caused difficulty, since it is generally uncertain whether they belonged to individual ecclesiastics or to their churches. The information about the pontifical of Roger de Martival, bishop of Salisbury, now Bodleian Library, MS. Rawlinson C.400, is exceptionally definite; on the death of each bishop it was to be restored to the church for the use of his successor.

Arrangement. The list is arranged in alphabetical order of the medieval libraries. The spelling of the name of each of these conforms to that given in Bartholomew's *Survey Gazetteer of the British Isles* (8th edn, 1932), the one-inch ordnance-survey maps and Ekwall's *Oxford Dictionary of English Place-names* (1936). Older spellings and alternative or medieval names have been given in parentheses after the main name, whenever it seemed useful to do so.

The smaller print below the heading refers to special studies of each medieval library, medieval book-lists (excluding lists of small gifts of less than about a dozen books), notes of books in the library by John Leland and John Bale about the time of the Dissolution, the usual forms of press-mark found in books from the library, and the usual forms of *ex libris* inscriptions.

The description of each book and the evidence for its provenance are necessarily stated very briefly indeed. The details given are:

(1) The name of the library in which the book is at present. The name is given in a short form, but fuller titles and addresses are in the index.

(2) The reference mark in the modern library. The mark given is that adopted in the most recent catalogue of each library. Marks which differ from those in the catalogues, but which are actually in use in the libraries, are given in the index, whenever it seemed that it would be useful to do so. The Bodleian Library forms an exception to this rule: here the arrangement under the various sub-collections, Bodley, Digby, etc., is followed in the main list, and the continuous numbering of the Summary Catalogue is referred to in the index. The obsolete system of reference to the important collection at Corpus Christi College, Cambridge, has been given in the index, since it was in use fairly recently.

(3) Short title or author's name, and language, if not Latin. This is often an inadequate guide to the contents of a book, but it is intended to give the reader a preliminary indication, and, if possible, enough to identify other references to the same book.

(4) An italic letter preceding the short title or author's name, to denote the kind of evidence on which the book is assigned to a particular medieval library. In some instances it can do little more than show the reader what to look for if he has access to the book itself.

b Evidence from binding (*see* p. xxii) or from leaves used in binding, for example Bodl. 751 (Bermondsey, end-leaves from Bermondsey accounts), Bodl. 730 (Buildwas, bosses provide supporting evidence), Jesus College, Oxford, 51, 54, 93 (Evesham, chain-staple), 102 (Winchcomb, label), MSS at Eton College (distinctive style of binding, s.xv/xvi).

c Evidence from contents, including obits, scribbles, etc.

e Evidence from an *ex libris* inscription or note of gift (*see* pp. xvi, xxv).

g Evidence from an inscription consisting of a title or, in Norwich books, a pressmark followed by a personal name in the genitive case (*see* p. xvii).

i Evidence from an inscription of ownership by an individual member of a religious house.[4] Such an inscription may only connect the book with the house under which it appears because the individual is known from other sources to belong to that house. Books marked *i* need not ever have formed part of the monastic library, and in some cases may not ever have been kept at the house to which the owner belonged. On the other hand the inscription of individual ownership may have the value of an *ex dono* inscription (*see* p. xviii).

l Liturgical evidence.

m Evidence from marginalia, for example the marks found commonly in Christ Church, Canterbury, and Salisbury manuscripts (*see* pp. 31, 171), and those in Royal 5 D.iv-vii (Bath, *see* p. 7).

s Evidence from character of script (*see* p. xx) or illumination, including the script and lay-out of tables of contents, which help to fix the provenance of manuscripts from certain houses, for example Gloucester and St Albans.

Normally only the main kind of evidence is shown, but occasionally it seemed desirable to use more than one letter. The evidence has sometimes defied classification within the limits of the scheme of letters, and among the books which have not been seen a few are not fully enough described in modern catalogues to warrant the use of a letter. No letter is used when the only evidence is supplied by (6) below.

(5) The date. This is given in the following form: 's.xiii in.' for first half of the thirteenth century, 's.xiii ex.' for second half of the thirteenth century, 's.xiii med.' for mid-thirteenth century, 's.xii/xiii' for late-twelfth or early-thirteenth century, 's.xii–xiii' for twelfth and thirteenth centuries.

(6) Medieval pressmarks and identifications with entries in medieval catalogues and in Leland's and Bale's lists, in square brackets after the date.

(7) A query at the end of the entry if the provenance is doubtful.

Books of which the present whereabouts is unknown and books which have been ascribed to a particular medieval library on evidence which seems to be insufficient or which is demonstrably wrong are listed below the main list of books from each medieval library and marked *untraced* and *rejected* respectively. Readers interested in a 'reject' will do well to turn to the index, which may point to a more acceptable ascription. The untraced books are arranged under the last known owner.

The descent of the books. About six thousand library-books and service-books of religious houses, cathedrals, and colleges are listed here,[5] and

[4] See also p. xxvi.
[5] The figure given in the 1941 edition was 'about four thousand two hundred' (*see* p. xxvii).

x

about five hundred medieval libraries are represented by one book or more. By the fallacious test of surviving books fourteen libraries appear vastly more important than all the others.[6] They are the libraries of the great Benedictine houses at Bury, Christ Church and St Augustine's at Canterbury, Durham, Norwich, Reading, Rochester, St Albans, and Worcester, of the secular cathedrals of Exeter, Hereford, Lincoln, and Salisbury, and of the comparatively unimportant Augustinian priory of Lanthony in the suburbs of Gloucester. We have over five hundred and fifty extant books from Durham, over three hundred and fifty from Worcester, about three hundred from Christ Church, Canterbury, about two hundred and fifty from Bury and St Augustine's, over two hundred from Salisbury, and over one hundred from each of the other seven libraries. On the other hand there are over four hundred libraries from which we have only between one and ten identifiable books. They include all the nunneries, all the Cluniac, Premonstratensian, and Gilbertine houses, and all the convents of Trinitarian and Austin friars which occur in the list at all. Between these extremes come Syon with over ninety identifiable books, the college of Windsor (81), Winchester (76), Eton College (62), Ely (47), and Westminster (41), twenty-five libraries with between twenty-one and forty books,[7] and twenty-seven libraries with between eleven and twenty books.[8] The number of surviving manuscripts from Scotch libraries—ninety-two are listed here[9]—is much less than the total number of surviving printed books. Statistics of this sort have, however, little bearing upon the actual size of any medieval library. Survival has been usually a matter of chance. For example, a large part of the Lanthony library has been preserved, but only a small part of the collections listed in the medieval catalogues of Dover, Leicester, Syon, and the Austin friars of York. An attempt is made in this part of the preface to illustrate briefly some of the workings of chance in the preservation of medieval books since the Dissolution of the monasteries.

There was one systematic attempt to preserve books at the time of the Dissolution. The manuscripts in King Henry VIII's library were mainly of English monastic provenance.[1] Out of more than four hundred of the king's books now in the Royal Collection in the British Museum, about two hundred and fifty can be assigned to fifty-five medieval libraries. As many as ninety-nine are from Rochester, and a good many others are from St Albans, St Augustine's, Canterbury, Ramsey, the Augustinian priory of Merton, and Worcester. No library north of Lincolnshire is represented. The collection is of an unusual character. There are no

---

[6] The libraries of Oxford and Cambridge colleges and Cambridge University are excluded from the following calculations.
[7] Abingdon, Battle, Chester, Dover, Evesham, Glastonbury, Gloucester, Hyde, Osney, Peterborough, Ramsey, Winchcomb, St Mary's, York; Buildwas, Byland, Fountains; London Charterhouse, Sheen; Cirencester, Merton, Southwark, Waltham; Cambridge and Hereford Franciscans; St Paul's Cathedral.
[8] Bath, Burton-upon-Trent, Coventry, Crowland, St Guthlac's, Hereford, Malmesbury, Tewkesbury, Thorney, Tynemouth; Hailes, Holmcultram, Rievaulx, Warden; Leicester, Lessness, St Osyth, Southwick; Canterbury and Lincoln Franciscans; London Dominicans; London Carmelites; Ashridge; Chichester Cathedral and York Minster; Oxford University; London Guildhall.
[9] This figure includes fifteen of Elphinstone's manuscripts at Aberdeen, for which see p. 2.
[1] A catalogue of some of them was drawn up as early as 1542: cf. G. F. Warner and J. P. Gilson, *Catalogue of Royal MSS in the British Museum* (1921), p. xiv.

early books, few finely illuminated books, and (except from Rochester) few of the handsome, clearly-written, twelfth-century patristic texts which were the usual choice of the early private collector. Instead the main interest is in works by or supposedly by English authors, in commentaries on the Bible and on the Sentences of Peter Lombard, and in Canon Law.[2] The brief list of theological and historical manuscripts in Lincolnshire libraries, based probably on notes by John Leland, the prime mover in this royal book collecting, and now in Royal MS. Appendix 69,[3] gives some insight into the actual process of selection. Thirty-five out of eighty-six books in this list are marked with crosses. Twenty-four of those marked are now in the Royal library, one is among a small collection of King Henry's books in the Bodleian, and one, a stray from the Royal library, was bought back by the British Museum in 1950 and is now Egerton 3668. The entry of three books from the Gilbertine house of St Catherine at Lincoln is marked, probably in the king's hand, *vel omnes vel antiquior istorum*. None of the unmarked books is to be found in the Royal library.

Some great national store-house of ancient manuscripts may have been dreamt of by Leland, but the reality was a rather small collection of selected books, not truly of the first interest and drawn from a restricted area. Local collectors up and down the country were actually much more effective than the king in preserving monastic books. Most of them were people of little importance. Some are merely names to us and others are entirely unknown. They were to be found in most parts of England, except, it seems, in the south-west, where there was no one willing to rescue the ancient treasures of Glastonbury, Wells, Malmesbury, and Sherborne. The last prior of Monk Bretton seems to have been in possession of his priory library in 1558; it has not survived.[4] Sir John Prise (1502–55), one of the commissioners appointed to visit the religious houses, collected theological manuscripts from libraries in the west of England, especially Cirencester and, almost certainly, St Guthlac's, Hereford (they are now at Hereford Cathedral and Jesus College, Oxford), and some choice historical manuscripts from Bury, one of the houses which he visited officially.[5] Southwick manuscripts were given by Sir John White, the purchaser of the priory, to the new foundation of St John's College in Oxford. The Burdet family of Sonning got many books from Reading, most of which are now in the Bodleian. Some books from the now extraordinarily scattered library of St Augustine's, Canterbury, are known to have belonged to John Twyne (1501–81), master of the grammar school, M.P., and mayor of Canterbury. Nearly all the extant books from Warden seem to have belonged to one R. Manley in s.xvi. In these and some other instances we know or can guess how the books have come down to us. More often, however, we can trace back their post-Dissolution history only to the period 1560–1640, the golden age of the English private collector and the great formative period of the modern public

[2] For example, the following came from St Augustine's: four glossed books of the Bible, a commentary on the Sentences, five legal books, two chronicles, the 'Prophetia Brydlyngton', the Summa of John Dumbleton, works of Giraldus Cambrensis, and a volume containing Juvencus and Aldhelm.

[3] Printed by J. R. Liddell, ' "Leland's" Lists of Manuscripts in Lincolnshire Monasteries', *Eng. Hist. Rev.*, liv (1939), pp. 88–95.

[4] See p. 131.

[5] N. R. Ker, 'Sir John Prise', *The Library*, Fifth Series, x (1955), pp. 1–24.

and college collections of manuscripts. Some collectors of this date had a good many books from a single monastic source. For example, William Smart of Ipswich gave over a hundred Bury manuscripts to Pembroke College, Cambridge, in 1599; Archbishop Whitgift (†1604) bequeathed sixteen Buildwas manuscripts to Trinity College, Cambridge; books from Rievaulx, Fountains, Byland, and from Yorkshire generally were numerous in the library of Henry Savile of Banke, near Halifax (1568–1617), and books from St Augustine's, Canterbury, in the library of John Dee (1527–1608);[6] Lord Lumley (1534?–1609) had a group from Bury, now among the Royal Manuscripts in the British Museum; and George Willmer (†1626) gave six Leicester manuscripts to Trinity College, Cambridge. On the other hand, the two greatest libraries of the period had little local character. Archbishop Matthew Parker (1504–1575), who was probably not collecting manuscripts before the sixties of the sixteenth century, and Sir Robert Cotton (1571–1631) assembled books from all parts of the country, and their collections, now at Corpus Christi College, Cambridge, and in the British Museum, became in a way substitutes for the national library which Cotton wanted and which he and others proposed to Queen Elizabeth, without success, perhaps in 1602.[7] We do not know what happened for a quarter of a century after the Dissolution, or longer, to the monastic books which found their way to these libraries, but it is possible that some at least were lying about in the monasteries for years, waiting to be picked up, like Cotton MS. Cleopatra B.xiii, fos 59–90, which was found at St Augustine's in 1565, according to a note by John Joscelyn on the first leaf of the manuscript.

The Durham and Roche books among Archbishop Laud's manuscripts, now in the Bodleian, the Worcester and Stafford books among Lord Hatton's, now also in the Bodleian, and the books from the west of England among John Theyer's, now in the British Museum, give some local character to collections formed in the seventeenth century. The Bodleian got a batch of a dozen Bury manuscripts in 1653. Later still, wholesale collectors like Sir Robert Harley (1661–1724) and Sir Thomas Phillipps (1792–1872) occasionally acquired a block of manuscripts which had belonged to a particular English religious house before the Dissolution. Thus Harley had a dozen Durham books from the library of Sir Thomas Tempest and Phillipps a group of Reading books which were in the hands of James Bowen in the middle of the eighteenth century. Usually, however, manuscripts have been bought and sold singly during the last three hundred years. Collections have been formed piecemeal in sale-rooms and such local groups as continued to exist in country-house libraries have been broken up one after another and scattered. The chances have been heavily against their survival intact. Some of the Reading-Bowen-Phillipps books are now at Berlin, Chicago, Eton, Harvard, and New York; others are untraced. The three Waltham and the three Bury books in the Holt-Wilson sale in 1910 are now in Dublin, Harvard, London, and Princeton. Of nine Fountains books in the Ingilby sale in 1920, one is now in London, another in Manchester, a

[6] Savile's and Dee's libraries were broken up, but catalogues survive; see J. P. Gilson, 'The Library of Henry Savile, of Banke', *Trans. Bibl. Soc.*, ix (1908), p. 127, and M. R. James, *Manuscripts formerly owned by Dr John Dee* (*Trans. Bibl. Soc.*, Suppl. 1, 1921).

[7] C. E. Wright in *The English Library before 1700*, ed. F. Wormald and C. E. Wright (London, 1958), p. 189.

third in New York, a fourth in Oxford, a fifth in Princeton, and a sixth is untraced; three went to Studley Royal, there to rejoin other Fountains books. When Lord Tollemache sold three of his five St Osyth books in 1961, one went over the border into its home county, Essex, but the other two are now in New York and San Marino. The Fountains books belonging to Mr Vyner and Mr Bradfer-Lawrence, the St Osyth books belonging to Lord Tollemache and Miss Foyle, and the Stamford, Pipewell, and Ramsey books in Mr Brudenell's library at Deene are among the last survivors of the old order of things. One monastic book, that at Lacock, appears never to have moved at all.

The libraries of cathedrals, of cathedral monasteries, of those religious houses which were converted into cathedrals in 1540 and 1541, of colleges at Oxford and Cambridge, and the ancient schools at Eton and Winchester, should in theory have been more fortunate than others, since their guardians were not suddenly expelled at the Dissolution. And in fact some of them have been more fortunate. There are still over three hundred medieval Durham manuscripts at Durham and over two hundred Durham manuscripts and printed books are to be found now in other libraries, alienated, chiefly it seems in the seventeenth century, but not lost outright. The large number of surviving books, their generally good condition, and the very fact that they were thought worth taking away cast doubt on Robert Hegge's statements that the library had been given over to pigeons and jackdaws and was 'now rather a βιβλιοτάφιον than a library: rather a place of a Sepulchre than a place to conserve bookes'.[8] Excluding fragments, only twenty-one books assignable to the medieval library of Christ Church are now at Canterbury, but the total of nearly three hundred books removed in one way and another and now divided among more than thirty modern libraries is impressive; a great many were acquired by Archbishops Parker and Whitgift and Dean Nevile and are now at Corpus Christi College and Trinity College, Cambridge. Over two hundred and fifty manuscripts remain at Worcester; of over a hundred which we have been able to identify elsewhere, some were in the king's library by 1542, a good many others, including most of the pre-conquest books, were obtained by Archbishop Parker, Lord Hatton and John Theyer, and yet others were looked upon as cathedral property out on loan in 1586 and 1590.[9] When Dr John Dee visited Worcester in February 1565/6 the dean gave him a nice pre-conquest manuscript of Ethicus, now Cotton MS. Vespasian B.x, which may be the one Leland saw in the monastery library. Out of 387 books listed in the catalogue of the Exeter Cathedral Library drawn up in 1506, 101 are identifiable today: 90 of them are in the Bodleian Library by gift of the dean and chapter in 1602.[1] Parker got some of the pre-conquest books, and sixteen volumes remain at Exeter. A large number of Rochester books were the property of the king by 1542,

[8] [Robert Hegge], *The Legend of St Cuthbert* (1663), p. 43. The book was written in 1626, as appears from the manuscript copy in the Bodleian Library, MS. Eng. hist. d.92 (*Sum. Cat.*, 36593).

[9] Notes to this effect are in Brit. Mus., Royal MSS 2 D.xxvi, 2 E.xi, 2 F.i, 3 A.viii, Bodleian MSS Auct. D.inf.2.4, Bodl. 861 ('. . . inde desumptus Mar. 22, 1590, et illuc restituendus').

[1] Service-books and some other books were kept in the church and not in the library and so are not included in these figures. The cataloguer also omitted books in Old English, no doubt 'quia nullius valoris reputantur', to borrow words from the earlier Exeter catalogue.

as we have seen. The history of the Norwich library is obscure, but many Norwich books are now in Cambridge University Library and others were procured by Parker. The cathedral library of Salisbury still retains over 175 of its medieval manuscripts, and the cathedral libraries of Lincoln and Hereford have over 90. The remains of the St Paul's library would be important, but for the accident of the Great Fire; some St Paul's books were fortunately in private hands by 1666 and are now at Aberdeen, but many others, including some identifiable with books seen by Leland, were burnt then, not at St Paul's, but at Sion College. There is no evidence that the books of the other cathedral libraries were kept together after the Dissolution. The remains of the libraries of Winchester, Ely, Westminster, Peterborough, and Gloucester are scattered, but not entirely insignificant. We have, however, very few books from Wells, where Leland saw much of value, York, where he noted 'jam fere bonorum librorum nihil est', Lichfield, Coventry, Carlisle, and the Scotch and Welsh cathedrals.

Of college libraries, Peterhouse, Gonville and Caius, and Pembroke at Cambridge, and Merton, Balliol, New College, Oriel, Lincoln, All Souls, and Magdalen at Oxford have still an appreciable number of their medieval books. The visitors appointed by King Edward VI are blamed, commonly, for the spoliation of these libraries, but it is better to suppose that there are various reasons why, for example, very many of the books noticed in college libraries by Bale in his collections compiled between 1547 and 1557[2] are not there now.[3] Shelves became overcrowded and new printed books pushed out old manuscripts. Over a dozen Oxford college books found their way to Antwerp some time during the sixteenth century and are now in the Plantin-Moretus Museum there. The Exeter College copy of the life and miracles of St Thomas, now Douai MS. 860, was rescued from 'amonge a caos of caste bookes and waste papers'[4] in the same century. A date in the histories of the college libraries is the year 1600, when Thomas James, Bodley's first librarian, published his *Ecloga Oxonio-Cantabrigiensis*, containing lists of the manuscripts in Oxford and Cambridge libraries. We can see from these lists that not much has been lost since then.[5] The University Library at Cambridge has a continuous history from the fifteenth century and retains some of its medieval books, but the public library at Oxford was not in existence for fifty years from the middle of the sixteenth century, and the books now in the Bodleian which belonged to the University in the Middle Ages are comparatively recent acquisitions. Eton College has still a fair number of its old books and Winchester College has a few.

The evidence of provenance. The means at our disposal for finding out where medieval books come from are obviously of many kinds. The

---

[2] *Index Britanniae Scriptorum*, ed. R. Lane Poole and M. Bateson (Oxford, 1902).
[3] *Cf.* N. R. Ker in *Bodleian Library Record*, vi (1959), pp. 489–92.
[4] From the preface to the anonymous English translation of this manuscript, Bodleian, MS. Eng. misc. c.322.
[5] For seven Merton manuscripts and three Balliol manuscripts see N. R. Ker, 'Thomas James's Collation of Gregory, Cyprian, and Ambrose', *Bodleian Library Record*, iv (1952), pp. 16–30, and for four New College manuscripts see the *Summary Catalogue* descriptions of MSS Bodl. 238, 310, 563, 798 (*Sum. Cat.*, 2050, 2121, 2347, 2656).

evidence derived from the contents or the liturgical character of a manuscript does not call for comment here, although it is often dubious and difficult to assess. Other main kinds of evidence are described in the following notes, roughly in the order of their importance.

'*Ex libris*' *inscriptions.* The practice of marking ownership by means of a formal inscription seems to have been widespread in England only in the late-twelfth century and in the thirteenth century, and then only in Cistercian and Augustinian houses. Inscriptions, and especially early inscriptions, often consist simply of the word *Liber*, the name of the patron saint in the genitive case and the place-name either in the genitive case or preceded by *de*: for example *Liber sancti Andree de Hextildesham* (Hexham), *Liber sancte Marie Rievallis* (Rievaulx).[6] This simple form was almost invariable throughout the Middle Ages in books from English Cistercian houses and usual before the fourteenth century in books from Augustinian houses, except Lessness, Newark, Southwick, and St Denis, Southampton, where the formula regularly begins *Hic liber est ecclesie*. After 1300 we have not many books and not many inscriptions from either Cistercians or Augustinians. The evidence of books from Benedictine houses shows that inscriptions were written in many books and in set forms before 1300 at Bury, Durham, Reading, and St Albans and its cells, and after 1300 at Bury, the two great Canterbury houses, Dover, Durham, Ely, Westminster, Worcester, and a few other places, but the form of the inscription varies from house to house and does not seem to have been dictated by any general custom of the Order. Before *c.* 1300 the vocabulary of the *ex libris* inscription was extremely limited and does not include such words as *pertinere, constare, monachus* (except occasionally in books from Cistercian houses), *libraria, monasterium,* or *domus*, which are common later. *Domus* was affected especially by Carthusians, Gilbertines and the Bonshommes of Ashridge, *communitas* especially by Franciscans, whose inscriptions commonly begin (*Iste liber est*) *de communitate fratrum . . .* and *conventus* by Franciscans and Dominicans. We have very little evidence for the usage of other orders of friars or of Cluniacs, Premonstratensians or Gilbertines.[7] The nunnery of Campsey appears to be alone in having a regular form in French, 'Cest livre est a covent de Campisse'. A form consisting of the words *Liber monasterii*, followed immediately by the place-name and omitting the name of the patron saint, is rare and late (s.xv, xvi). A form consisting merely of the place-name is probably in most instances not a monastic inscription at all, but a memorandum entered in books which were transferred immediately from a religious house to the Royal library at the Dissolution. Thus we find 'Bardenay' in Royal 13 A.vii, 'Barlinges' in Royal 3 B.xv, 'Cirencester' in Royal 7 F.vi, 'Lanthony' in Royal 5 B.i, 'Parshar' or the like in Royal 4 A.viii, 8 D.iv, 10 A.iv, 11 B.iv, Bodl. 209, 'Collegium de Tateshall' in Royal 8 G.vi, 11 A.xiii, 11 B.vi, 12 E.xxv, Bodl. 419, all manuscripts which are known to have belonged to King Henry VIII.

---

[6] The names of larger towns are usually in the genitive; so are the names of Abingdon, Lanthony, Jervaulx, Rievaulx, and Hurley, the last probably influenced by the Westminster usage. All other place-names are preceded by *de*.

[7] We list only 34 books from Cluniac, 44 from Premonstratensian, and 14 from Gilbertine houses, and only 35 from Carmelite and 25 from Austin friaries.

The common positions for the inscription are the flyleaf facing the first page of text or the head or foot of the first page. On the whole the flyleaf is the usual position before 1300, especially in Cistercian books, and the first page later. The inscription is regularly found in a certain position in books from certain houses; for example, on the flyleaf facing the first page of text in Reading books, at the head of the first page in Bury, Durham, and St Albans books, at the foot of the first page in Rochester books. In several books from Southwick it is written across a double opening, and a double opening is used also in three books coming respectively from Merevale, Titchfield, and Winchester, the last two being neighbours of Southwick.[8] The late Ely inscription tends to be written both at the beginning and at the end of the text. Some Buildwas books have the inscription at the end of the table of contents.

Red ink was commonly used for inscriptions at St Albans and its cells and by the Cistercians. Inscriptions in two different coloured inks occur in books from the Cistercian houses at Bordesley, Buildwas, Coggeshall, and Kingswood.

An anathema or curse on thieves and careless borrowers accompanies the inscription regularly or commonly in books from Bridlington, Lessness, Newark, Reading, St Albans and its cells, Southwick, Waltham, Winchester, and the earlier Lanthony and Rochester inscriptions. Elsewhere anathemas are not common and there are very few indeed from Christ Church and St Augustine's, Canterbury, Durham, Norwich, and the Cistercian houses. Where they occur they tend to be in a set form, a knowledge of which can be useful in fixing the provenance of books with partially illegible inscriptions. Thus the form of the anathema allows Royal MS. 12 B.xii to be assigned certainly to Newark and Corpus Christi College, Cambridge, MS. 319 certainly to Lessness.

'Ex dono' inscriptions. Inscriptions recording in unambiguous language the gift of a particular book to a particular library are commoner late than early. They are especially frequent in cathedral books and especially infrequent in Cistercian books, and inevitably vary a good deal in form. The circumstances of the gift may also be very various, but we seldom get any certain information about this. St Albans used a regular formula: 'Hunc (*or* istum) librum dedit . . . Deo et ecclesie Sancti Albani'. Other forms contain the words *ex adquisicione, ex perquisito, ex provisione, ex collacione, ex assignacione, ex impetracione.* The plain *Ex dono . . .* is usually late medieval. Some Syon books have simply *Ex dono . . .* , without naming the recipient, and can only be assigned certainly to that house on other evidence. In Rochester books the name of the donor in the genitive case or preceded by *per* follows the *ex libris* of the house, and in Norwich books it follows the pressmark.

An important form of *ex dono* inscription consists of the title of the book followed by the name of the donor in the genitive case, for example 'Psalterium Radulphi' in a manuscript from St Augustine's, Canterbury,

---

[8] Winchester College 6; Bodl. 249; Balliol College 15. A three-page inscription is written in one and the same hand in a handsome Decretum in the Bodleian, MS. Douce 218, in a bible belonging to the King Edward VI Grammar School, Southampton, and in a bible in Cambridge, Trinity College O.2.9, but it is damaged in each MS. and we know only the first eight of the nine words, 'Liber iste est / de almario ecclesie / sancte Marie'.

belonging to Dr Eric Millar.[9] It is the common form of inscription at Christ Church and St Augustine's, Canterbury, especially before *c.* 1300, when it almost takes the place of the *ex libris* inscription. It occurs also in some books from the important Benedictine houses of Peterborough, Ramsey, and Rochester,[1] and in a few books from other places.[2] It was a convenience to librarians in identifying books if they recorded the donor in this way. Out of 41 bibles listed at the beginning of the late-medieval catalogue of St Augustine's, Canterbury, 38 are distinguished by being called the bible of such and such a person. Eight of these 38 bibles are still extant, and all except one of them are inscribed in this form, as required by the customs of the house.[3] In the period before cataloguers adopted the method of recording the opening words of the second leaf of each book,[4] the arrangement of a catalogue by donors instead of by subjects, as in the early-fourteenth-century catalogue of Christ Church, Canterbury, and in the Ramsey catalogue of about the same date, would provide a quick and effective method of identification, if each book was also marked with the name of its donor. This arrangement is an extension of a method of distinguishing service-books, vestments, and other objects which was, no doubt, much used in inventories.[5] Later it caused trouble to bibliographers. Benedict of Peterborough owes his place in Tanner's *Bibliotheca Britannico-Hibernica* to the inscription in British Museum, Cotton MS. Julius A.xi, 'Gesta Regis H. secundi Benedicti abbatis', and gifts by Martin de Cliva to Christ Church, Canterbury, and by Gregory of Huntingdon and Robert de Dodford to Ramsey caused Bale to include them in his *Scriptores*.

Liber followed by a personal name in the genitive case is ambiguous. If the name is that of a monk, early inscriptions in this form may have the value of *ex dono* inscriptions. 'Liber Anselmi abbatis' and 'Liber Gilleberti prioris' in Pershore books indicate the donors. Late inscriptions, however, have the same value as *constat* or *possidet*, marking books in the temporary keeping of individual monks.[6]

Pressmarks[7] are useful indications of provenance just in so far as they are distinctive. The pressmark consisting of a letter followed by an arabic number may be taken as an example. It is the commonest of all forms,

[9] In the list the italic letter *g* marks all books with this form of inscription, unless the letter *e* can be used (*see* p. x).
[1] The inscription in Royal MS. 4 D.vii, from St Albans, 'Titulus istius libri in dorso Scolastica hystoria W. abbatis', suggests that inscriptions in this form were written on the bindings of St Albans books.
[2] Peterborough, 6; Rochester, 5; Chichester Cathedral, 4; Chester Dominicans, Ramsey, and St Mary's, York, 2 each; Manchester Collegiate Church, Spalding, Waltham, Worcester, 1 each. *Cf.* p. xxvi.
[3] The books a deceased monk had from the library 'et alii libri de acquisicione sua, omnia ista liberentur precentori; et ipse scribere faciet nomen fratris in quolibet libro de sua adquisicione, antequam portentur in librarium' (*Customary of St Augustine's, Canterbury, and St Peter's, Westminster*, i (Henry Bradshaw Soc., xxiii, 1902), p. 362).
[4] See below, p. xix, for the different kinds of catalogues.
[5] For example in the inventory of St Paul's Cathedral, A.D. 1295, 'Vestimentum Rogeri capellani', 'Passionarium Roberti de Clifford'.
[6] See p. xxvi.
[7] The term 'pressmark' is used here to cover both the form of mark which actually gives the position of a book in a press and the form of mark which refers to a catalogue. Most so-called 'pressmarks' are of the latter kind.

and the best-known house using it is Bury St Edmunds. Many manuscripts have been assigned to Bury for no better reason than that they contain this kind of pressmark in the correct position, but also the commonest position for a pressmark, the top right-hand corner of the first page of text. In fact, however, the pressmark must be related to the subject or author of the book if it is to be claimed for Bury, where bibles were marked with the letter B, sermons with the letter S, etc. Nor is agreement on this point necessarily enough. The mark C.4 borne by the famous copy of William of Malmesbury's *Gesta Pontificum*, now Magdalen College, MS. lat. 172, may be a Bury mark, but was no doubt used by many houses. On the other hand Bodleian, MS. Laud misc. 291, containing commentaries on St Matthew and St Mark, and marked B.241, can be claimed confidently for Bury, since we can see from the extant books that the letter B followed by numbers from 40 to 207 was used for glossed books of the Bible and the letter B followed by numbers from 220 to 252 was used for commentaries on the Bible. Most friaries from which we have pressmarks used this common form, but usually with the addition of a superscript *m* after the arabic number. Houses with really distinctive marks appear to be few, but our information is certainly most imperfect on this point, since the outside of the binding was probably a common position for the pressmark, and comparatively few medieval bindings survive. The pressmark alone is sufficient to distinguish books from St Augustine's, Canterbury, Christ Church, Canterbury, Chester, Dover, Durham, Fountains, St Guthlac's, Hereford, Hinton, Syon (but few remain), Titchfield (sometimes), Waltham, and St Mary's, York.[8] The lettermarks used at Christ Church, Canterbury, in s.xii, xiii, appear also to be distinctive in form and position. A form of pressmark used in many Franciscan convents consists of an author's name or subject title followed by a letter or number.[9]

Medieval catalogues. The primitive stage was of short titles and arrangement roughly by subjects, without any means of identifying a particular book from the catalogue description. This is found in the oldest catalogues of Durham and Lincoln (s.xii ex.), the Bury and Reading catalogues (s.xii ex.), the Glastonbury catalogue (s.xiii med.), the second Rochester catalogue (A.D. 1202), and other shorter lists. The first Rochester catalogue (s.xii med.) is on similar lines, but the contents of each book are listed fully. The late-twelfth-century Christ Church catalogue is the first to give reference letters, which, by corresponding to letters entered in the books themselves, act as a means of certain identification. Thirteenth- and fourteenth-century catalogues show improvements either by grouping the books by donors[1] or by recording the opening words,[2] or by arranging the catalogue according to the actual arrangement of the books on the shelves and recording the several presses or shelves,[3] or by recording pressmarks.[4] The earliest considerable catalogues to record the opening

---

[8] For descriptions of the marks see the headings under each house.

[9] For examples see under Bristol, Cambridge, Chester, Coventry, Norwich, Shrewsbury, Worcester, and York; also, for Oxford, Thomas Gascoigne's notes printed by Miss W. A. Pronger in *Eng. Hist. Rev.*, liii (1938), pp. 621–22. Guisborough and Selby used the same form of pressmark.

[1] Christ Church, Canterbury (except the first five hundred books), Ramsey.

[2] Exeter, A.D. 1327, but probably based on a catalogue of *c.* 1200.

[3] Lanthony.　　　　　　　　[4] Peterborough, Titchfield.

words of the second leaf of each book ('secundo folio') are those of Dover (A.D. 1389) and Durham (A.D. 1391). This very good method of distinguishing the books became the almost universal one, both for full library catalogues,[5] and for short lists of gifts by private persons.

The catalogues, being so diverse, are of very unequal value for identifying extant books. Those which give bare titles are only useful when a work is very rare or when an unusual title agrees with that of an extant manuscript; for example, the title 'Excepciones Roberti de Braci' in the Lanthony catalogue identifies Royal MS. 8 D.viii as a Lanthony book. Those which group by donors or record pressmarks are useful if, as is usually the case, the donors' names or the pressmarks are entered in the books themselves. Those which note the opening words of the second leaf provide an almost infallible means of identification, but one which is very difficult to apply if it is the only means at our disposal; in fact few books have been identified because their 'second folio' agrees with that of an entry in a catalogue, without the assistance of some pointer, even if it is only the name of a post-medieval owner.[6] The most useful catalogues are those which give both 'second folios' and pressmarks, like the admirable Dover catalogue, or 'second folios', pressmarks, and donors' names, like the St Augustine's and Syon catalogues. But even here we are in difficulties if the pressmarks or donors' names have been erased or otherwise removed, as often in Syon books. Part of the value of the Dover system of cataloguing is due to the care taken to note the pressmark of each volume (together with other details), in a distinctive form and not only on the outside of the binding and on a flyleaf, where it would be subject to loss in rebinding, but also on the second or another leaf near the beginning of the book. It is safe to say that any book which in fact comes from Dover but which we are not in a position to identify as a Dover book is in a very mutilated condition.

Script. We have seldom felt justified in assigning a manuscript to a particular house because of its script and for no other reason, both because the varieties of writing practised in English scriptoria have been little studied as yet and because the character of the script can only reveal the scriptorium in which a manuscript was written, not the library to which it belonged.[7] There are, however, a number of varieties of script which belong to particular regions, if not to particular scriptoria, and the character of the writing sometimes supports an identification which is probable for other reasons. A type of script which is regional, being

[5] St Augustine's, Canterbury, s.xv ex.; Lincoln, s.xv med.; Exeter, A.D. 1506; Syon, A.D. 1520; Leicester, s.xv ex.

[6] Identification by 'second folio' has its dangers. Two psalters of approximately the same format and with the same number of lines to a page may easily have the same words at the beginning of the second leaf. Sometimes, too, the opening words of the second leaf are in fact the opening words of the text, the first leaf being occupied by prefatory matter or a table of contents. When this occurred the medieval cataloguer would usually, but not always, be careful to note the first words of the third leaf. See also R. A. B. Mynors, *Durham Cathedral Manuscripts*, p. 3.

[7] Some work on English script in the eleventh and twelfth centuries has been done since 1941 by Mr T. A. M. Bishop in *Trans. Cambridge Bibliog. Soc.*, i (1949–53), pp. 432–41, ii (1954–58), pp. 185–99, 323–36, iii (1959–63), pp. 93–95, and by the present writer in *English MSS in the Century after the Norman Conquest* (Oxford, 1960), pp. 22–39, and a few more manuscripts have been added to *Medieval Libraries* solely because of their script.

common to a number of writing centres in the west of England in the first half and middle of the twelfth century, is shown in the facsimile of the 'Hereford Pontifical' (Oxford, Magdalen College, MS. lat. 226) by H. A. Wilson, *Pontifical of Magdalen College* (Henry Bradshaw Soc., xxxix, 1910), pl. 1. The so-called 'Lanthony' hand is of this kind. It is not peculiar to Lanthony—or, if peculiar, it is so in small details which have not yet been worked out—but the claim that certain manuscripts at Lambeth Palace, Corpus Christi College, Oxford, and Trinity College, Oxford, are from Lanthony, is much strengthened by the fact that they are in this kind of script. The distinctive 'Exeter' script of the middle and second half of the eleventh century may be regional or really peculiar to Exeter.[8] A late-eleventh-century script seen in some Worcester manuscripts is probably peculiar to the Worcester scriptorium, but all the manuscripts can be assigned probably or certainly to Worcester for other reasons.[9] The well-known prickly script found in many manuscripts from Christ Church, Canterbury, of the first half of the twelfth century is in its most pronounced form probably peculiar to the Canterbury scriptorium, but script of generally similar character was written at St Augustine's, Canterbury, and Rochester, and perhaps elsewhere in the south-east at the same period. The Rochester script is in fact a recognizable variant, probably though not certainly peculiar to Rochester.[1] Other houses, *e.g.* Bury, Durham, St Albans, and Reading, used distinctive forms of script in s.xii, and a few manuscripts in our lists have been assigned to these houses solely because of their script.

Occasionally a manuscript so closely resembles another that it can be assigned safely to the same scriptorium or to the same scribe.[2]

Binding. There is much to regret. The British Museum, the Cambridge University Library, most cathedral and college libraries, and most of the big private collectors of the past have rebound their collections wholesale, and often surely quite unnecessarily, in the seventeenth, eighteenth and nineteenth centuries. Of big libraries only a few, notably the Bodleian, Pembroke College and Gonville and Caius College, Cambridge, All Souls College and Jesus College, Oxford, Hereford Cathedral, and Worcester Cathedral, have allowed a good proportion of their manuscripts to remain

---

[8] Part or all of Cambridge, U.L. Ii.2.11, Corpus Christi College 190, 191, 196, 201 (fos 179–272), London, B.M., Add. 28188, Harley 863, 2961, Oxford, Bodleian, Bodl. 579 are in the 'Exeter' script, but these manuscripts can be assigned to Exeter also for other reasons. Some of them were certainly written for Exeter. Cambridge, U.L. Ii.2.4, Corpus Christi College 421 (part), London, B.M., Cotton Cleop. B.xiii, Lambeth Palace 489, in the same type of script, cannot be dissociated from this group. For these and other MSS and the single-sheet documents in this script, see Bishop, *Trans. Cambridge Bibliog. Soc.*, ii, pp. 192–99.

[9] Manuscripts which contain writing in this script are Cambridge, Corpus Christi Coll. 9, 178, 265, 391 (facsimile by E. S. Dewick and W. H. Frere, *Leofric Collectar*, ii (Henry Bradshaw Soc., lvi, 1921), pl. 2), London, B.M., Cotton Nero E.1, Oxford, Bodleian, Bodl. 223, Hatton 23, 113, 114, Junius 121. Some of them were certainly written for Worcester.

[1] For Canterbury and Rochester script see Ker, *op. cit.*, pp. 25–32, and C. R. Dodwell, *The Canterbury School of Illumination* (Cambridge, 1954), p. 119.

[2] Examples are Lambeth Palace 144 and Oxford, Bodleian, Hatton 86, which are assigned to Lessness and to Stafford because of their resemblance to Lambeth Palace 147 and Hatton 26 respectively, and Bodleian, Bodl. 134 and 387, the work of two well-known Rochester scribes.

in their old bindings. In consequence we have a number of old bindings from certain medieval libraries, notably Bury, Cirencester, Hereford, and Worcester, and very few from others, for example only six from Rochester, out of nearly 140 surviving manuscripts,[3] and only one from Dover.[4] We have still much to learn about medieval binding, but it is likely that there are not enough old bindings left for us to make really useful observations about the details of medieval binding-styles, and it is only in details that the practice of one library or workshop differed from that of another.[5] For example, we can note that surviving Buildwas bindings carried bosses on the corners—some of the rebound books too show the marks of the bosses on the flyleaves—and that Bury, Cirencester, Hereford, and Worcester bindings did not, but we know nothing at all about the practice of hundreds of other libraries. At the same time such a detail may have confirmatory value in assigning a manuscript to Buildwas. Old flyleaves have often been discarded with bindings—not however at Lambeth Palace —and with both bindings and flyleaves countless *ex libris* inscriptions have disappeared.[6] In the later Middle Ages, when books were commonly laid on their sides on desks, the outside of the exposed cover, usually the end cover, was a favourite place for a pressmark or for a title, perhaps with donor's name and 'second folio' added, on a label under a strip of horn secured by small nails.[7] Labels survive, for example, on books from Syon, Winchcomb, Worcester, and a number of college libraries, some *in situ* and some pasted by the rebinder on a flyleaf. We know that there was a pressmark on Dover bindings from the preface to the medieval catalogue, but no specimen survives. A manuscript of William of Malmesbury in the library of the Canterbury Franciscans is described in a note of s.xv in Register O at Canterbury as 'habens in dorso super ligamento tales figuras, P.15'.[8] One of the few Lanthony manuscripts in medieval binding, Lambeth Palace 349, has a pressmark on the end cover, and the fifteenth-century binding of Bodleian, Laud misc. 374, bears a label in this position, enclosed in a metal frame, which is continuous, except for a space at the top containing the word HIDA. Part of the interest of these bindings is that they help to explain why so few of the Lanthony books contain pressmarks, and that they provide a possible reason for the absence of anything which can properly be called an *ex libris* inscription in books from Hyde. The bindings are gone, and the inscriptions with them.

The thanks of the editor are due in a quite special degree to his four collaborators.[9] But a work of this kind entails inevitably a heavy debt of gratitude to many people, librarians, private collectors, booksellers, and scholars, who have helped in one way and another, and especially to Mr Francis Wormald for his constant advice about service-books, to Dr Robin Flower for answering numerous questions about British Museum manuscripts, questions which war conditions have made all the more

[3] Berlin; Cambridge, St John's 89, Trinity 1238; Bodleian, Bodl. 134, 387, Laud misc. 40.
[4] Bodleian, Bodl. 678.
[5] *Cf.* now H. G. Pollard, 'The Construction of English Twelfth-Century Bindings', *The Library*, 5th Series, xvii (1926), pp. 1–22.
[6] For a recent loss, see p. 137, n. 3.
[7] Earlier bindings often have a title, but very rarely a pressmark, on the spine, which was exposed as the book lay in a cupboard.
[8] See *Historical Manuscripts Commission, Ninth Report* (1883), Appendix, p. 108.
[9] This paragraph remains as in 1941. See p. xxix.

numerous and all the more inconvenient to answer, to Dr A. G. Little for correcting and adding to the list of Franciscan books, to Mr E. Dring for help in tracing books which have passed through the hands of Messrs Quaritch, to Mr C. E. Wright for help with Harleian manuscripts, to Mr H. Pink of the Cambridge University Library, to Mrs Rose-Troup and Miss Crighton for checking and adding to the list of manuscripts from Exeter, and, not least, to the fetchers and carriers of the many heavy books ordered for our use, especially at the Bodleian, the British Museum, and Lambeth Palace. Miss Maude Clarke was engaged, at the time of her death, on a full list of medieval English catalogues and book-lists; her materials for this list have been of use to us. In the past one man has made the subject of the provenance of English manuscripts peculiarly his own. Dr M. R. James has been before us almost everywhere and his discoveries are on nearly every page of this book.

Errors and omissions are, no doubt, many. We shall be grateful to those who send new information to the editor, Magdalen College, Oxford.

N. R. KER

OXFORD
May 1941; revised July 1962

PREFACE TO THE SECOND EDITION

THE new edition differs from the edition of 1941 in several respects. (1) It lists the manuscripts and printed books belonging to the medieval libraries of the cathedrals of Durham, Hereford, Lincoln, Salisbury, and Worcester, and of the colleges of Eton and Winchester, which still remain *in situ*. (2) It lists (*a*) persons who gave, wrote or were in other ways concerned before 1540 with the books recorded on pp. 1–224; (*b*) words used in inscriptions of gift, etc. (3) It does not list printed books from medieval libraries in Scotland. (4) Some 930 additional books have been listed. (5) The number of entries under the heading *Rejected* has increased by about 130. (6) Seventy-nine books have changed owners since 1941. (7) Twenty-one of the fifty-two untraced books listed in 1941 have been located. I will take these seven points in order.

(1) *Manuscripts and printed books in situ in the cathedral libraries of Durham, Hereford, Lincoln, Salisbury, and Worcester, and in the libraries of Eton College and Winchester College.* It is often difficult to distinguish between the books of the medieval library and the books added after 1540. Only at Durham, where librarians wrote *ex libris* inscriptions and press-marks in nearly all the books, can the distinction be made easily. Labels on Worcester books and price-marks in Hereford books assist the construction of the lists. So, also, do the catalogues of the manuscripts at Salisbury and Worcester made by Patrick Young in or about 1622. Sometimes books can be assigned to the medieval library on the evidence of the script of marginalia, the identity of which might not be noticed if the books had been dispersed, or on evidence which could not be used if a library had not had a continuous history since medieval times. For example the four books at Lincoln belonging to Thomas Salisbury, archdeacon of Bedford (†1460), are there presumably because he gave them to his cathedral library; one would presume the opposite if they were elsewhere. Special sigla have been used in the Hereford list to show the evidence for provenance.[1]

(2) *Persons who gave, wrote or were in other ways concerned before* 1540 *with the books recorded on pp. 1–224.* In the lists on pp. 225–325 an attempt has been made to give the principal details of the inscriptions in the books marked with the sigla *g* and *i* and in such of the books marked with the siglum *e* as contain information about donors and users.[2] Most of the inscriptions show either how a book was acquired or what happened to it after it was acquired. The institutions themselves are of three kinds: secular cathedrals, colleges and hospitals; monasteries; friaries. In books belonging to secular institutions the inscriptions are usually of

[1] See p. 96, n. 8.   [2] For the sigla, see p. x.

a simple kind, generally either *ex dono* or *ex legato*, with sometimes a direction about chaining or putting in a particular place or reserving use to a particular office-holder. In descriptions of the donors the word *quondam* is common.

There is much more variety of inscriptions in books belonging to monasteries. Many phrases besides *ex dono* are used to express gift. In some books, almost all of them from Benedictine houses, an inscription of the first half of the fourteenth century or earlier consisting of the title of the book, or a pressmark (at Norwich), or an *ex libris* (at Rochester), followed by a personal name in the genitive case shows that the book was considered to be a gift to the house from the person named.[3] Many late-medieval inscriptions are concerned with the use made of the books by individual monks. Sometimes the terms used are easily understood, *cujus usus conceditur* or *in custodia* followed by a personal name. Often, however, they are the same terms as are used by absolute owners, *liber* followed by a personal name in the genitive case; the words *constat, pertinet*, or *possidet*; and phrases which show that monks gave and sold books to other monks.[4] All this movement of books took place under the absolute ownership of the religious house, an ownership which was so obvious to the writers that we should not be surprised that only one of them entered in the book he was conveying to a colleague the words *quantum ad se pertinuit* and only a few recorded that they and the houses to which they belonged were joint owners.[5]

The inscriptions in the books of friars are in a class by themselves. They expose the unsatisfactory nature of *Medieval Libraries* as a record of books which do not contain an *ex libris* or some other definite evidence that they belonged to a particular friary as distinct from a particular friar. The books individual friars had the use of might be the property of the order, or of the province, or of the custody, and were carried from house to house. Hence books marked in the lists with the siglum *i* are attached to the convent under which they are entered by weak links, usually only because the friar 'owner' is known to have been a member of the convent at some time. The four books containing the name of Friar Ambrose Kelle, O.F.M., may be taken as examples. One of them, Oxford, Corpus 182, is in the Cambridge Franciscan list, because it is inscribed 'fratris Ambrosii Kelle, O.F.M., Custodie Cantabrigiensis'; two, Bodl. 429 and Douce 239, are in the London Franciscan list, because in both Kelle is referred to as cursor in theology at London; the fourth, Laud misc. 545, also in the London list, has only Kelle's name in the genitive case. Friar Thomas Man, who bought Bodl. 429 from Kelle at London in 1514, was *custos* at Winchelsea in 1526.[6] Evidently there is room for a list of friars' books arranged under the names of persons, instead of under the names of places.

Personal names written in the books in the nominative case, or of which only the surname, or only the surname and an initial are given, so that the case form cannot be determined (**CANTERBURY**, Chelmington, Dover), are a source of difficulty. Some are owners' marks, no doubt, and some are mere scribbles. I have tried to include the former, but not the latter.

[3] See above, p. xviii, and the entries marked *g* in the lists on pp. 1–224.
[4] See pp. 327–28, **dare** and **emere**.
[5] See pp. 328, 330, **liber** and **pertinere**.
[6] C. L. Kingsford, *Grey Friars of London* (Aberdeen, 1915), p. 67.

Some attempt, but not a thorough attempt, has been made to record inscriptions giving the names of scribes. The words *scripsit propriis manibus* (or the like) look reliable, but *scripsit* by itself may perhaps sometimes mean no more than *scribi fecit*. Similarly, *scriptus per* and *scriptus de industria* may mean that the actual scribe was not the person named, but his employee. In the fifteenth century, scribes often wrote the word *quod* and their name at the end of texts they had written, but the same form of words was sometimes added by irresponsible scribblers and may sometimes, like *scripsit*, have been taken over from the exemplar.

Ideally, each name should have a date attached to it, assigned either on palaeographical grounds or by reference to records. I should have done more dating than I have done. Dating on palaeographical grounds, however, has its limitations. In books from Chichester and Rochester, inscriptions recording the names of donors were entered in the books long after they were acquired: some Rochester inscriptions cannot be right, because the reputed donors, *e.g.* Bishop Siward, lived before the books with which they are credited were written.

(3) *Printed books from medieval libraries in Scotland.* Several hundred books belonging to libraries in Scotland before *c.* 1560 are recorded by Durkan and Ross, *Early Scottish Libraries.*[7] It seemed unnecessary to repeat the information about these books. References to *Early Scottish Libraries* will be found in the heading under each house.

(4) *Additions*, excluding those noticed above under (1), number about 930, a comparatively large proportion of them being printed books, for which no wide search was made before 1941. The lists to which ten or more additions have been made are the following: Durham (70), Worcester (36), Christ Church, Canterbury (29), Syon (25), St Augustine's, Canterbury (24), Norwich and St Albans (21), Bury (17), Lanthony and Winchester (15), Chester and Winchcomb (14), Salisbury (13), Rochester and London Guildhall (12), Exeter (11), Burton, Ramsey, and Reading (10). The Burton, Durham, and Winchcomb additions are mainly printed books. The Worcester and Salisbury additions are mainly the result of the discovery, since 1941, of early-seventeenth-century catalogues of these two libraries. Chester is included because eight manuscripts were mistakenly attributed in 1941 to the Dominican convent in Chester instead of to St Werburg's. On the whole the additions emphasize the obvious fact that the medieval libraries about which we may hope to discover more are those about which we already know something. Thirty-nine libraries now included did not figure at all in 1941.[8] The books from them are mainly printed: those which are manuscripts tend to be in the less well-known modern collections.[9]

(5) *Rejects.* Nearly all the new rejects are books which were included wrongly in the main lists in 1941. The number of rejects from three of the

[7] J. Durkan and A. Ross, *Early Scottish Libraries* (Glasgow, 1961); pp. 5–167 of this book are identical with *Innes Review*, ix (1958), pp. 5–167; pp. 169–88 contain addenda, and pp. 189–96, an index of titles.
[8] See, for example, AXHOLME, STOKE BY CLARE, THREMHALL.
[9] See, for example, DARLINGTON, HARROLD, WINCHELSEA *Franciscan convent.*

longer lists is considerable (Canterbury, 13; Bury, 12; Norwich, 10). Some books rejected in 1941 have now been restored to the main lists.

(6) *Changes of ownership.* Of the seventy-four books which have changed ownership, otherwise than by inheritance, since 1941, six have been rejected. Fifty-one of the remaining seventy-three are now in institutional libraries. The main events have been: the purchase of the remainder of the Phillipps collection by Messrs Robinson, finally completed in 1947; the bequest of Robert Garrett's collection to Princeton in 1942; the bequest of all James P. R. Lyell's manuscripts of known English provenance to the Bodleian Library in 1949; the transfer of the manuscripts of Mr C. H. St John Hornby (†1946) to Major Abbey and Dr Eric Millar; and the dispersal by sale of the Cockerell (1957), Davies-Cooke (1959), and Dyson Perrins (1958–60) collections, and of part of the Helmingham collection (1961). Together these account for thirty-nine changes of ownership. Only one book recorded in 1941 has moved from an institutional library, the Campsey book formerly in the Shipdham parochial library.

(7) *Untraced books.* Eighteen of the fifty-two untraced books listed in 1941 were known from pre-1870 sources. Only three of these eighteen books have now been located, a Bury book formerly in Coventry Grammar School and now in Cambridge University Library, a St Albans book which had, in fact, been acquired by the British Museum as long ago as 1838, and the breviary of Penwortham church recorded by Bernard in 1697 and, after an interval of 265 years, in a Sotheby sale catalogue of 1962.[1] Of the other thirty-four books, all last heard of at various dates between 1872 and 1937, eighteen have been located. It is surprising that books like the twelfth-century Bede from Byland and the twelfth-century Bede from Kirkham have not been seen, apparently, for over fifty years.

Many hundreds of English monastic manuscripts are not recorded in *Medieval Libraries.* Some have no obvious history at all. Others have a vague association with a particular place, for example British Museum, Cotton Titus C.xx, with Abingdon, because of the word 'Abyndonia' written in capitals on what was probably once the cover, but is now the first leaf. Others bear names or pressmarks or some incomplete indication of their history. A list of thirty-four manuscripts of this kind now in the Royal Collection in the British Museum was sent to me by Mr Richard Hunt about the time that *Medieval Libraries* was first published. A provenance has now been found for five of these thirty-four. Of the remainder, several have medieval pressmarks of an ordinary sort, but one, Royal 2 D.xxvii, has the mark 'xxxviii liber tercii gradus', a form not precisely the same as any recognized pressmark,[2] and another, Royal 13 B.xiv, has the pressmark V.59, not only in a usual position, the recto of the first leaf, but also in an unusual position, the verso of the last leaf. Royal 2 D.xxvii may be from the same library as Chetham Libr., Manchester, MS. 6722, which bears the mark 'Decimus octavus liber tercii gradus'. Royal 13 B.xiv is probably from the same large library as Royal 15 B.ii

---

[1] E. Bernard, *Catalogi MSS Angliae et Hiberniae,* ii (Oxford, 1697), p. 22, no. 7159; Sotheby sale, 10 Dec. 1962, lot 137; now B.M., Add. 52359.

[2] Facsimile in *New Pal. Soc.,* i, pl. 17, no. 10 *c.*

(R.164) and Magdalen College, Oxford, lat. 31 (P.145). The libraries of some important houses seem to have disappeared almost completely. We should beware of thinking that they really have disappeared.

After the publication of the first edition of *Medieval Libraries*, typescript lists of additions and corrections were deposited from time to time in the Bodleian Library and in the British Museum. I recorded the names of contributors to the typed list sent out at the end of 1941: Ivor Atkins, W. P. Blore, C. R. Cheney, Sydney Cockerell, S. L. Greenslade, R. W. Hunt, Clifford Maggs, R. A. B. Mynors, Otto Pächt, J. S. Purvis, K. F. Sisam, W. E. Tate, J. B. L. Tolhurst. Graham Pollard and E. H. W. Meyerstein figure in the second list; Hope Emily Allen, Bernard Payne, and Aelred Watkin in the third. I am sorry that I did not continue to record names. My obligations have not been only to contributors of additions and corrections. The many people who have helped to make the second edition more complete and accurate than the first include all the librarians and booksellers who have answered my questions; of booksellers, Mr Dring of Messrs Quaritch, and Mr Clifford Maggs have given me an especially large amount of help. My largest debts are to three of my collaborators in the first edition, Professor Christopher Cheney, Mr Richard Hunt and Professor Sir Roger Mynors, and to Mr Pierre Chaplais, Literary Director of the Royal Historical Society, Mr Ian Doyle, and Mr David Rogers. My indebtedness to Dr A. B. Emden will be apparent from the numerous references I have made to his two *Biographical Registers*. I fear that I have not dealt faithfully with all the suggestions made to me, and that some corrections and additions I ought to know about have not found their way into the new edition.

N. R. KER

February 1963

PRINCIPAL ABBREVIATIONS
AND CONVENTIONAL SIGNS

A.C.	Anno Christi
A.D.	Anno Domini
Aug.	Augustinian
B.M.	British Museum
B.N.	Bibliothèque Nationale
B.R.U.C.	A. B. Emden, *Biographical Register of the University of Cambridge*
B.R.U.O.	A. B. Emden, *Biographical Register of the University of Oxford*
Bale	J. Bale, *Index Britanniae Scriptorum*, ed. R. L. Poole and M. Bateson (Oxford, 1902)
Ben.	Benedictine
Cambr.	Cambridge
Cant.	Canterbury
Carm.	Carmelite
Carth.	Carthusian
cat.	catalogue
Ch.	Church
Cist.	Cistercian
Coll.	College
conv.	convent
Dom.	Dominican
dom.	dompnus
Durkan and Ross	J. Durkan and A. Ross, *Early Scottish Libraries* (Glasgow, 1961). *Cf.* above, p. xxvii.
fr.	frater
Fran.	Franciscan
Leland	*J. Lelandi de rebus Britannicis Collectanea*, ed. T. Hearne (1715; 2nd edn, 1774). [Vol. iv of the second edition, to which there are references *passim*, has the same contents and pagination as vol. iii of the first edition.]
libr.	library
Lond.	London
mag.	magister
N.L.	National Library
N.S.	New Series
Oxf.	Oxford
pr. bk	printed book
Prem.	Premonstratensian
P.R.O.	Public Record Office

Proc.	*Proceedings*
s.	saeculo
s.a.	sine anno
s.l.	sine loco
s.n.	sine numero
Trans.	*Transactions*
U.L.	University Library
Univ.	University

The italic letters *b, c, e, g, i, l, m, s* are used to indicate the evidence of provenance. For an explanation of these signs and of the method of denoting dates, medieval pressmarks, etc., see above, p. x. On pp. 225–325, * and ** are used as a means of reference to *B.R.U.O.* and *B.R.U.C.* (*see* above), and caret marks (ˎˏ) show insertions *secunda manu*. In the indexes, * and ** mark deposited manuscripts, and † marks rejects (*see* p. 332). For the † used in the list of Worcester Cathedral books, see p. 205, and for the sigla *p* and *r* used in the list of Hereford Cathedral books, see p. 96. In the index of personal names, the names of scribes are in italics.

ADDENDA

p. xx, n. 7: See also T. A. M. Bishop's article in *Trans. Cambridge Bibliog. Soc.*, iii, pp. 412–23.

p. xxvi, n. 6: On books belonging to friars see H. W. Humphreys, *The Book Provisions of the Mediaeval Friars* (Amsterdam, 1964).

p. 22 (BYLAND):
London, Lambeth Palace, 1510, nos 20, 21. *c*Antiphonale (1 fo.). s.xiv.

p. 33 (CANTERBURY):
Cambridge, Trinity Coll., 1135.[1] *s*Prosper, etc. s.x ex. ?

p. 121 (LONDON. *Cathedral church of St Paul*):
London, St Paul's Cathedral, 4 fos iv, v. 'Liber sermonum diversorum. Liber despensationum' (flyleaves only). [*Cat.* O(8)].

p. 126:
LONDON. *Priory of Knights Hospitallers of St John of Jerusalem, Clerkenwell.*
Dublin, Trinity Coll., 500 (E.2.33). *c*Brut Chronicle (in French). s.xiv. ?

p. 151 (PETERBOROUGH):
Oxford, Bodleian, Rawl. C.677. *g*Logica. s.xv. ?

p. 186 (SYON):
Cambridge, U.L., Add. 7634. *l*Breviarium (fragm.). s.xv.

p. 221:
LONDON, ST SEPULCHRE, HOLBORN.
London, B.M., Harley 2942. *ce*Processionale Sarisb. s.xv in.

p. 293 (PETERBOROUGH):
Exton, W., prior (*?*W. E., prior P. 1447*):
Oxford, Bodleian, Rawl. C.677 (g.).

p. 324:
LONDON, St Sepulchre, Holborn.
Lorde, mag. Johannes, Curie Cantuarie procurator generalis et Ursula uxor ejus.
London, B.M., Harley 2942 (Orate pro animabus —— et — , Simonis Briggeman, Marione uxoris ejus et omnium benefactorum eorundem cum quorum bonis iste liber conparatus fuit et datus huic ecclesie per media Willelmi Taylard).

[1] Trinity Coll., Cambridge, 1135 should be removed from the list of rejects, p. 39.

MEDIEVAL LIBRARIES OF
GREAT BRITAIN

LIST OF SURVIVING BOOKS

ABBOTSBURY, Dorset. *Ben. abbey of St Peter.*

Books noted by J. Leland, *Collectanea,* iv. 149.

Camarillo (Cal.), Doheny Libr., 7. *e*Zach. Chrysopolitanus. s.xii ex.
Cambridge, U.L., Hh.3.11. *c*Statuta Anglie. s.xiv. ?
London, B.M., Cotton Cleop. B.ix. *l*Treatise on chess (in French), etc.
    s.xiii ex.

ABERBROTHOCK. *See* **ARBROATH.**

ABERCONWAY. *See* **CONWAY.**

ABERDEEN. *Cathedral Church of B.V.M.*

Catalogues of 1436 and 1465 printed from Aberdeen U.L., MSS 247, 249, in *Registrum Episcopatus Aberdonensis,* ed. Cosmo Innes (Spalding Club, 1845), ii. 127, 154; second folios given. The 1465 cat. printed also by M. R. James, *Cat. of Med. MSS in Aberdeen U.L.* (Cambridge, 1932), p. 80.

9 printed books with *ex libris* or *ex dono* inscriptions listed by Durkan and Ross under Arthur Boece, 1-3; Alexander Galloway, 3, 15, 18, 20, 21; Duncan Shearer, 1.

Aberdeen, U.L., 22. *c*Epistolare. A.D. 1527.
Edinburgh, U.L., 27. *l*Breviarium, etc. s.xiv. ?
Oxford, Bodleian, Ashmole 1474. *e*Bartholomeus Anglicus. s.xiii/xiv.
    [*Cat. 1436,* 25; *1465,* 23].

ABERDEEN. *Hospital of the Visitation of B.V.M.*

Edinburgh, N.L., Adv. 18.8.14. *l*Psalterium. s.xv.

ABERDEEN. *Franciscan convent.*

'List of Books and MSS which belonged to the Franciscan Convent in Aberdeen at the time of the Reformation', printed in *Archaeologia Scotica,* II. ii (1831), 466-68, has no value: see W. M. Bryce, *Scottish Grey Friars,* ii. 237-44.

6 printed books with *ex libris* or *ex dono* inscriptions listed by Durkan and Ross, p. 164, and under Alexander Arbuckle, 7; Alexander Galloway, 14; John Scott, 3; Alexander Symson, 2; John Tullideff, 1.

Aberdeen, U.L., 278. *c*Obituarium. s.xvi med.

ABERDEEN. *Dominican convent.*

A printed book with *ex libris* inscription listed by Durkan and Ross, p. 164.

ABERDEEN. *Carmelite convent.*

2 printed books with *ex libris* inscriptions listed by Durkan and Ross under Alexander Galloway, 14; Andrew Storour, 1.

ABERDEEN. *King's College.*

M. R. James, *Cat. of Med. MSS in Aberdeen U.L.*, pp. xi, 122. *List of fifteenth-century Books in the U.L. of Aberdeen*, Edinburgh Bibliog. Soc., xiii (1925).

List of service books in inventory of 1542 printed in *Fasti Aberdonenses* (Spalding Club, 1854), pp. 568–70; second and penultimate folios given.

3 printed books have the *ex dono* of the founder William Elphinstone, bishop of Aberdeen, dated 1510 and 1512, and 8 have the *ex dono* of Hector Boece, first principal: see Durkan and Ross, pp. 34, 77–78 (William Elphinstone, 19–21; Hector Boece, 1, 2, 4, 5, 7, 9, 11, 16). Durkan and Ross list also 15 manuscripts and 3 printed books belonging to Elphinstone, but without his *ex dono*, now in Aberdeen U.L. The manuscripts are fifteenth-century commentaries on canon and civil law (MSS 12–17, 184, 195–98, 201, 202, 262) and a copy of L. Valla, Elegantiae (MS. 222).

Aberdeen,
    U.L., 214. *e*Orosius. s.xv.
        263. *e*Boethius, etc. s.xv.
        264. *e*J. Irlandus. s.xv/xvi.
Cambridge, Trinity Coll., 1421. *e*Scotichronicon. s.xv ex.
Edinburgh, N.L., Adv. 18.3.11. *e*Historia trium regum, etc. s.xv ex.

ABINGDON (Abbendonia), Berkshire. *Ben. abbey of B.V.M.*

Books written in the time of Abbot Faricius (†1117) listed in *Chronicon Monasterii de Abingdon*, ed. J. Stevenson (Rolls Series, 1858), ii. 289. Books noted by J. Leland, *Collectanea*, iv. 57.

Antwerp, Plantin-Moretus, 47.[1] *c*Excerptiones de Prisciano. s.xi in. ?
                  190.[1] *m*Boetius. s.x/xi. ?
Berlin, Staatsbibliothek, th. lat. fol. 579. Sermones Augustini, etc. s.xiii.
Brussels, Bibl. royale, 1520.[1] *m*Aldhelmus. s.xi in. ?
Cambridge, U.L., Dd.2.5. *c*Chronicon Anglie. s.xiv.
           Kk.1.22. *c*Martyrologium, etc. s.xiv.
           Kk.3.21. *c*Boetius. s.x/xi. ?
      Corpus Christi Coll., 25. *e*Cyprianus. s.xiv. ?
               28. *e*Origenes. s.xii.
               57. *c*Regula S. Benedicti, etc. s.x/xi.
      Emmanuel Coll., (pr. bk).[2] Portiforium. A.D. 1528.
      Pembr. Coll., 4.18.8 (pr. bk). *i*Primasius. Lyon, A.D. 1537.
      Trinity Coll., 993. *c*Chronicon Anglie. s.xiv in.
Edinburgh, U.L., O.18.17 (pr. bk). *i*Euclides (in Latin). Paris, A.D. 1516.
Leyden, U.L., Vulcanius 96. *i*Itinerarium J. Mandeville. A.D. 1390.
London,
    B.M., Add. 32246.[1] *c*Excerptiones de Prisciano. s.xi in. ?
        Add. 42555. *e*Apocalypsis glo. s.xiii.
        Arundel 326. *c*Annales Abbendonie, etc. s.xii–xiii ex.

---

[1] B.M., Add. 32246 is a fragment detached from Plantin-Moretus 47. The two Plantin-Moretus manuscripts and Brussels, Bibl. royale, 1520 probably formed one volume. Bodleian MS. Facs. d.76 is a facsimile of Add. 32246 and Plantin 47, and MS. Film 5 is a microfilm of Plantin 190.

[2] Printed at the abbey by J. Scolar, 'ad usum nigrorum monachorum Abendonie'.

London (*contd*)
 B.M., Cotton Tib. B.i.   *c*Anglo-Saxon chronicle, etc. (in English).   s.xi.
  Claud. B.vi.   *c*Cartularium et consuetudinarium.   s.xiii
   ex.
   C.ix, fos 105–202.   *c*Cart. et consuet.   s.xii ex.
  Vit. A.xiii, fos 83–90.   *c*Historia Abbendonie.   s.xiii in.
 Harley 209.   *c*Misc. theologica (partly in French).   s.xiii.
  3061.   *e*Paschasius, etc.   s.xii.
 Lambeth Palace, 42.   *e*Florentius Wigorn.   s.xii ex.   [liber lxxxviii in
   inventorio almarioli claustri].
Oxford, Bodleian, Digby   39.   *e*Vite sanctorum.   s.xi/xii.
   96.   Meditationes Godwini.   s.xii. [*Leland*].   ?
   146.   *e*Aldhelmus.   s.xi in.
   227.   *l*Missale, pars estiv.   A.D. 1461.
  Lyell 21.   *e*Polychronicon.   s.xv.
  Rawl. C.940.   *i*Psalterium, etc.   s.xiii.
   D.235.   *i*Duns Scotus.   s.xiv.
 Exeter Coll., 9M 15792 (pr. bk).[2]   Psalterium.   A.D. 1528.
 Pembr. Coll., 2.   *l*J. de Mirfeld, etc.   s.xv.
 Trinity Coll., 75.   *l*Missale, pars hiem.   s.xv.
Paris, B.N., lat. 1792.   *e*Jeronimus, etc.   s.xii.
Rejected: Oxford, Bodleian, Bodl. 874 and Wood empt. 23.

ACONBURY (Acornebury), Herefordshire.   *Priory of Holy Cross, of Aug.
 nuns.*
Rejected: Oxford, Bodleian, Laud lat. 114.

ALCESTER (Alencestria), Warwickshire.   *Ben. abbey of B.V.M. and St
 John the Baptist.*
Rejected: Cambridge, Trinity Coll., 143.

ALNWICK, Northumberland.   *Prem. abbey of B.V.M.*
London, B.M., Harley 217.   *e*Bonaventura, etc.   s.xv.

AMESBURY (Ambrosii burgum, Ambresberia), Wiltshire.   *Priory (cell of
 Fontevrault) and later abbey of B.V.M. and St Meilor, of Ben. nuns.*
Cambridge, U.L., Ee.6.16.   *l*Horae B.V.M.   s.xiv.   ?
London, B.M., Add. 18632.   *e*J. Lydgate, etc. (in English).   s.xv.
Oxford,
 Bodleian, Add. A.42.   *c*Exhortation to nuns (in English).   s.xv ex.   ?
   Liturg. misc. 407.   *l*Psalterium, etc.   s.xiii in.–xiv.   ?
Windsor Castle.   *l*Breviarium (4 fos).   s.xiii.   ?
Rejected: Oxford, All Souls Coll., 6.

ANGLESEY, Cambridgeshire.   *Aug. priory of B.V.M. and St Nicholas.*
 List of books in the keeping of certain monks, A.D. 1314, printed in English
translation from P.R.O., Ancient Deeds A.14502, by E. Hailstone, *Hist. and
Antiq. of Bottisham* (Camb. Antiq. Soc., 8vo publ. no. 14, 1873), p. 247; see also
Victoria County History, Cambridgeshire, ii. 231.
Cambridge, Corpus Christi Coll., 136.   *e*Summa Raymundi, etc.   s.xiii.

[2] See p. 2, n. 2.
3

ANKERWYKE, Buckinghamshire. *Ben. nunnery of St Mary Magdalen.*

Cambridge, Gonv. and Caius Coll., 390. *i*Horologium sapientie, etc. (in English). s.xv.

ARBROATH (Aberbrothock), Angus. *Ben. (orig. Tironensian) abbey of St Thomas the Martyr.*

List of thirty-four 'libri mag. Ricardi Guthre quos reliquit in abbatia de Aberbr' . . . 1473' in Aberdeen, U.L., 105, fo. 137ᵛ, printed by J. Durkan, 'An Arbroath Book Inventory of 1473', *The Bibliotheck*, iii (1961), 144–46: Guthrie was abbot 1450–55, 1470–72 (?).
For printed books see Durkan and Ross under Walter Baldowy and David Black.

Aberdeen, U.L., 105. *i*Albertus Magnus, etc. s.xv. [Guthrie 19].
London, B.M., Add. 8930, fos 1–3. *l*Kalendarium. s.xiii.
Wolfenbüttel, Ducal Libr., Helmst. 499. *e*Claudianus. s.xiii.
                  1006. *e*Misc. theol. et jur. s.xv.

ARBUTHNOTT, Kincardineshire. *Collegiate church of St Ternan.*

For a printed book see Durkan and Ross, p. 126.

Paisley, Free Libr. and Museum. *e*Psalterium. A.D. 1482.
                          *e*Missale. A.D. 1491.
                          *c*Horae. s.xv ex.

ARUNDEL, Sussex. *Collegiate church of Holy Trinity.*

120 books, of which 75 were service-books, are listed in an inventory of 1517, in roll form, belonging to the Duke of Norfolk at Arundel Castle, printed by W. H. St John Hope, 'On an Inventory of the Goods of the Collegiate Church of the Holy Trinity, Arundel', *Archaeologia*, lxi, part 1 (1908), pp. 82–96: second folios given.
Inscription and volume number of the Royal MS. are reproduced in *New Pal. Soc.*, i, pl. 147, no. 10, wrongly assigned to a college at Chichester.

London, B.M., Royal 10 A.xi. *e*G. Tornacensis, etc. s.xiv in. [xii vol.; *Cat*. 107].

ASHRIDGE (Esserugge), Buckinghamshire. *House of Bonshommes of B.V.M. (and of the Holy Blood).*

H. C. Schulz, 'The Monastic Library and Scriptorium at Ashridge', *Huntington Libr. Quarterly*, i (April 1938), 305.

Cambridge, Fitzwilliam Mus., 16. *l*Psalterium. s.xv med.
Kew, Mr B.S.Cron (pr. |bk). *i*J. Frobenii concordantie. Basel, A.D. 1516.
London, B.M., Royal 3 D.vi. *e*P. Comestor. s.xiii ex.
                  7 F.xi. *e*Florarium Bartholomei, etc. s.xv.
                15 C.xvi.[3] P. Berchorius, etc. s.xiv ex.
Oxford, Bodleian, Bodl. 415. *e*Handlyng synne (in English). s.xv.
           Trinity Coll., 18. *e*W. de Pagula, etc. s.xiii–xiv.

[3] From the hospital of St Thomas of Acon, London, 'caucio . . . exposita penes ven. virum rectorem de Ashrugge' (fo. ii).

San Marino,
   Huntington, EL 7 H.8. *i*J. de Deo, etc. A.D. 1368.
         EL 9 H.3. *i*Summa summarum. s.xiv ex. ?
         EL 9 H.9. *i*Egidius Romanus; Boetius. s.xiv ex. ?
         EL 9 H.15. *c*Statuta ordinis, etc. s.xiv.
Stonyhurst Coll., 44. *l*Breviarium. s.xiv ex. ?

ATHELNEY, Somerset. *Ben. abbey of St Saviour, St Peter, and St Paul.*

London, B.M., Royal 12 B.xvi. *e*Practica Alexandri. s.xiii ex. ?

AXHOLME, Lincolnshire. *Charterhouse of the Visitation of B.V.M.*

Lincoln, Cathedral, SS.2.15 (pr. bk). *e*A. de Clavasio. Nuremberg,
   A.D. 1488.
Oxford, Bodleian, Wood empt. 14.[4] *i*Statuta ordinis Carthus. s.xv. ?

AYLESBURY, Buckinghamshire. *Franciscan convent.*

Durham, Cathedral, Inc. 37, a, b (pr. bks). *e*Biblia. Naples, A.D. 1476.

AYLESFORD, Kent. *Carmelite friary.*

   The missing cartulary (*cf.* G. R. C. Davis, *Medieval cartularies of Great Britain,*
1958, no. 16) listed *c.*75 volumes in the library, A.D. 1381: extracts from it by
Roger Twysden, s.xvii, include the first 14 titles (MS. Phillipps 8130, now belonging to Mr F. T. Allen of Ramsey, Hunts., p. 523).

AYR. *Franciscan convent.*

   A printed book is listed by Durkan and Ross, p. 137.

AYR. *Dominican convent.*

   A printed book with *ex libris* inscription is listed by Durkan and Ross, p. 164.

BABWELL (Bury St Edmunds), Suffolk. *Franciscan convent.*

Cambridge, U.L., Add. 6866. *e*Euclides, etc. s.xiii–xiv.
            Ii.1.1. *e*B. de Gordonio, etc. s.xiv.
         Gonv. and Caius Coll., 111. *c*Philaretus, etc. s.xiii–xiv
           in. ?
         Trinity Coll., 919. *e*Platearius, etc. s.xiii in.–xiv ex.
London, B.M., Burney 5. *e*Biblia. s.xiii.
         Royal Astronomical Soc., QB. 7/1021. *e*Tabule planetarum.
         s.xiv.
         Oxford, Bodleian, Lat. th. d.1.[5] Sermones. s.xv.
Rome, Vatican, Ottobon. lat. 352, fos 1–86. *e*Isidorus, etc. s.xiv. ?
Rejected: Cambridge, Gonv. and Caius Coll., 464.

BANGOR, Caernarvonshire. *Cathedral church of St Daniel.*

Bangor, Cathedral, 1. *e*Pontificale. s.xiii.
Philadelphia, Pennsylvania U.L., 3. *e*J. de Burgo. s.xv. ?

   [4] Wood empt. 14 bears the name of a monk, John Chamberlayne, who was
successively at Axholme and Hinton, *q.v.*
   [5] A note in Lat. th. d.1 written at Norwich in 1538 records that it was to go
to Babwell after the death of Fr. Thomas Goddard: it belonged earlier to a friar
of Lynn.

BARDNEY, Lincolnshire. *Ben. abbey of St Peter, St Paul, and St Oswald.*

Note of books seen by J. Leland, printed from B.M., Royal MS. App. 69, fo. 5ᵛ, in *Eng. Hist. Rev.*, liv. 92; *cf. Collectanea*, iv. 33.

Lincoln, Lincolnshire Archives Committee, Monson Misc. 52 (deposit). *e*Constitutiones Clementine. s.xiv.

London, B.M., Cotton Vit. E.vii, fos 13–70. *e*Ailredus, etc. s.xiii–xiv. [*Leland*].

Royal 7 A.iii. *e*Theologica. s.xii ex. [*Leland*].
    9 B.ix. *e*P. Lombardus. s.xiii in. [*Leland*].
    10 A.vii. W. de Monte, etc. s.xiii. [*Leland*].
    13 A.vii. *e*Martinus Polonus, etc. s.xiii ex. [*Leland*].

Oxford, Bodleian, Douce 158 (pr. bk). *e*R. de Sabunde. Deventer, s.a.
    Rawl. C. 504.⁶ Collect. theol. s.xiii.
    C.510.⁶ Collect. theol. s.xiii.
    D.893, fos 19–26, 105–6, 113.⁶ *c*Collect. theol. s.xiii.

BARKING (Berking), Essex. *Abbey of B.V.M. and St Ethelburga, of Ben. nuns.*

M. R. James, 'MSS from Essex Monastic Libraries', *Trans. Essex Archaeol. Soc.*, N.S., xxi (1933), 35.   N. R. Ker, 'More MSS from Essex Monastic Libraries', *Trans. Essex Archaeol. Soc.*, N.S., xxiii (1945), 301, 310.

Beeleigh Abbey, Miss C. Foyle. *i*Mirror of Life of Christ (in English). s.xv in.

Cambridge, Trinity Coll., 1226. *l*Hymnarium. s.xv.

Cardiff, Central Public Libr.,
    1.381, fos 81–146. *cm*Vitae sanctorum. s.xii in.–xii med.   ?
    3.833. *em*Defensor, etc. s.xiii ex.   ?

London,
    B.M., Add. 10596, fos 25–83. *i*Tobie, etc. (in English). s.xv.
        Cotton Otho A.v. *l*Kalendarium. s.xiv ex.

Oxford, Bodleian, Bodl. 155. *c*Evangelia. s.x/xi.
    923. *i*The clensyng of mannes soule (in English). s.xiv.
        Laud lat. 19. *e*Cantica, etc., glo. s.xii. [B. iii].
    Magdalen Coll., lat. 41. *e*Bernard, Augustine, etc. (in French). s.xv.
    Univ. Coll., 169. *e*Ordinale. s.xiv/xv.

Paris, B.N., Fr. 1038. *i*Vies des saints pères, etc. (in French). s.xiii/xiv.

Rejected: Cambridge, Trinity Coll., 1133.

BARLINGS, Lincolnshire. *Prem. abbey of B.V.M.*

Note of books seen by J. Leland, printed from B.M., Royal MS. App. 69, fo. 3ᵛ, in *Eng. Hist. Rev.*, liv. 91.

Cambridge, Emmanuel Coll., 17. *e*Augustinus. s.xii.

El Escorial, d.iii.11. *e*Itinerarium Jerosolim., etc. s.xiii.

London, B.M., Royal 3 B.xv. *e*Unum ex quatuor glo. s.xiii. [*Leland*].

---

⁶ Bodleian, Rawl. C.504, C.510, D.893, fos 19–26, 105–6, 113, formed one volume.

Oxford, Magdalen Coll., lat. 199. *c*Chronica. s.xiv. ?
Wentworth Woodhouse, Lord Fitzwilliam. *e*Seneca. s.xii.

BARNWELL (Bernewell), Cambridgeshire. *Aug. priory of St Giles.*
Books noted by J. Leland, *Collectanea*, iv. 15.

Cambridge, U.L., Add. 6865. *e*J. de S. Paulo, etc. s.xiii. ?
       Gonv. and Caius Coll., 204. *l*Kalendarium, etc. s.xiii–
               xv. ?
       Trinity Coll., 1232. *e*Alex. Nequam. s.xiii.
London, B.M., Harley 3601. *c*Liber memorandorum. A.D. 1295–96.
       Coll. of Arms, Arundel 10. *c*Chronica, etc. s.xiii.
Oxford, Univ. Coll., 177. *m*Polychronicon. s.xiv ex.
Rejected: Cambridge, Gonv. and Caius Coll., 356.

BASINGWERK, Flintshire. *Savigniac and (1147) Cist. abbey of B.V.M.*

Aberystwyth, N.L., 7006 D. *c*Dares Phrygius, etc. ('Black book of
    Basing', partly in Welsh). s.xiv–xv. ?

BATH, Somerset. *Ben. cathedral priory of St Saviour, St Peter, and St Paul. (Cf.* cell at **DUNSTER**.)

Books noted by J. Leland, *Collectanea*, iv. 156; *cf.* Leland, *De Scriptoribus Britannicis*, p. 160.

Cambridge,
    Corpus Christi Coll., 111, pp. 3–6, 9–54. *c*Legenda, etc. s.xi–xiii.
                111, pp. 7–8, 55–56.[7] *c*Manumissions, etc. (in
                     English). s.xi.
                140.[7] *c*Gospels (in English). s.xi.
London, B.M., Arundel 86. *i*Polychronicon. s.xiv/xv.
       Cotton Claud. B.v. *e*Acta concilii Constantinop. s.ix.
                [*Leland*].
       Royal 3 B.xvi.[8] *s*Jeronimus. s.xii in.
           5 B.ii.[8] *s*Augustinus. s.xii in. ?
           5 B.xiv.[8] *c*Augustinus. s.xii.
           5 D.iv, v.[8] *m*Augustinus. s.xii in.
           5 D.vi.[8] *m*Augustinus. s.xii in.
           5 D.vii.[8] *m*Augustinus. s.xii in. ?
           6 B.i.[8] *c*Gregorius. s.xii.
           6 C.xi.[8] *c*Jeronimus. s.xii.
       Lincoln's Inn, Add. xliv. *c*Registrum; misc. historica. s.xiv.

BATTLE (de Bello), Sussex. *Ben. abbey of St Martin. (Cf.* cells at
    BRECON and **EXETER**, *St Nicholas*.)

Books noted by J. Leland, *Collectanea*, iv. 68.
The pressmark consists of a pair of letters in red ink placed usually at the head of the first page of text.

    [7] Pp. 7–8, 55–56 of MS. 111 appear to have belonged to MS. 140.
    [8] The nine Royal manuscripts belonged to Cranmer. 3 B.xvi is probably in the same hand as 6 C.xi. The marginalia in 5 D.iv, 5 D.v, 5 D.vi, and perhaps 5 D.vii are in the same hand as marginalia in 6 C.xi. 5 B.ii resembles 6 B.i in script and decoration.

Berlin, Staatsbibl., lat. 147. *c*Chronica, etc. s.xiii ex.
Cambridge,
    U.L., Kk.6.15. Hist. Jerosolim., etc. s.xii ex. [MT]. ?
        Inc. 1982 (pr. bk). *i*Cicero. Venice, A.D. 1494.
    Trinity Coll., 1359. *l*Breviarium. s.xv/xvi.
Chicago, Univ. of Chicago, 254. *i*Brut (in English). s.xv med.
Hereford, Cathedral, H.ii.7 (pr. bk). *i*Augustinus. Basel, A.D. 1489.
        P.v.1.[9] Beda, etc. s.xii.
London,
    B.M., Add. 22719.[1] Constantinus Africanus. s.xii. [CN].
        Burney 282. *s*Ambrosius. s.xiii in. [CO].
        Cotton Tib. B.v, part i, fos 2–73, 77–88.[2] *c*Kalendarium, etc.
                s.x/xi.
            Nero D.ii, fos 238–41.[2] *c*Annales. s.xii–xiii.
            Domit. ii, fos 8–130. *c*Historia mon. de Bello. s.xii in.–
                xii ex.
        Lansdowne 358. *e*Bernardus, etc. s.xii/xiii. [FX].
        Royal 4 C.xi. *e*Jeronimus, etc. s.xii in.–xiii in. [CQ].
            6 B.xiv. Recognitiones Clementis, etc. s.xii/xiii. [BR]. ?
        Sloane 4031. *e*J. Lydgate (in English). s.xv.
    The Robinson Trust (Phillipps 8517). *e*Chronicon Anglie, 1066–1306.
                s.xv in. [IN].
Oxford, Bodleian, Bodl. 724. Ricardus Pratellensis. s.xii ex. [FZ]. ?
            Digby 157. Josephus Iscanus, etc. s.xii/xiii. [GZ]. ?
            Lat. misc. c.16. *e*J. Saresberiensis. s.xii ex. [GS].
            e Mus. 93.[9] Relatio de Willelmo conquestore. s.xii. ?
    St John's Coll., 202. *e*Historie de sanctis. s.xiii.
    Univ. Coll., 104. Julianus Toletanus. s.xi. [CL]. ?
Untraced: Earl of Carlisle no. 37 (E. Bernard, *Catalogi* (1697), ii. 15, no.
    647). *i*Historia Britannie. s.xv. ?
Rejected: Cambridge, U.L., Ff.3.35. London, B.M., Royal 8 D.xviii.

BATTLEFIELD, Shropshire. *Collegiate church of St Mary Magdalen.*

Cambridge, Trinity Coll., 1285. *c*Grammatica, etc. s.xv. ?

BAYHAM (Begham), Sussex. *Prem. abbey of B.V.M. and St Lawrence,*
    removed from Otham.

Cambridge, Gonv. and Caius Coll., 458. *c*Aristoteles. s.xiii ex. ?
Eton Coll., 43. *e*Matheus glo. s.xiii.

BEAUCHIEF (de Bello Capite), Derbyshire. *Prem. abbey of B.V.M. and*
    St Thomas the Martyr.

Cambridge, St John's Coll., 86. *e*P. Alfonsi. s.xiii in.
London, B.M., Cotton Calig. A.viii, fos 4–47. *c*Kalendarium, etc.
                s.xiii–xv.

---

   [9] Hereford P.v.1 and Bodleian, eMus. 93, formed one volume later at the cell
of **BRECON,** *q.v.* Cf. N. R. Ker, 'Sir John Prise', *The Library*, 5th Series, x (1955),
7.
   [1] Add. 22719 was later at the cell of **EXETER,** *q.v.*
   [2] Nero D.ii, fos 238–41, was originally part of the same volume as Tib. B.v,
part i, fos 2–73, 77–88.

BEAULIEU (de Bello Loco Regis), Hampshire. *Cist. abbey of B.V.M.*
Books noted by J. Leland, *Collectanea*, iv. 149.

Oxford, Bodleian, Barlow 49, fos 58–114. *c*Compotus, etc. s.xiv.

BEAULY, Inverness-shire. *Priory of B.V.M. and St John the Baptist of the order of Vallis Caulium.*

Edinburgh, N.L., Adv. 3.1.12. *e*Gratianus. s.xiii in.

BEAUVALE (Gresley, de Pulchra Valle), Nottinghamshire. *Charterhouse of Holy Trinity.*

Cambridge, U.L., Mm.5.37. *e*R. Rolle. s.xiv/xv.
      Trinity Coll. (pr. bk). *e*Bonaventura, Opuscula. Strasbourg, A.D. 1495.
Oxford, Bodleian, Douce 114. *e*Lives of saints, etc. (in English). s.xv.

BEDDGELERT (de Valle S. Marie), Caernarvonshire. *Aug. priory of B.V.M.*

London, B.M., Add. 34633. *e*Steph. Langton, etc. s.xiii. ?

BEDFORD. *Franciscan convent.*

Oxford, Bodleian, Arch. G.e.5 (pr. bk). *i*Vulgaria Terentii. Oxford, ? A.D. 1483. ?
      Laud misc. 176. *e*Rogerus Computista. s.xiv.

BEELEIGH, Essex. *Prem. abbey of B.V.M. and St Nicholas* (formerly **MALDON**).

Oxford, Bodleian, Auct. D.inf.2.6. *e*Lucas glo. s.xiii in.

BEGHAM. *See* **BAYHAM.**

BELVOIR (de Bello Vero), Lincolnshire. *Ben. priory of B.V.M.; cell of St Albans.*

Cambridge, Trinity Coll., 317. *e*Odonis isagoge. s.xiii in.
            1437. *c*Martyrologium, etc. s.xiii/xiv.
Dublin, Trinity Coll., 432, fos 23–58. *e*Comment. in Decretum. s.xiii.
Eton Coll., 48, ii. *e*Notule super Genesim, etc. s.xii–xiii.
London, B.M., Cotton Claud. A.v, fos 46–134*a*. *e*W. Malmesburiensis. s.xii.
Oxford, Bodleian, Bodl. 755. *e*Gesta Francorum. s.xii.
      e Mus. 249. *e*Epp. G. Foliot, etc. s.xii ex.

BERMONDSEY, Surrey. *Cluniac priory and (1399) abbey of St Saviour.*

Imperfect library-catalogue, perhaps of this house, s.xiv in., printed from MS. Bodley 751, fo. 1, by N. Denholm-Young, *Eng. Hist. Rev.*, xlviii (1933), 440.

London, B.M., Harley 231. *c*Annales. s.xv in. ?
      Royal 11 B.vii. *e*Isidorus. s.xii. [Grad. B].

Oxford, Bodleian, Ashmole 342, fos 69–94. *i*J. Campanus, etc. s.xiv in.
> Bodl. 751. *b*Ambrosius. s.xiii in. ?
> 918. *e*'Donatus devocionis'. s.xv.
> Rawl. C.86, fos 2–30. *i*Poem on the Passion (in English). s.xv.

BEVERLEY, Yorkshire. *Minster (collegiate church) of St John of Beverley.*

London, B.M., Add. 39676. *l*Diurnale. s.xv in.
Manchester, J. Rylands, Lat. 186. Missale. s.xii–xv. ?
Ripon, Mr H. L. Bradfer-Lawrence. *c*Folcardus, etc. s.xiv ex.

BEVERLEY. *Dominican convent.*

Oxford, Corpus Christi Coll., 225. *i*Questiones de anima, etc. s.xiv.
> Univ. Coll., 6. *e*Gregorius, etc. s.xii–xiv.
> 67. *e*Alphabetum narracionum. s.xiv.
> 113, fos 166–69.[3] De tabernaculo (in Latin and Hebrew). s. xiii ex.
> 190.[3] *e*P. Comestor, etc. s.xiii.

BICESTER, Oxfordshire. *Aug. priory of St Edburga.*

Brussels, Bibl. royale, 1420. *e*H. de S. Victore, etc. s.xiii.

BIDDLESDEN (Bethlesdena, Bitlesden, etc.), Buckinghamshire. *Cist. abbey of B.V.M.*

Cambridge, U.L., Ii.3.9. *e*Augustinus, etc. s.xiii.
> Mm.4.28. *e*Vitas patrum. s.xii.
Hendred House, Mr T. Eyston (pr. bk). *i*Biblia. (Speier), A.D. 1489.
New York, Pierpont Morgan, 757 (pr. bk). *e*Promptorium puerorum.
> London, A.D. 1499.

BILSINGTON, Kent. *Aug. priory of B.V.M.*

Oxford, Bodleian, Bodl. 127. *e*T. de Chabham. s.xiv.

BISHAM (Bustleham), Berkshire. *Aug. priory and (1536) abbey of St Saviour and B.V.M., or of Holy Trinity.*

Rejected: Oxford, Bodleian, Lat. th. f.8.

BISHOP AUCKLAND, co. Durham. *Collegiate church of St Andrew.*

Book-list of 1499 in *Register of Bishop Richard Fox, Bishop of Durham* (Surtees Soc., 1932), p. 93; also printed in *Wills and Inventories* (Surtees Soc., 1835), i. 101, and by P. S. and H. M. Allen, *Letters of Richard Fox* (1929), pp. 163–66; second folios given.

BODMIN, Cornwall. *Ben. (later Aug.) priory of St Petroc.*

London, B.M., Add. 9381. *c*Evangelia. s.x in.
> Harley 2399, fos 47–64. *i*Infantia Salvatoris, etc. (in English). s.xv.
Oxford, Bodleian, Douce 22. *l*Manuale. s.xv in. ?

---

[3] Oxford, Univ. Coll. 190, and 113, fos 166–69, formed one volume.

BODMIN. *Franciscan convent.*

London, B.M., Royal 7 A.x. *e*P. Comestor. s.xiii ex.
Oxford, Bodl., Ashmole 360, fos 49–88, 113, 114. *i*Albumazar, etc.
s.xv. ?
Winchester, The Presbytery (pr. bk). *i*R. de Mediavilla. Paris (?)
A.D. 1517.

BOLTON, Yorkshire. *Aug. priory of B.V.M.*

London, B.M., Harley 212. *e*Mandeville (in French). s.xiv/xv.
Oxford, Bodleian, Fairfax 24. P. Langtoft, etc. s.xiv. ?
27. Liber correctorius, etc. s.xiii–xiv. ?
Princeton, Mr R. H. Taylor. *e*William of Nassington (in English). s.xv.

BORDESLEY, Worcestershire. *Cist. abbey of B.V.M.*

List of 27 books given by Guy de Beauchamp in 1305 printed by M. Blaess in *Romania*, lxxviii (1958), 512–14, from a transcript by H. Wharton (Lambeth Palace, MS. 577, fo. 18ᵛ).

London, B.M., Add. 37787. *i*Preces; poems (in English). s.xiv ex.
Oxford, Bodleian, Bodl. 168. *e*Bernardus. s.xii.
Laud misc. 606. *e*Cassiodorus. s.xii ex.
Untraced: Abednego Seller (E. Bernard, *Catalogi* (1697), ii. 96, no. 3772).
  Martyrologium, etc.

BOSTON, Lincolnshire. *Dominican convent.*

Note of books seen by J. Leland, printed from B.M., Royal MS. App. 69, fo. 7, in *Eng. Hist. Rev.*, liv. 94.

London, B.M., Royal 13 A.v. Martinus Polonus, etc. s.xiv in. [*Leland*]. ?
Oxford, St John's Coll., 198, fos 176–183. *i*Logica. s.xiv.

BOSTON. *Gild of Corpus Christi.*

London, B.M., Harley 4795. *c*Registrum, kalendarium, etc. s.xiv.

BOURNE (Brunne), Lincolnshire. *Aug. (Arrouaisian) abbey of St Peter and St Paul.*

A book (Nennius) noted by J. Leland, *Collectanea*, ii. 45.

London, B.M., Add. 38819. *l*Psalterium, etc. s.xii. ?
Lambeth Palace, 327. *e*Henr. Huntendonensis. s.xii/xiii.
Rejected: Lambeth Palace, 9 and 473.

BOXGROVE, Sussex. *Ben. alien priory of B.V.M. (? and St Blaise); cell of Lessay.*

Oxford, Bodleian, Rawl. A.411. *e*Omelie. s.xiii.

BOXLEY, Kent. *Cist. abbey of B.V.M.*

Cambridge, Corpus Christi Coll., 37. *e*Astronomica, etc. s.xiv in.
Oxford, Corpus Christi Coll., Φ.A.3.4 (pr.bk). *i*M. Ficinus. Venice,
A.D. 1495.

11

BRADENSTOKE, Wiltshire. *Aug. priory of B.V.M.*

Cambridge, Trinity Coll., 1298. *e*Gratianus. s.xiii.
London, B.M., Royal 6 E.iv. *e*Gregorius. s.xiii.

BRADSOLE. See **DOVER**, *St Radegund.*

BRECON (Brechinnium, Brecknock). *Ben. priory of St John the Evangelist; cell of Battle. Cf.* Appendix, **BRECON.**

Cambridge, Fitzwilliam Mus., 269. *i*Pictor in carmine. s.xiii in. [A.xii; M.35].
Hereford, Cathedral, P.v.1.⁴ Beda, etc. s.xii.
Oxford, Bodleian, e Mus. 93.⁴ Relatio de Willelmo conquestore. s.xii.

BRECON. *Dominican convent.*

London, B.M., Sloane 441.⁵ Pseudo-Dionysius, etc. s.xv.

BRIDGEND (de ponte Aslaci, Hollandbridge), Lincolnshire. *Gilbertine priory of St Saviour.*

Rejected: Oxford, Bodleian, Laud misc. 662.

BRIDGNORTH, Shropshire. *Franciscan convent.*

Rejected: London, B.M., Royal 3 A.xi.

BRIDGWATER, Somerset. *Franciscan convent.*

London, B.M., Royal 3 A.xi. *e*P. Comestor. s.xiii. [M.23 *altered to* A.18].
Oxford, Magdalen Coll., 174. *e*Albertus magnus. s.xiii ex.

BRIDLINGTON (Berlintona, Brellintona, Brillinctuna), Yorkshire. *Aug. priory of B.V.M.*

List of 'libri magni armarii', s.xiii in., printed from B.M., Harl. MS. 50, fo. 48ᵛ, by H. Omont in *Centralblatt für Bibliothekswesen*, ix (1892), 203, may come from this house. Books noted by J. Leland, *Collectanea*, iv. 35; *cf.* Leland, *De Scriptoribus Britannicis*, pp. 202–3.

Cambridge, Gonv. and Caius Coll., 406. *e*G. Monemutensis. s.xii–xiii.
Durham, U.L., Cosin V.v.19. *i*Misc. theol. s.xvi in.
London, B.M., Harley 50. *c*Marcus glo.; Catalogus librorum. s.xii–xiii. ?
Oxford, Bodleian, Bodl. 357. *e*W. Malmesburiensis, etc. s.xii. [littera J].
Digby 53. *e*Versus Serlonis, etc. s.xii.
Fairfax 15. *e*Lucas glo. s.xii. [littera D].
Merton Coll., 325. *e*P. Riga. s.xiv. [littera G].

⁴ Hereford P.v.1 and Bodleian, e Mus. 93, formed one volume, earlier probably at **BATTLE**, *q.v.* Sir John Prise found it 'in Brechonia Demetarum . . . urbe . . . ex coenobio Monachorum, quod ibidem erat Benedictini, quem vocant, ordine desumptum' (J. Prise, *Historiae Brytanniae Defensio*, 1573, p. 114).
⁵ Part of Sloane 441 was written by Bartholomew Texerii, O.P., 'degentem pro eo tempore Brechonie ejusdem ordinis conventu'.

Ripon, Cathedral, xvii.D.2.[6]   *e*Apocalypsis, etc., glo.   s.xii.   [littera D].
         xvii.D.3.[6]   Comment. in Apocalypsim, etc.   s.xii.
Rejected: London, B.M., Cotton Claud. A.v, fos 46–135; Royal 15 C.xii.
  Oxford, Bodleian, Lat. th. d.17.   New York, Pierpont Morgan, 766.

BRISTOL, Gloucestershire.   *Aug. (Victorine) abbey of St Augustine.*
  Books noted by J. Leland, *Collectanea*, iv. 68.
Bristol, Cathedral.   Graduale (fragment).[7]   s.xiv.   ?
    Central Public Libr., 2.   *l*Missale.   s.xv in.
London, B.M., Royal 2 D.x.   *e*Actus apost. glo.   s.xiii.
           5 E.ix.   *e*Prosper, etc.   s.xiii in.
           8 F.v.   *e*Ephraim Syrus, etc.   s.xiii in.
    Lambeth Palace, 355.   *e*Ivo Carnotensis, etc.   s.xii–xiii.   [*Leland*].
Oxford, Jesus Coll., 49.   *e*Unum ex quatuor glo., etc.   s.xii–xii/xiii.

BRISTOL.   *Gild of Kalendars in the church of All Saints.*
Rejected: Eight books in the library of All Saints' Church, Bristol.

BRISTOL.   *Hospital of St John the Baptist in Redcliffe.*
Oxford, Bodleian, Auct. QQ. supra 2.15 (pr. bk).   *e*Vitas patrum (in English).   Westminster,
                    A.D. 1495.

BRISTOL.   *Hospital of St Mark of Billeswick, otherwise Gaunt's hospital, of Aug. canons.*
Bristol, Central Public Libr., 6.   *e*Expo. verborum difficilium, etc.   s.xvi in.
Oxford, Bodleian, Bodl. 618.   *i*Albertus Magnus, etc.   s.xvi in.
        Lyell 38.   *i*R. Rolle.   s.xvi in.
    St John's Coll., 165.   *e*Anselmus, etc.   s.xiii in.
         173.   *e*Augustinus, etc.   s.xvi in.

BRISTOL.   *Franciscan convent.*
Bristol, Central Public Libr., 3.   *e*Isidorus, etc.   s.xiii in.   [ff.19 Ysidorus; F.24].
Cambridge, St John's Coll., 144.   *i*J. de Voragine.   A.D. 1381.
    Sid. Sussex Coll., 49.   *e*Exodus glo.   s.xiii in.
London, B.M., Royal 5 E.iv.   Isidorus, etc.   s.xii ex.   ?

BROMFIELD, Shropshire.   *Ben. priory of B.V.M.; cell of Gloucester.*
Oxford, Brasenose Coll., UB., S.II.51 (pr. bk).   *i*J. Damascenus.   Paris,
                    A.D. 1512.

BROMHOLM, Norfolk.   *Cluniac priory of St Andrew.*
Oxford, Bodleian, Ashmole 1523.   *l*Psalterium.   s.xiv in.–xiv ex.

  [6] Ripon Cathedral xvii.D.2 and xvii.D.3 formed one volume.
  [7] Sixteen leaves used as wrappers of account-books of Bristol Cathedral, 1557–68.

BRUISYARD, Suffolk. *Abbey of the Annunc. of B.V.M., of Franciscan nuns.*

London, B.M., Sloane 2400. *e*Psalterium, etc. s.xiii. ?
Oxford, Bodleian, Tanner 191 (pr. bk). *i*The Royal Book (in English). (London, A.D. 1507).

BRUTON, Somerset. *Aug. priory (later abbey) of B.V.M.*

London, B.M., Cotton Otho A.iv, fos 1–66. *c*Annales. s.xv. ?

BUCKFAST, Devon. *Savigniac and (1147) Cist. abbey of B.V.M.*

Books noted by J. Leland, *Collectanea*, iv. 152.

London, B.M., Sloane 513. *i*Miscellanea. s.xv.

BUCKLAND, Devon. *Cist. abbey of B.V.M.*

London, B.M., Harley 2931. *l*Kalendarium; consuetudinarium. s.xiv. ?

BUCKLAND MINCHIN, Somerset. *Priory of St John the Baptist, of nuns of St John of Jerusalem.*

London, Soc. of Antiquaries, 713. *e*Psalterium. s.xiii. ?

BUILDWAS (Bildewas), Shropshire. *Savigniac and (1147) Cist. abbey of B.V.M. and St Chad.*

The common forms of *ex libris* inscription are 'Liber sancte Marie de Bildewas' and 'Liber monachorum sancte Marie de Bildewas', often in red ink.

Cambridge, Pembr. Coll.,	154.	*e*Cyprianus, etc. s.xii ex.
St John's Coll.,	77.	*e*Ailredus, etc. s.xii.
Trinity Coll.,	1.	*e*Jeremias, etc., glo. s.xiii.
	2.	*e*Gregorius. s.xii.
	3.	*e*Gregorius. s.xii.
	10.	*e*Matheus et Marcus glo. s.xiii in.
	27.	*e*Jeronimus, etc. s.xi–xiii in.
	29.	*e*Leviticus glo. s.xiii.
	32.	*e*Actus apost. glo. s.xiii in.
	33.	*e*Numeri glo. s.xiii.
	34.	*e*Johannes glo. s.xii–xiii.
	37.	*e*Jeronimus, etc. s.xii–xiii in.
	49.	*c*Exodus glo. s.xii/xiii.
	58.	*e*Esaias glo. s.xii/xiii.
	87.	*e*Jeronimus, etc. s.xii.
	94.	*e*Libri regum glo. s.xii–xiii.
	117.	*e*XII prophete glo. s.xii.
	291.	*e*Gregorius. s.xii.
	1337.	*e*P. Comestor. s.xii–xiii.

London,
B.M., Harley 3038. *e*Leviticus glo. A.D. 1176.
Lambeth Palace, 73. *c*W. de Novoburgo, etc. s.xiii in. ?
107. *e*Hugo de Folieto. s.xii.
109. *e*Gregorius. s.xii.

London (*contd*)
    Lambeth Palace, 456, fos 1–106.[8] Priscianus, etc. s.xiii ex.–xv.
            457, fos 193–254.[8] 'Seneca ad Lucillum', etc. s.xiii.
            477. *c*Concordancie bibl., etc. s.xiii.
            488, fos 89–117.[8] *e*Sermones, etc. s.xiii.
Oxford, Bodleian, Bodl. 371. *e*P. Cantor. s.xiii in.
            395. *e*Isidorus. s.xii ex.
            730. *bs*J. Cassianus. s.xii ex. ?
    Balliol Coll., 35A. *e*Psalterium glo. s.xiii.
            39. *s*A. Nequam. s.xiii in. ?
            40. *s*A. Nequam. s.xiii in. ?
            150. *e*Bernardus. s.xiii in.
            173B. *e*Epp. Pauli glo. s.xii–xiii.
            229. *e*Jeronimus. s.xiii.
    Christ Church, lat. 88. *e*Augustinus. A.D. 1167.
Shrewsbury School, XII. *e*Apocalypsis glo., etc. s.xii ex.
Rejected: Cambridge, Pembr. Coll., 177–79; Trinity Coll., 11–13, 30, 31,
    95, 96, 357. Oxford, Bodleian, Auct. D.3.11.

BULLINGTON, Lincolnshire. *Gilbertine priory of B.V.M.*

    Note of books seen by J. Leland, printed from B.M., Royal MS. App. 69, fo. 5,
in *Eng. Hist. Rev.*, liv. 92.

BURNHAM, Buckinghamshire. *Abbey of B.V.M. of Aug. nuns.*

Rejected: Oxford, Bodleian, Lat. liturg. f.11 and Rawl. G.18.

BURNHAM NORTON, Norfolk. *Carmelite convent.*

London, B.M., IC.29955–56 (pr. bk). *i*Nicolaus de Horto Caeli, etc.
                              Padua, s.a.

BURTON-UPON-TRENT, Staffordshire. *Ben. abbey of B.V.M. and St
    Modwenna.*

    Catalogue, s.xii ex., printed from B.M., Add. MS. 23944, fo. 157, by H.
Omont, *Centralblatt für Bibliothekswesen*, ix (1892), 201.

Aberystwyth, N.L., Peniarth 390 C. *c*Summa m. Bernardi, etc. s.xiii ex.
Cambridge,
    U.L., Inc. 3057 (pr. bk). *i*Libellulus secundarum intentionum logica-
                       lium. Paris, s.a.
    Corpus Christi Coll., 281. *e*G. Monemutensis, etc. s.xii–xiv. ?
                     353. *e*P. de Vineis. s.xiv. ?
    St John's Coll., A.2.1 (pr. bk). *i*Theodolus, etc. London, A.D. 1497,
                       etc.
    Trinity Coll., 1411. *c*Alchemica. s.xvi in. ?
London, B.M., Add. 23944. *c*Augustinus, etc. s.ix.
            Cotton Vesp. E.iii, art. 1. *c*Annales, etc. s.xiii.
                 Cleop. A.ii. *i*Vita S. Modwenne. s.xii.
Norwich, City Libr. (pr. bk). *i*J. de Sacro Bosco, etc. Cologne, A.D.
                       1508, etc.

  [8] Lambeth Palace 456 (fos 1–106), 457 (fos 193–254) and 488 (fos 89–117)
formed one volume.

Oxford, All Souls Coll., i.12.15 (pr. bk).   *i*J. Wallensis.   Lyon, A.D. 1511.

v.2.13   (pr. bk).   *e*Sermones   thesauri   novi.
Paris, A.D. 1497.

v.4.12 (pr. bk).   *i*Gul. Pepin.   Paris, A.D. 1534.

LR.4.e.10 (pr. bk).   *i*N. de Orbellis, etc.   Paris,
A.D. 1498, etc.

SR.62.a.2 (pr. bk).   *i*J. de Trittenhem.   Paris,
A.D. 1512.

SR.77.g.13 (pr. bk).   *i*P. Lombardus.   Basel,
A.D. 1502.

Rejected: MS. (Vita S. Modwenne, etc.) belonging to Prof. F. Wormald.

BURWELL, Lincolnshire.   *Ben. alien priory; cell of La Sauve-Majeure.*

Rejected: Cambridge, Gonv. and Caius Coll., 376.

BURY ST EDMUNDS, Suffolk.   *Ben. abbey of St Edmund, King and Martyr.*

M. R. James, *On the Abbey of St Edmund at Bury: i, The Library, ii, The Church* (Cambridge Antiq. Soc., 8vo publ. no. 28), 1895.   M. R. James, 'Bury St Edmunds Manuscripts', *Eng. Hist. Rev.*, xli (1926), 251–60, enlarges the list given in 1895.   M. R. James, 'Description of the Ancient MSS in the Ipswich Public Libr.', *Proc. Suffolk Inst. of Archaeol. and Nat. Hist.*, XXII. i (1934), 86–103.

List of service-books, s.xi, printed from Oxford, Corpus Christi Coll., MS. 197, fo. 107, and a fragmentary catalogue, s.xii and s.xii/xiii, printed from Cambridge, Pembr. Coll., MS. 47 *ad fin.*, and notices of books read in refectory and of gifts by abbots, priors, etc., in James, *On the Abbey of St Edmund*, pp. 6, 23, 111, 181–82.   Books noted by J. Leland (*Collectanea*, iv. 162), *ibid.*, p. 10.   *Cf.* also Leland, *De Scriptoribus Britannicis*, p. 215.

The pressmark, which is written at the top of the outer margin of the first leaf of text, is reproduced from B.M., Royal 6 C.ii, 7 C.v and 8 E.x in *New Pal. Soc.*, i, pl. 17, no. 8 *a–c*, and from the Harvard MS. by E. G. Millar, *The Library of A. Chester Beatty* (1927), pl. 73.   The letter in the pressmark has reference to the contents, so that, *e.g.*, MSS of Augustine and Anselm are marked A, bibles B, chronicles C, sermons S.   'Liber Sancti Ædmundi regis et martyris' is the usual thirteenth-century form of *ex libris* inscription.   'Liber monachorum Sancti Edmundi' is common later.   The inscription is regularly at the head of the first leaf of text.   Six MSS (Cambridge, Pembroke Coll., 16, 44, 105; B.M., Royal 6 C.ii; Bodleian, e Mus. 7, 8) are marked 'De armario claustri' or 'De claustro', three (B.M., Egerton 2782, St John's Coll., Cambridge, 35, and Wisbech 1) are 'De refectorio', and B.M., Cotton Tib. B.ii is 'Liber feretrariorum'.

Bury St Edmunds, Cathedral, 4, fos 1–119.   Bernardus, etc.   s.xiii.   [B. 357].[9]

4, fos 120–165.   *e*Medica etc.   s.xii–xiii.
[M.27].[9]

Grammar School.   *l*Psalterium, etc.   s.xv.

Cambridge,
U.L., Add.   850.[1]   *c*Chronica.   s.xiv.

6006.   *e*Consuetudinarium, etc.   s.xiii/xiv.   [C.63].

6190.   *i*J. de Janduno, etc.   A.D. 1441.

6860.   *e*Imago mundi, etc.   s.xiv in.   [A.229].

Ff.1.27, pp. 249–642.[2]   Misc. historica.   s.xiv.

[9] B.357 and M.27 form one volume in fifteenth-century binding.
[1] Cambridge, U.L., Add. 850, Oo.6.110 (fos 84–90), and Oo.7.48 (fos 16–26) formed one volume.
[2] Cambridge, U.L., Ff.1.27, pp. 249–642, and Corpus Christi Coll., 66, ii, formed one volume.

Cambridge (*contd*)
U.L., Add. Ff.3.5.   Apuleius, etc. s.xii. [A.130].
         Ii.6.5.³ *e*Viaticum Constantini, etc. s.xiv–xv. [U.].
         Oo.6.110, fos 84–90.¹ De prosodia, etc. s.xv.
         Oo.7.48, fos 16–26.¹ T. de Chabham. s.xiv.
Corpus Christi Coll.,   2. Biblia, pars i. s.xii. [B.1; *cf. cat.* ii].
          66, ii.² *e*Misc. historica. s.xiv. [J.90].
         135. *e*Anselmus, etc. s.xii. [A.83; *cat.* xxviii].
         251. *c*Chronicon Buriense. s.xv in. [? E.43].
         404. *e*Prophetie. s.xiv. [P.163].
Gonv. and Caius Coll., 113. *i*Egidius Romanus. s.xv.
         145. *e*H. de S. Victore. s.xii/xiii. [H.31].
         154. Hist. Alexandri, etc. s.xii/xiii. [P.162].
         225. *e*W. de Conchis, etc. s.xiii. [V.12].
         480. *e*Canon Avicenne. s.xiii. [A.200].
Jesus Coll., 18. *c*Formulare. s.xv.
King's Coll., 3. Augustinus, etc. s.xii. [*Cf. cat.* xxviiij]. ?
       7. *e*Beda. s.xii. [B. 292; *cat.* xl].
Pembr. Coll., 1. *e*Anselmus, etc. s.xiv. [A.92].
       2. *e*W. Altissiodorensis (I, II). s.xiii. [A.109].
       3. *e*W. Altissiodorensis (III). s.xiii. [A.110].
       4. *s*W. Altissiodorensis (IV). s.xiii.
       5. *e*Ric. Armachanus. s.xiv ex. [A.143].
       7. *e*Glosa super psalt. s.xiii. [B.231].
       8. Concordancie bibl. s.xiv in. [B.276].
       9. *e*Bernardus, etc. s.xii ex. [B.305].
      10. Bonaventura. s.xiii–xiv. [B.385].
      11. *e*N. de Lyra. s.xiv/xv.
      12. *e*Claudius Clemens. s.xii. [C.16; *cat.* lxviii].
      15. *s*Gregorius. s.xii. [*Cf. cat.* 174].
      16. *e*Gregorius. s.xii. [G.8; *cat.* 177].
      17. *e*Jeronimus. s.ix/x. [J.6; *cat.* iii].
      18. *e*J. Chrysostomus. s.xii. [J.28; *cat.* xxxviiij].
      19. *e*J. Chrysostomus. s.xiv. [J.32].
      20. *e*J. Damascenus, etc. s.xiii ex. [J.57].
      21. *e*J. de Rupella. s.xiv. [M.93].
      22. Mariale. s.xiv. ?
      23. *e*Omelie de tempore. s.xi. [O.52].
      24. *e*Omelie de sanctis. s.xi. [O.54].
      25. *e*Omelie. s.xi. [O.55].
      26. *e*P. Comestor. s.xii/xiii. [P.11].
      27. *e*P. Comestor, etc. s.xiii. [P.25].
      28. *e*P. Lombardus. s.xiii in. [P. 64].
      29. *e*Rad. Flaviacensis. s.xii ex. [R.14].
      30. *e*Rob. de Cricklade. s.xiii. [R.54].
      31. *e*P. Berchorius. s.xv.
      32. P. Lugdunensis. s.xiv in. [S.71].
      33. *e*T. Aquinas. s.xiv. [T.1].
      34. *e*T. Aquinas, etc. s.xiv. [T.7].⁴

¹ See p. 16, n. 1.   ² See p. 16, n. 2.
³ Formerly bound with S.62 (Sermones), now gone.
⁴ The pressmark T.7 is on the medieval binding of MS. 34, now kept separately.

Cambridge (*contd*)

Pembr. Coll., 35.   T. Aquinas.   s.xiv.   ?
- 36.   T. Aquinas.   s.xiv.   [T.10].
- 37.   *e*T. Aquinas.   s.xiv.   [T.12].
- 38.   *e*T. Aquinas.   s.xiv in.   [T.16].
- 39.   *e*Tabule.   s.xiv.   [T.25].
- 40.   *e*Tabula Martini.   s.xiv.   [T.47].
- 41.   *e*Augustinus.   s.xi.   [A.31; *cat*. 191].
- 42.   *e*Ambrosius.   s.xii.   [A.61; *cat*. xlvi].
- 43.   Alex. de Hales.   s.xiii.   [A.114].
- 44.   *e*Amalarius, etc.   s.xii.   [A.121; *cat*. 251].
- 45.   *e*Andreas de S. Victore.   s.xiii.   [A.124].
- 46.   *e*Liber Catonis (in French), etc.   s.xiii.   [A.222].
- 47.   *e*Genesis et Cantica glo.   s.xii in.   [B.40; *cat*. cxxx].
- 48.   *s*Exodus glo.   s.xii.   [*Cf. cat*. c].   ?
- 49.   *e*Leviticus glo.   s.xii.   [B.48; *cf. cat*. 221].
- 50.   *m*Leviticus glo.   s.xii.
- 51.   *e*Numeri glo.   s.xii.   [B.50].
- 52.   *e*Numeri et Deut. glo.   s.xii.   [B.51; *cat*. 146].
- 53.   Deut. glo.   s.xii.   [B.52; *cf. cat*. 219].
- 54.   Josue glo.   s.xii.   [B.54; *cf. cat*. 227].
- 55.   *e*Ruth, etc., glo.   s.xiii.   [B.57].
- 56.   *e*Libri regum glo.   s.xii.   [B.58; *cf. cat*. 226].
- 57.   *e*Paralipom., etc., glo.   s.xiii.   [B.59].
- 58.   *e*Esaias glo.   s.xii.   [B.60; *cf. cat*. 163].
- 59.   *e*Esaias glo.   s.xii/xiii.   [B.61].
- 60.   *e*Esaias glo.   s.xiii.   [B.62].
- 61.   *e*Ezechiel glo.   s.xiii.   [B.66].
- 62.   *e*Daniel glo.   s.xii.   [B.68; *cf. cat*. 228].
- 63.   *e*Daniel, etc., glo.   s.xii.   [B.69].
- 64.   Parabole, etc., glo.   s.xii.   [B.80; *cat*. cxxvii].
- 65.   *e*XII prophete, etc., glo.   s.xii.   [B.70].
- 66.   *e*Matheus et Marcus glo.   s.xiii.   [B.90].
- 67.   Matheus glo., etc.   s.xii.   [B.92; *cat*. 150].
- 68.   *e*Matheus glo.   s.xii.   [B.93; *cat*. cxxxv].
- 69.   *e*Matheus glo., etc.   s.xii–xiii.   [B.95].
- 70.   *e*Matheus glo.   s.xii.   [B.97; *cat*. cxxxv].
- 71.   Marcus glo.   s.xiii.   [B.99].
- 72, i.   *e*Marcus glo.   s.xii.   [B.101; *cat*. 235].
- 72, ii.   *e*Pars Hugonis super decreta, etc.   s.xiii.   [L.].
- 73.   Lucas glo.   s.xii.   ?
- 74.   *e*Lucas et Johannes glo.   s.xii.   [B.105; *cat*. cxxxi].
- 75.   Postille super Lucam et Joh.   s.xiii.   ?
- 76.   *e*Johannes glo.   s.xii.   [B.109].
- 77.   Epp. Pauli, etc., glo.   s.xiii.   [B.204].
- 78.   *e*Epp. Pauli glo.   s.xii.   [B.205; *cf. cat*. 236].
- 79.   *e*Epp. Canonice et Pauli glo.   s.xii in.   [B.207].
- 80.   *e*Super Threnos et Cantica, etc.   s.xiii–xiv.   [B.225].
- 81.   *e*Beda.   s.ix in.   [B.282; *cat*. 156].
- 83.   *e*Beda.   s.ix/x–xiii.   [B.287; *cat*. 212].
- 84.   *e*Boetius, etc.   s.xii.   [B.319].
- 85, i.   *e*Tabula super S. Thomam.   s.xiii ex.   [T.65].

Cambridge (*contd*)
  Pembr. Coll., 85. ii.   P. Lombardus, etc.   s.xiii/xiv.   [P.92].
              85, iii.   *e*Berengaudus, etc.   s.xii/xiii.   [B.340].
              87.   *e*Sermones, etc. (partly in French).   s.xiii–xiv.
                    [E.11].
              88.   *e*Gregorius.   s.ix.   [G.18].
              89.   *i*Gregorius.   s.xv.   [G.129].
              90.   H. de S. Victore.   s.xii ex.   [H.19].
              91.   Jeronimus.   s.ix/x.   [J.3; *cat*. 193].
              92.   *e*J. Cassianus.   s.xiv.   [J.35].
              94.   *e*Origenes, etc.   s.xii–xiii.   [O.2; *cat*. xxxviiij].
              95.   *e*Origenes.   s.xii.   [O.4; *cat*. cv].
              96.   *e*P. Pictaviensis.   s.xii/xiii.   [P.35].
              97.   *e*P. Lombardus.   s.xiii.   [P.81].
              98.   *e*Sermones, etc.   s.xiv/xv.   [P.185].
              99.   *e*N. de Gorran, etc.   s.xiv.   [S.38].
              100.   *e*Distinctiones et sermones.   s.xiii.   [S.57].
              101.   Sermones, etc.   s.xiii in.   [S.65].
              102, i.   *e*Formulare.   s.xiv.
              102, ii.   *e*Distinctiones.   s.xiii.   [S.68].
              104.   *e*Tabule super Augustinum.   s.xiv.   [T.26].
              105.   *e*Valerius Maximus.   s.xiii in.   ?   [V.1].
              107.   *e*Bonaventura.   s.xiii ex.   [B. 328].
              108.   Justinianus, etc.   s.ix.   [F.12; *cat*. 168].
              109.   *e*H. de S. Victore.   s.xiii in.   [H.32].
              111.   *e*Jeronimus, etc.   s.xii–xiii.   [J.20].
              114.   *e*Sallustius.   s.xii.   [S.1; *Leland*].
              115.   *e*Collecta Samuelis.   s.xii ex.   [S.2].
              118.   *e*Isidorus, etc.   s.xii–xiii.   [Y.12].
              120.   *e*Novum testamentum.   s.xi–xii.
  Peterhouse, 163.   Manipulus florum.   s.xiv.   [M.4].   ?
  St John's Coll.,   35.   *e*Gregorius.   s.xi.   [G.6; *cat*. 202].
              92.   *b*Epp. Pauli glo.   s.xii.   ?
              94.   *e*Ivo Carnotensis.   s.xii.   [Y.24].
              138.   *e*Summa Peraldi.   s.xiii.   [S.26].
              140.   Distinctiones.   s.xiii.   [E.24].   ?
              149.   *e*Duns Scotus.   s.xv.
              170.   *e*H. de S. Victore, etc.   s.xiv/xv.   [H.56].
  Sid. Sussex Coll., 102.   Beda.   s.xv.   [B.295].
  Trinity Coll., 623.   *e*Virgilius.   s.xii/xiii.
              906.   *e*Constantinus Africanus.   s.xii.   [M.37].
  Mr F. J. Norton (pr. bk).   *i*P. Tataretus.   Paris, A.D. 1514, etc.
Cambridge (U.S.A.), Harvard University, Houghton Libr., W. K. Richard-
    son 26.   *e*Augustinus.   s.xii.   [A.6; *cat*. lxvii].
Dublin, Chester Beatty Libr., W.26.   *e*Augustinus.   s.xii.   [A.10; *cat*.
                    xlii].
              Trinity Coll., 492.   Beda.   s.xii.   [B.296].
Durham, U.L., Cosin V.iii.20.   *e*Isidorus, etc.   s.xiii.   [Y.28].
                    V.v.3.   *e*Sermones.   s.xiv.   [S.78].
Edinburgh, U.L., 163.   *e*Johannicius, etc.   s.xii.   [M.48].
Glasgow, U.L., Hunterian 209.   *e*Barth. Anglicus.   s.xiv.   [B.332].
Hereford, Cathedral, P.iii.1.   *e*J. Beleth, etc.   s.xiii.   [J.47].

Ipswich, Central Libr., 4. *e*Mariale. s.xiv. [M.xi].
  6. *c*Misc. theol. s.xiii–xv.
  8, i. *e*Ric. de S. Victore. s.xiii. [B.240].
  8, ii. *e*Josue et Judicum glo. s.xii/xiii. [B.55].
Laon, Bibl. mun., 238. *l*Missale. s.xii in. ?
London,
  B.M., Add. 24199. Prudentius. s.x–xii. [P.123].
  Campbell Roll xxi.1. *c*Chronologica. A.D. 1356 (?).
  Cotton Jul. E.vii.[5] *e*Ælfric (in English). s.xii in. [*Cf. cat.* 169].
    Tib. B.ii, fos 2–85.[5] *e*Vita S. Edmundi, etc. s.xi.
        [S. 155].
    Claud. A.xii, fos 81–192. *c*Registrum hostilarie; misc.
        hist. s.xv.
    Galba E.iv, fos 187–244. *e*Medica. s.xii. [M.21].
    Vit. C.viii, fos 91–130. *m*Boncompagnus. s.xiii.
        D.xv, fos 1–28. *c*Jocelinus de Brakelonde, etc.
        s.xiv.
    Titus A.viii, fos 65–145. *e*Vita S. Edmundi. s.xiii. [S.
        153].
  Egerton 2782. *e*Haymo. s.xii. [H.l; *cat.* xxcv].
  Harley 51. *e*Guido de Columna, etc. s.xv. [? B.555].
    76. *c*Evangelia. s.xi.
    447. *e*W. Malmesburiensis, etc. s.xiii. [C.49].
    1005. *e*Jocelinus de Brakelonde, etc. s.xiii–xiv. [C.68].
    2977. *l*Rituale. s.xv. ?
    3977. *c*Consuetudinarium. s.xiv.
    4968. *e*Cilium oculi sacerdotis, etc. s.xv. [O.28].
    4971. *e*Grammar (in French), etc. s.xiv–xv.
    5334. *e*Breviarium. s.xiv.
  Royal 2 E.ix. *e*J. de Abbatisvilla. s.xiii. [J. 40].
    5 A.viii. *e*Augustinus, etc. s.xiii. [A.52].
    6 B.x. *e*Anselmus, etc. s.xiii. [A.88].
    6 C.ii. *e*Gregorius. s.xii. [G.16; ? *cat.* 176].
    7 B.ix. *e*Pseudo–Dionysius, etc. s.xiii. [D.6].
    7 C.ii. Rob. Melodunensis, etc. s.xii–xiii. [R.40].
    7 C.v. *e*Distinctiones, etc. s.xiii in. [V.3].
    7 C.xi. *e*P. Cantor. s.xiii. [V.21].
    7 E.i. *c*Barth. Exoniensis, etc. s.xiii. [P.1000].
    8 B.iv. *e*Alexandreis, Suidas, etc. s.xii–xiv. [S.184].
    8 C.iv, fos 1–156. *e*R. Grosseteste etc. s.xiii.
        [R. 42].
    8 C.iv, fos 157–210. *e*Medica. s.xii ex. [M.35].
    8 E.x. *e*Meditationes. s.xiv med. [M.12].
    8 F.xiv. *e*Gregorius, etc. s.xiii–xiv. [G.15].
    10 B.xii. *e*P. Alfonsi, etc. s.xiii–xiv. [D.].
    11 B.iii. *e*Misc. theol. s.xiv in. [V.18].
    12 C.vi. *e*Misc. s.xiii–xiv. [M.83].
    12 F.xv. *e*Sermones, etc. s.xiii–xiv. [S.55].
    IB.40248 (pr. bk). *i*Aristoteles. Paris, s.a.
  Coll. of Arms, Arundel 30. *c*Collectanea J. de Everisden, etc. s.x in.–
        xiv.
[5] Jul. E.vii and Tib. B.ii (fos 2–85) perhaps formed one volume.

London (*contd*)
  Lambeth Palace, 67. *e*Boetius. s.xii. [B.318].
           90. *i*Biblia. s.xiii.
          105, fos 1–133. Ric. Barre in bibliam, etc. s.xiii.
             [R.36].
          120. *c*Hugutio, etc. s.xiv–xv. ?
          218, fos 89–114. *e*J. Cassianus. s.xiv. [J.23].[6]
          218, fos 115–208. Alcuini Epp. s.x. [E.43; *Leland*].[6]
          362. *c*Abbo Floriacensis, etc. s.xi. ?
  Sion Coll., Arc. L.40.2/L.9. Suetonius. s.xii/xiii. [S.18].
  Dr E. G. Millar. *e*Jeronimus. s.xii. [J.7; *cat*. xxxiv].
  The Robinson Trust (Helmingham 58). Medica. s.xiii. [M.36].
New York, Pierpont Morgan, 736. *c*Miracula S. Edmundi, etc. s.xii
  med.
Norwich, Castle Museum, 158.926.4g(4). *l*Processionale. s.xv.
Oswestry, Lord Harlech. *e*Liber epistolaris Ric. de Bury. s.xiv in.
Oxford,
  Bodleian, Add. C.181. *e*Augustinus. s.xii. [A.27; *cat*. lx].
      Auct. 7.Q.7.24 (pr. bk). *e*J. Nyder, etc. Paris, A.D. 1478.
      Bodl. 130. *e*Herbarium, etc. s.xi/xii. [M.44].
          216. *e*Simon de Boraston. s.xiv ex. [B.46].
          225. *e*Sermones Guidonis. s.xiv. [S.30].
          240. *e*Historia aurea. s.xiv ex. [H.55].
          297. *e*Flor. Wigorniensis. s.xii. [C.53].
          356. Alex. Nequam. s.xiii. [A.162; *Leland*].
          412. *e*Postille super Lucam. s.xiii. [B.252].
          426, fos 119–263.[7] P. Blesensis. s.xv.
          715. *e*Explanatio in Ruth, etc. s.xii. [B.220].
          716. *e*Postille super N. T. s.xv in.
          737. *e*Haymo. s.xii. [B.232].
          860. *e*W. de Monte. s.xiii. [B.233].
      Digby 109. *c*Abbo Floriacensis, etc. s.xii/xiii.
      Holkham misc. 37. *e*Guido de Columnis. s.xv.
      Lat. misc. c.26. *e*Jeronimus, etc. s.xii. [J.16; *cat*. cviiij].
      Laud misc. 233. *e*Isidorus, etc. s.xii. [Y.7].
          291. Postille (P. Comestoris). s.xiii in. [B.241].
          742. *e*Leges Langobardorum. s.xii. [L.393;
              Leland].
      or. 174. *e*Psalter (in Hebrew). s.xiii/xiv.
    e Mus. 6. *e*Augustinus. s.xi/xii. [A.8; *cat*. 191a].
          7. *e*Augustinus. s.xi/xii. [A.3; *cat*. 186].
          8. *e*Augustinus. s.xi/xii. [A.2; *cat*. 185].
          9. *e*Florus diaconus. s.xii. [B.290; *cat*. lvii].
         26. *e*Jeronimus. s.xii. [J.10; *cat*. 194].
         27. *e*Ambrosius. s.xii. [A.67; *cat*. xxv].
         31. *e*Augustinus, etc. s.xii. [A.31; *cat*. lxii].
         32. *e*Augustinus. s.xii. [A.24; *cat*. xxxvii].
         33. *e*Augustinus, etc. s.xii. [A. ; *cat*. xiii].
         34. Le livre de Sydrac (in French). s.xiv. ?

---

[6] J.23 and E.43 formed one volume by s.xv.
[7] MS. Bodl. 426 has the arms of the abbey in the initial on fo. 119 and W. B.
twice repeated in the margins, probably for William Babington, abbot 1446–53.

Oxford (*contd*)
 Bodleian,e Mus. 36. *e*Pseudo-Beda. s.xii. [B.280; *cat*. vi].
      112. *e*Jeronimus. s.xii. [J.13; *cf*. *cat*. 196].
   Rawl. C.697. *e*Aldhelmus, etc. s.xi. [A.119; *Leland*].
   Seld. sup.31. *e*Alcoran. s.xiii. [M.10].
 All Souls Coll., 49. *e*Digestum vetus. s.xiii. [L.289].
 Balliol Coll., 175. *e*Beda. s.xii. [B.283; *cf*. *cat*. vii].
 Corpus Christi Coll., 197. *e*Reg. S. Benedicti (in Lat. and Eng.).
                 s.x–xi. [R.70; *cat*. 258].
 St John's Coll., 43. *e*P. Lombardus. s.xii. [P.58].
      209. *c*Chronica. s.xv.
 Trinity Coll., 74. *c*Biblia. s.xiii. [B.15].
Rome, Vatican, Reg. lat. 12. *l*Psalterium, etc. s.xi in.
Wisbech, Museum, 1. *e*Prosper. s.xii. [P.119; *cat*. *after* cix].
Untraced: Sale at Christie's, 25 April 1949, lot 16, to Maggs Bros.
   *i*Boethius (in English). s.xv in.
Rejected: Bury St Edmunds, Cathedral, 3. Cambridge, U.L., Ee.1.14,
   Ff.3.7, Ii.2.16; Corpus Christi Coll., 322, 408; Jesus Coll., 49;
   King's Coll., 21; Pembr. Coll., 6, 13, 14, 82, 86, 93, 106, 110, 113, 116,
   117, 119, 195, 213, 298; St John's Coll., 66, 181. Ispwich, Central
   Libr., 1, 2, 3, 5. London, B.M., Add. 37472(1), Arundel 69, Harley
   1132, 2278, Royal 15 B.ii, 15 C.vi; Victoria and Albert Mus., 661.
   Malvern, Dyson Perrins, 1 (sold 1 Dec. 1959, lot 55). New York,
   Pierpont Morgan, 521, 724. Oxford, Bodleian, Auct. D.3.14,
   Bodl. 387, 582, 816, Digby 112, Laud misc. 85, 357; Magdalen Coll.,
   lat. 172. San Marino, Huntington, EL 9 H. 11. Wisbech, Museum,
   2–7, 9.

BURY ST EDMUNDS. *Franciscan convent.* See **BABWELL.**

BUTLEY, Suffolk. *Aug. priory of B.V.M.*

Ipswich, Central Libr. (pr. bk). *i*W. Lyndwood. Paris, A.D. 1505.
London, B.M., IB.55315 (pr. bk). *i*Alexander de Alexandria. Oxford,
   A.D. 1481.
Rejected: MS. in the Nicholson Museum, University of Sidney.

BYLAND (de Bella Landa), Yorkshire. *Cist. abbey of B.V.M.*

   Books noted by J. Leland, *Collectanea*, iv. 38. *Cf*. Leland, *De Scriptoribus
Britannicis*, p. 291. The common form of *ex libris* inscription is 'Liber sancte
Marie de Bella Landa.'
Cambridge, U.L., Res. b.162 (pr. bk). *e*Missale Ebor. Rouen, s.a.
      Gonv. and Caius Coll., 440. *c*Sermones. s.xiii. ?
      Trinity Coll., 1076. *e*Expositio misse. s.xii.
         1214. *e*Palladius, etc. s.xii ex.
Dublin, Trinity Coll., 45, fos 22 ff. *e*Genesis glo. s.xii ex.
Edinburgh, N.L., Adv. 18.8.19. *e*Arator. s.xii ex.
London,
   B.M., Add. 35180. *e*P. Cantor, etc. s.xiii in.
      38816, fos 18–20.[8] *e*Theodulfus Aurel. s.xii.

   [8] Add. 38816, fos 18–20, are flyleaves of a manuscript containing works of
Hugh of St Victor which belonged to Westminster Abbey in s.xvii and was burnt
in 1694 (M. R. James, *MSS of Westminster Abbey*, p. 43, no. 35).

London (*contd*),
    B.M., Arundel 368. *e*P. Comestor. s.xiii in.
        Cotton Julius A.xi, fo. 114. *e*Versus de contemptu mundi.
            s.xii ex.
        Cleop. B.iv, fos 2–30. *e*H. Huntendonensis. s.xii.
        Faust. B.i, fos 2–11.[9] Epp. Alexandri III pape, etc.
            s.xii ex.
            B.iv, fos 180–82. *e*Vita S. Alexis. s.xii.
      Harley 3641. *e*W. Malmesburiensis. s.xii ex.
      Royal 5 E.xxii. *e*Gregorius Nazianzenus. s.xii.
        8 F.xv.[9] *e*Bernardus. s.xii/xiii.
        15 A.xx. *e*Cicero, etc. s.xii–xiii.
Manchester, J. Rylands, Lat. 153. *e*R. Grosseteste, etc. s.xiii ex.
Oxford, Bodleian, Bodl. 842. *e*Theinredus Doverensis, etc. s.xiv/xv.
        Laud. misc. 149. *e*Steph. Langton. s.xiii.
    St John's Coll., 46. *e*Rob. de Bridlington. s.xii.
Ripon, Mr H. L. Bradfer-Lawrence. *e*Concordancie bibl. s.xiii.
York, Minster, xvi.I.7. *e*Psalterium glo., etc. s.xii.
Untraced: R. Thoresby MS. 99.[1] *e*Letania S. Bernardi, etc.
      Rob. Hoe Sale, Anderson Galleries, 1–5 May 1911, lot 2115 to
        G. D. Smith for T. J. Coolidge. *e*Beda. s.xii ex.

CAERLEON (Kairlion), Monmouthshire.   *Cist. abbey of B.V.M.*

London, B.M., Add. 48984. *e*Gregorius. s.xii ex.
Mostyn Hall, Lord Mostyn. Annales Cestrienses. s.xv/xvi. ?

CAMBRIDGE.   *Gilbertine priory of St Edmund.*

Cambridge, U.L., Ee.6.31.[2] *e*J. de Voragine. s.xiv.
        Trinity Coll., 1395.[2] *e*J. de Voragine. s.xiv.
London, B.M., Add. 18899. *e*P. Lombardus. s.xiv in.

CAMBRIDGE.   *Hospital of St John the Evangelist.*

Cambridge, Corpus Christi Coll., 21. *e*Polychronicon. s.xiv ex.

CAMBRIDGE.   *Franciscan convent.*

  'Notice of some MSS of the Cambridge Friars now in the Vatican', *Collectanea Franciscana*, i (Brit. Soc. for Fran. Studies, v, 1914).
  Books noted by J. Leland, *Collectanea*, iv. 16.
Cambridge,
    Gonv. and Caius Coll., 348. *i*Psalter (in Greek). s.xiv.
           403. *i*New Testament (in Greek). s.xii/xiii.
                ?
Ipswich, Central Libr. (pr. bk). *i*Epp. Eneae Silvii. Nuremberg,
    A.D. 1481. ?
London, B.M., Cotton Cleop. C.ix, fos 63–165. *i*Lamentationes Matheoli.
    s.xv.
          Sloane 1726. *e*P. Riga. s.xiii.
      Middle Temple (pr. bk). *i*Plotinus. Florence, A.D. 1492. ?

---

[9] Cotton Faust. B.i, fos 2–11, formed part of Royal 8 F.xv.
[1] Belonged later to Richard Gough, according to a manuscript note in Gough's
copy of *Ducatus Leodiensis* (Bodleian, Gough Yorks. 60), p. 529.
[2] Trinity Coll. 1395 is the second part of U.L., Ee.6.31.

Oxford, Bodleian, Bodl. 355, fos 159–223.[3] *e*T. Aquinas. s.xiv.
    Balliol Coll., 133. *i*Bonaventura. s.xiv in.
              214.[3] *e*H. de Gandavo. s.xiii ex.
    Corpus Christi Coll., 182.[3] *i*J. Pecham, etc. s.xiv. ?
Rome, Vatican, Ottob. lat.   69. *i*Greg. Ariminensis. ?
                  71. *e*Hugo de S. Caro. s.xiii.
                  96. *e*Hugo de S. Caro.
                101. *e*Eusebius. s.xiv.
                325. *e*P. Comestor. s.xiii.
                352, fos 1–86. *e*Isidorus, etc. s.xiv.
                611. *e*Bonaventura. [4tus bon. ff.].
                623. Nic. Ockham. s.xiv in. [f]. ?
              1126. Ric. Conington, etc. s.xiv. ?
              2048. *e*Aristoteles. s.xiv. [littera f].
              2088. *i*W. Ockham. ?
Salisbury, Cathedral, M.1.27 (pr. bk). *i*Pelbartus de Themeswar.
    Hagenau, A.D. 1521. ?
Untraced: Mostyn sale (Sotheby, 13 July 1920), lot 38, to Maggs, who sold
    to S. Babra of Barcelona in 1923. *i*Euclides. s.xiv. ?
Rejected: Dublin, Trinity Coll., 115. Leicester, Old Town Library, 20.
    Rome, Vatican, Ottob. lat. 1565.

CAMBRIDGE.   *Dominican convent.*
   'Notice of some MSS of the Cambridge Friars now in the Vatican', *Collectanea
Franciscana*, i (Brit. Soc. for Fran. Studies, v, 1914).
   Books noted by J. Leland, *Collectanea*, iv. 15.
London, B.M., Royal 10 B.vii. *e*R. Fishacre. s.xiii. ?
Rome,
    Vatican, Ottob. lat.   99. *e*Anselmus, etc.
              150, i. *e*Gregorius, etc. s.xiii.
              159, fos 1–120. *i*Ces. Arelatensis, etc. s.xiii. ?
              277. *e*H. de S. Victore, etc. s.xiii in.
              442. *e*Bernardus. s.xiii. ?
              640. *e*T. Aquinas. s.xiii.
              758. *i*Barthol. de S. Concordio.
              862. *e*Metaphysica. s.xiv ex.
            2055. *e*Q. Curtius.

CAMBRIDGE.   *Carmelite convent.*
York, Minster, xvi.K.5. *i*W. Hilton. s.xiv/xv. ?

CAMBRIDGE.   *Convent of Austin friars.*
   Books noted by J. Leland, *Collectanea*, iv. 15.
Dublin, Trinity Coll., 115. *i*Misc. theol. s.xiv ex.
Rome, Vatican, Vat. lat. 4954. *e*Augustinus.
            Ottob. lat. 746. *i*P. Riga, etc.

CAMBRIDGE.   *University.*
   [C. Hardwick, etc.], *Cat. of the MSS preserved in the Libr. of the University of
Cambridge*, 5 vols and index (Cambridge, 1856–67). 'Two lists of books [1473
and before 1424] in the U.L.', printed from a MS. in the University Registry by

---

[3] Belonged to the Cambridge custody.

H. Bradshaw, Cambridge Antiq. Soc., *Communications*, ii (1864), 239–78, reprinted in *Coll. Papers of H. Bradshaw* (Cambr., 1889), pp. 16–54; second folios given. For gifts of books between 1415 and 1528 see C. Sayle, *Annals of Cambridge U.L.* (1916), pp. 11–42; for Tunstall's books, also Charles Sturge, *Cuthbert Tunstal* (1938), pp. 392–95. Books noted by John Leland, *Collectanea*, iv. 15, 16–17, and *De Scriptoribus Britannicis*, p. 262, and by J. Bale, *Index* (p. 575).

Books from the medieval library now in the U.L. are not listed here; for them *cf.* N. R. Ker in *Trans. Cambridge Bibliog. Soc.*, i (1949–53), 1–5, and J. C. T. Oates and H. L. Pink, *ibid.*, 310–11.

Cambridge,

Corpus Christi Coll., 68.[4]   Cassiodorus, etc.   A.D. 1432.

King's Coll., 9, ii.[4]   Isidorus, etc.   A.D. 1432.   [*Cat. 1473*, 99].

Trinity Coll., 813.   *e*Polyaeni Strategemata (in Greek).   s.xv/xvi.   ?

Paris, B.N., Lat. 4928.   Rad. de Marham.   s.xiv ex.   [*Cat. 1473*, 72).

Shrewsbury School, E.VI.10 (pr. bk).   *e*T. Gaza.   Venice, A.D. 1495.
[*Tunstall* 13].

CAMBRIDGE.   *Christ's College.*

Thomas Colier, fellow of Michaelhouse, bequeathed 12 specified volumes in 1506 (Cambridge Univ. Wills, 1501–58, fos 16ᵛ–17ᵛ).
Books noted by J. Bale, *Index* (p. 575).

CAMBRIDGE.   *Clare College.*

M. R. James, *Descriptive Cat. of Western MSS in the Libr. of Clare Coll., Cambridge* (Cambr., 1905).   An imperfect catalogue (*c.* 1440) and a list of 'libri non ligati' (1496)—second folios given in both—and other references to books in the Master's Old Book and by Leland (*Collectanea*, iv. 19) and Bale printed by R. W. Hunt, 'Medieval inventories of Clare College Libr.', *Trans. Cambridge Bibliog. Soc.*, i (1949–53), 105–25.   List of books bequeathed by the Lady Elizabeth de Clare, 1360, printed in *Royal Wills*, ed. J. Nichols (London, 1780), p. 31, from the register of Archbishop Islip.   *Cf.* also Leland, *De Scriptoribus Britannicis*, pp. 233, 471.

London, The Robinson Trust (Helmingham 15).   *e*Rasis, etc.   s.xii/xiii.   ?
Oxford,

Bodleian, Bodl. 300.   *e*Astrologica, etc.   s.xv in.   [*Leland*].

Digby 178, fos 15–87.   Ric. Wallingford, etc.   s.xv.
[*Leland*].   ?

183.   Albertus Magnus, etc.   s.xiv ex.   [*Leland*].

Corpus Christi Coll., 150.   *e*Alhacen.   s.xiii.

235.   W. de Northfeld.   s.xv.   [*Bale*].

Magdalen Coll., lat. 195.   *e*Summa Dumbleton.   s.xiv.   [*Bale*].

CAMBRIDGE.   *Corpus Christi College, formerly often called Benet College.*

M. R. James, *Descriptive Cat. of the MSS in the Libr. of Corpus Christi Coll., Cambridge*, 2 vols (Cambr., 1912).   List of about 55 books, A.D. 1376, printed from J. Botener's register among the College records by M. R. James, 'The earliest Inventory of Corpus Christi College', Cambr. Antiq. Soc., *Proc.*, xvi (1912), 89–104, and in abbreviated form by James, *Descriptive Cat.*, I, ix–xi; second folios given.   List of 76 books bequeathed by T. Markaunt, fellow, in 1439, printed by M. R. James, *Sources of Archbishop Parker's Collection* (Cambr. Antiq. Soc., 8vo publ. no. 32, 1899), pp. 76–82, from Corpus Christi College, MS. 232, fos 5–10ᵛ, and list of 12 books given by J. Tyteshale, Master, in 1458, printed by James, *Descriptive Cat.*, i. 533 from the same MS.; second folios given.

---

[4] Corpus Christi Coll., 68, and King's Coll., 9, ii, formed one volume.

MS. 232 contains also a list of books distributed among the fellows in each year from 1439 to 1517 (fos 18–123) and a list of books in the library, apparently in desk order, s.xvi in. (fos 12–14). The latter list is printed by J. M. Fletcher and J. K. McConica, 'A sixteenth-century Inventory of the Library of Corpus Christi College, Cambridge', *Trans. Cambridge Bibliog. Soc.*, iii (1961), 191–99.

Books noted by J. Leland, *Collectanea*, iv. 17, and by J. Bale, *Index*, p. 159. A few MSS probably from the medieval library are catalogued by M. R. James, *Descriptive Cat.*

Cambridge, Univ. Registry. Liber statutorum Univ. Cant. [*Markaunt list* 76].

CAMBRIDGE. *Gonville Hall.*

M. R. James, *Descriptive Cat. of the MSS in the Libr. of Gonville and Caius Coll.*, 3 vols (Cambr., 1907–14). Books noted by J. Leland, *Collectanea*, iv. 29, and by J. Bale, *Index* (p. 575). MSS from the medieval library now in the College library are catalogued by James, *op. cit.*

Cambridge, U.L., Inc. 3856 (pr. bk). *e*J. Sarisburiensis. Brussels, s.a.
London, B.M., Harley 531. *e*Mathematica. s.xii–xiv. ?

CAMBRIDGE. *Jesus College.*

M. R. James, *Descriptive Cat. of the MSS in the Libr. of Jesus Coll., Cambridge* (London, 1895). Books noted by J. Leland, *Collectanea*, iv. 16.

Cambridge, U.L., Ff.6.20. *e*Biblia. s.xiii.

CAMBRIDGE. *King's College* (Collegium regale Beate Marie et Sancti Nicholai).

M. R. James, *Descriptive Cat. of the MSS other than Oriental in the Libr. of King's Coll., Cambridge* (Cambr., 1895). Catalogue (1452) printed from MS. inventory in the college muniments by M. R. James, *op. cit.*, pp. 72–83; second folios given. For the library in the fifteenth century and the early sixteenth century see A. N. L. Munby, 'Notes on King's College Libr. in the fifteenth century', *Trans. Cambridge Bibliog. Soc.*, i (1949–53), 280–86, and W. D. J. Cargill Thompson, 'Notes on King's College Libr., 1500–1570', *ibid.*, ii (1954–58), 38–54. Books noted by J. Bale, *Index* (p. 575).

MSS from the medieval library now in the College library (1(?), 21(?), 27, 40) are catalogued by James, *op. cit.*

Cambridge, U.L., AB.4.54.2 (sel.d) (pr. bk). *e*Solinus. Paris, A.D. 1503.
Leyden, U.L., Scal. Hebr. 8.[5] *e*Psalterium hebraicum. s.xii.
London, B.M., Royal 15 B.iii. *e*Boetius. s.xiv. ?
Oxford, Bodleian, Jones 41. *e*Augustinus. s.xv in.

CAMBRIDGE. *King's Hall.*

C. E. Sayle, 'King's Hall Library', Cambr. Antiq. Soc., *Proc.*, xxiv (1923), 54–76. Lists of 1361/2, 1386, 1391, etc., printed from College muniments and P.R.O., Exch. K.R., Acc. Var. 335/17 by Sayle, *op. cit.*; second folios sometimes given. Books noted by J. Leland, *Collectanea*, iv. 17.

London, B.M., Cotton Claudius B.ix, fos 2–263. Helinandus. s.xv.
    [*Cat.*, p. 72; *Leland*].
    Royal 12 C.xxi. *e*Frontinus. A.D. 1458.

CAMBRIDGE. *Michaelhouse.*

Ampleforth Abbey (pr. bk). *e*T. Aquinas. Venice, A.D. 1493.

[5] The Leyden psalter was earlier at **CANTERBURY,** *St Augustine's, q.v.*

Cambridge, St John's Coll., Qq.3.15 (pr. bk). *e*T. Aquinas. Paris, A.D. 1518.

Trinity Coll., C.15.2 (pr. bk). *e*P. Comestor, etc. Strasbourg, A.D. 1503, etc.

London, Lambeth Palace, **H.1970 (pr. bk). *e*Durandus. Lyon, A.D. 1515.

CAMBRIDGE. *Pembroke College* (Aula Valence S. Marie).

M. R. James, *Descriptive Cat. of the MSS in the Libr. of Pembroke Coll., Cambridge* (Cambr., 1905). G. E. Corrie, 'A list of Books presented to Pembroke Coll., Cambridge, by different donors, during the fourteenth and fifteenth centuries', Cambr. Antiq. Soc., *Communications*, ii (1864), 11–23, printed from a college register; reprinted by M. R. James, *op. cit.*, p. xiii. Books noted by J. Leland, *Collectanea*, iv. 17, and by J. Bale, *Index* (p. 575).

MSS from the medieval library now in the College library are catalogued by James, *op. cit.*

Cambridge, Gonv. and Caius Coll., 467, flyleaf[6] (table of contents).

Colchester, Harsnett Libr., H.f.28 (pr. bk). *e*Aug. de Ancona. (Lyon), s.a.

Leyden, U.L., Lipsius 24. *e*Seneca. s.xiv ex.

London, B.M., Cotton Claudius A.xiv. *e*Nich. de Dacia. s.xv.

Oxford, Bodleian, Laud misc. 85. H. de Costesay, etc. s.xiv ex. [*Cf. Bale*]. ?

Rejected: Cambridge, Gonv. and Caius Coll., 145.

CAMBRIDGE. *Peterhouse* (Collegium Sancti Petri).

M. R. James, *Descriptive Cat. of the MSS in the Libr. of Peterhouse* (Cambr., 1899). Catalogue (1418, with additions s.xv) printed from the oldest College register by M. R. James, *op. cit.*, pp. 3–26; second folios given. List of books bequeathed by John Newton, Master 1381–95 and treasurer of York (†1414), printed from a York register by J. Raine, *Testamenta Eboracensia*, i (Surtees Soc., 1836), 370. Books noted by Leland, *Collectanea*, iv. 21, and *De Scriptoribus Britannicis*, pp. 214, 274, 418, 426, 431, and by J. Bale, *Index* (p. 575).

MSS from the medieval library now in the College library are catalogued by James, *op. cit.*

Cambridge, Magdalene Coll., Pepys 2329. *e*Arithmetica Jordani, etc. s.xv. [*Cat.*, p. 23].

St John's Coll., 55. *e*Quintilianus, etc. s.xiv. [*Cat.* 157].

91. Quintilianus, etc. s.xii–xiv. [*Cat.* 160].

London, B.M., Egerton 889. *e*Astronomica. s.xv. [*Cat.* 210; *Leland*].

Harley 531. *e*Mathematica. s.xiii–xiv. ?

Sloane 59. *e*Medica. s.xv.

Lambeth Palace, 32. *e*Bradwardine. A.D. 1385. [*Cat.* 111].

Royal Coll. of Physicians, 390. *e*J. Aschendon. s.xiv. [*Cat.* 202].

Oxford, Bodleian, Ashmole 424. *e*Witelo. s.xiv. [*Cat.*, p. 23].

Corpus Christi Coll., 151. *e*Haly Abenragel. A.D. 1380. [*Cat.* 204].

CAMBRIDGE. *Queens' College.*

M. R. James, *Descriptive Cat. of the Western MSS in the Libr. of Queens' Coll., Cambridge* (Cambr., 1905). Catalogue (1472, with additions) printed from the

---

[6] The flyleaf of Gonv. and Caius Coll. 467 belongs to Pembroke Coll. 227.

college muniments by W. G. Searle, Cambr. Antiq. Soc., *Communications*, ii (1864), 168–81; second folios given. Books noted by J. Leland, *Collectanea*, iv. 17, and by J. Bale, *Index* (p. 575).

Winchester Coll., 7. *e*P. Lombardus. s.xiii.

CAMBRIDGE. *St Catherine's College.*

M. R. James, *Descriptive Cat. of the MSS in the Libr. of St Catherine's Coll., Cambridge* (Cambr., 1925). Catalogue (1475) printed by G. E. Corrie, Cambr. Antiq. Soc., 4to publ. i (1846), no. 1, reprinted by M. R. James, *op. cit.*, pp. 4–7; second folios given.

CAMBRIDGE. *St John's College.*

Ushaw Coll., XVIII.F.4.18 (pr. bk).[7] *e*Missale Sarisb. Paris, A.D. 1503. ?

CAMBRIDGE. *Trinity Hall.*

M. R. James, *Descriptive Cat. of the MSS in the Libr. of Trinity Hall* (Cambr., 1907). List of books given by the founder (*c.* 1350), printed by G. E. Corrie, Cambr. Antiq. Soc., *Communications*, ii (1864), 74–78.

CAMBRIDGE. *Gild of All Saints.*

Oxford, Bodleian, Rawl. C.541. *c*Statuta, etc. A.D. 1473.

CAMBUSKENNETH, Stirlingshire. *Aug. abbey of B.V.M.* (*Cf.* cell at **INCHMAHOME.**)

For printed books see Durkan and Ross, pp. 132–33.

Glasgow, U.L., BE.8.y.7. *e*Biblia. s.xiii.
Wemyss Castle, Capt. M. J. Erskine-Wemyss. Wyntoun's Chronicle (in English). s.xv in. ?

CAMPSEY, Suffolk. *Priory of B.V.M., of Aug. nuns.*

Cambridge, U.L., Add. 7220. *e*Psalterium. s.xii/xiii. [O.E.; 94].
        Corpus Christi Coll., 268. *i*W. Hilton (in English). s.xv.
London, B.M., Add. 40675. *e*Psalterium, etc. s.xiv. [D.D.; 141].
        Arundel 396. *e*Capgrave (in English). s.xv.
Welbeck Abbey, Duke of Portland, I.C.I.[8] *e*Lives of saints (in French). s.xiv.
Untraced: pr. bk listed in *Catal. Bibliothecae Harleianae* (1744), iii, no. 1560. *i*Chastising of God's children, etc. (in English). London (W. de Worde), A.D. 1493.

CANONS ASHBY (Esseby canonicorum), Northamptonshire. *Aug. priory of B.V.M.*
Hereford, Cathedral, P.iii.1. *i*J. Beleth, etc. s.xiii.

CANONSLEIGH, Devon. *Abbey of B.V.M., St John the Evangelist, and St Etheldreda, of Aug. nuns.*

---

[7] The Marian *ex libris* of Ushaw Coll., XVIII.F.4.18 suggests that this missal was at St John's Coll. earlier in the sixteenth century.
[8] On deposit in the British Museum, loans no. 29/61.

London, B.M., Cotton Cleop. C.vi. *e*Ancrene Riwle (in English). s.xiii in.

Rejected: Oxford, Bodleian, Bodl. 9.

CANTERBURY (Cantuaria), Kent. *Ben. cathedral priory of Holy Trinity or Christ Church. (Cf.* cells at **DOVER** and **OXFORD,** *Canterbury College.)*

M. R. James, *The Ancient Libraries of Canterbury and Dover* (Cambr., 1903), prints a fragmentary cat. (s.xii) from Cambridge, U.L., MS. Ii.3.12; Henry of Eastry's cat. (s.xiv in.) from London, B.M., Cotton MS. Galba E.iv; list of H. of Eastry's books (1331) from Canterbury, Ch. Ch., MS. 52 (extracts given by J. Leland, *Collectanea*, iv. 120); list of missing books (1337) from Canterbury, Ch. Ch., Registrum L; list of Thomas Chillenden's books (1411) from Canterbury, Ch. Ch., MS. C.166 (also printed in *Litterae Cantuar.* (Rolls Series), iii. 121); W. Ingram's list of 293 books (1508) from Canterbury, Ch. Ch., MS. 27 (second folios given);[9] Leland's notes of books from *Collectanea*, iv. 10. To the lists printed by M. R. James add a list of liturgical books (s.xii ex.) in London, B.M., Cotton MS. Aug. ii.32; the inventory of 'textus' (1316) printed from Cotton MS. Galba E.iv by J. Dart, *Hist. and Antiq. of the Cath. Ch. of Canterbury* (London, 1726), appendix vi, p. iv, and in *Inventories of Ch. Ch., Canterbury*, ed. J. Wickham Legg and W. H. St John Hope (London, 1902), pp. 78–79; lists of books found in the 'cubiculum' of Richard Stone (s.xvi in.), of books liberated for the use of Robert Holingbourne (*c*.1495 and *c*.1508), Thomas Goldwell (*c*.1496), and John Dunstone (1501–2), and of books formerly belonging to Robert Eastry, Warden of Canterbury College (*c*.1496), printed from records at Canterbury Cathedral by W. A. Pantin, *Canterbury Coll., Oxford,* i (Oxf. Hist. Soc., N.S., vi, 1947), 80–88. Manuscripts illuminated at Christ Church between 1050 and 1200 are listed and discussed by C. R. Dodwell, *The Canterbury School of Illumination* 1954.

References to the fragmentary cat. appear as 'old cat.', to Henry of Eastry's cat. as 'cat.'; other lists are referred to as 'H. of Eastry', 'Chillenden', and 'Ingram' respectively.

The common form of pressmark, which records the *Distinctio* and *Gradus* numbers (for these terms see M. R. James, *op. cit.*, pp. xxxviii–xliv), is reproduced from B.M., Cotton Vesp. B.xix and Royal 12 D.iv in *New Pal. Soc.*, i, pl. 17, no. 2 *a, b.* In some MSS the number of the *Demonstratio* (or *Monstratio*) is also entered. Many of the older MSS contain a mark consisting of a letter or letters or of a symbol, written at the top right-hand corner of the first page of text. Similar marks are written against the entries in the catalogues of s.xii, and the marks in Cambridge, Corpus Christi Coll., 260, and Trinity Coll., 289 and 944, correspond to these catalogue-marks (see M. R. James, *op. cit.*, pp. xxxii, xxxiii). The letters, but not the symbols, are recorded below. Common forms of *ex libris* inscription are 'de claustro ecclesie Cristi Cant.' and 'liber ecclesie Cristi Cant.', but many MSS have only a personal name in the genitive case following the short title, *e.g.* Cambridge, Corpus Christi Coll. 76, i, 'Annales Stephani Archiepiscopi'.

Ampleforth Abbey (pr. bk). *i*Joannes Franciscus, Brixianus. Venice,
A.D. 1500.

Cambridge,
    U.L., Dd.1.4.[1] *e*Josephus. s.xii. [*Cat.* 339, *Ingram* 149].
    Dd.2.7. *e*Jeronimus. s.xii. [.L.; *cat.* 211, *Ingram* 110].
    Dd.8.15. Haymo. s.xi/xii. [*Cat.* 164, *Ingram* 73].
    Ff.3.9. Gregorius. s.xii. [*Cat.* 144, *Ingram* 130].
    Ff.3.19. *g*P. Lombardus. s.xiv. [*Cat.* 1554, *Ingram* 35].
    Ff.3.20. *e*Augustinus. s.xiv. [*Cat.* 13 *or* 14, *Ingram* 95].
    Ff.3.28. *g*Epp. Pauli glo. s.xiii. [*H. of Eastry* 4].

[9] In *The Library*, N.S., xxiii (1942), 10–11, I suggested that Ingram's is a complete or almost complete list of the collection of chained books.
[1] Part ii is Cambridge, St John's Coll. 8.

Cambridge (*contd*).
U.L., Ff.3.29.   Isidorus.   s.xii.   [*Cat*. 195, *Ingram* 59; *Leland*].
     Ff.4.43.   Smaragdus.   s.ix.   [*Cat*. 118, *Ingram* 268].
     Ff.5.31.   *e*J. de Voragine.   s.xiii ex.
     Gg.4.17.   *e*P. Cantor, etc.   s.xiii in.   (*Cat*. 988, *Ingram* 280].
     Ii.1.41.   Prosper, etc.   s.xii.   [D.v. G.ii Dem.i; *cat*. 232, *Ingram* 293].
     Ii.2.1.   *m*Priscianus.   s.xii in.   ?
     Ii.3.1.   *i*Polychronicon.   s.xiv.
     Ii.3.12.   *e*Boetius.   s.xii.   [*Cat*. 354].
     Ii.3.33.   Gregorius.   s.xi/xii.   [*Cat*. 152, *Ingram* 128].
     Kk.1.20.   Warnerius, etc.   s.xiii.   [.Wa., D.iiii G.ii; *cat*. 156, *Ingram* 143].
     Kk.1.23.   Ambrosius.   s.xii.   [.T., D.ii G.vii: *cat*. 59, *Ingram* 136].
     Kk.1.28.   *i*Isidorus, etc.   s.xiii.   [.Sy., D.xiiii G.xi; *cat*. 1166, *Ingram* 61].
Corpus Christi Coll.,   19.   *e*Ivo Carnotensis.   s.xii.   [*Cat*. 351].
     46.   *g*J. Sarisberiensis.   s.xii–xv.   [D.ii G.x; *cat*. 853, *Ingram* 176].
     51.   *g*Eusebius.   s.xii.   [D.vi G.xiii Dem.i; *cat*. 282, *Ingram* 152].
     63, i–iii.   *g*Anselmus, etc.   s.xiii–xiv.
     63, iv.   Bernardus.   s.xiii.   [D.iii G.xiii].
     76, i.   *g*Rad. de Diceto.   s.xiii in.   [*Cat*. 1438].
     137.   *e*Philosophia monachorum.   s.xiv.
     158.[2]   Cicero.   s.xv.   ?
     173.   Anglo-Saxon chronicle (in English), Seldulius, etc.   s.viii–xi.   [? *Cat*. 311].
     187.   Eusebius.   s.xi/xii.   [? *Cat*. 186, *Ingram* 155].
     192.   Amalarius.   s.x.   [*Cat*. 74].
     200.   Baldewinus.   s.xii ex. [*Cat*. 94].
     222.[3]   Ric. de S. Victore.   s.xiii.
     226.[3]   *i*Simon Langton, etc.   s.xiii.   [*Cat*. 1310].
     260.   Musica Hogeri, etc.   s.x.   [TT.; *old cat*. 44].
     263.   Hon. Augustodunensis.   s.xiii.   ?
     272.   *b*Psalterium, etc.   s.ix ex.   ?
     288.   *i*Alanus prior, etc.   s.xii–xiii.   [*Cat*. 1389].
     295.   *e*T. Becket.   s.xiii in.   [? *Cat*. 358].
     298, i–ii.   *c*Collectanea.   s.xvi in.
     304.   *ms*Juvencus.   s.viii in.   [*Old cat*. 152].
     326.   Aldelmus.   s.x/xi.   [dc., D.ii G.iiii Dem.i; *cat*. 47].
     337.   *g*Scintillarium.   s.xiii.   ?
     341 (inserted leaf).   *s*Eadmerus.   s.xi ex.
     345.   Hilarius.   s.xii.   [*Cat*. 886, *Ingram* 125; *Leland*].
     371.   Eadmerus.   s.xii in.   [*Cat*. 257].

---

[2] A sixteenth-century note wrongly connects this volume with Archbishop Theodore of Canterbury. *Cf*. M. R. James, in *The Library*, vii (1927), 350.
[3] Corpus Christi Coll. 222 and 226 appear to have formed one volume originally; the flyleaves of 226 are in 222.

Cambridge (*contd*)

Corpus Christi Coll., 375.[4] Passio S. Katerine, etc. s.xii/xiii. [D.vii
G.viii; *Cat.* 281, *Stone* 10].

400, iv. *c*Versus. s.xiii ex.

403.[5] Euripides (in Greek). s.xv. ?

411. Psalterium. s.x. ?

417. *c*J. Stone chronica, etc. s.xv ex.

438. *c*Gerv. Cantuariensis. s.xiii–xv.

441. *g*Miscellanea. s.xiii. [*Cat.* 1420].

452. Eadmerus. s.xi. [*Cat.* 188 or 189].

457. *e*Alex. Cantuariensis. s.xii in. [.AN.;
? *cat.* 114].

S.P.71.[6] *m*Binding leaf in *Opus historiarum* (Basel,
A.D. 1541). s.xii.

Pembr. Coll., 148. Daniel glo. s.xii. [.Da.; *cf. cat.* 874]. ?

149. XII prophete glo. s.xiii. [*Prop.*; *cf. cat.* 875]. ?

210. Numeri glo. s.xii. [.NV., D.iii G.ii; *cat.* 862].

St John's Coll., 5, i. Ambrosius. s.xii. [.V.; *cat.* 51 *or* 52, *Ingram*
138].

8, i.[7] Josephus. s.xii. [J–C; *cat.* 340, *Ingram* 148].

30. *g*P. Cantor. s.xiii in. [D.vii G.v Dem.ii; *cat.*
1182].

51. *e*Concordancie bibl. s.xiii/xiv. [*Ingram* 5].

52. *g*T. Aquinas. s.xiv. [*H. of Eastry* 7, *Ingram* 10].

130. H. de S. Victore. s.xii. [D.iii G.xi; *cat.* 173].

Trinity Coll., 16. Jeronimus. s.xii. [.K.; *cat.* 208, *Ingram* 113].

20. Ambrosius. s.xiii in. [*Cat.* 60, *Ingram* 135].

23. H. de S. Victore. s.xii. [D.iiii G.vii Dem.i; *cat.*
176, *Ingram* 270].

45. *e*J. Chrysostomus. s.xiv. [*Ingram* 66].

46. Beda. s.xii. [*Cat.* 87, *Ingram* 121].

47. Rabanus. s.xii. [D.v G.xii; *cat.* 240, *Ingram*
53].

52. Hesychius. s.xii. [D.iii G.xi (?) Dem.i; *cat.* 123,
Ingram 64].

68. *e*R. Holcot. s.xiv ex. [*Ingram* 139].

74. *g*Pseudo-Dionysius, etc. s.xii. [Je, D.iii G.xi;
cat. 888, *Ingram* 107].

76. Augustinus, etc. s.xii. [*Cat.* 17, *Ingram* 88].

77. Jeronimus. s.xii in. [.M.; *cat.* 197, *Ingram* 114].

79. J. Chrysostomus, etc. s.xii–xiii. [.ph., D.v G.iii;
cat. 213, *Ingram* 74].

83. Jeronimus. s.xii. [.A.; *cat.* 199, *Ingram* 115].

84.[8] Jeronimus. s.xii. [.h., D.v G.i; *cat.* 206–7,
Ingram 117].

[4] The flyleaf of Corpus Christi Coll. 375, bearing the pressmark, is at Canterbury Cathedral in 'Scrapbook B'.

[5] A sixteenth-century note wrongly connects this volume with Archbishop
Theodore of Canterbury. *Cf.* M. R. James, in *The Library*, vii (1927), 350.

[6] Assigned on the evidence of marks in the margins, for which see N. R. Ker in
Brit. Mus. Quarterly, xiv (1940), 85.

[7] Part i is Cambridge, U.L., Dd.1.4.

[8] Part i is Cambridge, Trinity Coll. 107.

Cambridge (*contd*)
Trinity Coll.,
85. *g*Matheus et Marcus glo. s.xiii.
88. Ambrosius. s.xii. [D.ii G.v (?); *cat.* 49, *Ingram* 134].
89. Ambrosius. s.xii. [.y.; *cat.* 61, *Ingram* 133].
90. XII prophete glo. s.xii/xiii. [.*pro.*; ? *cat.* 797 *or* 875, *Ingram* 54].
91. Josue, etc., glo. s.xiii in. [.an.; *Ingram* 36].
92. *e*Angelomus. s.xii. [D.ii G.v; *cat.* 46, *Ingram* 49].
93.⁹ Ric. Pratellensis. s.xii. [D.v G.) ix; *cat.* 226].
98. *sm*Postille in Danielem, etc. s.xiii ex. [*Cat.* 924, *Ingram* 109].
100. J. Chrysostomus. s.xv ex. [*Ingram* 69].
104. Augustinus. s.xi. [*Cat.* 33, *Ingram* 96].
107.¹ Jeronimus. s.xii/xiii. [*Cat.* 205, *Ingram* 116].
108. Esaias glo. s.xii ex. [.BN.; ? *cat.* 792 *or* 871, *Ingram* 41].
109. Jeremias glo. s.xii ex. [.aa.; ? *cat.* 793 *or* 872, *Ingram* 40].
110. Augustinus. s.xii. [? *Cat.* 10 *or* 11, *Ingram* 91].
111. Augustinus, etc. s.xii. [.p., D.i G.xi; *cat.* 19, *Ingram* 86].
112. *e*Augustinus. s.xii. [.F., D.i G.xii; *cat.* 23, *Ingram* 97].
116. Augustinus. s.xi/xii. [*Cat.* 6, *Ingram* 89].
118. Libri Salomonis glo. s.xiii. [? *Cat.* 1390, *Ingram* 50].
119.² Florus diaconus. s.xii. [*Cat.* 8, *Ingram* 118].
120. Origenes. s.xii. [A; *cat.* 220, *Ingram* 75].
123. *e*Gregorius. s.xii. [*Cat.* 332, *Ingram* 131].
132. T. Aquinas. s.xiv in. [*Cat.* 1777 *or H. of Eastry* 3, *Ingram* 15].
133. T. Aquinas. s.xiv in. [*Cat.* 1778 *or H. of Eastry* 2, *Ingram* 16].
135. Ric. Pratellensis. s.xii/xiii. [*Ingram* 63].
137. *g*Epp. Pauli glo. s.xii/xiii. [*Cat.* 1339, *Ingram* 90].
139. Augustinus. s.xii. [? *Cat.* 1 *or* 2, *Ingram* 85].
140. *e*Augustinus. s.xii. [Dem.i D.i; *cat.* 34, *Ingram* 99].
141. Isidorus. s.x. [*Ingram* 60].
142. Jeronimus. s.xii. [.B.; *cat.* 203, *Ingram* 101].
144. Libri regum glo. s.xii/xiii. [? *Cat.* 100, *Ingram* 34].
150.³ Psalterium glo. s.xii ex. [*Cat.* 854, *Ingram* 56].
151. Evangelia glo. s.xii/xiii. [.ab.; ? *cat.* 799, *Ingram* 48].

⁹ Part i is Lambeth Palace 62.
¹ Part ii is Cambridge, Trinity Coll. 84.
² Part ii is Oxford, Bodleian, Bodl. 317.
³ Part ii is Oxford, Bodleian, Auct. E.inf.6.

Cambridge (*contd*)
Trinity Coll., 152–53. Epp. Pauli glo. s.xii ex. [Bos, D.ii G.xii;
cat. 856–57, *Ingram* 45–46].
154. *e*Augustinus. s.xiv ex. [*Ingram* 92].
154 (flyleaves). *g*Johannes in collectario. s.xv in.
[*Chillenden* 5, *cf. Ingram* 223].
163. *e*Paralipomenon, etc., glo. s.xiii. [*Cat.* 1325,
Ingram 58].
164. Augustinus. s.xv. [*Ingram* 79].
164 (flyleaf). Gregorius. [D.iiii G. ; *cf. cat.* 143,
Ingram 131].
168. Jeronimus. s.xii. [.C.; *cat.* 202, *Ingram* 103].
169. *e*Jeronimus. s.xii. [.D.; *cat.* 200, *Ingram* 100].
170. *e*Jeronimus. s.xii. [.E.; *cat.* 201, *Ingram* 102].
172. *e*Augustinus. s.xii in. [*Cat.* 324, *Ingram* 76].
174. *e*Augustinus. s.xii in. [*Cat.* 326, *Ingram* 78].
222.[4] Psalter (in Greek). s.xiv/xv. [? *Leland*]. ?
289. Arator. s.x/xi. [FF, D.ii G.xiii; old cat. 106,
cat. 79].
342. *g*P. Comestor. s.xii/xiii. [Dem.ii; *cat.* 1084].
346.[5] *m*H. de S. Victore. s.xii. [? *Cat.* 172].
377.[5] *m*A. de Hales. s.xv.
382. *e*T. Aquinas. s.xiv. [*Cat.* 1671, *Ingram* 11].
383. P. Lombardus. s.xiii. [*Cat.* 1649, *Ingram* 23].
384. *e*T. Aquinas. s.xiv. [*Cat.* 1666, *Ingram* 12].
385. T. Aquinas. s.xiii/xiv. [*Cat.* 1670, *Ingram* 9].
386. *e*Egidius Romanus. s.xiv. [*Cat.* 1676].
391. *g*Odo Morimundensis. s.xii. [D. G.v; *cat.* 833].
405. *e*Collectio Lanfranci. s.xi ex. [Dem.ii; *Ingram*
202].
407. *g*Hostiensis. s.xiii. [*H. of Eastry* 41, *Ingram*
234].
637. *e*T. Livius. s.xii. [*Cat.* 816, *Ingram* 154].
644. *c*Gerv. Cantuariensis. s.xiv. ?
729. *e*Gerv. Cantuariensis. s.xiv/xv. ?
829. *i*Miscellanea. s.xv.
944. *e*Boetius, etc. s.xii in. [.EE.; old cat. 39, cat.
438].
969. *e*Barth. Anglicus. s.xiv. [*Ingram* 266].
987.[6] *l*Psalterium ('Canterbury psalter'). s.xii med.
[*Cat.* 323].
990–91. Jeronimus. A.D. 1477–78. [*Ingram* 112, 111].
1155 (flyleaves).[7] Passionale S. Ignacii. s.xii. [*Cat.*
360].

[4] A sixteenth-century note wrongly connects this volume with Archbishop
Theodore of Canterbury.
[5] Assigned on the evidence of marks in the margins: *cf.* p. 31, n. 6.
[6] Four leaves containing biblical illustrations, now London, B.M. Add.
37472(1), Victoria and Albert Mus., 661, and New York, Pierpont Morgan
Libr., 521 and 724, may have formed part of Trinity Coll., 987: see C. R. Dodwell, *The Canterbury School of Illumination* (1954), pp. 99–102.
[7] Two flyleaves of Trinity Coll. 1155 belong to London, B.M., Cotton Otho
D.viii, fos 8–173.

Cambridge (*contd*)
Trinity Coll., 1264.   Orosius. s.xii in. [BY.; *cat.* 221].
         1266.[8] Ethicus, etc. [*Cat.* 221].
         1438. *c*Statuta, etc. s.xiv.
         1480.[9] *s*Eutropius, etc. s.xii in. ?
         1483.[9] *s*Victor Vitensis, etc. s.xii in. ?
Cambridge (U.S.A.), Harvard University, Houghton Libr. Typ. 3.
  *i*Biblia, pars i. s.xiii. [D.iii G.iiii].
Canterbury,
  Cathedral, 1. *i*Egidius Romanus. s.xv. [*Ingram* 269].
            11. J. de Baro. s.xv. [*Ingram* 242].
            13. Otto et Ottobonus glo. s.xv. [*Ingram* 221].
            14. *i*Decretales, etc. s.xiv ex. [*Ingram* 235].
            15. *g*Summa decretalium. s.xiii ex. [Dem.ii; *cat.* 1493,
                  Ingram 217].
            16. *e*Samson de Calvo Monte. s.xiv. [*Chillenden* 23,
                  Ingram 250].
            17. *e*J. Hispanus, etc. s.xiii. [Dem.i; *cat.* 628, *Ingram*
                  237].
            26. *i*Memoranda T. Cawston. s.xv ex.
            37. *i*T. de Chabham, etc. s.xiv.
            42. *i*Hugo de S. Caro. s.xiii. [*Cat.* 1597, *Ingram* 20].
            43. *i*W. Ingram. s.xv ex.
            45. *i*Steph. Langton. s.xiii. [*Cat.* 1214–16, *Ingram*
                  37–39, *Leland*].
            46.[1] *m*Passionale. s.xii. [*Cat.* 359, 360, 364, 365].
            53. *i*Misc. jur. s.xiv in.–xiv ex.
            57, ii. De primatu Romane eccl. s.xi ex.
            57, iii. *g*Sermones. s.xii. [D.xiiii G.ii; *cat.* 1122].
            62. *i*Preces. s.xiv/xv.
            65. *e*Ric. de Mediavilla. s.xiv. [*Ingram* 22].
            67. *g*Sermones. s.xiii in. [*Cf. Cat.* 577].
            74. *g*Duns Scotus. s.xiv.
            75. Duns Scotus. s.xiv. [*Ingram* 29].
          100. Tabula speculi historialis. s.xiv. [*Ingram* 141].
          104. *g*W. Northwicensis. s.xiii/xiv. [*Cat.* 1810].
        Add. 6. *lc*Breviarium, etc. s.xiv.
        Add. 17. *c*Chronicle (in French; 9 fos). s.xiv.
        Add. 25. Gregory, Dialogues (in English; 4 fos). s.x ex.
                [*Cf. cat.* 306]. ?
        Box ABC. Cassiodorus, In Psalmos (1 fo.). s.xii. [*Cf.*
                cat. 329]. ?
        Box CCC, no. 19a. Regula Chrodegangi (in Latin and
                English; 2 fos). s.xi ex. [*Cf. cat.*
                371]. ?
        Box CCC, no. 23. *s*Ivo Carnot., Epp. (3 fos). s.xii in.
                [*Cf. cat.* 126]. ?

---

[8] Destroyed in Mommsen's fire; originally one with the preceding volume.
[9] Trinity Coll. 1480 and 1483 formed one volume and were probably part of Trinity Coll. 1264 and 1266.
[1] Fragments (72 fos) recovered from bindings of books of the archdeacon's court.

Canterbury (*contd*)
    Cathedral, Chart. Antiq. A.42.[2] *c*Vite paparum et archiepiscoporum
                     Cantuar. s.xiii ex.
        Register J. *c*W. de Henley (in French), etc. s.xiv.
        Register P. *c*W. de Henley (in French), etc. s.xiii–xiv.
Chichester, Cathedral (pr. bk). *i*Gregorius, Moralia. Paris, A.D. 1495.
Douai, Bibl. mun., 202. *g*Joh. Scotus. s.xii. [D.iii G.xii; *cat.* 887,
                    Ingram 108].
Dublin, Trinity Coll., 98. *s*Pontificale. s.xii. ?
           124. *g*Gilb. Altissiodorensis. s.xii/xiii. [.OG.;
                 cat. 1096].
          371.[3] Ethicus, etc. s.xii. [D.iii G.xiiii; *cat.* 137].
Eton Coll., 78. *l*Psalterium. s.xiii.
          91.[4] Ovidius; De mirabilibus mundi. s.xiii. [*Cf. cat.*
             632]. ?
London,
    B.M., Add. 6159. *c*Walter de Henley (in French), etc. s.xiii–xiv.
          6160. *c*Kalendarium, etc. s.xiii–xiv.
        37517. *l*Psalterium ('Bosworth psalter'). s.x. ?
        45103. Historia Trojanorum, etc. s.xiii ex. [*Ingram* 161].
    Arundel 16. Osbernus. s.xii. ?
          68. *c*Martyrologium, etc. s.xiv–xvi.
        155. *i*Psalterium, etc. s.xi in.
    Cotton Aug. ii.32. *c*Catalogus librorum. s.xii ex.
        Tib. A.ii.[5] *e*Evangelia, etc. s.ix.
             A.iii, fos 2–173. Reg. S. Benedicti, etc. (Lat. and
                Eng.). s.xi. [? *Cat.* 296].
             A.iii, fos 174–77.[6] *c*Regularis concordia (Lat. and
                Eng.). s.xi.
             B.iii, fos 2–11. *l*Kalendarium, etc. s.xii ex.
             B.iv, fo. 87.[7] Charters (in English). s.xi in.
        Calig. A.xiv, fos 1–92. *l*Troparium. s.xi–xii. ?
             A.xv, fos 120–53. *c*Computistica, etc. (Lat. and
                Eng.). s.xi ex.
        Claud. A.iii, fos 2–7, 9*.[8] Charters (Eng. and Lat.).
                s.xi.
             A.iii, fos 9–18, 87–105. *l*Benedictionale. s.xi. ?
             A.iii, fos 19–29. *s*Ordo coronationis. s.xii. ?
             C.vi, fos 170–203.[9] *c*Miscellanea. s.xii. [*Cat.*
                291].
        E.v. *s*Pseudo-Isidorus. s.xii. [*Cat.* 352, *Ingram*
             197].

   [2] A roll of six membranes.
   [3] Dublin, Trinity Coll. 371, and London, B.M., Cotton Domit. v, fos 2–14,
formed one volume.
   [4] Eton Coll. 91 was later at Winchester Coll., *q.v.*
   [5] Claud. A.iii, fos 2–7, 9*, and Faust. B.vi, part 1, fos 95, 98–100, were parts
of Tib. A.ii.
   [6] Tib. A.iii, fos 174–77, was part of Faust. B.iii, fos 159–98.
   [7] Tib. B.iv, fo. 87, was part of Lambeth Palace 1370.
   [8] Claud. A.iii, fos 2–7, 9*, and Faust. B.vi, part 1, fos 95, 98–100, were parts
of Tib. A.ii.
   [9] Claud. C.vi, fos 170–203, was part of Royal 7 E.vi.

London (*contd*)

Cotton Nero A.viii, fos 1–86. *m*Annales, etc. s.xii.
C.vii, fos 29–79.[1] *c*Passionale. s.xii. [*Cat.* 362].
C.ix, fos 3–18. *c*Martyrologium. s.xiii.
C.ix, fos 19–21.[2] *c*Obituarium. s.xii. [D.viiG.ii; *cat.* 292].
Galba A.xix.[3] Proverbs of Alfred (in English). s.xiii in. [*Cat.* 954].
E.iii. *c*Chronica. s.xiii ex.
E.iv, fos 1–186. *g*Memoriale. s.xiv. [*H. of Eastry* 69].
Otho D.viii, fos 8–173.[4] Passionale S. Ignacii. s.xii. [*Cat.* 360].
Vit. C.iii. Herbal (in English). s.xi. [? *Cat.* 308]. ?
Vesp. B.xix. Gerv. Cantuar. s.xiii. [D.vi G.xiiii; *cat.* 284].
B.xxv. *i*Solinus, etc. s.xii. [D.v G.xiiii (?); *cat.* 244].
D.xix. *e*Versus Nigelli, etc. s.xii ex. [D.vi G.xi.i.; *cat.* 278].
Domit. v, fos 2–14.[5] Ep. Radulfi archiepiscopi, etc. s.xii. [*Cat.* 137].
viii, fos 30–70. *s*Chronicle (Lat. and Eng.). s.xi/xii. [*Cat.* 318].
Cleop. E.i, fos 16–55. *c*Professiones episcoporum, etc. s.xii.
Faust. B.iii, fos 159–98.[6] *c*Regularis concordia. s.xi.
B.vi, part 1, fos 95, 98–100.[7] Epp. paparum. s.xii in.

Egerton 2867. *e*Biblia. s.xiii.
3314. *c*'Ædthelardus de compoto', etc. s.xi–xii. [*Cf. cat.* 287].
Harley 315, fos 1–39.[8] *cm*Passionale. s.xii. [*Cat.* 362].
624, fos 84–143.[8] *c*Passionale. s.xii. [*Cat.* 362].
636. *e*Brut (in French). s.xiv. [*Ingram* 281].
1587, fos 1–188. *i*Grammatica, etc. A.D. 1396–s.xv/xvi.
Royal 1 A.xiv. Gospels (in English). s.xii in. [D.xvi G.iiii; *cat.* 314].
1 D.ix. *c*Evangelia. s.x. ?
1 E.vii–viii. *e*Biblia. s.x ex. [? *Cat.* 321]. ?

[1] Nero C.vii, fos 29–79, Harley 315, fos 1–39, and Harley 624, fos 84–143, are fragments of one volume.
[2] Nero C.ix, fos 19–21, and Lambeth Palace 430, flyleaves, are fragments of one volume.
[3] Galba A.xix and Oxford, Bodleian, Digby 4 formed one volume.
[4] Otho D.viii, fos 8–173, and Cambridge, Trinity Coll. 1155, flyleaves, are fragments of one volume.
[5] Dublin, Trinity Coll. 371 and Domit. v, fos 2–14, formed one volume.
[6] Tib. A.iii, fos 174–77, was part of Faust. B.iii, fos 159–98.
[7] Faust. B.vi, part 1, fos 95, 98–100, and Claud. A.iii, fos 2–7, 9*, were parts of Tib. A.ii.
[8] Nero C.vii, fos 29–79, Harley 315, fos 1–39, and Harley 624, fos 84–143, are fragments of one volume.

London (*contd*)

    Royal 2 D.xxxii. Ailredus, etc. s.xiii. [.SS., D.ii G.xii; *cat.* 78, *Ingram* 278, *Leland*].

          7 C.iv. *e*Defensor (Lat. and Eng.). s.xi. [*Cat.* 246].

          7 E.vi, fos 2–103.[9] Martyrologium, etc. s.xii. [D.vii G.xiii; *cat.* 291].

         10 A.xiii. *i*Smaragdus. s.xii/xiii. [D.iii G.xii; *cat.* 139].

         10 B.ix. *i*Epistole, etc. s.xv.

         12 D.iv. Helpericus, etc. s.xii in. [D.iii G.ii; *cat.* 91, *Ingram* 123].

    IB.48104 (pr. bk). *i*Bonaventura. Zwolle, A.D. 1479.

Coll. of Arms, Arundel 20. *e*Chronica. s.xiv.

Inner Temple, 511.10. Macrobius. s.xii in. [D.viii G.ix M⁰.i; *old cat.* 54, *cat.* 421].

Lambeth Palace, 20. *c*Martyrologium, etc. s.xvi in.

         59, fos 1–190. *e*Anselmus, etc. s.xii. [D.ii G.x, Dem. i; *cat.* 71, *Ingram* 145].

         62.[1] Ric. Pratellensis. s.xii. [*Cat.* 225].

         78. *e*W. Chartham. s.xv med.

         142, fos 153–204. *g*Unum ex quatuor glo. s.xii. [D.ii G.xii; *cat.* 1184].

         159, fos 1–271. *i*Vite sanctorum. s.xvi in. [*Cf. Stone* 42].

         180. *e*Russell super cantica, etc. s.xiv in.

         194. *e*De sedacione scismatis, etc. s.xiv ex. [*Ingram* 172].

         303. *g*Gerv. Cantuar., etc. s.xv. ?

         399. *g*Summa Raymundi, etc. s.xiii ex.

         415. *e*Epp. Cantuarienses. s.xiii in. [D.iii G.xiii, Dem.i (ii); *cat.* 134 *or* 135, *Leland*].

         430 (flyleaves).[2] *l*Obituarium. s.xii.

         558. *i*Psalterium, etc. s.xiii ex. –xv in.

         1212.[3] *c*Miscellanea. s.xiii–xiv.

         1370.[3] *e*Evangelia ('Macdurnan Gospels'). s.ix.

Public Record Office, Exch. T.R., Misc. Bks 196, pp. 31–66. *c*De anno jubileo S. Thome martyris, 1420.

Sion Coll., Arc. L.40.2/L.2. *g*Psalterium, etc. s.xiv in. ?

         Arc. L.40.2/L.31. Johannes Andreae. s.xiv. [*Ingram* 201, ? *Chillenden* 2].

         Arc. L.40.2/L.32. J. Lathbury. s.xv. [*Ingram* 186].

Manchester, Northwestern Congregational Coll., 1. *b*Biblia. s.xiii.

Oxford,

    Bodleian, Add. C.260. *l*Kalendarium. s.xii.

         Ashmole 1525. *c*Psalterium, etc. s.xiii. ?

         Auct. D.2.2. *e*Psalterium, etc. s.xiv.

         E.inf.6.[4] Psalterium glo. s.xii/xiii. [BOS., D.ii G.xi; *cat.* 855, *Ingram* 57].

---

[9] Claud. C.vi, fos 170–203, was part of Royal 7 E.vi.
[1] Part ii is Cambridge, Trinity Coll. 93.
[2] Nero C.ix, fos 19–21, and Lambeth Palace 430, flyleaves, are fragments of one volume.   [3] Tib. B.iv, fo. 87, was part of the Macdurnan Gospels.
[4] Part i is Cambridge, Trinity Coll. 150.

Oxford (*contd*)
  Bodleian, Auct. E.inf.7. Pentateuchus glo. s.xii ex. [.to.; *cat.* 784].
      Bodl. 1. Alcuinus, etc. s.xiii. [*Cf. cat.* 77].
          97. Aldhelmus. s.xi. [sx, D.ii G.v; *cat.* 48].
        160. Beda, etc. s.xii. [O; *cat.* 88, *Ingram* 124].
        161. Beda, etc. s.xii. [*Cat.* 85, *Ingram* 122].
        196. *m*Ambrosius, etc. s.xiii–xiv.
        214. *e*T. Aquinas. s.xiii/xiv. [*Cat.* 1668, *Ingram* 7].
        217. Beda. s.xii. [R; *cat.* 89, *Ingram* 120].
        251. *e*N. de Lyra. s.xiv ex. [*Ingram* 1].
        271. Anselmus. s.xii–xv. [D.ii G.viii, i Dem.i; *cat.*
               62, *Ingram* 144].
        281. W. de Alvernia. s.xv in. [*Ingram* 164].
        317.[5] Florus diaconus. s.xii in. [*Cat.* 9, *Ingram* 119].
        336. *g*Legenda sanctorum. s.xiv in. [Dem.i; *cat.*
               1793].
        345. H. de S. Victore. s.xii ex. [.hu.; *cat.* 808,
               Ingram 193].
        379. *e*H. de S. Victore. s.xiii/xiv. [*Cat.* 1661, not
               Ingram 177].
        385. Jeronimus, etc. [.F.; *cat.* 204, *Ingram* 104].
        648. *i*Miscellanea. s.xv ex.
        827. Ambrosius. s.xii in. [R, D.ii G.vi; *cf. cat.* 51,
               52].
    Canonici gr. 35. *e*Octateuch (in Greek). s.xiii.
    Digby 4.[6] *g*Tractatus super canonem misse, etc. s.xii–
             xiii. [*Cat.* 954].
        5, fos 1–72. *i*Seneca. s.xii. [? *Old cat.* 220]. ?
        13. Marbodus. s.xii. [.CE.]. ?
        28. *c*Compotus, etc. s.xiv. ?
        92. *c*Astronomica. s.xiii–xiv. ?
        222.[7] *m*H. de Bracton. s.xiv in.
    Junius 11. Genesis (in English). s.x/xi. [? *Cat.* 304]. ?
    Lat. misc. b.12, fo. 8. *i*J. Andreae. s.xiv/xv. [? *Chillenden*
             16].
        d.13.[8] *m*Chronica. s.xii. [? *Cat.* 283].
        d.14. *c*Chronicon. s.xiii in.
        d.30.[8] *m*Chronica. s.xii. [? *Cat.* 283].
    Laud. misc. 160. *g*Postille super xii proph. s.xiii ex.
               [*Cat.* 922, *Ingram* 44].
        161. *s*Postille super pentateuchum. s.xiii ex.
               [*Cat.* 921, not *Ingram* 32].
        165. *e*W. Nottingham. s.xiv. [*Ingram* 47].
        412.[9] R. Tuitiensis. s.xii. [Y].
        444. *g*Pseudo-Chrysostomus, etc. s.xiv ex.
        576. *e*P. Riga. s.xiii. [? *Cat.* 1245].
        730. *b*P. de Ickham. s.xv. ?

---

[5] Part i is Cambridge, Trinity Coll. 119.
[6] B.M., Cotton Galba A.xix and Bodleian, Digby 4 formed one volume.
[7] Assigned on the evidence of marks in the margins: *cf.* p. 31, n. 6.
[8] Lat. misc. d.13 and Lat. misc. d.30 are fragments of one volume.
[9] Laud misc. 412 was later at Canterbury College, Oxford, *q.v.*

Oxford (*contd*)
  Bodleian, Lyell 19. *i*Reg. S. Benedicti, etc. s.xv.
      Rawl. B.188. *i*G. Cambrensis. s.xiii.
           B.191.[1] *m*Polychronicon. s.xiv.
           C.168, fos 45–108.[2] *e*Missale. s.xv.
           C.269. *i*R. Rolle, etc. s.xv.
      Tanner 15. *i*J. Capgrave. A.D. 1499. ?
           165. *c*Registrum W. Molassh, etc. s.xv.
  Corpus Christi Coll., 189. *i*Constantinus Africanus, etc. s.xii/xiii.
           [*Cat.* 452].
  Magdalen Coll., lat. 166. Cassiodorus. s.xii. [sa., D.ii G.v; *cat.* 835].
  Merton Coll., 328, fos 1–60. *e*Index statutorum, etc. s.xv.
  New Coll., 300. *e*Misc. theologica. s.xvi.
  Pembr. Coll., 5. *g*T. Wallensis, etc. s.xiii–xv. [Jor; *cat.* 1305, *Ingram* 146, *Leland*].
      fragments.[3] *i*T. Wallensis (32 fos). s.xiv.
  St John's Coll., 89. Beda, etc. s.xi/xii. [D.iii G.i M°.i; *cat.* 90].
           194. *c*Evangelia. s.ix ex. [gl']. ?
  Univ. Coll., 68. *g*T. Aquinas. s.xiii/xiv. [Dem.i; *cat.* 1665, *Ingram* 8].
Paris, B.N., Lat. 770. *l*Psalterium, etc. s.xiii in.
           987. *l*Benedictionale. s.x/xi. ?
           10062, fos 162, 163. *l*Kalendarium. s.xi. ?
      nouv. acq. lat. 1670. *l*Psalterium, etc. s.xii/xiii.
  Bibl. Mazarine, 5. *e*Biblia. s.xiii.
Shrewsbury School, xxvi. Cyprianus, etc. s.xii. [AR(?); *cat.* 127].
Stockholm, Kungl. bibl. *e*Evangelia ('Codex aureus'). s.viii.
Tokyo, U.L., A.100.1300. *c*Formularium. s.xv med.
Utrecht, U.L., 32, fos 1–91. Psalterium ('Utrecht psalter'). s.ix.
Wellington (N.Z.), Alexander Turnbull Libr. 'Musica Boetii. Musica Guidonis inperfecta'. s.xii. [H.; *old cat.* 40 *cf. cat.* 438].
Windsor, St George's Chapel, 5. *e*Gregorius, etc. s.xii. [.F., D.iii G.xiii Dem.i; *cat.* 145].
Wisbech, Museum, Town Libr. C.3.8. (pr. bk). *i*Epistole Pii secundi. Lyon, A.D. 1497.
Rejected: Baltimore, Walters Art Gallery, 57. Cambridge, University Libr., Dd.4.25, Ff.1.23, Ff.1.29, Ff.4.32, Hh.1.10, Ii.2.26, Kk.3.18; Clare Coll., 18; Corpus Christi Coll., 11, 23 ii, 94, 123, 161, 214, 253, 274, 328 i, 330, 332, 424 v, 425; Gonv. and Caius Coll., 301, 308, 427; St John's Coll., 229; Trinity Coll., 15, 44, 63, 73, 147, 159, 173, 212, 250, 320, 379, 610, 629, 722, 1042, 1135, 1155, 1315, 1427; Trinity Hall, 5, 7, 21, 24, 26. London, B.M., Add. 6158, Arundel 87, 401, Cotton Jul. B.iii, Tib. B.i, Tib. B.xi, Claud. A.i, Galba A.ii, Galba A.iii, Otho A.i, Otho A.vi, Vit. A.iii, Vesp. D.xiv, Vesp. D.xxi, Vesp. E.iii, Titus A.ix, Cleop. C.vii; Harley 56, 322, 989; Royal 2 F.v, 5 B.iii, 7 D.xxiv, 10 B.iv, 11 C.ii. Manchester, J. Rylands, Lat. 109. Oxford,

---

[1] Assigned on the evidence of marks in the margins: *cf.* p. 31, n. 6.
[2] Given by Archbishop William Warham to his chantry in the cathedral church.
[3] The fragments at Pembr. Coll. are in the bindings of Jason Maynus, Lyon, 1526 (4 vols).

Bodleian, Bodl. 134, Bodl. 135, Bodl. 193, Bodl. 378, Bodl. 387, Digby 110, Digby 203, D'Orville 208, Hatton 48, Laud misc. 454; New Coll., 204.

CANTERBURY. *Ben. abbey of St Augustine (originally of St Peter and St Paul).*

M. R. James, *The Ancient Libraries of Canterbury and Dover* (Cambr., 1903), prints a catalogue (s.xv ex.) from Dublin, Trinity Coll., MS. D.1.19 (360); second folios and many pressmarks given; also several short lists, including books noted by J. Leland from *Collectanea*, iv. 7. *Cf.* also Leland, *De Scriptoribus Britannicis*, pp. 299–301.

The pressmark, which records the *Distinctio* and *Gradus* numbers (for these terms see M. R. James, *op. cit.*, p. lx), is reproduced from B.M., Harley 3644, Royal 6 C.i and Royal 4 A.xi, in *New Pal. Soc.*, i, pl. 17, no. 1 *a–c*. In some MSS there is also a letter-mark, preceded by *cum*. Common forms of *ex libris* inscription are 'Liber sancti Augustini Cant.', and 'de librario sancti Augustini Cant.' In many MSS a personal name in the genitive case follows the short title, as at Christ Church, Canterbury.

Brussels, Bibl. royale, 3097. *e*Polychronicon. s.xiv. [D.x G.iii; *cat.* 932].
Cambridge,
  U.L., Add. 3578. Chronica. s.xiv. [*Cat.* 925].
    Ee.6.37. *e*Priscianus. s.xii/xiii. [D.xi G.iv; *cat.* 1357].
    Ff.4.40. *e*Epp. Pauli glo. s.xii. [D.iii G.ii; *cat.* 204].
    Ff.6.16. *c*Preces. s.xv. ?
    Gg.5.35. *e*Juvencus, etc. ('Cambridge Songs'). s.xi. [D.xi G. ; *Leland*].
    Ii.1.15. *e*Astronomica. s.xiii–xiv in. [D.xiii G.iiii; *cat.* 1155].
    Ii.2.24. *i*Polychronicon. s.xiv/xv. [*Cat.* 934].
    Kk.1.17. *e*Jeronimus. s.xii. [D.iiii G.i; *cat.* 323].
    Kk.1.19. *i*P. Tarentasius. s.xiii. [D.iii G.iii; *cat.* 551].
  Christ's Coll., 1. *e*P. Lombardus. s.xiii/xiv. [D.vii G.i; *cat.* 530].
  Corpus Christi Coll., 13.[4] V. Bellovacensis. s.xiii/xiv. [*Cat.* 902].
    14.[4] *i*V. Bellovacensis. s.xiii/xiv. [*Cat.* 903].
    20. *e*Apocalypsis, etc. s.xiv in. [D.i G.iii; *cat.* 224].
    38. *e*Tabula super decreta, etc. s.xiv. [*Cat.* 1723].
    44. *l*Pontificale. s.xi. ?
    49. *g*Biblia. s.xiii. [*Cat.* 9].
    50. *e*Wace, etc. (in French). s.xiii ex. [*Cat.* 1516].
    81. Homer, etc. (in Greek). s.xv. ?
    94. *s*Collectio decem partium. s.xii. ?
    129. Eutropius, etc. s.xiii–xiv. [*Cat.* 910].
    144. *e*Glossaria. s.viii/ix. [D.xi G.i Retro].
    154. *e*Anselmus, etc. s.xiv. [D.vi G.i; *cat.* 457].
    189. *c*Chron. W. Thorne, etc. s.xii–xiv.
    267. *e*Freculphus. s.xi. [D.x G.ii; *cat.* 884].
    270. *l*Missale. s.xi.

[4] Cambridge, St John's Coll. 43 and Corpus Christi Coll. 13 and 14 belong to one series.

Cambridge (*contd*)
Corpus Christi., 271. *e*Decretales, etc. s.xiii–xiv. [D.xiiii G.iiii; *cat*. 1632].
274. Ambrosius. s.xi. [*Cat*. 383].
276. *e*Eutropius, etc. s.xi–xii. [D.x G.ii; *cat*. 892].
284. *l*Anselmus, etc. s.xiv ex. ?
286. *c*Evangelia ('Canterbury Gospels'). s.vi.
291. *e*Beda, etc. s.xi/xii. [D.6 G.i; *cat*. 444].
301. *e*Annales, etc. s.xiv in.
312. *e*Goscelinus, etc. s.xi/xii. [D.ix G.v; *cat*. 939].
314. Pseudo-Dionysius, etc. s.xiii/xiv. [*Cat*. 419].
352. *e*Boetius. s.ix/x. [*Cat*. 1008].
364. *e*Medica. s.xiii. [D.xiiii G.iii; *cat*. 1202].
382. *e*Ric. Armachanus. s.xiv ex. [*Cat*. 621].
389. *e*Vita Pauli, etc. s.x. [D.ix G.(iii) v].
466. *e*Medica. s.xii. [*Cat*. 1245].
Gonv. and Caius Coll., 144. *e*Glose super Sedulium, etc. s.ix ex. [D.xi G.ii; *cat*. 1467].
211. *c*Consuetudinarium, etc. s.xiii. [D.xiiii G.iii de officio sacriste].
238. *e*Miscellanea. s.xiii. [D.xvii G.iiii].
361. *e*Biblia. s.xiii. [D.i G.i; *cat*. 25].
435. *e*Priscianus, etc. (in Latin and French). s.xiii–xiv. [D.viii G.iii].
456. *e*Astronomica. s.xii–xiii. [D.xiii G.iii; *cat*. 1150].
Magdalene Coll., Pepys 2314. *c*Chronicon. s.xv med. ?
St John's Coll., 10. Augustinus. s.xiv. [*Cat*. 356].
43.[5] *i*V. Bellovacensis. s.xiii/xiv. [*Cat*. 901].
78. *e*Medica. s.xiii. [D.xiiii G.ii(i); *cat*. 1228].
97. *e*Valerius Maximus, etc. s.xiv. [D.x G.vi; *cat*. 937].
99. *e*Medica. s.xiii. [D.xiiii G.ii; *cat*. 1218].
142. *e*Formularium. s.xiv. [D.x G.iii].
164. *e*Miracula S. Benedicti. s.x. [D.ix G.v].
171. *e*W. de Conchis. s.xiii. [D.12 G.4; *cat*. 1485].
230. *e*H. de Victore, etc. s.xii–xiii. [D.6 G.i; *cat*. 482].
262. *l*Cantica, etc. s.xiv in.
Trinity Coll., 38. *e*Augustinus. s.xi/xii. [D.iiii G.iii; *cat*. 363].
40. Pentateuchus metrice. s.x. [*Cat*. 113].
115. *e*Epp. Pauli glo. s.xiii–xiv. [D.iii G.ii; ? *cat*. 196].
321. *e*Miracula S. Thome. s.xii/xiii. [*Cat*. 1543].
904. *e*Chirurgica. s.xii ex. [D.xii G.iii; *cat*. 1273].
939. Boetius. s.x. [*Cat*. 1007].
945. Hyginus, etc. s.xi. [*Cat*. 1157].
1155. *s*Prudentius, etc. s.x/xi–xi/xii. ?

[5] Cambridge, St John's Coll. 43 and Corpus Christi Coll. 13 and 14 belong to one series.

Cambridge (contd)
   Trinity Coll., 1179.   Boetius. s.x. [Cat. 993].
           1215.   ePalladius. s.xiii in. [D.xi G.iiii; cat. 1125].
           1241.   Juvenalis, etc. s.x. [Cat. 1439].
           1242.   Juvenalis, etc. s.x. [Cat. 1440].
   Trinity Hall, 1. cT. Elmham. s.xv.
Canterbury, Cathedral, 4. gBiblia, etc. s.xiii in. [D.i G.ii; cat. 17].
              34. Matheus glo. s.xii. [D.iii G.i; cat. 157].
              49. eVetus logica, etc. s.xiii. [D.xii; cat. 1286].
              58. eCorrectorium biblie, etc. s.xv. [Cat. 300].
              68. eAugustinus. s.xi/xii. [D.iiii G.iii; cat. 349].
           Add. 16.[6] Evangelia (1 fo.). s.viii ex.
           Archdeaconry Visitations Dioc. Cant., Detecta,
                1571–72. sJeronimus. (1 fo.). s.xii in. [Cf.
                cat. 327].
Dublin, Trinity Coll., 514. Dares Phrygius, etc. s.xiii in.–xiv. [D.x
                  G.ii; cat. 900].
          602, fos 1–62. eW. Malmesburiensis, etc. s.xiii
                  in. [Cat. 919].
   Chester Beatty Libr., W.27. eLucas glo. s.xii. [D.iii G.i; cat.
                  168].
Durham, U.L., Cosin V.ii.9. gRob. Kilwardy. s.xiii. [D.vii G.iii;
   cat. 616].
Edinburgh, N.L., Adv. 18.6.8. eConstantinus Africanus. s.xii/xiii.
   [D.xiiii G.ii; cat. 1193].
Elmstone, Rectory. sAugustinus in Psalmos (2 fos). s.xi/xii. [Cf. cat.
   336].
Eton Coll., 78. lPsalterium. s.xiii.
Exeter, Cathedral, 3529. eBoccaccius. s.xv ex.
Glasgow, U.L., Hunterian 253. eAlchemica,   etc.   s.xiii/xiv.   [D.xiii
                  G.iiii; cat. 1544].
          379. eT. Elmham. s.xv.
Leyden, U.L., Scaliger 69. sEthicus. s.x ex. [Cat. 1468].
          Hebr. 8.[7] ePsalterium Hebraicum. s.xii. [D.iii
                G.i; cat. 89].
London,
   B.M., Add. 6042. eClaudianus. s.xiii. [D.xi G.ii(iii); cat. 1444].
          26770. iJ. de Sacro Bosco, etc. s.xiii–xiv in. [Cat. 1552].
          33241. eGesta Cnutonis. s.xi. [D.x G.iii; cat. 907].
          35289. eChanson d'Aspremont (in French). s.xiii. [D.xvi
                G.iiii; cat. 1519].
          37517. lPsalterium ('Bosworth psalter'). s.x.   ?
          46352. eP. Blesensis, etc. s.xiii. [de camera abbatis,
                Dist. T. abbatis; cf. cat. after 950].
          48178. eMartinus Polonus, etc. s.xiv in. [D.x G.i; cat.
                916].
        Arundel 57. eAyenbite of inwyt (in English), etc. s.xiii–xiv.
                [D.xvi G.iiii; cat. 1536].
          91.[8] Vite sanctorum. s.xii.

[6] Canterbury Cathedral, Add. 16 is a detached leaf of B.M., Royal 1 E.vi.
[7] The Leyden psalter was later at King's Coll., Cambridge, q.v.
[8] B.M., Arundel 91 and Bodleian, Fell 2 are companion volumes.

London (*contd*)
B.M., Arundel 165. *e*Augustinus, etc. s.xiv.   ?
        282.[9] *e*Summa Raymundi. s.xiii. [D.ix G.ii; *cat.*
           1766].
        310. *e*Statuta Anglie, etc. s.xiii–xiv.
   Burney 3. *e*Biblia. s.xiii. [*Cat.* 10].
        11. *e*Biblia. s.xiii. [*Cat.* 44].
        36. 'Matheus glo. minori glo. cum B'. s.xii. [*Cat.*
          156].
   Cotton Jul. D.ii. *c*Annales, etc. s.xiii.
        D.xi, fos 85–93. *l*Kalendarium. s.xiii ex.   ?
        Tib. A.iii, fo. 178.[1] Genealogy of kings (in English).
          s.x.
        A.vi, fos 1–35.[1] Anglo-Saxon chronicle (in English).
          s.x.
        A.vii, fos 1–38. Martinus Polonus. s.xiv/xv.
          [*Cat.* 917].
        A.ix, fos 107–80. *c*Chronica T. Sprott. s.xiv.
          [*Cat.* 931].
        Calig. A.xv, fos 3–117. Jeronimus, etc. s.viii. [*Cat.*
          330].
        Claud. B.iv. Pentateuch and Joshua (in English).
          s.xi. [*Cat.* 95].
        Nero A.viii, fos 1–86. *c*Annales, etc. s.xii.   ?
        Otho E.xiii. *e*Corpus canonum. s.x/xi. [D.xv G.iii].
        Vit. A.ii, fos 3–19. *c*De sanctis Anglie, etc. s.xii.
        A.vi. *c*Gildas. s.x. [? *Cat.* 887].
        A.x, fos 1–18. *c*Annales. s.xiv in.
        C.xii, fos 114–57. *c*Martyrologium. s.xi/xii.
        D.xvi.[2] *e*Consuetudinarium. s.xiv ex.
        Vesp. A.i. Psalterium. s.viii. [? *Leland*].
        A.ii. *l*Rogerus Bacon, etc. s.xii–xiii.   ?
        B.xx. *e*Vita S. Augustini, etc. s.xii. [D.x G.i].
        D.vi, fos 2–77. Parabole Salomonis, etc. s.x.
          [D.ii G.iii; *cat.* 131].
        E.xi, fos 46–132.[3] P. Blesensis. s.xiii.
       Titus A.xxvii. G. Monemutensis, etc. s.xii/xiii. [*Cat.*
          895].
        Domit. 1, fos 2–55. Isidorus, etc. s.x–xi. [D.v G.iv;
          cat. 434, *Leland*].
        Cleop. A.xii, fos 79–144. Penitentiale. s.xiii in. [D.ix
          G.i; *cat.* 640].
        B.xiii, fos 59–90. Vita S. Dunstani. s.xi in.
        D.i, fos 1–128. Vitruvius, etc. s.xi. [*Cat.* 1123].
       Faustina C.xii. *c*Consuetudinarium. s.xiv in.
   Egerton 823.[4] Astronomica. s.xii. [? *Part of cat.* 1599].   ?

---

[9] B.M., Arundel 282 and Cotton Vesp. E.xi, fos 46–132, formed one volume.
[1] Tib. A.iii, fo. 178, was part of the same volume as Tib. A.vi, fos 1–35.
[2] Badly burnt. *Ex libris* inscription preserved in the transcript in Oxford, Jesus Coll., MS. 75, fo. 329.
[3] B.M., Arundel 282 and Cotton Vesp. E.xi, fos 46–132, formed one volume.
[4] Egerton 823 and 840a formerly formed Cambridge, Trinity Coll., R.15.15.

London (*contd*)
B.M., Egerton 840a.[4] Theophilus, etc. s.xiii. [? *Part of cat.* 1599] ?
        874. *e*Augustinus. s.ix. [D.iiii G.ii(iii); *cat.* 345].
Harley 1.[5] *i*Mathematica. s.xiii–xiv. [*Cat.* 1147].
        13. *e*Astronomica. s.xiii. [D.13 G.4; *cat.* 1166].
        105. *c*Goscelinus, etc. s.xii. ?
        603. *s*Psalterium. s.xi in. ?
        641, fos 1–115. *e*Chronica. s.xiv. [Dist. T. abbatis; *cat.* 926].
        647. Aratus. s.x in. [*Cat.* 1164].
        652. *l*Omeliarium. s.xi–xii. [D.x G.ii].
        1524. Epp. Pauli glo. s.xiii. [D.iii G.ii; *cat.* 197].
        3224. *e*Alanus de Insulis, etc. s.xiv ex. [D.xi G.i; *cat.* 964].
        3644. *e*Britton (in French). s.xiv. [D.xvi G.iii].
        3908, fos 1–100. *cs*Vita S. Mildrethe, etc. s.xii.
        4132. *e*P. Comestor. s.xiii.
        5369. *e*Gesta Romanorum. s.xv. [*Cat.* 1484].
        5431. *e*Reg. S. Benedicti, etc. s.x–xiv. [D.xiiii G.i; *cat.* 462].
Lansdowne 359. *e*Sermones. s.xiv. [D.8 G.3].
Royal 1 A.vii. Biblia. s.xiii. [*Cat.* 31].
        1 A.xviii. *e*Evangelia. s.x in.
        1 B.xi. *c*Evangelia. s.xii.
        1 E.vi.[6] Evangelia. s.viii ex. [D.i G.iii].
        3 A.i. *e*Numeri glo. s.xiii. [D.i G.ii; *cat.* 109].
        3 A.ii. *g*Leviticus glo. s.xiii. [D.i G.ii; *cat.* 105].
        4 A.x. *e*Genesis glo. s.xiii. [D.i G.ii; *cat.* 98].
        4 A.xi. *e*Esaias glo. s.xii/xiii. [D.ii G.ii; *cat.* 143].
        5 B.xv. Augustinus, etc. s.xi/xii. [*Cat.* 358].
        6 C.i. *e*Isidorus. s.xi. [D.v G.iiii; *cat.* 427].
        7 D.ii. Miscellanea. s.xii. [D.vi G.i; *cat.* 415].
        8 A.vi. *e*Grammatica. s.xiii. [D.7(ix) G.5(i); *cat.* 820].
        8 C.xvii. *e*J. de Bridlington. s.xiv ex.
        9 B.i. *g*Jacobus de Viterbo. s.xiv. [D.vi G.iiii; *cat.* 544].
        9 C.vi. *e*Summe juris civilis. s.xiii ex. [D.15 G.2; ? *cat.* 1810].
        9 E.vii. J. Faventinus. s.xiii. [*Cat.* 1692].
        10 B.xiv. *e*J. Dumbleton. s.xiv. [D.xii G.iii; *cat.* 1324].
        11 A.vi. *e*T. de Chabham. s.xiii/xiv. [D.ix G.ii; *cat.* 1785].
        11 A.xii. Flores dictaminum. s.xiv. [D.x G.iii; *cat.* 958].
        11 B.xiv. *i*Misc. juris civilis. s.xiii. ?
        12 B.ix. *e*Medica. s.xiii in. [D.xiiii G.iii; *cat.* 1244].
        12 D.ix. *e*Constantinus Africanus. s.xiii.

[4] See p. 43, n. 4.
[5] B.M., Harley 1 and Oxford, Corpus Christi Coll. 254, fos 191–96, formed one volume.
[6] Canterbury Cathedral, Add. 16 is a detached leaf of B.M., Royal 1 E.vi.

London (*contd*)
B.M., Royal 12 E.xxiii.　*e*Q. Serenus.　s.xiii ex.　[D.xiiii (xiii) G.iii; *cat*. 1196].
　　13 A.xxii.　*e*Paulus Diaconus.　s.xi ex.　[D.x G.ii; *cat*. 893].
　　13 A.xxiii.　*e*Chronica Adonis, etc.　s.xii.　[D.x G.i; *cat*. 912].
　　13 B.viii.　*e*G. Cambrensis, etc.　s.xii/xiii–xiii.　[*Cat*. 906].
　　15 A.vi.　*e*Cicero.　s.xii.　[D.x G.iii; *cat*. 1011].
　　15 A.xvi.　*e*Juvencus, etc.　s.ix–x.　[D.xi G.ii; *cat*. 1438].
　　15 B.vi.　*e*Virgilius.　s.xiii.　[D.xi G.ii; *cat*. 1476].
　　Stowe 378.　*e*Gratianus.　s.xiii.　[D.xv G.iii (iiii); *cat*. 1619].
Lambeth Palace,　　3.[7]　*c*Biblia, pars i.　s.xii.　?
　　49.　*e*W. Durandus, etc.　s.xiii–xiv.　[D.xv G.4; *cat*. 1809].
　　116, fos 1–131.　*e*De nominibus hebraicis, etc.　s.xiv. [Dist. T. abbatis; *cat*. 299].
　　144, fos 1–163.　*e*Gregorius, etc.　s.xiv.　[D.viii G.v; *cat*. 1551].
　　179, fos 99–196.　*e*Statuta Anglie.　s.xiii/xiv.
　　185.　*e*Sermones.　s.xii/xiii.　[D.viii G.ii; *cat*. 708].
　　414,　fos 1–80.　*e*Theologica.　s.x.　[D.iiii G.iii; *cat*. 851].
　　419.　*e*Chronica.　s.xiv.　[D.x G.　; *cat*. 929].
　　430.　*e*Decretales.　s.xiii.　[D.xiiii G.iiii; *cat*. 1651].
　　498.　*e*Liber voc. Paupertas.　s.xiv.　[D.9 G.6; *cat*. 845].
　　522.　Château d'amour, etc.　(in French).　s.xiii. [D.xvi G.iiii; *cat*. 1510].
　　1213.　*ic*Miscellanea.　s.xiii–xiv.
Public Record Office, Exch. K.R., Misc. Bks 1.27.　*e*Chronicon, etc. s.xiv in.
Dr E. G. Millar.　*g*Psalterium glo.　s.xiii.　[D.ii G.i; *cat*. 71].
Longleat, Marquess of Bath, 177.　*e*Beda, etc.　s.xii.　[D.vi G.i; *cat*. 447].
Maidstone, Museum, 1.[8]　Biblia, pars ii.　s.xii.　?
New York, Public Libr., 8.　*e*J. de Abbatisvilla.　s.xiii/xiv.　[*Cat*. 665].
　　Mr G. M. Crawford.　*e*Biblia.　s.xiii ex.　[D.i G.ii; *cat*. 29].
　　Mr W. S. Glazier, 18.　*e*Biblia.　s.xiii.　[D.i G.i; *cat*. 14].
　　53.　*il*Psalterium.　s.xiv in.
Norwich, Castle Museum, 158.926.4g(2).　*e*Liber voc. Paupertas.　s.xiv ex.　[D.9 G.6; *cat*. 844].
Oxford,
Bodleian, Ashmole 341.　Astronomica.　s.xii–xiii.　[*Cat*. 1130].
　　1431.　*e*Apuleius Barbarus.　s.xii in.　[D.14 G.2; *cat*. 1264].
　　Auct. F.6.3.　*e*Medica.　s.xiii.　[D.xii G.iii; *cat*. 1240].
　　Barlow 32.　*e*Manuale, etc.　s.xiv.　[D.xiiii G.iiii].
　　Bodl. 97.　*e*Aldhelmus.　s.xi.　[*Not cat*. 1431].
　　144.　*i*Ric. Armachanus.　s.xv.　?

[7] Part ii is at Maidstone Museum.
[8] Part i is Lambeth Palace 3.

Oxford (*contd.*)
Bodleian, Bodl. 299. *e*J. de Friburgo, etc. s.xiv. [D.x G.i; *cat.* 1812].
381.[9] *e*Vita S. Gregorii. s.xi. [D.ix G.v.].
391. *e*Theologica. s.xi/xii. [D.iiii G.i; *cat.* 329].
426, fos 1–118. *e*Philippus in Job. s.viii/ix. [D.iii
G.iv; *cat.* 137, *Leland*].
464. *e*Astrologica, etc. s.xiv in. [*Cat.* 1156].
507. *i*Computistica. s.xv med.
521. *bc*Chronicon Anglie. s.xiv ex. ?
572. *c*Theologica. s.ix–x. [*Part in cat.* 129].
596, fos 175–214. *e*Vita S. Cuthberti, etc. s.xi/xii.
[D.ix G.v (iii); *cat.* 443].
600. *e*Collectiones Roberti infirmarii. s.xiii. [D.viii
G.vi; *cat.* 1562].
679. *e*Collectiones J. de London. s.xiii ex.
746. P. Lombardus. s.xiii. [D.vi G.ii; *cat.* 507].
826. Augustinus. s.xii. [D.iiii G.iiii; *cat.* 364].
Digby 174. *e*Boetius, etc. s.xii–xiv. [D.xi G.i; *cat.* 987].
Douce 88, fos 68–154. Bestiarium, etc. s.xiii. [*Cat.* 870].
89. *i*Collectiones J. Pistoris. s.xiii in. [D.viii G.v;
cat. 1565].
Fell 2.[1] *c*Vite sanctorum. s.xii. ?
Hatton 94. *e*Himbertus Prulliacensis. s.xiv. [D.vii G.ii;
cat. 588].
Lat. bib. b.2(P).[9] Actus apostolorum. s.viii/ix.
Lat. liturg. a.6, fo. 38. *c*Prosarium. s.xiii in. ?
Lat. th. b.2, fo. 2. Augustinus. s.xii in. [*Fo. 1 of cat.* 357].
Laud lat. 65. *e*Johannicius, etc. s.xiii. [D.14 G.ii; *not
cat.* 1200].
Laud misc. 125. *e*Sermones. s.xii ex. [D.viii G.ii; *cat.*
676].
296. *e*J. Waldeby. s.xv.
300. Jeronimus. s.xii ex. [*Cat.* 325].
385. *g*Flores Bernardi, etc. s.xiii. [D.vi G.i;
cat. 468].
Lyell 1. Johannes glo. s.xii. [*Cat.* 182].
Marshall 19. *e*Philo Judeus. s.ix. [D.xi G.i retro].
e Mus. 66. *s*Beda, etc. s.xii. [*Cat.* 441].
223. *e*Rogerius de Barone, etc. s.xiii. [*Cat.* 1222].
Rawl. C.7. *e*Epistole. s.xiv. [*Cat.* 953].
C.117. *e*Astronomica. s.xiii/xiv. [D.xiii G.4; *cat.*
1140].
C.159. *e*H. de Bracton. s.xiii.
C.570. Arator. s.x/xi. [*Cat.* 1433].
Selden supra 25. Mathematica. s.xi–xiii. [D.13 G.3; *cat.*
1019].
26.[2] *e*Mathematica (in Lat. and Fr.). s.xii
ex.–xiii. [D.xii(xi) G.iii (v *or* vi)].

[9] Bodleian, Lat. bib. b.2 (P) is one leaf which was used as a flyleaf for Bodl. 381.
[1] London, B.M., Arundel 91 and Bodleian, Fell 2 are companion volumes.
[2] Selden supra 90, fos 30–37, probably formed one volume with Selden supra
26.

Oxford (*contd*)

Bodleian, Selden supra 30. Actus Apostolorum. s.viii. [D.i G.iii; *cat.* 222].

90, fos 30–37.[2] *sl*Tabule; Kalendarium. s.xii ex.

4⁰ B.2 Art. Seld. (pr. bk). *i*Boetius. (Lyon), s.a.

Wood empt. 13. *e*Alex. Nequam. s.xiii. [D.viii G.ii; *cat.* 675].

All Souls Coll., 1. *e*Biblia. s.xiii. [D. G.i; *cat.* 12].

Corpus Christi Coll., 41. *e*Augustinus, etc. s.xiii–xiv. [D.4 G.3; *cat.* 374].

65. *e*Tacuinus. s.xiv. [D.14 G.2; *cat.* 1197].

125. *e*Alchemica. s.xiii–xv. [D.10 G.1; *cat.* 1277].

130. *e*W. de Alvernia. s.xv. [D.12 G.4].

221. *i*Miscellanea. s.xii–xiv. [D.xiii G.3; *cat.* 1170].

248. *e*Albumazar. s.xiii ex. [D.xiii G.v; *cat.* 1145].

254, fos 191–96.[3] Alkindus. s.xiv.

283. *e*Euclides, etc. s.xii–xiii. [D.xi G.ii (8); *cat.* 1009].

Queen's Coll., 307. *e*Polychronicon. s.xv in. [*Cat.* 936].

St John's Coll., 66B. *e*Vitruvius. A.D. 1316. [D.x G.iiii; *cat.* 1124].

152. *e*Priscianus, etc. s.xiii. [D.xi G.4; *cat.* 1390].

Trinity Coll., 4. *e*Augustinus, etc. s.xi. [D.iiii G.iii; *cat.* 367].

Univ. Coll., 19. *i*Clemens Lanthon. s.xiii ex. [D. T. abbatis, D.iii G.iiii; *cat.* 286].

21. *e*Summa Raymundi. s.xiv. [D.ix G.ii; *cat.* 1763].

117. *e*Augustinus, etc. s.xii–xiii. [D.iiii G.iii; *cat.* 351].

Mr M. B. Parkes. *s*Beda, De templo (2 fos). s.xii. [*Cf. cat.* 439].

Paris, B.N., nouv. acq. lat. 873. *e*Remigius Autissiodor., etc. s.xii. [D.vii G.4; *cat.* 758].

Redlynch, Major J. R. Abbey. *e*Epp. Pauli glo., etc. s.xi. [D.iii G.ii; *cat.* 205].

Wolfenbüttel, Ducal Libr., Helmst. 481. *i*Gervas. Tilleberiensis. [D.x G.iii; *cat.* 933].

York, Minster, xvi.D.6. *e*H. de Bracton. s.xiv in. [D.16 G.3].

Rejected: Cambridge, Corpus Christi Coll., 130, 197 (pp. 245–316), 280, 374; Trinity Coll., 320, 1368. Cambridge (U.S.A.), Harvard Univ., Houghton Libr., Typ. 3. Cardiff, Public Libr., 381. Leyden, U.L., B.P.L.190. London, B.M., Cotton Jul. D.xi, Aug. ii.2 (*rectius* 3), Tib. B.vii, Claud. B.ix, Galba A.i, Otho A.viii, Otho A.xii, Otho C.v; Royal 2 D.xxxiv; Lambeth Palace, 209, 362. Manchester, J. Rylands, Lat. 155. Oxford, Bodleian, Hatton 47, 48, Laud lat. 18, Laud misc. 299; Merton Coll., 122; St John's Coll., 17; Univ. Coll., 138.

CANTERBURY. *Aug. priory of St Gregory.*

Book noted by J. Leland, *Collectanea*, iv. 10.

Cambridge, Trinity Coll., 387. *e*P. Lombardus. s.xii.

[2] See p. 46, n. 2.

[3] B.M., Harley 1 and Oxford, Corpus Christi Coll. 254, fos 191–96, formed one volume.

CANTERBURY. *Franciscan convent.*
The pressmarks in Royal 3 D.ii are reproduced in *New Pal. Soc.*, i, pl. 17, no. 3.
Hereford, Cathedral, P.v.10, fos 80–124. *e*T. Gallus. s.xiii.
Lincoln, Cathedral, 36. *e*Philippus Cancellarius Paris. s.xiii. [I.13].
            195. *e*Vita S. Francisci, etc. s.xiv. [A; N(?).3].
London,
  B.M., Cotton Galba E.xi. *e*G. Monemutensis, etc. s.xiii ex. [P.8].
  Royal 2 D.xxiv. *e*Marcus et Matheus glo. s.xiii. [D.23].
  3 C.vi.[4] *b*Job, etc., glo. s.xiii. ?
  3 C.xi.[4] *e*Evangelia glo. s.xiii.
  3 D.ii.[4] *e*Esaias, etc., glo. s.xiii. [.B. *and* C.4].
  3 D.iv.[4] *e*P. Lombardus. s.xiii.
  3 E.ix.[4] *e*Genesis, etc., glo. s.xiii.
  4 C.i.[5] *e*Lucas et Johannes glo. s.xiii. [B.] ?
Lambeth Palace, 1483.5 (pr. bk). *e*W. Ockham. [Urach], A.D. 1483.
Oxford, Bodleian, Digby 153. *e*Albertus Magnus. s.xiv.
          Rawl. poet. 137.[6] *e*Piers Plowman (in English).
                        s.xv in.
    Trinity Coll., 37. *e*Anselmus. s.xiii.

CARDIFF (Kerdif), Glamorgan. *Ben. priory of B.V.M.; cell of Tewkesbury.*
London, B.M., Royal 6 B.xi. *c*Bernardus, etc. s.xiv in. ?

CARLISLE. *Aug. cathedral priory of B.V.M.*
Durham, Cathedral, B.IV.38. *e*J. Wallensis. s.xv.
Oxford, Bodleian, Bodl. 728. *e*Pseudo-Clemens. s.xii.

CARLISLE. *Dominican convent.*
Edinburgh, U.L., 1. *e*Biblia. s.xiii.

CARMARTHEN (Kermerdinia). *Aug. priory of St John the Evangelist.*
Aberystwyth, N.L., Peniarth 1. Poems in Welsh ('Black Book of Carmarthen'). s.xiii. ?

CARMARTHEN. *Franciscan convent.*
Oxford, Bodleian, Bodl. 36. *e*R. Grosseteste, etc. s.xiii.

CARROW, Norfolk. *Priory of B.V.M. and St John, of Ben. nuns.*
Baltimore, Walters Art Gallery, 90. *e*Psalterium, etc. s.xiii med.

CASTLE ACRE, Norfolk. *Cluniac priory of B.V.M.*
Books noted by J. Leland, *Collectanea*, iv. 29.

---

[4] These five volumes and Royal 3 D.viii, 4 C.v, and 4 E.vi were treated as an eight-volume set in s.xvi.
[5] *Ex libris* inscription on flyleaf of Royal 3 C.vi (fo. 312) probably belongs to this volume.
[6] The pastedowns used in the medieval binding of Rawl. poet. 137 are now Rawl. D.913, fos 86–89 (Guy of Warwick, in French, s.xiv in.): the *ex libris* is on fo. 87[v].

CERNE (Cernelium), Dorset. *Ben. abbey of B.V.M., St Peter and St Ethelwold.*

Cambridge, U.L., Hh.3.11. *e*Statuta Anglie. s.xiv.
    Ll.1.10. *c*Liber precum, etc. ('Book of Cerne').
       s.ix–xv.
  Trinity Coll., 317. *e*Odonis isagoge. s.xiii in.
      1149.[7] *cl*Miscellanea. s.xiii.
London, B.M., Egerton 843.[7] J. de Sacro Bosco. s.xiii.
Oxford, Bodleian, Auct. D.4.13. *e*Theologica. s.xii–xiii.
  Merton Coll., 189. *b*J. Lathbury. s.xv. ?

CHERTSEY (Certeseia), Surrey. *Ben. abbey of St Peter.*

London, B.M., Add. 24067. *e*H. de Bracton. s.xiv.
    Royal 6 D.i. *e*Jeronimus. s.xii ex.
  Westminster Abbey, 7. *e*Epp. Pauli glo. s.xii ex.
Oxford, Bodleian, Lat. liturg. e.6.[8] *l*Breviarium. s.xiv med.
      e.37.[8] Breviarium. s.xiv med.
    D.13.5 Linc. (pr. bk). *i*J. Herolt. Rouen, A.D. 1511.
  Trinity Coll., 67. *e*Aristoteles. s.xiv.
Untraced: Sotheby sale, 29 July 1946, lot 108, to Francis Edwards.[8]
*l*Breviarium. s.xiv.

CHESTER (Cestria). *Ben. abbey of St Werburg.*

 *c.*20 books bequeathed by Richard of Chester, canon of York († 1347), are listed in York Minster, Acts of Chapter 1343–68, fo. 17.
 The pressmark is written on a flyleaf, immediately after and in the same hand as a note of contents.

Aberystwyth, N.L., DN 4923 (pr. bk). *e*Polychronicon (in English).
  Westminster, A.D. 1482.
Berlin, Staatsbibl., lat. 194. *c*Misc. grammatica, etc. s.xiv. ?
Cambridge, U.L., Ff.6.9. Pontificale. s.xiii. [xviii⁰ loco].
    Gg.5.34. Anselmus. s.xii/xiii. [vii⁰ loco].
Dublin, Trinity Coll., 46. Exodus et Deut. glo. s.xii ex. [iiii⁰ loco].
    271.[9] Speculum spiritalium. s.xv.
London, B.M., Cotton Otho B.iii, fos 1, 2. *c*Annales Cestrienses.
       s.xiv. ?
    Royal 4 E.viii. *e*Epp. Pauli glo. s.xii. [v⁰ loco].
     8 F.ix. *e*Nominum hebr. expo., etc. s.xiii/xiv.
      [primo loco].
    11 B.xiii. Ivo Carnotensis, etc. s.xiii. [xii⁰ loco].
  Gray's Inn, 3. Passionale. s.xi/xii. [xi⁰ loco].
     14, fos 1–138. Isidorus, etc. s.xiii in. [viii⁰ loco].
     19. Smaragdus. s.xii in. [xi⁰ loco].
Mostyn Hall, Lord Mostyn. *c*Annales Cestrienses. s.xv/xvi. ?
Oxford,
 Bodleian, Bodl. 373. P. Cantor. s.xiii ex. [vii⁰ loco].

----

[7] B.M., Egerton 843 was abstracted from Cambridge, Trinity Coll. 1149 about the year 1838.
[8] Three portions of one manuscript.
[9] The provenance of Trin. Coll. 271 is recorded by Bernard, *Catalogi* (1697), II. ii, no. 735. There does not seem to be any evidence for it now in the MS.

Oxford (*contd*)
   Bodleian, Bodl. 672. *c*Liber Luciani. s.xii ex.
                843.[1] Ambrosius, etc. s.xii–xiii in.
         Tanner 169*. *l*Psalterium, etc. A.D. 1193.
   All Souls Coll., 8. Matheus, etc., glo. s.xiii. [v⁰ loco].
   Balliol Coll., 57. R. Fishacre. s.xiii ex. [vii⁰ loco].
San Marino, Huntington, HM 132. *c*Polychronicon. s.xiv.
Shrewsbury School, VII. Gregorius, etc. s.xiii. [viii⁰ loco].
Rejected: Manchester, J. Rylands, Lat. 217.

CHESTER. *Priory of B.V.M., of Ben. nuns.*

San Marino, Huntington, EL 34 B. 7. *i*Processionale. s.xv.

CHESTER. *Franciscan convent.*

London, Gray's Inn, 1. *e*J. Cassianus. s.xii. [Johannes Cassianus A].
                2. *e*R. Holcot, etc. s.xiii–xiv.
                5. *e*Beda, etc. s.xiii. [Beda A].
                7. *e*P. Blesensis, etc. s.xiii.
               11. *e*Speculum religiosorum, etc. s.xiv.
               12. *e*Sermones, etc. s.xiv. [Summa de viciis et
                     virtutibus A].
Oxford, Bodleian, Lat. misc. d.74. *i*Panormia Ivonis. s.xii. ?
Rejected: London, Gray's Inn, 6.

CHESTER. *Dominican convent.*

Shrewsbury School, I. *e*Sapientia glo. s.xiii in.
                XXIV. *e*P. Comestor. s.xiii.
                XXXV. *e*Lucas glo. s.xiii.

CHESTER-LE-STREET. *Seat of bishopric of* **LINDISFARNE** *from 883,
   removed to* **DURHAM** *in 995, q.v.*

CHICH. *See* **ST OSYTH.**

CHICHESTER, Sussex. *Cathedral church of Holy Trinity.*

   The pressmark, together with the title, name of donor and first words of second
leaf, which regularly precede it, is reproduced from Emmanuel Coll., 25 ('Jeronimus contra Ruffinum Seffridi episcopi ii^do fo. magistrum H. xxv.') and Cambridge, U.L., Dd.10.20 in *New Pal. Soc.*, i, pl. 147, no. 11 *a, b*; the inscription is
written sometimes at the head and sometimes at the foot of the first leaf of text.
Cambridge, U.L., Dd.10.20. Hugo Floriacensis. s.xii. [I.xiiii].
               Emmanuel Coll., 16. Augustinus. s.xii. [H.xiiii].
                        25. *g*Jeronimus. s.xii in. [H.xxv].
                        26. Jeronimus. s.xii in. [H.xxiiii].
                        28. *g*Boetius. s.xii/xiii. [H.xxxvi].
               Trinity Coll., 1207. Ambrosius. s.xi. [H.xxviii].
Glasgow, U.L., Hunterian 20. Egesippus. s.xii ex. [I.xi].
Lincoln, Cathedral, 216. Liber florum. s.xii. [H.xliii].

   [1] Bodley 843 was rebound in s.xix and contains now no evidence of its provenance. Langbaine records that it was 'olim monasterii Cestriæ' (Bodleian,
MS. Langbaine 6, p. 60).

London, B.M., Cotton Vit. A.xvii, fos 1–16. cAnnales. s.xii med.
   Harley 6. Isidorus, etc. s.xiii. [I.vi].
  Coll. of Arms, s.n. Beda. s.xii. [L.xiii].
Oxford, Bodleian, Auct. D.3.14. gJob glo. s.xii ex. [C.xxix].
    Bodl. 142. Augustinus. s.xii. [H.xxi].
     374. Augustinus. s.xii ex. [H.vi].
   Laud lat. 95. lPsalterium, etc. s.xiii. ?
   Laud misc. 607. Avicenna. s.xiii med. [I.iiii].
  St John's Coll., 49. gP. Lombardus. s.xii ex. [F.xxiiii].
     88. Rabanus Maurus. s.xii. [I.x].
     95. Orosius. s.xii. [I.xvii].
  Univ Coll., 148. eStatuta ecclesie, etc. s.xiii–xiv.
Paris, B.N., lat. 15170, fos 126–62. cKalendarium, etc. s.xii in.
Rejected: Cambridge, Emmanuel Coll., 27.

CHICHESTER. *Dominican convent.*

Oxford, St John's Coll., 198. iSophismata Heytisbury, etc. s.xiv.

CHICKSANDS, Bedfordshire. *Gilbertine priory of B.V.M.*

Cambridge, St John's Coll., 216. eAugustinus. s.xii.
   Sid. Sussex Coll., 85. iBarlaam et Josaphat, etc. s.xiv.
London, B.M., Arundel 83. ePsalterium, etc. s.xiv in. ?
Oxford, Bodleian, Auct. E.infra 4. eOrigenes. s.xii ex.

CHRISTCHURCH (Twinham), Hampshire. *Aug. priory of Holy Trinity or Christ Church.*

Books noted by J. Leland, *Collectanea*, iv. 149, and *De Scriptoribus Britannicis*, p. 38.

Cambridge, U.L., Ff.1.31. cEusebius, etc. s.xiii–xiv.

CIRENCESTER, Gloucestershire. *Aug. abbey of B.V.M.*

Books noted by J. Leland, *Collectanea*, iv. 158. The *ex libris* inscription is 'Liber (ecclesie) sancte Marie de Cirencestria'.

Hereford, Cathedral, O.i.3. eGregorius, etc. s.xii.
    O.i.6. eJulianus Tolet., etc. s.xii in.
    O.i.10. eGregorius. s.xii in.
    O.ii.4.[2] G. Porretanus. s.xii/xiii. ?
    O.iii.10. Rob. Cricklade. s.xii. [? *Leland*]. ?
    O.v.10. eJ. Cassianus. s.xii med.
    O.v.14. eJ. Chrysostomus. s.xii med.
    O.vi.10. eAugustinus. s.xii in.
    P.i.12. eAugustinus. s.xii in.
    P.i.17. eAldhelmus, etc. s.xii–xiii.
    P.ii.14. eAugustinus. s.xii med.
    P.ii.15. eIvo Carnotensis. s.xii.
    P.iii.7. eAugustinus. s.xii med.
    P.iv.8. eRob. Cricklade. s.xiii. [*Leland*].
    P.iv.9. eH. de S. Victore. s.xii–xiii.

[2] Hereford, Cathedral, O.ii.4, All Souls Coll. 82 and Jesus Coll. 26 are inscribed 'Liber Magistri Aluredi', s.xii/xiii (?).

Hereford, Cathedral (*contd*)

P.v.3. *e*Augustinus. s.xii in.

P.v.4. *e*Augustinus. s.xii med.

P.v.9. *e*Augustinus, etc. s.xiii–xiv.

London, B.M., Cotton Vesp. A.xv. *e*Epp. Clementis, etc. s.xii in.

Royal 3 A.xii. *e*Beda. s.xii med. [*Leland*].

5 E.xviii. *e*Isidorus, etc. s.xii.

7 F.i. Alex. Nequam. s.xiii in. [? *Leland*]. ?

7 F.vi. *e*Paterius. s.xii med.

Oxford, Bodleian, Barlow 48. *e*J. Saresberiensis. s.xii/xiii.

Bodl. 284. *e*Psalterium cum comment. s.xiii/xiv.

Laud lat. 17. *c*Psalterium glo. s.xii. ?

All Souls Coll., 82.[2] *e*Virgilius. s.xii.

Jesus Coll., 3.[3] Greg. Nazianzenus, etc. s.xii in. ?

26.[2] Ivo, Panormia. s.xii. ?

34. *e*Orosius. s.xiii in.

48. *e*Cantica cum comment., etc. s.xii.

52. *e*Beda. s.xii med.

53. *e*Beda. s.xii med.

62. *e*Orosius. s.xii.

63. *e*Egesippus. s.xii med.

67. *e*Beda. s.xii med.

68. *e*Beda. s.xii med.

70. *e*Beda. s.xii med.

94. *e*Alex. Nequam. s.xiii in.

Rejected: Hereford, Cathedral, P.ii.10.

CLARE, Suffolk. *Convent of Austin friars.*

Oxford, Bodleian, Bodl. 797.[4] *e*Misc. theol. s.xv.

CLATTERCOTE, Oxfordshire. *Gilbertine priory of B.V.M. and St Leonard.*

Oxford, Bodleian, Rawl. A.420. *e*Bernardus, etc. s.xiii.

COBHAM, Kent. *Collegiate church of St Mary Magdalen.*

Inventory of books, etc. (s.xiv ex.), in London, B.M., Harley Roll C. 18.

COCKERSAND, Lancashire. *Prem. abbey of B.V.M.*

Oxford, Bodleian, Rawl. C.317. *c*Theologica. s.xiii. ?

COGGESHALL, Essex. *Savigniac and (1147) Cist. abbey of B.V.M.*

M. R. James, 'MSS from Essex Monastic Libraries', *Trans. Essex Archaeol. Soc.*, N.S., xxi (1933), 36. Books noted by J. Leland, *Collectanea*, iv. 162; *cf.* Leland, *De Scriptoribus Britannicis*, p. 212.

[2] See p. 51, n. 2.

[3] Jesus Coll. 3 belonged to Sir John Prise (†1555), who had many MSS from Cirencester, and it appears to have been seen at Cirencester by the compiler of the thirteenth-century list of books in monastic libraries, B.M., Royal 3 D.i.

[4] Bodl. 797 was later at **SHEEN,** *q.v.*

Cambridge, U.L., Ii.2.25. *e*Cassiodorus. s.xiii in.
    Corpus Christi Coll., 31. *e*Steph. Langton. s.xiii.
              54. *e*Odo Cantuariensis. s.xii ex.
                 [*Leland*].
              89. *e*Steph. Langton, etc. s.xiii.
London, B.M., Cotton Vesp. D.x, fos 4–128. *c*Chronicon Rad. de
                           Coggeshall, etc. s.xiii.
      Royal 5 B.ix. *e*Ailredus, etc. s.xiii.
         6 D.vi. *e*Jeronimus. s.xiii in.
    Coll. of Arms, Arundel 11. *c*Chronica. s.xiii. ?
San Marino, Huntington, HM 27186.[5] Statuta (in roll form). s.xiii
                      ex.–xiv. ?
Rejected: Cambridge, Corpus Christi Coll., 30.

COLCHESTER, Essex. *Ben. abbey of St John the Baptist.* (*Cf.* cell at
SNAPE.)

    M. R. James, 'MSS from Essex Monastic Libraries', *Trans. Essex Archaeol.
Soc.*, N.S., xxi (1933), 37. N. R. Ker, 'More MSS from Essex Monastic Libraries', *ibid.*, xxiii (1945), 303.
    Books noted by J. Leland, *Collectanea*, iv. 162.

Leyden, U.L., Voss. lat. F.18.[6] Orosius; Justinus. s.xiii.
London, B.M., Harley 1132. *c*Annales. s.xiv.
Oxford, Bodleian, Gough Essex 1. *c*Chronicon. s.xvi in. ?
Rejected: Oxford, Queen's Coll., 54.

COLCHESTER. *Aug. priory of St Botolph.*

    M. R. James, 'MSS from Essex Monastic Libraries', *Trans. Essex Archaeol.
Soc.*, N.S., xxi (1933), 37. N. R. Ker, 'More MSS from Essex Monastic Libraries', *ibid.*, xxiii (1945), 303.

Antwerp, Plantin-Moretus, 78. *e*Comment. in epp. Pauli. s.xiii.
Oxford, Balliol Coll., 182. *e*Haymo. s.xii.

COLCHESTER. *Franciscan convent.*

    N. R. Ker, 'More MSS from Essex Monastic Libraries', *Trans. Essex Archaeol.
Soc.*, N.S., xxiii (1945), 303.

Oxford, Bodleian, Lat. misc. f.37. *i*Dictionarium ('campeflore'). s.xiv.

COLDINGHAM, Berwickshire. *Ben. priory of B.V.M.; cell of Durham.*

    Lists of books kept in the church in inventories of 1362, 1371, 1372, 1446
printed from Durham Muniments in *Correspondence . . . of the Priory of Coldingham* (Surtees Soc., xii, 1841), App., pp. xl, lxiv, lxvii, lxxxiii.

Durham,
    Cathedral, A.II.8. *c*Epp. can., etc., glo. s.xiii. [*Cat. vet.*, p. 53 A]. ?
            B.II.32. *e*Gregorius. s.xiii. [*Cat. vet.*, p. 63 A].
London, B.M., Add. 24059. *c*Historia Dunelm. s.xiv. ?
         Harley 4664. *l*Breviarium. s.xiii/xiv. ?
           4747. *c*Kalendarium, etc. s.xiii. ?

---

    [5] A hand of *c*.1600 records that this roll was 'found in the abbey of Coxall in
Essex at the tyme of the dissolution'.
    [6] The provenance of Voss. lat. F.18 is recorded in Gronovius's edition of
Justinus (edn 1760, sign. ††4ᵛ).

COMBE (Cumba), Warwickshire. *Cist. abbey of B.V.M.*

London, Gray's Inn, 13. *e*R. Grosseteste, etc. s.xiii.

COMBERMERE, Cheshire. *Savigniac and (1147) Cist. abbey of B.V.M. and St Michael.*

Dublin, Trinity Coll., 49. *e*Job glo. s.xii.
Stonyhurst Coll., S.2.5 (pr. bk). *e*Breviarium Cisterciense. Paris, s.a.

CONISHEAD, Lancashire. *Aug. priory of B.V.M.*
Rejected: Carlisle, Tullie House Museum (Augustinus).

CONWAY, Caernarvonshire. *Cist. abbey of B.V.M.*

London, B.M., Harley 3725. *c*Chronicon, etc. s.xv.

COTTINGHAM. *See* **HALTEMPRICE.**

COUPAR ANGUS (de Cupro), Perthshire. *Cist. abbey of B.V.M.*

For printed books see Durkan and Ross, pp. 81 (Donald Campbell), 104, 112 (Thomas Hamilton), 123, 173, 188. Another (Augustinus Datus, etc.) belongs, Mr Durkan tells me, to the Edinburgh Royal High School.

Edinburgh, N.L., Adv. 35.1.7. *e*Scotichronicon. s.xv.
    U.L., 126. *e*Kalendarium, etc. s.xv.
Rome, Vatican, Pal. lat. 65. *e*Psalterium glo. s.xii.
    Regin. lat. 694. *e*Beda, etc. s.xii/xiii.
Wolfenbüttel, Ducal Libr., Helmst. 927. *e*Pseudo-Turpinus. s.xv.

COVENTRY, Warwickshire. *Ben. cathedral priory of B.V.M.*

List of books written for the church by John de Bruges 'monachus Coventr.' *c.*1240, edited by C. Eyston from Bodleian, Digby MS. 104, fo. 171 (also in Bodleian, MS. Auct. F.5.23, fo. 166ᵛ), in T. Hearne, *Hist. and Antiq. of Glastonbury* (Oxford, 1722), pp. 291–93; reprinted in *Monasticon*, iii. 186.

Cambridge, Magdalene Coll., 26. *c*Isidorus, etc. s.xiii. ?
    Trinity Coll., 1088. *e*Beda. s.xii.
London, B.M., Royal 12 G.iv. *i*Gilbertus Anglicus, etc. s.xiv in.
Oxford, Bodleian, Auct. F.3.9. *e*Grammatica. s.xv.
     F.5.23. *c*Miscellanea. s.xiii–xiv.
    Bodl. 901. *e*Pontificale. s.xv.
    Digby 33. *e*Bonaventura, etc. s.xii–xv.
     104, fos 169–74. *c*Beda, etc. s.xiii.
     115. *e*W. Hilton, etc. s.xv.
   Douce 139.[7] Statuta Anglie, etc. s.xiii.
  New Coll., 123. *e*T. Aquinas, etc. s.xiv–xv.

COVENTRY. *Charterhouse of St Anne.*

List of books brought thither from London (A.D. 1500), printed from P.R.O., Exch. K.R., Eccl. docs 2/44 by E. Margaret Thompson, *Carth. Order in England*, p. 326; second folios given.

---

[7] Twenty leaves containing documents relating to St Mary's, Coventry, detached from the end of Digby 139, were in the Staunton collection burnt in the fire at Birmingham Reference Library in 1879.

Cambridge, Christ's Coll., 11. *e*Comment. in Psalterium. s.xv.
   Peterhouse, 276. *e*Psalterium. s.xv in.
London, B.M., Royal 5 A.v. *e*Augustinus, etc. s.xv.

COVENTRY. *Franciscan convent.*

Cambridge, Trinity Coll., 940. *e*Boetius. s.xii. [Boethius A].
Colchester, Harsnett Libr., H.h.14 (pr. bk). *i*Pontificale romanum.
   Lyon, A.D. 1511.
London, B.M., Harley 5116. *e*Josephus. s.xiii. [Josephus A].
Oxford, Bodleian, Rawl. D.238. *l*Astronomica, etc. s.xiv.
Rejected: Eton, Coll., 108, ii.

COVENTRY. *Carmelite convent.*

Berlin, Staatsbibl., Hamilton 503. *e*P. Comestor. s.xiii.
Durham, Cathedral, A.IV.9. *e*Misc. theologica. s.xiv.
Oxford, Merton Coll., B.8.G.17 (pr. bk).[8] *i*Antonius Andreas, etc.
   Venice, A.D. 1496.

COVERHAM, Yorkshire. *Prem. abbey of B.V.M.*

London, B.M., Sloane 1584. *i*Misc. theol., etc. (mainly in English).
 s.xvi in.
New York, Mr W. S. Glazier, 39. *i*Liber precum (in roll form). s.xv ex.

CREDITON, Devon. *Collegiate church of Holy Cross.*

Oxford,
 Bodleian, Bodl. 159[9] Augustinus, etc. s.xiii–xv.
     383.[9] R. Holcot, etc. s.xiv–xv.
     390.[9] 'Exposicio super Job', etc. s.xiii–xiv.
     793.[9] Acta S. Germani, etc. s.xii in. –xii.
     863.[9] Haimo, etc. s.xiv–xv.
 Christ Church, 90.[9] Comment. in Danielem. s.xv.
     91.[9] N. de Aquavilla, etc. s.xiii ex. –xv.
 Univ. Coll., 91. *e*W. Peraldus. s.xiii.

CRENDON. *See* **NOTLEY.**

CROSSRAGUEL, Ayrshire.

For a printed book which traditionally belonged to Quintin Kennedy, abbot
(†1564), see Durkan and Ross, p. 120.

CROWLAND, Lincolnshire. *Ben. abbey of B.V.M., St Bartholomew,*
 and St Guthlac. (Cf. cell at **FREISTON.**)

A list of books 'apud Croylande in abathia', s.xiii/xiv, printed from Berlin,
Staatsbibl., MS. Hamilton 30, fo. 123, by H. Boese, 'Ein mittelalterliches
Bücherverzeichnis von Croyland Abbey', *Bibliothek, Bibliothekar, Bibliothekswis-
senschaft, Festschrift Joris Vorstius*, 1954, pp. 286–95. Books noted by J.
Leland, *Collectanea*, iv. 30. The *ex libris* inscription is 'Liber Croylandie'.

Bristol, Baptist Coll., Z.e.38. *i*Biblia. s.xiii.

---

[8] Belonged to a Carmelite who was earlier at the Newcastle convent, *q.v.*
[9] For the provenance of these seven manuscripts see *Bodleian Library Record*,
ii (1941–49), 91.

Cambridge, Magdalene Coll., 5. *i*Apocalypsis. s.xiv–xv. ?
      Sid. Sussex Coll., 73. *e*Excepciones monachi Croylandie.
      s. xiii.
Detroit, Public Libr., 2. *e*Polychronicon. s.xiv ex.
Douai, Bibl. mun., 852. *e*Heraclides, etc. s.xii–xiii.
Dublin, Trinity Coll., 370.[1] *e*Ric. Armachanus, etc. s.xiv.
London, B.M., Add. 35168. *e*Chronicon. s.xiii.
      Arundel 230. *l*Psalterium (Lat. and Fr.), etc. s.xii–xiii. ?
      Egerton 3759. *l*Graduale. s.xiii in.
      Lansdowne 338. *e*Summa Reymundi. s.xiii.
    Lambeth Palace, 145, fos 138–255. *e*J. Chrysostomus. s.xii.
                          [*Cat.* 43–49].
         873. *l*Kalendarium, etc. s.xii–xv.
Oslo, Riksarkivet, Lat. fr. 145. *c*Kalendarium. s.xii in. ?
Oxford, Bodleian, Douce 296. *l*Psalterium, etc. s.xi. ?
      Rawl. C.531. *e*Augustinus, etc. s.xiii.
Paris, B.N., Lat. 5557. *e*Pseudevangelium Nicodemi, etc. s.xiii.
Princeton, U.L., R. Garrett 119. *i*W. de Insulis. s.xiv ex.
Spalding, Gentlemen's Soc., M.J.B.13. *e*Statuta Anglie, etc. s.xiii/xiv.
Untraced: MS. belonging to Lewis Baillardeau: *cf.* T. Hearne, *Collections*
(Oxf. Hist. Soc.), ix. 46, 55, 85. Historica.

CROXDEN (de valle S. Marie de Crokesdene), Staffordshire. *Cist. abbey
of B.V.M.*

Cambridge, U.L., Gg.1.22. *e*Expo. in Psalmos 1–134. s.xiv.
Dublin, Archbishop Marsh's Libr., Q.4.16 (pr. bk).[2] *e*R. Holcot. Lyon,
A.D. 1497.
London, B.M., Add. 34633. *e*Steph. Langton, etc. s.xiii. ?
      Cotton Faust. B.vi, part 1, fos 41–94. *c*Annales, etc. s.xiv.

CULROSS, Fife. *Cist. abbey of B.V.M. and St Serf.*

Edinburgh, N.L., Adv. 18.8.11. *i*Psalterium. s.xv ex.
Traquair Ho., Mr P. Maxwell Stuart. *e*Biblia. s.xiii.

DALE (de Parco Stanley), Derbyshire. *Prem. abbey of B.V.M.*

Oxford, Bodliean, Don.e.598 (pr. bk). *i*P. de Herentals. Rouen,
A.D. 1504.

DARLEY (Derleya), Derbyshire. *Aug. abbey of B.V.M.*

Cambridge, Gonv. and Caius Coll., 84. *bi*Medica, etc. (partly in English).
s.xiv–xv.
Oxford, Bodleian, Auct. D.infra 2.8. *e*Haymo. s.xiii.
      Laud gr. 28. *e*Basilian Liturgy (in Greek). s.xii ex.
      e Mus. 222. *e*Sermones, etc. s.xiii.
Untraced: John Cochran cat. (1837) no. 108.[3] *c*P. Lombardus. s.xii.

---

[1] The flyleaves, part of an office of St Guthlac, s.xii in., are kept separately as
MS. D.1.25a.
[2] Belonged also to Holme Cultram (*q.v.*).
[3] Presumably the same as lot 1203 in the Van Mildert sale, 21 July 1838, sold
to the bookseller Thomas Rodd.

DARLINGTON, co. Durham. *Collegiate church of St Cuthbert.*

List of 17 books 'in isto librario' in 1487 on flyleaf at end of Mr Smith's manuscript.

Leicester, Mr H. F. Smith. *e*P. Comestor, etc. s.xiii in. –xv in.

DARTFORD, Kent. *Priory of B.V.M. and St Margaret, of Dom. nuns.*

Downside Abbey, 26542. *i*Stimulus amoris, etc. (in English). s.xv.
Dublin, Trinity Coll., 490. *e*Brut (in English). s.xv.
London, B.M., Harley 2254. *i*W. Hilton, etc. (in English). s.xv.
      Soc. of Antiquaries, 717. *i*Officium mortuorum, etc. s.xv.
Oxford, Bodleian, Douce 322. *e*J. Lydgate, etc. (in English). s.xv.
Taunton, Castle Mus., 2. *e*Horae. s.xv.

DEEPING, Lincolnshire. *Ben. priory of St James; cell of Thorney.*

List of books (s.xiv med.) printed from B.M., Harley MS. 3658, fo. 75ᵛ, in *Monasticon*, iv. 167.

London, B.M., Cotton Jul. B.xiii, fos 2–47. *e*Chronologica. s.xii ex.

DEER, Aberdeenshire. *Cist. abbey of B.V.M.*

For 4 printed books see Durkan and Ross, pp. 82, 101, 120, 165.

Cambridge, U.L., Ii.6.32. *c*Evangeliarium ('Book of Deer'). s.x.
Edinburgh, Scottish Record Office, Murray of Ochtertyre Muniments,
    Sect. 1, no. 428A. Ordinale Cist., from binding of Deer Rentale.
St Andrews, U.L., PA.3895.P.6. *i*Aristoteles. s.xv.
Rejected: Cambridge, Trinity Coll., 1335. Edinburgh, N.L., Adv.
    18.8.8.

DENNY, Cambridgeshire. *Abbey of St James and St Leonard, of Franciscan nuns.*

Oxford, Bodleian, Hatton 18. *i*W. de Nassington (in English). s.xv.

DERBY. *Priory of B.V.M., King's Mead, of Ben. nuns.*

London, B.M., Egerton 2710. *e*Theologica (in French). s.xiii.

DERBY. *Collegiate church of All Saints.*

List of ten 'bokes in our Lady chapell tyed with chenes', probably *c*.1527, printed by J. C. Cox and W. H. St John Hope, *Annals of the Collegiate Church of All Saints* (1881), p. 175.

DEREHAM, WEST, Norfolk. *Prem. abbey of B.V.M.*

Cambridge, U.L., Kk.1.11. *e*Odo Cheritonensis. s.xiii. ?
Dublin, Trinity Coll., 51. *e*Biblia (pars ii). s.xii/xiii.

DIEULACRES (Deulacresse), Staffordshire. *Cist. abbey of B.V.M. and St Benedict.*

London, Gray's Inn, 9, fos 88–147. *c*Misc. historica. s.xiii–xv.

DONCASTER, Yorkshire. *Franciscan convent.*

Oxford, Bodleian, Savile 20. *e*Boetius. s.xii.
Untraced: R. Thoresby (†1725) MS. 104.[4] Chronicon Martini.
Rejected: Oxford, Bodleian, Savile 15, 18, 19.

DORCHESTER, Oxfordshire. *Aug. (Arrouaisian) abbey of St Peter.*

Dublin, Trinity Coll., 65. *c*Concordancie bibl. s.xiv med.

DORE (Vallis Dore), Herefordshire. *Cist. abbey of B.V.M.*

The usual form of *ex libris* inscription is 'Liber (monachorum) sancte Marie vallis Dore'.

Cambridge, Trinity Coll., 1272. *e*Regula S. Basilii, etc. s.xiii in.
Hereford, Cathedral, P.i.13. *c*Abbreviacio Justini, etc. s.xii/xiii. ?
             P.v.5. *e*Osbernus Gloucestr. s.xiii in.
London, B.M., Cotton Vesp. D.xi. *e*Laur. Dunelmensis. s.xii.
             Cleop. C.xi. *e*Eadmerus, etc. s.xiii.
             Egerton 3088. *c*Beda, etc. s.xiii.
             Harley 4981. *e*XII prophete glo. s.xii.
Oxford, Bodleian, Laud misc. 138. *e*Augustinus. s.xiii.
             e Mus. 82. *e*Theologica. s.xii–xiii.
        Exeter Coll., 1. *c*Regula monachorum Cist. s.xiii. ?

DOVER, Kent. *Ben. priory of B.V.M. and St Martin; cell of Canterbury.*

M. R. James, *The Ancient Libraries of Canterbury and Dover* (Cambr., 1903), prints a catalogue (A.D. 1389) from Bodleian, Bodl. 920 (second folios given), and reprints J. Leland's note of two books seen there from *Collectanea*, iv. 11. C. R. Haines, 'The Library of Dover Priory, its Catalogue and Extant Volumes', *The Library*, N.S., viii (1927), 97–118, and *Dover Priory* (Cambr., 1930), pp. 383–401, with facsimile of a page of the catalogue.

The pressmark, in which the arabic number is written inside the capital letter, seems usually to have been entered twice, once with the *ex libris* and table of contents on a flyleaf, and again at the foot of the second, third or fourth leaf of text, where it is followed by the short title, the opening words of the leaf, the number of leaves in the volume and the number of items in the volume (see M. R. James, *op. cit.*, pp. xcii, xciii, 408, and the reproduction of the entry in the Advocates MS. by C. R. Haines, *op. cit.*, p. 365). The pressmark only of Royal 15 A.xii is reproduced in *New Pal. Soc.*, i, pl. 17, no. 4.

Cambridge,
     Corpus Christi Coll., 3–4. Biblia. s.xii. [A.I.1; *cat.* 2 *and* 3].
                42. *i*Vita S. Martini, etc. s.xii. [D.II; *cat.* 129].
                365. R. Rolle. s.xv ex. [A.V].
                366. P. Blesensis. s.xiii. [D.III.3; *cat.* 133].
                462. Recapit. biblie, etc. s.xii. [J.II.7; *cat.* 385].
     Pembr. Coll., 280. Ovidius. s.xii. [J.III.8; *cat.* 397].
     St John's Coll., 59. Psalterium (Irish glosses). s.x ex. [A.V.1; *cat.* 18].
                87. *e*Statius, etc. s.xi–xiii. [J.III.2; *cat.* 391].
     Trinity Coll., 624. *i*Galfridus Vinsauf, etc. s.xiii in. [J.III.5; *cat.* 394].
                825. Priscianus. s.xii. [J.(V.3); *cat.* 423].

[4] Belonged later to Richard Gough, according to a MS. note in Gough's copy of Thoresby's *Ducatus Leodiensis* (Bodleian, Gough Yorks. 60), p. 529. The MS. was lot 44 in the 1764 Thoresby sale.

Canterbury, Cathedral, 71. *i*Reg. S. Benedicti glo. A.D. 1380.
Cardiff, Public Libr., 1.381, fos 1–80. Vita S. Wingualei. s.xiii in. [D.VII.6; *cat.* 169].
Edinburgh, N.L., Adv. 18.5.12. *e*Statius, etc. s.xii. [J.III.7; *cat.* 396].
Glasgow, U.L., Hunterian 467. *i*Helpericus, etc. s.xii–xv. [C.VII.8; *cat.* 124].
London,
B.M., Arundel 16. Vita Dunstani, etc. s.xii. [D.VII.4; *cat.* 167].
Cotton Jul. D.v, fos 14–68. Chronica. s.xiii ex. [H.VII.11; *cat.* 374].
Vesp. B.xi, fos 72–79. *c*Chronica. s.xv.
Cleop. A.xii, fos 4–62. Chronicon. s.xiv. [H.VII.8; *cat.* 371].
Egerton 2867. *l*Biblia, etc. s.xiii med.
Harley 550. Statuta Anglie. s.xiv. [G.II.7; *cat.* 273].
Royal 15 A.xii. Terentius. s.xii. [J.III.16; *cat.* 405].
Oxford, Bodleian, Bodl. 678. Elucidarium, etc. s.xiii. [C.VII.3; *cat.* 119].
Digby 13. Marbodus, etc. s.xii. [J.IIII.9; *cat.* 415].
Trinity Coll., 59. Augustinus. s.xiv. [C.VI.6; *cat.* 113].

DOVER. *Prem. abbey of St Radegund at Bradsole.*

Catalogue (s.xiii ex.) printed by A. H. Sweet in *Eng. Hist. Rev.*, liii (1938), 88–93, from Bodleian, Rawl. B.336, fos 189–93.

DROITWICH (Wichia), Worcestershire. *Convent of Austin friars.*

Oxford, Brasenose Coll., 13. *i*Seneca, etc. s.xiii.

DRYBURGH, Berwickshire. *Prem. abbey of B.V.M.*

For a printed book see Durkan and Ross, p. 134.

DUNDEE, Angus. *Dominican convent.*

For a printed book see Durkan and Ross, p. 75.

DUNFERMLINE, Fife. *Ben. abbey of Holy Trinity.*

For a printed book see Durkan and Ross, p. 137.

Boulogne, Bibl. mun., 92. *e*Psalterium. s.xv ex.
Edinburgh, N.L., Adv. 1.1.1. Biblia. s.xiii. ?
U.L., 72. *i*Compendium theologice veritatis. s.xv ex.
Glasgow, U.L., BE.7.b.8.[5] 'Liber Pluscardensis'. s.xv ex.
Rejected: Oxford, Bodleian, Fairfax 8.

DUNKELD, Perthshire. *Cathedral church of St Columba.*

Edinburgh, N.L., Adv. 18.2.6. *e*Gregorius. s.xv.
U.L., 64. Antiphonarium. s.xvi in. ?

DUNKESWELL, Devon. *Cist. abbey of B.V.M.*

Book noted by J. Leland, *Collectanea*, iv. 150.

[5] Written at Dunfermline for William Schevez, archbishop of St Andrews.

DUNSTABLE, Bedfordshire. *Aug. Priory of St Peter.*

Cambridge, U.L., Ff.6.55. *i*Pore Caitiff, etc. (in English). s.xv. ?
London, B.M., Cotton Tib. A.x, fos 5–59. *c*Annales. s.xiii.
Inner Temple, Barrington 83. *c*Placita, etc. s.xiv in. ?
Manchester, Chetham, 6709. *i*Lydgate (in English). A.D. 1490.

DUNSTABLE. *Dominican convent.*

Cambridge, U.L., Add. 2770.[6] *ic*Collectarius. s.xv.

DUNSTER, Somerset. *Ben. priory of St George; cell of Bath.*

London, B.M., Add. 10628. *l*Kalendarium, etc. s.xiv ex.

DUREFORD, Sussex. *Prem. abbey of B.V.M. and St John the Baptist.*

Lincoln, Cathedral, 179. *e*Vocabularium, etc. s.xv.

DURHAM (Dunelmum). *Ben. cathedral priory of St Cuthbert, including the temporary settlements of the community at* **LINDISFARNE** *and* **CHESTER-LE-STREET.** (*Cf.* cells at **COLDINGHAM, FARNE ISLAND, FINCHALE, JARROW, LINDISFARNE, OXFORD,** *Durham College,* **STAMFORD.**)

Thomas Rud, *Codicum MSS Ecclesiae Cath. Dunelm. Catalogus Classicus* (Durham, 1825, compiled early xviii cent.). *Catalogi Veteres Librorum Ecclesiae Cath. Dunelm.,* ed. J. Raine, with preface by B. B[otfield] (Surtees Soc., 1838), referred to hereafter as *Cat.* C. H. Turner, 'The earliest List of Durham MSS', *Journal of Theol. Studies,* xix (1918), 121–32. H. D. Hughes, *Hist. of Durham Cathedral Library* (Durham, 1925). R. A. B. Mynors, *Durham Cathedral MSS to the end of the twelfth century* (Durham, 1939).

For five books given to Chester-le-Street by King Athelstan, see Arnold, *Symeon of Durham* (Rolls Series), i. 211. List of books given by Bishop William of St Carilef (†1096) printed in *Wills and Inventories* (Surtees Soc., 1835), p. 1, and in *Cat.,* pp. 117–18. Catalogue (s.xii ex.) printed from Durham, Cathedral, MS. B.IV.24, fos 1–2, in *Cat.,* pp. 1–9. Incomplete catalogue (s.xii) printed from Durham, Muniments of Dean and Chapter, Misc. Ch. 7143, by Mynors, *op. cit.,* p. 10. Books given by Bishop Hugh du Puiset (†1195) printed in *Wills and Inventories,* pp. 4–5, and in *Cat.,* pp. 118–19. Incomplete catalogue (s.xiv ex.) printed from Muniments of Dean and Chapter, Misc. Ch. 7144, by Mynors, *op. cit.,* p. 11. Another incomplete catalogue (s.xiv ex.) in Misc. Ch. 2475 described by Mynors, *op. cit.,* p. 11 (letters and second folios given). Catalogue of books in the Spendement (s.xiv ex. and additions of 1416) printed from MS. B.IV.46 in *Cat.,* pp. 85–116 (letters and second folios given); another copy (dated 1391) printed *ibid.,* pp. 10–39. Catalogues of books in the cloister, for the refectory, and for novices (1395) printed in *Cat.,* pp. 46–84 (letters and second folios given). Catalogue of books (mainly registers) in the Chancery (1421) printed from Muniments of Dean and Chapter, Registrum II, fo. 156ᵛ, in *Cat.,* pp. 123–24 (letters and second folios given). New acquisitions of the common library (s.xv) printed in *Cat.,* pp. 41–45 (letters and second folios given). List of *c.*20 books bought at Oxford (for Durham ?), s.xiv, by Thomas de Wyniston (this name in *Liber Vitae,* fo. 59ᵛ), printed by M. R. James, *Catalogue of MSS of Jesus Coll., Cambridge* (1895), pp. 91–92, from Jesus Coll. 57. Books noted by J. Leland, *Collectanea,* iv. 41; see also Leland, *De Scriptoribus Britannicis,* p. 205. See also lists of books sent to Oxford, under **OXFORD,** *Durham College.*

The fifteenth-century library pressmark and the earlier letter-mark, which corresponds nearly always to the letter in the catalogues of s.xiv, xv, are reproduced from Lambeth Palace 325 and B.M., Cotton Jul. A.vi, in *New Pal. Soc.,* i,

---

[6] Cambridge, U.L., Add. 2770 belonged to the Dominicans of Smithfield in Marian times.

pl. 147, no. 2 *a–c* (part of a Durham mark is shown also in no. 4 *a*, but ascribed wrongly to Norwich). The marks are written commonly at the head of the first leaf of text in the right-hand corner (see Mynors, *op. cit.*, pl. 19, 21, 28, 30, 34, 38, 45, 47, 56). The *ex libris* inscriptions are also written at the head of the first leaf of text and usually in the form 'Liber sancti Cuthberti (de Dunelmo)' (s.xii/xiii and later) or 'De communi libraria monachorum Dunelm.' (s.xv in.). Marks consisting of a letter and, below it, an arabic number were written on the flyleaf (usually) of some manuscripts, *c.*1500: these marks are reproduced here thus: a/12 (York, xvi.D.9).

Ampleforth Abbey, C.v.72 (pr. bk).   *i*Hadrianus Sextus.   Paris, A.D. 1527.
Birdsall House, Lord Middleton.[7]   *e*Biblia.   s.xiii.
Bristol, Central Public Libr. (pr. bks; 5 vols).   *i*Duns Scotus.   Venice, A.D. 1506.
Cambridge,
U.L., Add. 3303 (6).   *l*Kalendarium.   s.xii.   ?
 Ff.4.41.   *i*Ivo Carnotensis.   s.xii/xiii.
 Gg.3.28.   Ælfric (in English).   s.x/xi.   [1ª.8¹.L; *cat.*, p. 5].
 Gg.4.33.   *e*Epp. Pauli, etc.   s.xii.   [C; *cat.*, pp. 18, 93 H].
 Kk.5.10.   *e*Biblia, etc.   s.xiii.
 Mm.3.14.   *e*J. de Voragine.   s.xiv.   [*Cat.*, p. 75 G].
 Inc. 1049 (pr. bk).   *i*L. Pruthenus.   Nuremberg, A.D. 1498.
 Rel. b.51.3 (pr. bk).   *i*Postille majores.   Lyon, A.D. 1519.
  c.50.8 (pr. bk).[8]   *i*Epistole ex registro beatissimi Gregorii. Paris, A.D. 1508.
Corpus Christi Coll., 183.   *c*Beda, etc.   s.x in.   [*Æthelstan*].
  EP.S.3 (pr. bk).   *i*J. F. de Panvinis, etc.   Paris, A.D. 1503.
Fitzwilliam Mus., McClean 169.   *i*Miscellanea.   s.xv.
Jesus Coll., 1.   *e*Decretales glo.   s.xiii.   [*Cat.*, p. 47 E].
 6.   *e*Decretales glo.   s.xiii–xiv.   [M].
 13.   *e*Sermones.   s.xiv–xv.   [N/ii].
 14.   *e*Beda.   s.xii.   [A].
 15.   P. Lombardus.[9]   s.xiv.   [*Cat.*, pp. 22, 99 P].
 20.   Summa de vitiis.   s.xiii.   [*Cat.*, pp. 24, 100 C].
 22.   *l*Graduale.   s.xiii–xiv.   ?
 23.   *e*Psalterium.   s.xii–xv.
 24.   *cl*Theologica.   s.xiv.
 25.   Astronomica, etc.   s.xii.   [A, a/22; *cat.*, p. 75 A].
 28.   *e*Priscianus.   s.xi ex.   [*Cat.*, p. 49 N].
 29.   Constit. Clementine.   s.xv in.   [H].   ?
 41.   *c*Speculum religiosorum, etc.   s.xiii–xv.
 44.   *e*Medica.   s.xii.   [O, 2ª.7¹.ffe; *cat.*, pp. 8, 33, 111 O].
 45.   *e*Repertorium super Speculum hist.   s.xv.   [L].
 48.   Boethius.   s.xiii–xv.   [O/ii].
 50.   Esaias, etc., glo.   s.xii.   [E; *cat.*, pp. 15, 90 E].
 52.[1]   *s*Sermones, etc.   s.xii in.
 53.[1]   *s*Ivo Carnotensis.   s.xii in.
 54.   *e*T. Aquinas, etc.   s.xiii–xv.

[7] Lord Middleton's manuscripts are deposited at Nottingham University Library.
[8] Two binding leaves of Rel. c.50.8 are kept separately as MS. Add. 2751 (7).
[9] The binding leaves (20) contain English sermons, s.xi.
[1] Jesus Coll. 52, 53, and Bodleian, Laud misc. 52, formed one volume.

Cambridge (*contd*)
Jesus Coll., 57. T. Aquinas, etc. s.xiii/xiv. [N; *cat.*, p. 73 N].
  59. *e*W. de Alvernia, etc. s.xiv. [C; *cat.*, p. 72 C].
  61. *e*Reg. S. Benedicti, etc. s.xiv–xv.
  64. *e*Boetius, etc. s.xii. [B; *cat.*, p. 71 B].
  65. Expo. misse, etc. s.xii–xiii. [*Cat.*, pp. 25, 101 D].
  67. J. Wallensis. s.xiv. [G; *cat.*, p. 77 G].
  69. *e*Summa Raymundi. s.xiii–xiv.
  70. *i*W. de Conchis, etc. s.xv.
  71. *e*Ric. de S. Victore, etc. s.xii/xiii. [B; *cat.*, p. 75 B].
  76. Jeronimus, etc. s.xii. [D; *cat.*, pp. 19, 94 D].
King's Coll., 22. *e*H. de S. Victore. s.xii. [C; *cat.*, pp. 21, 37, 41 F,
  97 H].
Magdalene Coll., Pepys 1662. *l*Kalendarium. s.xv.
  2981, nos 18–19.[2] Evangelia. s.viii.
Pembr. Coll., 241. *e*Isidorus. s.xiv.
Peterhouse, 74. *e*Pseudo-Isidorus. s.xi ex. [E, 2ª.8¹.S; *cat.*, pp. 35,
  112 E].
St John's Coll., 112. *e*T. Aquinas, etc. s.xiii ex.–xv. [G; *cat.*, p. 68 G].
  172. *e*Antidotarium. s.xii ex. [C, 2ª.7¹. G; *cat.*,
  pp. 33, 110 C].
Sid. Sussex Coll., 32.[3] Florus. s.xii ex. [C; *cat.*, p. 64 A].
  51. Hildebertus, etc. s.xii. [P; *cat.*, pp. 24, 101 P].
  56. *e*Galfridus Vinsauf, etc. s.xv. [K].
  100, ii. *e*Pontificale. s.xi.
  101. *e*Decreta non glo. s.xii. [1ª.8¹.F; *cat.*,
  pp. 35, 112 F].
Trinity Coll., 8. *e*Tract. de vitiis, etc. s.xiii. [F; *cat.*, p. 72 F].
  216.[4] Epp. Pauli glo. s.viii. [L; *cat.*, pp. 18, 93 L].
  365. *bs*T. de Chabham, etc. s.xiii/xiv–xv. ?
  1194. *e*Claudianus. s.xii ex. [A, 2ª.7¹.C; *cat.*, pp. 32,
  109 A, 119].
  1227. *e*Beda, etc. s.xii. [B; *cat.*, pp. 30, 107 B].
Deene Park, Trustees of the late Mr G. Brudenell, XVIII.B.3.[5] *e*Biblia.
  s.xiii.
Downside Abbey, 960 (pr. bk). *i*Augustinus, Epistole. Basel, A.D. 1493.
  970 (pr. bk). *i*Jeronimus. Venice, A.D. 1497.
  18274 (pr. bk). *i*Bernardus, etc. Paris, A.D. 1508.
Dublin, Trinity Coll., 349, fos 67–102. *e*Augustinus, etc. s.xii/xiii. [G].
  440. *i*N. Wireker. s.xiv/xv.
  Ff.dd.4–6 (pr. bks). *i*Biblia cum expo. N. de Lyra
  (ii–iv). Basel, A.D. 1498.
Durham,
  Cathedral, A.I.1. W. de Nottingham. s.xiv/xv. [D].
  A.I.2. *e*Concordancie Bibl. s.xiv. [C; *cat.*, p. 53 C].
  A.I.3. *e*Nicholaus de Lyra. A.D. 1386. [K, 1ª.2¹.M; *cat.*
  p. 51 K].

---

[2] Two slips cut from leaves of Durham, Cathedral, A.II.16 and A.II.17
respectively.
[3] The second volume of this work is Durham, Cathedral, B.II.34.
[4] B.M., Cotton Vit. C.viii, fos 85–90, was part of Cambridge, Trinity Coll. 216.
[5] Mr Brudenell's bible was later at the cell of Stamford, *q.v.*

Durham (*contd*)

Cathedral, A.I.4. *e*Nicholaus de Lyra. s.xiv ex. [M, 1ª.2¹.N; *cat.*, p. 51 M].

A.I.5. *e*Nicholaus de Lyra. s.xiv ex. [1ª.2¹.O; *cat.*, p. 119].

A.I.6. *i*Postille. s.xv. [S].

A.I.7. *e*S. Langton. s.xiii in. [B, 1ª.2¹.Q; *cat.*, p. 50 B].

A.I.8. *e*H. de S. Caro. s.xiii. [I, [1ª].2¹.F; *cat.*, pp. 44 I, 51 I].

A.I.9. Postille super Bibliam. s.xiii in. [E, 1ª.2¹.5; *cat.*, p. 52 E].

A.I.10. *e*Berengaudus, etc. s.xii in. [D; *cat.*, pp. 2(?), 76, 81].

A.I.11. *e*T. Aquinas. s.xiv. [Q, 1ª.2¹.A; *cat.*, p. 73 Q].

A.I.12. *e*H. de S. Caro. s.xiii. [H, 1ª.2¹.B; *cat.*, p. 43 C].

A.I.13. H. de S. Caro. s.xiii ex. [Q, 1ª.2¹.I; *cat.*, pp. 44 Q, 51 Q].

A.I.14. *e*H. de S. Caro. s.xiii. [L; *cat.*, p. 41 L].

A.I.15. *e*H. de S. Caro. s.xiii. [F, 1ª.2¹.D; *cat.*, pp. 44 F, 52 F].

A.I.16. *e*H. de S. Caro. s.xiii. [1ª.2¹.E; *cat.*, pp. 45 E, 53 E].

A.II.1. *e*Biblia (4 vols). s.xii ex. [*Cat.*, pp. 10, 118].

A.II.2. Biblia, pars ii. s.xii ex. [K].

A.II.3. Biblia. s.xiii ex. [E; *cat.*, p. 50 E].

A.II.4. *e*Biblia, pars ii. s.xi ex. [H; *cat.*, pp. 1, 50 H, 80 H, 117].

A.II.5. Pentateuchus glo. s.xiii. [A, 1¹.A; *cat.*, p. 50 A].

A.II.6. *e*Libri Regum, etc., glo. s.xiii. [1¹.B; *cat.*, pp. 12 A, 87 A].

A.II.7. *e*Libri Regum, etc., glo. s.xiii in. [E; *cat.*, pp. 12 C, 87 C].

A.II.8. *e*Epp. Cath., etc., glo. s.xiii in. [A; *cat.*, p. 53 A].

A.II.9. *e*P. Lombardus. s.xii ex. [H, 1¹.E; *cat.*, p. 51 H].

A.II.10. *e*P. Lombardus. s.xiii in. [A; *cat.*, pp. 13 A, 88 A].

A.II.11–13. *e*Comment. on Psalms (in French; 3 vols). s.xiii in. (vols 1, 2); s.xiii med. (vol. 3). [N, 1ª.5¹.S (vol. 1); R, 1ª.5¹.T (vol. 3); *cat.*, pp. 13 N, O, R, 88 N, O, R].

A.II.14. *e*Isaias, etc., glo. s.xiii. [1¹.F; *cat.*, p. 51 O].

A.II.15. *e*Evangelia glo. s.xii/xiii. [A; *cat.*, p. 52 A].

A.II.16. *c*Evangelia. s.viii. [*Cat.*, pp. 16 D, 92 D].

A.II.17. *e*Evangelia. s.vii/viii. [C].

A.II.18. *e*Matheus et Marcus glo. s.xiii in. [F; *cat.*, p. 52 F].

A.II.19. *e*P. Lombardus. s.xii ex. [B; *cat.*, pp. 17 B, 93 B, 118].

A.II.20. W. Brito. s.xiii/xiv. [1ª.1ᵉ.G; *cat.*, p. 49 G].

A.II.21. Comment. in Psalterium, etc. s.xiii. [C; *cat.*, pp. 27 C, 103 C].

Durham (*contd*)
Cathedral, A.II.22.   *e*Alexander de Hales. s.xiii. [G, 1ª.3¹.D *altered to* 2ª.2¹.D; *cat.*, p. 52 G].
   A.III.1.   *e*Genesis glo. s.xii. [D; *cat.*, pp. 11 D, 86 D].
   A.III.2.   *e*Leviticus, etc., glo. s.xii. [C; *cat.*, pp. 11 C, 86 C].
   A.III.3, fos 1–62. *e*Deuteronom. glo. s.xii ex. [C; *cat.*, pp. 12 C, 87 C].
   A.III.3, fos 63–173. *e*Job glo. s.xii ex. [A; *cat.*, pp. 12 A, 88 A].
   A.III.4.   *e*Libri Regum glo, etc. s.xii ex. [D; *cat.*, pp. 12 D, 87 D].
   A.III.5.   *e*Paralipom., etc., glo. s.xii ex. [A; *cat.*, pp. 12 A, 88 A].
   A.III.7.   *e*P. Lombardus. s.xii ex. [K; *cat.*, p. 51 K].
   A.III.8.   Psalterium glo., etc. s.xiii in. [B; *cat.*, pp. 13 B, 88 B].
   A.III.9.   *e*Psalterium glo. s.xii ex. [AA; *cat.*, pp. 13 AA, 89 AA].
   A.III.10.   *e*G. Porretanus. s.xii med. [1¹.L; *cat.*, pp. 3, 13 L, 88 L].
   A.III.11.   *e*Misc. theol. s.xiii–xiv.
   A.III.12.   *e*Misc. theol. s.xiii. [G, 2ª.6¹.F; *cat.* pp. 26 G, 103 G].
   A.III.13.   *e*N. de Gorran. s.xiii ex. [A, 2ª.2¹.N.2; *cat.*, p. 68 A].
   A.III.14.   *e*Parabole, etc., glo. s.xiii. [L, 1ª.1ᵉ.C.1; *cat.*, p. 51 L].
   A.III.15.   *e*Parabole, etc., glo. s.xiii in. [M; *cat.*, p. 51 M].
   A.III.16.   *e*Ecclesiasticus, etc., glo. s.xii ex. [B; *cat.*, pp. 14 B, 90 B].
   A.III.17.   *e*Isaias glo. s.xii ex. [F; *cat.*, pp. 2(?), 15 F, 90 F].
   A.III.18.   *e*Isaias, etc., glo. [A; *cat.*, pp. 15 A, 90 A].
   A.III.19.   *e*Jeremias, etc., glo. s.xii ex. [B, 1ª.1ᵉ.F (*altered to* G); *cat.*, pp. 15 B, 91 B].
   A.III.20.   Jeremias glo. s.xiii in. ?
   A.III.21.   *e*H. de Sancto Caro. s.xiii. [[1]ª.2¹.C; *cat.*, pp. 44 A, 51 A].
   A.III.22.   *e*Ezechiel et Daniel glo. s.xiii. [B; *cat.*, pp. 15 B, 91 B].
   A.III.23.   *e*Daniel et Esdras glo. s.xii ex. [A; *cat.*, pp. 15 A, 91 A].
   A.III.24.   Proph. minores glo. s.xii ex. [E, 1ª.1¹.G; *cat.*, pp. 16 E, 91 E].
   A.III.25.   *m*Matheus et Johannes glo. s.xiii in.
   A.III.26.   *s*Postille in Vet. Test. s.xiii in. [V].
   A.III.27.   *e*R. Holcot. s.xiv ex. [1ª.5¹.A].
   A.III.28.   *e*S. Langton. s.xiii. [A, F; *cat.*, pp. 15 F, 90 F].
   A.III.29.   *e*Omeliarium. s.xi.
   A.III.30.   *e*Postille super Matheum. s.xiv. [D; *cat.*, pp. 16 D, 92 D].

Durham (*contd*)
Cathedral, A.III.31. *e*N. Gorham. s.xiv. [*C*, 2ª.2¹.O; *cat.*, p. 68 C].
A.III.35. *e*Tabula super Bibliam. s.xiv. [P; *cat.*, p. 51 P].
A.IV.1. *e*Leviticus glo. s.xii ex. [D; *cat.*, pp. 11 D, 87 D, 118].
A.IV.2. *e*Psalterium glo., etc. s.xii ex. [X; *cat.,* pp. 13 X, ·89 X].
A.IV.3. *e*Glose super Psalterium. s.xiii in. [I; *cat.*, pp. 14 II, 89 II].
A.IV.4. *e*P. Pictaviensis. s.xii ex. [F, 1ª.5¹.X; *cat.*, pp. 13 FF, 89 FF].
A.IV.5. *i*P. de Herenthals, etc. s.xiv. [A].
A.IV.7. *e*Isaias glo. s.xii ex. [G; *cat.*, p. 15 G].
A.IV.8. *e*Evangelia, etc. s.xiii–xiv.
A.IV.10. *e*Matheus glo. s.xii ex. [B; *cat.*, pp. 16 B, 92 B, 118].
A.IV.11. *e*Marcus glo. s.xii ex. [D; *cat.*, pp. 16 D, 92 D].
A.IV.12. *e*Marcus glo. s.xii ex. [C; *cat.*, pp. 16 C, 92 C].
A.IV.13. *e*Lucas glo. s.xii ex. [D; *cat.*, pp. 17 D, 92 D].
A.IV.14. *e*Lucas glo. s.xii/xiii. [B; *cat.*, pp. 16 B, 92 B].
A.IV.15. *e*Johannes glo., etc. s.xii in.–xii med. [D (*altered to* A); *cat.*, pp. 17 D, 93 D].
A.IV.16. *e*Johannes glo., etc. s.xii in.–xiii. [G; *cat.*, pp. 17 G, 93 G].
A.IV.17. Misc. theol. s.xii ex. [*Cat.*, p. 62 AD].
A.IV.19. *c*'Rituale Dunelmense'. s.x in.
A.IV.23. Summa Biblie. s.xiv. [1ª.5¹.Q].
A.IV.28. *e*Beda. s.xii. [A; *cat.*, pp. 18 A, 94 A].
A.IV.34. *e*Notule in Cantica Canticorum. [C; *cat.*, pp. 14 C, 90 C].
A.IV.35. Beda, etc. s.xii ex. [*Cat.*, pp. 30 A, 107 A,
A.IV.36. *e*Simeon Dunelmensis, etc. s.xiii in. [*Cat*]. p. 56 M].
B.I.1. *e*P. Lombardus. s.xiii ex. [B/25; *cat.*, p. 54 B].
B.I.2. *e*P. Lombardus. s.xiii ex. [D; *cat.*, p. 54 D].
B.I.3. *e*P. Lombardus. s.xiii ex. [A, 1ª.6¹.M; *cat.*, p.54 A].
B.I.4. P. Lombardus. s.xiii. [2ª.6¹.M].
B.I.5. *e*T. Aquinas. s.xiv in. [R; *cat.*, p. 73 R].
B.I.6. *e*T. Aquinas. s.xiv in. [N, 1ª.6¹.S; *cat.*, p. 74 N].
B.I.7. *e*T. Aquinas. s.xiii/xiv. [A; *cat.*, pp. 23 C, 99 C].
B.I.8. *e*T. Aquinas. s.xiii/xiv. [G,O; *cat.*, p. 72 C].
B.I.9. *e*T. Aquinas. s.xiv in. [T; *cat.*, p. 73 T].
B.I.10. *e*T. Aquinas. s.xiii/xiv. [B; *cat.*, p. 72 B].
B.I.11. *e*T. Aquinas. s.xiii ex. [E, 1ª.6¹.T; *cat.*, p. 72 E].
B.I.12. T. Aquinas. s.xiii/xiv. [E; *cat.*, pp. 23 E, 99 E].
B.I.13. *e*T. Aquinas. s.xiii ex. [O; *cat.*, p. 73 O].
B.I.14. *e*T. Aquinas. s.xiv. [1ª.6¹.R; *cat.*, p. 74 A].
B.I.15. *s*T. Aquinas. s.xiii/xiv. [*Cat.*, pp. 23, 100].
B.I.16. *e*T. Aquinas. s.xiv in. [D, 1ª.6¹.F; *cat.*, p. 72 D].
B.I.17. *e*T. Aquinas. s.xiii/xiv. [L, 1ª.6¹.E; *cat.*, p. 73 L].
B.I.18. *i*Summa de viciis. s.xiv. [G].
B.I.19. *e*T. Aquinas. s.xiv. [K, 1ª.6¹.G; *cat.*, p. 73 K].

G

Durham (*contd*)

Cathedral, B.I.20.   *e*T. Aquinas.   s.xiv in.   [I; *cat.*, pp. 23 I, 99 I].

B.I.21.   *e*T. Aquinas.   s.xiv.   [I/36; *cat.*, p. 73 I].

B.I.22.   *e*T. Aquinas.   s.xiv in.   [H, 1ª.6¹.H; *cat.*, p. 73 H].

B.I.23.   *s*T. Aquinas.   s.xiii/xiv.

B.I.24.   *e*Bonaventura.   s.xiv.   [D; *cat.*, p. 74 D].

B.I.25.   *e*Bonaventura.   s.xiii/xiv.   [E; *cat.*, p. 74 E].

B.I.26.   *e*H. de Gandauo.   s.xiv.   [A, K, 2ª.6¹; *cat.*, p. 74 A].

B.I.27.   P. Tarentasius.   s.xiii ex.   [*Cat.*, pp. 17 F, K, 98 F, K].

B.I.28.   *e*P. Pictaviensis, etc.   s.xiii in.   [V, N; *cat.*, pp. 22 N, 98 N].

B.I.29.   *e*R. de Peniaforte, etc.   s.xiv.   [P; *cat.*, p. 47 P].

B.I.30.   *e*J. de Friburgo.   s.xiv.   [P, 2ª.8¹.Q; *cat.*, p. 48 P].

B.I.31.   J. de Balbis.   s.xiv.   [B; *cat.*, p. 49 B].

B.I.32.   *e*V. Bellovacensis.   A.D. 1448.   [N].

B.I.33.   *e*P. Comestor.   s.xiii in.   [A; *cat.*, p. 53 A].

B.I.34.   *e*P. Comestor.   s.xii/xiii.   [B; *cat.*, p. 53 B].

B.II.1.   *e*Josephus.   s.xii med.   [A; *cat.*, p. 56 A].

B.II.2.   Omelie.   s.xi ex.

B.II.3.   Opus imperfectum in Matheum, etc.   s.xiv. [1ª.3¹.X.1].

B.II.4.   *e*J. Chrysostomus, etc.   s.xiv in.   [A, 1ª.3¹.Y; *cat.*, p. 68 A].

B.II.5.   *e*J. Chrysostomus.   s.xiv in.   [1ª.3¹.V].

B.II.6.   *e*Ambrosius.   s.xi ex.   [E, 2ª.2¹.Q; *cat.*, pp. 3, 57 E, 118].

B.II.7.   *e*Jeronimus.   s.xii med.   [F, 1¹.V; *cat.*, p. 58 F].

B.II.8.   *e*Jeronimus.   s.xii in.   [A, 1¹.R; *cat.*, p. 57 A].

B.II.9.   *e*Jeronimus.   s.xi ex.   [G (*altered to* T), 1¹.T; *cat.*, p. 58 G].

B.II.10.   *e*Jeronimus.   s.xi ex.   [C, 1¹.X; *cat.*, pp. 1, 57 C, 117].

B.II.11.   *e*Jeronimus.   s.xi ex.   [E, 1¹.Y; *cat.*, pp. 1, 58 E, 117].

B.II.12.   *e*Augustinus.   s.xiv in.   [AB, 2ª.2¹.G; *cat.*, p. 62 AB].

B.II.13.   *e*Augustinus.   s.xi ex.   [K, 2ª.2¹.X; *cat.*, pp. 1, 60 K, 117].

B.II.14.   *e*Augustinus.   s.xi ex.   [L, 2ª.2¹.Y (1¹.N *canc.*); *cat.*, pp. 1, 60 L, 117].

B.II.15.   *e*Augustinus.   s.xiv.   [M; *cat.*, p. 60 M].

B.II.16.   *e*Augustinus.   s.xi med.   [G; *cat.*, pp. 59 G, 117].

B.II.17.   *e*Augustinus.   s.xi ex.   [F, 2ª.2¹.E; *cat.*, pp. 59 F, 117].

B.II.18.   *e*Augustinus.   s.xii in.   [AA, 2ª.2¹.F; *cat.*, p. 63 AA].

B.II.19.   *e*Augustinus.   s.xiv in.   [H, 1ª.3¹.I; *cat.*, p. 60 H].

B.II.20.   *e*Augustinus, etc.   s.xiv in.   [X; *cat.*, p. 61 X].

B.II.21.   *e*Augustinus.   s.xi ex.   [N, 1ª.3¹.H; *cat.*, pp. 2, 60 N, 117].

Durham (*contd*)
Cathedral, B.II.22. *e*Augustinus.   s.xi ex.   [D, 1ª.3¹.A; *cat.*, pp. 1, 59 D, 117].

B.II.23. *e*Augustinus.   s.xiv in.   [AD, 1ª.3¹.B(?)].
B.II.24. *e*Augustinus.   s.xiv ex.   [C; *cat.*, p. 59 C].
B.II.25. *e*Augustinus.   s.xiii ex.   [E; *cat.*, p. 59 E].
B.II.26. *e*Augustinus.   s.xii in.   [A; *cat.*, p. 59 A].
B.II.27. *e*Augustinus.   s.xiv.   [AC; *cat.*, p. 63 AC].
B.II.28. *e*Augustinus.   s.xiv in.   [B; *cat.*, p. 59 B].
B.II.29. *e*Augustinus.   s.xiv.   [2ª.2¹.K; *cf. cat.*, p. 63 AD].
B.II.30. Cassiodorus.   s.viii.   [E, 1ª.2¹.K(?); *cat.*, pp. 3, 13 H, 88 H].
B.II.31. *e*Omelie.   s.xiv.   [C; *cat.*, p. 76 C].
B.II.32.[6] Gregorius.   s.xiii in.   [A, 1ª.3¹.M; *cat.*, p. 63 A].
B.II.33. *e*Isidorus, etc.   s.xiii in.   [A; *cat.*, p. 65 A].
B.II.34.[3] *e*Florus.   s.xii ex.   [B, 2ª.3¹.N; *cat.*, p. 64 C].
B.II.35. *e*Beda, etc.   s.xi ex.–xv.   [*Cat.*, pp. 3, 56 G].
B.II.36.[7] *e*P. Comestor.   s.xiii ex.
B.III.1. *e*Origenes.   s.xi ex.   [1¹.Q; *cat.*pp. 2, 72 A, 118].
B.III.2. *e*Didymus, etc.   s.xii ex.   [K, 1¹.Z; *cat.*, p. 59 K].
B.III.3, fos 1–56. *e*Augustinus.   s.xii in.   [S; *cat.*, p. 61 S].
B.III.4, fos 1–162. *e*Augustinus, etc.   s.xiii ex.   [2ª.2¹.I; *cat.*, p. 63 AE].
B.III.4, fos 163–253. *e*Tabula Martiniana.   s.xiv.   [K].
B.III.5. *e*Augustinus.   s.xii.   [P, 1ª.3¹.K; *cat.*, p. 60 P].
B.III.6. *e*Augustinus.   s.xiv ex.   [Ab, 1ª.3¹.E; *cat.*, p. 63 Ab].
B.III.7. *e*Eugippius, etc.   s.xiii/xiv.   [V, 1ª.3¹.F; *cat.*, p. 61 V].
B.III.8. *e*Cassianus, etc.   s.xiv in.   [D; *cat.*, p. 69 D].
B.III.9. *e*Gregorius.   s.xi ex.   [D, 1ª.3¹.O; *cat.*, pp. 2, 63 D, 117].
B.III.10. *e*Gregorius.   s.xi ex.   [C; *cat.*, pp. 2, 63 C, 117].
B.III.11. *e*Gregorius, etc.   s.xi ex.   [F; *cat.*, pp. 63 F, 117].
B.III.12. *e*Gregorius.   s.xiv in.   [F].
B.III.13. *e*Warnerius.   s.xii ex.   [G, 1ª.3¹.K; *cat.*, p. 63 G].
B.III.14. *e*Isidorus, etc. s. xii in.   [E; *cat.*, p. 66 E].
B.III.15. *e*Isidorus.   s.xiii in.   [D; *cat.*, p. 66 D].
B.III.16. *e*Rabanus Maurus.   s.xi ex.   [A; *cat.*, pp. 3, 67 A, 117].
B.III.17. *e*Jeronimus.   s.xiii in.   [A, 2ª.3¹.B; *cat.*, p. 70 A].
B.III.18. *e*Bernardus, etc.   s.xiv ex.   [G/8].
B.III.19. *e*R. Grosseteste, etc.   s.xiv ex.   [2ª.5¹.C].
B.III.20. *i*P. Comestor.   s.xiii.
B.III.21. *e*W. Peraldus, Summa de vitiis.   s.xiii ex.   [B, 4¹.B; *cat.*, p. 71 B].
B.III.22. *e*Bonaventura, etc.   s.xiv.   [E, 2ª.6¹.Q; *cat.*, p. 71 I].
B.III.23. *e*Johannes Lector.   s.xiv.   [O; *cat.*, p. 47 O].

[6] B.II.32 was earlier at **COLDINGHAM**, *q.v.*   [3] See p. 62, n. 3.
[7] B.II.36 was earlier at the Franciscan Convent at York.

Durham (*contd*)
Cathedral, B.III.24.   *e*Egidius Romanus, etc. s.xiv ex. [S, 1ª.7¹.R; *cat.*, p. 43 S].

B.III.25.   *e*J. de Abbatisvilla. s.xiii ex. [M; *cat.*, pp. 27 M, 104 M].

B.III.26.   *e*Anselmus, etc. s.xiii ex. [F].

B.III.27.   *e*Tabule. s.xiv in. [Z; *cat.*, p. 83 Z].

B.III.28.   *b*Tabule. s.xiv. [1ª.3¹.S(?)].

B.III.29.   *i*Tabule. A.D. 1438. [A].

B.III.30.   *i*Vitas Patrum, etc. s.xiii–xiv ex. [B].

B.III.31.   *e*Tabule. s.xiv. [F; *cat.*, pp. 42 AF, 84 F].

B.IV.1.   Gregorius Nazianzenus. s.xii in. [C; *cat.*, pp. 2, 20 C, 96 C].

B.IV.2.   *e*J. Chrysostomus. s.xii ex. [B; *cat.*, pp. 3, 69 B].

B.IV.3.   *e*J. Chrysostomus. s.xiv. [1ª.3¹.Z].

B.IV.4.   *e*Ambrosius. s.xii in. [C, C/15; *cat.*, p. 57 C].

B.IV.5.   *e*Ambrosius. s.xii in. [B, 2ª.2¹.T; *cat.*, p. 57 B].

B.IV.6.   *e*Augustinus, etc. s.xii in. [Q; *cat.*, pp. 1, 61 Q].

B.IV.7.   *e*Augustinus, etc. s.xii in. [R, 2ª.2¹.D; *cat.*, p. 61 R].

B.IV.8.   Augustinus, etc. s.xii in. [B; *cat.*, p. 19 B].

B.IV.9.   *e*Prudentius. s.x. [A, 1ª.7¹; *cat.*, pp. 2, 32 A, 109 A].

B.IV.10.   Cassianus, etc. s.xii ex. [G, G/4; *cat.*, pp. 24 G, 101 G].

B.IV.11.   *e*Cassianus, etc. s.xii ex. [C, C/4; *cat.*, p. 69 O].

B.IV.12.   *e*Augustinus, etc. s.xii in. [O, 2ª.2¹. ; *cat.*, pp. 2, 60 O].

B.IV.13.   *e*Gregorius. s.xi ex. [I; *cat.*, pp. 2, 64 I, 118].

B.IV.14.   *e*Vite sanctorum. s.xii in. [L; *cat.*, pp. 54 L, 118].

B.IV.15.   *e*Isidorus. s.xii in. [C; *cat.*, p. 65 C].

B.IV.16.   *e*Beda, etc. s.xii in. [G; *cat.*, p. 65 G].

B.IV.17.   Decretum Burchardi, etc. [H; *cat.*, pp. 35 H, 112 H].

B.IV.18.   Collectanea Juris Canonici. s.xii in. [T, 2ª.8¹.K; *cat.*, pp. 35 T, 112 T].

B.IV.19.   Anselmus, etc. s.xiv. [H, H/15].

B.IV.20.   Bernardus, etc. s.xii/xiii. [F; *cat.*, p. 21 F, 97 F].

B.IV.21.   Bernardus. s.xiii. [B].

B.IV.22.   *e*Bernardus, etc. s.xii ex. [B; *cat.*, p. 66 B].

B.IV.23.   *e*Bernardus. s.xiii in. [A; *cat.*, p. 66 A].

B.IV.24.   *e*Martyrologium, etc. s.xi ex.–xii. [A; *cat.*, pp. 30 A, 107 A].

B.IV.25.   *e*Ailredus, etc. s.xii ex.–xii/xiii. [B, B/2; *cat.*, pp. 25 B, 101 B].

B.IV.26.   *e*Regula S. Benedicti, etc. s.xiv ex.

B.IV.27.   H. de S. Victore, etc. s.xii/xiii. [P].

B.IV.28.   *e*P. Riga, etc. s.xiii. [R, 4¹.Q.2; *cat.*, pp. 11 R, 85 R].

B.IV.29.   *e*P. Aureolus. s.xiv. [2ª.5¹.I].

Durham (*contd*)
Cathedral, B.IV.30. *e*N. de Hanapis, etc. s.xiv. [T/12].
B.IV.31. *e*Egidius Romanus. s.xiv. [T, T/57].
B.IV.32.[8, 9] *e*R. Armachanus, etc. s.xiv in.–xv in. [S, 2ª.6¹.G].
B.IV.34. *i*Uthredus Boldon. s.xiv. [T].
B.IV.36. *e*R. Higden, Speculum curatorum. s.xiv/xv. [H].
B.IV.37. Excerpta patrum, etc. s.xii in. [M, 2ª.9¹.K, 1ª.9¹.I; *cat.*, pp. 35 M, 112 M].
B.IV.39A.[1] *e*J. de Voragine, etc. s.xiv. [Q, Q/4].
B.IV.39B.[1] Vita S. Oswaldi, etc. s.xiii in. [D; *cat.*, pp. 29 D, 106 D].
B.IV.40. *e*Mariale. s.xv. [P].
B.IV.41. *i*Constitutiones Clementine, etc. s.xiv in.–xv in.
B.IV.42. *e*Tabule, etc. s.xiv/xv.
B.IV.43. *e*Tabule, etc. s.xiv. [AH; *cat.*, p. 83 AH].
C.I.2. Digestum inforciatum. s.xiii in. [2ª.9¹.C].
C.I.3.[2] *e*Digestum novum. s.xiii ex. [A, 2ª.9¹.K; *cat.*, pp. 36 A, 114 A].
C.I.4.[2] *e*Parvum volumen. s.xiii ex. [B, 2ª.9¹.I; *cat.*, pp. 36 B, 114 B].
C.I.5. Parvum volumen. s.xiv. ?
C.I.6. *e*Codex Justiniani. s.xiii ex. [A; *cat.*, pp. 36 A, 114 A].
C.I.7. *e*Decretum Gratiani. s.xii/xiii. [B, 2ª.8¹.P; *cat.*, pp. 34 B, 112 B].
C.I.8. Decretum Gratiani. s.xii/xiii. [N].
C.I.9.[2] Decretales Gregorii noni. s.xiii ex.
C.I.11. *i*Bernardus Compostellanus, etc. s.xiv.
C.I.12. *e*Odofredus. s.xiv in. [2ª.9¹.A; *cat.*, pp. 36 C, 114 C].
C.I.13. *e*H. de Segusio. s.xiii ex. [T; *cat.*, p. 48 T].
C.I.14. *e*Sextus liber decretalium, etc. s.xiv in. [1ª.9¹.M; *cat.*, p. 47 I).
C.I.16. *e*Logica vetus et nova. s.xiv in. [Q, 2ª.10¹.A].
C.I.17.[3] Aristoteles. s.xiv. [*Cf. cat.*, p. 77 B]. ?
C.I.18. *e*Aristoteles. s.xiv in. [D, 1ª.10¹.O; *cat.*, p. 77 D].
C.I.19, fos 1–233.[4] Constantinus; Bernardus de Gordonio. s.xiii. [2ª.7¹.K; *cat.*, p. 79 K].
C.I.19, fos 234–324. *e*Avicenna. s.xiv. [B, 2ª.7¹.X; *cat.*, p. 78 B].
C.I.20. *e*Huguitio, etc. s.xiii ex.–xiv. [4¹.M].
C.II.1. *e*Decretum Gratiani. s.xii ex. [C; *cat.*, p. 46 C].

[8] B.IV.32, fos 1–49, and fos 50–181, originally 2 vols, were bound together by s.xvi in.
[9] The fly leaves of B.IV.32 are B.IV.39B, fos 2–4.
[1] B.IV.39A and B were originally 2 vols, as at present, but were bound in one vol. by s.xvi in.
[2] C.I.3, C.I.4, and C.I.9 are companion volumes.
[3] C.I.17 is now bound in two volumes.
[4] C.I.19, fos 1–127, and fos 128–233, originally 2 vols, were bound together by s.xvi in.

Durham (*contd*)
   Cathedral, C.II.2.   *e*Decretales Gregorii noni, etc. s.xiii ex. [A; *cat.*,
                     p. 47 A].

          C.II.3.   *e*Decretales Gregorii noni, etc. s.xiii. [D; *cat.*,
                     p. 47 D].

          C.II.4.   Decretales Gregorii noni, etc. s.xiii ex. [$2^a.8^1$. P
                     (*altered to* O)].

          C.II.5.   *e*Decretales Gregorii noni, etc. s.xiii ex. [C; *cat.*,
                     p. 47 C].

          C.II.6.   *e*P. de Salinis. s.xiv in. [H, $1^a.9^1$.D; *cat.*, p. 46 H].

          C.II.7.   *e*H. de Segusio. s.xiv. [$2^a.8^1$.N].

          C.II.8.   *e*H. de Segusio. s.xiv. [$2^a.8^1$.N2].

          C.II.9.   *s*J. Andree. s.xiv in. [X(?)].

          C.II.10. *e*Summa Goffredi, etc. s.xiv in. [Y; *cat.*,
                     p. 36 X].

          C.II.11. *e*W. Durandus. etc. s.xiv in. [AD; *cat.*,
                     p. 48 AD].

          C.II.12. W. Durandus. s.xiii/xiv. [*Cat.*, p. 48 AC].

          C.II.13. *e*W. de Pagula, etc. s.xiv. [L; *cat.*, p. 47 L].

          C.III.1.   *e*Decretum Gratiani. s.xiii ex. [K, $2^a.8^1$.T; *cat.*,
                     p. 35 K].

          C.III.2.   *e*Decretales Gregorii IX. s.xiii. [N, $1^a.8^1$.B; *cat.*,
                     p. 35 D].

          C.III.3.   'Decretales antique'. s.xiii in. [H, $1^a.8^1$.H; *cat.*,
                     p. 35 H].

          C.III.4.   'Decretales antique'. s.xiii. [E, $1^a.8^1$.I; *cat.*,
                     p. 35 E].

          C.III.5.   *e*Bartholomeus Brixensis. s.xiv in. [R, $1^a.9^1$.E;
                     cat., p. 35 R].

          C.III.6.   *e*N. de Tudeschis, etc. s.xiii/xiv. [P, $1^a.9^1$.G].

          C.III.7.   J. Faventinus. s.xiii in. [Q, $2^a.8^1$.D; *cat.*,
                     p. 35 Q].

          C.III.8.   Glossa Palatina super Decreta. s.xiii in. [V,
                     $2^a.8^1$.C; *cat.*, p. 112 V].

          C.III.9.   *e*Innocentius IV. s.xiii/xiv. [B].

          C.III.10. *e*Summa Goffredi. s.xiv in. [D].

          C.III.11. *e*Bartholomeus de S. Concordio, etc. s.xv in.
                     [Q, $1^a.9^1$.P].

          C.III.12. Summa Goffredi, etc. s.xiii ex. [$2^a.9^1$.G].

          C.III.13. *e*Tabule. s.xiii–xiv. [$1^a.9^1$.O].

          C.III.14. Aristoteles, etc. s.xiii. [S, $2^a.10^1$.M; *cat.*,
                     p. 32 S].

          C.III.15. *e*Averroes, etc. s.xiii. [C, $1^a.10^1$.P; *cat.*,
                     p. 77 C].

          C.III.16. *e*Averroes. s.xiv in. [K, $1^a.10^1$.E].

          C.III.17. *i*Aristoteles. s.xiii ex. [$2^a.10.^1$K].

          C.III.18. *e*Suetonius. s.xi ex. [AG/9].

          C.III.20.[5] Evangelia (2 fos). s.vii/viii.

          C.IV.1.   Decreta non glosata. s.xii/xiii. [G; *cat.*, p. 35 G].

          C.IV.4.   *e*Medica quedam. s.xiii in. [V, $2^a.7^1$.Be].

---

[5] Binding leaves. Six other leaves of the same MS. are in A.II.10 and two are in C.III.13.

Durham (*contd*)
    Cathedral, C.IV.5.   Cicero. s.xii. [C, $2^a.7^1.$P; *cat.*, pp. 31 C, 108 C, 119].

    C.IV.7.   Glose in Ciceronem, etc. s.xii in. [*Cat.*, pp. 31 F, 108 F].

    C.IV.10.   Comment. in Boetium. s.xii in. [F; *cat.*, pp. 4, 30 F, 108 F].

    C.IV.11.   Alexander Trallianus. s.xii ex. [L; *cat.*, p. 33 L].

    C.IV.12.   *e*Constantinus Africanus. s.xii. [H, h/95; *cat.*, p. 78 H].

    C.IV.13.   *e*Isaac Judeus. s.xiii in. [$2^a.7^1.$E4; *cat.*, p. 111].

    C.IV.15.   Chronica, etc. s.xii in. [$1^a.7^1.$E(?); *cat.*, p. 30 O, 107 O].

    C.IV.16, fos 1–166.   Aristoteles. s.xiii ex. [$2^a.10^1.$F].

    C.IV.16, fos 167–304.   Aristoteles. s.xiii ex. [$1^a.10^1.$G].

    C.IV.17.   *e*Aristoteles. s.xiii ex. [$2^a.10^1.$C].

    C.IV.19.   Aristoteles. s.xiii ex. [G, $2^a.10^1.$D; *cat.*, pp. 32 G, 109 G].

    C.IV.20A.   J. de Ditneshale. s.xiii ex. [M, $1^a.10^1$(?). [ ]; *cat.*, p. 32 M].

    C.IV.20B.   *e*Tabule in Aristotelem. s.xiv ex. [N, $1^a.10^1.$H].

    C.IV.21.   *e*Tabule. s.xv in. [EM].

    C.IV.22.   *e*N. Bonetus, etc. s.xv.

    C.IV.23, fos 67–128^v.   *i*G. de Vinosalvo. s.xv.

    C.IV.24.   *e*P. de Vineis, etc. s.xiii/xiv. [AG; *cat.*, p. 48 AG].

    C.IV.25.   *i*Registrum litterarum. s.xv in. [*Cat.*, p. 124 L].

    C.IV.29.   *e*Note super Priscianum et super Rethoricam Tullii. s.xii in. [*Cat.*, p. 33 P].

    Hunter 100.   Medica quedam. s.xii in. [*Cat.*, pp. 33 A, 110 A].

        101.   *c*Reginaldus Dunelm. s.xii ex.

Inc. 1a–d (pr. bks). *i*N. de Lyra (4 vols). Strasbourg, s.a.

    1f (pr. bk). *e*N. de Lyra. s.l.et a. [q].

    2 (pr. bk). *i*P. Comestor. Strasbourg, A.D. 1483.

    3 (pr. bk). *i*Bartholomeus Anglicus. Strasbourg, A.D. 1491.

    4a (pr. bk). *e*J. Duns Scotus. s.l., A.D. 1473.

    11 (pr. bk). *e*Gregorius, Moralia. s.l.et a. [H].

    13a, b (pr. bks). *e*Omeliarium (2 vols). s.l. et a.

    14c (pr. bk). *e*J. Duns Scotus. Nuremberg, A.D. 1481. [Ia].

    20a (pr. bk). *e*N. de Tudeschis. Venice, s.a. [S].

    20b (pr. bk). *e*N. de Tudeschis. Venice, s.a. [T].

    21b (pr. bk). *i*J. Duns Scotus. Venice, s.a.

    22 (pr. bk). *e*P. de Abano. s.l. et a. [sa].

    25 (pr. bk). *i*A. de Rampengolis. Venice, A.D. 1496.

    32–34 (pr. bks). *e*Bartholus de Saxoferrato (3 vols). Venice, A.D. 1483.

    35 (pr. bk). *e*J. M. Parthenopeus. Treviso, A.D. 1480.

    43 (pr. bk). *e*N. de Tudeschis. Basel, s.a.

    44 (pr. bk). *i*Augustinus in Psalmos. Basel, A.D. 1489.

Durham (contd)
Cathedral, Inc. 45 (pr. bk). iAugustinus super Johannem. s.l. et a.
47a (pr. bk). eH. Bohic. Lyon, A.D. 1498.
47b (pr. bk). iW. Lindwood. Paris, A.D. 1501.
48 (pr. bk). iJ. de Turrecremata. s.l., A.D. 1484.
53 (pr. bk). eA. de Montalvo. Louvain, A.D. 1486.
62 (pr. bk). eW. Lindwood. (Oxford), s.a.
B.V.58 (pr. bk). eJ. Dytenbergius. Cologne, A.D. 1524.
D.VII.23–24 (pr. bks). eAmbrosius (2 vols). Basel,
A.D. 1527.
P.V.16, 17 (pr. bks). iOrigenes (2 vols). Paris, A.D. 1512.
U.L., Cosin V.i.4. P. Lombardus. s.xii ex. [Cat., pp. 13, 89 BB].
V.i.8. eAnselmus, etc. s.xiv in. [D; cat., p. 71 D].
V.ii.1. Numeri glo. s.xii ex. [A; cat., pp. 12, 87 A].
V.ii.2. eRuth, etc., glo., etc. s.xii ex. [D; cat., p. 50 D].
V.ii.5. iSpeculum amicitie, etc. s.xiv.
V.ii.6. eSimeon Dunelm. s.xii in. [O; cat., pp. 4, 124 O].
V.ii.8. Odo Cantuar. s.xiii in. [O; cat., p. 75 O].
V.iii.1. Laurent. Dunelm. s.xii ex. [1ª.7¹.Z; cat.,
pp. 26, 102; Leland, De Script. Brit., p. 205].
V.v.6. lSequentiae. s.xi/xii. ?
Mickleton and Spearman, 89. eP. Limovicensis. s.xiv in.
[9.v.g].
S.R.2.B.12 (pr. bk). iJ. Sprenger. s.l. et a.
Edinburgh,
N.L., Adv. 18.4.3. eParadysus, etc. s.xii. [1ª.7¹. T; cat., p. 67 C].
18.6.11. eMedica. s.xii. [Cat., pp. 7, 33, 110 H].
Glasgow, U.L., Hunterian 85. Kalendarium, etc. s.xii. [F, 2ª.3¹.T;
cat., p. 64 F].
Gouda, Messrs Koch and Knuttel (pr. bk). iSermones sensati. Gouda,
A.D. 1482.
Hawkesyard Priory (pr. bk). iR. Holcot. (Paris), A.D. 1489.
Hereford, Cathedral, A.ix. 2, 3 (pr. bks). eV. T. polyglot. complutens.
(Alcala), A.D. 1517.
Lincoln, Cathedral, 162. eHugucio, etc. s.xv. [V].
F.1.14 (pr. bk). eBiblia complutens., vol. v.
(Alcala), A.D. 1517.
London,
B.M., Add. 6162. cLaurent. Dunelm., etc. s.xv. ?
16616. Marcus glo. s.xii ex. [A; cat., pp. 16, 92 A,
118].
28805. iOpusculum rhetorice preceptionis, etc. s.xv/xvi.
38666, fo. 4. eProsper (flyleaf only).
Arundel 332. eR. Grosseteste, etc. s.xiii.
507. Theologica (partly in English). s.xiii–xiv.
Burney 310. eEusebius, etc. A.D. 1381. [N, . . . 7¹.Q; cat.,
pp. 56, 65 N].
Cotton Jul. A.vi. Hymnarium (gloss in English). s.xi in. [A;
cat., pp. 33, 111 A].
D.iv. cChronicon Anglie. s.xiv.
D.vi. cChronicon Anglie, etc. s.xiii ex. [Cat.,
p. 124 K].
72

London (*contd*)
  Cotton Claud. D.iv. *i*Historia Dunelm. s.xv in.
    Nero D.iv. *e*Evangelia ('Lindisfarne Gospels'). s.viii in.
    Otho B.ix. *e*Evangelia. s.ix. [*Æthelstan*].
    Vit. A.ix. *c*Collectiones J. Washington. s.xv. ?
      C.viii, fos 85–90.[6] Epp. Pauli. s.viii. [L; *cat.*,
          pp. 18, 93 L].
      D.xx. *c*Misc. de S. Cuthberto. s.xii. ?
      E.xii, fos 55–113. *c*Miscellanea. s.xv med.
    Vesp. A.vi, fos 61–89. *c*Chronicon Dunelm., etc. s.xiv. ?
      B.x, fos 1–23.[7] Vita S. Brendani (partly in
          French), etc. s.xiv in.
    Titus A.ii. *c*Misc. Dunelm. s.xiv. ?
      A.xviii.[8] *e*G. Monemutensis, etc. s.xiv. [Q].
      D.xix, fo. 170. *i*(flyleaf only).
    Domit. vii. *c*Liber vite. s.ix–xvi.
    Fragments xxix, fos 36–39.[8] *e*(endleaves only).
  Harley 491. *e*W. Gemmeticensis. s.xii. [L; *cat.*, p. 56 L].
    1804. *cl*Horae, etc. s.xv ex.
    1924.[9] *c*Beda. s.xii. [D]. ?
    3049. *e*Ambrosius, etc. s.xv med. [2ª.2¹.Q].
    3100. Suidas (in Greek). s.xv.
    3858. *e*Opus vii custodiarum. s.xv in. [I, 2ª.5ᵗ¹.G;
        cat., p. 79 I].
    3864. *e*Beda. s.xii. [D; *cat.*, p. 64 D].
    4657. *c*Poemata (partly in French). s.xiv.
    4664. *i*Breviarium. s.xiii/xiv.
    4688. Beda. s.xii in. [F; *cat.*, pp. 20, 96 D].
    4703. *e*Sermones. s.xiv. [H; *cat.*, pp. 27, 104 H].
    4725. *i*Bonaventura, etc. s.xii–xiv.
    4843. *i*Miscellanea. s.xvi in.
    4894. Sermones R. Ripon. s.xiv. [M; *cat.*, p. 76 R].
    5234. *e*Isidorus, etc. s.xiii.
    5289. *c*Missale. s.xiv.
  Lansdowne 397. *i*Ric. de Pophis, etc. s.xiv. [P; *cat.*, p. 124 P].
  Royal 6 A.v. Fulgentius. s.xi med. [A, 2ª.3¹.H; *cat.*, pp. 24,
      101 A].
    7 A.vi. *b*Mariale, etc. s.xiv.
  Yates Thompson 26 (formerly Add. 39943). *e*Beda. s.xii ex.
    [*Cat.*, pp. 29, 107 O].
  British Records Association, 481. *e*(flyleaf only).
  Coll. of Arms, Arundel 25. *c*Hist. Dunelm., etc. s.xiv. ?
  Dulwich College, 23. *e*W. Brito. s.xiv.
  Lambeth Palace, 10–12. Historia aurea (3 vols). s.xiv. [D; *cat.*,
      p. 56 D–F].
    23. Alex. Nequam, etc. s.xiv/xv. [1ª.5ᵗ¹.M].

---

[6] Cotton Vit. C.viii, fos 85–90, was part of Cambridge, Trinity Coll. 216.
[7] Cotton Titus A.xviii and Vesp. B.x (fos 1–23) formed one volume, of which Cotton fragments xxix (fos 36–39) were the endleaves.
[8] See above, n. 7.
[9] Bodleian, Digby 41, fos 91, 91*, 92, 101, was part of B.M., Harley 1924.

London (*contd*)
  Lambeth Palace, 325. Ennodius. s.x in. [A, 1ª.7¹.O.i; *cat.*, pp. 32, 109 A].
           483. *e*Pseudo-Grosseteste, etc. s.xiv.
  Law Society, 107.d (pr. bk). *e*W. Durandus. Strasbourg, A.D. 1493.
  Lincoln's Inn, Hale 104. *c*Misc. Dunelm. ('Liber rubeus'). s.xv–xvi.
  Soc. of Antiquaries, 7. *e*Anselmus, etc. s.xii in. [*Cat.*, p. 63 Y].
Longleat, Marquess of Bath, 13. 'De officiis divinis que pertinent ad episcopum'. s.xiii. [A *altered to* T, de cancellaria T; *cat.*, pp. 34, 111 A].
Oxford,
  Bodleian, Auct. 1. Q.5.1 (pr. bk). *i*Joannes Franciscus, Brixianus. Venice, A.D. 1500.
      Bodl. 819. *s*Beda. s.viii.
      Digby 41, fos 91, 91*, 92, 101.⁹ *c*Reliquie Dunelm., etc. s.xii. ?
        81, fos 133–140. Misc. computistica. s.xi in. [C].
      Douce 129. *i*J. de Sacro Bosco, etc. s.xv.
        270. *cl*Sermones, etc. (in French); Kalendarium. s.xii ex.–xiii. ?
      Fairfax 6.¹ Vita S. Cuthberti, etc. s.xiv. [P; *cat.*, p. 55 P].
      Lat. liturg. f.5.² Evangelistarium. s.xi. ?
      Laud lat. 12. *e*Biblia. s.xiii. [B *corr. from* C; *cat.*, pp. 10, 85 C].
        36. *e*Psalterium glo. s.xiii. [I, 1ª . . . F; *cat.*, p. 51 I].
      misc. 52.³ Ivo Carnotensis, etc. s.xii in. [E; *cat.*, pp. 24, 101 E].
        262. *e*Sermones. s.xiv. [K; *cat.*, p. 75 K].
        277. H. de S. Victore, etc. s.xii. [1ª.5ᵗˡ. F; *cat.*, p. 67 D].
        344. *e*H. de S. Victore, etc. s.xii ex.–xiii in. [2ª.3¹.D; *cat.*, pp. 16, 91 C].
        345. Miscellanea. s.xiii–xiv. [R].
        359. *e*Jeronimus, etc. s.xii. [D; *cat.*, p. 57 D].
        368. *e*P. Blesensis, etc. s.xiii–xv.
        389. *e*Pera peregrini abbrev. s.xiv. [*Cat.*, p. 71 G].
        392. *e*H. de S. Victore, etc. s.xii. [A; *cat.*, pp. 21, 97 A].
        402. Dictamina, etc. s.xiii–xv. [2ª.5ᵗˡ.P].
        413. *e*Vita S. Godrici. s.xii. [L, 1ª.7¹.V; *cat.*, pp. 29, 106 L].
        489. *e*J. de Voragine. s.xiii ex. [F].
        491. *s*Beda, etc. s.xii. ?
        546. *e*Julianus Tolet. s.xi ex. [A; ? *cat.*, pp. 3, 118].

⁹ See p. 73, n. 9.
¹ Laud misc. 700 is probably copied from Fairfax 6, whence also passages were copied in B.M., Harley 4843.
² *Cf.* H. H. E. Craster in *Bodleian Quarterly Record*, iv. 201.
³ Jesus Coll. 52, 53 and Bodleian, Laud misc. 52 formed one volume.

Oxford (*contd*)
Bodleian, Laud misc. 603. *e*Martinus Polonus, etc. s.xiv. [I,
1ᵃ.7ᵐ¹.F, 2ᵃ.7¹.F; *cat.*, p. 56 I].
641. *e*P. Chrysologus. s.xiii. [F, 2ᵃ.5ᵗ¹.T;
cat., pp. 75, 118 F].
700.¹ Chronica Dunelm. s.xiv. ?
748. *i*Hist. Dunelm. s.xv.
Lyell 16. *i*'Petrus Ruffensis in summula viciorum'. s.xiv.
Rawl. C.4. *e*Enchiridion penitentiale. s.xiv. [*Cat.*,
p. 72 AH].
D.338. *e*Jeronimus, etc. s.xii. [L, 1¹. M; *cat.*,
p. 59 L].
Wood empt. 24. *i*Augustinus, etc. s.xii. [K; *cat.*,
p. 202 K].
Brasenose Coll., 4. *e*Biblia. s.xiii. [A].
Magdalen Coll., lat. 162. *i*W. Milverley, etc. s.xv.
Oriel Coll., C.e.20 (pr. bk). *i*Lactantius, etc. Venice, A.D. 1509, and
Paris, A.D. 1515.
St John's Coll., 14. *e*P. de Herentals. s.xiv/xv. [G ?].
97. *e*R. de Hoveden. s.xiii in. [K; *cat.*, p. 56 K].
154. *e*Ælfric (Lat. and Eng.). s.xi in. [E, 2ᵃ.7¹. H;
cat., pp. 33, 111 E].
P.4.46 (pr. bk). *i*N. Dorbellus. Basel, A.D. 1494.
Univ. Coll., 86. *e*Gratianus. s.xiii. [Q].
Stonyhurst College, s.n. *e*Evangelium Johannis. s.vii.
Tollerton, St Hugh's Coll. (pr. bk).⁴ *i*Epp. Hieronymi. Basel, A.D. 1524.
(pr. bk).⁴ *i*Repertorium in postillam N. de
Lyra. Nuremberg, A.D. 1494.

Ushaw College,
XVII.E.4.1 (pr. bk).⁵ *i*T. Aquinas. Basel, A.D. 1495.
E.4.2 (pr. bk).⁵ *i*Bonaventura. Strasbourg, A.D. 1495.
E.4.6–10 (pr. bks).⁵ *i*Nicholaus de Lyra (5 vols). Lyon,
A.D. 1520.
E.5.4 (pr. bk).⁵ *i*J. Sarisburiensis. Paris, s.a.
F.4.1 (pr. bk).⁵ *i*T. Aquinas, etc. Venice, A.D. 1500, etc.
F.4.3 (pr. bk).⁵ *i*P. Lombardus. Basel, A.D. 1516.
F.4.4 (pr. bk).⁵ *i*L. de Saxonia. Paris, A.D. 1517.
F.4.5 (pr. bk).⁵ *i*Destructorium viciorum. Paris, A.D. 1521.
F.4.12 (pr. bk).⁶ *i*Augustinus. Basel, A.D. 1489.
F.4.13 (pr. bk).⁵ *i*J. Damascenus (in Latin). Paris, A.D. 1512.
G.4.1–2 (pr. bks).⁶ *e*Origenes (in Latin; 2 vols).
G.4.3 (pr. bk).⁶ *i*M. Vigerius. Fano, A.D. 1507.
G.4.5 (pr. bk).⁵ *i*F. de Puteo. Paris, A.D. 1530.
XVIII.A.3.4–5 (pr. bks). *i*V. Ferrerius (2 vols). Strasbourg, A.D.
1493–94.
A.3.12 (pr.bk). *i*Augustinus. Basel, A.D. 1495.
A.3.15 (pr. bk). *i*Dictionarius pauperum. Paris, A.D. 1498.

¹ See p. 74, n. 1.
⁴ The books at Tollerton are on deposit from Hassop Catholic Church.
⁵ On permanent loan to Ushaw Coll. from St Mary's Catholic Church,
Yealand Conyers, Lancs.: *cf. Ushaw Magazine*, no. 184 (1952), pp. 41–47.
⁶ Deposited at Ushaw Coll. in 1952 by the trustees of the Silvertop heirlooms,
from the library at Minsteracres, Shotley Bridge, co. Durham.

Ushaw College (*contd*)
    XVIII.B.1.2 (pr. bk). *i*A. de Spina, Fortalicium fidei. s.l. et a.
        B.3.5–11 (pr. bks). *i*H. de S. Caro (7 vols). Basel, A.D. 1502.
        B.4.4 (pr. bk). *i*Gesta Romanorum. s.l. et a.
        B.4.24 (pr. bk). *m*B. de Bustis. Lyon, A.D. 1502.
        B.5.15 (pr. bk). *i*Augustinus. Paris, A.D. 1515.
        B.6.7 (pr. bk). *i*J. Major. Paris, A.D. 1529.
        B.7.6 (pr. bk). *i*B. de Bustis. Lyon, A.D. 1513.
        C.2.9 (pr. bk). *i*P. Comestor. Basel, A.D. 1486.
        C.3.13 (pr. bk). *i*Ægidius Romanus, etc. Venice, A.D. 1502,
            etc.
        C.4.11 (pr. bk). *m*H. de S. Victore, etc. Paris, A.D. 1507.
        C.5.2 (pr. bk). *i*P. Berchorius. Basel, A.D. 1515.
        C.5.10–11 (pr. bks). *i*J. Chrysostomus (2 vols). Basel,
            A.D. 1517.
        C.5.15 (pr. bk). *i*P. Tateretus. Paris, A.D. 1520.
        G.3.11–12 (pr. bks).[7] *i*Ambrosius (2 vols). Basel, A.D. 1516.
Winchester, Cathedral, 10. *ic*Vita S. Godrici. s.xv in.
York,
    Minster, vii.G.4 (pr. bk). *i*W. Burley, etc. Venice, A.D. 1485, etc.
        x.A.7 (pr. bk). *i*Duns Scotus. Nuremberg, A.D. 1481.
        x.G.13 (pr. bk). *i*J. Trithemius. Strasbourg, A.D. 1516.   ?
        xi.G.4 (pr. bk). *i*Psalterium quincuplex. Paris, A.D. 1509.
        xii.J.22 (pr. bk). *i*P. Comestor. Basel, A.D. 1486.
        xiv.B.22 (pr. bk). *e*Panormitanus. Basel, A.D. 1488.
        xv.A.12 (pr. bk). *i*G. de Baysio. s.l., A.D. 1495.
        xvi.D.9. *e*W. de Alvernia. s.xv. [a/12].
        xvi.I.1. *i*Theologica. s.xv ex.
        xvi.I.12. *c*Misc. Dunelm. s.xiii ex.–xv.   ?
        xvi.K.4. Augustinus, etc. s.xiv. [H; *cat.*, pp. 19, 95 H].
        xvi.N.8. *e*Psalterium, etc. s.xiv. [H].
        xvi.Q.5. Ezechiel glo. s.xii ex. [A; *cat.*, pp. 15, 91 A].
        xix.C.5 (pr. bk). *e*J. de Voragine. s.l. et a. [T].
Untraced: Phillipps sale (Sotheby, 21–26 March 1895), lot 136 to Quaritch,
    who sold to Harrassowitz. *e*Cassiodorus, etc. s.xiii.
        Messrs Quaritch in 1961 (sold then to E. Rossignol, bookseller,
    Paris, who sold to an unknown customer). *i*Biblia. s.xiii.
Rejected: Cambridge, Gonv. and Caius Coll. 159; Jesus Coll. 35, 66, 68;
    Sid. Sussex Coll. 30, 50, 55. Oxford, Bodleian, Douce 293, Laud
    misc. 720. Vienna, Nazionalbibl. 1274. York, Minster, xiv.K.3
    (pr. bk).

EASBY, Yorkshire. *Prem. abbey of St Agatha.*

Cambridge, Jesus Coll., 55. *bi*Ordinale premonstr. s.xv ex.

EDINBURGH. *Franciscan convent.*

For printed books see Durkan and Ross, pp. 71–72 (Arbuckle, nos 4, 9),
141 (John Scott, nos 2, 4), 165.

---

[7] On permanent loan to Ushaw Coll. from Hexham Catholic Church.

EDINBURGH. *Dominican convent.*

For printed books see Durkan and Ross, pp. 47, 49(?), 66–67, 86 (James Crichton, no. 4), 122, 147, 153, 154, 158, 165, 172, 186–87.

For pressmarks in the form 'De primo ambone' followed sometimes by a capital letter, see Durkan and Ross, pp. 66–67 and pl. XXVII.

EDINBURGH. *Convent of Dominican nuns, of St Catherine of Siena.*

For a printed book see Durkan and Ross, p. 86.

Edinburgh, U.L., 150. *c*Evangeliarium, etc. s.xvi. ?

EDINBURGH. *Collegiate church of St Giles.*

Edinburgh, N.L., Adv. 18.1.2. Biblia. s.xiii. ?

EDINGTON (Edyndon), Wiltshire. *House of Bonshommes, of St James, St Catherine, and All Saints.*

Cambridge, Pembr. Coll., C.48 (pr. bk). *e*Cicero, De officiis. Louvain. (A.D. 1483).

Oxford, Bodleian, Auct. D.5.14. *e*Biblia. s.xiii.

Bodl. 565. *e*Pilgrimages of W. Wey (in Lat. and Eng.), *c.* A.D. 1470.

Univ. Coll., 95.[8] *be*Rosarium theologie. s.xv.

Salisbury, Cathedral, L.5.10 (pr. bk). *e*W. Alvernus. Paris, A.D. 1478.

ELGIN. *Cathedral church of Holy Trinity.*

Edinburgh, U.L., 50. *c*Kalendarium, etc. s.xvi.

ELGIN. *Franciscan convent.*

For a printed book see Durkan and Ross, p. 112.

ELGIN. *Dominican convent.*

For 5 printed books see Durkan and Ross, pp. 94, 144–45, 165.

ELSHAM, Lincolnshire. *Aug. priory of B.V.M. and St Edmund.*

Note about books by J. Leland, printed from B.M., Royal MS. App. 69, fo. 5, in *Eng. Hist. Rev.*, liv. 92.

ELSTOW, Bedfordshire. *Abbey of B.V.M. and St Helen, of Ben. nuns.*

London, B.M., Royal 7 F.iii. *e*P. Comestor, etc. A.D. 1191–92.

ELY, Cambridgeshire. *Ben. abbey and (1109) cathedral priory of St Peter and St Etheldreda.*

Books noted by J. Leland, *Collectanea*, iv. 163.

A distinctive mark, consisting of a cross on a single or double-limbed base, occurs in Cambridge, U.L., Ii.2.15; Corpus Christi Coll. 44, 393, 416; Pembroke Coll. 308; Trinity Coll. 1105; B.M., Harley 1031; Bodleian, Bodl. 582, Rawl. Q.f.8, and is reproduced from the Harleian MS. in *New Pal. Soc.*, i, pl. 17, no. 5; the mark is usually written near the top of the outer margin of the first leaf of text. The common form of *ex libris* inscription 'Iste liber pertinet ecclesie Eliensi' (s.xv) is written at the end as well as at the beginning of the MS.

---

[8] The leaf of an Edington register formerly used as stiffening of the front cover of MS. 95 is now kept separately as MS. 192, fo. 30.

Cambridge, U.L., Gg.1.21. *e*Actus apost. glo. s.xii.

    Ii.2.15. Constitutiones provinciales, etc. s.xiv.

    Ii.4.3. *e*Rogerus Dymmok. s.xv.

    Ii.4.20. *l*Breviarium, etc. s.xv.

    Kk.1.24.[9] Evangelia. s.viii. ?

    Ll.2.10. *l*Pontificale. s.xii. ?

  Corpus Christi Coll., 44. *e*Pontificale. s.xi.

      335. *e*Tractatus de Mahometo, etc.
        s.xv.

      393. *e*Historia Eliensis. s.xii.

      416. Amalarius. s.xii. [108].

  Pembr. Coll., 308. *e*Rabanus Maurus. s.ix.

  St John's Coll., 23. *i*R. Rolle. s.xv.

     103.** *l*Psalterium. s.xiv. ?

  Trinity Coll., 249. *l*Pontificale. s.xii. ?

    1105. *c*Kalendarium, etc. s.xii ex.

    1145. *c*Kalendarium, etc. s.xii.

Ely, Cathedral, s.n. Historia Eliensis. s.xii–xiii. [G (*or* C) 60].

London,

  B.M., Add. 33381. *c*Miscellanea. s.xiii–xv.

  Arundel 377. *l*Kalendarium. s.xii/xiii. ?

  Cotton Tib. B.v, fo. 74.[9] *c*Ely documents (in English). s.x ex.

    Tib. B.v, fo. 76.[9] *c*Evangelia. s.viii. ?

    Calig. A.viii, fos 59–191. *i*Vite sanctorum. s.xii.

    Nero A.xv, xvi, fos 1–92. *c*Chronicon ecclesie. s.xv.

    Vesp. A.xix, fos 2–27. *c*Libellus operum Æthelwoldi.
        s.xii. ?

    Titus A.i, fos 3–56. *c*Historia Eliensis, etc. s.xii/xiii.

    Domit. xv. *c*Chronica, etc. s.xiii–xv.

  Harley 547. *l*Psalterium, etc. s.xiii ex.

    985. *i*Philomena, etc. s.xiv–xv.

    1031. *e*W. Peraldus. s.xiv.

    3721. *c*Chronicon Eliense. s.xvi in.

  Sloane 1044, fo. 2.[9] Evangelia. s.viii.

    1609, fos 5–10. *l*Kalendarium. s.xiii.

  Lambeth Palace, 204. *i*Gregorius, etc. s.x/xi.

     448. *c*Chronica Eliensia, etc. s.xv–xvi.

Milan, Braidense, A.F. xi. *l*Psalterium. s.xii ex.

Oxford, Bodleian, Bodl. 582. *e*Jeronimus, etc. s.xii. [M.23].

     762. *c*Ambrosius, etc. s.xii. [G.32]. ?

    Laud lat. 95. *l*Psalterium, etc. s.xiii.

    misc. 112. *e*Augustinus, etc. s.xiii.

     647. *c*Historia Eliensis. s.xiv.

     698. *c*Vite episcoporum Eliensium.
       s.xv.

   Rawl. Q.f.8. *e*Epp. T. Becket, etc. s.xii ex.

  Balliol Coll., 49. *e*T. Aquinas. s.xiii/xiv. [8.17].

  New Coll., 98. *c*W. de Monte, etc. s.xiii.

  Trinity Coll., 7. *c*Hymni, etc. (in Lat. and Eng.). s.xv. ?

  [9] Cotton Tib. B.v, fo. 76, and Sloane 1044, fo. 2, are leaves from Cambridge, U.L., Kk.1. 24; Cotton Tib. B.v, fo. 74, containing Ely documents, was probably originally a blank leaf of the same volume.

Trier, Stadtbibliothek, 9. *l*Psalterium, etc. s.xii in. ?
Ushaw College, XVIII.B.2.13.[1] *l*Missale (1 fo.). s.xii in. ?
Untraced: T. Thorpe, cat. for 1838, no. 169. *i*Horae. s.xv.
Rejected: London, Lambeth Palace, 40, 214. Oxford, Bodleian, Douce 296.

ELY. *Bishopric.*

Cambridge, U.L., Add. 3468. *c*Misc. jur. s.xv–xvi.

ETON, Buckinghamshire. *Royal College of B.V.M.*

M. R. James, *Descriptive Cat. of MSS in the Library of Eton College* (Cambr., 1895). Lists of service-books in 1445 and 1531 (?), and of library books and service-books in 1465 printed from Eton College muniments by M. R. James, 'Chapel inventories', *Etoniana*, 25–28 (1920–21), 391, 442–47; second folios given. Books noted by J. Bale, *Index* (p. 576).

Eton College,
  5. *e*Ambrosius. s.xii ex.
  6.[2] Augustinus. s.xv.
  14. *b*P. Cantor. s.xii/xiii. [*Inv. 1465,* ix].
  15. R. Flaviacensis. s.xii ex. [*Inv. 1465,* vi].
  16. *b*Rabanus Maurus, etc. s.xii/xiii. [*Inv. 1465,* xxii].
  19. P. Cantor. s.xii/xiii. [*Inv. 1465,* viii].
  20. *b*Haymo. s.xii.
  22.[2] Jeronimus. s.xiii. [*Inv. 1465,* iv].
  24. Berengaudus, etc. A.D. 1455.
  28, 29. *e*Vetus testamentum, cum glosa. s.xiii ex.
  30. *b*J. Athon. s.xv. ?
  32. *b*Bernardus, etc. s.xiv.–xv.
  33.[3] Gregorius, etc. s.xii/xiii.
  34. *b*Gregorius, etc. s.xv.
  37. *b*Gregorius, etc. s.xii/xiii.
  39. Bernardus, etc. s.xiii. ?
  42. *e*Opus imperfectum in Matheum. s.xv.
  44. Albertus Magnus. s.xv. ?
  47. Augustinus, etc. s.xv. ?
  48. *e*Augustinus. s.xii–xiii.
  76. *e*Jeronimus, etc. s.xii–xv.
  79. *e*P. de Palma. s.xv.
  80. *e*Jeronimus. s.xii.
  83.[4] Pascasius Radbertus, etc. s.xii–xiii. ?
  84. *b*Alanus de Insulis. s.xiv/xv.
  97[5]. Decreta pontificum. s.xii.
  98. *e*W. Lyndwode. s.xv.
  99. *b*P. de Nathalibus. s.xiv.
  101[5]. Augustinus, etc. s.xiv–xv.
  103. N. Gorran. s.xv. [*Inv. 1465,* xv].

---

[1] A leaf formerly in the binding of Ushaw Coll., XVIII.C.3.10, *Sermones Socci de Sanctis*, Strasbourg, A.D. 1484.
[2] MSS 6, 22, 97, 101 have a common form of inscription, s.xv, consisting of the title and secundo folio linked by the words 'et incipit in 2° folio'.
[3] See R. Birley, 'Eton College Library', *The Library*, 5th Series, xi, p. 233.
[4] *Ibid.*, pp. 239, 241.   [5] See above, n. 2.

Eton College (contd)
105. Augustinus. s.xii/xiii.
106. eAugustinus. s.xi/xii.
107. bAugustinus. s.xiii in.
108. bAugustinus, etc. s.xiv–xv.
109. J. de Ford, etc. s.xiii in. [Bale, Index, p. 202].
114. eP. Lombardus. s.xiii ex.
116.⁶ bT. Aquinas. s.xiii/xiv.
119. beGregorius, etc. s.xiii/xv.
120. eAugustinus, etc. s.xiv.
122. Aristoteles. s.xiv.
126. bJoh. filius Serapionis. s.xiv.
127. eMedica quedam. s.xiv.
131. eCassiodorus, etc. s.xiv.
132. Galienus. s.xiii. [Inv. 1465, xxxiii].
134. Rob. Cricklade. s.xii. [Bale].
145. bAmbrosius. s.xii.
178. Liber antiphonarum. s.xvi in. [Inv. 1531 (?), fo. 4ᵛ].
219, pp. 27–46.⁶ T. Aquinas. s.xiii/xiv.
Am.4.2 (pr. bk). beJ. Reuchlin. Pforzheim, A.D. 1506.
By.1.3 (pr. bk). eOrigenes contra Celsum. Rome, A.D. 1481.
By.1.9 (pr. bk). eQuintilianus. Venice, A.D. 1494.
By.2.1 (pr. bk). eT. Aquinas. Venice, A.D. 1493.
By.2.5 (pr. bk). bCassianus. Basel, A.D. 1485. ?
Ee.1.6 (pr. bk). beSimon de Cassia. (Strasbourg, c. A.D. 1487).
Ef.4.6 (pr. bk). eA. de Ghislandis. Lyon, A.D. 1508.
Eh.1.1, 2 (pr. bk). eReynerius de Pisis (2 vols). Nuremburg, A.D. 1477.
En.1 (pr. bk). eLudolphus de Saxonia. Cologne, A.D. 1487.
Fc.5.12 (pr. bk). e Silius Italicus. Venice, A.D. 1483.
Ga.3.11 (pr. bk). beG. de Zerbis. Venice, A.D. 1502.
Ge.1.5 (pr. bk). eM. A. Sabellicus. Venice, A.D. 1487.
Gloucester, Cathedral, 3. eAugustinus. s.xiii ex.
London, B.M., Cotton Titus A.xxii. eBiblia. s.xiii.
Harl. 3643. eChronica. s.xv. ?
Winchester Coll., 2. eTabula, etc., in Psalterium. s.xvi in.

EVESHAM, Worcestershire. Ben. abbey of B.V.M. and St Egwin. (Cf. cell at **PENWORTHAM.**)

Lists of books obtained by Thomas of Marlborough (abbot, †1236) and Nicholas Hereford (prior, †1392) printed from B.M., Harley 3763 in Monasticon, ii. 5, 7 n., the former also in Chron. Abb. de Evesham (Rolls Series), pp. 267–68, the latter also by W. A. Hulton, Priory of Penwortham (Chetham Society, xxx, 1853), p. 94. Books noted by J. Leland, Collectanea, iv. 160.

Aberystwyth, N.L., Peniarth 119D, pp. 503–741. Epistole R. Joseph monachi Eveshamensis. s.xvi in.
Evesham, Almonery Museum. lPsalterium, etc. s.xiv in.
London,
B.M., Add. 44874. lPsalterium, etc. s.xiii med.
Cotton Vit. E.xii, fos 1–54. cMartyrologium, etc. s.xii.
Vit. E.xvii, fos 224–50. cMiscellanea. s.xiv–xv.

⁶ MS. 219, pp. 27–46, are detached leaves of MS. 116.

London (*contd*)
B.M., Cotton Vesp. A.vi, art. 10. *c*Miracula Simonis Montisfortis.
s.xiii ex. ?
Appendix xiii. *e*Ambrosius, etc. s.xii–xiii. ?
Harley 229, fos 1–47. *e*Chronica. s.xiv.
3763. *c*Cartularium; Chronicon. s.xv.
Lansdowne 451. Pontificale. s.xiv.
Royal 4 E.ii. *e*W. de Nottingham. A.D. 1381.
8 G.iv. *e*Pseudo-Dionysius. s.xiii ex.
10 D.vi. *e*H. de Gandavo. s.xiv.
Mr Philip Robinson (pr. bk). *i*Bible (in English). (Antwerp),
A.D. 1537.
Manchester, J. Rylands, Lat. 122. *e*Novum testamentum. s.xiii.
Oxford, Bodleian, Auct. D.1.15. *e*Job, etc., glo. s.xiii.
Barlow 7. *i*Pontificale. s.xiii/xiv.
41. *l*Breviarium (pars hiemalis), etc. s.xiii.
Gough Missals 33 (pr. bk).[7] *e*Missale. Basel, ?
A.D. 1489.
Rawl. A.287. *c*Haymo, etc. s.xiii. [*Marlborough
list*].
G.16. *e*Biblia. s.xiii.
Jesus Coll., 51.[8] *b*Beda. s.xii. ?
54.[8] *b*Beda. s.xii. ?
93.[8] *b*Augustinus. s.xii. ?
103. *i*Matheus, etc., glo. s.xiii in.
Magdalen Coll., lat. 22. *e*Seneca. s.xii ex.
Queen's Coll., 302. *e*P. Lombardus. s.xiv.
Worcester Cathedral, Add. 68 (5). *l*Missale (6 fos). s.xv.
Rejected: London, B.M., Royal 6 C.ix, 6 D.iii. Oxford, Bodleian, Laud
lat. 31, Laud misc. 529.

EWELME, Oxfordshire. *Domus Dei.*

Inventory of books (A.D. 1466) printed from muniments of Ewelme Almshouse
A.47 in *Hist. MSS Comm., Eighth Report*, i. 629.

EXETER (Exonia), Devon. *Cathedral church of St Peter.*

Records of gifts of Bishop Leofric (†1072) printed from Exeter, Cathedral,
MS. 2501, fos 1–3, Oxford, Bodleian, MS. Auct. D.2.16, fos 1–2, and Exeter,
Cathedral, charter 2570, by Max Förster in *The Exeter Book* (London, 1933),
pp. 10–32; also in *Monasticon*, ii. 527–28, Kemble, *Codex Diplomaticus*, no. 940,
etc. Catalogue (incipits given) in inventory of 1327 printed from Exeter,
Cathedral, MS. 3671 by G. Oliver, *Lives of the Bishops of Exeter, etc.* (1861),
pp. 301–10; supplementary gifts, pp. 317–19. Catalogue (second folios given)
in inventory of 1506 printed by G. Oliver, *op. cit.*, pp. 366–75; service-books, etc.,
kept outside the library, listed pp. 323, 330–34, 350–54, 356–65. Note of sale
in 1383 of 11 books given 'ad fabricam ecclesie' printed from the chapter Act-
book, i, p. 32, in *Hist. MSS Comm. Rep., Var. Coll.*, iv. 37; second folios given.
Books noted by J. Leland, *Collectanea*, iv. 151, and *Itinerary* (ed. L. Toulmin
Smith), i. 230. The letter-marks in Bodleian, MSS Bodl. 494 and 482 are
reproduced in *New Pal. Soc.*, i, pl. 147, no. 8 *a, b*.

---

[7] Belonged to the Chapel of the Battle Well.
[8] See N. R. Ker, 'Sir John Prise,' *The Library*, 5th Series, x (1955), 18.

Cambridge,
    U.L., Ii.2.4. *s*Gregory, Pastoral Care (in English). s.xi. ?
        Ii.2.11.[9] *e*Gospels (in English), etc. s.xi. [*Leofric*].
    Corpus Christi Coll., 41. *e*Bede (in English). s.xi.

                190. Penitential, etc. (in Lat. and Eng.). s.xi.
                      [? *Leofric*; *cat.*, p. 309].
                191.[1] Regula canonicorum (in Lat. and Eng.).
                      s.xi. [? *Leofric; cat.*, pp. 304, 367].
                196.[1] Martyrology (in English). s.xi. [? *Leofric*].
                201, fos 179–272.[2] Theodulf of Orleans (in Lat.
                      and Eng.). s.xi.
                419.[2] Homilies (in English). s.xi. ?
                421.[2] *s*Homilies (in English). s.xi. ?
    Trinity Coll., 241. *e*Amalarius. s.x. [*Leofric; cat.*, pp. 303, 368].
             1475. *e*Gregorius Turonensis. s.xii in. [*Cat.*, p. 371].
Edinburgh, N.L., Adv. 18.5.1. Beda. s.xiv in. [*Cat.*, p. 369].
Eton College, 97. *m*Pseudo-Isidorus. s.xii. [*Cat.*, p. 304].
Exeter, Cathedral, 3501, fos 0–7.[9] List of Bishop Leofric's gifts, etc. (in
                      English). s.xi ex.

                fos 8–130. Poems (in English). s.x ex. [*Leofric*].
              3502. *l*Ordinale. s.xv.
              3503. *e*Euclides, etc. s.xiii. [*Cat.*, p. 367].
              3504–5. *e*Legenda Exon. s.xiv. [*Cat.*, p. 350].
              3507. Rabanus Maurus, etc. s.x ex. [*Cat.*, p. 303].
              3508. *c*Psalterium, etc. s.xiii. [*Cat.*, p. 333].
              3509. Polychronicon. s.xiv ex. [*Cat.*, p. 368].
              3510. *l*Missale. s.xiii.
              3512. *e*Excerpta ex decretis. s.xii. [*Cat.*, pp. 304,
                    369].
              3513. Pontificale. s.xv. [*Cat.*, p. 331].
              3516. W. Woodford, etc. s.xv. [*Cat.*, p. 370; *Leland*].
              3518. *c*Martyrologium. s.xii in.
              3520. Anselmus, etc. s.xii. [*Cat.*, pp. 303, 371].
              3548(D). *e*Legenda ex dono W. Poundestoke. s.xv.
              3625. *c*Kalendarium, etc. s.xiv.
London,
    B.M., Add. 28188. *ls*Benedictionale. s.xi ex. [? *Leofric; cat.*, p. 351 (?)].
        Cotton Tib. B.v, fo. 75. *c*Evangelium (and documents in Eng.).
                      s.viii–x.

        Vesp. D.xv, fos 2–67. *c*Pontificale. s.xii. ?
        Cleop. B.xiii, fos 1–58.[3] *s*Homilies, etc. (in English).
                      s.xi. ?

[9] Exeter, Cathedral, 3501, fos 0–7, are detached leaves of Cambridge, U.L., Ii.2.11.

[1] Corpus Christi Coll. 191, 196, 201 (fos 179–272) are companion volumes. Transcripts from the first two by John Joscelyn in Cotton Vit. D.vii are said to be from Exeter MSS.

[2] Corpus Christi Coll. 419 and 421 are companion volumes.

[3] Cotton Cleopatra B.xiii, fos 1–58, and Lambeth Palace 489 perhaps formed one volume.

London (*contd*)
  B.M., Harley 863. *l*Psalterium, etc. s.xi. [? *Leofric; cat.*, p. 334].
    2961. Collectarium ('Leofric collectar'). s.xi med.
      [? *Leofric*].
  Royal 6 B.vii. *c*Aldhelmus. s.xi/xii–xii. ?
  Lambeth Palace, 104, fos 1–208.[4] *e*Polychronicon, etc. s.xiv–xv.
    149, fos 1–138. Beda, etc. s.x. [*Leofric; cat.*,
      pp. 303, 367; *Leland*].
    188, fos 168–74.[4] *m*Memoranda historica. s.xiii.
    203. *e*Augustinus, etc. s.xii–xiv. [*Cat.*,
      p. 368].
    489.[3] *s*Homilies (in English). s.xi. ?
Manchester, J. Rylands, Lat. 24. Missale. s.xiii. [*Cat.*, p. 350].
Oxford,
  Bodleian, Auct. D.1.7. *e*Lucas et Joh. glo. s.xii ex. [*Cat.*, pp. 307,
      368].
    D.1.9. *e*Lucas et Joh. glo. s.xiii in. [*Cat.*, pp. 308,
      373].
    D.1.12. *e*Actus apost. glo. s.xiii. [*Cat.*, pp. 308 (?),
      373].
    D.1.13. Epp. Pauli glo. s.xii. [*Cat.*, p. 368].
    D.1.18. *e*Biblia. s.xiii/xiv. [*Cat.*, p. 367].
    D.2.8. *e*Psalterium glo. s.xii ex. [*Cat.*, pp. 307 (?),
      373].
    D.2.16. *e*Evangelia. s.x. [*Leofric; cat.*, p. 323].
    D.3.10. Genesis glo. s.xiii.
    D.infra 2.9. J. Cassianus. s.x–xi. [*Cat.*, pp. 304,
      367].
    F.1.15. *e*Boetius, etc. s.xi. [*Leofric*].
    F.3.6. *e*Prudentius. s.xi. [*Leofric; cat.*, pp. 307,
      368].
    F.3.7 Solinus, etc. s.xii. [*Cat.*, pp. 304, 368].
  Bodl. 92. Ambrosius. s.xii. [*Cat.*, pp. 303, 372].
    93. Augustinus. s.xii ex. [*Cat.*, pp. 302, 373].
    94. Ambrosius. s.xii. [*Cat.*, pp. 303, 372].
    135. Augustinus. s.xii. [*Cat.*, pp. 302, 372].
    137. Ambrosius. s.xii. [*Cat.*, pp. 303, 372].
    147. Pseudo-Athanasius. s.xii. [*Cat.*, pp. 303, 370].
    148. *e*Augustinus. s.xii. [*Cat.*, pp. 301, 372].
    149. Augustinus. s.xii. [*Cat.*, pp. 302, 373].
    150. Augustinus. s.xiii. [*Cat.*, p. 372].
    162. *e*Bonaventura, etc. s.xiv. [*Cat.*, p. 372].
    190. *e*Gregorius. s.xii. [*Cat.*, pp. 302, 371].
    193. Gregorius. s.xii. [*Cat.*, pp. 302, 371].
    201. Augustinus. s.xii. [*Cat.*, pp. 302, 373].
    206. Ambrosius. s.xii. [*Cat.*, pp. 303, 374].
    229. Augustinus. s.xi. [*Cat.*, pp. 302, 372].
    230. *e*Gregorius. s.xii. [*Cat.*, p. 367].
    237. Florus diaconus. s.xii. [*Cat.*, pp. 302, 373].

[4] Lambeth Palace 188, fos 168–74, was part of Lambeth Palace 104, fos 1–208.
[3] See p, 82, n. 3.

Oxford (*contd*)
Bodleian, Bodl. 239. Isidorus. s.xii. [*Cat.*, pp. 303, 367].
    253.[5] Gregorius. s.xii. [*Cat.*, pp. 302, 371].
    256. Johannes in novella, pars ii. s.xiv. [*Cat.*, p. 366].
    268. *e*Pera peregrini, pars ii. s.xv. [*Cat.*, p. 371].
    272.[6] *e*Augustinus. s.xii. [*Cat.*, pp. 301, 372].
    273.[6] *e*Augustinus. s.xii. [*Cat.*, pp. 301, 372].
    274. Augustinus. s.xii. [*Cat.*, pp. 302, 372].
    279. *e*R. Holcot. s.xiv ex. [*Cat.*, p. 373].
    286. *e*Duns Scotus. s.xiv. [*Cat.*, p. 370].
    287. *e*V. Bellovacensis. s.xiv. [*Cat.*, p. 368].
    289.[6] *e*Augustinus. s.xii. [*Cat.*, pp. 301, 372].
    290. Gratianus glo. s.xiv. [*Cat.*, p. 369].
    291. Decreta. s.xii ex. [*Cat.*, pp. 304, 369].
    293. Summa summarum. s.xiv. [*Cat.*, p. 369].
    301. Augustinus. s.xii. [*Cat.*, pp. 302, 373].
    311. Gregorius. s.x. [R; inv. 1327;[7] *cat.*, p. 368].
    314. *e*Gregorius. s.xii. [*Cat.*, pp. 302, 370].
    315. *e*J. Sarisberiensis, etc. s.xv. [*Cat.*, p. 371].
    318. Lethbertus. s.xiv. [*Cat.*, p. 371].
    319. Isidorus. s.x. [? *Leofric; cat.*, pp. 303, 367].
    320. Jac. de Voragine. s.xv. [*Cat.*, p. 370].
    333. *e*Rob. Kilwardby. s.xiv–xv. [*Cat.*, p. 372; *Leland*].
    335. *e*P. Lombardus. s.xiii/xiv. [*Cat.*, p. 370].
    338. Somnium viridarii. s.xv. [*Cat.*, p. 369].
    377.[8] *e*T. Aquinas. s.xiv. [*Cat.*, pp. 309 (?), 373].
    380.[8] T. Aquinas. s.xiv. [*Cat.*, pp. 309 (?), 373].
    382. Jeronimus, etc. s.xii. [*Cat.*, pp. 302, 372].
    389. Legenda sanctorum. s.xv. [*Cat.*, p. 370].
    393. Isidorus, etc. s.xv. [*Cat.*, p. 371].
    394. Isidorus, etc. s.xi–xii. [*Cat.*, pp. 302, 303, 372].
    449. Sermones. s.xii. [*Cat.*, pp. 305, 371].
    463. *e*Astrologica. s.xiv. [*Cat.*, p. 368].
    473.[9] Sermones. s.xiii in. [*Cat.*, pp. 309, 370].
    479. Beda. s.xii. [*Cat.*, pp. 303, 371; *Leland*].
    482. *e*Barth. Exoniensis. s.xiii. [G.; *cat.*, pp. 305, 367; *Leland*].
    494. *e*P. Comestor, etc. s.xii/xiii. [H.; *cat.*, pp. 308, 36
    579. *e*Missale ('Leofric missal'), etc. (Lat. and Eng.). s.x–xi. [*Leofric*].
    683.[1] Gregorius. s.xii. [*Cat.*, pp. 302, 371].
    691. *e*Augustinus. s.xii. [*Cat.*, pp. 302, 372].

[5] Bodl. 683 and 253 form one set.
[6] Bodl. 289, 272 and 273 form one set.
[7] The last entry under 'Libri Gregorii' in the 1327 inv., 'Duo penitenciales Gregorii qui sic incipiunt in ordinacione', was left out in Oliver's edition (p. 302).
[8] Bodl. 377 and 380 form one set.
[9] Bodl. 734 and 473 form one set.
[1] Bodl. 683 and 253 form one set.

Oxford (*contd*)
  Bodleian, Bodl. 707. *e*Gregorius. s.xi. [*Cat.*, pp. 302, 370].
            708. *e*Gregorius. s.xi. [*Leofric*; *cat.*, pp. 302, 367 *or*
                     371].
            717. *e*Jeronimus. s.xii. [*Cat.*, pp. 302, 372].
            718. Penitentiale, etc. s.x.
            720. *e*Gilbertus Anglicus. s.xiv. [*Cat.* p. 368;
                     Leland].
            722. R. Holcot. s.xv. [*Cat.*, p. 370].
            725. *e*Epp. Pauli glo. s.xii ex. [*Cat.*, pp. 307 (?),
                     373].
            732. *e*Beda, etc. s.xii ex. [*Cat.*, p. 370].
            734.[9] Sermones. s.xiii in. [*Cat.*, p. 370].
            736. Barth. Pisanus. s.xv in. [*Cat.*, p. 367].
            738. *e*Nic. Trivet. s.xiv. [*Cat.*, p. 373].
            739. Ambrosius. s.xii. [*Cat.*, pp. 303, 372].
            744. *e*Ric. de Mediavilla. s.xiv. [*Cat.*, p. 370].
            748. *e*P. Comestor. s.xiv. [*Cat.*, p. 373].
            749. *e*Barth. Anglicus. s.xiv ex. [*Cat.*, p. 370].
            783. *ms*Gregorius. s.xi/xii. [*Cat.*, pp. 302, 367 *or*
                     371].
            786. *e*Medica. s.xiii. [*Cat.*, p. 368].
            792. Julianus Toletanus. s.xii. [*Cat.*, pp. 303, 372].
            804. Augustinus. s.xii. [*Cat.*, pp. 302, 373].
            808. Jeronimus. s.xii. [*Cat.*, pp. 302, 372].
            810. *e*Canones apostolorum, etc. s.xii. [*Cat.*
                     pp. 304, 369].
            813. Augustinus. s.xii. [*Cat.*, pp. 302, 373].
            815. Augustinus. s.xi ex. [*Cat.*, pp. 302, 373].
            829. *e*Ric. [*sic*] Ringstede. s.xv in. [*Cat.*, p. 373;
                     Leland].
            830. *e*R. Grosseteste. s.xiv ex. [*Cat.*, p. 371].
            849. Beda. A.D. 818. [? *Leofric*; *cat.*, pp. 303, 371;
                     Leland].
            859. *e*Epp. Gilberti Stone, etc. s.xiii ex.–xv in.
            865, fos 1–88. *e*Ric. Armachanus. s.xv. [*Cat.*,
                           p. 369].
                fos 89–115. Theodulf of Orléans, etc. (in Lat.
                        and Eng.). s.xi. [*Cf. cat.*,
                        p. 304].
        Bodl. Or. 135. *e*Grammar, etc. (in Hebrew). s.xiii.
        Wood empt. 15. *e*Herbarium, etc. s.xv med. [*Cat.*, p. 368].
  All Souls Coll., 6. *m*Psalterium. s.xiii. [*Cf. cat.*, p. 333]. ?
Rejected: Cambridge, Corpus Christi Coll., 93; Trinity Coll., 255. Exeter,
    Cathedral, 3506, 3514, 3519, 3525–26, 3533, 3549B (Bishop Grandi-
    son's Isidore). London, B.M., Add. 16412. Oxford, Bodleian,
    Auct. D.2.7. Wells, Cathedral, s.n. (Isidorus).

EXETER. *Ben. priory of St Nicholas; cell of Battle.*
London, B.M., Add. 22719. *e*Constantinus Africanus. s.xii. [CN].

[9] See p. 84, n. 9.

EXETER. *Hospital of St John the Baptist.*

Exeter, Cathedral, 3511. *e*Sermones J. Januensis. s.xiv in.
London, B.M., Add. 38129. *e*W. Malmesburiensis. s.xv in. [FA].
        Harley 3671. *e*Polychronicon. s.xiv/xv. [F.2].
Oxford, Bodleian, Laud misc. 156. *e*Figure et tabule. s.xv. [A.27].

EXETER. *Franciscan convent.*

List of fourteen books assigned to the use of the convent (1267) by Roger de Thoriz, archdeacon of Exeter, in *Register of Walter Bronescombe*, ed. F. C. Hingeston-Randolph, p. 79.

Oxford, Bodleian, Bodl. 62. *c*Horae B.V.M. s.xiv. ?

EXETER. *Dominican convent.*

Books noted by J. Leland, *Collectanea*, iv. 151.
The inscription and pressmark in B.M., Royal 19 C.v are reproduced in *New Pal. Soc.*, i, pl. 147, no. 9.

London, B.M., Royal 19 C.v. *e*Comment. on Psalms 51–100 (in French). s.xiii. [F.1].

EYE, Suffolk. *Ben. alien priory of St Peter; cell of Bernay.*

The 'ruber liber de Eya', a gospel-book 'scriptus litteris majusculis Longobardicis', is noticed by Leland, *Collectanea*, iv. 26, and in an inventory of 1536 'an old Masse boke callyd the redde boke of Eye garnysshed with a lyttel sylver on the one side, the residewe lytell worth', printed in *Proc. Suffolk Inst. Archaeol.*, viii (1894), 106.[2]

Norwich, City Libr., F.c.18 (pr. bk). *i*Expo. hymnorum et sequentiarum. London, A.D. 1497.
Oxford, Magdalen Coll., lat. 170. *e*G. Monemutensis. s.xii/xiii.

EYNSHAM (Egnesham), Oxfordshire. *Ben. abbey of B.V.M., St Benedict and All Saints.*

Books noted by J. Leland, *Collectanea*, iv. 161.
The pressmark in Laud lat. 31 is in red at the top of the first leaf of the text in the centre. Closely similar marks are in three MSS without *ex libris* inscriptions.

Bristol, All Saints' Church, 5 (pr. bk). *i*T. Aquinas. Bologna, A.D. 1481.
Cambridge, U.L., Gg.4.15. Beda. s.xi/xii. [D.XX]. ?
London, B.M., Cotton Tib. A.xii. *e*Alex. Nequam, etc. s.xiii. [*Leland*].
Oxford, Bodleian, Bodl. 269. Augustinus. s.xii. [B.IIII]. ?
        435. *c*Consuetudinarium. s.xiv.
        700. Ambrosius. s.xii ex. [C.XV]. ?
        Laud lat. 31. *e*Augustinus. s.xii. [B.IX].

FARNE ISLAND, Northumberland. *Ben. priory; cell of Durham.*

For English translations and abstracts of lists of books in inventories of 1394, 1436, 1451 and 1513/14 from Durham Muniments, see J. Raine, *North Durham* (1852), pp. 347–57.

---

[2] Two traditions regarding this book are (1) that it is represented by Corpus Christi College, Cambridge, 197, pp. 245–316, and (2) that it was comparatively recently (before 1848) in the possession of the corporation of Eye. A report that it was cut up for game labels at Brome Hall is referred to by M. R. James, *Suffolk and Norfolk* (1930), p. 12.

FAVERSHAM, Kent. *Ben. abbey of St Saviour.*

Books noted by J. Leland, *Collectanea,* iv. 6.

Cambridge, Emmanuel Coll., 10–11. *c*Haymo. s.xii. ?
Grenoble, Bibl. de la ville, 985. *c*P. Comestor. s.xiii in.
Lampeter, St David's Coll. (pr. bk). *e*Virgilius. Nuremberg, A.D. 1492.
Oxford, Bodleian, Jones 9. *c*Martyrologium. s.xvi in.
    Corpus Christi Coll., 31. *e*Hilarius. s.xii ex.

FAVERSHAM. *Corporation of the borough.*

London, B.M., Add. 37488. Liber precedentium, etc. s.xv ex.

FEARN, Ross and Cromarty. *Prem. abbey of St Ninian.*

Dunrobin, Duke of Sutherland. *c*Kalendarium. s.xv.

FELIXSTOWE (Walton St Felix, Filchestowe), Suffolk. *Ben. priory of St Felix; cell of Rochester.*

Catalogue of 'libri prioris Rodberti de Waletune' (supplement to Rochester catalogue of 1202) printed from B.M., Royal MS. 5 B.xii, in *Archaeologia Cantiana,* iii (1860), p. 61.

London, B.M., Royal 7 A.vii. *e*P. Blesensis. s.xii/xiii.

FERRIBY, NORTH, Yorkshire. *Aug. priory of B.V.M.*

London, B.M., Harley 114. *e*P. Langtoft (in French). s.xiv.

FINCHALE, co. Durham. *Ben. priory of St John the Baptist and St Godric; cell of Durham.*

London, B.M., Add. 35283. *l*Psalter, etc. (in Lat. and Fr.). s.xiii. ?
Oxford, Bodleian, Laud misc. 546. *e*Julianus Toletanus. s.xi ex.
Rejected: Cambridge, Trinity Coll., 365.

FINESHADE (de Castro Hymel), Northamptonshire. *Aug. priory of B.V.M.*

London, B.M., Cotton Cleop. D.ix, fos 84–88. *c*Chronicon. s.xiv. ?
Rejected: New York, Columbia Univ., Plimpton 76.

FLANESFORD, Herefordshire. *Aug. priory of St John the Baptist.*

Oxford, Bodleian, Lat. th. e.9. *c*Hon. Augustodunensis, etc. s.xii. ?

FLAXLEY, Gloucestershire. *Cist. abbey of B.V.M.*

Catalogue (s.xiii in.) printed from Phillipps MS. 1310 (*cf.* 19745), transcript (s.xix) of a cartulary roll, B.M., Add. 49996, in *Cartulary . . . of Flaxley,* ed. A. W. Crawley-Boevey (Exeter, 1887), pp. 183–85, and in *Centralblatt für Bibliothekswesen,* ix (1892), 205–7, and in *Trans. Bristol and Glouc. Archaeol. Soc.,* xxxi (1908), 113–15.

Hereford, Cathedral, O.iii.3. *e*Summa Raymundi. s.xiii.

FLIXTON, Suffolk. *Priory of B.V.M. and St Catherine, of Aug. nuns.*

Cambridge, U.L., Ee.3.52. *e*Old Testament (Genesis–Job; in French) s.xv.

FORD, Devon. *Cist. abbey of B.V.M.*

Books noted by J. Leland, *Collectanea,* iv. 150.

Chicago, Newberry Libr., 344984. *e*Augustinus. s.xii.
Eton Coll., 119, fos 1–182. *e*Gregorius. s.xiii.
Oxford, Bodleian, Laud misc. 450. *e*Eusebius. s.xii.
Rejected: London, B.M., Add. 17003. Oxford, Bodleian, Laud misc. 606.

FOTHERINGHAY (Fodringhey), Northamptonshire. *Collegiate church of B.V.M. and All Saints.*

Cambridge, St John's Coll., 135. *c*Martyrologium. s.xiv.
London, Lambeth Palace, 1500.91 (pr. bk). *e*Revelationes S. Brigitte. Nuremberg, A.D. 1500.

FOUNTAINS (de Fontibus, de Fontanis), Yorkshire. *Cist. abbey of B.V.M.*

Books noted by J. Leland, *Collectanea,* iv. 44.
The fifteenth-century pressmark, written usually inside the front cover or on a flyleaf, is reproduced from Dublin, Trinity Coll. 114 ('Theca 8ª in novis armariis liber 17') and Trinity Coll. 167 ('Theca suprema liber 4 in antiquis') in *New Pal. Soc.,* i, pl. 147, no. 3 *a, b.* The forms below have been normalized and the word *armariis,* which does not always occur, has been omitted. Three MSS contain an earlier form of pressmark, consisting of a number and letter. The common form of *ex libris* inscription is 'Liber sancte Marie de Fontibus'.

Berlin, Staatsbibl., lat. 172. *e*Ennodius. s.xii. ?
Brussels, Bibl. royale, 149. *e*Marcus glo. s.xii/xiii.
Cambridge, Gonv. and Caius Coll., 126. *e*Augustinus, etc. s.xii ex.
        [J.7, Th.3 in ant. lib.35].
    Trinity Coll., 54. *e*Beda. s.xii. [Th.3 lib.4].
    1054. *e*Divisio scientiarum, etc. s.xiii.
    1104. *c*Hugo de Kirkestall. s.xv ex.
    Union Soc., Fairfax Rhodes Libr. (pr. bk). *e*Biblia glo., pars
        iii. s.l. et a.
Clongowes Wood Coll. *e*Ivo Carnotensis. s.xii/xiii. [C.XI, Th.1 in ant. lib.38].
Dublin, Trinity Coll., 114.³ *e*Clemens Lanthoniensis, etc. s.xiv in.–xv in. [Th.8 in nov. lib.17].
    167. Vita S. Marie. s.xiv/xv. [Th. suprema in ant. lib.4].
London,
    B.M., Add. 24203. *i*Prick of conscience (in English). s.xiv ex.
    Arundel 217. *e*Cyprianus, etc. s.xii. [C.XIII].
    231. *e*J. de Abbatisvilla, etc. s.xiv ex. [Th.4 in nov. lib.27].
    Cotton [Galba A.iii, art. 2.⁴ Causa regis Stephani. ?]
    Vit. A.x, fos 19–138. *e*Brut (in French). s.xiii. [Th.8 lib.3].
    Faust. A.v.³ *e*Hist. Dunelmensis, etc. s.xii–xiv/xv.
    B.i, fos 192–205. *c*Itinerarium iii monachorum. s.xii ex.

³ Dublin, Trinity Coll. 114, and London, B.M., Cotton Faust. A.v formed one volume.
⁴ Galba A.iii was burnt in 1731.

London (*contd*)
 B.M., Harley 3173. *e*Expo. misse, etc. s.xii. [Th. E.10].
  6551. *e*Meditationes et preces. s.xiv.
 Mr H. Davis. *e*Ezechiel glo. s.xii.
 Manchester, J. Rylands, Lat. 365. *i*Sermones. s.xiv. [Th.6 in nov.
  lib.2].
 New York, Pierpont Morgan Libr., M.890. Bestiarium. s.xiv. ?
 Oxford,
  Bodleian, Ashmole 1398, pp. 217–52. *e*Misc. theologica. s.xiii.
   1437. *e*Medica. s.xv ex.
  Laud misc. 310. *e*H. de S. Victore. s.xii.
   619. *e*Polychronicon. s.xv.
   Lyell 8. *e*Sermones. s.xiv.
 Christ Church, e.8.29 (pr. bk).[5] *i*Breviarium. Paris, A.D. 1516 (?).
 Corpus Christi Coll., 209. *e*Augustinus, etc. s.xii/xiii. [Th.3 in ant.
  lib. 38].
 Univ. Coll., 124. 'Tertius liber florum'. s.xiii in. [Th.1 in nov. lib.13].
  167. *c*Registrum; privilegia ordinis Cist. s.xv.
 Princeton, U.L., R. Garrett 94. *e*Theologica. s.xiii. [Th.1 in nov. lib.22].
 Ripon, Cathedral, xvii. C.15 (pr. bk). *e*Vincentius Ferrer. Leyden,
  A.D. 1497.
   xvii.E.16–18 (pr. bk). *e*P. Berchorius. s.l. et a.
 Studley Royal, Mr H. Vyner. *e*Bernardus de Gordonio.[6] s.xiv.
   *e*Basilius, etc.[6] s.xii–xiii. [Th.[ ] in
   nov. lib.16].
   *e*Parabole, etc.[6] s.xiii. [Th.3 in nov.
   lib.16].
   *e*Collectanea H. de Knarresburc.[6] s.xiii.
   [Th.2 in nov. lib.36].
   *e*Grammatica, etc.[6] s.xiv–xv.
 Untraced: T. Martin sale, 18–21 May 1774, lot 245. W. Peraldus.
 Rejected: Oxford, Bodleian, Laud misc. 730. San Marino, Huntington,
  HM 3027.

FRIESTON (Frestuna), Lincolnshire. *Ben. priory of St James; cell of
 Crowland.*
 Note of MSS seen by J. Leland, printed from B.M., Royal MS. App. 69,
 fo. 7, in *Eng. Hist. Rev.*, liv. 93.
 Ripon, Cathedral, xvii.B.29. *e*Bonaventura. s.xv. ?

FURNESS, Lancashire. *Savigniac and (1147) Cist. abbey of B.V.M.*
 Oxford, Bodleian, Jones 48. *e*G. Monemutensis. s.xiv in.
 Rejected: London, B.M., Cotton Cleop. A.i.

GARENDON (Geroldonia), Leicestershire. *Cist. abbey of B.V.M.*
 The *ex libris* inscription is 'Liber sancte Marie de Geroldonia'.
 Oxford, Bodleian, Ashmole 1516. *e*Rabanus Maurus. s.xii.
  Bodl. 706. *e*S. Langton. s.xiii.
 Wells, Vicars Choral Hall. *e*Ivo Carnotensis, Chronicon. s.xii.

 [5] Christ Church e.8.29 has the arms of Abbot Marmaduke Huby.
 [6] These MSS are on permanent loan to the Archives Department of Leeds
 Public Libraries and are referenced there VR 6109, VR 6107, VR 6108, VR 6106
 and VR 6120 respectively.

GATESHEAD, co. Durham. *Hospital of St Edmund.*

List of 16 service-books in inventory of A.D. 1325 printed in *Reg. Pal. Dunelm.* (Rolls Series), iii. 84, and in *Wills and Inventories* (Surtees Soc., 1835), i. 22.

GLASGOW. *Cathedral church of St Mungo.*

Catalogue of 1432 printed from the Registrum Glasguense by John Dillon in *Archaeologia Scotica*, ii, part 2 (1831), pp. 328–49; also in *Registrum Episcopatus Glasguensis* (Bannatyne Club, 1843), pp. 334–39, and in *Inventory of the Ornaments of the Cathedral Church of Glasgow* (Maitland Club, 1831), pp. 8–22.

London, B.M., Cotton Tib. B.viii, fos 1–34, 81–197. *c*Pontificale. s.xii.

GLASGOW. *Franciscan convent.*

For two printed books see Durkan and Ross, pp. 125, 166.

GLASGOW. *Dominican convent.*

For two printed books see Durkan and Ross, pp. 118 (Hunter, 1), 138 (Ritchie).

GLASGOW. *University library.*

Lists of books given in 1475, 1483 and other years, printed from the Annales Facultatis Artium 1451–1555, pp. 45–47, 73, in *Munimenta Alme Universitatis Glasguensis*, ed. Cosmo Innes (1854), iii. 403–6.

For a printed book given by Archbishop James Beaton, see Durkan and Ross, p. 26 (Beaton, 23). Other books of Beaton's, without *ex dono*, were probably pre-Reformation gifts, alienated after 1560 and finally returned by James Boyd in 1581 (Durkan and Ross, pp. 24–28, 169).

GLASTONBURY, Somerset. *Ben. Abbey of B.V.M.*

Catalogue (A.D. 1247) printed from Cambridge, Trinity Coll., MS. 724, fos 102–4, by T. Hearne, *J. Glaston. Chronica* (Oxford, 1726), pp. 423–44 (thence by T. W. Williams, *Somerset Mediaeval Libraries* (Som. Arch. Soc., 1897), pp. 55–78). For lists of books written for or acquired by abbots, etc., s.xii ex.-xiv in., see T. Hearne, *op. cit.*, pp. 252, 262, 265, and T. Hearne, *Adami de Domerham Historia* (1727), pp. 317, 441, 574. List of books given by Abbot Walter de Monyton, 1341–74, in Cambridge, Trinity Coll., 711; second folios given. Books noted by J. Leland, *Collectanea*, iv. 153–55; *cf.* Leland, *De Scriptoribus Britannicis*, pp. 38, 41, 131, 172. Extracts 'ex registro librorum Glasconiensis monasterii' by Bale, *Index*, pp. 513–14 (*cf.* also p. 576).

Brinkley, Sir G. Keynes.   *s*W. Malmesburiensis (fragm.), cum tabula J. Merylynch. A.D. 1411.
Bristol, Central Public Libr., 5.   *e*Jac. de Voragine. s.xv in.
Cambridge, U.L., Kk.5.32.   *l*Boetius, etc. s.xi in.–xii in. ?
      St John's Coll., Ii.3.39 (pr. bk).   *i*Augustinus de Ancona. Cologne, A.D. 1475.
      Trinity Coll.,   86.   *e*Steph. Langton. s.xv in.
               167.   *e*P. Riga, etc. s.xiii.
               711.   *c*J. Glaston. chronica. s.xiv.
               724.   *c*W. Malmesburiensis, etc. s.xiii–xiv.
               727.[7]   W. Malmesburiensis. s.xii.
              1450.   *c*Collectanea. s.xv/xvi.
              1460.   *e*Augustinus, etc. s.xiv. [*Monyton list*].
London,
   B.M., Add. 10105.   *i*Polychronicon. s.xiv.

[7] Borrowed from Malmesbury by the abbot of Glastonbury in 1411/12.

London (*contd*)
    B.M., Add. 21614. *e*H. de Bracton. s.xiv. [*Monyton list*].
          22934. *c*W. Malmesburiensis, etc. s.xiv.
      Cotton Tib. A.v. *c*Historia Glastonie, etc. s.xv. ?
          Titus D.vii, fos 2–13. *c*Catalogus reliquiarum. s.xiv. ?
          Cleop. C.x, fos 71–100. *c*Chronicon. s.xv.
      Harley 641, fos 118–206.[8] *i*Martinus Polonus. s.xv.
          651, fos 185–91.[8] *i*Provinciale episcopatuum. s.xv.
          1916.[9] Augustinus. s.xii. ?
          1918. Clemens Lanthoniensis. s.xii. [? *Leland*]. ?
          5958, fo. 87.[9] Augustinus. s.xii. ?
      Lansdowne 212. Chronicon Anglie. s.xv. ?
Oxford,
    Bodleian, Ashmole 790. *ci*J. Glaston. chronica. s.xv.
        Auct. F.4.32. Ars Euticis, etc. s.ix–xi. [*Cat.* p. 441;
          Leland].
             4.Q.6.83 (pr. bk). *i*Cicero, etc. Paris, s.xvi in.
        Bodl. 80. *i*Sinesius Cyrenensis. s.xv ex.
        Hatton 30. *i*Augustinus. s.x.
        Lat. hist. a.2.[1] *c*Collectanea Glaston. s.xv.
        Laud lat. 4. *e*J. Saresberiensis, etc. s.xv.
          misc. 128. *i*T. Wallensis, etc. s.xv.
          misc. 497. *b*J. Wallensis, etc. s.xiii–xv. ?
          misc. 750. *c*Chronicon Glastonie, etc. s.xiii ex.
        Wood empt. 1. *e*Chronicon, etc. s.xiv. [*Monyton list*].
    Oriel Coll., 15.[2] R. Holcot, etc. A.D. 1389 (?). ?
    Queen's Coll., 304. *i*Chronica. s.xv in.
Paris, B.N., Lat. 4167A. *e*Ric. de Pophis, etc. s.xiv.
Princeton, U.L., R. Garrett 153. *e*J. Glaston. chronica. s.xv in.
Upholland College, 98. *l*Psalterium, etc. s.xv in.
Wells, Cathedral, Liber ruber (binding leaves). *l*Collectarium. s.xii. ?
Rejected: Cambridge, U.L., Dd.1.17; Trinity Coll., 822, 1042. London,
    B.M., Cotton Tib. B.v, part 1, fos 2–73, 77–88. Oxford, Bodleian,
    Hatton 42, 43. Phillipps 9328.

GLOUCESTER. *Ben. abbey of St Peter.* (*Cf. cells at* **BROMFIELD,**
HEREFORD, *St Guthlac,* **OXFORD,** *Gloucester College.*)

    Dugdale, *Monasticon*, i. 537 prints a list of seven books given by Richard
de Stowa (s.xiii) from B.M., Harley MS. 627. M. R. James, *Cat. of MSS
of Corpus Christi Coll., Cambridge*, ii. 439, prints a list of 41 'libri Ricardi de
Aldesworth' (probably his gifts to Gloucester) from Corpus 485. Books noted
by J. Leland, *Collectanea*, iv. 159. The common form of *ex libris* inscription is
'Liber (monasterii) sancti Petri Gloucestrie'. A table of contents in a distinctive
hand, s.xii, occurs in Hereford Cathedral, O.iii.1, P.i.5, B.M., Harley 2659,
Bodl. 210 and Jesus Coll., Oxford, 43.

---

    [8] Harley 651, fos 185–91, was possibly part of Harley 641, fos 118–206.
    [9] Harley 5958, fo. 87, is a detached leaf of Harley 1916. At its foot is a note,
s.xiii, designed to help the 'lector refectorii' to find his place. After 'refectorii'
the words '(scilicet Abbatiae Glastoniensis)' have been added in the hand of
Humfrey Wanley.
    [1] A 'tabula' consisting of six sheets of parchment pasted on swinging
wooden frames.
    [2] Oriel Coll. 15, or its exemplar, was written in 1389 by a Glastonbury monk.

Belmont Abbey (pr. bk). *i*P. Lombardus. Paris, A.D. 1508.
Cambridge, Corpus Christi Coll., 485. *i*Biblia. s.xiii.
        Gonv. and Caius Coll., 309. *m*Boethius, etc. s.xii–xiv. [BT].
        Trinity Coll., 75. *i*Beda. s.xi/xii. ?
               160. *e*Haymo. s.xiii.
               161. *e*Haymo. s.xiii.
               166. *e*Epp. Pauli glo. s.xii.
Cambridge (U.S.A.), Harvard Law School, 26. *i*Registrum Brevium.
    s.xv.
Dublin, Trinity Coll., 184. *e*Ivo Carnotensis, etc. s.xii.
Gloucester, Cathedral, 34. *c*Historia W. Frowcester, etc. s.xv in.
Hereford, Cathedral, O.i.2. *i*Misc. theologica. s.xiii in.
                O.iii.1. *e*Prosper, etc. s.xii in.
                P.i.5. *s*Augustinus. s.xii in.
                P.i.6. *e*Didimus, etc. s.xii–xiv.
                P.i.10. Didimus, etc. s.xii. ?
London,
    B.M., Cotton Domit. viii, fos 120–61. *c*Chronicon. s.xv.
        Harley 613. *e*Biblia. s.xiii.
             627. *e*P. Riga. s.xiii in.
           2659. *i*Seneca. s.xii.
        Royal 2 C.xii. *e*Isidorus. s.xiii in.
             3 B.x. Gervasius Cicestrensis. s.xii/xiii. [*Leland*]. ?
             5 A.xi. *e*Augustinus; Milo. s.xii.
            10 C.vi. *e*R. Holcot, etc. s.xiv ex.
            11 D.viii. *e*Canones. s.xii.
            13 C.v. *e*Beda. s.xi ex.
    Lambeth Palace, 179, fos 1–98. *m*H. Huntendonensis, etc. s.xiii in. ?
New York, Pierpont Morgan, 99. *cl*Horae, etc. s.xv in.
Oxford, Bodleian, Bodl. 210. *s*Cyprianus. s.xii.
           Laud misc. 123. *i*Augustinus, etc. s.xii. [AM].
               706. *ib*Sermones, etc. (partly in English).
                  s.xv.
        Rawl. liturg. f.1. *l*Horae. s.xv.
    Corpus Christi Coll., 89. *e*Polychronicon. s.xv.
    Jesus Coll., 10. *l*Antiphonale. s.xii–xv.
           42. *e*Gregorius. s.xiii/xiv.
           43. *s*Pseudo- Athanasius, etc. s.xii.
           65. *is*Beda, etc. s.xii.
    Queen's Coll., 367. *c*Chronicon. s.xv.
    Trinity Coll., 64. *e*Rabanus Maurus, etc. s.xiii. [? *Leland*].
           66. *e*Steph. Langton. s.xiii.
Williamstown, Williams Coll., Chapin Libr.[3] *i*Fragm. operis incerti.
Rejected: Cambridge, Trinity Coll., 159. London, B.M., Royal 6 D.ix,
    8 A.xxi. Munich, Staatsbibl., lat. 835.

GLOUCESTER. *Aug. priory of St Oswald, King and Martyr.*

Oxford, Bodleian, Tanner 170. *c*Polychronicon. s.xiv.

   [3] Binding leaves in pr. bk, Martial, *Epigrammata* (Venice, A.D. 1485), and
Juvenal, *Satyrae* (Venice, A.D. 1494).

GLOUCESTER. *Franciscan convent.*

Hereford, Cathedral, O.v.5. *e*Gregorius. s.xiii.
$\left[\dfrac{)}{)}\text{C } 16^m\right]$.

London, Lambeth Palace, 151, fos 1–209. *e*Augustinus, etc. s.xiii.
$\left[\dfrac{)}{)}\text{C } 2^m\right]$.

GLOUCESTER. *Dominican convent.*

Longleat, Marquess of Bath, 2A. *e*Biblia. s.xiii ex.

GODSTOW, Oxfordshire. *Abbey of B.V.M. and St John the Baptist, of Ben. nuns.*

Manchester, Chetham, 6717. *e*Psalterium. s.xv.
Oxford, Bodleian, Rawl. B.408. *c*Cartulary, etc. (in English). s.xv med.

GORING (Garinges, etc.), Oxfordshire. *Priory of B.V.M., of Aug. nuns.*

Cambridge, Trinity Coll., 241. *e*Psalterium. s.xiii.

GRACEDIEU, Leicestershire. *Priory of B.V.M. and Holy Trinity, of Aug. nuns.*

Rejected: Oxford, Bodleian, Liturg. misc. 6.

GRANTHAM, Lincolnshire. *Franciscan convent.*

Lincoln, Cathedral, 207. *e*W. de Alvernia, etc. s.xv.

GREENFIELD, Lincolnshire. *Priory of B.V.M., of Cist. nuns.*

Rejected: London, B.M., Royal 15 D.ii.

GREENWICH, Kent. *Franciscan convent.*

London,
    B.M., Sloane 1617. *e*Bonaventura, etc. s.xv. ?
    St Paul's Cath., 13.D.16 (pr. bk). *e*Sermones discipuli. Strasbourg,
                A.D. 1495.
    Lambeth Palace, 1494.2 (pr. bk). *e*Bernardus. Paris, A.D. 1494. ?
Rejected: London, B.M., Arundel 71, fo. 9.

GRIMSBY, Lincolnshire. *Franciscan convent.*

Note about books seen by J. Leland, printed from B.M., Royal MS. App. 69, fo. 6, in *Eng. Hist. Rev.,* liv. 92.
Belvoir Castle, Duke of Rutland, Mun. Room. *e*Cassiodorus. s.xiii.
                              [P.8].

GRIMSBY. *Convent of Austin friars.*

Note about books seen by J. Leland printed from B.M., Royal MS. App. 69, fo. 6, in *Eng. Hist. Rev.,* liv. 93.

GUILDFORD, Surrey. *Dominican convent.*

Books noted by J. Leland, *Collectanea,* iv. 148.

Cambridge, U.L., Ll.2.9. *c*Martyrologium, etc. s.xiv.

GUISBOROUGH (Giseburn, etc.), Yorkshire. *Aug. priory of B.V.M.*

Books noted by J. Leland, *Collectanea,* iv. 41. The common form of *ex libris* inscription is 'Liber sancte Marie de Gyseburn'.

Cambridge, Gonv. and Caius Coll., 109. *i*Avicenna, etc. s.xiii.
　　　　　　St John's Coll., 74. *e*Biblia. s.xiii/xiv.
Dublin, Chester Beatty Libr., W.45. *e*Cassiodorus. s.xii ex. [Historia ii].
London,
　　B.M., Add. 35285. *c*Missale, etc. s.xiii–xv.
　　　　Arundel 218. *e*Alcuinus, etc. s.xii–xiii. [Originalia 7, in quarta fenestre (*sic*) tercii gradus].
　　　　Cotton Vit. E.i.[4] Beda, etc. s.xii. ?
　　　　Vit. E.vii, fos 1, 2.[4] Beda. s.xii.
　　　　Royal 3 A.xiii. *e*Sermones dominicales. s.xiii/xiv. [Collectar' 3].
Oxford, Bodleian, Laud lat. 5. *l*Psalterium. s.xiii.
Woolhampton, Douai Abbey, 4. *l*Breviarium; Missale. s.xiv in. ?
Rejected: Oxford, Bodleian, Seld. sup. 87.

GUTHRIE, Angus. *Collegiate church.*

Edinburgh, N.L., Adv. 18.2.8. *e*J. de Irlanaia (in Scots). s.xv ex.

HAGNABY, Lincolnshire. *Prem. abbey of St Thomas the martyr.*

Note of five books received by Arthur Wadington in B.M., Cotton Vesp. B.xi. Note about books seen by J. Leland printed from London, B.M., Royal MS. App. 69 in *Eng. Hist. Rev.,* liv. 93.

Cambridge, Gonv. and Caius Coll., 190. *i*J. Arderne. s.xv. ?
London,
　　B.M., Cotton Vesp. B.xi, fos 1–61. *c*Chronicon. s.xiv.
　　　　Royal 5 F.v. *e*Adalberti speculum, etc. s.xiii.
　　　　Royal 13 A.xxi, fos 13–150. *e*Imago mundi, etc. (partly in French). s.xiv in.

HAILES (Heyles), Gloucestershire. *Cist. abbey of B.V.M.*

Cambridge, Trinity Coll., 373. *e*Miscellanea. s.xiii.
Edinburgh, Theological Coll., Forbes e.34 (pr. bk). *e*Speculum exemplorum. Strasbourg, A.D. 1495.
Insch, Mr C. A. Gordon (pr. bk). *e*Duns Scotus (2 vols). Venice, A.D. 1516.
London,
　　B.M., Add. 5667. *i*De vitiis et virtutibus, etc. s.xiii.
　　　　48984. *e*Gregorius. s.xii ex.
　　　　Cotton Cleop. D.iii, fos 1–72. *c*Chronicon. s.xiv in.

---

[4] Provenance inferred from note of s.xvii in Oxford, Bodleian, Lat. misc. c.52, fo. 216. Vit. E.vii, fos 1, 2, is a misplaced fragment of Vit. E.i. Five small fragments are kept as Cotton Misc. Burnt Fragments, Bundle I (12).

London (*contd*)
    B.M., Harley 3725, fos 1–37. *c*Chronicon. s.xv. ?
        Royal 5 A.xiii. *e*J. Wallensis, etc. s.xv.
           8 A.v. *ec*Sermones. s.xiv in.
           8 D.xvii. *e*Sixtus papa, De sanguine Christi. s.xv ex.
           12 E.xiv. *c*Formularium, etc. s.xiv–xv.
      C.37.c.44 (pr. bk). *e*Libellus sophistarum ad usum Oxon, etc.
           London, s.a., etc.
Manchester, Chetham, 19495 (pr. bk). *i*Jeronimus. Lyon, A.D. 1518.
Oxford, Balliol Coll. (pr. bk). *e*Beda. Paris, A.D. 1521.
      Corpus Christi Coll., Z.12.6 (pr. bk). *e*Biblia. Paris, A.D. 1532.
Wells, Cathedral, s.n. *e*Chrysostomus. A.D. 1514.
           s.n. *e*Psalterium. A.D. 1514.
           G.1.3–8 (pr. bks). *e*Augustinus (6 vols). Paris,
                A.D. 1531.
Windsor, St George's Chapel, III.c. (2 vols; pr. bks). *e*Dionysius Car-
    thus. Cologne, A.D. 1533.
Untraced: Lt-Col. W. E. Moss sale (Sotheby, 8 Mar. 1937), lot 1134 to
    Maggs (pr. bk). *i*P. Lombardus. Lyon, A.D. 1527.
Rejected: Bible at Wells Cathedral.

HALESOWEN, Worcestershire. *Prem. abbey of B.V.M. and St John the Evangelist.*

London, Soc. of Antiquaries, 134. J. Lydgate, etc. (in English). s.xv. ?
              544. Magna Carta, etc. s.xiii in. ?

HALTEMPRICE (or **COTTINGHAM**), Yorkshire. *Aug. priory of B.V.M. and Holy Cross.*

Leicester, Bernard Halliday. Breviarium. s.xiv.

HAMPOLE, Yorkshire. *Priory of B.V.M., of Cist. nuns.*

San Marino, Huntington, EL 9 H. 17. *e*Psalterium. s.xiv med.

HARROLD, Bedfordshire. *Priory of St Peter, of Aug. nuns.*

Bristol, Baptist Coll., Z.c.23. *c*Psalterium, etc. s.xii ex.

HARTLAND, Devon. *Aug. (Arrouaisian) abbey of St Nectan.*

Books noted by J. Leland, *Collectanea*, iv. 153.
London, B.M., Cotton Vesp. D.xii, fo. 157. *l*Officium de S. Nectano.
                s.xiv/xv.
        Harley 220. *e*Constitutiones P. Quivil, episcopi Exon.,
            etc. s.xv.
Stonyhurst Coll., 9. *e*Evangelia glo. s.xiii.

HATFIELD PEVEREL, Essex. *Ben. priory of B.V.M.; cell of St Albans.*

M. R. James, 'MSS from Essex Monastic Libraries', *Trans. Essex Archaeol. Soc.*, N.S., xxi (1933), 37. N. R. Ker, 'More MSS from Essex Monastic Libraries', *ibid.*, xxiii (1942–45), 303, 306.

Berlin, Staatsbibl., Th. lat. oct. 167.[5] eJ. de Mantua, etc. s.xi–xii.
London, B.M., Royal 5 C.x, xi.[5, 6] Augustinus (2 vols). s.xii ex.
Oxford, Bodleian, Rawl. B.189. eG. Monumutensis, etc. s.xv.
Untraced: Towneley sale (Sotheby, 27 June 1883), lot 56 to Jackson.[5]
eAnselmus, etc. s.xii.

HATFIELD REGIS, Essex. *Ben. alien priory of B.V.M.; cell of St Melaine, Rennes; independent in 1254 (?).*

Oxford, Bodleian, Bodl. 602, fos 67–171. eJ. Cassianus, etc. s.xiii in.   ?

HAUGHMOND (Hagemon'), Shropshire. *Aug. abbey of St John the Evangelist.*

London, B.M., Add. 37785. eIsidorus, etc. s.xii/xiii.
           Harley 622.[7] eGraduale. s.xiii.
           1712. eP. Comestor. s.xii/xiii.
Oxford, Bodleian, Bodl. 188. eHugo de Folieto, etc. s.xiii ex.
           Auct. 1.Q.6.9 (7) (pr. bk). iJ. Gerson. (Venice,
                                       A.D. 1485).
        Univ. Coll., 77. eMatheus et Lucas glo. s.xiii.   ?
Spalding, Gentlemen's Society, B.96. eBiblia. s.xiii.

HAVERFORDWEST, Pembrokeshire. *Dominican convent.*

Eton Coll., 90. eCicero, etc. s.xii ex.

HAVERHOLME, Lincolnshire. *Gilbertine priory of B.V.M.*

Note about books seen by J. Leland printed from B.M., Royal MS. App. 69 in *Eng. Hist. Rev.,* liv. 95.

HEDON. *Hospital of St Sepulchre.* See **PRESTON.**

HENTON. See **HINTON.**

HEREFORD. *Cathedral church of St Ethelbert.*

A. T. Bannister, *Descriptive Catalogue of MSS in the Hereford Cathedral Library* (Heref., 1927).
Books given by Bishop Charles Bothe (†1535) and the incunabula are listed by F. C. Morgan, *Hereford Cathedral Library,* 1952, pp. 16–28; the former also in *Registrum Bothe* (Canterbury and York Soc., xxviii, 1921), p. ix.

Cambridge, Pembr. Coll., 302. cEvangeliarium. s.xi.
Hereford, Cathedral,[8]
    A.vi.5–8 (pr. bks). eBiblia glo. (parts ii–v). Venice, A.D. 1495.
    C.viii.14 (pr. bk). eAugustinus, Sermones. Basel, A.D. 1494.

---

[5] Perhaps from Hatfield Regis rather than Hatfield Peverel.
[6] The provenance is recorded in a catalogue of Theyer manuscripts, Public Record Office, S.P.9/13.
[7] Harley 622 was removed to Haughmond at the suppression of **RANTON,** *q.v.,* in 1537.
[8] In the following list the siglum *r* before a title shows the presence of an inscription 'Rad: Arch: Me: Dedit: Inter XX[ti]', except in O.i.5, which has only 'Magistri Rad' '; the siglum *p* that there is a pricemark at the beginning or at the end; the siglum *2p* that there is a pricemark both at the beginning and at the end; *p* and *2p* are only used if no other siglum is appropriate.

Hereford, Cathedral (*contd*)
E.ii.6, 7 (pr. bks). *e*Bartolus de Saxoferrato.   Milan, A.D. 1490.
E.ii.8 (pr. bk).   *e*Digestum vetus.   Venice, A.D. 1490.
E.ii.9 (pr. bk).   *e*Digestum infortiatum.   Venice, A.D. 1489.
E.ii.10 (pr. bk).   *e*F. de Zabarellis, etc.   Turin, A.D. 1492, etc.
E.iv.1 (pr. bk).   *e*Angelus de Perusio, etc.   Venice, A.D. 1489, etc.
E.iv.3 (pr. bk).   *e*Angelus de Gambiglionibus.   Louvain, A.D. 1475.
E.iv.5 (pr. bk).   *e*W. Lyndwood.   Oxford, A.D. 1483.
E.v.5 (pr. bk).   *e*J. A. de Sancto Georgio.   Venice, A.D. 1493, etc.
E.v.8 (pr. bk).   *e*Extravagantes communes, etc.   Paris, A.D. 1501.
E.v.9 (pr. bk).   *e*J. Koelner de Vanckel.   Cologne, A.D. 1484.
E.vi.5 (pr. bk).   *e*Decretum Gratiani.   Venice, A.D. 1487.
E.vi.6 (pr. bk).   *e*Codex Justiniani.   Venice, A.D. 1490.
E.vi.7–9 (pr. bks).   *e*Baldus de Ubaldis.   Milan, A.D. 1477.
H.ii.9 (pr. bk).   *e*Augustinus.   Louvain, A.D. 1488.
I.i.10 (pr. bk).   *e*Hieronymus.   Lyon, A.D. 1508.
L.viii.6.   *e*Terentius, etc.   s.xv ex.
M.i.1 (pr. bk).   *e*P. Lombardus.   Venice, A.D. 1489.
N.i.5 (pr. bk).   *e*Aristoteles, etc.   Louvain, A.D. 1475, etc.
N.vii.2 (pr. bk).   *e*Ludolphus de Saxonia.   Paris, A.D. 1502.
N.vii.3–6 (pr. bks).   *e*Antoninus archiepisc. Florent.   Basel, A.D. 1511.
O.i.5.   *r*Honorius.   s.xii.
O.i.8.   *p*Evangelia.   s.xii.
O.i.9.   *e*J. Ridevall.   s.xv.
O.ii.1.   *e*Lucas glo.   s.xii.
O.ii.2.   *r*Johannes glo.   s.xii.
O.ii.7.   *p*Canones conciliorum, etc.   s.xii.
O.ii.9.[9]   *p*Origenes, etc.   s.xii.   [xxi].
O.iii.2.   *e*Jeronimus, etc.   s.ix.
O.iii.7.   *r*Job glo.   s.xii.
O.iii.13.   2*p*'Omelie quedam Crisostomi'.   s.xii ex.
O.iv.1.   2*p*Numeri glo.   s.xiii.
O.iv.3.[1]   Josue, etc., glo.   s.xiii.
O.iv.4.   *r*Numeri, etc., glo.   s.xii.
O.iv.5.   2*p*Excerpta ex decretis Romanorum Pontificum.   s.xii.
O.iv.7.   *r*Ezechiel, etc., glo.   s.xii.
O.iv.8.   *e*Augustinus.   s.xii.
O.iv.14.   *e*Vita S. Thome, etc.   s.xiv.
O.v.4.   *e*Amalarius.   s.xii.
O.v.7.   *p*Johannes glo.   s.xii.
O.v.8.[1]   *r*Actus apostolorum, etc., glo.   s.xii.
O.v.9.   *e*Omelie in Orationem Dominicam.   s.xv.
O.v.13.   *e*Jac. de Voragine.   s.xiv.
O.v.15.   *e*Bartholomeus Anglicus.   s.xv.
O.vi.1.   *r*Lucas glo.   s.xii.
O.vi.3.   *e*Pseudo-Dionysius, etc.   s.xii/xiii.   [xix].
O.vi.4.   *p*Matheus glo.   s.xii.
O.vi.5.   *r*Marcus glo.   s.xii.

[9] O.ii.9, O.viii.8, P.iv.11, P.vii.6 contain annotations in one hand of s.xiv.
[1] O.iv.3, O.v.8, O.viii.11, O.ix.1, P.ii.11, P.ii.13, P.iv.2, P.iv.13, P.v.13, P.ix.4 contain annotations by one hand of s.xv, perhaps—see P.ix.4—that of John Castyll, penitentiary 1414–30.

Hereford, Cathedral (*contd*)

O.vi.6.   *p*Epp. Pauli glo.   s.xii.
O.vi.7.   *e*Formula noviciorum, etc.   s.xv.
O.vi.9.   *2p*Exodus glo.   s.xii.
O.vi.12.   *2p*'Psalterium de parva glosur' Anselmi'.   s.xii.
O.vi.13.   *2p*Ivo Carnot.   s.xii ex.
O.vii.3.   *e*P. Comestor.   s.xiii in.
O.vii.4.   *p*'Omelie Bede et aliorum'.   s.xii.
O.vii.6.   *e*J. Bromyard.   s.xv.
O.vii.8.   *e*J. Januensis.   s.xiv.
O.viii.1. *e*R. Rolle.   s.xiv/xv.
O.viii.5. *e*Comment. in Constitutiones Clementinas.   s.xiv.
O.viii.8.[2] *p*Excerpta ex decretis Romanorum Pontificum.   s.xi/xii.
O.viii.9. *r*P. Lombardus, etc.   s.xii.
O.viii.10. *c*T. Aquinas.   s.xiv.   ?
O.viii.11.[3] *e*Augustinus.   s.xii.
O.ix.1.[3]   *er*Libri Regum glo.   s.xii ex.
O.ix.7.   *e*Paralipomena, etc., glo.   s.xii ex.   [xi].
O.ix.9.   *p*P. Lombardus.   s.xii ex.
O.ix.11.   *2p*Jeremias, glo.   s.xii ex.   [vii].
P.i.2.   *e*Evangelia.   s.viii ex.
P.i.4.   *p*Cicero, etc.   s.xii.
P.i.7.   *p*Prophete minores glo.   s.xii.
P.i.8.   *e*Apocalypsis, etc., glo.   s.xii.
P.ii.7.   *e*Isidorus.   s.xiv.
P.ii.8.   *2p*Canones apostolorum.   s.xii in.
P.ii.9.   *e*Job glo.   s.xii ex.
P.ii.11.[3]   *2p*Leviticus glo.   s.xii.   [xvi].
P.ii.13.[3]   Job glo.   s.xii.
P.iii.6.   *e*De arte rhetorica, etc.   s.xv.
P.iii.8.   *2p*Exodus glo.   s.xii.
P.iii.9.   *p*Sermons (in French).   s.xiv.   ?
P.iii.10. *e*P. Lombardus.   s.xiii.
P.iii.11. *e*P. Lombardus.   s.xiv.
P.iv.1.   *e*Decretales.   s.xiv.
P.iv.2.[5]   N. de Lyra.   s.xiv.
P.iv.3.   *e*Prophete minores glo.   s.xii.
P.iv.7.   *e*J. de Burgo.   s.xiv/xv.
P.iv.11.[4]   *e*Ambrosius.   s.xii.
P.iv.12.   *2p*Psalterium glo.   s.xii.
P.iv.13.[5]   *e*Prophete minores glo.   s.xii.
P.v.6.   *e*Azo.   s.xiv.
P.v.7.   *e*Egidius Romanus.   s.xiv.
P.v.11.   *e*P. de Crescentiis.   s.xv.
P.v.12.   *2p*Hugo de Folieto, etc.   s.xiv.
P.v.13.[5]   *p*P. Lombardus.   s.xiii.
P.v.14.   Azo.   s.xiii.   ?
P.v.15.   *e*P. Comestor.   s.xiii in.
P.vi.3.   *e*Augustinus.   s.xii.   [xviii].
P.vi.7.   Constitutiones Clementine cum apparatu.   s.xiv ex.   ?

[2] See p. 97, n. 9.   [3] See p. 97, n. 1.
[4] See p. 97, n. 9.   [5] See p. 97, n. 1.

Hereford, Cathedral (*contd*)
   P.vi.9. *e*P. Lombardus. s.xiii ex.
   P.vi.10. *e*Jeronimus. s.xii ex.
   P.vi.11. *e*Gregorius. s.xii.
   P.vii.2. *e*Codex Justiniani. s.xiv.
   P.vii.4. *e*Lapus de Castellione, etc. s.xv.
   P.vii.5. *e*Digestum vetus. s.xiv.
   P.vii.6.[5] *e*Vite sanctorum. s.xii.
   P.vii.7. *e*Constitutiones Anglicane, etc. s.xiv.
   P.viii.1.[6] Codex Justiniani. s.xiv. ?
   P.viii.2. *o*Collectanea ex jure canonico. s.xv.
   P.viii.5. *e*Jeronimus. s.xii ex. [i liber].
   P.viii.7. *s*Omeliarium. s.xii.
   P.viii.8. *e*Justinianus s.xiv.
   P.viii.9.[7] Glosa super decretales. s.xv. ?
   P.viii.11. *e*Digestum novum. s.xiii/xiv.
   P.ix.1.[7] Digestum inforciatum. s.xiii/xiv. ?
   P.ix.2. *e*Decretum Gratiani. s.xiv.
   P.ix.4.[8] *m*Genesis et Exodus glo. s.xiii in.
   P.ix.6. *p*Augustinus. s.xii ex.
London, B.M., Add. 39675. *l*Missale. s.xiv ex. ?
               Harley 2983. *l*Ordinale. s.xiii ex.
Oxford, Bodleian, Rawl. B.328. *c*Martyrologium. s.xiv.
                     C.67. *e*Misc. theologica. s.xiii. ?
     Balliol Coll., 321. *l*Collectarium. s.xiv. ?
Rejected: Cambridge, Peterhouse, 112, 119; Trinity Coll., 255.

HEREFORD. *Cathedral of St Ethelbert, Vicars Choral.*

Dublin, N.L., 700. *e*G. Cambrensis. s.xiii in.
Oxford, Bodleian, Rawl. C.427. *e*Steph. Langton. s.xiii.

HEREFORD. *Diocesan Registry.*

Oxford, Bodleian, Ashmole 789. *e*Epp. Thome Bekyngton, etc. s.xv.

HEREFORD. *Ben. priory of St Peter, St Paul, and St Guthlac; cell of Gloucester.*

    N. R. Ker, 'The Medieval Pressmarks of St Guthlac's Priory, Hereford, and of Roche Abbey, Yorks.', *Medium Ævum*, v (1936), 47–48. The pressmark is written inconspicuously above the opening words of the second leaf.

Hereford, Cathedral, O.iv.12. XII prophete glo. s.xiii in. [xliii].
                 O.v.1. *e*Genesis glo. s.xii. [iii].
                 O.vi.11. Epp. Jeronimi. s.xi. [xxix].
                 P.iii.2. *e*Epp. Pauli, etc. s.xii. [viii].
                 P.iii.5. *e*Misc. theologica. s.xii–xiii. [xxxi].
                 P.iv.5. *e*Steph. Langton. s.xiii. [xvii].
                 P.vi.1. *e*Gregorius. s.xii. [iiii].
Oxford, Jesus Coll., 10. *l*Antiphonale. s.xii–xv.
                37. Johannes Levita. s.xi. [xxiiii].

---

[5] See p. 97, n. 9.
[6] P.viii.1, P.viii.9 and P.ix.1 are inscribed 'Grene'; *cf.* p. 268.
[7] See above, n. 6.   [8] See p. 97, n. 1.

Oxford, Jesus Coll. (*contd*)
          66. *e*Matheus glo. s.xii. [xlv].
          105. *e*Lucas glo. s.xii. [xxvi].
          106. *e*Johannes glo. s.xii. [xx].
York, Minster, xvi.K.10. Ambrosius. s.xii. [xxxvi]. ?

HEREFORD. *Franciscan convent.*

M. R. James, 'The Library of the Grey Friars of Hereford', *Collectanea Franciscana*, i (Brit. Soc. for Franc. Studies, v, 1914).
The pressmark of B.M., Royal 7 A.iv is reproduced in *New Pal. Soc.*, i, pl. 17, no. 6.

Cambridge, St John's Coll., 90. *e*Gregorius, etc. s.xii/xiii. [E.5^m].
                      157. *e*Gregorius. s.xiii. [E.8].
                      169. *e*Historia tripertita. s.xiii. [D.17].
        Trinity Coll., 749. G. Cambrensis. s.xiii in. [F.37].
Hereford, Cathedral, O.i.1. *e*Esaias glo. s.xiii. [B.23].
                 O.i.4. *e*Bernardus. s.xiii. [F.6^m].
                 O.ii.11. *e*Adalberti speculum. s.xiii ex. [F.39].
                 O.iii.6. *e*Isidorus. s.xii. [F.25].
                 O.v.12. *e*Bernardus, etc. s.xii. [F.65^m].
                 O.vii.7. *e*Decretales Gregorii ix, etc. s.xiii/xiv.
                 O.viii.12. Postille super Esaiam, etc. s.xiv. [C.18].
                 P.i.15. *e*Ivo Carnotensis, etc. s.xii ex. [F.34].
                 P.iii.12. *i*P. Blesensis, etc. s.xiii–xiv. [F.8].
                 P.v.8. *e*Actus apost., etc., glo. s.xiii. [B.46].
                 P.v.10. *e*Pseudo-Dionysius, etc. s.xiii. [F.4^m].
London,
    B.M., Add. 46919. *i*Misc. poetica (partly in French and English).
                    s.xiv in. ?
    Burney 325. *e*Josephus. s.xiii.
    Cotton Jul. A.xi, fos 115–52. *e*Vita T. Becket. s.xii/xiii.
          Nero A.ix, fos 75–103.[9] *e*Misc. franciscana. s.xiii–xiv.
          Vesp. A.xiii, fos 94–147. *c*Turpinus, etc. s.xv. ?
    Egerton 3133.[9] T. de Eccleston. s.xiii ex.
    Royal 7 A.iv. *e*Hildebertus, etc. s.xii ex. [F.35].
        7 F.vii. *m*Rog. Bacon. s.xiii ex. ?
        7 F.viii. *i*Rog. Bacon. s. xiii ex. ?
Oxford, Bodleian, Bodl. 897. *e*Hugo de Folieto. s.xiii. [F.21].
               Hatton 102. *e*Misc. theol. s.xiii–xiv. [E.27].
               Rawl. C.308. *e*Beda. s.xiii. [C.15].
      New Coll., 285, fos 194–257. *e*Comment. in Aristotelem.
                            s.xiii/xiv.
Shrewsbury, School, xv. *e*Gregorius. s.xiii. [E.7^m].
Rejected: Cambridge, Trinity Coll., 348. Hereford, Cathedral, O.iii.8,
    O.iii.9, O.iii.12, P.i.7.

HEREFORD. *Dominican convent.*

Hereford, Cathedral, O.iv.10. *e*Jeronimus. s.xiv.
Oxford, Magdalen Coll., lat. 226. *l*Pontificale. s.xii. ?

[9] Egerton 3133 was originally part of Cotton Nero A.ix, fos 75–103; *cf. Eng. Hist. Rev.*, xlix. 299 and *B.M. Quarterly*, ix. 116.

HERTFORD. *Ben. priory of B.V.M.; cell of St Albans.*

List of 16 books sent from Hertford to St Albans (s.xv ex.) printed from Lambeth Palace, MS. 420 by M. R. James, *Descriptive Cat. of MSS in the Library of Lambeth Palace* (1932), p. 580; St Albans pressmarks given.

Glasgow, U.L., Hunterian 4.   *e*Josephus.   s.xii.   ?
London, Lambeth Palace, 420.   *e*Mariale, etc.   s.xii–xiii.
        443.   *e*Laurent. Dunelm.   s.xii.

HEXHAM (Hagustaldensis, Hextildesham), Northumberland.   *Aug. priory of St Andrew.*

The *ex libris* inscription is 'Liber sancti Andree de Hextildesham'.

Cambridge, Corpus Christi Coll., 149.   *e*Hegesippus.   s.xi.   ?
     Jesus Coll., 38.   *e*Gregorius Nazianzenus.   s.xii.
     St John's Coll., 46.   *e*Augustinus.   s.xii.
Durham, Cathedral, Hunter 57.   *e*Augustinus.   s.xii.
Newcastle, Cathedral.   *e*Biblia.   s.xiii.
Oxford, Bodleian, Bodl. 236.   *e*Augustinus.   s.xii ex.
     Corpus Christi Coll., 134.   *l*Vita S. Oswini.   s.xii.
Rejected: Cambridge, Corpus Christi Coll., 139.

HEYNINGS, Lincolnshire.   *Priory of B.V.M., of Cist. nuns.*

Lincoln, Cathedral, 199.   *e*Honorius Augustodun., etc.   s.xii.

HICKLING, Norfolk.   *Aug. priory of B.V.M., St Augustine and All Saints.*

London, B.M., Egerton 3142.   *c*G. Monemutensis, etc.   s.xiii/xiv–xv.

HIGHAM FERRERS, Northamptonshire.   *College of B.V.M., St Thomas the Martyr and St Edward the Confessor.*

Gloucester, Cathedral (pr. bk).   *e*T. Aquinas.   Venice, A.D. 1494.
Oxford, Trinity Coll., 23.[1]   *e*Evangeliarium.   s.xv.

HINTON (domus loci Dei de Hentone), Somerset.   *Charterhouse of B.V.M., St John the Baptist and All Saints.*

List of books lent to another house in 1343 printed in abstract, from an indenture in the Phillipps Library, by Joseph Hunter, *English Monastic Libraries* (London, 1831), pp. 16–17, reprinted in *Cat. Vet. Eccl. Dunelm.* (Surtees Soc.), p. xxxviii, and by E. Margaret Thompson, *Carthusian Order in England* (London, 1930), p. 323.   List of books sent to Hinton from London, s.xvi, printed from P.R.O., Exch. K.R., Eccl. Docs 2/45, by E. M. Thompson, *op. cit.*, p. 329.

Aberdeen, U.L., 154.   *e*Sermones.   s.xiv.   [liber xxi in H].
Cambridge, St John's Coll., 125.   *e*Excerpta theologica.   s.xv.
London, B.M., Royal   2 F.iii.   *e*Rad. Flaviacensis.   s.xiii.
          [liber xi in E].
      12 B.iv.   *i*Scintillarium; Smaragdus.   s.xii ex.
     Lambeth Palace, 410.   *e*Augustinus, etc.   s.xv.
          [liber xxxv in G].
Oxford, Bodleian, Wood empt. 14.[2]   *i*Statuta ordinis Carthus.   s.xv.

---

[1] The name of Higham Ferrers College has been erased and that of All Souls College, Oxford, *q.v.*, substituted, probably in s.xvi.
[2] *Cf.* **AXHOLME.**

HOLME ST BENETS (Hulme), Norfolk. *Ben. abbey of St Benedict.*

Books noted by J. Leland, *Collectanea*, iv. 29.

Colchester, Harsnett Libr., K.f.11 (pr. bk). *i*P. Lombardus. Basel, A.D. 1498.

Douai, Bibl. mun., 171. *i*Psalterium. s.xiv in. ?

London,
    B.M., Cotton Nero D.ii, fos 215–37. *c*J. de Oxenedes. s.xiv. ?
        Egerton 3142. *c*G. Monemutensis, etc. s.xiii/xiv–xv.
        Royal 14 C.vi. *c*Flores historiarum. s.xiv. ?
Longleat, Marquess of Bath, 2. *c*Apoc. cum comment. Berengaudi. s.xii. ?

HOLME CULTRAM (Holmcoltran), Cumberland. *Cist. abbey of B.V.M.*

The pressmark, consisting of the word 'liber' followed by a number, is written at the head of the first page of text. The *ex libris* inscription is 'Liber sancte Marie de Holmcoltran (*or* de Holmo)'.

Cambridge,
    Emmanuel Coll., 86. *e*Sermones. s.xii–xiii. [liber clxvii primus].
    Trinity Coll., 609. *e*Alanus de Monte Pessulano, etc. s.xiii in.
Cambridge (U.S.A.), Harvard Coll., Lat. 27. *e*Vite sanctorum. s.xii ex.
Carlisle, Cathedral, F.III. 10 (pr. bk). *e*J. Damascenus. Paris, A.D. 1519.
Dublin, Archbishop Marsh's Libr., Q.4.16 (pr. bk). *e*R. Holcot. Lyon, A.D. 1497.
London,
    B.M., Add. 17511. *e*J. Chrysostomus, etc. s.xiii. [liber xlvi].
        Cotton Claud. A.v, fos 135–99. *s*Vite sanctorum. s.xii/xiii.
                                                              [liber cciii primus].
        Faust. B.iv, fos 3–179. *e*Vite sanctorum. s.xiii in.
                                                              [liber cxl].
        Nero A.v, fos 1–82. *e*Bestiarium. s.xii.
Oxford, Bodleian, Hatton 101. *e*Sermones. s.xiii. [liber lxxxvi].
        Lyell 2. *e*Jeronimus. s.xii ex. [liber lxxviii].
        Univ. Coll., 15. *e*Sermones. s.xii/xiii.
San Marino, Huntington, HM 19915. *e*Augustinus, etc. s.xiii in.
                                                              [liber lxxvi].
Untraced: Yarmouth (I.O.W.), Mr F. Rowley (in 1941). *e*Biblia. s.xiii.
Rejected: Cambridge, St John's Coll., 134.

HOLYROOD, Midlothian. *Aug. abbey of Holy Cross, B.V.M., and All Saints.*

Edinburgh, N.L., 5048. *l*Kalendarium. s.xiii.
        Holyrood House. *c*Ordinale. s.xv.
London, Lambeth Palace, 440. *c*Chronica. s.xii.

HORSHAM ST FAITH, Norfolk. *Ben. alien priory of St Faith; cell of Conches.*

Cambridge, Trinity Coll., 884. *c*Dares Phrygius, etc. s.xii–xv. ?
London, B.M., Royal 12 F.iv. *e*Remigius super Focam, etc. s.xii ex.

HORTON, Dorset. *Abbey of St Wolfrida, of Benedictine nuns.*

El Escorial, e.ii.1.[3] *e*Boethius. s.xi in.

HOUNSLOW, Middlesex. *Trinitarian convent.*

Untraced: F. Edwards Ltd, cat. 700 (1950), no. 323 (pr. bk). *i*Michael de Insulis. s.l. et a.

HULL. *See* **KINGSTON-UPON-HULL.**

HULNE, Northumberland. *Carmelite convent.*

An imperfect catalogue of 1443 (second folios given) and an inventory of *c.*1365 printed from the cartulary, B.M., Harley MS. 3897, in *Cat. Vet. Eccl. Dunelm.* (Surtees Soc.), pp. 128, 131.

HUMBERSTONE, Lincolnshire. *Ben. (? originally Tironensian) abbey of B.V.M. and St Peter.*

Oxford, Balliol Coll., 13. *e*Rob. de Tumbalena, etc. s.xii.

HUNTINGDON. *Aug. priory of B.V.M.*

Cambridge, U.L., Kk.4.21. *e*XII prophete glo. s.xii.
London, Lambeth Palace, 1106, fos 111–20. *c*Annales. s.xiii. ?

HURLEY, Berkshire. *Ben. priory of B.V.M.; cell of Westminster.*

Oxford, Bodleian, Lat. th. c.23. *e*P. Comestor. s.xiii in.
St John's Coll., 50. *e*P. Lombardus. s.xiii.

HYDE (Hida, formerly New Minster, Winchester), Hampshire. *Ben. abbey of Holy Trinity, B.V.M., and St Peter.*

Books noted by J. Leland, *Collectanea,* iv. 148: cf. Leland, *De Scriptoribus Britannicis,* p. 131.

Cambridge, St John's Coll., 12, vol. i. *e*Polychronicon. s.xiv ex. ?
        Trinity Coll., 215. *s*Evangelia. s.xi in.
           945, pp. 13–36. *sl*Kalendarium. s.xi in.
Compton Church, Surrey. *c*Processionale (fragm.). s.xv ex.[4]
London,
  B.M., Add. 34890. *c*Evangelia. s.xi in. ?
        49598. *b*Benedictionale S. Æthelwoldi. s.x. ?
     Arundel 60. *l*Psalterium (glossed in English). s.xi ex. ?
     Cotton, Vit. E.xviii. *l*Psalterium (glossed in English).
                  s.xi med. ?
        Vesp. A.viii. *c*Carta regis Eadgari. s.x (?).
        Titus D.xxvi, xxvii. *sl*Liber precum, etc. (partly in English). s.xi in.
        Domit. xiii, fos 1–87 (and ? fos 88–127). *c*Annales, etc.
                          s.xiii. ?
            xiv, fos 1–20. *c*Chronicon. s.xiii.
  Harley 960. *l*Psalterium. s.xiv–xv.

---

[3] Bodleian, MS. Film 4 is a microfilm of this manuscript.
[4] For this fragment, in binding of churchwardens' accounts beginning at 1570, cf. *Victoria County History, Surrey,* iii. 23.

London (*contd*)
    B.M., Royal 2 B.v.[5] *c*Psalterium (glossed in English). s.x. ?
           4 A.xiv.[5] *s*Expositio psalterii. s.x. ?
           8 A.xviii. *i*Misc. philosophica et canonica. s.xv in.
      Stowe 944. *c*Liber vite (partly in English). s.xi in.–xvi in.
Madrid, Biblioteca Nacional, V.3.28. *l*Psalterium, etc. s.xii. ?
New York, Mr W. Glazier, 19. *l*Psalterium, etc. s.xiv.
Oxford, Bodleian, Bodl. 91. *c*H. de S. Victore, etc. s.xii–xiv.
           Gough liturg. 8.[6] *l*Psalterium. s.xiii/xiv.
           Laud misc. 374. *be*R. Grosseteste. s.xv.
           Rawl. liturg. e.1*.[6] *l*Breviarium. s.xiii/xiv.
Rouen, Bibl. municipale, 369. *l*Benedictionale. s.x ex. ?
Shirburn Castle, Earl of Macclesfield. *c*Liber de Hyda. s.xiv–xv.
Rejected: Cambridge, Corpus Christi Coll., 422. Rouen, Bibl. munici-
    pale, 274. Winchester Coll., 22. Worcester, Cathedral, F.173.

ICKLETON, Cambridgeshire. *Priory of St Mary Magdalen, of Ben. nuns.*

Cambridge, St John's Coll., T.9.1 (MS. and pr. bk). *i*Psalterium, etc.
    A.D. 1516.

ILCHESTER (Ivelcestre), Somerset. *Dominican convent.*

Hereford, Cathedral, O.iv.11. *e*Psalterium cum comm. Nic. Trivet.
    s.xiv.

INCHCOLM (Emonie), Fife. *Aug. abbey of St Columba.*

    For 3 printed books see Durkan and Ross, pp. 160, 175, 179.
Cambridge, Corpus Christi Coll., 171. *e*Scotichronicon. s.xv.
Darnaway Castle, Earl of Moray. *e*Scotichronicon. s.xv.
Edinburgh, U.L., 211 iv. *l*Antiphonale (fragm.). s.xiv. ?

INCHMAHOME (Insula S. Colmoci), Stirlingshire. *Aug. priory of St
    Colmoc; cell of Cambuskenneth.*

Insch, Mr C. A. Gordon. *e*Psalterium. s.xiv.

IPSWICH (Gipeswic), Suffolk. *Franciscan convent.*

    List of books given to the convent(?), with donors' names (*c*.1300 and later
additions), on flyleaf of Ipswich Central Libr. MS. printed with facsimile in
List 30 (1938) of E. P. Goldschmidt and Co. Ltd; English transl. printed with
facsimile in *Ipswich Library Journal*, no. 46 (1939), 14–17.

Cambridge, Peterhouse, 49. *i*T. Aquinas. s.xiii–xiv. ?
Ipswich, Central Libr., Suffolk Collection 1. *b*Albertus de Saxonia.
    s.xv in. ?

JARROW and **MONKWEARMOUTH,** co. Durham. *Ben. abbey of St
    Paul; later cell of Durham.*

    For the library of the original house see M. L. W. Laistner, 'The Library of
the Venerable Bede', *Bede, his Life, Times and Writings*, ed. A. Hamilton Thompson (Oxford, 1935).

---

    [5] Royal 4 A.xiv (*cf.* under **WORCESTER**) is a companion volume to Royal
2 B.v.
    [6] Gough liturg. 8 and Rawl. liturg. e.1* probably formed one volume.

Inventories of service-books in use at the cell of Jarrow, s.xiv in.–xv ex., printed from MSS of Durham in *Inventories and Account Rolls . . . of Jarrow and Monk-Wearmouth* (Surtees Soc., 1854).

London, B.M., Add. 37777.[7] *s*Biblia (1 fo.). s.vii/viii.
     45025.[7] *s*Biblia (11 fos). s.vii/viii.
Rejected: Oxford, Bodleian, Laud gr. 35.

JERVAULX (Girevallis, Jorevallis), Yorkshire. *Cist. abbey of B.V.M.*

 Books noted by J. Leland, *Collectanea*, iv. 44. The common form of *ex libris* inscription is 'Liber sancte Marie de Jorevalle (*or* Jorevallis)'.

Cambridge, Corpus Christi Coll., 96. *e*Chronicon. s.xv.
Dublin, Trinity Coll., 171. *e*Vite sanctorum. s.xiii.
Lincoln, Cathedral, 231. *e*Sermones. s.xiii.
London, B.M., Cotton Tib. C.xiii. *c*Chronicon. s.xv.   ?
    Harley 1620. *e*Flores historiarum. s.xiii/xiv.
    Royal 3 E.vi. *e*Evangelia glo. s.xiii.
    Lambeth Palace, 210. *e*Baldewinus Cant. s.xiii in.
Oxford, Bodleian, Bodl. 514. *e*G. Monemutensis. s.xiii.
    Lat. th. f.3. *e*Beda. s.xii/xiii.
    St John's Coll., 99. *e*Beda, etc. s.xii.

KELSO (Kalchou), Roxburghshire. *Ben. (orig. Tironensian) abbey of B.V.M.*

Dublin, Trinity Coll., 226. *e*Augustinus, etc. s.xii.

KENILWORTH, Warwickshire. *Aug. priory of B.V.M.*

Berlin, Staatsbibl., lat. qu. 503. *e*Gesta Francorum, etc. s.xii/xiii.
Chichester, Cathedral. *c*Missale, etc. s.xiii.
London, B.M., Add. 35295. *c*Misc. historica. s.xv in.
    38665. *c*Miscellanea. s.xii–xv.
Oxford, Bodleian, Auct. F.3.13. *e*Euclides, etc. s.xiii ex.

KEYNSHAM, Somerset. *Aug. abbey of B.V.M., St. Peter, and St Paul.*

 Books noted by J. Leland, *Collectanea*, iv. 68.

Dublin, Trinity Coll.,   48. *i*Paralipom. glo. s.xii.
     187. Sermones. s.xii/xiii.   ?
Taunton, Somerset Archaeol. and Nat. Hist. Soc., 1. *e*Polychronicon.
 s.xiv ex.
Rejected: Oxford, Bodleian, Tanner 3.

KINGS LANGLEY, Hertfordshire. *Dominican convent.*

 Numerous books bequeathed by Bishop Robert Rede of Chichester 1415 (*Reg. Henr. Chichele*, ii. 38).

London, Middle Temple (pr. bk). *i*H. Schedel. Nuremberg, A.D. 1493.
Oxford, Blackfriars. *i*Collectarium. A.D. 1523.   ?

---

 [7] Add. 37777 and Add. 45025 are fragments of one volume written in the same type of uncial and in the same format as the Codex Amiatinus (Florence, Laurenziana, MS. Amiatino 1), and therefore to be identified with one of the two bibles written for Wearmouth-Jarrow at the time that Amiatinus was written for presentation to St Peter's, Rome (Bede, *Hist. Abbatum*, ed. Plummer, i. 379–80). For other MSS written in the scriptorium of Wearmouth-Jarrow see E. A. Lowe, *English Uncial* (Oxford, 1960), pp. 8–13.

KING'S LYNN. *See* **LYNN, KING'S.**

KINGSTON-UPON-HULL (domus Cartus' prope Hull), Yorkshire. *Charterhouse of B.V.M., St Michael, and St Thomas the Martyr.*

List of books taken thither from London, s.xv ex., printed from P.R.O., Exch. K.R., Eccl. Docs 2/58 by E. Margaret Thompson, *Carthusian Order in England* (London, 1930), pp. 324–26; second folios given.

Copenhagen, Kongelike Bibl. (pr. bk). *i*Bonaventura. (Paris), s.a.
Heythrop College (pr. bk). *i*J. Gerson. Strasbourg, A.D. 1502.
London, Middle Temple (pr. bk). *i*T. Aquinas. Nuremberg, A.D. 1496.
      Mr C. Hohler (pr. bk). *e*J. Capgrave. Westminster, A.D. 1516.
Oakham, Church, 59 (pr. bks). *i*T. Aquinas (2 vols). Nuremberg, A.D. 1496.

KINGSWOOD, Gloucestershire. *Cist. abbey of B.V.M.*

The *ex libris* inscription is 'Liber monachorum sancte Marìe de Kingeswde'.
Bristol, Central Public Libr., 12. *e*Psalterium. s.xii ex.
Cambridge, Sid. Sussex Coll., 77. *e*Jeronimus. s.xii.
Oxford, Bodleian, e Mus. 62. *e*Ric. de S. Victore, etc. (partly in French). s.xiii ex.
      Trinity Coll., 34. *e*Berengaudus, etc. s.xii.

KINGTON ST MICHAEL, Wiltshire. *Priory of B.V.M., of Ben. nuns.*

Cambridge, U.L., Dd.8.2. *c*Obituary, etc. (in English). s.xv ex.

KINLOSS, Moray. *Cist. abbey of B.V.M.*

For printed books see Durkan and Ross under Robert Reid, Thomas Brown, James Burt, John Cameron, Thomas Chrystall, Adam Elder, Giovanni Ferreri, William Forsyth, Thomas Hastie, James Pont, and their addenda, p. 176.
Cambridge, U.L., Ee.4.21. *i*Regiam Majestatem. s.xvi in.
Edinburgh, U.L., 80. *e*Seneca, etc. s.xiv.
London, B.M., Harley 2363. *c*Chronicon, etc. s.xvi.

KIRBY BELLARS (Kirkby super Wrethek), Leicestershire. *Aug. priory of St Peter.*

Cambridge, Trinity Coll., 1144. *i*Secreta philosophorum, etc. s.xv ex. ?
London, Lincoln's Inn, Hale 68. *e*Chronica, etc. s.xiv.

KIRKHAM, Yorkshire. *Aug. priory of Holy Trinity or Christ Church.*

Books noted by J. Leland, *Collectanea,* iv. 36. The *ex libris* inscription in MSS of s.xii is 'Liber sancte trinitatis de Kirkham'.
Cambridge, U.L., Dd.9.6. *i*Augustinus. s.xii ex.
      Emmanuel Coll., 65. *c*Miscellanea. s.xv. ?
      Sid. Sussex Coll., 36. *c*Liber precum. s.xiii–xiv.
            62. *l*Breviarium. s.xiii/xiv. ?
London B.M., Add. 38817. *e*Beda, etc. s.xii.
      Arundel 36. *e*Possidius, etc. s.xii.
      Harley 1770. *e*Psalterium (Lat., Fr., and Eng.). s.xiv.
Oxford, Bodleian, Rawl. D.938. *c*Kalendarium. s.xiv.
Untraced: Brooke sale (Sotheby, 25 May 1921), lot 840, to Davis and Orioli. *e*Beda super Tobiam, etc. s.xii.

KIRKSTALL, Yorkshire. *Cist. abbey of B.V.M.*

J. Taylor, *The Kirkstall Abbey Chronicles* (Thoresby Soc., xlii, 1952), pp. 30–40.

Cambridge, Jesus Coll., 75. *e*Oculus spiritalis, etc. s.xiii/xiv.
    Sid. Sussex Coll., 85. *i*Barlaam et Josaphat, etc. s.xiv.
Liège, U.L., 369 C. *ec*Eutropius, etc. s.xii.
Oxford, Bodleian, Dodsworth 140, fos 98–108.[8] *c*Chronicon. s.xv in.
    Laud lat. 69. *e*Hugucio. s.xiii.
     misc. 216. *e*Beda, etc. s.xii.
      722.[8] *c*Vita S. Germani, etc. s.xv.
   e Mus. 195. *e*Smaragdus. s.xii.
  Corpus Christi Coll., Δ.10.4 (pr. bk). *e*P. Crinitus. Paris,
         A.D. 1508.

KIRKSTEAD (de loco ecclesie, de loco Christi), Lincolnshire. *Cist. abbey of B.V.M.*

Note about books seen by J. Leland printed from B.M., Royal MS. App. 69, fo. 8, in *Eng. Hist. Rev.*, liv. 94.

Beaumont College, VI. *ic*Psalterium. s.xiii–xiv.
Cambridge, U.L., Dd.7.16. *s*Florus Diaconus, etc. s.xii ex. ?
    8.13.[9] Rabanus Maurus. s.xii ex.
    13.4.[9] *e*Rabanus Maurus. s.xii in.
   Ff.4.1. *e*Rabanus Maurus. s.xiii in.
Leyden, U.L., Lipsius 41.[1] Seneca. s.xii ex.
London, B.M., Royal 3 D.ix. *e*Rad. Flaviacensis. s.xii. [*Leland*].
   7 F.v. *e*H. de S. Victore. s.xii/xiii.

KNARESBOROUGH, Yorkshire. *Trinitarian convent.*

Cambridge, Trinity Coll., 943. *e*Liber cosmographie, etc. s.xv in.
London, B.M., Egerton 3143. *c*Vita S. Roberti, etc. (in Lat. and Eng.).
  s.xv. ?
Oxford, Bodleian, Rawl. D.938. *c*Kalendarium. s.xiv.

KYME, Lincolnshire. *Aug. priory of B.V.M.*

Note about books seen by J. Leland printed from London, B.M., Royal MS. App. 69, fo. 9, in *Eng. Hist. Rev.*, liv. 95.

Oxford, Bodleian, Auct. D.4.15. *e*Berengaudus. s.xii.
Wisbech, Museum, Town libr. A.5.15 (pr. bk). *i*W. Lyndwood. Paris,
  A.D. 1501.

LACOCK, Wiltshire. *Abbey of B.V.M. and St Bernard, of Aug. nuns.*

Lacock Abbey, Mrs A. D. Burnett-Brown. *b*W. Brito. s.xiv–xv.
Oxford, Bodleian, Laud lat. 114. *l*Psalterium, etc. s.xiii ex.–xv. ?

LANCASTER. *Dominican convent.*

Aberdeen, U.L., Inc. 90 (pr. bk). *e*M. A. Sabellicus. Venice, A.D. 1487.
Bristol, Central Public libr. (pr. bks). *e*Antoninus archiep. Florent.
  (3 vols). Basel, A.D. 1491.
Cambridge, Sid. Sussex Coll., 48. *e*Albertanus Brixiensis. s.xv.

---

[8] Dodsworth 140, fos 98–108, was part of Laud misc. 722.
[9] Dd.8.13 and Dd.13.4 are companion volumes.
[1] Lent to a monk of Kirkstead by the Dominicans of Lincoln.

LANERCOST, Cumberland. *Aug. priory of St Mary Magdalen.*

Cambridge, Peterhouse, 247. *e*Misc. medica. s.xii–xiii.

London, B.M., Cotton Claud. D.vii. *c*Chronicon, etc. s.xiv. ?

LANGDON, WEST, Kent. *Prem. abbey of B.V.M. and St Thomas the Martyr.*

Cambridge, Corpus Christi Coll., 59. *c*Miscellanea. s.xiv in. ?

LANGLEY, Norfolk. *Prem. abbey of B.V.M.*

Oxton Hall, Rear-Adm. R. St V. Sherbrooke. *c*Biblia. s.xiii.

LANTHONY (prima), Monmouthshire. *See* **LLANTHONY.**

LANTHONY (secunda), Gloucestershire. *Aug. priory of B.V.M. and St John the Baptist.*[2]

Catalogue, s.xiv in.–xiv ex., printed from B.M., Harley MS. 460 by H. Omont in *Centralblatt für Bibliothekswesen*, ix (1892), 207, and reprinted by T. W. Williams in *Trans. Bristol and Glouc. Archaeol. Soc.*, xxxi (1908), 141, lists the contents of five book-cupboards, shelf by shelf. 56 volumes bequeathed by John Leche (died by Sept. 1361) are listed in a Lanthony Register, P.R.O., C.115/A.2, fo. 281 (second folios given): *cf.* A. B. Emden, *B.R.U.O.*, ii, p. 1119. Books noted by J. Leland, *Collectanea*, iv. 159.

The most usual form of *ex libris* inscription is 'Liber Lanthonie juxta Gloucestriam'. In five MSS there is a pressmark referring to a shelf of the first cupboard.

The prior of the Irish cell at Duleek, Meath, owned Lambeth Palace, MS. 60.

Bristol, Baptist Coll., Z.d.5. *s*Augustinus, etc. s.xiv.

Cambridge,U.L., Dd. 10.25. *e*Isidorus, etc. s.xiii–xiv.

       Fitzwilliam Mus., McClean 145. *c*H. de Bracton. s.xiii ex.

London,

    B.M., Add. 24061. *c*H. Huntendonensis. s.xiv. ?

        Cotton Jul. D.x. *c*Vita Roberti episcopi Hereford., etc.
             s.xiii. ?

           App. xx.[3] H. de Folieto. s.xiii.

                  xxiv. *c*De vitiis capitalibus. s.xiii. [*Cf. cat.*
                      289]. ?

        Harley 459.[4] Officium S. Marthe. s.xii ex. ?

             460.[4] Catalogus librorum. s.xiv in.–xiv ex.

             461.[4] R. de S. Victore super Ezechielem. s.xii. ?

             462.[4] Omelie. s.xiv. ?

             463.[4] J. de Vitriaco. s.xiv. ?

        Lansdowne 387. *l*Liturgica. s.xiv/xv.

        Royal 2 C.x.[5] *s*Claudius Clemens. s.xii. [*Leland*].

             2 D.v. Clemens Lanthon. s.xii. [*Cat.* 108].

---

   [2] See note to **LLANTHONY (prima).**

   [3] For evidence that this book is from Lanthony, see Bodleian, MS. Twyne xxii, p. 419.

   [4] Harley 459–63 formed one volume in s.xvi.

   [5] B.M., Royal 2 C.x; Lambeth Palace 30; 80, fos 168–246; 101; 138, fos 1–44; 148; 153, fos 156–79; 165, fos 102–90; 195; 200, fos 114–63; 208; 215; 218, fos 1–88; 227; 231; 345, fos 98–227; 360, fos 1–118; 365, fos 1–119; 377; 378, fos 1–56, 122–64; 390; 394; 397; 398; 409; 449; 452; 481; Oxford, Bodleian, Bodl. 839, Hatton 49; Corpus Christi Coll. 33, 43; Trinity Coll. 39: have a note of contents in the hand of 'Morganus canonicus de Kermerden' (s.xv), who has written his name in many of the books.

London (*contd*)
B.M., Royal 5 B.i. *e*Augustinus, etc. s.xiii in. ?
        8 D.viii. *l*'Excepciones Rob. de Braci'. s.xii. [*Cat.* 225].
      11 A.x. *c*Ivo Carnotensis. s.xii ex. ?
Lambeth Palace, 13. *e*Liber decretalium. s.xiv. [*Leche*, 16].
      21. *e*Innocentius IV. s.xiv.
      30.[5] Decretales nove. s.xiii ex.
      37. *e*Digestum vetus. s.xiii ex.
      39. *e*Leges Langobardorum, etc. s.xiii–xiv. [*Leche*, 25].
      55, fos 1–156, 162. *i*Aristoteles. s.xiii/xiv.
      56. *s*Gregorius. s.xii. ?
      58. *e*T. Aquinas. s.xiii ex.
      63. *e*Psalterium glo. s.xii/xiii. [*Cat.* 51 *or* 52].
      68. *e*W. Durandus. s.xiv. [*Leche*, 42].
      70. *e*W. Burley, etc. s.xiv.
      71, fos 1–118. P. Cantor. s.xiii. [de i armario primi gradus; *cat.* 53].
         fos 119–222. *c*Steph. Langton. s.xii/xiii. [*Cf. cat.* 146].
      74. *e*W. Burley. A.D. 1391.
      80, fos 168–246.[5] Bernardus Papiensis, etc. s.xiii.
      81.[6] Job et Daniel glo. s.xii/xiii. [*Cf. cat.* 15].
      83. *e*P. Comestor. s.xiii.
      85.[6] Libri regum glo. s.xii ex.
      95. *s*Augustinus. s.xii. ?
      97. *e*T. Aquinas. s.xiii ex.
      101.[7] J. Cassianus. s.xii.
      103. *e*Decretales, etc. s.xiii ex.
      106. *es*Cyprianus. s.xii. [*Cat.* 199].
      111. *e*Egidius Romanus. s.xiii ex.
      115.[8] P. Lombardus. s.xiv in.
      119. J. Lanthoniensis. s.xii ex. [*Cat.* 130].
      122.[9] *e*P. Cantor, etc. s.xiii in.
      128. *e*J. Monachus. s.xiv.
      129.[8] *e*J. Damascenus, etc. s.xiv.
      138, fos 1–44.[7] Seneca. s.xii ex.
      141. *i*Augustinus. s.xiii.
      142, fos 120–22.[9] Tabula super bibliam. s.xiii.
      145, fos 1–137. *e*J. Chrysostomus. s.xv.

[5] See below, n. 7.
[6] Lambeth Palace 81, 85, 208, 343, 349 are associated by the script of the title (s.xii/xiii).
[7] B.M., Royal 2 C.x; Lambeth Palace 30; 80, fos 168–246; 101; 138, fos 1–44; 148; 153, fos 156–79; 165, fos 102–90; 195; 200, fos 114–63; 208; 215; 218, fos 1–88; 227; 231; 345, fos 98–227; 360, fos 1–118; 365, fos 1–119; 377; 378, fos 1–56, 122–64; 390; 394; 397; 398; 409; 449; 452; 481; Oxford, Bodleian, Bodl. 839, Hatton 49; Corpus Christi Coll. 33, 43; Trinity Coll. 39: have a note of contents in the hand of 'Morganus canonicus de Kermerden' (s.xv), who has written his name in many of the books.
[8] Lambeth Palace 115 and 129 formed one volume.
[9] Lambeth Palace 142, fos 120–22, probably formed part of Lambeth Palace 122.

London (*contd*)

Lambeth Palace, 146. *s*Ambrosius. s.xii. ?

147, fos 60–179. *s*Beda. s.xii. ?

148.⁷ *s*Beda. s.xii.

149, fos 139–240. Augustinus, etc. s.xii/xiii. [*Cat.* 186].

150. *e*Egidius Romanus, etc. s.xiv in. [*Leche*, 13].

151, fos 210–335. Augustinus, etc. s.xiii. [*Cat.* 175].

153, fos 156–79.⁷ Lucas glo. s.xiii.

161.¹ Bernardus. s.xii/xiii.

165, fos 102–90.⁷ Sermones G. Babion. s.xiii in.

170.² Psalterium glo. s.xii ex.

189. *es*H. de S. Victore. s.xii. [*Cf. cat.* 218].

195.⁷ Priscianus. s.xii.

196. *e*Priscianus. s.xii. [*Cf. cat.* 372].

200, fos 114–63.⁷ Dist. super psalterium, etc. s.xiii–xiv.

200, fos 164–67.² *l*Letanie, etc. s.xii–xiii.

208.⁷, ³ Esaias glo. s.xii.

215.⁷ *e*Vigilius Thapsensis. s.xii.

217, fos 86–126. Matheus glo. s.xiii. [de V gradu primi armarii; *cf. cat.* 66].

218, fos 1–88.⁷ Gregorius. s.xii.

227.⁷ Comment. in psalterium. s.xiii in.

231.⁷ Matheus glo. s.xii.

239. Clemens Lanthon. s.xii ex. [*Cat.* 109].

335, fos 33–228. Cantica, etc., glo. s.xiii. [de primo armario 4 gradus; *cat.* 84].

336. *s*Augustinus. s.xii. ?

337. *s*Augustinus. s.xii. ?

339. *e*Logica. s.xii.

343.³, ⁴ Deut. et Josue glo. s.xii ex. [*Cf. cat.* 22].

345, fos 98–227.⁷ Gregorius. s.xii.

349.³, ⁴ Genesis glo. s.xii. [de tercio gradu primi armarii; *cat.* 29 *or* 30].

356, fos 176–283. *s*Anselmus. s.xii.

357. *c*R. Rolle, etc. s.xv. ?

360, fos 1–118.⁷ Note super bibliam, etc. s.xii–xiii.

365, fos 1–119.⁷, ⁵ Augustinus. s.xii in.

365, fos 120–228. *s*Augustinus. s.xii.

370. *e*Rob. Cowton. s.xv in.

372. *s*Augustinus. s.xii–xii/xiii. ?

---

⁷ See p. 109, n. 7.

¹ The marginal signs used in Lambeth Palace 161 are identical with those in 452.

² Lambeth Palace 200, fos 164–67, formed part of 170.

³ Lambeth Palace 81, 85, 208, 343, 349 are associated by the script of the title (s.xii/xiii).

⁴ Lambeth Palace 343 and 349 are in identical medieval bindings. The pressmark is on the outside of the end cover of MS. 349.

⁵ Lambeth Palace 392 (fos 116–31) and 431 (fos 161–82) formed part of 365 (fos 1–119).

London (*contd*)

Lambeth Palace, 375. *e*Albertanus Brixiensis. s.xiv. [*Leche*, 48].

377.[6] Isidorus. s.x.

378, fos 1–56, 122–64.[6] Alcuinus, etc. s.xii–xiii.

380, fos 121–228. *e*Isidorus, etc. s.xii.

389. Jeronimus, etc. s.xii/xiii. [*Cf. cat.*, p. 150, n. 1]. ?

390.[6] W. Peraldus, etc. s.xiii ex.

391. *e*Sermones G. Babion. s.xii. [*Cf. cat.* 215].

392, fos 29–58.[7] R. de Wetherset. s.xiii in.

fos 116–31.[8] De significacionibus rerum. s.xii ex.

393. *e*Universalia Penbygull, etc. s.xv in.

394.[6] Innocentius III, etc. s.xiii.

395, fos 1–52, 141–78. Hester, etc., glo. s.xii/xiii. [*Cat.* 38].

396. *e*J. Sharp, etc. s.xv in.

397.[6] *s*Ailredus Rievall., etc. s.xii.

398.[6] Sermones, etc. s.xiii.

408, fos 20–141.[9] Sermones. s.xii. [*Cat.*, p. 145, n. 2].

409.[6, 7] Medica. s.xiii ex.–xiv.

411.[1] S. de Bisigniaco. s.xiii. ?

427. *e*Psalterium (glossed in English). s.x/xi.

431, fos 146–60[9]. *e*De viciis et virtutibus. s.xi.

fos 161–82.[8] Anselmus, etc. s.xii ex.

437, fos 43–72.[1] Bernardus. s.xiii. ?

449.[6] Decretum Gratiani. s.xii ex.

451, fos 83–192. *s*Bernardus, etc. s.xii. ?

452.[6] *s*Bernardus. s.xii.

475, fos 109–80. *c*Vita Rob. episcopi Hereford. s.xii. ?

481.[6] H. de S. Victore, etc. s.xiii.

540. Psalterium Ivonis. s.xii. [de v gradu primi armarii; *cat.* 61].

Lincoln's Inn, Hale 85. *e*P. Comestor. s.xiii.

Westminster Abbey, H.1.31 (pr. bk). *iJ.* Major. Paris, A.D. 1509.

Oxford,

Bodleian, Bodl. 839.[6] Ambrosius, etc. s.xii.

Hatton 49.[6] Flores Bernardi. s.xiii. [*Cf. cat.* 141].

---

[6] B.M., Royal 2 C.x; Lambeth Palace 30; 80, fos 168–246; 101; 138, fos 1–44; 148; 153, fos 156–79; 165, fos 102–90; 195; 200, fos 114–63; 208; 215; 218, fos 1–88; 227; 231; 345, fos 98–227; 360, fos 1–118; 365, fos 1–119; 377; 378, fos 1–56, 122–64; 390; 394; 397; 398; 409; 449; 452; 481; Oxford, Bodleian, Bodl. 839; Hatton 49; Corpus Christi Coll. 33, 43; Trinity Coll. 39: have a note of contents in the hand of 'Morganus canonicus de Kermerden' (s.xv), who has written his name in many of the books.

[7] Lambeth Palace 392 (fos 29–58) and 409 formed one volume.

[8] Lambeth Palace 392 (fos 116–31) and 431 (fos 161–82) formed part of 365 (fos 1–119).

[9] Lambeth Palace 408 (fos 20–141) and 431 (fos 146–60) probably formed one volume.

[1] Lambeth Palace 411 and 437 (fos 43–72) formed one volume with a now missing 'Fructus sive pensiones quas Hibernia tenebatur solvere Monasterio Lanthoniæ' (*cf.* Bodleian MS. Tanner 258, fo. 158).

Oxford (*contd*)
Bodleian, Rawl. A.374. *s*Augustinus. s.xii.
Corpus Christi Coll., 33.[6] Sermones, etc. s.xiii.
            36. M. de Sully, etc. (in French). s.xiv in.
                  [*Cat.*, p. 141, n. 5].
            42.[2] *e*Mariale, etc. s.xiii/xiv.
            43.[6] W. de Monte, etc. s.xii ex.–xiii in.
            59. *c*Alanus de Insulis, etc. s.xii ex.–xiii.
          139. *s*Cassiodorus, etc. s.xii.
          154. *c*Decretum Gratiani, etc. s.xiii.
          159. *e*P. Comestor. s.xiv in.
          192. *l*Collectarium. s.xiv/xv.
          194. *s*Augustinus, etc. s.xii. [*Cf. cat.* 180]. ?
Queen's Coll., 309. *e*Augustinus. s.xii.
Trinity Coll., 33. *s*Jeronimus. s.xii.
         39.[6] Gregorius. s.xii.
         51. *s*Paschasius, etc. s.xii.
         69. *e*Jeronimus. s.xii.

M. R. James suggests, often tentatively and often no doubt correctly, that the following MSS are also from Lanthony: Lambeth Palace 18, 28, 29, 44, 45, 61 (fos 1–117), 76 (fos 148–238), 77, 80 (fos 1–167), 88, 102, 110, 112, 114, 133, 139, 142 (fos 1–119), 152, 154, 164, 165 (fos 1–101), 173, 176 (fos 1–120), 201, 213, 217 (fos 1–85 and 127–272), 220, 228–30, 240, 335 (fos 1–32), 338 (fos 1–96), 346, 373, 376, 378 (fos 57–121), 380 (fos 1–120), 385, 387, 388, 395 (fos 55–138), 425 (fos 1–21), 442, 451 (fos 1–82); Oxford, Trinity College 40, 68. Brian Twyne in Bodleian, MS. Twyne xxii, pp. 162–67, assigns London, B.M., Cotton Tib. B.xiii, Domit.xi (fos 107–79); Oxford, Corpus Christi Coll. 32, 55, 116, to Lanthony; these MSS, like the nine Corpus Christi MSS listed above, belonged to Henry Parry (†1629).

Untraced: 'MS. penes Henr. Parry' (Tanner, *Bibl. Brit.*, p. 641).[3] Rog. Sarisberiensis.

Rejected: London, B.M., Royal 3 B.ii. Oxford, Bodleian, Bodl. rolls 21.

LAUNCESTON, Cornwall. *Aug. priory of St Stephen.*

Cambridge, U.L., Kk.2.2. *e*Zach. Chrysopolitanus. s.xiii.
Little Malvern, W. Berington. *l*Horae. s.xiv/xv.
Oxford, Bodleian, Tanner 196. *c*Misc. jur., etc. s.xv.

LAUNDE (de Landa), Leicestershire. *Aug. priory of St John the Baptist.*

Books noted by J. Leland, *Collectanea,* iv. 47.

Eton Coll., 120. *i*Augustinus, etc. s.xiv. ?
Oxford, Bodleian, Douce 302. *i*Poems of J. Awdelay (in English). s.xv.

LEEDS, Kent. *Aug. priory of B.V.M. and St Nicholas.*

Dublin, Trinity Coll., Q.cc.30 (pr. bk). *i*Cicero. Lyon, A.D. 1499.
London, B.M., Royal 5 F.xvii. *i*Nic. de Aquavilla. s.xv.
Oxford, Bodleian, Bodley 406. *e*Sermones. A.D. 1291.
        Corpus Christi Coll., 251. *e*Euclides, etc. s.xiii ex.

---

[6] See p. 111, n. 6.
[2] The flyleaf of MS. 42, with table of contents, is bound up with MS. 38.
[3] Unless this is Bodleian, Hatton 37 (*Sum. Cat.* 4091), rebound.

LEICESTER. *Aug. abbey of B.V.M. de Pratis.*

M. V. Clarke, 'Henry Knighton and the Library of Leicester Abbey', *Eng. Hist. Rev.*, xlv (1930), 103–7, reprinted in M. V. Clarke, *Fourteenth-century Studies* (Oxford, 1937), pp. 293–99. Books identified by Miss R. Bressie in *Times Lit. Supp.*, 24.x.35, p. 671, from the second folios. Catalogue (s.xv/xvi) of more than 940 books in Bodleian, MS. Laud misc. 623, edited by M. R. James, 'Catalogue of the Library of Leicester Abbey', *Trans. Leics. Archaeol. Soc.*, xix (1936–37), 118–61, 378–440; xxi (1939–41), 1–88. 228 books 'in libraria' and 21 books 'in scriptoria' are listed again separately. Books noted by J. Leland, *Collectanea*, iv. 46.

Cambridge, King's Coll., 2. *e*Biblia. s.xiv in.
      Queens' Coll., 2. Ambrosius, etc. s.xii. [*Cat.* 163, *Libraria* 64].
          8. Comment. in Pentateuchum. s.xii ex. [*Cat.* 35].
      Trinity Coll., .7. Flores Bernardi, etc. s.xiii. [*Cat.* 185, *Libraria* 68].
         65. Gregorius. s.xii in. [*Cat.* 174].
       106. Ambrosius. s.xiii in. [*Cat.* 162, *Libraria* 65].
       293. Bonaventura, etc. s.xiv in. [*Cat.* 243].
       315. Augustinus, etc. s.xii in. [*Cat.* 150].
       381. P. Lombardus. s.xii. [*Cat.* 276, *Libraria* 116].
Edinburgh, N.L., Adv. 18.5.13. *i*Ovidius, etc. s.xii ex. [*Cat.* 595].
London, B.M., Cotton Tib. C.vii. Chronicon H. Knighton. s.xiv ex. [*Cat.* 368, *Libraria* 188].
Oxford, Bodleian, Bodl. 57. *c*Miscellanea. s.xiii/xiv. ?
      Rawl. A.445. *e*Sermones. s.xv. ?
York, Minster, xvi.M.6.[4] *e*Cicero. s.xii. [*Cat.* 604, *Libraria* 225].
      xvi.M.7.[4] Expo. super Ciceronis rhetorica. s.xii. [*Cat.* 604a].

LEICESTER. *Collegiate church of B.V.M.*

Leicester, Museum, Wyggeston Hospital 11. *e*S. Boraston. s.xiv/xv.
Rejected: Leicester, Museum, Wyggeston Hospital 6.

LEICESTER. *Dominican convent.*

Oxford, Bodleian, Bodl. 140. *i*T. Aquinas, etc. s.xiv-xv.
    St John's Coll., 198, fos 1–175. *i*W. Heytisbury. s.xiv.

LEISTON, Suffolk. *Prem. abbey of B.V.M.*

Cambridge, Corpus Christi Coll., 27. *e*Zach. Chrysopolitanus. s.xii/xiii.
London, B.M., IB.24866 (pr. bk). *i*Cicero. Venice, A.D. 1480.

LEITH, Midlothian. *Hospital of St Anthony.*

Edinburgh, N.L., Adv. 34.5.5. *c*Officia liturgica. s.xvi in.

LENTON, Nottinghamshire. *Cluniac priory of Holy Trinity.*

Shrewsbury, School, xxix. *c*Beda. s.xii.
Rejected: London, Dr Williams's Library, Anc.3. New York, Pierpont Morgan, 103.

---

[4] York xvi.M.6, M.7 formed one volume in s.xvi in.

LEOMINSTER, Herefordshire. *Ben. priory of St Peter; cell of Reading.*

Catalogue of s.xiii in B.M., Egerton MS. 3031 printed in *Eng. Hist. Rev.,* iii (1888), 123. For the book-list in Bodleian, MS. Bodl. 125, see under **READING**.

London, B.M., Harley 1246. *s*Omeliarium. s.xii. [*Cf. cat.* p. 124, 1.9].
Royal. 8 E.xviii. *c*Smaragdus. s.xii. [*Cf. cat.* p. 124, 1.41].
Oxford, Bodleian, Bodl. 125. *c*Odo Cluniacensis. s.xii. [*Cf. cat.,* p. 124]. ?
Univ. Coll., d.6 (pr. bk). *i*Speculum spiritualium, etc. Paris, A.D. 1510.

Rejected: London, B.M., Harley 2253.

LESSNESS or **WESTWOOD,** Kent. *Aug. abbey of St Thomas the Martyr.*

The common form of *ex libris* inscription, 'Hic liber est ecclesie beati Thome martiris de Liesnes', followed by the anathema 'quem qui ei abstulerit aut super eo fraudem fecerit nisi eidem ecclesie plene satisfecerit anathema sit maranatha', is written at the head or foot of the first leaf of text.

Cambridge, Corpus Christi Coll., 319. *e*P. Comestor, etc. s.xii–xiii.
387. *i*R. Rolle (in English). s.xv.
Gonv. and Caius Coll., 121. *e*H. de Folieto. s.xii ex.
135. *e*P. Comestor, etc. s.xii–xiii.
151. *e*Barth. Exoniensis, etc. s.xii–xiii.
426. *e*Sermones. s.xii.
Trinity Coll., 1236. *e*Gregorius. s.xii ex. ?
London,
B.M., Royal 8 F.xvii. *e*P. Blesensis, etc. s.xiii.
Lambeth Palace, 144, fos 164–314.[5] *s*Gregorius. s.xii.
147, fos 1–59.[5] *e*Beda. s.xii.
207. *e*Epp. Pauli glo. s.xii.
Victoria and Albert Mus., L.404.1916. *c*Missale. s.xiii in.
Oxford,
Bodleian, Bodl. 656. *e*P. Riga, etc. s.xii/xiii.
Douce 287. *e*W. filius Stephani, etc. s.xiii.
330. *e*Berengaudus, etc. s.xii.
St John's Coll., 19. *e*Augustinus. s.xiv.
31. *e*P. de Cornubia. s.xii/xiii.
134. *e*Sermones. s.xiii.

LETHERINGHAM (Crew), Suffolk. *Aug. priory of B.V.M.; cell of St Peter's, Ipswich.*

Cambridge (U.S.A.), Harvard Law School, 25. *c*Registrum Brevium. s.xv ex. ?

LETLEY. *See* **NETLEY.**

LEWES, Sussex. *Cluniac priory of St Pancras.*

Cambridge, Fitzwilliam Mus., 369. *l*Breviarium, etc. s.xiii–xiv.
Copenhagen, Royal Libr., Ny Kgl. S.172.8⁰. *c*Chronicon. s.xv.
Edinburgh, N.L., Adv. 18.4.2. *e*Tabula super Bibliam. s.xv in.

---

[5] Lambeth Palace 144 (fos 164–314) and 147 (fos 1–59) formed one volume.

Oxford, Bodleian, Douce 296. cPsalterium. s.xi. ?
Rome, Vatican, Reg. lat. 147, fos 61–69. cAnnales. s.xii–xiv. ?
Rejected: London, B.M., Harley 4978.

LEWES. *Franciscan convent.*

Colchester, Harsnett Libr., K.d.2 (pr. bk).[6] *i*M. Marulus. Cologne,
A.D. 1529.
Worcester, Cathedral, Inc. 12, i–iii (pr. bks). *e*P. Berchorius (3 vols).
Nuremberg, A.D. 1499.

LICHFIELD, Staffordshire. *Cathedral church of B.V.M. and St Chad.*

List of about 60 books, chiefly service-books, in inventory of the sacristy,
A.D. 1345, printed by J. C. Cox, *Catalogue of the Muniments and MSS Books
pertaining to the Dean and Chapter of Lichfield* (Wm Salt Archaeol. Soc., VI (ii),
1886, p. 204). Catalogue of c.1622, listing 79 MSS, printed by N. R. Ker,
'Patrick Young's Catalogue of the Manuscripts of Lichfield Cathedral', *Medieval
and Renaissance Studies,* ii (1950), 151.

Lichfield, Cathedral. cEvangelia ('Codex S. Ceadde'). s.viii in.
eDecretales. s.xiii ex.
cChronica, etc. ('Magnum registrum album').
s.xiii.
London, B.M., Cotton Cleop. D.ix, fos 5–79. cChronica, etc. s.xiv.
Harley 5249. eProcessionale. s.xv in.
Oxford, Bodleian, Bodl. 956. eW. Malmesburiensis, etc. s.xv in.
Rawl. A.389.[7] R. Rolle, etc. (partly in English). s.xv
in. [*Young* 73].
Rejected: Cambridge, Corpus Christi Coll., 369. London, B.M.,
Cotton Claudius B.vii. Oxford, Bodleian, Ashmole 1518.

LICHFIELD. *Cathedral chantries.*

New York, Mr and Mrs Gordan, 24. eSpeculum humane salvationis.
s.xv.

LICHFIELD. *Franciscan convent.*

London, B.M., Royal 3 D.i. eTabula vii custodiarum. A.D. 1452.

LILLESHALL, Shropshire. *Aug. abbey of B.V.M.*

Cambridge, Corpus Christi Coll., 339, ii. cP. de Ickham. s.xiv. ?

LINCOLN. *Cathedral church of B.V.M.*

J. W. Clark, 'The Libraries at Lincoln, Westminster, and St Paul's', *Cambr.
Antiq. Soc. Proc.,* ix (1896–98), 37. R. M. Woolley, *Catalogue of the MSS of
Lincoln Cathedral Chapter Library* (Oxford, 1927).
Catalogues of s.xii and xv (the latter with second folios, referred to below as
Cat.) printed from MSS at Lincoln by Woolley, *op. cit.,* pp. v–xiv; the former
also, better, by J. F. Dimock, *Opera Giraldi Cambrensis,* vii (Rolls Series, 1877),
165. 14 books borrowed from the library, s.xiii in., noted in Lincoln Cathedral,
201, fo. 109 (printed, incorrectly, Woolley, *op. cit.,* pp. ix–x). 12 law books
given by Robert Newton in 1526 (*Chapter Acts 1520–36* (Lincoln Rec. Soc., xii,
1915), p. 72). Inventory of service books in the revestry in 1536 printed from
a register of the cathedral in *Monasticon,* vi. 1281; second folios given. Note

---

[6] See also under **WESTMINSTER.**
[7] Rawl. A.389 belonged to two prebendaries of Lichfield in s.xv ex.

of books seen by J. Leland printed from B.M., Royal MS. App. 69, fo. 2, by Woolley, *op. cit.*, p. xvi, and in *Eng. Hist. Rev.*, liv. 89. The common form of *ex libris* inscription in twelfth-century MSS is 'liber sancte Marie Linc' '.

Cambridge,
    U.L., Add. 3571. *e*W. Woodford, etc. s.xiv ex.
    Fitzwilliam Mus., McClean 109. *e*Beda. s.xv.
    Gonv. and Caius Coll., 667. *e*Collectio missarum. s.xvi in. ?
    Trinity Coll., 148.[8] Biblia, pars ii. s.xi ex. [*Cat.* 1; *old cat.* 1].

Lincoln, Cathedral,	1.[8]	*e*Biblia, pars i. s.xi ex. [*Cat.* 1; *old cat.* 1].
	2.	Huguitio. s.xiv. [*Cat.* 44].
	3.[9]	Decretales Gregorii IX. s.xiii/xiv.
	4.	*e*Gregorius. s.xii med. [*Cat.* 53; *old cat.* 58].
	7.	Passionarius, etc. s.xii in.–xii ex. [*Old cat.* 19].
	8.	Jo. Chrysostomus, etc. s.xv. [*Cat.* 28].
	9.	*e*Augustinus. s.xii. [*Cat.* 63; *old cat.* 3].
	11.	Odo de Cantia. s.xiv. [*Cat.* 65].
	12.	T. Bradwardine. s.xiv. [*Cat.* 67].
	13.	*e*Augustinus. s.xi. [*Cat.* 59; *old cat.* 27].
	15.	Radulfus Niger. s.xiii in. [*Cat.* 86].
	16.	*e*Ambrosius. s.xii ex. [*Cat.* 62; *old cat.* 36].
	18.	Psalterium triplex glo. s.xii. [*Cat.* 3; *old cat.* 85].
	19–22.	N. de Lyra (4 vols). s.xiv. [*Cat.* 6–9].
	23–27.	*e*Radulfus Niger. s.xiii in. [*Cat.* 12, 13, 15–17; *old cat.* 73].
	28.	Libri regum, etc., glo. s.xiii. [*Cat.* 20].
	29.[9]	Decretales antique. s.xiii/xiv.
	31.	*e*P. Lombardus. s.xii. [*Cat.* 84; *old cat.* 61].
	32.	Constitutiones Ottonis et Octoboni, etc. s.xiv. [*Cat.* 52].
	33.	T. Aquinas. s.xiii/xiv. [*Cat.* 38].
	35.	Flores doctorum, etc. s.xiii. [*Cat.* 70].
	37.	T. Aquinas. s.xiii/xiv. [*Cat.* 34].
	39.	P. Lombardus. s.xiii. [*Cat.* 33].
	42.	Ezechiel, Daniel, et Proph. Min. glo. s.xiv. [*Cat.* 25].
	43.	P. Lombardus. s.xiv. [*Cat.* 88].
	45.	*e*Opus imperfectum in Matheum. s.xiv in.
	63.[9]	Johannes Andree, etc. s.xv.
	67.	Origenes. s.xi/xii. [*Cat.* 99; *old cat.* 70].
	68.	*e*Dieta salutis, etc. s.xv.
	72.	*e*Augustinus. s.xiii ex. [*Cat.* 75].
	74–76.	*e*Gregorius. s.xii. [*Cat.* 94–96; *old cat.* 28].
	77.	Basilius, etc. [*Cat.* 71].
	79.	Tobit, etc., glo. s.xiii. [*Cat.* 22].
	80.	*e*P. Comestor. s.xii. [*Cat.* 47; *old cat.* 40].
	81.	Job et Daniel glo. s.xiii. [*Cat.* 30].
	83.	*e*Jacobus de Altavilla. s.xv in.
	86.	*e*P. Comestor. s.xiii. [*Cat.* 5].

---

[8] Lincoln Cathedral 1 and Trinity Coll. 148 are the two parts of one Bible.
[9] MSS 3, 29, 63, 198 belonged to Canon Thomas Salysbury (†1451).

Lincoln, Cathedral (*contd*)

89. Gregorius. s.xii med. [*Cat.* 74; *old cat.* 6 (*or* 72)].
90. *e*Augustinus. s.xii. [*Cat.* 73; *old cat.* 4].
96. *e*Liber omeliarum. s.xii. [*Cat.* 76; *old cat.* 62].
105.[1] *e*Dares Phrygius, etc. s.xiii–xiv.
107. *e*Vitas patrum. s.xii. [*Cat.* 79].
116. Isaias, etc., glo. s.xiii. [*Cat.* 24].
121. Summa de decretis, etc. s.xiii. [*Cat.* 45].
134. Ambrosius, etc. s.xii. [*Cat.* 77; *old cat.* 4].
135. *e*Evangelia glo. s.xiv. [*Cat.* 10].
137. Decretum Gratiani. s.xiii. [*Cat.* 137].
138. Decretum Gratiani. s.xiii. [*Cat.* 43].
139. P. Lombardus. s.xiii. [*Cat.* 26].
141. Jeronimus. s.xii. [*Cat.* 55; *old cat.* 24].
145. Josephus. s.xii med. [*Cat.* 54; *old cat.* 59].
146.[2] Libri regum glo. s.xii.
147. P. Lombardus. s.xii. [*Cat.* 98; *old cat.* 55(?)].
152. P. Lombardus. s.xiii. [*Cat.* 100].
153. Bernardus, etc. s.xiii. [*Cat.* 93].
154. Bartholomeus Anglicus. s.xv. [*Cat.* 81].
155. *e*Augustinus. s.xii med. [*Cat.* 56; *old cat.* 25].
156. Augustinus. s.xiv. [*Cat.* 57].
157. Augustinus. s.xii med. [*Cat.* 58; *old cat.* 63].
159. Matheus glo., etc. s.xiv/xv. [*Cat.* 108].
160. P. Lombardus. s.xiii. [*Cat.* 90].
161. *e* Excerpta ex decretis Romanorum Pontificum. s.xii. [*Cat.* 50; *old cat.* 16; *Leland*].
163. Decretales antique. s.xiv. [*Cat.* 101?].
164. T. Aquinas. s.xiv. [*Cat.* 29].
165. Beda. s.xii. [*Cat.* 72; *old cat.* 69].
170. *e*P. Lombardus. s.xii. [*Cat.* 91].
171. *e*Haimo. s.xii. [*Cat.* 27].
172. *e*Isaias glo. s.xii. [*Cat.* 23; *cf. old cat.* 86].
174. *e*G. Porretanus. s.xii ex. [*Cat.* 174; *old cat.* 80].
176. *e*P. Lombardus. s.xii. [*Cat.* 82].
182. Beda. s.x/xi. [*Cat.* 78; *old cat.* 13].
183. *e*Avicenna. s.xv in. [*Cat.* 39].
186. Augustinus. s.xiv/xv. [*Cat.* 61].
187. *e*Paralipomena, etc., glo. s.xii. [*Cat.* 21; *old cat.* 87].
190. Glosa in Pentateuchum. s.xiii. [*Cat.* 18].
191. *e*Manipulus florum, etc. s.xiv. [*Cat.* 64].
193. *e*Decreta pontificum, etc. s.xii. [*Cat.* 46; *old cat.* 38].

[1] MS. 105 belonged to the chantry of Nicholas Cantilupe.
[2] MS. 146 has a title and pricemark like those in other glossed books of the Bible (MSS 176, 187, 190).

117

Lincoln, Cathedral (*contd*)

        198.[3] Sextus liber decretalium, etc. s.xv.

        201. *c*Sermones lxv. s.xii. [*Cf. cat.* 85 *and old cat.* 61].

        203. *e*Compendium theologice veritatis, etc. s.xiv.
              [*Cat.* 31].

        205. *e*Summa Raymundi. s.xiii.

        217. *e*Honorius, Gemma anime. s.xii. [*Cat.* 103; *old cat.* 39].

        219. *e*Jeronimus. s.xii med. [*Cat.* 87; *old cat.* 71].

London,

  B.M., Royal 8 G.iii. *e*P. de Aureolis. s.xv in. [*Cat.* 4; *Leland*].

          11 B.i. *e*R. Cowton. s.xv in. [*Cat.* 32; *Leland*].

          11 D.vii. *e*Ivo Carnotensis. s.xii/xiii. [*Old cat.* 15(?); *cat.* 60; *Leland*].

          13 E.i. *e*Polychronicon. s.xiv ex. [*Cat.* 102; *Leland*].

Oxford, Balliol Coll., 36. *e*G. Porretanus. s.xii. [*Cf. old cat.* 60].

LINCOLN. *Episcopal registry.*

Oxford, Univ. Coll., 156. *e*Excerpta de opere sacramentali fratris Thome Waldensis. A.D. 1491.

LINCOLN. *Gilbertine priory of St Catherine.*

List of MSS seen by J. Leland printed from London, B.M., Royal MS. App. 69, fo. 2[v], in *Eng. Hist. Rev.*, liv. 90.

Lincoln, Cathedral, 115. *l*Missale. s.xii–xiii. ?

London, B.M., Royal 4 B.viii. *ec*Threni, etc., glo.; sermones, etc. s.xiii. ?

LINCOLN. *Franciscan convent.*

Note about books seen by J. Leland printed from B.M., Royal MS. App. 69, fo. 3, in *Eng. Hist. Rev.*, liv. 90. Nine MSS (Cambridge, St John's Coll., 17; Lincoln Cathedral, 41, 82, 208; Lambeth Palace, 57; Westminster Abbey, 17; Millar; Bodleian, Lyell 11; Salisbury, Cathedral, 127) contain a mark like the figure 2 with a long horizontal tail, transected by two vertical strokes. This mark is placed in front of the note of contents or *ex libris* inscription and appears to be peculiar to this house.

Cambridge, Peterhouse, 89. *e*Gregorius. s.xiii. [149].

        St John's Coll., 17.[4] Patristica. s.xiii. [J.1]. ?

              47.[4] Patristica. s.xiv. ?

Lincoln, Cathedral, 41. *e*P. Lombardus. s.xiii. [C.13].

           82. R. Tuitiensis. s.xiii. [99.O].

          208. *e*Augustinus. s.xiv. [M.25; 120].

          221. *e*W. de Alvernia, etc. s.xiii. [10(?).71; Y.3; 22].

London, Lambeth Palace, 57. *e*Epp. Pauli glo. s.xiii.

      Wesmintster Abbey, 17. *e*Arator, etc. s.xi/xii. [20.31.25].

      Dr E. G. Millar. Pentateuchus glo. s.xiii in.

Oxford, Bodleian, Lyell 11. Augustinus. s.xiii/xiv. [M.16; 70].

Princeton, U.L., R. Garrett 102. *e*Aristoteles. s.xiv.

Salisbury, Cathedral, 127. *e*Biblia. s.xiii. [3060; 8].

---

[3] MSS 3, 29, 63, 198 belonged to Canon Thomas Salysbury (†1451).
[4] St John's Coll. 47 was formerly part of St John's Coll. 17.

LINCOLN. *Dominican convent.*

Note about books seen by J. Leland printed from London, B.M., Royal MS. App. 69, fo. 3, in *Eng. Hist. Rev.*, liv. 90.

Leyden, U.L., Lipsius 41. *i*Seneca. s.xii ex.

London, B.M., Royal 13 B.vi. *e*H. Huntendonensis. s.xiv. [*Leland*].

LINCOLN. *Carmelite convent.*

Note about books seen by J. Leland printed from London, B.M., Royal MS. App. 69, fo. 2ᵛ, in *Eng. Hist. Rev.*, liv. 90.

London, B.M., Egerton 3668. *e*H. Huntendonensis. s.xii. [*Leland*].

    Royal 6 D.ix. Osbernus Gloucestrensis. s.xii/xiii.
        [*Leland*].

    13 C.iv. *e*Paulus diaconus. s.xiv. [2ᵐV;
        Leland].

LINDISFARNE (Holy Island), Northumberland. *Ben. priory of St Peter; originally seat of bishopric, later cell of Durham.*

For English translations and abstracts of book-lists in inventories of 1348, 1362, 1367, 1401, 1409, 1416, 1437, 1533 from Durham muniments see James Raine, *North Durham* (1852), pp. 93–125.

See under **DURHAM** for books belonging to Lindisfarne before removal of the bishopric in 883.

London, B.M., Cotton Nero D.iv. Evangelia ('Lindisfarne Gospels'). s.viii in. [*Cf. inv. 1367*].

LINDORES (Lundores), Fife. *Ben. (orig. Tironensian) abbey of B.V.M. and St Andrew.*

For a printed book see Durkan and Ross, p. 159.

London, Gray's Inn, 5. *e*Beda, etc. s.xiii.

LINGFIELD, Surrey. *Collegiate church of St Peter.*

List of 21 books in inventory, s.xvi, of goods 'yeven by the founders', printed in *Surrey Archaeol. Soc. Coll.*, xxiv. 12.

LITTLEMORE, Oxfordshire. *Priory of B.V.M. and St Nicholas, of Ben. nuns.*

Oxford, Bodleian, Auct. D.2.6, fos 1–155. *i*Psalterium, etc. s.xii.

LLANDAFF, Glamorganshire. *Cathedral church of St Peter and St Teilo.*

Aberystwyth, N.L., 17110 E. *c*'Liber Landavensis'. s.xii.

Lichfield, Cathedral. *c*Evangelia ('Codex S. Ceadde'). s.viii in.

LLANTHONY (prima), Monmouthshire. *Aug. priory of St John the Baptist; cell of Lanthony (secunda) from A.D. 1481.*[5]

The Irish cell of Greatconnell, co. Kildare, owned Hereford, Cathedral, MS. P.iv.14.

---

[5] The occurrence of books from Llanthony (prima) at Lambeth Palace and Corpus Christi Coll., Oxford, suggests that at the time of the Dissolution they were kept at Lanthony (secunda), Gloucestershire. Some of the books listed under Lanthony (secunda) may have belonged to Llanthony (prima).

London,
   Lambeth Palace, 96, fos 113–243. *e*Gregorius. s.xii.
                200, fos 114–163. *i*Distinct. super Psalterium, etc.
                           s.xiii–xiv.
                356, fos 75–125.[6] Jeronimus, etc. s.xiii.
                380, fos 1–120.[6] *c*Isidorus, etc. s.xii ex.
                425, fos 1–21.[7] Cicero. s.xii/xiii.
                431, fos 1–7, 16–88.[7] *i*Misc. theol. s.xii.
   Oxford, Corpus Christi Coll., 83. *e*Polychronicon. s.xiv/xv.

LLANTHONY (secunda), Gloucestershire. *See* **LANTHONY.**

LLANVAES, Anglesey. *Franciscan convent.*
London, Dr E. G. Millar. *e*Biblia. s.xiii in.

LOCH LEVEN, Kinross-shire. *Aug. priory of St Serf.*
    List of 17 books, transferred at foundation (s.xii med.) from the Culdees of
Loch Leven, printed in *Liber Cartarum Prioratus S. Andree*, ed. J. Thomson
(Bannatyne Club, 1841), p. 43, and by Haddan and Stubbs, *Councils and Ecclesi-
astical Documents*, II, i. 228.
London, Lambeth Palace, 440. *e*Ivo Carnotensis, Chronicon, etc. s.xii.

LONDON. *Cathedral church of St Paul.*
    J. W. Clark, 'The Libraries at Lincoln, Westminster and St Paul's', *Cambr.
Antiq. Soc. Proc.*, ix (1896–98), 37.
    Book-lists included in the inventory of the treasury A.D. 1245 printed from
St Paul's MS. W.D.9 by W. Sparrow Simpson in *Archaeologia*, l(ii), 496–500,
and A.D. 1295 printed by Dugdale, *Hist. of St Paul's* (edn 1818), pp. 310 ff., from
St Paul's MS. W.D.16: collation and corrections by Simpson, *loc. cit.*, pp. 360–64.
The earlier list is truncated in MS. W.D.9, but exists in full in MS. W.D.4
('Liber L'), fos 131–34. Another text, A.D. 1295, in Bodleian, MS. Ashmole
845, fos 174, 181–84. List of service-books, A.D. 1445, printed from a St Paul's
MS. by Simpson, *loc. cit.*, p. 523; second folios given. Catalogue of the new
library in 1458 printed by Dugdale, *op. cit.*, pp. 392 ff., from B.M., Cotton Roll
xiii.11; second folios given. List of 52 books, mainly service-books, in the
treasury in 1486 printed by Dugdale, *op. cit.*, pp. 399 ff., from B.M., Cotton Roll
xiii.24; second folios given. A list of 126 books bequeathed by Ralph de
Baldock, bishop of London (†1313), is printed from St Paul's Cathedral, Dean
and Chapter Libr., Mun. A, box 66, no. 17, by A. B. Emden, *Biographical
Register of the University of Oxford*, pp. 2147–48. A list of over 100 school-
books bequeathed by the almoner, William of Ravenston, to his successors,
A.D. 1358, is printed from Mun. A, box 67, no. 46, by E. Rickert, 'Chaucer at
School', *Modern Philology*, xxix (1932), 257–74. Books noted by Leland,
Collectanea, iv. 47 (see Dugdale, *op. cit.*, p. 399) and Leland, *De Scriptoribus
Britannicis*, pp. 216, 230, 328, 403; also by Bale, *Index* (p. 577). Many of the
MSS in the 1458 catalogue are listed in three post-medieval catalogues: (*a*) At St
Paul's, by Patrick Young, *c.*1622; (*b*) Bodleian, Rawl. D.888, fos 2–5, listing
164 MSS and 67 printed books removed from St Paul's in 1647 to Sion College,
London; (*c*) Sion College, MS. dated A.D. 1650. Nearly all the MSS removed
to Sion College were destroyed in the fire of London, A.D. 1666.

Aberdeen, U.L., 1. Gregorius. s.xii. [*Cat.* O.(3)].
                2. Esaias, etc., glo. s.xii ex. [*Cat.* M.(1)].
                3. Gregorius. s.xii/xiii. [*Cat.* O.(4)].

---

[6] Lambeth Palace 356 (fos 75–125) and 380 (fos 1–120) formed one volume.
[7] Lambeth Palace 425 (fos 1–21) and 431 (fos 1–7, 16–88) formed one volume.

Aberdeen, U.L. (*contd*)
- 4. *e*Augustinus. s.xii in. [*Cat*. M.(7)].
- 5. Augustinus. s.xii in. [*Cat*. M.(9)].
- 6. Augustinus. s.xiii. [*Cat*. M.(5)].
- 8. Augustinus. s.xiii. [*Cat* M.(6)].
- 9. Augustinus. s.xii in. [*Cat*. N.(2)].
- 10.[8] Gregorius. s.xiv in.–xv ex.
- 137. *e*Gregorius, etc. s.xiii.
- 205. Seneca, etc. s.xiii–xiv. [*Cat*. C.(1)].
- 219.[8] Augustinus. s.xii ex.
- 240.[8] Legenda aurea. s.xiv.
- 241. *e*Ric. de S. Victore, etc. s.xiii–xiv. [*Cat*. (Q.2)].
- 244.[8] Rufinus. s.xii ex.

Cambridge,
Corpus Christi Coll., 383. *c*Laws (in English). s.xi/xii. ?
Downing Coll. *c*Kalendarium (6 fos). s.xv.

London,
B.M., Royal 15 B.xvi. Eutropius, etc. s.xii. [*Cat*. G.(1)].
        15 C.iii. Suetonius. s.xii. [*Cat*. G.(3)].
St Paul's Cathedral, 1. Psalterium. s.xiii in. [*Cat*. *1486* (23)].
         2. *e*Psalterium cum glosa H. de Bosham. s.xiii in. [*Cat*. *1486* (33)].
         3. *e*Avicenna. s.xiii ex. [*Cat*. D.(1)].
Lambeth Palace, 8. *e*R. de Diceto. s.xii. [*Cat*. F.(1)].
        1106,i. *c*Flores historiarum, etc. s.xiv.

Oxford,
Balliol Coll., 45, 46.[9] T. Aquinas. s.xiii ex.–xiv. ?
Oriel Coll., 30. A. de Hales. s.xiii ex. [*Baldock* 15].

Rejected: Aberdeen, U.L., 7, 11, 215, 218. London, B.M., Add. 34652, fos 11–12; Lambeth Palace, 188, i.

LONDON. *St Peter's, Westminster. See* **WESTMINSTER.**

LONDON. *Priory of St John the Baptist, of Aug. canonesses in Holywell (Shoreditch).*

Oxford, Bodleian, Douce 372. *e*Lives of Saints (in English). s.xv.

LONDON. *Cist. abbey of St Mary of Graces.*

For nine books valued at 44 shillings, pledged by the abbot in 1429/30, see *Calendar of Plea and Memoranda Rolls of the City of London 1413–37* (1943), p. 248.

Berlin, Staatsbibl., lat. qu. 487. *e*Rog. de Waltham. s.xiv.
London, B.M., Harley 4711, fo. 299. *i*(flyleaf only).
        Lambeth Palace, 1484.2 (pr. bk). *e*Sermones Socci.   Strasbourg, A.D. 1484.

[8] Aberdeen MSS 10, 219, 240, 244 contain the name of Thomas Graunt (treasurer of St Paul's, 1454–74).
[9] Thomas Gascoigne intended to bequeath Balliol Coll. 45 and 46 to St Paul's, according to erased inscriptions in each volume, but it is unlikely that the intention was carried out.

LONDON. *Charterhouse of the Salutation of the B.V.M.* (domus salutacionis matris Dei).

E. Margaret Thompson, *Carthus. Order in England* (London, 1930), pp. 323–30, prints lists of books sent to several Carthusian houses from the London Charterhouse, s.xv–xvi; second folios given. The most usual form of *ex libris* inscription is 'Liber domus salutacionis matris Dei ordinis Carthusiensis prope London'.'

Blackburn, Public Libr., 091.21038. *e*Biblia. s.xiii.
           091.21195. *c*Breviarium. s.xv in.
Cambridge, U.L., Ee.4.30. *e*W. Hilton (in English). s.xv.
      Ff.1.19.[1] *i*Liber spiritualis gracie S. Matildis.
      A.D. 1492.
      Inc. 634+1121+3901+3948 (pr. bks).[1] *m*Albertanus
      Brixiensis, etc. Antwerp, A.D. 1487, etc.
Corpus Christi Coll., S.P.21. *e*(flyleaf only).[2]
Gonv. and Caius Coll., 433. *e*Augustinus. s.xv.
Jesus Coll., 12. *c*Consuetudines ordinis Carth. s.xv.
King's Coll., 4. *e*Vitas patrum. s.xv.
Pembr. Coll., 309. *i*W. Lyndwood. s.xv ex.
St John's Coll., 71. *e*Mirror of simple souls (in English).
      s.xv.
Douai, Bibl. mun., 269. *e*Augustinus, etc. s.xv.
London,
  B.M., Cotton Calig. A.ii, fos 144–210. *c*Statuta ordinis. s.xv–xvi.
  Egerton 3267. *l*Graduale. s.xv.
  Harley 6579. *e*W. Hilton (in English). s.xv.
  Sloane 2515. *e*Ars moriendi, etc. s.xv. ?
  Charterhouse, s.n. *e*Sermones Ade Carthusiensis, etc. s.xv.
  Public Record Office, Aug. Office Misc. Bks 490. *c*Index statutorum
                    ordinis. s.xv ex. ?
Oxford,
  Bodleian, Bodl. 277. *e*Bible (in English). s.xv.
        505. *e*Chastising of God's children, etc. (in English).
        s.xv in.
    Douce 262. *e*Cloud of unknowing (in English, etc.).
        s.xv–xvi.
    Rawl. D.318, fos 73–167. *e*Varia ad ordinem pertinentia.
        s.xv.
Paris, B.N., Lat. 10434.[3] Psalterium. s.xiii.
Partridge Green, St Hugh's Charterhouse. *e*Preces, etc. s.xv.
                     *e*Cloud of unknowing (in
                     English). s.xvi in.
Yale, U.L., 286. *e*Missale. s.xiv ex.
Untraced: MS. of W. Hilton belonging to John Murray noted by T. Hearne, *Collections*, vii (Oxford Hist. Soc.), 339.[4]

---

[1] Cambridge, U.L., Inc. 634, 1121, 3901, 3948 formed one volume with Ff.1.19.
[2] Part of a leaf with *ex libris* and table of contents used as a strip in the binding of *Vocabularius utriusque juris* (Paris, 1538).
[3] Lent in 1426 to William Bernham of the Charterhouse by Rob. Lucas, priest, of London.
[4] Perhaps identical with Harley 6579.

Untraced: Earl of Clarendon, Theol. 12 (E. Bernard, *Catalogi* (1697), II, ii, no. 110). *i*Liber spiritualis gracie S. Matildis, etc. A.D. 1513.[5]

LONDON. *Aug. priory of Holy Trinity, Aldgate.*

Cambridge, Emmanuel Coll., 252, ii. *c*Kalendarium. s.xii ex.
London,
    B.M., Add. 10053. *i*Speculum religiosorum, etc. (in English). s.xv.
    Lambeth Palace, 51. P. Londiniensis. s.xiii in. [de vi ordine xlii]. ?

LONDON. *Aug. priory of St Bartholomew, Smithfield.*

Cambridge, U.L., P*.10.43 (pr. bk). *i*Hieronymus de S. Marco. Cologne, A.D. 1507.
London,
    B.M., Cotton Vesp. B.ix. *c*Liber fundationis prioratus (Lat. and Eng.). s.xv.
    Harley 631. *i*Marsilius de Padua, etc. s.xv.
    Royal 7 C.vii. *e*Misc. theol. s.xiii.
          10 E.iv. *e*Decretales glo. s.xiv in.
          17 D.xxi. *c*Brut (in English). s.xv. ?
St Bartholomew's Hospital, s.n. *i*Unum ex quatuor. s.xiv ex.

LONDON. *Franciscan convent.*

Books noted by J. Leland, *Collectanea*, iv. 49.

London, B.M., Royal 4 D.iv. *e*Bertrandus de Turre. s.xiv. [29].
        Lambeth Palace, 33. *e*T. Ringstead. s.xv.
                450.[6] Laur. Gul. Traversanus. s.xv ex.
    Middle Temple (pr. bk). *i*Bonaventura, vol. 2. Strasbourg, A.D. 1495. ?
Oxford, Bodleian, Bodl. 429. *i*Fr. de Maronis. s.xv in.
             Douce 239. *i*Summa Britonis. s.xv ex.
             Laud misc. 545. *i*Polychronicon. s.xv in.
Paris, B.N., Lat. 3757.[7] J. de Hoveden. s.xiv.
Rome, Vatican, Ottob. lat. 1565. Ric. de Mediavilla. [? *Leland*].

LONDON. *Abbey of B.V.M. and St Francis, without Aldgate, of Franciscan nuns.*

Cambridge, Trinity Coll., 301. *e*The doctrine of the heart (in English). s.xv in.
London, B.M., Harley 2397. *e*W. Hilton. s.xv.
Oxford, Bodleian, Bodl. 585, fos 48–104. *c*Rule for minoresses (in English). s.xv. ?
Reigate, Church, 2322. *i*Horae. s.xv ex.
Wellington (N.Z.), Bible House. *i*Psalterium. s.xv in.
Untraced: Meade Falkner sale (Sotheby, 12 Dec. 1932), lot 387 to Tregaskis. *e*Pore caitif (in English). s.xv.

---

[5] Written by John Whetham, see *Librorum MSS in Bibl. Jacobi Waraei, Eq. Aur. Catalogus* (Dublin, 1648).
[6] Written in the convent for presentation to William Waynflete, bishop of Winchester.
[7] Apparently borrowed by Charles d'Orléans: his inventory A.D. 1436, no. 104: De Laborde, *Les Ducs de Bourgogne*, iii. 330.

LONDON. *Dominican convent.*

Extracts by J. Bale 'ex inventario bibliothece fratrum predicatorum Londini per provincialem eorum Ricardum de Winkele, A.D. 1339' printed by R. L. Poole and M. Bateson in Bale's *Index Britanniae Scriptorum* (Oxford, 1902), p. 513. Books noted by J. Leland, *Collectanea*, iv. 51, and *De Scriptoribus Britannicis*, pp. 201–2, 214, 260.

The pressmark is reproduced from Cambridge, Corpus Christi Coll., 306 in *New Pal. Soc.*, i, pl. 147, no. 6.

Cambridge, U.L., Add. 2991. *e*Cicero. s.xiii.

      Corpus Christi Coll., 299. *i*Ivo Carnotensis, etc. s.xiii.

                  306. *e*Albertanus Brixiensis. s.xiv in. [ff.8].

                  316. *e*H. de S. Victore, etc. s.xiii in.

    Trinity Coll., 1154. *e*W. Burley, etc. s.xiv/xv. [Q.P^m].

London, B.M., Royal 3 E.i–v.[8] Vetus testamentum glo. s.xiii.

               3 E.vii. *e*P. Lombardus. s.xiii.

               3 E.viii. Evangelia glo. s.xiii.

               5 C.vii. *e*Augustinus, etc. s.xiii.

               9 B.x. *e*P. Lombardus. s.xiv.

             12 G.vi. *e*Avicenna. s.xiv.

Oxford, Bodleian, Laud misc. 728. *i*Averroes, etc. s.xiv. [I.12].

Rome, Vatican, Ottobon. lat. 862. *i*Tractatus metaphysici. s.xiv.

Rejected: Cambridge, Gonv. and Caius Coll., 378; Magdalene Coll., 13.

LONDON. *Carmelite convent.*

Books noted by J. Leland, *Collectanea*, iv. 52. *Cf.* Leland, *De Scriptoribus Britannicis*, p. 441.

The pressmark is reproduced from B.M., Royal 13 A.xviii and 13 C.vii in *New Pal. Soc.*, i, pl. 147, no. 5 *a*, *b*, wrongly assigned to the Cistercians of London. Somewhat similar marks occur in books from other houses of friars.

Cambridge, U.L., Ee.3.51. *c*Rabanus Maurus. s.xv. [I.28^m]. ?

      Corpus Christi Coll., 266. P. Blesensis. s.xiii in. [M.57^m]. ?

      St John's Coll., 221. *e*Computistica. s.xii. [I.79^m; *Leland*].

Edinburgh, N.L., 6121. Jeronimus, etc., s.xii ex. [M.51^m]. ?

Glasgow, U.L., BD.19 h.9.[9] Missale (fragm.). s.xiv ex.

Lincoln, Cathedral, 58. *e*H. de S. Victore, etc. s.xiii. [I.13^m].

London,

    B.M., Add. 29704, 29705, 44892.[9] *l*Missale. s.xiv ex. ?

    Harley 40. *i*Martinus Polonus. s.xiv. [P.9^m].

    Royal 2 D.xxxvi. *i*P. de Aureolis. s.xiv.

            5 F.i. Bernardus, etc. s.xiv in. [M.13^m]. ?

            7 B.v. *e*Ivo Carnotensis. s.xiii. [I.54^m]. ?

          11 B.xii. J. Baconthorpe. s.xiv. [F.18^m]. ?

          13 A.xii. Rad. Niger. s.xiii. [S.7^m].

         13 A.xviii. *i*Ivo Carnotensis, etc. s.xiv–xv. [M.39^m].

         13 C.vii. *i*Freculphus, etc. s.xiv ex. [M.40].

---

[8] Sixteenth-century notes in Royal 3 E.i and 3 E.ix show that 3 E.i and six other volumes 'all bounde in white lether' and identifiable with 3 E.ii–v, vii, viii, formed a 'set' of glossed books of the greater part of the bible (*cf. Cat. Royal MSS*, i, p.xl). The fact that 3 E.i–v, viii belonged to the London Dominicans is now recorded only on the outside of the eighteenth-century bindings.

[9] The three British Museum manuscripts have been reconstructed as one. The Glasgow manuscript was part of the same book.

Oxford, Bodleian, Bodl. 730. *e*J. Cassianus. s.xii ex. [I.66ᵐ].
Laud lat. 87. *e*Biblia. s.xiii. [A.1ᵐ].
Trinity Coll., 58. *e*Clemens Lanthon. s.xii. [C.24ᵐ].
Rejected: Dublin, Trinity Coll., 194.

LONDON. *Convent of Austin friars.*

Books noted by J. Leland, *Collectanea*, iv. 54, and *De Scriptoribus Britannicis*, p. 470, and by J. Bale, *Index*, p. 186.

Dublin, Trinity Coll., 486. *e*Polychronicon. s.xv.
Glasgow, U.L., Dp.e.6 (pr. bk). *i*Biblia. Venice, A.D. 1484.
Helmingham Hall, Lord Tollemache, 8.[1] Martinus Polonus. s.xiv ex.
London, B.M., Add. 34652, fos 11–12.[2] *e*Epp. Sidonii. s.xiii.
Royal 3 A.x. *i*Clemens Lanthoniensis, etc. s.xiii.
Oxford, Bodleian, Lat. misc. d.80.[2] Epp. Sidonii. s.xiii.
Rome, Vatican, lat. 11438. *l*Psalterium, etc. s.xv med.
San Francisco, John Howell.[1] *i*Archimatheus, etc. s.xiv ex.
Untraced: Thomas Rawlinson sale, March 1733/4, lot 541, to Lord Coleraine. *e*'Expositio Magistri Hugonis super lamentationes Jeremie'.

LONDON. *Convent of friars of the Holy Cross* (Crutched friars).

An inscription in Westminster Abbey, CC.18, records that Mag. Gerard [*blank*] gave this book and more than thirty others in 1496.

Bury St Edmunds, Cathedral (pr. bk). *e*W. Durandus. Strasbourg, A.D. 1486.
Cambridge, U.L., Ee.1.7. *e*Manuale sacerdotum. s.xvi.
E.9.24 (pr. bk). *e*Albertus magnus. Basel, A.D. 1506.
London, Westminster Abbey, CC.18 (pr. bk). *e*Lanfrancus de Oriano. Cologne, A.D. 1488.
New York, Columbia U.L., Plimpton collection (pr. bk). *e*A. Dathus, etc. Paris, A.D. 1508, etc.
Oxford, Bodleian, Auct. I.Q.2.10 (pr. bk). *e*P. Comestor, Basel, A.D. 1486.
8⁰ B.115 Th. (pr. bk). *e*S. Baron. London, s.a.

LONDON. *Hospital of B.V.M., without Bishopsgate.*

Cambridge, Corpus Christi Coll., 194. *e*Miscellanea. s.xiv–xv.

LONDON. *Hospital of B.V.M., near Cripplegate* (Elsyng spital).

Inventory of 1448 in London, B.M., Cotton Roll xiii.10, printed by J. P. Malcolm, *Londinium Redivivum* (1803), i. 27 ff.

Dublin, Trinity Coll., 436. *e*Pseudo-Aristoteles. s.xv.
Oxford, Bodleian, e Mus. 113. *e*Vita S. Marie Magdalene, etc. s.x–xii.

LONDON. *Hospital of St Thomas of Acon, Cheapside.*

London, B.M., Royal 3 A.ix. *e*J. de Abbatisvilla. s.xv.
3 E.x, xi. *e*Nic. de Gorran. s.xv.
4 C.vii. *e*Nic. de Gorran. s.xv.

[1] Helmingham Hall 8 and the Howell MS. (formerly Helmingham Hall 57) formed one volume.
[2] B.M., Add. 34652, fos 11–12, and Bodleian, Lat. misc. d.80, formed one volume.

London, B.M., Royal (*contd*)
   7 D.v. *e*Franciscus de Maronis. s.xv.
   13 C.xi. *e*Eusebius, etc. s.xii.
   14 C.xii. *e*Polychronicon. s.xiv.
   15 C.xvi. *e*P. Berchorius, etc. s.xiv ex.
Rejected: London, Lambeth Palace, 433.

LONDON. *Collegiate church of St Michael, in Crooked Lane.*
London, B.M., Royal 1 C.i. *e*Biblia. s.xiii.

LONDON. *Whittington college.*
Cambridge, St John's Coll., 150. *e*Gregorius. s.xv.
Oxford, Bodleian, H.1.14 Art. Seld. (pr. bk). *e*Martinus de Magistris,
 etc. Paris, A.D. 1511, etc.

LONDON. *Gray's Inn.*
London, B.M., Add. 34901. *e*Registrum Brevium. s.xv in. ?

LONDON. *Lincoln's Inn.*
London, Lincoln's Inn, 1. *e*Biblia. s.xiii. ?

LONDON. *Guildhall.*

 E. M. Borrajo, 'The Guildhall Library: its history and present position',
Library Assoc. Record, x (1908), 382. W. S. Saunders, introduction and appendix
to *Catalogue of Engraved Portraits* . . . *exhibited at the opening of the new Library
and Museum of the Corporation*, ed. W. H. Overall (1872). N. R. Ker, 'Liber
Custumarum and other Manuscripts formerly at the Guildhall', *Guildhall Mis-
cellany*, iii (1954), 37–45.
 For books bequeathed by Andrew Horn, fishmonger, in 1328 see R. R. Sharpe,
Calendar of Wills proved and enrolled in the Court of Husting (1889), i. 344,
from Husting roll 57(16).

Cambridge, Corpus Christi Coll., 70.[3] Leges Anglorum. s.xiv in.
            [*Horn* 2].
      258.[3] Speculum justitiariorum, etc.
         s.xiv in. [*Horn* 2].
London,
 B.M., Add. 14252.[4] *c*Leges Henrici II, etc. s.xiii in.
   Cotton Claudius D.ii, fos 1–24, 31–115, 124–35, 266–77.[5] Leges
    Anglorum, etc. s.xiv in.
   D.ii, fos 116–23.[6] Statuta Anglie. s.xiv.
   D.ii, fos 136–265.[7] Statuta Anglie (in Latin
    and French). s.xv in.
 Harley 32. *e*T. Aquinas. s.xiv in.

---

 [3] Corpus Christi Coll. 70 and 258 formed one volume.
 [4] B.M., Add. 14252, and Rylands, lat. 155, formed one volume.
 [5] Cotton Claudius D.ii, fos 1–24, 31–115, 124–35, 266–77, 'Liber Custumarum', fos v, 1–102, 173–86, and Oriel Coll. 46, fos 109–211, formed one
volume. Fos 16–39 of the Corporation's 'Liber Albus' was originally part of this
manuscript, but was removed from it in the Middle Ages.
 [6] Cotton Claudius D.ii, fos 116–23, 'Liber Custumarum', fos 103–72, 187–
286, and Oriel Coll. 46, fos 1–108, formed one volume.
 [7] Cotton Claudius D.ii, fos 136–265, and 'Statuta antiqua Angliæ' formed one
volume.

London (*contd*)

Guildhall Libr., 244.[8]   Croniques de France (in French).   s.xiv ex.

        3042.   *e*P. Riga.   s.xiii.

Corporation of London, Records Office.

  *c*Chronica, etc. ('Liber de Antiquis Legibus').   s.xiii ex.

  *c*Statuta Anglie, etc. ('Liber Horn').   A.D. 1311.   [? *Horn* 4].

  *c*Statuta Anglie, etc. ('Liber Ordinationum').   s.xiv in.

  *c*Magna Carta, etc. ('Liber Custumarum', fos v, 1–102, 173–86).[5]
    s.xiv in.

  *c*Statuta Anglie, etc. ('Liber Custumarum', fos 103–72, 187–286).[6]
    s.xiv in.

  *e*Statuta Anglie ('Cartæ Antiquæ': in French and English).   s.xv ex.

  'Statuta antiqua Angliæ' (in French).[7]   s.xv.   ?

Manchester, J. Rylands, Lat. 155.[4]   Leges Anglie.   s.xiii in.

Oxford, Oriel Coll., 46, fos 1–108.[6]   Leges Anglie.   s.xiv in.

             fos 109–211.[5]   Statuta Anglie, etc.   s.xiv in.

LOUTH PARK (de Parco Lude), Lincolnshire.   *Cist. abbey of B.V.M.*

Notes about books seen by J. Leland printed from B.M., Royal MS. App. 69, fo. 6ᵛ, in *Eng. Hist. Rev.*, liv. 93.   The *ex libris* inscription is in the form 'Liber sancte Marie de Parco Lude'.

Cambridge, U.L., Dd.1.29.   *e*Beda.   s.xii.

           Ff.6.15.   *c*Annales, etc.   s.xiii/xiv.

           Kk.4.15.   *e*Origenes.   s.xii.

Flackwell Heath, Mr R. W. Allison.   *c*Chronicon abbatie.   s.xv.

Lincoln, Cathedral, 47.   *e*Jeronimus.   s.xiii.

Oxford, Bodleian, Fairfax 17.   *c*Misc. theologica.   s.xii.   ?

LUFFIELD, Northamptonshire.   *Ben. priory of B.V.M.*

Cambridge, U.L., Ee.1.1.   *e*Misc. jur.   s.xiii/xiv.

LYNN, KING'S, Norfolk.   *Ben. priory of St Margaret; cell of Norwich Cathedral Priory.*

Cambridge, Gonv. and Caius Coll., 136.   *i*A. Nequam, etc.   s.xiii ex.

LYNN, KING'S.   *Franciscan convent.*

London, B.M., Add. 47214.   *c*Annales, etc.   s.xiv.   ?

Oxford, Bodleian, Lat. th. d.1.   *i*Sermones.   s.xv.

LYNN, KING'S.   *Carmelite convent.*

Oxford, Bodleian, Ashmole 1398, pp. 1–214.   *i*Misc. medica, etc.   s.xiii.

LYNN, KING'S.   *Hospital of St Mary Magdalen.*

Ripon, Mr H. L. Bradfer-Lawrence.   *c*Liber vite.   s.xiv–xvi.

---

[8] Guildhall 244 belonged to the library 3 July 1516 (**Repertory** 3 of the Court **of** Aldermen, fo. 93ᵛ).

[5] See p. 126, n. 5.   [6] See p. 126, n. 6.

[7] See p. 126, n. 7.   [4] See p. 126, n. 4.

MAIDSTONE, Kent. *Collegiate church of St Peter and St Paul.*

London, B.M., Cotton Claudius A.xi. *e*Anselmus. s.xiii.
    Wellcome Historical Medical Mus. (pr. bk). *e*Anselmus.
    Nuremberg, A.D. 1491.
Oxford, Bodleian, Bodl. 794. *e*Constitutiones provinciales. s.xiv–xv.

MALDON. *See* **BEELEIGH.**

MALLING, Kent. *Abbey of B.V.M. and St Andrew, of Ben. nuns.*

Blackburn, Publ. Libr., 091.21040. *i*Horae, etc. s.xv in.

MALMESBURY, Wiltshire. *Ben. abbey of B.V.M. and St Aldhelm.*
    (*Cf.* cell at **PILTON.**)

Books noted by J. Leland, *Collectanea*, iv. 157. *Cf.* Leland, *De Scriptoribus
Britannicis*, pp. 100–1, 134–35.

Beeleigh Abbey, Miss C. Foyle. *em*Ezechiel glo. s.xii. ?
Cambridge,
    Corpus Christi Coll., 23, fos 1–104. *e*Prudentius. s.x/xi.
                330, fos 1–87.[9] Martianus Capella. s.xii in.
                361. *e*Gregorius. s.xi.
    Trinity Coll., 727. *e*W. Malmesburiensis. s.xii.
                740. *c*Eulogium historiarum, etc. s.xiv.
                1301.[9,1] Joh. Scotus, De divisione nature; Evangelium
                    S. Luce. s.xii.
London,
    B.M., Cotton, Cleop. B.iii, fos 2–35. *e*Aelredus Rievallensis. s.xiv ex.
            Otho B.x, fo. 51.[2] Gospels (in English). s.xi. ?
            C.i, part 1.[2] *c*Gospels (in English). s.xi. ?
            Vit. A.x, fos 158–60. *c*De abbatibus Malm. s.xii/xiii.
    Lambeth Palace, 224.[9] *s*Anselmus. s.xii in.–xiii. [xxvi].
Oxford,
    Bodleian, Arch. Seld. B.16.[9] *s*Misc. hist. et jur. s.xii in.
            Auct. F.3.14.[9,1] *sc*Computistica. s.xii in.
            Barlow 6. *c*J. Saresberiensis. s.xii ex.
            Bodl. 852. *e*Vite sanctorum. s.xi. [xxxix].
            Marshall 19. *e*Philo Judeus. s.ix.
            Wood empt. 5. *c*Alcuinus, etc. s.xiii in. [*Leland*].
    Lincoln Coll., lat. 100.[9] Vegetius, etc. s.xii in.
    Magdalen Coll., lat. 172.[9] *s*W. Malmesburiensis. s.xii in. [C.4].
    Merton Coll., 181.[9] *b*Beda, etc. s.xii in. [xvi].
    Oriel Coll., 42.[9] *s*Canones conciliorum, etc. s.xii in.

---

[9] Cambridge, Corpus Christi Coll., 330, fos 1–87; Trinity Coll., 1301; Lambeth
Palace, 224; Bodleian, Arch. Seld. B.16, Auct. F.3.14; Lincoln Coll., lat. 100;
Magdalen Coll., lat. 172; Merton Coll., 181, fo. 230 (binding leaf); Oriel Coll.,
42: contain writing in a hand identified as that of William of Malmesbury; for
nos 3–7 *cf.* N. R. Ker in *Eng. Hist. Rev.*, lix (1944), 371–76.
[1] Trinity Coll., 1301 and Auct. F.3.14 are to be identified with volumes returned
to the abbot of Malmesbury by the abbot of Glastonbury after the death of
Roger Swyneshead, monk of Glastonbury, 12 May 1365 (B.M., MS. Arundel 2,
fo. 80[v]).
[2] Otho B.x, fo. 51, is a detached leaf of Otho C.i, part 1.

Rejected: Cambridge, U.L., Kk.4.6; Corpus Christi Coll. 380. London, B.M., Cotton Galba E.vii. Philadelphia (U.S.A.), Free Library, J. F. Lewis 123.

Untraced: James West MS. (T. Hearne, *Collections* (O.H.S.), x. 79, 96, 292). *c*Chronicon, etc. s.xiv.

MALVERN, GREAT, Worcestershire. *Ben. priory of B.V.M. and St Michael; cell of Westminster.*

Helmingham Hall, Lord Tollemache, 49.[3] *e*Compendium theologice veritatis. s.xiii/xiv.
Oxford,
 Bodleian, Hatton 23. *c*J. Cassianus. s.xi/xii. ?
 Corpus Christi Coll., 157. *i*Florentius Wigornensis. s.xii. ?
 Queen's Coll., 362. *c*T. de Chabham. s.xiii. ?

MANCHESTER, *Collegiate church of B.V.M.*

San Marino, Huntington, HM 26560. *g*Mariale. s.xiv.

MARGAM, Glamorganshire. *Cist. abbey of B.V.M.*

Cambridge, Trinity Coll., 1108. *c*Chronica abbatie. s.xiii.
London, B.M., Arundel 153. *e*Domesday abbrev. s.xii. ?
 Royal 13 D.ii. *e*W. Malmesburiensis, etc. s.xii.

MARKBY, Lincolnshire. *Aug. priory of St Peter.*

 Notes of books seen by J. Leland in B.M., Royal MS. App. 69, fo. 7, printed in *Eng. Hist. Rev.,* liv. 93.

London, B.M., Royal 14 C.xi. *e*Godefridus Viterbiensis. s.xiv. [*Leland*].

MARKYATE, Hertfordshire. *Hermitage, later priory of Ben. nuns.*

Hildesheim, S. Godehards Bibl. *c*Psalterium. s.xii in.
Sürth bei Köln, Dr J. Lückger.[4] Preces (1 fo.). s.xii in.

MARLBOROUGH, Wiltshire. *Carmelite convent.*

Untraced: Kerslake cat. (noticed by W. Carew Hazlitt in Item 2462 in *The Bibliographer,* vi (1884), 140). *e*Bartholomeus Anglicus, *De proprietatibus rerum* (pr. bk). s.l., A.D. 1488.

MARRICK, Yorkshire. *Priory of B.V.M. and St Andrew, of Ben. nuns.*

New York, Publ. Libr., Spencer 19. *e*The dream of the pilgrimage of the soul (in English). s.xv in.

MAXSTOKE, Warwickshire. *Aug. priory of Holy Trinity, B.V.M., St Michael and All Saints.*

Cambridge, U.L., Kk.2.18. *m*Epp. Pauli glo. s.xii ex.
Oxford, Bodleian, Bodl. 182. *e*Compendium pupille oculi. s.xv.

---

[3] Helmingham Hall, 49 belonged earlier to the Worcester Dominican convent, *q.v.*
[4] Dr Lückger's leaf was formerly part of the psalter at Hildesheim.

MAY, ISLE OF, Fife. *Ben. and (s.xiv) Aug. priory of All Saints; cell of Reading, later cell of St Andrews and transferred to Pittenweem.*

Oxford, St John's Coll., 111. *e*Matheus glo. s.xii.

MEAUX (Melsa), Yorkshire. *Cist. abbey of B.V.M.*

Catalogue of s.xv in. printed from B.M. Cotton MS. Vit. E.vi in *Chronica Mon. de Melsa* (Rolls Series, 1866–68), iii, pp. lxxxiii–c.

Chicago, Univ. of Chicago, 654. *e*Sermones, etc. s.xiii–xiv. [Y.xviiii; *cat.*, p. xciv].

Manchester, J. Rylands, Lat. 219. *c*Chronicon abbatie. s.xiv ex.

Oxford, Bodleian, Digby 77, fos 109–49. *i*R. Grosseteste. s.xiv.

Rawl. C.415. *e*Augustinus. s.xii.

Wolfenbüttel, Herzog-August-Bibl., 4447 (Gudianus lat. 143). *e*M. Polonus. s.xv.

MEDMENHAM, Buckinghamshire. *Cist. abbey of B.V.M.*

Oxford, All Souls Coll., SR.68.g.10 (pr. bk). *e*Biblia. Lyon, A.D. 1520.

MELROSE, Roxburghshire. *Cist. abbey of B.V.M.*

For a printed book see Durkan and Ross, p. 111.

London, B.M., Cotton Faust. B.ix, fos 2–75. *c*Chronicon abbatie. s.xii–xiii.

MENDHAM, Suffolk. *Cluniac priory of B.V.M.*

Rejected: New York, Pierpont Morgan, M.43.

MEREVALE (Mirevallis, etc.), Warwickshire. *Cist. abbey of B.V.M.*

Cambridge, U.L., Add. 3097. *e*Statuta. s.xiv.

London, B.M., Add. 31826. *e*Statuta. s.xiii–xiv.

Harley 324. *e*Breton (in French). s.xiv in.

Oxford, All Souls Coll., 33. *e*W. Malmesburiensis. s.xii ex. ?

Winchester, College, 6. *e*Josephus. s.xii. ?

MERSEA, Essex. *Ben. alien priory of St Peter; cell of St Ouen, Rouen.*

Cambridge, St John's Coll., 132. *e*Medica. s.xiii. ?

MERTON, Surrey. *Aug. priory of B.V.M.*

Ampleforth Abbey, C.v.23a (pr. bk). *i*Athanasius. Paris, A.D. 1519.

Cambridge, U.L., Ee.6.26. *e*Biblia. s.xiv.

Eton Coll., 123. *c*Flores historiarum. s.xiii–xiv.

Glasgow, U.L., Eg.6.a.9 (pr. bk). *i*G. Odonis. Venice, A.D. 1500.

London, B.M., Add. 45568. *e*J. de Abbatisvilla. s.xiii.

Royal 4 B.xiv. Misc. theologica. s.xii ex. ?

5 F.xvi. *e*Basilius, etc. s.xii ex.

6 E.v. *e*R. Grosseteste. s.xv.

8 E.ix. *e*A. Nequam. s.xv.

9 E.vi. *e*P. Lombardus. s.xiii ex.

9 E.xii. *e*Simon Tornacensis. s.xiii in.

11 A.v. *e*P. Abaelardus, etc. s.xii–xiii.

London (*contd*)
    B.M., Royal 11 B.v. *e*Constitutiones, etc. s.xiii–xiv.
             15 A.xxxii. *e*B. Silvestris, etc. s.xiii.
    Coll. of Arms, Arundel 28. *c*Historia fundationis prioratus,
                      etc. s.xiv/xv.
    Lambeth Palace, 118. *e*H. Huntendonensis. s.xii.
              **H890.B6, B7 (pr. bks: 2 vols). *i*Stephanus
                Brulefer. Basel, A.D. 1507.
    Soc. of Antiquaries, 47. *i*Isidorus, etc. s.xv.
Oxford, Bodleian, Ashmole 1522. *e*Misc. mathematica. s.xiv.
            Bodl. 555. *c*Purg. S. Patricii, etc. s.xiv/xv.
            Digby 147. *e*Miscellanea. s.xv.
            Laud misc. 723. *c*Tabule cyclorum decennovenalium,
                      etc. s.xiii–xv.
            Seld. supra 39. *i*Penitentiale. s.xiv.
            4⁰ Z.33 Th. (pr. bk). *e*Erasmus. Basel, A.D. 1519.
    St John's Coll., c.3.5 (pr. bk). *e*H. Bouhic. Lyon, A.D. 1498.
            K.3.9 (pr. bk). *i*W. Lyndwood. Paris,
                    A.D. 1505. ?
            U.2.16 (pr. bk). *e*A. Corsetus. Lyon, A.D. 1505.
            Φ.1.32 (pr. bk). *e*Dionysius Carthus., *Opera*,
                    vol. 1. Cologne, A.D. 1532.
Shrewsbury, School, A.x.15 (Inc. 31: pr. bk). *i*Bernardus. Basel,
    A.D. 1494.
Rejected: Cambridge, Corpus Christi Coll., 59.

METTINGHAM, Suffolk. *Collegiate church of B.V.M.*
Rejected: London, B.M., Egerton 1066.

MISSENDEN, Buckinghamshire. *Aug. (Arrouaisian) abbey of B.V.M.*
Chicago, Art Institute, 23. 420. Speculum humane salvationis. s.xv in.
Oxford, Bodleian, Auct. D.1.10. *e*Augustinus. s.xii/xiii.
            Bodl. 729. *e*Beda, etc. s.xiii.
Rejected: Medieval MSS belonging to the Fleetwood family of Missenden
    Abbey, advertised as the 'Antient conventual-library of Missenden-
    Abbey' in the sale catalogue of the Fleetwood MSS (S. Paterson, 5
    Dec. 1774): *cf.* Bodleian, MS. Tanner 268, fo. 178.

MONK BRETTON, Yorkshire. *Cluniac priory of St Mary Magdalen.*
    The library catalogue by the late prior in 1558 printed by Jos. Hunter, *Engl.
Monastic Libraries* (London, 1831) and in his *South Yorkshire* (1831), ii. 274,
from a cartulary formerly at Woolley Hall, near Wakefield (see J. W. Walker,
'Abstracts of the Chartularies of the Priory of Monkbretton', *Yorks. Arch.
Soc., Record Series,* lxvi, 1924), and now B.M., Add. MS. 50755.

London, B.M., Royal 1 A.xix. *e*Biblia. s.xiii.
Oxford, Univ. Coll., 101. *e*Breviarium. s.xiii.

MONKS KIRBY, Warwickshire. *Ben. alien priory of St Nicholas; cell of
St Nicholas, Angers.*
Oxford, Balliol Coll., 240. *c*Miracula B.V.M. s.xii–xiv in.

MONKTON FARLEIGH, Wiltshire. *Cluniac priory of St Mary Magdalen; cell of Lewes.*

An inventory of goods, probably of A.D. 1338, mentions 'cxxx libros in libraria quorum nomina continentur in una tabula ibidem' (P.R.O., C.47/18/1/17, noted by R. Bressie in *Modern Language Notes*, liv (1939), 250).

MONTACUTE, Somerset. *Cluniac priory of St Peter and St Paul.*

Book noted by J. Leland, *Collectanea*, iv. 150.

MONYMUSK, Aberdeenshire. *Aug. priory of B.V.M.*

For two printed books see Durkan and Ross, p. 95.

MOTTENDEN, Kent. *Trinitarian convent.*

Cambridge, Corpus Christi Coll., E.P.D.Par.4 (pr. bk). *e*Legenda aurea. Cologne, A.D. 1485.
Oxford, Bodleian, Auct. D.2.20. *i*Matheus et Marcus glo. s.xiii. ?
                Bodl. 643. *e*W. Burley, etc. s.xv.
        Corpus Christi Coll., Δ.15.5 (pr. bk). *e*Gratianus. Paris, A.D. 1508.
        Hertford Coll., Mr C. A. J. Armstrong (pr. bk). *e*W Lyndwood. Paris, A.D. 1501.
Richmond (U.S.A.), Virginia State Libr., 1. *i*J. Gerson. s.xv.

MOTTISFONT, Hampshire. *Aug. priory of Holy Trinity.*

Oxford, Bodleian, Rawl. G.183–84. *e*Pentateuchus glo. (2 vols). s.xiii in.

MOUNT GRACE (in East Harlsey), Yorkshire. *Charterhouse of the Assumption of the B.V.M.*

E. Margaret Thompson, *Carthusian Order in England* (London, 1930), pp. 330–31.

Cambridge, U.L., Add. 6578. *e*Mirror of life of Christ (in English). s.xv.
           Trinity Coll., 1160. Opera R. Methley. s.xv ex. ?
Dublin, Trinity Coll., 318. *e*Gregorius, etc. s.xiv in.
London, B.M., Harley 237. *e*Misc. theologica. s.xv.
                2373. *m*Cloud of unknowing, etc. (in English). s.xv.
Mayfield, Capt. M. Butler-Bowden. *e*Margery Kempe (in English). s.xv.
Oxford, Bodleian, Antiq. d.F.1512/1 (pr. bk). *e*Biblia. Rouen, A.D. 1512.
                AA.61 Th. Seld. (pr. bk). *e*Fortalicium fidei. Nuremberg, A.D. 1494.
Ripon, Cathedral, xvii.B.29. *e*Bonaventura. s.xv.
        Mr H. L. Bradfer-Lawrence. *e*Gregorius, etc. s.xv.
York, Minster, xvi.I.9. *e*Speculum spiritalium. s.xv.
Untraced: T. Rawlinson sale, A.D. 1733/34, lot 822 to Barker. *e*Speculum discipulorum Christi. A.D. 1474.
Rejected: Cambrai, Bibl. com., 255. Oxford, Brasenose Coll., 9.

MUCH WENLOCK. *See* **WENLOCK.**

MUCHELNEY, Somerset. *Ben. abbey of St Peter and St Paul.*

London, B.M., Add. 43405–6. *cl*Breviarium. s.xiii/xiv.
        Royal 7 A.ii. *e*J. Cassianus, etc. s.xiii.
Oxford,
  Bodleian, Ashmole 189, fos 70–115. *i*Hymns, etc. (in English). s.xv.
  Magdalen Coll., lat. 182, fos 1–53, 60–105. *i*Tabule astronomice. s.xv.

NEATH, Glamorgan. *Savigniac and (1147) Cist. abbey of B.V.M.*

Hereford, Cathedral, P.viii.11. *e*Digestum novum. s.xiii/xiv.

NETLEY (Letus locus *or* Locus S. Edwardi, Letley), Hampshire. *Cist. abbey of B.V.M. and St Edward.*

Book noted by J. Leland, *Collectanea*, iv. 149.

London, B.M., Arundel 69. *e*R. de Hoveden. s.xiii. ?

NEW ABBEY. *See* **SWEETHEART.**

NEWARK (de novo loco, Aldbury *or* New Place), Surrey. *Aug. priory of B.V.M. and St Thomas the Martyr.*

The *ex libris* inscription is 'Hic liber est ecclesie sancte Marie et beati Thome martiris de Novo Loco' followed by the anathema 'quem qui furto abstulerit vel sine conscientia ejusdem ecclesie conventus quocumque modo alienaverit sit anathema maranatha. Amen.'

London, B.M., Royal 12 B.xii, fos 228–80. *e*Macer. s.xiii.
Oxford,
  Bodleian, Auct. D.inf.2.10.[5] *e*P. Lombardus. s.xiii in.
        Bodl. 207.[5] Mirror of life of Christ (in English). s.xv. ?
            398.[5] Isidorus, etc. s.xii. ?
            602, fos 1–66. *i*Bestiarium. s.xii–xiii.
      Laud lat. 15. *c*Kalendarium, etc. s.xv.
        misc. 548. *e*W. Malmesburiensis. s.xii ex.
  Balliol Coll., 85. *e*W. Altissiodorensis. s.xiii.
  Keble Coll., A.62 (pr. bk). *i*Biblia. Venice, A.D. 1478.

NEWBATTLE, Midlothian. *Cist. abbey of B.V.M.*

For 3 printed books see Durkan and Ross, pp. 100, 154.

Edinburgh, N.L., Adv. 18.4.1. *i*Carta caritatis, etc. A.D. 1523.
Untraced: Sir J. Home-Purves-Hume-Campbell sale at Marchmont House, Berwickshire, in 1913. *e*'Liber Pluscardensis'. s.xv ex.

NEWBURGH (de novo burgo), Yorkshire. *Aug. priory of B.V.M.*

Book noted by J. Leland, *Collectanea*, iv. 37.

London, B.M., Arundel 252. *e*Ivo Carnotensis. s.xiii in.
        Stowe 62. *e*W. de Novo Burgo, etc. s.xii/xiii.
Winchester Coll., 20. *e*Augustinus. s.xii.

NEWCASTLE-UPON-TYNE, Northumberland. *Convent of Austin friars.*

London, B.M., Add. 35110. *e*Vite sanctorum. s.xii ex.

---

[5] The provenance of Bodl. 207 and 398 is inferred from the similarity of the medieval bindings to that of Auct. D.inf.2.10.

NEWCASTLE-UPON-TYNE. *Dominican convent.*

Ripon, Cathedral, xvii.D.19. *e*Anselmus, etc. s.xiii.
Southwell, Minster, 5. *e*Biblia. s.xiii. [a.3⁰].

NEWCASTLE-UPON-TYNE. *Carmelite convent.*

Oxford, Merton Coll., B.8.G.17 (pr. bk). *i*Ant. Andreas, etc. Venice,
A.D. 1496.

NEWCASTLE-UPON-TYNE. *Reclusory.*

Oxford, Bodleian, Rawl. C.258. *i*New Testament (in English). s.xv in.

NEWENHAM, Devon. *Cist. abbey of B.V.M.*

List of books given by the first abbot, John Godard (1246–48), printed by
J. C. Russell, *Dictionary of Writers of thirteenth-century England* (1936), p. 65,
from the cartulary, B.M., MS. Arundel 17, fo. 53ᵛ.

NEWHOUSE. *See* **NEWSHAM.**

NEWMINSTER (Novum monasterium), Northumberland. *Cist. abbey
of B.V.M.*

London, B.M., Add. 25014. *c*Beda. s.xii. ?
           Harley 3013. *e*Aldhelmus. s.xii ex.

NEWNHAM (Neweham), Bedfordshire. *Aug. priory of St Paul.*

  Book noted by J. Leland, *Collectanea*, iv. 12.

Cambridge, Pembr. Coll., 143. *i*Exodus glo. s.xii.
          St John's Coll., 119. *b*Miscellanea. s.xii in.–xiii. [liber 53].
Copenhagen, Royal Libr. (pr. bk). *i*R. Higden, Polychronicon. West-
minster, A.D. 1495.
London, B.M., Royal 5 B.xi. *i*Flores Bernardi, etc. s.xiv.
Oxford, Univ. Coll., 181. *i*Pilgrimage of the Soul (in English). s.xv in.

NEWSHAM (Newhouse), Lincolnshire. *Prem. abbey of B.V.M. and
St Martial.*

  Note about books seen by J. Leland printed from B.M., Royal MS. App. 69,
fo. 4, in *Eng. Hist. Rev.* liv. 91.

Grimsthorpe Castle, Earl of Ancaster.[6] *c*W. de Monte, etc. s.xiii.

NEWSTEAD (de novo loco juxta Stamfordiam *or* ad portam de Uffing-
tone), Lincolnshire. *Aug. priory of B.V.M.*

Oxford, Bodleian, Laud misc. 428.[7] *e*Gregorius. s.xii. ?

NEWSTEAD (de novo loco in Schirewode), Nottinghamshire. *Aug.
priory of B.V.M.*

London, Lambeth Palace, 261. *e*W. de Monte, etc. s.xiii in.

---

[6] Deposited with the Lincolnshire Archives Committee, Exchequer Gate,
Lincoln, Ancaster 16/1.
[7] Bodleian, Laud misc. 428 may have belonged to Newstead, Lincs., or more
probably, Newstead, Notts., since it came to Laud from William le Neve, like
Laud lat. 34.

Newbury, Prof. H. A. Ormerod.[8] *b*Meditaciones Anselmi, etc. s.xiii ex.
Oxford, Bodleian, Auct. D.3.6. *i*Biblia. s.xiv.
   Laud lat. 34. *e*Psalterium glo. s.xii.
      misc. 428.[9] *e*Gregorius. s.xii/xiii. ?

NEWSTEAD (de novo loco super Ancholme), Lincolnshire. *Gilbertine priory of Holy Trinity.*

Note about books seen by J. Leland printed from B.M., Royal MS. App. 69, fo. 4ᵛ, in *Eng. Hist. Rev.*, liv. 91.

NOCTON PARK (de parco Noctone), Lincolnshire. *Aug. priory of St Mary Magdalen.*

Note about books seen by J. Leland printed from B.M., Royal MS. App. 69, fo. 9ᵛ, in *Eng. Hist. Rev.*, liv. 95.

Insch, Mr C. A. Gordon. *e*Anselmus, etc. s.xii.
Lincoln, Cathedral, 73. *e*Origenes. s.xii/xiii.
Untraced: T. Thorpe, cat. for 1831, no. 4110. *e*Augustinus, etc.

NORTHAMPTON. *Cluniac priory of St Andrew.*

Oxford,
   Bodleian, Auct. D.1.8. *e*Unum ex quatuor glo. s.xiii in. [E.z].
      Laud misc. 372. *e*Defensor, etc. s.xiii ex. [D.b]. ?
      e Mus. 60. Liber sextus. s.xiv in. [E.b]. ?
   Balliol Coll., 32. *s*Augustinus, etc. s.xiii in. [B.b].
         307. Excerpta patrum. s.xii. [D.o]. ?
   Oriel Coll., 53. *e*Steph. Langton, etc. s.xiii-xiv. [E.w].
         60. *s*Gregorius, etc. s.xiii in. [X].
         63. *s*Gregorius. s.xiii in. [A.b].
   St John's Coll., 20. Haymo. s.xii. [B.g]. ?
         39. Matheus et Marcus glo. s.xiii. [E.y]. ?
Rejected: Maidstone, Museum, A.13.

NORTHAMPTON. *Aug. abbey of St James.*

Rejected: London, B.M., Royal 8 F.x.

NORTHAMPTON. *Franciscan convent.*

Oxford, Bodleian, Auct. D.4.11. *e*Biblia. s.xiii.

NORTHAMPTON. *Dominican convent.*

London, Sion Coll., Arc.L.40.2/L.21. *e*Suetonius, etc. s.xii.

NORWICH. *Ben. cathedral priory of Holy Trinity.* (*Cf.* cells at **NORWICH**, St Leonard, **YARMOUTH**.)

H. C. Beeching and M. R. James, 'The Library of the Cathedral Church of Norwich and Priory MSS now in English Libraries', *Norfolk Archaeology*, xix (1917), 67, 174. N. R. Ker 'Mediaeval Manuscripts from Norwich Cathedral

---

[8] Deposited in Nottingham Public Library.
[9] Bodleian, Laud misc. 428 may have belonged to Newstead, Lincs., or more probably, Newstead, Notts., since it came to Laud from William le Neve, like Laud lat. 34.

Priory', *Trans. Cambr. Bibl. Soc.*, i (1949–53), 1–28. A list of the books of Prior Simon Bozoun printed from B.M., Royal MS. 14 C.xiii, fo. 13ᵛ, in *Giraldi Cambrensis Opera* (Rolls Series), v, p. xxxix n., and in facsimile in *New Pal. Soc.*, i. 143. Books noted by J. Leland, *Collectanea*, iv. 27, and *De Scriptoribus Britannicis*, p. 247, and by J. Bale, *Index* (p. 578). Cardinal Adam de Eston (†1397) bequeathed six barrels of books: *cf.* Rymer, *Foedera*, viii. 501, A.D. 1407.

The pressmark which is written commonly at the head of the first leaf of text, often in the middle, is reproduced from Cambridge, U.L, Ii.1.32, Ii.2.19, Ii.3.11, Kk.4.12, Kk.4.13, and Bodleian, Douce 366, by S. Cockerell and M. R. James, *The Ormesby and Bromholm Psalters* (Roxburghe Club, 1926), pl. 34, and from Cambridge, U.L., Ii.1.21 and Ii.1.22, in *New Pal. Soc.*, i, pl. 147, no. 4 *b, c*) (4 *a* is a Durham, and not a Norwich mark).

Austin (U.S.A.), U.L., 2. Gesta Alexandri. s.xiv. [N.lxi]. ?
Avignon, Bibl. de la ville, 996. *e*B. de Gordonio, etc. s.xiv. [X.cliii].
Cambridge,
   U.L., Dd.13.5. *s*Jeremias, etc., glo. s.xiii.
      Ee.1.4. *e*Pseudo-Dionysius, etc. s.xiii.
         6.11. Légende de Ste Marguerite, etc. (in French). s.xiii. [Y.x].
      Ff.5.28. *g*J. Beleth, etc. s.xiii. [D.li].
         6.44. Pseudo-Augustinus, etc. s.xv. [M.lxviiii].
      Gg.1.33. *e*Nic. de Gorran. s.xiii/xiv. [S.lxxiii].
         6.3. Astronomica. s.xiv. [X.clxx].
      Ii.1.18. Bonaventura, etc. s.xiv. [C.liiii].
         1.20. Jac. de Losano. s.xiv. [N.xxxviii].
         1.21. Origenes. s.xii ex. [X.cxx].
         1.22. *g*H. de S. Victore, etc. s.xiii. [E.liiii].
         1.23.[1] N. de Lyra. s.xiv. ?
         1.30. *e*Januensis tabula. s.xv.
         1.31. *i*Bernardus, etc. s.xv. [Q.lxviii].
         1.32. *g*Flores Bernardi. s.xiv. [F.xxxi, H.x *canc*.].
         1.34. *c*Rolandinus. s.xiii/xiv. ?
         2.2. Job, etc., glo. s.xiii. [G.xxxv].
         2.6. Tobias, etc., glo. s.xiii. [G.xxxiiii].
         2.7. Constitutiones, etc. s.xiv. [Y.xxiiii].
         2.14. *g*Esaias, etc., glo. s.xiii. [D.(?).xliiii, F.xliiii].
         2.19. Sermones. s.xi ex.–xii in. [A.vii].
         2.20. Augustinus, etc. s.xiii/xiv–xiv ex. [G.lxvi].
         2.22. Gregorius. s.xiv. [M.viii].
         2.27. *i*Walt. Wiburn, etc. s.xiv. [Q.lxiiii].
         3.6. Paterius. s.xii. [O.xxxviii].
         3.7. Martinus Polonus, etc. s.xiv. [M.xxvi].
         3.10. *i*Joh. XXII. s.xiv. [C.vi].
         3.11. Gregorius. s.xiii. [A.ix].
         3.16. Aristoteles. s.xiv. [G.15].
         3.22. *i*Sermones, etc. s.xv in. [C.lxvii].
         3.24. *e*P. Lombardus. s.xii. [R.lxxii].
         3.29. *i*J. Waldeby. s.xiv. [C.lxx].
         3.31. *i*Ludolphus. s.xv. [M.lxvii].
         3.32. Pseudo-Dionysius. s.xii. [X.ccxxvii].
         4.2. *g*Bonaventura. s.xiii ex. [F.xli].

[1] Ii.1.23 belonged like some other Norwich MSS to R. Catton, first subdean of Norwich.

Cambridge (*contd*)

U.L., Ii.4.8. *m*W. Peraodus, etc. s.xiv.?
- 4.12. *g*G. Monemutensis, etc. s.xiv. [G.lvii, J.lvii].
- 4.15. *g*Liber eruditionis religiosorum. s.xiv. [F.xxxv].
- 4.18. *m*Tractatus de virtutibus. s.xiii. ?
- 4.34. Priscianus. s.xii. [L.iiii]. ?
- 4.35. *g*Hugo de Folieto. s.xiii/xiv. [F.xlvii].
- 4.37. *i*Egidius Romanus. s.xiv/xv. [Z.xxxv].
- 4.38. P. Lombardus. s.xiv. [C.lxxviii].

Kk.2.8.   Matheus et Marcus glo. s.xiii. [X.ciiii].
- 2.13. *g*Isidorus, etc. s.xiii/xiv. [H.xix].
- 2.15. *e*Augustinus. s.xiv. [M.v].
- 2.19. Jeronimus, etc. s.xiv. [Y.xxxv].
- 2.20. *e*Haymo, etc. s.xiv ex. [H.lxxiiii].
- 2.21. Bern. Cassinensis. s.xiv. [N.lvii].
- 3.25. *i*Gregorius. s.xiv. [P.lxxviii].
- 3.26. Flores Bernardi, etc. s.xiii/xiv. [R.lxv].
- 4.3. *e*Josue, etc., glo. s.xiii. [G.xxxiii].
- 4.5. Augustinus, etc. s.xiv. [M.xiii].
- 4.10. Genesis et Exodus glo. s.xiii/xiv. ?
- 4.11. *g*Augustinus. s.xiv. [H.ii].
- 4.12.[2] *g*Egidius Romanus, etc. s.xiv. [K.xxxvii].
- 4.13. *g*Omelie. s.xi–xii. [A.viii].
- 4.20. *g*Summa Raymundi, etc. s.xiii–xiv. [C.iii].

Ll.5.21. *i*Cyrillus episcopus, etc. s.xv. [V.lxxviii].

Mm.3.16. *i*Avicenna. s.xiii–xiv. [Z.xxxi].

Corpus Christi Coll., 34. Anselmus, etc. s.xiii. [Y.xlix].
- 36. Vitas patrum, etc. s.xv in. [M.lxvi].
- 74. *e*Berengarius Biterrensis. s.xiv in. [X.xxxiiii].
- 138. *c*Chronica. s.xiv. ?
- 148. Memoriale presbyterorum. s.xiv in. [P.viii]. ?
- 180. *i*Ric. Armachanus. s.xiv. [X.xlvi].
- 252. *i*Stimulus amoris, etc. s.xiv in.
- 264. *i*Beda, etc. s.xiv. [*Bozoun cat.* 30].
- 278. Psalter (Eng. and Fr.). s.xiv in. [N.xlvii]. ?
- 325. *g*V. Bellovacensis, etc. s.xiii/xiv. [I.lviii].
- 347. *e*Tabule. s.xiv in.
- 370. *c*Gesta Alexandri, etc. s.xiv. ?
- 407. *i*Secreta secretorum, etc. s.xiv. [S.xxiii; *Bozoun cat.* 26].
- 465. *lg*Consuetudinarium. s.xiii ex. [J.iii].
- 470. *l*Hildebertus, etc. s.xii ex.–xiii. [N.lxix].

Emmanuel Coll., 91. Rabanus Maurus. s.xii/xiii. [V.xlix]. ?
- 142. *ci*Concilium Basiliense. s.xv.

Gonv. and Caius Coll., 161. Passionarius Galieni, etc. s.xii–xiv. [N.xliiii].[3] ?

---

[2] The flyleaf of Kk.4.12 is bound with Ii.4.2.

[3] The pressmark was on the lower cover of the medieval binding according to the catalogue printed in 1907. MS. 161 was rebound in 1909.

Cambridge (*contd*)
St John's Coll., 218. David Kimchi (in Hebrew). s.xiii (?).
[X.clxxxi].
Trinity Coll., 883. *g*Rule for nuns, etc. (in French). s.xiii–xiv in.
[I.ix].
Durham, U.L., Cosin V.ii.12. *i*Dares Phrygius, etc. s.xv.
Edinburgh, N.L., 6125. *i*'Cronica de regibus et pontificibus Anglie', etc.
s.xiv. [D.lxviii].
London,
B.M., Add. 15759.[4] R. Higden. s.xiv ex. [O.lxxxviii].
30079. *g*Genealogia regum Angl. s.xiii. [C.xii].
Arundel 292. *c*Purgatorium Patricii, etc. s.xiii ex. [C.x].
Cotton Claudius E.viii. *cm*Flores historiarum, etc. s.xiv.
Nero C.v, fos 162–285. *gc*Barth. Cotton. s.xiii/xiv.
[L.ix].
Harley 3634.[5] Chronicon Anglie. s.xiv ex. [C.lxv].
3950. *lc*Psalterium, etc. s.xiv.
Royal 14 C.i, fos 20–137.[6] Barth. Cotton. s.xiii/xiv.
14 C.xiii. *i*Polychronicon, etc. s.xiv. [P.lxi; *Bozoun
cat.* 29, ?26].
App. 85, fos 11–14. *c*De episcopis Norwic. s.xv.
Lambeth Palace, 188, fos 175–79.[4] *c*Misc. historica. s.xiv–xv.
[O.xcviii].
368. *l*Psalterium. s.xiii ex.
Messrs Maggs. *e*Summa Raymundi. s.xiii/xiv. [F.lxxviii].
Manchester, J. Rylands, Lat. 185.[7] T. Wallensis (fragm.). s.xiv.
226.[7] *c*Injunctiones W. Bateman episcopi.
s.xiv.
R.32528 (pr. bk).[7] *i*A· de Rampegollis.
(Cologne, A.D. 1487).
R.32548 (pr. bk).[7] T. Anguilbertus. Louvain,
s.a.
New York, Columbia U.L., Plimpton 269. New Testament (in English).
s.xv. [B.lxx]. ?
Norwich, Castle Mus., 99.20. *i*Liber glosarum. s.xiii ex. [H.xlv].
Cathedral. *e*Joh. Boccatius, etc. s.xv. [F.lxxv].
*gc*Barth. Cotton. s.xiii ex. [C.xi, C.xix].
Oxford,
Bodleian, Auct. D.4.8. *g*Biblia. s.xiii. [E.xliii].
Bodl. 151. *e*W. de S. Amore. s.xiv. [X.xlvi].
454. De suppressione templariorum. s.xiv.
[L.xliii]. ?
787. *e*Bernardus de Parantinis. s.xv. [M.lxxvi].
Canonici misc. 110. *e*Anticlaudianus, etc. s.xv in.

[4] Lambeth Palace 188, fos 175–79, has been detached apparently from B.M., Add. 15759.
B.M., Harley 3634 and Bodleian, Bodley 316 (*see under* Pleshey) formed one volume.
[6] B.M., Cotton Nero C.v, fos 162–285, and Royal 14 C.i, fos 20–137, formed one volume.
[7] Rylands R.32528 and R.32548 were formerly together in one binding. MSS Lat. 185 and 226 were binding leaves in this volume.

Oxford (*contd*)
Bodleian, Douce 366. *e*Psalterium ('Ormesby Psalter'). s.xiii/xiv.
[A.i, [ ].xlii].
    Fairfax 20. *i*Flores historiarum. s.xiv. [*Bozoun cat.* 27].
    Lat. liturg. f.19. *l*Psalterium. s.xiv ex. [A.xxiii].
    Laud misc. 675. *c*Barth. Cotton, etc. s.xiii ex. ?
    Vet. E.1.f.134 (pr. bk). *i*J. Faber Stapulensis. Paris,
A.D. 1521.
Balliol Coll., 300B. *e*J. Sarisburiensis. s.xiv–xiv/xv. [X.clxxxxiii].
Magdalen Coll., lat. 53, pp. 169–98. *gc*Annales, etc. s.xiii. [I.xxiii].
    180. *g*V. Bellovacensis. s.xiv. [C.xli].
Wadham Coll., s.n. *l*Psalterium, etc. s.xiv. [A.x].
Paris, B.N., Lat. 4922. *e*R. Higden. s.xiv ex. [I.lxii].
Ushaw Coll., 7. *c*Psalterium, etc. s.xiii ex. [A.xlii].
Untraced: Quaritch, cat. 196 (1900), no. 3417. *e*Biblia. [E.xxiii].
Rejected: Cambridge, U.L., Dd.12.67, Ee.5.11, Gg.2.18, Gg.3.28, Gg.4.15,
Ii.4.5, Ii.4.14, Ii.4.22, Ii.4.31; Corpus Christi Coll., 17, 30, 39, 64, 283,
344, 460; Trinity Coll., 1442. Eton Coll., 45. London, B.M.,
Cotton Faust. B.vi, fos 2 ff. Norwich Cathedral (Psalter). Nor-
wich, Church of St Peter Mancroft (Epp. Pauli glo.). Oscott Coll.,
1 (Missal).

NORWICH. *Ben. priory of St Leonard; cell of Norwich.*

Book-lists in inventories of *c.* 1422 and 1452–53 among Norwich muniments
printed by W. T. Bensly in *Norfolk Archaeology*, xii (1895), 196, 208–10, 216,
224–26; pressmarks given (letter K and number).

Oxford, Bodleian, Jones 46. *l*Horae. s.xv in. ?

NORWICH. *Franciscan convent.*

Book noted by J. Leland, *Collectanea*, iv. 28. *Cf.* J. Bale, *Index*, p. 220.

London, B.M., Harley 1034. *e*Biblia. s.xiii. [Biblia. M.].

NORWICH. *Dominican convent.*

Books noted by J. Leland, *Collectanea*, iv. 28.

Cambridge, U.L., Inc. 755 (pr. bk). *i*Questiones Versoris, etc. Cologne,
s.a.
Oxford, Hertford Coll., a.1.27 (pr. bk). *i*P. Lombardus. Venice,
A.D. 1489.
London, Middle Temple (pr. bk). *i*H. Schedel. Nuremberg, A.D. 1493.

NORWICH. *Convent of Austin friars.*

London, B.M., Harley 2386, fos 1–74. *c*Misc. historica. s.xv. ?

NORWICH. *Carmelite convent.*

Books noted by J. Leland, *Collectanea*, iv. 28. *Cf.* also J. Leland, *De Scriptori-*
bus Britannicis, pp. 365, 442; J. Bale, *Scriptores* (edn 1557), pp. 73, 553, 593;
J. Bale, *Index*, p. 479.

Cambridge, U.L., Ff.6.28. *i*Historia sancti Cyrilli, etc. (manu J. Bale).
s.xvi in.
London, B.M., Harley 211. *i*Orationes, etc. (partly in English). s.xv in.

Oxford,
  Bodleian, Bodl. 73.   Collectanea Carmelitica (manu J. Bale).   s.xvi in.
  e Mus. 86.   Fasciculi zizaniorum.   s.xv in.   ?
  Seld. supra 41.   Collectanea Carmelitica (manu J. Bale).
  s.xvi in.
Rejected: Cambridge, Trinity Coll., 1445.

NORWICH. *Hospital of St Giles.*
London, B.M., Royal 9 E.ii. *e*Sextus liber decretalium. s.xiv in. ?

NOTLEY (Nutley, de parco de Crendon), Buckinghamshire. *Aug. abbey*
of B.V.M. and St John the Baptist.
London, Lambeth Palace, 344. *i*J. Lydgate (in English). s.xv. ?
Oxford, Bodleian, Douce 383, fos 41–46. *e*Kalendarium. s.xiv/xv.

NOTTINGHAM. *Franciscan convent.*
London, Dr Williams's Libr., Anc.1. *e*Biblia. s.xiii.

NUN COTON, Lincolnshire. *Priory of B.V.M., of Cist. nuns.*
London, B.M., Harley 2409. *i*Pistil of love, etc. (in English). s.xv.

NUNEATON, Warwickshire. *Priory of B.V.M., of nuns of Fontevrault.*
Cambridge, Fitzwilliam Mus., McClean 123. *i*R. Grosseteste (in French),
etc. s.xiii ex.
Douai, Bibl. mun., 887. *e*G. Cambrensis, etc. s.xiii–xiv. ?

NUTLEY. *See* **NOTLEY.**

ORMSBY, Lincolnshire. *Gilbertine priory of B.V.M.*
Note about books seen by J. Leland printed from London, B.M., Royal MS.
App. 69, fo. 5, in *Eng. Hist. Rev.*, liv. 92.

OSNEY (Oseneia), Oxfordshire. *Aug. abbey of B.V.M.*
Books noted by J. Leland, *Collectanea*, iv. 57.
Cambridge,
  U.L., Ii.6.1 *i*Gesta Romanorum, etc. A.D. 1449.
  Gonv. and Caius Coll., 297, fos 66–219. *e*Hugo de Vienna. s.xiii.
                                   481. *s*Hugo de Vienna. s.xiii–xiv. [M].
  Trinity Coll., 952. *e*A. Nequam. s.xii ex.
                 1209. *e*Isidorus. s.xii. [S].
London,
  B.M., Cotton Tib. A.ix, fos 2–102. *c*Chronicon, etc. s.xiii–xiv.
        Vesp. B.vi, fos 111–82. *c*W. de Novoburgo. s.xiii in.
        Vit. E.xv, fos 1–3. *c*Chronicon. s.xii ex.
        Tit. A.xiv. *c*Chronicon. s.xiii ex. ?
Oxford,
  Bodleian, Auct. F.6.4. *i*Boetius. s.xii–xiv. ?
  Bodl. 477. *ib*H. de S. Victore. s.xii. [D].
  Digby 23,i. *e*Plato. s.xii. [168, 114].
         168, fos 147–80. *c*Annales. s.xiv in. ?

Oxford (*contd*)
Bodleian, Rawl. C.273.   *i*W. Lyndwood.   s.xv.
　　　　　　 939.   *c*Ordinale.   s.xiii.
Magdalen Coll., lat. 121.   *e*Genesis glo.   s.xii ex.   [F].
　　　　　　 122.   Exodus, etc. glo.   s.xii/xiii.   [G].
　　　　　　 123.   Numeri, etc. glo.   s.xii/xiii.   [I].
　　　　　　 124.[8]   *e*Josue, etc. glo.   s.xiii in.   [D; 31].
　　　　　　 125.   Paralipom., etc. glo.   s.xiii in.   [E; 40].
　　　　　　 126.   Libri sapientiales, glo.   s.xiii in.   [M; 54].
　　　　　　 127.   Job glo.   s.xii/xiii.   [45].
　　　　　　 128.   P. Lombardus in Psalterium.   s.xii ex.   ?
　　　　　　 129.   Proph. majores et minores, glo.   s.xiii in.
　　　　　　　　　[H; 67].
　　　　　　 130.[8]   *e*Evangelia glo.   s.xiii in.   [R].
　　　　　　 131.   P. Lombardus in Epp. Pauli.   s.xiii in.   [X].
　　　　　　 132.   Actus Apost., etc., glo.   s.xiii in.   [T].
St John's Coll., 109.   *i*J. Felton.   s.xv.   [M].

OTHAM, Sussex.   *Prem. abbey of B.V.M. and St Lawrence.*   Removed
to **BAYHAM,** *q.v.*

OTTERY ST MARY, Devon.   *Collegiate church of B.V.M.*

List of 137 books bequeathed in 1445 by John Exceter, clericus, in Register
of E. Lacy, bishop of Exeter, iii, fo. 513[v] : the books, mostly of the donor's own
writing, were to be chained 'in libraria'.

Berlin, Staatsbibl., lat. qu. 515.   *e*Joh. de Muris, etc.   s.xiv.
Cambridge, Corpus Christi Coll., 93.   Ordinale, etc.   s.xv.   ?
Exeter, Cathedral, 3521.   *c*J. Seward, etc.   s.xv in.   ?
Rejected: London, Lambeth Palace, 104, 221, fos 1–157.

OWSTON, Leicestershire.   *Aug. abbey of St Andrew.*

London, B.M., Campbell Roll xxi.2.   *c*Prognostications (in French).
s.xiv.

OXFORD.   *Aug. priory of St Frideswide.*

Paris, B.N., Fr. 24766.   *i*Dialogues and life of St Gregory (in French).
s.xiii in.

OXFORD.   *Franciscan convent.*

For the form of pressmark and references by Thomas Gascoigne (†1458) to
books in the library, see Miss W. A. Pronger, 'Thomas Gascoigne', *Eng. Hist.
Rev.,* liii (1938), 622.   Notes on the library by J. Leland, *Collectanea,* iv. 60,
and *De Scriptoribus Britannicis,* pp. 268, 286.   For 'Excerpta e libro fratrum
minorum Oxon. qui intitulatur Speculum laicorum versibus' at Hamburg, see
Foedera, App. A. (1869), p. 110.   A. G. Little, *The Grey Friars in Oxford* (Oxf.
Hist. Soc., 1891), p. 59; R. W. Hunt in *Robert Grosseteste,* ed. D. Callus (1955),
pp. 130–38.

---

[8] Magdalen Coll., lat. 121–32 are a series of glossed books of the Bible
collected by one John Grene in s.xv and all, except perhaps 128, evidently in the
possession of one religious house at an earlier date.   Traces of the place-name
in 124 and 130 suggest Osney and this is confirmed by the letter-marks and
numbers.

Cambridge,
    Corpus Christi Coll., 315. *e*Ric. de S. Victore, etc. s.xiii.
    Gonv. and Caius Coll., 403. *e*New Testament (in Greek). s.xii–xiii.
Florence, Laurenziana, Plut. xvii sin. cod. x.[9] Theologica. A.D. 1393.
Hereford, Cathedral, P.i.9. *e*Bonaventura, etc. s.xv.
London,
    B.M., Harley 3249. *e*Epp. Pauli glo. s.xiii.
    Mr E. M. Dring, A.34. *e*W. Alvernus, etc. (1 fo.). s.xiv.
Manchester, Chetham, 6681.[1] *ic*De situ universorum. s.xiv. ?
Oxford,
    Bodleian, Bodl. 198. *m*Augustinus, etc. s.xiii.
                703. *m*W. Woodford, etc. s.xiv/xv. ?
          Digby 11, fos 1–91.[2] Suidas, etc. s.xiv in. ?
              90.[1] *e*IV principalia musice. s.xiv.
           93, fos 1–8. *i*Theorica planetarum, etc. s.xiv.
        Laud misc. 746.[3] *m*Rabanus Maurus. s.xiii. ?
    Corpus Christi Coll., 227.[4] Duns Scotus, etc. s.xv ex.
              228.[4] Questiones de anima. s.xv ex.
    Lincoln Coll., lat. 33. *e*Bernardus, etc. s.xiii–xv.
            54. R. Grosseteste, etc. s.xiii. ?
    Merton Coll., 158.[5] Raynaldus de Piperno. s.xiv in. ?
          166, 168–72. N. de Gorran (6 vols). s.xiv in. ?
    Trinity Coll., 17.[2] *em*Boethius, etc. s.xii–xiii. ?
Rejected: Cambridge, Corpus Christi Coll., 480; Gonv. and Caius Coll.,
    348. London, B.M., Cotton Vit. C.viii.

OXFORD. *Dominican convent.*

    Books noted by J. Leland, *Collectanea*, iv. 59; also by Thomas Gascoigne in
Oriel Coll., MS. 30, fo. 111 (*cf.* Miss W. A. Pronger in *Eng. Hist. Rev.*, liii (1938),
622, where the books are said, wrongly, to have belonged to the Oxford Franciscan convent).

Cambridge, Trinity Coll., 347. *i*W. Woodford, etc. A.D. 1430.
Oxford, Merton Coll., 132. *m*P. Pictaviensis, etc. s.xiii in.
        Mr N. R. Ker.[6] Biblia, etc. s.xiii–xiv. ?

OXFORD. *Carmelite convent.*

    Books noted by J. Leland, *Collectanea*, iv. 59.

Cambridge, U.L., Ff.4.31. *e*Jeronimus, etc. s.xv.
Copenhagen, Royal Libr., G.K.S. 1653 4⁰. *i*Gynecia Muscionis, etc.
    s.xi. ?
Longleat, Marquess of Bath, 16. *bc*Martyrologium. s.xv.
Rejected: Oxford, Bodleian, Bodl. 706.

    [9] Written by Fr. J. Fey de Florentia in the Oxford Convent.
    [1] Chetham, 6681, and Digby 90 are in the same hand.
    [2] *Cf.* H. H. E. Craster in *Bodleian Quarterly Record*, iii. 51.
    [3] *Cf.* R. W. Hunt in *Bodleian Library Record*, iv (1953), 243.
    [4] MSS 227, 228 were written in the Oxford convent, but it is probable that
MS. 227 at least was at the York convent (*q.v.*) at the Dissolution.
    [5] Written under the supervision of William of Nottingham, who is perhaps
identical with William of Nottingham, O.F.M., regent in theology at Oxford
c. 1312. The fly-leaf of MS. 158 is in MS. 208.
    [6] The calendar contains the dedication of the church as an addition (June 15).

OXFORD. *Convent of Austin friars.*

In London, B.M., Royal MS. 10 A.xv, fo. 2, Thomas Gascoigne lists some books 'inter fratres Augustinenses . . . in communi libraria Oxonie in fine dormitorii anno Cristi 1430' (*cf.* Miss W. A. Pronger, 'Thomas Gascoigne', *Eng. Hist. Rev.*, liii (1938), 621).

Cambridge, U.L., Ii.2.30. *e*Hostiensis, etc. s.xiv.
       3.14. *e*Constitutiones. s.xiv/xv.
Stonyhurst Coll., 1.22 (pr. bk). *i*Opera Origenis. Paris, s.a. ?

OXFORD. *University.*

K. Vickers, *Humphrey, Duke of Gloucester* (1907), pp. 426–38. H. H. E. C[raster], 'Duke Humphrey's Gifts', *Bodl. Quart. Rec.*, iii (1920), 45. N. R. Ker, 'Chaining, Labelling and Inventory Numbers of MSS belonging to the old University Library', *Bodl. Libr. Rec.*, v (1955), 176–80.

Lists of Humphrey, duke of Gloucester's gifts in 1439, 1441, 1444, from Register F of the Univ., in *Epistolae Acad.*, ed. H. Anstey (Oxf. Hist. Soc., 1898), i. 179, 204, 232, and *Mun. Acad.*, pp. 758–72; H. H. E. C[raster], 'Index to Duke Humphrey's Gifts', *Bodl. Quart. Rec.*, i (1915), 131. Books noted by J. Leland, *Collectanea*, iv. 58. *Cf.* also J. Leland, *De Scriptoribus Britannicis*, pp. 334, 336, 432, 437, 443, and J. Bale, *Index* (p. 578).

London,
    B.M., Cotton Nero E.v.   Concilium Constanciense. s.xv. [Liber 318; *Dk.H.1444*, 47].
        Harley 33. W. Ockham. s.xv in. [Q.15; Liber 207; *Dk.H.1444*, 16].
        Royal 5 F.ii. Athanasius. s.xv. [*Dk.H.1444*, 21].
Oxford,
    Bodleian, Arch. Seld. B.50. *e*Omnibonus Leonicenus. s.xv.
        Bodl. 362.[7] *b*J. Gadesden, etc. A.D. 1448–55.
        Digby 40.[7] Rogerus Hereford., etc. s.xii ex.–xiii in. [Liber 360].
        Duke Humphrey b.1. J. Capgrave. s.xv. [*Dk.H.1444*, 20].
           d.1. Plinius secundus. s.xv. [*Dk.H.1444*, 74].
        Hatton 36. N. de Clamengiis. s.xv. [*Dk.H.1444*, 93, *Leland*].
        Laud misc. 558.[7] *b*Medica quedam. A.D. 1459–60.
    Magdalen Coll., lat. 37, fos 61–278. Ptolomeus. s.xv. [*Dk.H.1444*, 107].
    Merton Coll., 268. *e*Medica. A.D. 1458–59. ?
    Oriel Coll., 32. J. Capgrave. s.xv. [Liber 7; *Dk.H.1444*, 19].
    St John's Coll., 172. *e*R. de Bury, etc. s.xv.
Paris, B.N., Lat. 7805. Plinius secundus. s.xv. [Liber 163 in ordine; *Dk.H.1444*, 73].
        8537. Cicero. s.xv. [*Dk.H.1439*, 115].
Rejected: Oxford, Bodleian, Auct. F.5.27, Bodl. 215.

OXFORD. *All Souls College* (Collegium animarum omnium fidelium).

Catalogue of s.xv printed from All Souls Coll., Archives Misc. 210 by E. F. Jacob, 'Two Lives of Archbishop Chichele', *Bull. John Rylands Libr.*, xvi (1932), 469–81; second folios given. Another similar list is in Archives Misc. 209. List of 27 books given by King Henry VI in P.R.O. [Privy Seal Office, Warrants]

---

[7] *Cf. Bodl. Libr. Rec.*, v (1955), 176.

P.S.O. 1/8/404, printed from a modern transcript in B.M., Add. MS. 4608 by Nicolas, *Proceedings and Ordinances of the Privy Council* (1834–37), v. 117–19; second folios given. Five catalogues of s.xv ex. and s.xvi and lists of books given by Archbishop Warham, of law books given by Richard Andrew, of books 'inter socios concurrentes', etc., are in a damaged 'Vellum Inventory' among the archives. Books noted by J. Bale, *Index* (p. 578).

MSS from the medieval library now in the college library are catalogued by H. O. Coxe, *Cat. MSS Coll. Oxon.* (1852), i. The common form of *ex libris* inscription is 'Liber collegii animarum omnium fidelium defunctorum in Oxonia', written usually at the foot of the second leaf of text.

Antwerp, Plantin-Moretus, 12. *e*Innocentius IV. s.xiii ex.

        26. *e*Augustinus. s.xii. [*Cat.*, p. 478, line 13].

        30. *e*Gratianus. s.xiii. [*Cat.*, p. 480, line 22].

        107. *e*Bernardus, etc. s.xiii.

        110. *e*J. de Deo. s.xiii/xiv.

        144. *e*Decreta, etc. s.xii in.

Exeter, Cathedral, 3506. *b*J. Gadesden. s.xiv ex. [*Inv.*, fo. 25].

Glasgow, U.L., Bi.4.g.20 (pr. bk). *e*A. de Rampegollis, etc. Paris, A.D. 1513, etc. [*Warham* 64].

London, B.M., Sloane 280. *e*J. Gadesden. s.xv.

  The Robinson Trust (Phillipps 3119, fos 176–205). T. Rudborne. s.xiv/xv. [*Cf.* Bale, *Index*, p. 452].

Oxford, Bodleian, Auct. 1.Q.3.1 (pr. bk). *e*F. Savonensis. (Rome, A.D. 1473).

    Bodl. 741–42.[8] *e*Ludolphus, etc. A.D. 1444.

    Digby 44. *e*Questiones in physica. s.xv. [*Inv.*, fos 2ᵛ, 24].

    Rawl. G.47. *e*Lactantius, etc. A.D. 1441. [*Inv.*, fos 23ᵛ, 27ᵛ].

  Pembr. Coll., 2. *e*J. de Mirfeld, etc. s.xv.

  Trinity Coll., 23. *e*Evangeliarium. s.xv.

Tokyo, U.L., A.100.1300. *e*Formulare. s.xv.

Winchester, Coll., 60A.[9] R. Flaviacensis (2 fos). s.xiii in.

OXFORD. *Balliol College* (Domus de Balliolo).

  Books noted by J. Leland, *Collectanea*, iv. 60 and by J. Bale, *Index* (p. 578). MSS from the medieval library now in the college are catalogued by H. O. Coxe, *Cat. MSS Coll. Oxon.*, i, and by R. A. B. Mynors, *Catalogue of the MSS of Balliol College, Oxford*, 1963 (see there pp. 375–83 for the 20 MSS listed below).

Antwerp, Plantin-Moretus, 52. *e*Gregorius. s.xii.

        57. *e*Sermones. s.xv in.

        77.[1] *e*Ric. de S. Victore, etc. s.xiii.

        106. *e*Gilb. de Tornaco. s.xiii.

        131. *e*Augustinus, etc. s.xiv.

        341, fos 8–11.[1] Fragm. questionum. s.xiii/xiv.

Brussels, Bibl. royale, 1557. *e*Baldewinus Cant. A.D. 1453. [*Leland*].

Cambridge, U.L., Dd.13.2. *e*Cicero. A.D. 1444.

---

[8] A gift by reversion which probably did not take effect.

[9] Winchester Coll. 60A is a detached fragment of All Souls Coll. 13: *cf.* N. R. Ker, *Pastedowns in Oxford bindings*, pp. xi, 109.

[1] Plantin-Moretus 341, fos 8–11, formed flyleaves of Plantin-Moretus 77.

Cambridge (*contd*)
       U.L., Ff.4.11. *e*Steph. Langton. s.xiii in.
       Ii.2.10. *e*Aristoteles. s.xiv.
       Kk.4.2. *i*Thucydides. s.xv.
Douai, Bibl. mun., 750. *e*Priscianus. s.xii.
London, B.M., Royal 7 F.xii. *e*W. Ockham. s.xv.
       Lambeth Palace, 759. *e*Sallustius. s.xv.
Oxford,
  Bodleian, Auct. Q.2.2.29 (pr. bk). *e*Augustinus. s.l. et a.
      Bodl. 252. *e*Gregorius, etc. s.xii/xiii.
          312, fos 117–85. R. Grosseteste. s.xv. [*Leland*]. ?
          753. Gregorius, etc. s.xv.
      Digby 29. *e*Misc. medica, etc. s.xv in.
      Laud misc. 209. *e*Berengaudus. s.xii.
      Savile 106, fos 5–8. *s*M. Vegius (4 fos). s.xv. [*Leland*]. ?
      A.2.8 Th. Seld. (pr. bk). *e*Augustinus. Louvain, A.D. 1488.

OXFORD. *Brasenose College* (Aula regia et collegium de Brasenose).

Books noted by J. Bale, *Index* (p. 578).

MSS from the early sixteenth-century library now in the college library are catalogued by H. O. Coxe, *Cat. MSS Coll. Oxon.*, ii.

London, B.M., Royal 7 E.ii. *e*J. Waldby, etc. s.xiv ex.
St Albans, School, Y.4 (pr. bk). *e*J. Duns Scotus. Venice, A.D. 1481.

OXFORD. *Canterbury College; cell of Christ Church, Canterbury.*

List of 292 books at Canterbury College in 1524 printed from a roll among the Muniments of Canterbury Cathedral by M. R. James, *Ancient Libraries of Canterbury and Dover* (1903), pp. 165–72; second folios given. Other lists of 1443, 1459, 1501 (two), 1510 and 1534 at Canterbury are printed by W. A. Pantin, *Canterbury College, Oxford* (Oxf. Hist. Soc., N.S., vi, 1947). *Cf.* J. Leland, *De Scriptoribus Britannicis*, pp. 168, 249.

Cambridge, Trinity Coll., 61. Mirror of life of Christ (in English), etc. s.xiv–xv. ?
London, B.M., Add. 22572. *e*J. Felton. s.xv. [*List 1501*, 50; etc.].
Oxford,
  Bodleian, Laud misc. 412. R. Tuitiensis. s.xii. [*List 1501*, 165; etc.].
      Selden supra 65. Artes dictandi. s.xv in. [*List 1501*, 311].

OXFORD. *Corpus Christi College.*

Books noted by J. Bale, *Index* (p. 578).
MSS from the early sixteenth-century library now in the college library are catalogued by H. O. Coxe, *Cat. MSS Coll. Oxon.*, ii.

London, B.M., IA.17393 (pr. bk). *e*Guido, *Accessus*. Rome, A.D. 1483.

OXFORD. *Durham College; cell of Durham cathedral priory.*

Lists of books sent there from Durham in 1315, *c.* 1400, and in 1409, printed from rolls in the Durham Cathedral Muniments by H. E. D. Blakiston, *Oxf. Hist. Soc. Collectanea*, iii (1896), 36–41; second folios given in the second and third lists, which are printed also in *Cat. Vet. Eccl. Dunelm.*, pp. 39–41. Another list, *c.*1390–1400, is printed by W. A. Pantin in H. E. Salter, *Oxford Formularies* (Oxford Hist. Soc., N.S., iv, 1942), pp. 241–44.

Cambridge, King's Coll., 22.² H. de S. Victore. s.xii. *Cat. 1409*, F].
London, B.M., Harley 1924.³ *c*Beda. s.xii. [D; ? *Cat. 1315*, 22]. ?
Oxford,
    Bodleian, Digby 41, fos 91, 91*, 92, 101.³ *c*Reliquie Dunelm., etc.
                                               s.xii. ?
            Laud lat. 12.² *e*Biblia. s.xiii. [B *corr. from* C].
Rejected: Oxford, Bodleian, Aubrey 31.

OXFORD. *Exeter College.*

    Books noted by J. Bale, *Index* (p. 578).
    MSS from the medieval library now in the college library are catalogued by
H. O. Coxe, *Cat. MSS Coll. Oxon*, i.
Douai, Bibl. mun., 860. *e*Vite S. Thome Cant. s.xii ex.
Oxford,
    Bodleian, Auct. D.4.9. *m*Biblia. s.xiii.
            Bodl. 42. *e*Misc. theologica. s.xiv–xv.
    St John's Coll., 77. *e*Augustinus, etc. s.xv.

OXFORD. *Gloucester College; cell of Gloucester.*

London, B.M., Royal 8 G.x.⁴ *e*T. Netter. s.xv.
Oxford,
    Bodleian, Auct. F.inf.l.l. *e*Dionysius de Burgo. s.xv.
    Worcester Coll., LRA 6.⁴ *e*T. Netter, etc. s.xv.
Rejected: Oxford, Bodleian, Bodl. 692.

OXFORD. *Lincoln College.*

    R. Weiss, 'The earliest Catalogues of the Library of Lincoln College', *Bodl.
Quart. Rec.*, viii (1937), 343–59, prints a cat. of 1474 and a list of books 'in
communi eleccione sociorum' in 1476, from the Registrum vetus; second folios
given. Books noted by J. Bale, *Index* (p. 578).
    MSS from the medieval library now in the college library are catalogued by
H. O. Coxe, *Cat. MSS Coll. Oxon.*, ii.
Cambridge, Trinity Coll., 303. *e*R. Holcot. s.xv. [*Cat*. 26].
London, B.M., Cotton Otho A.xiv. *m*Chronicon Ivonis, etc. s.xii. [*Cf.
cat*. 52].
            Royal 10 A.xv. *e*Marsilius de Padua. s.xv. [*Cat*. 51].
Oxford,
    Bodleian, Bodl. 198. *e*Augustinus, etc. s.xiii.
            Rawl. G.14. *e*Biblia. s.xiii. [*Cat*. 1].

OXFORD. *St Mary Magdalen College.*

    Books noted by J. Leland, *De Scriptoribus Britannicis*, p. 236, and by J. Bale,
Index (p. 578).
    MSS from the medieval library now in the college library are catalogued by
H. O. Coxe, *Cat. MSS Coll. Oxon.*, ii.
London, B.M., Cotton Cleop. C.ix, fos 1–62.⁵ Gesta Ricardi I. s.xiv.
                                  [*Bale, Index*, p. 468].
            Royal 6 E.iii. *e*Misc. theologica. s.xv ex.

  ² King's Coll. 22 and Laud lat. 12 were earlier at Durham, *q.v.*
  ³ Bodleian, Digby 41 (fos 91, 91*, 92, 101) was part of B.M., Harley 1924.
The MS. was used by T. Gascoigne, perhaps at Oxford.
  ⁴ Worcester Coll., LRA 6 is the second part of B.M., Royal 8 G.x and was,
until recently, Merton College, MS. 318.
  ⁵ Cotton Cleopatra C.ix, fos 1–62, is no. 139 in the list of Magdalen College
manuscripts printed by T. James, *Écloga*, 1600.

Oxford, Bodleian, H.3.3–7 Th. (pr. bks). *e*Opera Hieronymi. Basel, A.D. 1516.

OXFORD. *Merton College* (Domus scolarium de Mertone).

F. M. Powicke, *The Medieval Books of Merton College* (Oxford, 1931). P. S. Allen, 'Early Documents connected with the Library of Merton College, Oxford', *The Library*, Fourth Series, iv. (1924), 249–76. Powicke prints catalogues of philosophical (s.xiv in.) and theological (*c*.1360) books, *electiones* of books (s.xiv–xvi), etc.; second folios given. A contemporary list of 100 books given to the college by William Rede († 1385) was acquired by Merton College in 1941; second folios given. Books noted by J. Leland, *Collectanea*, iv. 59, and *De Scriptoribus Britannicis*, pp. 54, 261, and by J. Bale, *Index* (p. 578). The usual form of *ex libris* inscription is 'Liber domus scolarium de Merton' in Oxonia'.

MSS from the medieval library now in the college library are catalogued by H. O. Coxe, *Cat. MSS Coll. Oxon.*, i, and see Powicke, *op. cit.*

Dublin, Trinity Coll., 517, fos 1–49. *e*Prosper, etc. s.xiii.
London,
    B.M., Add. 38666, fo. 178.[6] *e* . s.xv.
        Harl. 3753. *e*Codex Justiniani. s.xiii/xiv.
        Royal 12 B.iii. *e*Medica. s.xiv.
            12 E.xxv. *e*Augustinus, etc. s.xiii/xiv. [*Cat. T*.205].
    Westminster Abbey, 36, nos 4, 5.[7] Alhasen (4 fos). s.xiv.
Oxford,
    Bodleian, Bodl.   4. Distinctiones theologie. s.xiv. [*Reg. Coll.*, sub anno 1496].
              50. *e*Sermones, etc. s.xiv.
              52. *e*Collect. J. Maynsforth. s.xv in.
           365, fos 1–92. Augustinus, etc. s.xiii. [*Cat. T*.184].
          688. *e*Gregorius, etc. s.xv in. [li. 7].
          689. *e*Pseudo-Ambrosius. s.xii. [B lib. 14].
          696. *e*Gregorius. s.xii–xv.
          700. *e*Ambrosius. s.xiii.
          751. *e*Ambrosius. s.xii.
          752. *e*Ambrosius. s.xii ex. [*Cat. T*.228].
          757. *e*Ambrosius, etc. s.xv.
        Digby 10. *c*Ailredus. s.xii.
           61, fos 1–20.[8] *e*Gernardus. s.xii/xiii.
           67, fos 85–116. *e*Varia philosophica. s.xiv. [*Cat. D*.28].
           77, fos 150–197.[9] J. Chylmark, etc. s.xv in. [*Bale, Index*, p. 192].
          155. *e*Questiones Parisiensis. s.xiv.
          176, fos 1–86. *e*Varia astronomica. s.xiv.
          190, fos 90–127.[1] Ric. de Wallingford, etc. s.xiii–xiv.
          191, fos 1–78.[1] *e*Euclides, etc. s.xiii–xiv.

---

[6] B.M., Add. 38666, fo. 178, is a flyleaf bound up with unrelated MSS.
[7] Westminster Abbey 36 (nos 4, 5), Bodleian 4° C.95, and the fragments at Corpus Christi Coll. are leaves from the same MS. used in binding: *cf.* N. R. Ker, *Pastedowns in Oxford Bindings*, 1954, p. xi. Four more leaves are at Merton Coll.
[8] Digby 61, fos 1–20, contained a Merton *ex libris*, now missing, but recorded by Langbaine in Bodleian MS. Wood F.26, p. 36.
[9] Digby 77, fos 150–97, was formerly part of Merton Coll. 251.
[1] Digby 190, fos 90–127, was formerly part of Digby 191, fos 1–78.

Oxford (*contd*)
Bodleian, Digby 212. Rob. de Leicestria, etc. s.xiv. [*Cf. Bale, Index*, p. 384].
      216. *e*Questiones theologice.
      218, fos 70–91. Ailredus, etc. s.xiv. [*Cf. Bale, Index*, p. 13]. ?
      e Mus. 19. *e*Cyrurgia Rogeri, etc. s.xiv. [*Rede* 26].
      Savile 19. *e*Misc. geometrica. s.xiii ex. [*Cat. D*.22].
      4° C.95 Art.[7] Alhasen (2 fos). s.xiv.
Ball. Coll., 211. *e*Godefridus de Fontibus. s.xiv. [*Cat. E*.120].
Corpus Christi Coll., 489, no. 86; 490, nos 7, 8, 33, 115 (7 fos).[7]
      *e*Alhasen. s.xiv. [*Cat. P*.49].
Lincoln Coll., lat. 62. *e*'Exposicio super prologum scripture sacre cum variis sermonibus'. s.xv.
Rejected: Cambridge, Pembroke Coll., 256.

OXFORD. *New College* (Collegium beate Marie Winton' in Oxonia).

List of books given by Wm of Wykeham and of other gifts of s.xiv–xvi contained in the Registrum primum of the college, printed, incompletely, in *Oxf. Hist. Soc. Collectanea*, iii. 223–44; second folios given. For books bequeathed by Nicholas de Wykeham to John Wykeham, with reversion to New College, A.D. 1407, see A. B. Emden, *B.R.U.O.*, p. 2111. Books noted by J. Leland, *Collectanea*, iv. 66, and by J. Bale, *Index* (p. 578).

MSS from the medieval library now in the college library are catalogued by H. O. Coxe, *Cat. MSS Coll. Oxon.*, i.

Oxford,
Bodleian, Auct. D.3.7. *c*Biblia. s.xiii ex. ?
      F.5.29. *e*Varia astronomica. s.xiii–xiv.
      Bodl. 238. Ambrosius, etc. s.xiv. [*Cat.*, p. 228].
      310, fos 146–300. *e*'Memoriale milicie'. s.xiv.
      809. *e*P. Blesensis, etc. s.xiv.
      Digby 31. *c*Jacobus de Cressolis. s.xv. ?
Exeter Coll., 29. *e*Innocentius IV. s.xiv.
Winchester Coll., 12. *e*P. de Crescentiis. s.xv.

OXFORD. *Oriel College* (Domus beate Marie seu collegium regale Oxon' vocat' Oryall').

A 'Catalogue of Oriel College Library'(A.D. 1375), printed from a roll belonging to the college by C. L. Shadwell in *Oxf. Hist. Soc. Collectanea*, i (1885), 66–70; second folios given. Part of the original was destroyed by fire in 1954. Books noted by J. Bale, *Index* (p. 578).

MSS from the medieval library now in the college library are catalogued by H. O. Coxe, *Cat. MSS Coll. Oxon.*, i.

Bern, Stadtbibl., 69. *e*Martinus Polonus, etc. s.xiv.
London,
B.M., Sloane 3884, fo. 70.[2] *e*Duns Scotus. s.xv. [*Cf. cat.*, p. 69].
Lambeth Palace, 1106, fos 111–20. Annales. s.xiii.
Sion Coll., Arc.L.40.2/L.21. *e*Suetonius, etc. s.xii.

[7] See p. 147, n. 7.
[2] Sloane 3884, fo. 70, is a leaf with the *explicit* of Duns Scotus on the first book of the Sentences and the Oriel inscription, used apparently as a binding leaf.

Oxford,
    Bodleian, Auct. F.5.28, fos ii–xlii, 1–144, 226–27. *e*Misc. geometrica,
                                   etc. s.xiii. [*Cat*., p. 67].
                 fos 145–225. *c*Misc. theologica, etc. s.xiii.
      Bodl. 637.[3] *e*Processionale. s.xv. ?
      Digby 37, fos 98–141. Cicero, etc. s.xii–xiii.
            161, fos 24–93.[4] P. Aponensis, etc. s.xiv/xv.
            190, fos 128–210.[5] Tract. de arithmetica, etc. s.xiv.
            191, fos 79–167.[5] *e*Astronomia Arzachelis, etc. s.xiv.
                         [*Cat*., p. 68].
      e Mus. 121. W. de Conchis. s.xiii. [*Cat*., p. 70]. ?
    Lincoln Coll., lat. 33. *e*Bernardus, etc. s.xiii–xv.
    St John's Coll., 112, fos 115–210. Itinerarium Petri. s.xii/xiii. [*Cat*.,
                         p. 69].

OXFORD, *Queen's College.*

    A list of twenty-four books returned to the college in 1378 printed in *Stonor
Letters and Papers*, i (Camden Third Series, xxix, 1919), 13, from P.R.O., Ancient
Deeds C.1782, and by J. R. Magrath, *The Queen's College*, i. 126, from the copy
in the college archives; second folios given. Books noted by J. Bale, *Index*
(p. 578).

London, B.M., Harley 1751. R. Higden. s.xiv. [*Cf. Bale, Index*,
                        p. 399]. ?
      Royal 8 A.xiii. *e*W. de Conchis, etc. s.xv.
    The Robinson Trust (Phillipps 3119, fos 55–121).[6] T. de
      Eccleston, etc. s.xiii ex.–xiv ex. [*Cf. Bale, Index*,
      p. 238, etc.] ?

OXFORD. *St Edmund Hall.*

Oxford, Bodleian, Rawl. C.900.[7] *e*Sermones. s.xiv. ?

OXFORD. *Staple Hall.*

Oxford, Bodleian, Ashmole 748. *e*Biblia. s.xiv.

OXFORD. *University College* (Aula magna universitatis).

    List of 18 books given by William Asplyon in 1473 contained in W. Smith's
MS. Collections, vol. ii, p. 223 (copy of *c*.1700) among the college archives,
printed by R. W. Hunt in *Bodl. Libr. Rec.*, iii (1950), 30; second folios given:
the original, in the archives, Pyx 11.3.a, is damaged. Books noted by J. Bale,
Index (p. 578).
    MSS from the medieval library now in the college library are catalogued by
H. O. Coxe, *Cat. MSS Coll. Oxon.*, i.

Antwerp, Plantin-Moretus, 41. *e*H. de S. Victore, etc. s.xiii–xiv.

PAISLEY (Pasletum), Renfrewshire. *Cluniac priory and from 1219 abbey
    of St James and St Mirren.*
    For a printed book see Durkan and Ross, p. 121.

---

    [3] The inscription of ownership is post-medieval.
    [4] Digby 161, fos 24–93, formed one volume with Oriel Coll. 28.
    [5] Digby 190, fos 128–210, and Digby 191, fos 79–167, formed one volume.
    [6] For Phillipps 3119, fos 55–121, see N. R. Ker in *Bodl. Libr. Rec.*, vi (1959),
491.
    [7] The inscription of ownership and gift from King Henry VIII, A.D. 1422 [*sic*],
is seventeenth century.

London, B.M., Royal 13 E.x. *e*Scotichronicon, etc. (Black book of Paisley). s.xv.

PENWORTHAM, Lancashire. *Ben. priory of B.V.M.; cell of Evesham. See* Appendix, **PENWORTHAM** Church.

PERSHORE, Worcestershire. *Ben. abbey of St Edburga* (*originally of B.V.M., St Peter, and St Paul*).

Books noted by J. Leland, *Collectanea*, iv. 160.

Cambridge, Emmanuel Coll., 38. *ic*Isidorus. s.xii.
London, B.M., Royal 2 D.ix. *i*Misc. theologica, etc. s.xiii in.
     4 A.viii. *e*P. Lombardus, etc. s.xiii.
     8 D.iv. *e*Misc. theologica. s.xiii–xiv.
     10 A.iv. *e*P. Pictaviensis, etc. s.xiii.
     11 B.iv. *e*P. Pictaviensis. s.xiii.
   Lambeth Palace, 761. *i*Ailredus. s.xiii. ?
Oxford, Bodleian, Bodl. 209. *ce*Zach. Chrysopolitanus. s.xiii.
    Laud. misc. 114. *sc*Augustinus, etc. s.xii.
    Rawl. C.81. *e*Medical tracts (in English). s.xv. ?
  Jesus Coll., 4. *i*Anselmus, etc. s.xii.
     47. *e*Beda, etc. s.xii.
  St John's Coll., 96. *ic*Vite sanctorum. s.xii.
Rejected: Oxford, Bodleian, Barlow 3, Laud misc. 664.

PERTH. *Charterhouse Vallis Virtutis.*

For 5 printed books see Durkan and Ross, pp. 97, 166.
Edinburgh, N.L., Adv. 25.5.10. *e*Regiam majestatem, etc. s.xv. [H.vj].

PERTH. *Franciscan convent.*

For two printed books see Durkan and Ross, pp. 108, 166.
Edinburgh, N.L., Adv. 18.2.6.[8] Gregorius. s.xv.
Wolfenbüttel, Ducal Libr., Helmst. 499[9]. *e*Claudianus. s.xiii.

PERTH. *Dominican convent.*

For two printed books see Durkan and Ross, pp. 79, 126.

PETERBOROUGH (Burgus S. Petri), Northamptonshire. *Ben. abbey of St Peter, St Paul, and St Andrew.*

M. R. James, 'Lists of MSS formerly in Peterborough Abbey Library', *Bibliog. Soc. Trans., Supplement*, v (1926) includes:
Gifts of Bishop Æthelwold of Winchester, printed from Soc. Antiq. MS. 60 (also printed in Dugdale, *Monasticon*, i. 382); gifts of abbots, s.xii–xiv, from B.M., Add. MS. 39758 (also printed by S. Gunton, *History of Church of Peterborough* (London, 1686), 25 ff., and by J. Sparke, *Hist. Angl. Scriptores* (London, 1723), ii. 98 ff.), here referred to as *Abbots*; catalogue, s.xii in., from Bodleian, MS. Bodl. 163, fo. 251 (also printed in *Neues Archiv*, ii (1877), 433; *Serapeum*, xxxviii (1877), 120; and Becker, *Catalogi*, p. 216); catalogue ('matricularium', with pressmarks), s.xiv ex., from MS. in Peterborough Cathedral Library (also printed by Gunton, *op. cit.*, p. 173; and in *Serapeum*, xii (1851), Intelligenz Blatt,

---

[8] Lent to the Franciscans by the cathedral church of Dunkeld in 1483.
[9] Lent to the Franciscans by the abbey of St Thomas the martyr, Arbroath.

nos 18–24; xiii (1852), Intelligenz Blatt, nos 1–5) here referred to as *Cat*. Books noted by J. Leland (also printed in his *Collectanea*, iv. 31).

Brussels, Bibl. royale, 593. *l*Psalterium. s.xiii ex.
Cambridge,
    U.L., Inc. 1344 (pr. bk). *i*Paulus scriptor. Tübingen, A.D. 1498.
    Corpus Christi Coll., 53. *g*Psalterium, etc. s.xiv.
                92. *e*Florentius Wigorn. s.xii ex.–xiv.
                134. *bs*Berengaudus. s.xii. ?
                160. *e*Beda. s.xi.
                459. Misc. theol. s.xiii. [*Cat*. X.11].
    Fitzwilliam Mus., 12. *l*Psalterium, etc. s.xiv. ?
    Gonv. and Caius Coll., 437. *i*J. Wallensis, etc. s.xiv in. [*Cat*. Y.xv].
                    454. *g*W. Peraldus. s.xiii ex. [*Abbots* 129].
    Magdalene Coll., 10. *e*Antiphonale. s.xiv in.–xv ex.
    St John's Coll., 81. *g*Psalterium. s.xiii. [*Abbots* 58].
Edinburgh, N.L., Adv. 18.5.16. *i*Macer, etc. s.xii. ?
Eton Coll., 21. Jeronimus. s.xii. [*Cf. cat.* C]. ?
Helmingham Hall, Lord Tollemache, 6. Rabanus Maurus, etc. s.xii.
    [*Cat*. P.ii].
London,
    B.M., Add. 39758. *i*Chronicon, etc. s.xiv in.
           47170. *g*'Cronica rotulata' (in Lat. and Fr.). s.xiii ex.
           Cotton Julius A.xi, fos 3–112. *g*Gesta Henrici II, etc. s.xii/xiii.
                            [*Abbots* 40].
              Tib. C.i, fos 2–42.[1] Aratus, etc. s.xii in. [*Cf. cat.* A.ii].
              Claudius A.v, fos 2–45. *e*Chronicon. s.xiv ex.
              [Otho A.xvii.[2] *c*Chronica, etc. (part in French)]. [*Leland*].
           Harley 3097. Jeronimus, etc. s.xii in. [*Cat*. I].
              3667.[1] *c*Annales, etc. s.xii in.
    Lambeth Palace, 5. *e*Concordancie sententiales, etc. s.xiv in.
                9. *c*N. de Lyra. s.xiv/xv.
              191. Beda, etc. s.xii. [*Cat*. B.ii].
              198, 198b. *l*Consuetudinarium. s.xiv.
              202. Isidorus, etc. s.xii ex. [*Cat*. O; ? *Leland*]. ?
              335, fos 229–76.[3] Epp. can. glo. s.xiii in. ?
              360, fos 119–58.[3] *c*Biblia versificata. s.xv ex. ?
              473. *c*W. Peraldus. s.xiii ex.
    Middle Temple (pr. bk). *i*R. Holcot. s.l. et a.
    Soc. of Antiquaries, 59. *i*Psalterium. s.xiii in. [*Abbots* 60].
                    60. *c*Chronicon abbatie; Cartularium. s.xii–xiii.
Oxford,
    Bodleian, Barlow 22. *ic*Psalterium. s.xiv.
           Bodl. 96. *i*Augustinus, etc. s.xiv.
              163. *ic*Beda, etc. s.xi. [*Cf. cat.* K.iii]. .
           Gough liturg. 17. *i*Diurnale. s.xiv/xv.
           Laud. misc. 636. *c*Chronicle (in English; 'Peterborough
                    Chronicle'). s.xii in.

[1] Cotton Tib. C.i, fos 2–42, and Harley 3667 are two fragments of a larger MS.
[2] Cotton Otho A.xvii was burnt in 1731.
[3] Lambeth Palace 335, fos 229–76, and Lambeth Palace 360, fos 119–58, appear to have formed one volume.

Peterborough,
Cathedral, 1. cChronica abbatie, etc. ('Liber R. de Swafham').
s.xiii.
3. Pharetra, etc. s.xiv in. [*Cf. cat.* F.ix]. ?
15. cCatalogus librorum, etc. s.xv.
Rejected: Cambridge, St John's Coll., 256. Copenhagen, Royal Libr., Ny
Kgl. Saml. 1854. London, Lambeth Palace, 96, fos 1–112; 182, fos
185–206; 367. Oxford, Bodleian, Douce 296, Laud misc. 247.

PILTON, Devon. *Ben. priory of B.V.M.; cell of Malmesbury.*

Cambridge, Trinity Coll., 727. W. Malmesburiensis. s.xii. ?
Oxford, Bodleian, Rawl. liturg. g.12. *l*Horae B.V.M. *c.* A.D. 1521. ?

PIPEWELL (Sancte Marie de Divisis), Northamptonshire. *Cist. abbey of
B.V.M.*

Cambridge, Corpus Christi Coll., 269. *e*Ivo Carnotensis. s.xii.
Deene Park, Trustees of the late Mr G. Brudenell, XVIII.B.6. *e*Sermones.
s.xii ex.
Dublin, Chester Beatty Libr., W.34. *e*Biblia. s.xiii.
London, B.M., Harley 5765. *e*Psalterium. s.xiii.
Oxford,
Bodleian, Bodl. rolls 22. Hymns (in English). s.xv. ?
Douce HH.252 (pr. bk). *i*Vulgaria W. Horman. London,
A.D. 1519.
Rawl. A.388. *e*H. de S. Victore, etc. s.xiii.
Peterborough, Cathedral, D.8.17 (pr. bk). *e*Speculum spiritualium.
Paris, A.D. 1510.
Untraced: Lt-Col. W. E. Moss sale (Sotheby, 8 March 1937), lot 1171 to
Marks. *i*Psalterium. s.xiii.

PITTENWEEM, Fife. *Aug. priory of B.V.M.*

For a printed book see Durkan and Ross, p. 103.

PLESHEY, Essex. *College of Holy Trinity.*

Book-list in inventory, A.D. 1527, printed from MS. in the muniment room of
King's College, Cambridge, by W. H. St J. Hope in *St Paul's Ecclesiological
Soc. Trans.,* viii (1917–20), 164, 165.
Cambridge, St John's Coll., 27. *e*Beda. s.xiv. [*Cat.* 14].
Oxford, Bodleian, Bodl. 316. *e*Polychronicon, etc. s.xiv ex. [*Cat.* 22].

PLUSCARDEN, Moray. *Ben. priory of St Andrew; cell of Dunfermline,
1454; earlier Valliscaulian.*

For a printed book see Durkan and Ross, p. 140.

PLYMPTON, Devon. *Aug. priory of St Peter.*

Robert, archdeacon of Totnes, s.xii ex., gave books in his lifetime and be-
queathed all his books 'præter libros phisicæ quorum nomina in catalogo
librorum nostrorum continentur expressa' (extract by R. James, s.xvii in., in
Bodleian, MS. James 23, p. 169, from a now missing cartulary).
Books noted by J. Leland, *Collectanea,* iv. 152.
London, B.M., Add. 14250. *e*Beda, etc. s.xii.

PONTEFRACT, Yorkshire. *Cluniac priory of St John the Evangelist.*
Books noted by J. Leland, *Collectanea*, iv. 46.

Boston, Church. *e*Augustinus. s.xii.
Cambridge, King's Coll., 31. *c*Missale. s.xv.
Oxford, Univ. Coll., 101. *l*Breviarium. s.xiii.

PRESTON, Yorkshire. *Hospital of St Sepulchre.*
New York, Public Library, Spencer 2. *c*Psalterium. s.xiv in. ?

PRITTLEWELL, Essex. *Cluniac priory of B.V.M.; cell of Lewes.*
M. R. James, 'MSS from Essex Monastic Libraries', *Trans. Essex Archaeol. Soc.*, N.S., xxi (1933), 37.
Rejected: London, Lambeth Palace, 345, fos 1–96.

QUARR (Quadraria, etc.), Isle of Wight. *Cist. abbey of B.V.M.*
Cambridge, U.L., Mm.6.4. *e*Manuel des pechez (in French), etc. s.xiv.
Eton Coll. 14.[4] *e*P. Cantor. s.xiii.
      16.[4] Rabanus Maurus, etc. s.xii/xiii.
      19.[4] P. Cantor. s.xii/xiii.
Rejected: Eton Coll. 23.

RADFORD. *See* **WORKSOP.**

RAMSEY, Huntingdonshire. *Ben. abbey of B.V.M. and St Benedict.* (*Cf.* cell at **ST IVES.**)
Fragment of catalogue, s.xiii ex., printed from Lambeth Palace, MS. 585, pp. 661–64, in *Chron. Abbatiae de Rameseia* (Rolls Series), pp. lxxxv–xci. Catalogue, s.xiv ex., imperfect at the beginning, printed from London, B.M., Cotton Rolls ii. 16, *ibid.*, pp. 356–67; other books mentioned *ibid.*, pp. 63, 65, 71, 74, n.2. A list of 12 books probably belonging to this house and on loan in s.xiv is in B.M., Royal 8 F.x, fo. 2 (*cf. Catalogue of Royal MSS*, where the list is assigned to St James, Northampton, and R. Bressie, in *Modern Language Notes*, liv (1939), 249). Books noted by J. Leland, *Collectanea*, iv. 47, and *De Scriptoribus Britannicis*, pp. 159, 172, 264, 322, 453; also by J. Bale, *Index* (p. 579). See also J. Bale, *Scriptores* (edn 1557), p. 708.

Cambridge,
    U.L., Hh.6.11. *e*H. de S. Victore, etc. s.xiii.
        Mm.5.30. *e*G. Cambrensis. s.xii/xiii. ?
    Corpus Christi Coll., 468. *gl*Psalterium lat.-grecum. s.xiii. [*Cf. cats*, pp. lxxxvi, 365].
    Gonv. and Caius Coll., 236. *c*A. Nequam. s.xiii ex. [*Cf. cat.*, p. lxxxviii]. ?
    Peterhouse, 10. *i*Decretales, etc. s.xiii–xiv.
           132. *e*J. de Voragine. s.xiii.
    St John's Coll., 209. *e*Beda, etc. s.xii.
Deene Park, Trustees of the late Mr G. Brudenell, XVIII.B. *c*H. Huntendonensis, etc. s.xiv in.
Holkham Hall, Lord Leicester, 26. *l*Psalterium. s.xiv.
Lavantal, Carinthia, Abbey of St Paul, xxv/2.19.[5] *lc*Psalterium. s.xiv in.

---

[4] Eton Coll. 14, 16, and 19 are companion volumes.
[5] New York, Pierpont Morgan 302 was part of the St Paul-in-Lavantal MS.

London,
   B.M., Add. 33350, fos 32, 33.   Gautier de Metz (in French). s.xiii.
        Cotton Galba E.x, fos 2–58. *c*Kalendarium, etc. s.xiii in.
            Otho D.viii, fos 234–54. *c*Chronicon. s.xv. ?
            Vit. A.vii, fos 1–112. *l*Pontificale. s.xi. ?
        Harley 649. *e*Beda, etc. s.xii in.
            2904. *l*Psalterium. s.x. ?
        Royal 2 C.xi. *e*A. Nequam. s.xiii.
            3 B.xi. *e*Comment. in psalterium. s.xii/xiii.
            5 D.x. *i*Augustinus, etc. s.xiii ex.
            5 F.xv. *gc*Augustinus, etc. s.xiii. [*Cat.*, p. 363].
            7 C.i. *i*Miscellanea. s.xiv.
            8 C.xvi. *e*L. de Sumercote, etc. s.xiv in. ?
            8 D.iii. *c*Miscellanea. s.xiii. [*Cat.*, p. 363].
            8 F.x. *ic*Isidorus, etc. s.xiii.
            14 C.iv. *e*P. Blesensis, etc. s.xiv.
            14 C.ix. *i*Polychronicon. s.xiv.
        Sloane 2397. *l*Kalendarium, etc. s.xv in.
   Lambeth Palace, 1106, fos 111–20. *c*Annales. s.xiii. ?
   Public Record Office, Exch. K.R., Misc. Books, i.28. *c*Chronicon, etc.
                                   s.xiv in.
   The Robinson Trust (Phillipps 3119, fos 144–175). Haymo Floriacensis,
        etc. s.xii. [*Cf. cat.*, p. 360; *Bale, Index*, p. 155].
New York, Pierpont Morgan, 302.[6] Psalterium (fragm.). s.xiv in.
Oxford,
   Bodleian, Bodl. 40. *m*A. Essebiensis, etc. s.xiii.
                285. *c*Vite sanctorum. s.xiii in. ?
                543. *c*Expo. super reg. S. Benedicti, etc. s.xii ex. ?
                833. *e*Eufrastica W. de Burgo. s.xiii. [*Leland, De*
                        Script. Brit., p. 264].
                851. *i*W. Mapes, etc. s.xiv–xv.
        Gough Missals 122 (pr. bk). *i*Expo. hymnorum, etc. Paris,
                      A.D. 1502.
        Rawl. B.333. *c*Chronicon abbatie. s.xiv.
        Tanner 110. *i*Bestiarium, etc. s.xii–xiv.
   Mr David Rogers (pr. bk). *i*H. de Sancto Marco. Cologne, A.D. 1507.
Wisbech, Museum, 5. *c*Innocentius III, etc. s.xiii. [*Cf. cat.*, p. 364].
Rejected: Cambridge, Corpus Christi Coll., 321. Mount Stuart, Marquess
   of Bute. Oxford, Bodleian, Laud misc. 371. Paris, B.N., Lat. 987.

RANTON (Ronton), Staffordshire. *Aug. priory of B.V.M.*

London, B.M., Harley 622. *e*Graduale. s.xiii.

READING, Berkshire. *Ben. abbey of B.V.M.* (*Cf.* cells at **LEO-MINSTER, MAY.**)

   J. B. Hurry, *Reading Abbey* (1901), pp. 103–26. J. R. L[iddell], 'Some Notes on the Library of Reading Abbey', *Bodl. Quart. Rec.*, viii (1935), 47–54.
   Catalogue of s.xii ex. printed in *Eng. Hist. Rev.*, iii (1888), 117–25, from Lord Fingall's cartulary of Reading, now London, B.M., Egerton 3031; facsim. of first page in M. R. James, *Abbeys* (1926), pl. facing p. 82. List of books for reading in church or in refectory, s.xv, in Oxford, St John's Coll. MS. 11, printed by J. R. Liddell, *loc. cit.*; second folios given. List of 14 books received by King John

---

   [6] New York, Pierpont Morgan 302 was part of the St Paul-in-Lavantal MS.

'per manus Gervasii sacriste de Rading.' in *Rot. Litt. Claus.*, i. 108 and in *Sussex Archaeol. Coll.*, ii (1849), 134. List of books copied by 'frater W. de Wicumbe' at Reading, or possibly at Leominster, s.xiii, printed from Bodleian, MS. Bodley 125 by F. Madan in *Bodl. Quart. Rec.*, iv (1924), 168.

The common form of *ex libris* inscription of s.xiii is 'Hic est liber Sancte Marie de Rading. Quem qui celaverit vel fraudem de eo fecerit anathema sit', written on a flyleaf (*cf.* C. H. Borland, *Cat. of Western Mediaeval MSS in Edinburgh Univ. Libr.*, pl. xxiv).

Belvoir Castle, Duke of Rutland. *e*Psalterium ('Rutland psalter'). s.xiii.

Berlin, Staatsbibl., th. lat. fol. 590. Gregorius in Ezech., etc. s.xiii. ?

Cambridge,

    U.L., Dd.9.38. *c*Constitutiones, etc. s.xiv.

        Inc. (pr. bk). *e*Sophilogium Jac. Magni. Lyon, A.D. 1495.

    Gonv. and Caius Coll., 177. *e*Alcuinus, etc. s.xii. [*Cat.*, p. 120].

    Pembroke Coll., 225. *e*P. Comestor, etc. s.xiii in.

              274. *e*Summa G. de Trano. s.xiii.

              275. *e*Miscellanea. s.xiii.

    St John's Coll., 22. *e*Beda, etc. s.xii. [*Cat.*, p. 120].

    Trinity Coll., 823.[7] Gaza de arte grammatica (in Greek). A.D. 1489.

Cambridge (U.S.A.), Harvard Law School, 64. Gratianus. s.xiii. ?

Chicago,

    Newberry Library, Ry. 24.[8] *e*Augustinus, De vera religione, etc. s.xii. [*Cat.*, p. 119].

                    Augustinus, De quantitate anime, etc. s.xii. [*Cat.*, p. 118].

                    Augustinus, De sermone domini, etc. s.xii. [*Cat.*, p. 119].

                    Augustinus, Super genesim. s.xii. [*Cat.*, p. 119].

                    Augustinus, Super Johannem, etc. s.xii. [*Cat.*, p. 119].

                    *e*Augustinus, Unde malum, etc. s.xii. [*Cat.*, p. 118].

                    *e*Augustinus, Confessiones. s.xii. [*Cat.*, p. 119].

Edinburgh, U.L., 100. *e*Basilius, etc. s.xii ex. [*Cat.*, p. 119].

            104.[9] *e*Anselmus; J. Chrysostomus. s.xii. [*Cat.*, p. 121].

Eton College, 225. Jeronimus. s.xii. [*Cf. cat.*, p. 119]. ?

           226. Gregorius. s.xii. [*List in B.Q.R.*, 21; *cf. cat.*, p. 119].

Glasgow, U.L., BE.7.e.24. *e*Aristoteles abbrev. s.xv.

Göttingen, U.L., Theol. 2. *e*Biblia. s.xiv.

London, B.M., Add. 48179. *c*Formularium, etc. s.xv in.

           Cotton Vesp. E.iv, fos 104–202. *c*Annales, etc. s.xiii ex.

           Egerton 2204. *e*Beda. s.xii. [*Cat.*, p. 120].

                2951. Rob. Partes, etc. s.xii ex. ?

---

[7] Cambridge, Trinity Coll. 823, and Oxford, Corpus Christi Coll. 23, 24, 106, New Coll. 240, 241, and 254 were written at Reading Abbey by John Serbopoulos of Constantinople.

[8] The MSS at Chicago are bound uniformly and formed one number in the Phillipps collection (MS. 241) and subsequently.

[9] Edinburgh, U.L., 104 has two *ex libris* inscriptions and was originally two volumes, entered separately in the catalogue.

London (*contd*)
  B.M., Harley 82, fos 1–34. *c*Martyrologium. s.xii. [*Cf. cat.*,
                                  p. 122].
                    101. *e*Origines, etc. s.xii. [*Cat.*, p. 120].
                    330. *e*W. Hilton, etc. (partly in English). s.xv.
                    651, fos 4–177. *e*Chronica. s.xii. [*Cat.*, p. 119].
                    876.[1] R. de Sancto Victore, etc. s.xiii.
                    978. Versus, etc. (partly in French). s.xiii.
                    979. *e*Isagoge mag. Hugonis, etc. s.xiii.
           Royal 1 C.iii. *e*Bible (in French). s.xiv.
                  3 A.iv. *e*Paschasius Radbertus. s.xii. [*Cat.*,
                                  p. 121].
                  3 A.vi. *e*Michael Meldensis. s.xiii.
                  3 A.xiv. *e*R. Holcot. s.xiv.
                  4 C.vi. *e*Comment. super Sapientiam. s.xv in.
                  7 E.ix. *e*W. Durand. s.xiv.
                  8 C.ix. *e*P. Comestor, etc. s.xiii.
                  9 C.iii. *e*Decretum glo. s.xii ex.–xiv.
                  9 F.iii. *e*Innocentius IV. s.xiv.
                  9 F.v. *e*Sextus liber decretalium. s.xiv. ?
                  10 C.iii. *e*Distinctiones, etc. s.xiii.
                  10 D.x. *e*Summa summarum. s.xiv ex.
                  11 A.xvii. *e*T. de Capua. s.xiv.
                  11 C.ii. *e*J. Monachus. s.xv in.
                  11 C.iii. *e*Digestum vetus. s.xiii in.
                  11 C.xi. *e*Const. Clementine, etc. s.xiv.
                  12 F.xix. *e*W. Burley, etc. s.xiv.
       Lambeth Palace, 371. *c*Chronica, etc. s.xiii.
                    497. *e*Sermones. s.xii/xiii.
        Dr E. G. Millar. *s*Liber judicum, etc., glo. [*Cat.*, p. 117]. ?
Morcombelake, Mr J. S. Cox. *c*Tractatus de cartis, etc. s.xiv.
New York, Pierpont Morgan, 103. *l*Psalterium. s.xiii in.
Oxford,
    Bodleian, Auct. D.1.19. *e*Psalterium glo. s.xiii.
                    2.12. *e*XII prophete glo. s.xiii in. [*Cat.*, p. 119].
                    3.12. *e*Leviticus glo. s.xii ex. [*Cat.*, p. 117].
                    3.15. *e*Libri regum glo. s.xii ex. [*Cat.*, p. 117].
                    4.6. *c*Psalterium glo. s.xii. [*Cat.*, p. 117].
                    4.10. *e*Biblia. s.xiii.
                    4.18.[2] Epp. can. glo., etc. s.xii/xiii. ?
                  F.3.3.[3] Egidius Romanus, etc. s.xiv. ?
                    3.8.[1] *e*Misc. grammatica. s.xiii.
                  inf.1.2. *e*Collectarium theol. s.xiv.
         Bodl. 44. *i*Glosa super psalterium, etc. s.xiii.
                125. *c*Odo Cluniacensis. s.xii. [*Cf. cat.*, p. 120]. ?
                146. *s*W. Autissiodorensis, etc. s.xiii.
                197. *e*Ailredus, etc. s.xii.

---

[1] Harley 876 and Bodleian, Auct. F.3.8, formed one volume.
[2] The table of contents of Bodley 528 is bound up with Auct. D.4.18.
[3] The Reading provenance of Auct. F.3.3, Bodl. 396, 631, 639 is inferred from
the character of the binding, s.xvi(?), which resembles that of Auct. D.1.19,
D.2.12, D.3.12, D.3.15, D.4.18, Bodl. 200, 413.

Oxford (*contd*)
Bodleian, Bodl. 200.　*e*T. Aquinas.　s.xiii.
　　　　　241.　*e*Augustinus.　s.xii.　[*Cat.*, p. 118; *list in B.Q.R.*, 9].
　　　　　257.　*e*Augustinus.　s.xii.　[*Cat.*, p. 118; *list in B.Q.R.* 7].
　　　　　396.[3]　Isidorus.　s.xiii/xiv.　?
　　　　　397.　*e*Misc. theol.　s.xiii.
　　　　　409.　*s*Innocentius III, etc.　s.xiii.
　　　　　413.　*e*Adalberti Speculum.　s.xii ex.　[*Cat.*, p. 120].
　　　　　528.[2]　*e*A. Nequam, etc.　s.xiii.
　　　　　550.　*e*A. Nequam, etc.　s.xiii.
　　　　　570.　*e*P. Blesensis, etc.　s.xv.
　　　　　631.[3]　Concordancie biblie.　s.xiii.
　　　　　639.[3]　Decretales Gregorii IX.　s.xiii.　?
　　　　　713.　*e*P. de Tarantasia.　s.xiii/xiv.
　　　　　760.　*m*Comment. super psalmos, etc.　s.xiii.
　　　　　772.　*e*Comment. super psalmos, etc.　s.xiii in.
　　　　　781.　*e*Comment. super psalmos.　s.xii ex.
　　　　　848.　*e*Misc. theologica.　s.xiii.
　　　　　853.　P. Lombardus.　s.xiii.　?
Digby 148.　*e*H. de S. Victore.　s.xii ex.　[*Cat.*, p. 118].
　　　151.　*e*Actus apostolorum glo., etc.　s.xiii.
　　　158.　*e*Scintillarium, etc.　s.xii.　[*Cat.*, p. 119].
　　　184.　*ms*Jeronimus.　s.xii.　[*Cat.*, p. 119].
　　　200.　*e*Ric. de S. Victore.　s.xiii.
　　　214.　*s*Gregorius.　s.xii.　[*Cf. cat.*, p. 119].　?
Douce F.205 (pr. bk).　*e*D. Mancinus.　London, s.a.
Laud misc. 79.　*e*Haymo, etc.　s.xii.　[*Cat.*, p. 121?].
　　　　　91.　*e*Baldewinus Cantuariensis, etc.　s.xiii in.
　　　　725.　*e*J. Cassianus, etc.　s.xii.　[*Cat.*, p. 121].
Rawl. A.375.　*e*Distinctiones in psalterium.　s.xiii in.
　　　376.　*e*Ambrosius.　s.xii.　[*Cat.*, p. 120].
　　　416.　*c*Ambrosius, etc.　s.xii.　[*Cat.*, p. 120].
　　　C.118.　*s*Bernardus.　s.xii.　[*Cf. cat.*, p. 120].　?
Corpus Christi Coll., 23, 24.[4]　Chrysostomus (in Greek).　A.D. 1499, 1500.
　　　　　45.　*e*A. Nequam.　s.xiii in.
　　　　106.[4]　Comment. Eustratii (in　Greek).　A.D. 1495.
　　　　147.　*s*Cassianus.　s.xii.　[*Cf. cat.*, p. 119].　?
Magdalen Coll., lat. 25.　*e*Compendium theologice veritatis.　s.xv.
New Coll., 240, 241.[4]　Comment. in Aristotelem (in Greek).　A.D. 1497.
　　　254.[4]　Gaza de arte grammatica (in Greek).　A.D. 1494.
Queen's Coll., 317.　*e*Matheus et Marcus glo., etc.　s.xiii in.
　　　323.　*e*Lucas glo.　s.xii.　[*Cat.*, p. 122 *or* 123].
St John's Coll.,　1.　Augustinus.　s.xiii/xiv.　[*List in B.Q.R.*, 13].
　　　　5.　*e*Rabanus.　s.xii/xiii.

[3] See p. 156, n. 3.　　　　[2] See p. 156, n. 2.
[4] Cambridge, Trinity Coll. 823, and Oxford, Corpus Christi Coll. 23, 24, 106, New Coll. 240, 241, and 254 were written at Reading Abbey by John Serbopoulos of Constantinople.

Oxford (*contd*)
St John's Coll., 11. *c*Omelie. s.xii. [*List in B.Q.R.*, 15].
         21. *e*Libri Josue et Judicum glo. s.xiii.
         59. *e*T. Aquinas. s.xiv.
         73. *e*Berengaudus, etc. s.xii–xiii.
       104. *e*Deuteronomium glo. s.xii.
Trinity Coll., 19. *e*Sermones, etc. s.xii ex.
         63. *s*Augustinus. s.xii. [*Cf. cat.*, p. 118]. ?
Worcester Coll., 3.16 A. *e*Jeronimus, etc. s.xiii. [P].
Portsmouth,
    Roman Catholic Bishopric, Virtue and Cahill 8473. *e*Rodbertus de
    benedictionibus patriarcharum, etc. s.xii. [*Cat.*, p. 121].
Untraced: Phillipps sale (Sotheby, 21–26 March 1895), lot 420 to Quaritch,
       who sold to Harrassowitz. Hildwinus, etc. s.xii. ?
       Quaritch cat. 164 (1896), no. 78 (sold to H. White). Gregorius,
       Omel. in evangelia. s.xii. [*Cf. cat.*, p. 119]. ?
       Sale by Puttick and Simpson, 5 July 1877, lot 698, to Stark.
       *e*Julius Solinus.
       Stony Brook (N.Y.), Rev. A. C. Gaebelein. *e*Gregorius.
                           s.xii. [*Cat.*, p. 119].
Rejected: Cambridge, Trinity Coll., 1213. Oxford, Bodleian, Bodl. 32,
    186, 263, 408, 450, 730. Portsmouth, Roman Catholic Bishopric,
    Virtue and Cahill 8451.

READING. *Franciscan convent.*

    Books noted by J. Leland, *Collectanea*, iv. 57, and by J. Bale, *Index* (p. 579,
the entry given wrongly as *Reading abbey*).

London, B.M., Harley 493. Statuta. s.xiv.
Rejected: Oxford, Bodleian, Digby 221.

REDBOURN, Hertfordshire. *Ben. priory of St Amphibalus; cell of St
    Albans.*

London, B.M., Cotton Tib. E.i. *e*Sanctilogium J. Anglici. s.xiv.
         Royal 13 D.ix. *e*Sanctilogium Guidonis. s.xiv.

REPTON, Derbyshire. *Aug. priory of Holy Trinity.*

Oxford, Bodleian, Auct. D.inf.2.8.[5] Haymo. s.xiii in.

REVESBY, Lincolnshire. *Cist. abbey of B.V.M. and St Lawrence.*

    Note of MSS seen by J. Leland printed from B.M., Royal MS. App. 69, fo. 8[v]
in *Eng. Hist. Rev.*, liv. 94: *cf.* Leland, *Collectanea*, iv. 32.

London, B.M., Royal 7 D.xv. *e*R. Grosseteste. s.xiii ex. [*Leland*].
          8 F.i. *e*Ailredus, etc. s.xii/xiii. [*Leland*].
Rejected: Cambridge, U.L., Ii.4.26. Maidstone, Museum, A.13.

REWLEY, Oxfordshire. *Cist. abbey of B.V.M.*

Oxford, Trinity Coll., 59.[6] *e*Augustinus. s.xiii.

     [5] Lent by the abbot and canons of Darley to a canon of Repton.
     [6] Trinity Coll. 59 was earlier at Dover, *q.v.*

RICHMOND, Yorkshire. *Franciscan convent.*

Thomas Colier, fellow of Michaelhouse, Cambridge, bequeathed twelve specified books in 1506 (Cambridge Univ. Archives, Wills 1501–58, fos 16ᵛ–17ᵛ).

Oxford, Bodleian, Rawl. liturg. e.1, fos 9–14. eKalendarium. s.xv.

RIEVAULX, Yorkshire. *Cist. abbey of B.V.M.*

Catalogue of s.xiii printed by A. Hoste, *Bibliotheca Aelrediana* (Instrumenta Patristica, ii, 1962), pp. 150–76, and by M. R. James, *Cat. of MSS of Jesus Coll., Cambridge*, pp. 44–52, from Jesus Coll., MS. 34 (also by Th. Wright and J. O. Halliwell, *Reliquiae Antiquae*, ii (London, 1843), 180, and by E. Edwards, *Memoirs of Libraries*, i (London, 1859), 333). Books noted by J. Leland, *Collectanea*, iv. 38, and *De Scriptoribus Britannicis*, p. 201. The common form of *ex libris* inscription is 'Liber Sancte Marie Rievallis'.

Cambridge,
    Corpus Christi Coll., 86. eRabanus Maurus. s.xii. [*Cat.*, fo. 2].
    Jesus Coll., 34. eW. de Monte, etc. s.xii–xiii.
Dublin,
    Archbishop Marsh's Library, Z.4.5.17. eAmbrosius, etc. s.xiii in.
                                             [*Cat.*, fo. 2ᵛ].
    Trinity Coll., 279, fos 33–111. eH. de S. Victore, etc. s.xii ex.
London,
    B.M., Arundel 346.[7] eDe officiis eccles., etc. s.xii/xiii.
        Cotton Vit. C.viii, fos 4–22.[8] Versus P. Abaelardi, etc. s.xii ex.
                D.v.[9] Constitutiones provinciales Ebor., etc. s.xv.
                F.iii. Ailredus, etc. s.xii ex. [*Cat.*, fo. 1ᵛ; *Leland*].
            Vesp. D.v, fos 121–38.[7] Hildebertus, etc. s.xii/xiii.
        Harley 5273. eJob glo. s.xii. [*Cf. cat.*, fo. 5].
        Royal 6 C.viii.[8] eOrosius, etc. s.xii ex. [*Cat.*, fo. 3].
            8 D.xxii. sP. Chrysologus. s.xiii in. ?
            8 E.iv. Ennodius, etc. s.xii/xiii. [? *Leland*]. ?
    Inner Temple, 511.2. eR. de Hoveden. s.xiii in.
Manchester, J. Rylands, Lat. 196. W. Daniel, s.xii–xiii. [*Cat.*, fo. 3ᵛ; *Leland*].
Oxford,
    Corpus Christi Coll., 155.[9] eR. Grosseteste, etc. s.xv.
    Lincoln Coll., lat. 15. eApocalypsis glo., etc. s.xiii.
    Univ. Coll., 113, fos 1–165. eP. Lombardus. s.xiii.
Paris, B.N., Lat. 15157, fos 35–135. cMatheus Vindocinensis, etc. s.xiii in. ?
York, Minster, xvi.I.8. eJeronimus, etc. s.xii. [*Cat.*, fo. 4ᵛ].
Rejected: London, B.M., Add. 31826.

RIPON, Yorkshire. *Ben. abbey, later collegiate church, of St Peter, later St Wilfred.*

J. T. Fowler, 'Ripon Minster Library and its Founder', *Yorks. Archaeol. Journal*, ii (1871–72), 371, contains no information about the medieval library.

Rejected: New York, Pierpont Morgan, 23.

---

    [7] Cotton Vesp. D.v, fos 121–38, was part of Arundel 346.
    [8] Cotton Vit. C.viii, fos 4–22, was part of Royal 6 C.viii.
    [9] Cotton Vit. D.v was part of Corpus Christi Coll., Oxford, 155.

ROBERTSBRIDGE (de Ponte Roberti), Sussex. *Cist. abbey of B.V.M.*

Cambridge, St John's Coll., 113. *c*Speculum juniorum, etc. s.xiii. ?
Longleat, Marquess of Bath, 37. *c*Formularium, etc. s.xiv–xv.
London, Soc. of Antiquaries, 14. *c*Forma visitacionis, etc. s.xv.
Oxford, Bodleian, Bodl. 132. *e*Augustinus. s.xiii.
Rejected: Bodleian, Auct. D.2.10.

ROCHE, Yorkshire. *Cist. abbey of B.V.M.*

N. R. Ker, 'The Medieval Pressmarks of St Guthlac's Priory, Hereford, and
of Roche Abbey, Yorks.', *Medium Aevum*, v (1936), 47–48.

Cambridge, U.L., Gg.3.33. *e*Lethbertus, Flores psalterii (Pss 1–50). s.xii.
Manchester, J. Rylands, Lat. 186. Missale. s.xii–xv. ?
Oxford,
    Bodleian, Laud misc. 145. *m*Lethbertus, Flores psalterii (Pss 101–50).
            s.xiii in.
           241. Gregorius. s.xii. [VI.D].
           308. *e*Augustinus. s.xii ex. [III.E (F)].
           309. Augustinus. s.xii ex. [XVII.D].
      Rawl. C.329. *e*Ambrosius. s.xii. [XVII.F].
Yale University, Prof. N. H. Pearson. *b*G. Monemutensis, etc. s.xii ex.–
    xiii. [VIII.E].

ROCHESTER, Kent. *Cathedral priory of St Andrew.* (*Cf.* cell at
FELIXSTOWE.)

Catalogue, s.xii med., in the 'Textus Roffensis', fos 224–30, reproduced in
facsimile in *Textus Roffensis, part ii*, ed. P. Sawyer (Early English MSS in
Facsimile, xi, 1962), and printed in *Archaeologia Cantiana*, vi. 120 ff. (*Cat. I*).
A fragment of a catalogue like and contemporary with *Cat. I* is at Rochester
Cathedral, Muniments, B. 854 (*Cat. Ia*). Catalogue of A.D. 1202 printed from
B.M., Royal MS. 5 B.xii, fo. 2, *ibid.*, iii. 54 ff. (*Cat. II*). A list of books written
or acquired by Alexander the precentor, s.xiii in., printed, inaccurately, from
B.M., Royal MS. 10 A.xii, fo. 111ᵛ in the catalogue of Royal MSS. Notes about
gifts of books printed from B.M., Cotton Vesp. A.xxii in *Archaeologia Cantiana*,
iii. 62, 63, and by J. Thorpe, *Registrum Roffense* (1769), pp. 116–25.
An *ex libris* inscription of s.xiv is written in most MSS at the foot of the first
page of text and is in the form 'Liber de claustro Roffensi' followed usually by
a personal name introduced by *per* or in the genitive. In some MSS there is a
serial number, usually before or after the inscription.

Baltimore, Walters Art Gallery, 57. *c*Novum testamentum. s.xii. ?
Berlin, Staatsbibl., lat. 350. *e*Berengaudus. s.xii. [*Cf. cat. I*, p. 127].
Brussels, Bibl. royale, 1403. *e*Ernulfus, etc. s.xii.
Cambridge,
    U.L., Ff.4.32. *s*Augustinus. s.xii. [*Cf. cat. I*, p. 123; *II*.7].
        Inc. 2179 (pr. bk). *e*Iamblichus. Venice, A.D. 1497.
    Corpus Christi Coll., 62, fos 1–48. *e*Parabole, etc., glo. s.xiii.
                fos 49–208. *e*Bernardus, etc. s.xii. [*Cat.*
                      II.104].
                fos 209–74. *e*Beda. s.xii in. [*Cat. Ia;*
                      II.148].
           184. *m*Eusebius. s.xii. [*Cf. cat. I*, p. 126; *II*.96].
           318. *e*Vite sanctorum, etc. s.xii.
           332. *s*Augustinus, etc. s.xii in. [*Cat. I*, p. 128;
              II.18].

Cambridge (*contd*)
St John's Coll., 70. *e*Epp. Pauli glo. s.xii. [III].
         89. *e*Epp. Pauli glo. s.xii. [VI].
Trinity Coll., 610. *sc*Lucanus. s.xii in. [*Cf. cat. II*.186].
      1128. *e*Grammatica. s.xii in. [*Cat. I*, p. 126; II.98].
      1238. *e*Jeronimus. s.xii. [*Cat. I*, p. 124; *II*.46].
Dublin, Trinity Coll., 163. *e*Pseudo-Dionysius. s.xiii.
Edinburgh, N.L., Adv. 18.2.4. *c*Omelie. s.xii in. [*Cf. cat. I*, p. 127; *II*.57].
      18.3.9. *is*Egesippus. s.xii in. [*Cf. cat. I*, p. 126; *II*.74].
      18.5.18. *i*Boethius, etc. s.xiii.
Eton Coll., 80. *s*Jeronimus, s.xii. [*Cat. I*, p. 124; *II*.47].
London,
  B.M., Cotton Nero D.ii, fos 2–214, 242–51, 297–305. *c*Chronicon Roffense. s.xiv.
      [Otho A.xv.[1] Acta Pontificum]. [*Cf. cat. Ia*; *II*.135].
      Vit. A.xiii, fos 91–100.[2] Nennius, etc. s.xiii in.
      Vesp. A.xxii. *e*Chronica, etc. s.xiii in. [II].
      D.xxi, fos 1–17.[3] *s*Nennius, etc. s.xii in. ?
  Harley 23.[4] P. Comestor. s.xiii.
      261.[4] *e*W. Malmesburiensis. s.xii/xiii. [*Cat. II*.120].
      3680. *e*Beda. s.xii. [*Cf. cat.* I, p. 126; *II*.50].
  Royal 1 B.iv. *e*Parabole, etc. s.xiii in.
    1 D.iii. *e*Evangelia. s.xi. [III].
    2 C.i. *e*P. Comestor. s.xiii. [III].
    2 C.iii. *e*Omelie. s.xi ex. [*Cf. cat. I*, p. 127; *II*.57].
    2 C.v. *e*N. de Gorran. s.xiii/xiv.
    2 D.vi. *e*Flores psalterii, etc. s.xiii.
    2 D.xxx. *e*Summa R. Blundi, etc. s.xiii.
    2 E.i. *e*Job glo. s.xiii.
    2 E.vii. *e*G. Foliot. s.xiii in. [*Cat. II*.240].
    2 F.iv. *e*Evangelia glo. s.xiii ex.
    2 F.vi. *e*Esaias glo. s.xiii.
    2 F.xi. *e*Flores psalterii. s.xii/xiii. [*Cat. II*.237].
    2 F.xii. *e*XII prophete glo. s.xiii.
    3 B.i. *e*Isidorus, etc. s.xii. [*Cat. I*, p. 124; *II*.80].
    3 B.xiii. *e*Esaias glo. s.xiii.
    3 C.iv. *e*Gregorius. s.xii. [*Cat. I*, p. 125; *II*.24].
    3 C.vii. *e*Zach. Chrysopolitanus. s.xiii. [*Cf. cat. II*.241].
    3 C.viii. Leviticus, etc. glo. s.xii ex. [E.vi.m'].
    3 C.ix. *e*Leviticus, etc. glo. s.xii ex. [*Cat. II*.49].
    3 C.x. *e*Augustinus. s.xii in. [*Cat. II*.3].
    4 A.vii. *e*Lucas glo. s.xii ex. [E.iii.m'].

---

[1] Cotton Otho A.xv was burnt in 1731. It is ascribed to Rochester by T. Smith, *Catalogus Bibliothecae Cottonianae*, 1696. The Rochester *ex libris* is recorded by Richard James, Cotton's librarian, on a flyleaf of the copy of Anastasius Bibliothecarius, *Historia Romanorum Pontificum* (Mainz, 1602) in the library of Corpus Christi College, Oxford.
[2] Cotton Vitellius A.xiii, fos 91–100, was part of Royal 15 B.xi.
[3] Cotton Vesp. D.xxi, fos 1–17, probably formed part of Royal 15 A.xxii.
[4] Harley 23 was part of Harley 261.

London (*contd*)
B.M., Royal 4 A.xii. *e*Matheus, etc., glo. s.xii.
4 A.xv. *e*N. de Lyra. s.xiv ex.
4 A.xvi. *e*Comment. super Matheum. s.xii. [*Cat. II*.128].
4 B.i. *e*Gregorius. s.xii. [*Cat. I*, p. 125; *II*.28].
4 B.ii. *e*Epp. Pauli et catholice glo. s.xii.
4 B.vii. *e*Flores psalterii, etc. s.xiii. [X].
4 C.iv. *gs*Florus diaconus. s.xii. [*VII*; cf. cat. *II*.13].
4 C.x. *e*Pentateuchus glo. s.xii/xiii. [*Cat. II*.117, 200].
4 D.xiii. *e*Esaias, etc., glo. s.xiii.
4 E.v. *e*Concordancie bibl. s.xiv.
5 A.i. *e*Augustinus, etc. s.xiii.
5 A.iv. *e*Misc. theologica et grammatica. s.xii–xiii.
5 A.vii. *e*Paschasius Radbertus, etc. s.xii. [*Cat. I*, p. 125; *II*.83].
5 A.x. *e*Flores Bernardi, etc. s.xii–xiv.
5 A.xv. *e*Augustinus, etc. s.xii. [*Cat. I*, p. 122; *II*.9].
5 B.iv. *e*Augustinus. s.xii. [*II; cat. I*, p. 122, *II*.2].
5 B.vi. *e*Augustinus, etc. s.xii. [*Cat. I*, p. 122; *II*.12].
5 B.vii. *e*Augustinus, etc. s.xii. [*Cat. I*, p. 122; *II*.15].
5 B.x. *e*Augustinus. s.xii. [*Cat. I*, p. 122, *II*.8].
5 B.xii. *e*Augustinus. s.xii. [*III; cat. I*, p. 122; *II*.11].
5 B.xiii. *e*Augustinus. s.xii. [*Cat. I*, p. 123; *II*.19].
5 B.xvi. *e*Augustinus. s.xii. [4; *cat. I*, p. 123; *II*.21].
5 C.i. *e*Augustinus. s.xii. [6; *cat. II*.20].
5 C.viii. *e*Augustinus. s.xii. [*Cat. II*.5].
5 D.i. *e*Augustinus. s.xii in. [*Cat. I*, p. 122; *II*.6].
5 D.ii. *e*Augustinus. s.xii in. [*Cat. I*, p. 122; *II*.6].
5 D.iii. *e*Augustinus. s.xii in. [*Cat. I*, p. 122; *II*.6].
5 D.ix. *e*Augustinus. s.xii. [*Cat. I*, p. 122; *II*.1].
5 E.i. *e*Isidorus, etc. s.xii. [*Cat. II*.81].
5 E.ii. *e*Gregorius. s.xii. [II].
5 E.x. *e*Prosper. s.xii. [*Cat. I*, p. 125; *II*.93].
5 E.xx. *e*Anselmus, etc. s.xii.
6 A.i.[5] *e*Ambrosius. s.xii. [*Cat. I*, p. 125; *II*.34].
6 A.iv. *e*Ambrosius. s.xii. [*Cat. I*, p. 125; *II*.35].
6 A.xi. *e*Hon. Augustodunensis, etc. s.xii.
6 A.xii. *e*J. Chrysostomus, etc. s.xii. [*Cat. I*, p. 126; *II*.76].
6 B.ii. *e*Gregorius. s.xiii.
6 B.vi. *e*Ambrosius, etc. s.xii. [*Cat. I*, p. 125; *II*.30].
6 C.iv. *e*Ambrosius. s.xii. [*Cat. I*, p. 125; *II*.31].
6 C.vi. *e*Gregorius. s.xii in. [*Cat. I*, p. 125; *II*.24].
6 C.x. *e*Gregorius. s.xii. [*Cat. I*, p. 125; *II*.29].
6 D.ii. *e*Jeronimus. s.xii. [*Cat. I*, p. 123; *II*.37].
6 D.v. *e*Prosper, etc. s.xii. [*Cat. II*.94].
6 D.vii. *e*Gregorius. s.xiv.
7 A.v. *e*H. de Folieto. s.xiii ex. [III].
7 A.xi, fos 19–24.[5] Inventio sancte crucis. s.xii.

[5] Royal 7 A.xi, fos 19–24, formed part of Royal 6 A.i.

London (*contd*)
   B.M., Royal 7 B.xiii. *e*'Excepciones ex libris 23 auctorum', etc.
                  s.xiii–xiv.
           7 C.xiii, xiv.[6] *e*P. de Cornubia. s.xiii in.
           7 E.iv. *e*J. de Bromyard. s.xiv ex.
           7 E.viii.[6] *e*P. de Cornubia. s.xiii in.
           7 F.iv. *e*P. de Cornubia. s.xiii ex.
           7 F.x. *e*Sermones. s.xii ex. [*Cf. cat. II*.72].
           8 D.v*. *e*H. de S. Victore, etc. s.xii ex. [*Cat. II*.89].
           8 D.xvi. *e*J. Cassianus. s.xii. [*Cat. I*, p. 127; *II*.91].
           9 C.iv. *e*T. Aquinas. s.xiv.
           9 E.xi. *e*Alex. de Hales. s.xiii/xiv.
          10 A.xii. *e*Collect. theologice. s.xiii in.
          10 A.xvi. *e*P. Cantor. s.xiii.
          10 B.ii. *e*W. Peraldus, etc. s.xiii.
          10 C.iv. *e*Omnibonus. s.xiii in. [*Cat. II*.236].
          10 C.xii. *e*Bonaventura, etc. s.xiv in.
          11 B.xv. *e*Instituta, etc. s.xiii.
          11 C.i. *e*P. Lombardus. s.xiv in.
          11 D.i. *e*Volumen parvum. s.xiii–xiv.
          12 C.i. *e*Misc. theologica. s.xii. [*Cat. I*, p. 127; *II*.99].
          12 C.iv. *e*Hyginus, etc. s.xiii. [*Cat. I*, p. 127; *II*.92].
          12 D.xiv. *e*Aristoteles, etc. s.xiii ex.
          12 F.i. *e*Aristoteles, etc. s.xiii ex.
          12 F.viii. *e*Joh. Saresberiensis. s.xii/xiii. [*Cat. II*.239].
          12 F.xiii. *e*Bestiarium, etc. s.xiii in.
          12 G.ii. *e*Aristoteles. s.xiii ex.
          12 G.iii. *e*Aristoteles. s.xiii ex.
          13 D.iii. Cassiodorus. s.xiii in. ?
          15 A.xix.[7] P. Riga. s.xii/xiii. ?
          15 A.xxii.[8] *e*Solinus, etc. s.xii. [*Cat. I*, p. 127; *II*.100
                 (i)].
          15 B.xi.[9] *e*Solinus, etc. s.xiii in. [*Cat. II*. 100 (ii)].
          15 C.x. *e*Statius. s.x ex. [*Cat. II*.197].
          App. 10, fo. 1.[7] *e*P. Riga. s.xiii.
      IA.3420 (pr. bk). *i*Augustinus, etc. Cologne, s.a.
  Lambeth Palace, 76, fos 1–147. *e*Augustinus, etc. s.xii in.
  Messrs Maggs (pr. bk). *i*Ludolphus Carthus. Paris, A.D. 1506.
Manchester, J. Rylands, Lat. 109. *es*Epp. Pauli. s.xi/xii.
Oxford,
  Bodleian, Bodl. 134. *s*Augustinus. s.xii in. [*Cat. I*, p. 123; *II*.16].
               340. Homilies (in English). s.xi in. [*Cat. I*, p. 127;
                      II.112].
               342. Homilies (in English). s.xi in. [*Cat. I*, p. 127;
                      II.112].
               387. *es*Augustinus, etc. s.xii in. [*Cat. I*, p. 124;
                      II.45].
      Hatton 54. *c*W. Malmesburiensis. s.xiv in.

---

[6] Royal 7 C.xiii, 7 C.xiv are the second and third parts of Royal 7 E.viii.
[7] Royal App. 10, fo. 1, formed probably the first leaf of Royal 15 A.xix.
[8] See p. 161, n. 3.
[9] Cotton Vitellius A.xiii, fos 91–100, was part of Royal 15 B.xi.

Oxford (*contd*)
 Bodleian, Laud misc. 40. *e*Reginaldus, Vita Malchi, etc. s.xii.
 [*Cat. II*. 144].
 Wood B.3. *e*Juvenalis. s.xi.
 All Souls Coll., LR.4.a.8 (pr. bk). *i*Augustinus. Paris, s.a.
 St John's Coll., 4. *e*Biblia. s.xiii ex. [III].
 Worcester Coll., 273. *s*Vita S Rumboldi (1 fo.). s.xii in. [*Cf. cat. I*,
 p. 127; *II*.56].
Rochester,
 Cathedral. *e*Augustinus de consensu evangelistarum, etc. s.xii in.
 [*Cat. I*, p. 122; *II*.4].
 *e*Laws, etc., in English ('Textus Roffensis', fos 1–118).
 s.xii in. [*Cf. cat. I*, p. 126].
 *e*P. Lombardus. s.xiii ex.
Rome, Vatican, Lat. 4951. *e*Omeliarium. s.xii. [*Cf. cat. I*, p. 127; *II*.57].
San Marino (U.S.A.), Huntington, HM 62. *e*Biblia (2 vols). s.xi.
 [*Cat. I*, p. 124; *II*.48].
Rejected: Cambridge, Corpus Christi Coll., 253. London, B.M., Cotton
 Nero A.viii, fos 1–86.

ROMSEY, Hampshire. *Abbey of B.V.M. and St Elfleda, of Ben. nuns.*

London, B.M., Lansdowne 436. *e*Chronicon, etc. s.xiv in.
 Royal College of Physicians, 409. *i*Psalterium. s.xiii.
Rejected: London, B.M., Add. 28188, Cotton Vit. A.vii. Romsey, Parish
 Church (Psalterium).

RONTON. *See* **RANTON.**

ROTHERHAM, Yorkshire. *Jesus College.*

 Cat. of over 100 books bequeathed by Archbishop Rotherham (†1500) printed
from Cambridge, Sidney Sussex Coll., MS. 2, by M. R. James, *Descriptive Cat.
of MSS in the Libr. of Sidney Sussex College, Cambridge*, pp. 5–8; second folios
given.

RUFFORD, Nottinghamshire. *Cist. abbey of B.V.M.*

London, B.M., Cotton Titus D.xxiv. *e*Carmina misc., etc. s.xii ex.
Oxford, Bodleian, Rawl. B.192. *e*W. de Novo Burgo. s.xiii/xiv.

RUSHEN (Russin), Isle of Man. *Savigniac and (1147) Cist. abbey of
 B.V.M.*

London, B.M., Cotton Julius A.vii, fos 1–54. *c*Chronicon Mannie.
 s.xiii.

SAFFRON WALDEN. *See* **WALDEN, SAFFRON.**

ST ALBANS, Hertfordshire. *Ben. abbey of St Alban.* (*Cf.* cells at
 **BELVOIR, HATFIELD PEVEREL, HERTFORD, REDBOURN,
 TYNEMOUTH, WALLINGFORD, WYMONDHAM,** and depen-
 dent hermitage at **MARKYATE.**)

For books given or acquired by abbots, etc., see *Gesta Abbatum* (Rolls Series), i. 58, 94, 184, 233, 483; ii. 201, 363. A list of books acquired in the time of Abbot Whethamstede printed from B.M., Arundel MS. 34, fos 74–77 in *Annales J. Amundesham* (Rolls Series), ii. 268–71. For a list of books sent to St Albans from the cell at Hertford see **HERTFORD.** Burnt fragments of book-lists of Abbot Whethamstede in London, B.M., Cotton Otho B.iv, fos 12ᵛ–16. One leaf containing part of a list of books in the keeping of certain monks, s.xv in., is at Gonville and Caius Coll., Cambridge, among fragments taken from bindings; some pressmarks given. Books noted by J. Leland, *Collectanea*, iv. 163, and *De Scriptoribus Britannicis*, p. 166. Bale gives extracts from the lost 'indiculus' of Walter the chanter (s.xii ex.): see A. Wilmart, *Archives d'hist. doctr. et litt. du moyen âge*, ii (1927), 27–29.

The fifteenth-century pressmark, which refers to the cupboards (armariola) A, B, C, D, usually also to the number of the shelf in the cupboard and sometimes to the number of the book on the shelf, is reproduced from B.M., Royal 4 D.vii and 10 C.xiii in *New Pal. Soc.*, i, pl. 17, no. 10 *a*, *b* (10 *c* is not a St Albans mark). The shelf-number is sometimes written inside the cupboard-letter. Two liturgical books are marked 'de armariolo in choro' and eleven books 'de studio abbatis'. Common forms of *ex libris* inscription are 'Hic est liber sancti Albani quem qui ei abstulerit aut titulum deleverit anathema sit', often in red ink, and 'Hunc librum dedit . . . Deo et ecclesie sancti Albani', followed by an anathema.

Cambridge,
U.L., Dd.6.7. *e*G. Monemutensis, etc. s.xv.
7.7–10. *e*N. de Lyra (4 vols). s.xv.
8.6. *e*Jeronimus. s.xii.
11.78.[1] *e*H. Abrincensis. s.xiii.
Ee.1.9. *e*Biblia. s.xiii.
3.59. *s*'Estoire de S. Aedward' (in French). s.xiii. ?
6.28. *e*Ruth et Actus apost. glo. s.xiii.
Gg.4.11. *e*Bonaventura, etc. s.xv. [Studio abbatis specialiter deputatus].
Kk. 4.22. *e*Ambrosius. s.xii.
Clare Coll., 14. *b*T. de Capua, etc. s.xiv in. ?
27. *b*Turpinus, etc. s.xiv in. ?
Corpus Christi Coll., 5,6. *e*Historia aurea (2 vols). s.xv in.
7. *e*Chronica et registrum benefactorum. s.xiv ex.–xv in.
16.[1, 2] *cl*M. Paris. s.xiii.
26.[1, 2] *c*M. Paris. s.xiii.
48. *s*Biblia. s.xii. ?
71.[3] Macrobius, etc. s.xii.
77. *i*W. Durandus. s.xiv. [de studio dompni abbatis sancti Albani].
290. *e*Chronica Adonis. s.xi/xii.
385, pp. 89–212.[4] W. de Conchis. s.xiii.
Fitzwilliam Mus., 274. *l*Psalmi, etc. s.xiv ex.

[1] These manuscripts contain writing in the hand of Matthew Paris: see R. Vaughan, 'The Handwriting of Matthew Paris', *Trans. Cambr. Bibl. Soc.*, i (1953), 390–92.

[2] Corpus Christi Coll. 16 is the second part of Corpus Christi Coll. 26.

[3] The table of contents of Corpus Christi Coll. 71 is in the distinctive form found in B.M., Royal 12 F.ii, Bodleian, Laud misc. 363, 370, and Oxford, Christ Church 115.

[4] This manuscript contains writing in the hand of Matthew Paris: see above, n. 1.

Cambridge (*contd*)
> Gonv. and Caius Coll., 230. *c*Misc. theologica, etc. s.xv.
> King's Coll., 19. *e*Beda. s.xii in.
> Pembr. Coll., 180. *e*Hilarius. s.xii. [de armariolo A 4 et quarto gradu liber quartus].
> St John's Coll., 137**. *e*Nova officia ad usum S. Albani. s.xv ex. [de infirmitorio].
>> 183. *e*Novum Testamentum. s.xii.
> Trinity Coll., 149. *e*Evangelia glo. s.xii ex.
>> 317. *e*Odonis isagoge. s.xiii in.
>> 320. R. Grosseteste, etc. s.xv. [de studio abbatis]. ?
>> 847. *l*Psalterium. s.xiii–xv. ?
>> 1289. *e*Epp. Pauli glo. s.xii ex.
>> 1341. *e*Cassiodorus. s.xii ex. [de almariolo C].
>> 1446. *s*Romance of Alexander (in French). s.xiii. ?
>> Grylls 2.179 (pr. bk).[5] *i*Duns Scotus. Venice, A.D. 1490.
> Trinity Hall, 2. *e*Rad. Flaviacensis. s.xii/xiii.

Dublin,
> Trinity Coll., 177.[4] *e*Passio S. Albani, etc. s.xiii. [de armariolo A].
>> 444. *i*Tabule astron., etc. s.xiii. [de studio abbatis].

Durham, U.L., Cosin V.v.15, fos 44–86. *i*Macer. s.xiii–xv.

El Escorial, P.i.5. *e*Cassiodorus. s.xii.

Eton Coll., 26. *e*Biblia. s.xii/xiii. [de armario B].
> 103. *e*N. de Gorran. s.xv. [*Whethamstede list*, p. 268].

Hildesheim, S. Godehards Bibl.[6] *l*Psalterium. s.xii in.

Kew, Mr B. S. Cron. *l*Psalterium. s.xii in.

Leyden, U. L., B.P.L. 114B. *es*Priscianus. s.xii in. ?

London,
> B.M., Add. 16164. *e*W. de Monte, etc. s.xiii. [de almariolo et nono gradu almarioli A].
>> Arundel 201, fos 44–97. *c*Carmina. s.xiii in. ?
>> Cotton Jul. D.vii.[4] *c*Collectanea J. de. Wallingford. s.xiii.
>>> Claud. D.i. *c*Acta J. Whethamstede, etc. s.xv.
>>> D.vi.[4, 7] *c*M. Paris, etc. s.xiii–xiv in.
>>> E.iv, fos 34–377. *c*Gesta abbatum, etc. s.xv.
>>> Nero D.i.[4, 8] *c*Gesta abbatum, etc. s.xiii.
>>> D.v.[4] *m*M. Paris. s.xiii.
>>> D.vii. *c*Liber vite. s.xiv ex.
>>> Otho B.iv. *c*Gesta J. Whethamstede. s.xv.
>>> Vesp. B.xiii, fo. 133.[4, 8] *s*M. Paris. s.xiii.
>>> Titus D.xvi. *e*Prudentius, etc. s.xii. [D 9.11.l].
>> Egerton 633. *e*P. Lombardus. s.xiii ex.
>>> 654. *e*Seneca. s.xii.
>>> 1982. *e*J. Mandeville (in English). s.xv. ?
>>> 3721. *l*Kalendarium, etc. s. xii.
>> Harley 865. *b*Ambrosius, etc. s.xi/xii. ?

---

[5] Trinity Coll., Grylls 2.179 was earlier at Tewkesbury, *q.v.*
[4] See p. 165, n. 1.
[6] A detached leaf of the psalter at Hildesheim belongs to Dr J. Lückger, Sürth bei Köln.
[7] Royal 14 C.i, fos 1–19, was part of Cotton Claudius D.vi.
[8] Cotton Vesp. B.xiii, fo. 133, belongs with Cotton Nero D.i, fos 197, 197.*

London (*contd*)
B.M., Harley 2624. *e*Cicero. s.xii in. [D 11.5.l].
　　　　　　3737. *e*A. Nequam, etc. s.xii/xiii. [B].
　　　　　　3775, fos 100–139. *c*Misc. historica, etc. s.xv.
　　　Royal 2 A.x. *e*Breviarium. s.xii. [de armariolo in choro].
　　　　　　2 B.iv. *l*Troparium. s.xii.
　　　　　　2 B.vi. *e*Psalterium. s.xiii. [de almariolo in choro].
　　　　　　2 F.vii. *e*N. de Hanapis, etc. s.xv. [*Whethamstede list*, p. 268].
　　　　　　2 F.viii. *e*P. Lombardus. s.xiii.
　　　　　　3 C.v. *e*Ivo Carnotensis. s.xiii.
　　　　　　4 D.vii.⁹ *s*P. Comestor, etc. s.xiii in. [B 8.gra.]
　　　　　　6 D.x. *e*N. de Radclif, etc. s.xiv ex.
　　　　　　6 E.viii. *e*P. de Cornubia. s.xiii.
　　　　　　8 G.i. *i*Tabula originalium sacre scripture. s.xiv. [de studio abbatis].
　　　　　　8 G.xi. *e*J. de Friburgo. s.xiv in.
　　　　　　9 C.x. Innocentius IV. s.xiv. [de studio abbatis]. ?
　　　　　　10 C.xiii. *e*Decretales. s.xiii. [B gra. 9 lib. ii].
　　　　　　10 D.i. *e*Parvum volumen. s.xiv. ?
　　　　　　10 D.iii. Innocentius IV. s.xiv. [de studio abbatis].
　　　　　　10 E.vii. *e*Lectura Hostiensis. s.xiv in.
　　　　　　10 E.viii. *e*Summa de titulis decretalium. s.xiv ex.
　　　　　　11 D.ix. *e*Decretum glo. s.xiv in.
　　　　　　12 F.ii. *e*Helpericus, etc. s.xii.
　　　　　　12 G.xiv. *e*Rabanus Maurus. s.xii.
　　　　　　13 B.v. *e*Eusebius. s.xii. [de octavo gradu et almariolo B].
　　　　　　13 C.xiv. *e*Cassiodorus. s.xiii in. [de primo gradu et almariolo B].
　　　　　　13 D.iv. *e*J. Saresberiensis. s.xii ex.
　　　　　　13 D.v.⁹ *e*G. Monemutensis, etc. s.xiii in. [de almariolo B primus liber in primo gradu].
　　　　　　13 D.vi. vii. *e*Josephus (2 vols). s.xii.
　　　　　　13 E.vi.⁹ *c*R. de Diceto. s.xii/xiii. [A 6 gradus 2 p].
　　　　　　13 E.ix. *c*Misc. historica. s.xiv/xv. •
　　　　　　14 C.i, fos 1–19.¹ Misc. historica. s.xiv in.
　　　　　　14 C.vii.⁹ *ls*M. Paris, etc. s.xiii–xiv ex. [A 19].
Coll. of Arms, Arundel 3. *c*Gesta Joh. Whethamstede. s.xv.
Lambeth Palace, 102. *s*Lucas et Johannes glo. s.xii–xiii. ?
　　　　　　111. *e*Egidius in Aristotelem. s.xiii ex.
　　　　　　420.² Mariale, etc. s.xii–xiii.
Longleat, Marquess of Bath, 27. *e*W. de Conchis, etc. s.xii–xiii.
Manchester, Chetham, 6712.⁹,³ Flores historiarum. s.xiii–xiv.
Mount Stuart, Marquess of Bute. *c*Vita S. Albani, etc. s.xiv–xv. [de studio domini abbatis].

---

⁹ These manuscripts contain writing in the hand of Matthew Paris: see R. Vaughan, 'The Handwriting of Matthew Paris', *Trans. Cambr. Bibl. Soc.*, i (1953), 390–92.
¹ Royal 14 C.i, fos 1–19, was part of Cotton Claudius D.vi.
² Sent with other books from Hertford Priory to St Albans, s.xv ex.
³ Chetham 6712 belonged to Westminster by s.xiii ex.

Oxford,
Bodleian, Ashmole 304.⁹ *s*Bernardus Sylvestris, etc. s.xiii.
          1796. *e*Tract. de sphera, etc. s.xiv/xv.
        Auct. D.2.6, fos 2–8. *l*Kalendarium. s.xii. ?
        F.2.13. *e*Terentius. s.xii.
        Bodl. 292, fos 176–411. A. de Hales, etc. s.xiv ex.
                             [de studio abbatis].
             462, fos 1–325. *c*Chronicon. s.xv in.
             467. *e*R. Rolle (in English). s.xv.
             569. *e*Lanfrancus, etc. s.xii.
             752.⁴ *e*Ambrosius. s.xii in.
        Finch e.25. *e*Novum testamentum. s.xii.
        Laud lat. 67. *e*Glose super Priscianum, etc. s.xii/xiii.
        misc. 264. *e*Anselmus. s.xiv. [de studio abbatis].
             279. *e*Missale. s.xiv.
             358. *e*Graduale. s.xii.
             363. *e*Misc. theologica. s.xii.
             370. *e*H. de S. Victore, etc. s.xii.
             409. *e*H. de S. Victore, etc. s.xiii in.
                       [C 7 lib. 6].
        Rawl. C.31. *e*Sermones, etc. s.xii.
             D.358. *e*Pseudo-Aristoteles, etc. s.xv.
             G.99. *e*Donatus, etc. s.xii/xiii.
             liturg. c.1. *l*Sacramentarium. s.xii.
        Seld. supra 24. *e*Aristoteles, etc. s.xii–xiii.
Christ Church, 97. *e*Rupertus Tuitiensis. s.xii/xiii.
                 115. *e*P. Damianus, etc. s.xii.
Corpus Christi Coll., 2.⁵ *s*Biblia. s.xiii. ?
                     233. *e*Misc. grammatica, etc. s.xiii–xv.
Exeter Coll., 15. *e*V. Bellovacensis. s.xiii ex.
Magdalen Coll., lat. 53, pp. 145–68. *cs*Chronicon Anglie. s.xii in. ?
New Coll., 274. *e*Plinius. s.xiii in.
             358. *lc*Psalterium. s.xiii.
St John's Coll., 64. *e*P. de Harentals. A.D. 1414.
             130. *e*Bernardus, etc. s.xv.
Princeton, U.L., R. Garrett 73. *e*Haymo. s.xii in.
San Marino, Huntington, HM 27187. R. Holcot, etc. s.xiv ex.–xv in.
[de studio abbatis]. ?
Stonyhurst Coll., 10. *e*Gregorius. s.xii.
Sürth bei Köln, Dr J. Lückger.⁶ Preces (1 fo.). s.xii in.
Verdun, Bibl. mun., 70. *s*Anselmus. s.xii. ?
Untraced: Bollandists' MS. +73.⁷ Epp. H. de Losinga.
Rejected: Cambridge, U.L., Dd.7.11; Corpus Christi Coll. 33, 319.
        London, B.M., Cotton Claudius E.iii, Harley 3634, fos 137–63.
        Oxford, Bodleian, Bodl. 316, 948, Gough liturg. 18, Laud misc.
        215.

---

⁹ See p. 167, n. 9.
⁴ Bodl. 752 was later at Merton College, Oxford, *q.v.*
⁵ Corpus Christi Coll. 2 contains writing in the hand of Matthew Paris:
see p. 167, n. 9.
⁶ A detached leaf of the psalter at Hildesheim.
⁷ See Brussels, Bibl. royale, MS. 3723, fo. 243.

ST ANDREWS, Fife. *Aug. cathedral priory of St Andrew.*

For numerous existing printed books belonging to or in use by canons, see Durkan and Ross under the names Annand, Thomas Cranston, Cunningham, Duncanson, Goodfellow, John Hepburn, Hindmarsh, Inglis, Law, Mason, Preston, James Stewart, Alexander Young, and their addenda, pp. 174, 175, 185.

Paris, B.N., lat. 1218. cPontificale. s.xiii. ?
St Andrews, U.L., SwB. B 39 BL. eBinding leaf in pr. bk.
           BR 65. A 9. eAugustinus. s.xiii.
Wolfenbüttel, Ducal Libr., Helmst. 411. cCopiale S. Andree. s.xv.
                         538. eScotichronicon. s.xiv.
                         628. eHymni. s.xiv.
                       1029. cSermones. s.xiv ex. ?
                       1108. cMisc. theologica. s.xiii–
                                  xiv. ?

ST ANDREWS. *Franciscan convent.*

For 3 or 4 printed books see Durkan and Ross, pp. 108, 131, 135, 167.

ST ANDREWS. *Dominican convent.*

For about 24 printed books see Durkan and Ross, pp. 74, 104, 108–9, 126 (?), 142, 177.

ST ANDREWS. *University.*

For notices of gifts of books between 1456 and 1496 contained in the Acta Facultatis Artium, see J. R. Salmond and G. D. Bushnell, *Henderson's Benefaction* (Univ. of St Andrews, Libr. Publications, ii, 1942), pp. 29–31.

ST ANDREWS. *St Leonard's College.*

For printed books see Durkan and Ross, pp. 48, 86, 90, 148, 167.

ST ANDREWS. *St Mary's College.*

For printed books see Durkan and Ross, pp. 40–42.

ST ANDREWS. *St Salvator's College.*

For a printed book see, perhaps, Durkan and Ross, p. 136.

ST ASAPH, Flintshire. *Cathedral church.*

List of 22 books given by the Black Prince in 1358 is printed by M. E. C. Wallcott in *Archaeologia Cambrensis*, 4th Series, ii (1871), pp. iii–iv.

ST BEES (Sancta Bega), Cumberland. *Ben. priory of St Bee; cell of St Mary's, York.*

Oxford, Bodleian, Lat. liturg. g.1. *l*Psalterium. s.xv in. ?

ST DAVID'S (Menevia), Pembrokeshire. *Cathedral church of St David.*

Cambridge, Corpus Christi Coll., 199. Augustinus. s.xi. ?
London, B.M., Cotton Dom. i, fos 56–160.[8] Giraldus Cambrensis, etc. s.xiii.
Rejected: Cambridge, Corpus Christi Coll., 153.

[8] Cotton Dom. i, fos 56–160, was taken out of the treasury of St David's by the treasurer, John Lewis, and sent to Sir John Prise, s.xvi: *cf.* J. Prise, *Historiae Brytanniae Defensio* (1573), pp. 26, 128.

ST DOGMELLS, Pembrokeshire. *Ben. (orig. Tironensian) abbey of B.V.M.(?).*

Cambridge, St John's Coll., 5, ii. *c*Eusebius. s.xiii in.
Worcester, Cathedral, F.150. *e*Decretales glo. s.xiii ex.

ST GERMANS, Cornwall. *Ben. (afterwards Aug.) priory of St German.*

Rouen, Bibl. mun., 368. *c*Pontificale ('Lanalet Pontifical'). s.x ex. ?

ST IVES (S. Ivo de Selepe), Huntingdonshire. *Ben. priory of St Ives; cell of Ramsey.*

Cambridge, Gonv. and Caius Coll., 236. *c*A. Nequam. s.xiii ex. ?

ST MICHAEL'S MOUNT, Cornwall. *Archpresbytery.*

London, B.M., Cotton Julius A.vii, fos 124–33. *e*Revelatio S. Michaelis in monte tumba. A.D. 1489.

ST NEOTS, Huntingdonshire. *Ben. alien priory of St Neot; cell of Bec.*

Books noted by J. Leland, *De Scriptoribus Britannicis*, pp. 143, 152.

Cambridge, Trinity Coll., 770. Chronicon Anglie. s.xii. [*Leland, Script. Brit.*, p. 152].
London, Lambeth Palace, 563. *l*Psalterium. s.xiii in.
Oxford, Brasenose Coll., 21. *lc*Kalendarium, etc. s.xv.
　　　　Univ. Coll., 130. *e*Biblia, pars i. s.xii ex.

ST OSYTH (Chich), Essex. *Aug. abbey of St Peter, St Paul, and St Osyth.*

M. R. James, 'MSS from Essex Monastic Libraries', *Trans. Essex Archaeol. Soc.*, N.S., xxi (1933), 36. N. R. Ker, 'More MSS from Essex Monastic Libraries', *ibid.*, xxiii (1945), 298–310.

Beeleigh Abbey, Miss C. Foyle.[9] Bernardus, Apologeticum, etc. s.xii.
Edinburgh, U.L., 136. *e*J. Seward. s.xv.
Helmingham Hall, 2. *s*Ambrosius, Exameron, etc. s.xii. ?
　　　　　　　3. *e*Augustinus. s.xiii.
London, B.M., Lansdowne 382. *e*Marcus glo. s.xii ex. ?
　　　　　Sloane 1935. *l*Psalterium, etc. s.xiv ex.
New York, Mr W. S. Glazier, 65.[9] *e*Ambrosius, De officiis. s.xii.
　　　　　　　　　　　　　　　　　[R.B.].
Oxford, Bodleian, Laud misc. 329. *l*Processionale. s.xv.
　　　　　Lyell 6. *e*J. de Abbatisvilla. s.xiii in.
　　　　　Balliol Coll., 152. *ec*Bernardus, etc. s.xiii in.
　　　　　Trinity Coll., 82. *l*Psalterium. s.xiii. ?
San Marino, Huntington, HM 26052. Augustinus in Pss 101–150. s.xii. [B.B.]. ?
Rejected: Oxford, Bodleian, Laud misc. 240.

ST SERF'S. *See* **LOCH LEVEN.**

---

[9] The Beeleigh and New York MSS bear post-Dissolution inscriptions of ownership by former canons of St Osyth.

SALISBURY. *Cathedral church of B.V.M.; see removed from Sherborne in 1078.*

E. Maunde Thompson, 'Cat. of MSS in the Cathedral Libr. of Salisbury', *Cat. of the Libr. of the Cathedral Church of Salisbury* (1880), pp. 3–36. C. Wordsworth, 'Salisbury Cathedral Libr.', *Notes on the Cathedral Church of Salisbury*, by G. H. Bourne and J. M. J. Fletcher (1924), pp. 106–37. N. R. Ker, 'Salisbury Cathedral MSS and Patrick Young's Catalogue', *Wilts. Archaeol. and Nat. Hist. Magazine*, liii (1949), 153–83.
Legacy of Henry de la Wyle, chancellor, 1329, printed in *Hist. MSS Comm. Rep.*, *Var. Coll.*, i. 375–76, from his will in Salisbury D. and C. Muniments (Box W). Books noted by J. Leland, *Itinerary*, ed. L. Toulmin Smith, i. 263, and *De Scriptoribus Britannicis*, pp. 114, 227.

Aberdeen, U.L., 216.[1] *m*Beda, etc. s.xi/xii.
Cambridge,
    Trinity Coll., 717, fos 44–71. Vite sanctorum. s.xii. ?
                72–158. Gregory's Pastoral Care (in English).
                                s.x/xi. ?
        982. *s*Cicero, etc. s.xii in. [*Cf. Leland, Itin.*, i.263].
Dublin, Trinity Coll., 174. *m*Vite sanctorum. s.xi ex. [*Young* 160].
London,
    B.M., Cotton Tib. C.i, fos 43–203. *sl*Pontificale. s.xi.
        Harley 7026, fos 4–20. *e*Lectionarium. s.xv.
        Royal 5 E.xvi. Isidorus. s.xi ex. [*Cf. Young* 23].
              5 E.xix. Alcuinus, etc. s.xi/xii. [*Young* 31].
           15 B.xix, fos 200–205.[2] Enigmata Symphosii, etc.
                        (6 fos). s.xi/xii. ?
           15 C.ii. Seneca, etc. s.xii ex. [*Young* 154]. ?
           App. 1.[3] Augustinus, etc. (15 fos). s.xii. [*Young* 7].
        Sloane 1056A.[4] Rathramnus, etc. (10 fos). s.xiii. [*Young* 78].
Oxford,
    Bodleian, Arch. Seld. B.26, fos 35–94.[5] J. Tyssington, etc. s.xv in.
        Bodl. 32. *c*Ordinale. s.xiii.
              392.[6] *e*Sermones. s.xi ex.
              407. *e*Ivo Carnotensis. s.xii.
              444, fos 1–27.[6] *m*Isidorus. s.xii in.
              516.[7] *b*Augustinus, etc. s.x.
              698.[7] Ambrosius, etc. s.xii. ?
              756.[6, 7] *m*Ambrosius. s.xi ex.
              765.[6, 7] *m*Ambrosius, etc. s.xii in.
              768.[6, 7] *m*Ambrosius. s.xii.
              835.[6, 7] *m*Ambrosius, etc. s.xii.
        Digby 173.[5] *e*Innocentius III, etc. s.xiii–xv.

---

[1] The same scribe, s.xii, wrote the letters 'D.M.' as a 'nota bene' sign in the margins of Aberdeen, U.L., 216; Bodl. 392, 444 (fos 1–27), 756, 765, 768, 835; Fell 1, 4; Rawl. C.723; Salisbury Cath. 10, 24, 25, 37, 67, 78, 88, 106, 128, 129, 135, 140, 154, 159, 165.
[2] Royal 15 B.xix, fos 200–205, is probably a detached fragment of Salisbury Cathedral 115.
[3] Royal App. 1 is a detached fragment of Salisbury Cathedral 197.
[4] Sloane 1056A is a detached fragment of Salisbury Cathedral 62.
[5] Arch. Seld. B.26, fos 35–94, and Digby 173 formed one volume.
[6] See above, n. 1.
[7] Bodley 516 (*cf.* p. 175, n. 3), 698, 756, 765, 768, 835 belonged to Salisbury Cathedral in s.xvii in.

Oxford (*contd*)
Bodleian, Fell 1.[1, 4]   Vite sanctorum.   s.xi ex.   [*Young* 158].
           3.   Vite sanctorum.   s.xii in.   [*Young* 157].
           4.[1, 4]   *m*Vite sanctorum.   s.xi ex.   [*Young* 159].
    e Mus. 2.   *c*Breviarium.   s.xiv ex.   ?
    Rawl. C.400.   *e*Pontificale.   s.xiv in.
        C.723.[4]   *m*Jeronimus.   s.xi/xii.
Corpus Christi Coll., 222, fos 57–84.[2]   Philobiblon, etc.   s.xv.
Salisbury, Cathedral,[3]   1.   Benedictionale.   s.xii.   [*Young* 163].
           2.   *e*T. Aquinas.   s.xiv in.   [*Young* 134].
           3.   H. de Sancto Victore.   s.xiii.   [*Young* 84].
           4.   Hilarius.   s.xii in.   [*Young* 93].
           5.   Pelagius.   s.xii in.   [*Young* 126].
           6.   Augustinus.   s.xii in.   [*Young* 56].
           7.   Isidorus.   s.xii in.   [*Young* 72].
           8.   Filia matris, etc.   s.xv.   [*Young* 167].
           9.   Cyprianus, etc.   s.xii in.   [*Young* 24].
         10.[4]   *m*Cassianus.   s.xii in.   [*Young* 105].
         11.   *e*Pseudo-Clemens.   s.xii in.   [*Young* 172].
         12.   Smaragdus, etc.   s.xii in.   [*Young* 156].
         13.   *e*Sermones, etc.   s.xiv–xv in.   [*Young* 38].
         14.   Omeliarium.   s.xii.   [*Young* 2].
         15.   H. de Gandavo.   s.xiv in.   [*Young* 124].
         16.   Innocentius IV, etc.   s.xiv.   ?
         17.   Jeronimus.   s.xii.   ?
         18.   T. Aquinas.   s.xiv in.   ?
    19, 20.   *e*T. Aquinas (2 vols).   s.xiii.   [*Cf. Young* 145].
         21.   Sermones.   s.xiii.   [*Cf. Young* 146].
         22.   Augustinus.   s.xii.   [*Young* 90].
         23.   Bernardus.   s.xii/xiii.   [*Young* 37].
        24.[4]   *m*Jeronimus.   s.xii in.   [*Young* 59].
        25.[4]   *m*Jeronimus.   s.xii in.   [*Young* 75].
         26.   Gratianus, Decretum.   s.xiii ex.   ?
         27.   Vetus testamentum.   s.xiii.   [*Young* 83].
         28.   Concordantie bibl.   s.xiv in.   [*Young* 130].
         29.   P. Lombardus.   s.xiii.   [*Young* 45 *or* 152].
         30.   G. de Baysio.   s.xiv in.   ?
         31.   Constitutiones Clementine.   s.xiv.   ?
         32.   *e*Lucas et Johannes cum comment.   s.xiv/xv.
             [*Young* 57].
         33.   Gregorius.   s.xii in.–xii ex.   [*Young* 98].

[1] Fell 1 is the second part of Fell 4.
[2] Corpus Christi Coll., 222, fos 57–84, and Salisbury Cathedral 167 formed one volume.
[3] The following are listed: (*a*) manuscripts containing evidence, indicated here by sigla or in footnotes, that they belonged to Salisbury Cathedral Library before 1540; (*b*) manuscripts listed in Patrick Young's catalogue made in 1622 or 1623, concerning which there is no reason to suppose that they were added to the Library between 1540 and 1622; (*c*) manuscripts which are likely to have been at Salisbury before 1540, but which are not listed in Young's catalogue: these are queried.
[4] See p. 171, n. 1.

Salisbury, Cathedral (*contd*)

34.   Compendium veritatis theologice. s.xiii ex.
     [*Young* 5].

35.[5] *m*Augustinus. s.xii in. [*Young* 18].

36.   *e*Floretum. s.xv in. [*Young* 116].

37.[6] *m*Beda. s.xi/xii. [*Young* 51].

38.   Aldhelm. s.xi in. [*Young* 3].

39.[7] *e*J. Waldeby, etc. s.xv. [*Young* 168].

40.   *e*Jacobus de Voragine. s.xiv in. [*Young* 97].

41.   *e*Johannes glo., etc. s.xii. [*Young* 101].

42.   *e*P. Comestor. s.xiii in. [*Young* 119].

43.   Pentateuchus glo. s.xiii. [*Young* 120 *or* 143].

44.   *e*Numeri, etc., glo. s.xiii in. [*Young* 42].

45.   *e*Regum, etc., glo. s.xiii. [*Young* 68].

46.   *s*Threni, etc., glo. s.xiii in. [*Young* 41].

47.   *s*Isaias, etc., glo. s.xiii in. [*Young* 118].

48.[8] I Macchab., etc., glo. s.xiii in. [*Young* 43].

49.   Evangelia glo. s.xiii. ?

50.[8] Numeri glo. s.xiii. [*Young* 63].

51.[9] Jeremias, etc., glo. s.xii ex. [*Young* 121].

52.[9] Daniel et Ezechiel glo. s.xii ex. [*Young* 54].

53.   Prophete minores glo. s.xii ex. [*Young* 66].

54.   *e*'Flores Bernardi cum parvis concordanciis'.
     s.xiv in. [*Young* 1].

55.   *e*W. Peraldus, etc. s.xiv ex.

56.   Speculum spiritalium, etc. s.xv. [*Cf.*
     Young 19].

57.   Augustinus. s.xii. [*Young* 57].

58.   Augustinus. s.xii. [*Young* 111].

59.   Cassiodorus. s.xii in. [*Young* 142].

60.   *e*Omelie, etc. s.xiii.

61.   Augustinus, etc. s.xii in. [*Young* 112].

62.[1] Mariale. s.xiii. [*Young* 78].

63.   Augustinus. s.xii in. [*Young* 110].

64.   *e*Augustinus. s.xii in. [*Young* 81].

65.[2,3] *m*Augustinus. s.xii in. [*Young* 25 *or* 179].

66.   Augustinus. s.xiii ex. [*Young* 173].

67.[4] *m*Augustinus. s.xii in.–xiii. [*Young* 50].

68.   *e*Opus imperfectum in Matheum. s.xv.

[5] Salisbury Cathedral 35, 65, 106, 109, 115, 118, 168, 197 contain marking with letters 'vz' in pencil, by one hand, s.xiii (?).
[6] See p. 171, n. 1.
[7] Salisbury Cathedral 39 and 113 formed one volume.
[8] MSS 48, 50, and 107 were given by Ralph of York, chancellor 1288–1309, according to a nineteenth-century catalogue of the manuscripts, now at Salisbury, which may preserve inscriptions lost as a result of rebinding.
[9] MSS 51 and 52 are in the same hand.
[1] Salisbury Cathedral 62 and B.M., Sloane 1056A formed one volume.
[2] See above, n. 5.
[3] Salisbury Cathedral 65 appears to be the exemplar of 138.
[4] See p. 171, n. 1.

Salisbury, Cathedral (*contd*)

70. Digestum novum. s.xiv in. ?
71. *e*Innocentius IV. s.xiv in.
72. *e*H. de Gandavo. s.xiv in. [*Young* 133].
73-74. *e*Biblia. s.xiii/xiv.
75. P. Lombardus in Psalterium. s.xiii.
    [*Young* 9].
76. Paterius. s.xii med. [*Young* 64].
78.⁵ *m*'Excerpta ex decretis Romanorum Ponti-
    ficum'. s.xi ex. [*Young* 11].
79. Decretales Gregorii IX. s.xiii ex. ?
80. *e*Paulus Diaconus, etc. s.xii/xiii. [*Young* 26].
81. *e*Biblia. s.xiv in. [*Young* 139].
82. *e*Matheus, Lucas, Johannes, glo. s.xiii.
83. Parabole, etc., glo. s.xiii ex. ?
84. P. Comestor. s.xiii in. [*Young* 61 *or* 114].
85. *e*P Comestor. s.xiii. [*Young* 61 *or* 114].
86. *e*P. Lombardus. s.xii/xiii. [*Young* 141].
87. T. Aquinas. s.xiv–xiv ex. ?
88.⁵ *me*Cassiodorus, etc. s.xi ex. [*Young* 92].
89. Gregorius Nazianzenus. s.xi. [*Young* 22].
90. *e*Esdras, etc., glo. s.xiii. [*Young* 10].
91. *e*Johannes et Matheus glo. s.xiii. [*Young*
    65].
92. Papias. s.xiii in. [*Young* 103].
93. *e*Bonaventura. s.xiv in. [*Young* 181].
94. Gregorius. s.xii. [*Young* 149].
95. Gregorius. s.xii med. [*Young* 46].
96. Gregorius. s.x. [*Young* 47].
97. Sermones, etc. s.xiii in. [*Young* 150].
98. Willelmus de Melitona. s.xiii. [*Young* 180].
100. *e*Augustinus. s.xiii. [*Young* 60].
101. Isidorus, etc. s.x. [*Young* 12].
102. *e*Marcus et Lucas glo. s.xiii. [*Young* 100].
104. *e*Pentateuchus glo. s.xiii. [*Young* 120 *or*
    143].
105. Alex. de Hales. s.xiii. [*Young* 153].
106.⁶,⁸ *m*Augustinus. s.xii in. [*Young* 77].
107.⁷ Psalmi glo. s.xii ex. [*Young* 45 *or* 152].
108. Lucas glo. s.xii/xiii. [*Young* 53].
109.⁸ *m*Augustinus. s.xii in. [*Young* 36].
110. *s*Cosmographia Ethici. s.xii in.
111. Aristoteles. s.xiii. [*Young* 85].
112. Isidorus. s.xi ex. [*Young* 138].
113.⁹ *e*Chaucer (in English), etc. s.xv in.
    [*Young* 168].
114.¹ Augustinus. s.xii in. [*Young* 176].

⁵ See p. 171, n. 1.   ⁶ See p. 171, n. 1.
⁷ See p. 173, n. 8.   ⁸ See p. 173, n. 5.
⁹ Salisbury Cathedral 39 and 113 formed one volume.
¹ Flyleaves of Salisbury Cathedral 114 and 128 are from the same manuscript s.xiex.

Salisbury, Cathedral (*contd*)

115.[2]	Collectanea ex Augustino, etc. s.xii in. [*Young* 86].
116.	Augustinus. s.xii in. [*Young* 17].
117.[3]	Augustinus. s.x. [*Young* 29].
118.[2]	*m*Augustinus. s.xii in. [*Young* 40].
119.	Freculphus. s.xii in. [*Young* 32].
120.	Freculphus. s.xii. [*Young* 33].
122.	Constitutiones Clementine glo. s.xiv. ?
123.	T. de Chabham. s.xiv. ?
124.	Hilarius. s.xii in. [*Leland; Young* 87].
125.	Liber de differentiis. s.xii in. [*Young* 67].
126.	*e*J. de Burgo. s.xv in. [*Young* 123].
128.[4, 5]	*m*Augustinus. s.xii in. [*Young* 88].
129.[4]	*m*Augustinus. s.xii in. [*Young* 28].
130.	Pascasius Radbertus. s.xii in. [*Young* 169].
131.	Ephraem Syrus. s.xii in. [*Young* 144].
132.	Gregorius. s.xi ex. ?
133.	Alcuinus. s.ix. [*Young* 71].
134.	'Commentum Remegii super Sedulium'. s.x/xi. [*Young* 95].
135.[4]	Isidorus, etc. s.xii in. [*Young* 161].
136.	Beda. s.xii in. ?
137.	Jeronimus. s.xii in. [*Young* 58].
138.[6]	Augustinus. s.xii in. [*Young* 25 *or* 179].
139.	Eusebius. s.xii in. [*Young* 6].
140.[4]	Ambrosius. s.xii in. [*Young* 117].
142.	*e*Isidorus. s.xii–xiii in. [*Young* 27].
143.	*e*Jeronimus. s.xv ex. [*Young* 44].
144.	*e*Huguitio. s.xiii/xiv. [*Young* 125].
145.	*e*Ezechiel et Daniel glo. s.xiii. [*Young* 48].
148.	*c*Processionale. s.xv.
149.	Missale. s.xii. [*Young* 165].
150.	Psalterium. s.x ex. [*Young* 30].
151.	Sextus liber decretalium, etc. s.xiv in. ?
153.	*e*Lectionarium. s.xiii.
154.[4]	Amalarius. s.xii. [*Young* 175].
155.	Bernardus. s.xii ex. [*Young* 89].
156.	Epp. Canon. glo. s.xiii. [*Young* 99].
157.	Gregorius, etc. s.xi. [*Young* 14].
158.	Beda, etc. s.ix–xi. [*Young* 15].
159.[4]	*m*Origenes. s.xii in. [*Young* 136].
160.	*e*Comment. in Psalmos. s.xii. [*Young* 104].

[2] See p. 173, n. 5.
[3] Flyleaves of Oxford Bodleian, Bodl. 516, now kept separately as lat. bib. c.8 (P), and Salisbury Cathedral 117 are from the same manuscript, s.viii/ix. Another pair of leaves from this manuscript are now in the Bodmer collection in Geneva: they were formerly in use as binding leaves of a Salisbury manuscript, one of them bearing the inscription 'Iste liber est de almario Sarr', s.xiii/xiv.
[4] See p. 171, n. 1.
[5] The flyleaves of Salisbury Cathedral 114 and 128 are from the same manuscript, s.xi ex.
[6] Salisbury Cathedral 65 appears to be the exemplar of 138.

Salisbury, Cathedral (*contd*)

161. *e*Cantica Canticorum et Parabole glo. s.xii. [*Young* 108].
162. *e*Rufinus, etc. s.xii in. [*Young* 107].
163. Concordantie Biblie. s.xiii. [*Young* 122].
164. Ivo Carnot. s.xii in.–xii. [*Young* 171].
165.[7] *m*Augustinus, etc. s.xii in. [*Young* 35].
166. N. de Byard, Distinctiones. s.xiv. [*Young* 34].
167.[8] *e*J. Manduyt, etc. s.xv. [*Young* 151].
168.[9] Augustinus, etc. s.xii in. [*Young* 127].
169. Augustinus, etc. s.xii in. [*Young* 55].
170. *e*Compendium theologice veritatis, etc. s.xiv in. [*Young* 96].
171. Petrus Cantor, etc. s.xiii in. [*Young* 21].
172. Augustinus. s.x ex. [*Young* 74].
173. Augustinus, etc. s.x ex. [*Young* 13].
174. *e*Sermones. s.xiv. [*Cf. Young* 162].
176. T. Aquinas. s.xiv in. ?
177. Regum et Paralipomena glo. s.xiii. [*Young* 128].
178. Decretales Gregorii noni. s.xiv in. ?
179. Omelie. s.xi ex.–xii in. [*Young* 20].
180. Psalterium. s.x. [*Young* 106].
181. Rad. de Atton. s.xv. [*Young* 132].
182. Evangelia glo. s.xiii in. [*Young* 82].
183. Digestum vetus. s.xiii. ?
184. Biblia, pars ii. s.xii med. [*Young* 148].
185–86. Johannes Andree (2 vols). s.xiv/xv. [*Young* 174, 91].
187. Parvum volumen. s.xiv. ?
197.[9, 1] *m*Augustinus. s.xi ex. [*Young* 7].

Rejected: Cambridge, U.L., Ii.2.4; Emmanuel Coll., 27.

SALISBURY. *Franciscan convent.*

Colchester, Harsnett Libr., K.d.2 (pr. bk).[2] *i*M. Marulus. Cologne, A.D. 1529.

Oxford, Bodleian, Lat. th. e.39. *e*Augustinus, etc. s.xiii ex. [I.32].

SALISBURY. *Dominican convent.*

Books noted by J. Leland, *Collectanea,* iv. 67.

Göttingen, U.L., Theol. 3. *e*Biblia. s.xiv.
London, B.M., IB.26227 (pr. bk).[3] *i*P. Venetus. Milan, A.D. 1476.

---

[7] See p. 171, n. 1.
[8] Salisbury Cathedral 167 and Corpus Christi College, Oxford, 222, fos 57–84, formed one volume.
[9] See p. 173, n. 5.
[1] Royal App. i is a detached fragment of Salisbury Cathedral 197.
[2] Harsnett Libr., K.d.2 belonged also to a member of the Franciscan convent at Lewes.
[3] B.M., IB.26227 belonged also to a member of the Dominican convent at Warwick.

SAWLEY (Sallay, Salley), Yorkshire. *Cist. abbey of B.V.M.*

Cambridge, U.L., Ff.1.27, pp. 1–40, 73–252.[4] Misc. historica. s.xii ex.
      Corpus Christi Coll., 66, pp. 1–114.[4] *e*Misc. historica.
                                           s.xii ex.
                      139. *e*Simeon Dunelm., etc. s.xii ex.
London, B.M., Royal 12 F.vi. *e*T. Cantimpratensis. s.xiv.

SAWTRY, Huntingdonshire. *Cist. abbey of B.V.M.*

Books noted by J. Leland, *Collectanea*, iv. 47.

SCARBOROUGH, Yorkshire. *Grange or 'domus' dependent on the abbey
    of Cîteaux.*

Newbury, Prof. H. A. Ormerod.[5] W. Brito. s.xiii.

SCONE, Perthshire. *Aug. priory, later abbey, of B.V.M. and St Michael.*

For 2 printed books see Durkan and Ross, pp. 83, 135.
Edinburgh, N.L., Adv. 5.1.15. *i*Antiphonarium. s.xvi in.

SELBORNE, Hampshire. *Aug. priory of B.V.M.*

List of 7 service-books and 6 other books in an inventory of 1490, printed in
Charters of Selborne, ed. W. D. Macray, i. 145–46; second folios given.

SELBY, Yorkshire. *Ben. abbey of B.V.M. and St German.*

Cambridge, U.L., Dd.9.52. *e*Augustinus, etc. s.xiv.
Oxford, Bodleian, Fairfax 12. *e*Beda. s.xii. [Cronica xii].
Rejected: Cambridge, Emmanuel Coll., 143.

SEMPRINGHAM (Sempingham, Semplingham), Lincolnshire. *Gilb.
    priory of B.V.M.*

London, B.M., Royal 3 A.xv. *e*Paterius, etc. s.xiv.
                3 B.iii. *e*Concordancie bibl. s.xiii ex.
                5 C.v. *e*Augustinus, etc. s.xiii/xiv.
                8 G.v. *e*J. de Friburgo. s.xiv in.
Oxford, Lincoln Coll., lat. 27. *ce*Bernardus, etc. s.xii in.–xii ex.

SHAFTESBURY, Dorset. *Abbey of B.V.M. and St Edward, of Ben. nuns.*

Cambridge, Fitzwilliam Mus., 2–1957. *i*Horae, etc. s.xvi in.
London, B.M., Add. 11748. *e*W. Hilton, etc. (in English). s.xv. ?
           Cotton Nero C.iv. *l*Psalterium (in Lat. and French).
                              s.xii.
           Lansdowne 383. *l*Psalterium. s.xii.
Steyning, Sir Arthur Howard. *i*Psalterium. s.xv in.
Wellington, J. Hasson. *i*Psalterium. s.xv in.
Rejected: Bodleian, French e.22 (formerly Fox).

[4] Corpus Christi Coll. 66, pp. 1–114, was part of Cambridge, U.L., Ff.1.27,
pp. 1–40, 73–252.
[5] Belonged to Cîteaux, but brought to England temporarily *c.*1295, no doubt
to Scarborough, the only English cell of Cîteaux.

SHEEN, Surrey. *Charterhouse of Jesus of Bethlehem.*

E. Margaret Thompson, *Carthusian Order in England* (1930), pp. 331–34. Brussels, Bibl. royale, 2530; Cambridge, U.L., Inc. 1824, 4121; London, B.M., Add. 11303, Lansdowne 1201, 704 h̄.21 (pr. bk); Oxford, Bodleian, 8vo H.36 Th. BS. (pr. bk) appear to have belonged to the English community of Sheen Anglorum, settled in Flanders from 1568 to 1783. A copy of *Statuta Ordinis Carthusiensis*, Basel, A.D. 1510, now at St Hugh's Charterhouse, Partridge Green, contains the name of Maurice (Chauncey) as prior and has the word 'Shene' stamped on the binding: it belonged either to Sheen at the Marian restoration or to Sheen Anglorum.

Cambridge, U.L., Gg.1.6. *e*Speculum devotorum (in English). s.xv.
      Emmanuel Coll., 35.[6] *m*R. Rolle, etc. s.xv.
            241. *i*N. de Lyra, etc. A.D. 1474.
      Trinity Coll., 354.[6] *i*W. Hilton (in English). s.xv.
Chandlers Cross, Mr W. L. Wood. *e*J. Chrysostomus. A.D. 1496.
Colchester, Harsnett Libr., H.c.27–31 (pr. bks). *i*Biblia glo. (vols 1, 3–6). Basel, A.D. 1502.
Douai, Bibl. mun., 396. *e*R. Rolle. s.xv.
Dublin, Trinity Coll., 281. *e*R. Rolle, etc. s.xv.
Glasgow, U.L., Bn.6.b.11 (pr. bk). *i*Dionysius Carthus. Cologne,
                             A.D. 1531.
      Hunterian 77. *e*Mirror of life of Christ (in English).
                     A.D. 1474–75.
Lincoln, Cathedral, 64. *i*Officia carthusiana. s.xv.
London, B.M., Add. 22121. *e*Speculum christiani. s.xv/xvi.
      Cotton Vesp. D.ix, fos 44–49, 167, 168. *i*Miscellanea.
                             s.xv.
      Harley 4711, fos 304, 341 (pr. bk). *e*'Aurelii Augustini/ Opuscula plurima' (title-page and flyleaf only). (Strasbourg, A.D. 1489 *or* 1491).
      Royal 7 D.xvii. *e*Meditaciones, etc. s.xiii–xv.
Oxford,
    Bodleian, Bib. lat. c.1498. 1–5 (pr. bks). *e*Biblia cum glossa N. de Lyra (5 vols). Basel, A.D. 1498.
        Bodl. 117. *i*Miscellanea. s.xv.
        417. *e*Meditaciones. s.xv.
        797. *e*Misc. theologica. s.xv.
      Hatton 14. *e*Polychronicon. s.xiv.
      Lat. th. e.26. *e*W. Hilton, etc. s.xv.
      Rawl. C.57. *e*Chastising of God's children (in English). s.xv.
  St John's Coll., b.3.22(pr. bk). *i*Bernardus de Botone. Strasbourg, A.D. 1493.
  Trinity Coll., 46. Psalterium, etc. s.xv.
Paris, Mazarine, 34. *e*Biblia. s.xiv ex.
Philadelphia, Rosenbach Foundation, Inc. H491 (pr. bk).[6] *e*W. Hilton. Westminster, A.D. 1494.

---

[6] Cambridge, Emmanuel Coll. 35, Trinity Coll. 354, and the Hilton in Philadelphia contain notes in the hand of James Grenehalgh (professed 1495). Grenehalgh also annotated Bodleian, Douce 262 (see under **LONDON,** *Charterhouse*), B.M., Royal 5 A.v (see under **COVENTRY,** *Charterhouse*) and his monogram is in B.M., Add. 24461 and 37790 and probably Harley 2373 (see under **MOUNT GRACE**).

SHEEN, Surrey. *Reclusory.*

London, B.M., Harley 3820. *e*Misc. theologica. s.xv.
Oxford, Magdalen Coll., lat. 77. *e*Revelationes beate Brigitte. s.xv.

SHELFORD, Nottinghamshire. *Aug. priory of B.V.M.*

Oxford, Bodleian, Bodl. 386. *e*Vitas patrum. s.xii.

SHERBORNE, Dorset. *Ben. abbey of B.V.M.; seat of bishopric until*
A.D. *1078.*

Books noted by J. Leland, *Collectanea,* iv. 150, and *De Scriptoribus Britannicis,*
p. 165.

Alnwick Castle, Duke of Northumberland. *l*Missale. s.xiv/xv.
Cambridge,
    Corpus Christi Coll., 422. *l*Missale. s.xi. ?
    Trinity Coll., 751. *c*Chronicon, etc. s.xv. ?
London,
    B.M., Add. 46487. *c*Cartularium, Officia divina. s.xii.
        Cotton Tib. C.i, fos 43–203. *c*Pontificale. s.xi. ?
            Faust. A.ii. *l*Compotus, etc. s.xv.
Oxford,
    Bodleian, Auct. F.2.14. Vita S. Swithuni, etc. s.xi ex. [*Leland*]. ?
Paris, B.N., Lat. 943. *c*Pontificale. s.x ex.
Rejected: Cambridge, Corpus Christi Coll., 88, 277.

SHERBORNE, MONK, Hampshire. *Ben. alien priory of B.V.M. and St*
   John; cell of Cerisy.

Eton Coll., 33. *c*Gregorius, etc. s.xii/xiii. ?

SHERBURN-IN-ELMET, Yorkshire. *Hospital of St Mary Magdalen.*

York, Minster, xvi.I.11.[7] *e*Gemma ecclesie, etc. s.xii/xiii. ?

SHREWSBURY. *Ben. abbey of St Peter and St Paul.*

London,
    B.M., Hargrave 313. *c*Liber ruber scaccarii. s.xiii. ?
    Prof. F. Wormald. *c*Lectionarium, etc. s.xi–xii. ?

SHREWSBURY. *Collegiate church of St Chad.*

Oxford, Bodleian, Rawl. D.1225. *l*Martyrologium, etc. s.xii.

SHREWSBURY. *Franciscan convent.*

Leicester, Bernard Halliday. *e*Isidorus. s.xiv in.
Oxford,
    Bodleian, Bodl. 771. *e*Clemens Lanthon. (in English). s.xiv ex. ?
    Univ. Coll., 41. *e*Astronomica. s.xiv.
           77. *e*Matheus et Lucas glo. s.xiii.
Shrewsbury, School, XXXII. *e*R. de Pennaforte, etc. s.xiii. [Summa
   de casibus.a.].
Worcester, Cathedral, Q.75. *e*H. de S. Victore. s.xii/xiii. [Hugo a.].

---

[7] York, Minster, xvi.I.11 may have belonged to the hospital at Sherburn,
co. Durham.

SHREWSBURY. *Dominican convent.*
Rome, Vatican, Ottobon. lat. 191. *e*T. Aquinas. ?

SHULBREDE, Sussex. *Aug. priory of B.V.M.*
Cambridge, King's Coll., 18. *e*Ambrosius. s.xii/xiii.

SIBTON, Suffolk. *Cist. abbey of B.V.M.*
Oxford, Bodleian, Laud misc. 545. *e*Polychronicon. s.xv. ?

SNAPE, Suffolk. *Ben priory of B.V.M.; cell of St John's, Colchester (later independent).*
Cambridge, Trinity Coll., 1369. *m*Marianus Scotus. s.xi. ?

SOULSEAT, Wigtownshire. *Prem. abbey of St John the Evangelist.*
Edinburgh, U.L., 165. *i*Avicenna. s.xiii.

SOUTHAMPTON, Hampshire. *Aug. priory of St Denis.*
Books noted by J. Leland, *Collectanea*, iv. 148.
London, B.M., Royal 5 E.vii. *e*Omelie, etc. s.xiii.

SOUTHAMPTON. *Franciscan convent.*
London, B.M., Sloane 1617. *e*Bonaventura, etc. s.xv.
Paris, Ste Geneviève, 2809. *e*J. de Pecham (in French). A.D. 1297.

SOUTHWARK, Surrey. *Aug. priory of St Mary Overy.*
The usual form of *ex libris* inscription is 'Liber beate Marie Overey'.
Cambridge, U.L., Add. 6855. *e*Musica ecclesiastica. s.xv.
    Emmanuel Coll., 338.5.29 (pr. bk). *e*M. Vigerius. Paris, A.D. 1517.
    St John's Coll., 524. *e*Biblia. s.xiii.
    Trinity Coll., 1134, fos 1–128. *e*Isidorus, etc. s.xii.
Canterbury, Cathedral, 101. *e*R. Grosseteste, etc. s.xiii ex.
Glasgow, Mitchell Libr., 20611–13 (pr. bk). *e*Persius, etc. Venice, A.D. 1494, etc.
Guildford, Mrs F. E. O'Donnell. Psalterium, etc.[8] s.xiii ex.
London,
  B.M., Cotton Faust. A.viii, fos 40–178. *e*Annales, etc. s.xiii in.
    Egerton 272. *e*P. Comestor, etc. s.xiii.
    Royal 7 A.i. *e*Misc. theologica. s.xiv/xv.
       7 A.ix. *e*R. Grosseteste, etc. s.xiii.
       10 B.vii. *e*R. Fishacre. s.xiii.
  Westminster Abbey, G.4.30 (pr. bk). *e*A. de Clavasio. Strasbourg, A.D. 1513.
Oxford,
  Bodleian, Ashmole 1285. *e*Boetius, etc. s.xiii.
    Bodl. 423, fos 244–354. *i*Prick of conscience (in English). s.xv.
      924. *e*J. Wyclif. s.xiv/xv.

[8] Dedication added to the calendar at July 11.

Oxford (*contd*)
  Bodleian, Lat. th. e.8. *e*Speculum spiritalium, etc. s.xv.
      Rawl. B.177. *i*Flores historiarum. s.xiv.
      C.1.5 Linc. (pr. bk). *e*De vita et moribus sacerdotum. Paris,
        A.D. 1519.
  Trinity Coll., 31. *e*Isidorus. s.xii.
Paris, U.L., 153. *e*Genesis et Exodus glo. s.xiii.
Yale, U.L., s.n. *e*R. Rolle, etc. s.xv.
York, Minster, xv.P.8 (pr. bk). *e*Meditationes sanctorum. Paris,
    A.D. 1510.
Rejected: Oxford, Bodleian, Rawl. B.186.

SOUTHWELL, Nottinghamshire. *Collegiate church of B.V.M.*

Cambridge, Gonv. and Caius Coll., 449, ii. *e*Martinus Polonus, etc.
                               s.xiv in.
      St John's Coll., 4. *e*Guido de Baysio, etc. s.xiv in.
London, B.M., Royal 4 B.iii. Beda. s.xii. ?
Winchester, Cathedral, 9. *e*Dares Phrygius, etc. s.xiv.

SOUTHWICK (Suðwica, Suwicha), Hampshire. *Aug. priory of B.V.M.*

  Books noted by J. Leland, *Collectanea*, iv. 148. The *ex libris* inscription is regularly in the form 'Hic liber est ecclesie Sancte Marie de Suwica (Suthewyk, Suðwica, Suwicha)' followed by a long anathema, and is written usually at the foot of a page, not the first page. In eight MSS the inscription stretches over a double opening.

Cambridge, Corpus Christi Coll., 145. *e*Legendary (in English). s.xiv in.
London,
  B.M., Add. 34652, fo. 2.[9] Genealogy (in English). s.xi in.
      Arundel 48. *e*H. Huntendonensis. s.xii/xiii. [*Leland*].
      Cotton Otho B.x, fos 55, 58, 62.[9] Bede (in English). s.x.
             B.xi.[9] *e*Bede, etc. (in English). s.x–xi in. [*Leland*].
          Vit. A.xv, fos 4–93. *e*Augustine (in English). s.xii.
Oxford, Bodleian, Bodl. 719. *e*Gregorius. s.xii.
  St John's Coll. 62. *e*Bernardus. s.xiii.
             126. *e*Arnulfus Lexoviensis, etc. s.xiii in.
             153. *e*Gregorius. s.xiii.
             158. *e*Anselmus, etc. s.xii in.
             163. *e*Barth. Exoniensis, etc. s.xii/xiii.
             176. *c*Guido, De modo dictaminis, etc.
                    s.xiii–xiv.
             183. *e*J. Cassianus. s.xii/xiii.
             185. *e*Paterius. s.xi.
    Univ. Coll., 165. *e*Beda. s.xii in. ?
Rejected: London, B.M., Egerton 2863.

SPALDING, Lincolnshire. *Ben. priory of B.V.M. and St Nicholas; cell of Crowland, 1051, and of St Nicholas, Angers, 1074.*

  List of 12 books taken by a monk to Oxford *c.*1438 in *Visitations of Religious Houses of the Diocese of Lincoln*, ed. A. H. Thompson, iii (1929), 330. Books noted by J. Leland, *Collectanea*, iv. 32.

Cambridge, Gonv. and Caius Coll., 314. *e*Chronica, etc. s.xv in.

  [9] Add. 34652, fo. 2, and Cotton Otho B.x, fos 55, 58 and 62, were part of Cotton Otho B.xi.

London, B.M., Royal 3 B.viii. *e*Unum ex quatuor glo. s.xiii.
            6 B.xii. *e*J. Damascenus. s.xiv.
            6 D.viii. *e*Anselmus. s.xiv.
            8 D.xx. *e*Innocentius III. s.xiii in.
            8 E.vi. *e*Pharetra. s.xiii ex.

STAFFORD. *Aug. priory of St Thomas the Martyr.*

Cambridge, U.L., Add. 3572. *e*Consuetudines monastice. s.xv.
London, B.M., Royal 5 F.viii. *e*Innocentius III. s.xiii.
Oxford,
    Bodleian, Auct. F.3.10. *e*Compendium theol. veritatis, etc. s.xiii–xiv.
                5.17. *e*Epp. Senece. s.xiii.
        Hatton 26. *e*H. de S. Victore, etc. s.xiii in.–xiv ex.
              86. *s*R. Rolle. s.xiv ex. ?

STAFFORD. *Franciscan convent.*

Manchester, J. Rylands, Lat. 391. *e*Augustinus. s.xiii.
Oxford, Bodleian Auct. F.5.18. *e*Epp. Senece. s.xiii. [Epistole Senece
    10].

STAFFORD. *Collegiate church of B.V.M.*

Oxford, Bodleian, Hatton 74. *e*Chronicon Anglie. s.xiv.

STAINDROP, co. Durham. *Hospital of B.V.M.*

Oxford, Bodleian, Rawl. A.363, fos 19–65. *e*Innocentius III, etc. s.xiii.

STAMFORD, Lincolnshire. *Ben. priory of St Leonard; cell of Durham.*
    List of 'Libri Henrici Helaugh missi Stamfordiam in octavis S. Laurencii
A.D. MCCCCXXII' printed from Durham, Cathedral, MS. B.IV.46 in *Catalogi
Veteres Librorum Ecclesiae Cath. Dunelm.*, p. 116; second folios given.
Deene Park, Trustees of the late Mr G. Brudenell, XVIII.B.3. *e*Biblia.
    s.xiii.

STAMFORD. *Priory of St Michael, of Ben. nuns.*

Oxford, Bodleian, Arch. A.d.15 (pr. bk). *i*Rule of seynt Benet (in
    English). London, preface dated 1517.

STAMFORD. *Hospital of William Browne, of All Saints.*

London, B.M., Harley 2372. *e*Devotional tracts (in English). s.xv.

STAMFORD. *Franciscan convent.*

Cambridge, Magdalene Coll., 15. *e*Innocentius III, etc. s.xiii–xiv.

STAMFORD. *Carmelite convent.*

Durham, Cathedral, C.IV.22, fos 89–139. *i*Speculum naturale.
    A.D. 1449.
Yale, U.L., s.n. *e*Compendium theologice veritatis. s.xiv. [H.30]. ?

STANLEY (Stanlega, Stanleia), Wiltshire. *Cist. abbey of B.V.M.*
Oxford,
 Bodleian, Digby 11, fos 149–89. *c*Chronicon. s.xiii ex. ?
 All Souls Coll., 12.[1] *e*Comment. in pentatheucum. s.xii/xiii. ?

STANLOW (Locus benedictus), Cheshire. *Cist. abbey of B.V.M., removed in 1296 to* **WHALLEY,** *q.v.; later cell of Whalley.*
Stonyhurst Coll., 11. *e*Haymo. s.xiii.

STIRLING. *Royal collegiate chapel of B.V.M. and St Michael.*
 List of service-books in inventory of 1505 printed in English translation from the cartulary, Edinburgh, N.L., Adv. 34.1.5, by F. C. Eeles in *Trans. of the Scottish Ecclesiological Soc.,* III. iii (1912), 324.

STIRLING. *Franciscan convent.*
 For two printed books see Durkan and Ross, pp. 110, 139. A third, J. Pico della Mirandola, *Opera,* Venice, A.D. 1498, is in the Brechin Diocesan Library, deposited in Dundee University Library.
Edinburgh, N.L., Adv. 18.7.5 (partly pr. bk). *e*Dogma philosophorum, etc. s.xv ex.

STOKE-BY-CLARE, Suffolk. *College of St John the Baptist.*
Cambridge,
 Corpus Christi Coll., EP.C.Par.2–5 (pr. bks). *e*Biblia glo. (4 vols). Nuremberg, A.D. 1493.
  EP.G.Par.3 (pr. bk). *e*J. Boccaccius. Venice, A.D. 1472–73.
  SP.54 (pr. bk). *e*J. de Voragine. Cologne, A.D. 1483.

STONE, Staffordshire. *Aug. priory of St Wulfhad.*
London, B.M., Burney 323. *e*J. Januensis. s.xiv.

STONELEIGH (Stanlega, Stanleia), Warwickshire. *Cist. abbey of B.V.M.*
Cambridge, U.L., Ff.i.20. *i*J. Villan, Sermones. A.D. 1473.
Oxford, All Souls Coll., 12.[1] *e*Comment. in pentatheucum. s.xii/xiii. ?

STRATFORD LANGTHORNE, Essex. *Savigniac and (1147) Cist. abbey of B.V.M.*
 M. R. James 'MSS from Essex Monastic Libraries', *Trans. Essex Archaeol. Soc.,* N.S., xxi (1933), 38.
 Books noted (?) by J. Leland, *Collectanea,* iv. 161; *cf.* J. Leland, *De Scriptoribus Britannicis,* p. 249.
Cambridge, U.L., Inc. 124 (pr. bks). *e*Biblia glo. (4 vols). Strasbourg, s.a.
  Emmanuel Coll., 94. *i*T. a Kempis. s.xv ex.
Oxford, Corpus Christi Coll., 142. *e*J. Damascenus, etc. s.xiii ex.

---

[1] Oxford, All Souls Coll. 12 is from Stanley, Wiltshire, or Stoneleigh, Warwickshire.

STUDLEY, Warwickshire. *Aug. priory of B.V.M.*

London, B.M., Harley 2791. *e*Matheus et Marcus glo. s.xii.

SUDBURY (Sudbyrie, Sulbiria, Suthbur'), Suffolk. *Dominican convent.*

Cambridge, U.L., Kk.1.21. *e*'Postille super Epp. Pauli mag. Petri'. s.xiii.
        St John's Coll., 13. *e*Jeronimus, etc. s.xiv. [C.IIII]. ?
London,
  B.M., Harley 3241. *e*P. Lombardus. s.xii/xiii.
  Gray's Inn, 20. *e*W. Peraldus. s.xiii.
Oxford,
  Univ. Coll., 143. *e*P. Riga. s.xiii.

SWEETHEART (de dulci corde) or **NEW ABBEY,** Kirkcudbrightshire.
    Cist. abbey of B.V.M.

The *ex libris* inscriptions in all four MSS is 'Liber Sancte Marie de dulci corde'
(*cf.* C. H. Borland, *Cat. of Western Mediaeval MSS in Edinburgh Univ. Libr.*,
pl. xxiv).
    For a printed book see Durkan and Ross, p. 132.

Edinburgh, U.L., 101. *e*Gregorius. s.xii.
Oxford, Bodleian, Fairfax 5. *e*Jeronimus, etc. s.xii.
Princeton, U.L., R. Garrett 27. *e*Biblia (3 vols). s.xiii.
Untraced: R. Thoresby MS. 183 (= Bernard, *Catalogi* (1697), ii, 231,
    no. 7610). *e*Breviarium.

SWINE, Yorkshire. *Priory of B.V.M., of Cist. nuns.*

List of eleven books given by Peter, vicar of Swine, in s.xiv/xv printed from
Cambridge, King's Coll., MS. 18, fo. 104ᵛ, by M. R. James, *Descriptive Cat. of
MSS in the Library of King's Coll., Cambridge* (1895), pp. 34–35.

Cambridge, King's Coll., 18. Ambrosius. s.xii/xiii. ?
London, B.M., Harley 2409. *i*Pistil of love, etc. (in English). s.xv.

SWINESHEAD, Lincolnshire. *Savigniac and (1147) Cist. abbey of
    B.V.M.*

Cambridge, Corpus Christi Coll., 150. P. Cantor, etc. s.xiii. ?
        St John's Coll., 100. *e*Cicero, etc. s.xiii.
Oxford, Balliol Coll., 213. *e*H. de Gandavo. s.xiii/xiv.

SYON, Middlesex. *Bridgettine abbey of St Saviour, B.V.M., and St
    Bridget.*

Catalogue of the Library of Syon Monastery, Isleworth, ed. Mary Bateson
(1898). R. J. Whitwell, 'An Ordinance for Syon Library, 1482', *Eng. Hist.
Rev.*, xxv (1910), 121–23.
    Catalogue of s.xvi in. in Cambridge, Corpus Christi Coll., MS. 141, printed
by Mary Bateson, *op. cit.*; pressmarks and second folios given.
    The pressmark, which survives only in three MSS, was written in red on a
label under horn on the outside of the end cover; it is reproduced from B.M.,
Harley 42 (in modern binding, but the label is pasted on to a flyleaf) in *New Pal.
Soc.*, i, pl. 147, no. 7. Another label on the end cover bore the title, donor's
name, and opening words of second leaf.

Aberdeen, U.L., 134.² *i*Mirror of Our Lady (in English). s.xv ex.
Bristol, Baptist Coll., Z.d.40. *lc*Processionale. s.xv.

    ² Bodleian, Rawl. C.941 is the second part of Aberdeen, U.L., 134.

Bury St Edmunds, Cathedral, 1. *e*Beda, etc. s.xiii–xiv in. [*Cat.* K.59].
Cambridge,
   U.L., Add. 4081. *i*Sermo ad clerum, etc. (binding and endleaf only).
      Dd.2.33. *i*Formula noviciorum (in English). s.xvi in.
      Hh.6.8. Astronomica. s.xiii–xv. [*Cat.* B.2].
      Rit. c.351.1 (pr. bk). *c*Primer (in English). Paris, A.D. 1514.
   Magdalene Coll., 11. *l*Diurnale. s.xv in.
             12. *l*Diurnale. s.xv.
             13. *i*Liber precum, etc. s.xvi in. ?
             23. *lc*Martinus Polonus, etc. s.xv.
   St John's Coll., 11. *c*Regula ordinis, etc. s.xv.
           109. *i*Collectanea T. Betson. s.xv.
           131. Ric. de S. Victore, etc. s.xv. [*Cat.* N.49].
           139. *l*Processionale. s.xv.
           219. Gervasius Tilleberiensis, etc. s.xiii–xiv. [*Cat.* K.28].
   Sid. Sussex Coll., Bb.2.14 (pr. bk). *i*Chastising of God's Children, etc. (in English). Westminster, A.D. 1493.
   Trinity Coll., 339. Themata super Epistolas, etc. s.xv. [*Cat.* L.33].
          792. R. Grosseteste, etc. s.xv.
        1336. Epitome biblica J. Castellensis. s.xv. ?
        C.7.12 (pr. bk). *i*Tree of the Holy Ghost, etc. (in English). London, A.D. 1534–35.
Dublin, Archbishop Marsh's Libr., Z.4.4.3. *i*Psalterium, etc. s.xv.
Durham, Mr A. I. Doyle (pr. bk). *i*Pelbartus de Themeswar. Hagenau, A.D. 1501.
Edinburgh, U.L., 59. *l*Psalterium. s.xv. ?
Glasgow,
   U.L., Hunterian 136. *i*T. a Kempis (in English). A.D. 1502.
           332. Dares Phrygius. s.xiv. [K.11; *cat.* K.11].
           509. Medical treatises (in English). s.xv. [*Cat.* B.40].
Göttingen, U.L. (pr. bk). *i*Chastising of God's children, etc. Westminster, A.D. 1493.
Ipswich, Central Libr. (pr. bk). *e*Gratianus. Strasbourg, A.D. 1490.
Lincoln, Cathedral, 60. *e*W. de Alvernia. s.xv. [*Cat.* O.16].
         244. Concordancie Biblie. s.xv. [*Cat.* L.44].
London,
   B.M., Add. 5208. *c*Reg. S. Augustini, etc. s.xv. [*Cat.* M.72].
        22285. *c*Martyrologium, etc. s.xv.
        24661. *i*R. Rolle, etc. s.xv. ?
        30514. *l*Horae, etc. s.xv. ?
        40006. *e*Biblia. s.xiii/xiv. [*Cat.* E.1].
     Arundel 146. *c*Rules for the sisters (in English). s.xv.
     Cotton App. xiv. *i*Breviarium. s.xv ex.
     Harley   42. W. Woodford. s.xv. [d.41; *cat.* D.75].
           487. *i*Psalterium, etc. s.xv.
           612. *c*Revelationes S. Brigitte. s.xv. [? *Cat.* M.64].
           632. J. Wallensis. s.xv. [*Cat.* O.10].
           993. *i*W. Hilton, etc. (in English). s.xv.
        2387. *e*W. Hilton (in English). s.xv.
     Royal 2 A.xiv. *l*Breviarium. s.xiv/xv.
        13 D.viii. *i*V. Bellovacensis. s.xiv. ?

London (*contd*)
B.M., IB.55119 (pr. bk). Bonaventura (in English). Westminster, A.D. 1490.
Dutch Church (pr. bks).[3] *i*W. Parisiensis (2 vols). s.l., A.D. 1516. [*Cat*. N.84, 85].
Lambeth Palace, 546. *c*Devotions (in English). s.xv. ?
St Paul's Cathedral, 5. *c*Rules for the brethren, etc. (in English). s.xv/xvi.
Sion Coll., A.51.2.Aq.5Be (pr. bk). *i*P Bergomatis. Venice, A.D. 1497. [*Cat*. D.122].

Manchester,
Chetham, 27907. *l*Hymnarium. s.xv. ?
J. Rylands, English 81. *e*New Testament (in English). s.xiv ex.
Morcombelake, Mr J. S. Cox. *i*Sermones dominicales, etc. s.xv. [*Cat*. P.51].

New York,
Public Libr., Spencer, Eng. 1519. Catherine. Orcharde of Syon (pr. bk). *i*Orchard of Syon (in English). London, A.D. 1519.
Pierpont Morgan, 600 (pr. bk). *i*Boccaccio (in French). Lyon, A.D. 1483.

Oakly Park, Earl of Plymouth. *i*Psalterium, etc. s.xv ex.

Oxford,
Bodleian, Auct. D.3.1. Biblia. s.xiii ex. [r.1; *cat*. R.1].
D.4.7. *lc*Breviarium. s.xv in.
Barlow 49, fos 4–56.[4] R. Grosseteste. s.xv.
Bodl. 212. Chronica Eusebii, etc. s.xv. [*Cat*. K.9].
630. *e*Misc. theologica. s.xv. [*Cat*. N.64].
Douce N.300 (pr. bk). *i*P. de Natalibus. Venice, A.D. 1506. ?
Lat. th. f.20. W. Hilton, etc. s.xv. [*Cat*. M.95].
Laud misc. 416. *i*Cursor Mundi, etc. (in English). A.D. 1459.
Rawl. C. 781. *l*Ordinale. s.xv. ?
941.[5] Mirror of Our Lady (in English). s.xv ex.
D.403. *c*Misc. theologica. s.xv/xvi.
8° A.11 Th. (pr. bk). *ib*Agapetus, etc. Venice, A.D. 1509, etc.
4° W.2 Th. Seld. (pr. bk). *i*R. Whitford (in English). London, A.D. 1532.
All Souls Coll., 25. *i*W. Hilton (in English) s.xv. ?
Brasenose Coll., 15. R. Rolle, etc. s.xv. [*Cat*. M.44].
Corpus Christi Coll., 245.[4] A. Nequam. s.xv.
Jesus Coll., 39. *i*Disce mori (in English). s.xv. ?
Magdalen Coll., Arch. C.I.1.14 (pr. bk). *c*Breviarium Sarisb. Paris, s.a.
Merton Coll., 76.b.11 (pr. bk). *i*Biblical concordance (in Hebrew). Venice, A.D. 1524.
77.a.20 (pr. bk). *i*Grammatica hebraica. Basel, A.D. 1525.

[3] Deposited at Lambeth Palace.
[4] Barlow 49, fos 4–56, and Corpus Christi Coll. 245 are parts of the manuscript entered in the medieval catalogue under N.16.
[5] Bodleian, Rawl. C.941 is the second part of Aberdeen, U.L., 134.

Oxford (*contd*)
St John's Coll., 167. *c*Processionale. s.xv.
          A.9.5–7 (pr. bks). *b*P. Berchorius (3 vols). Nurem-
                 berg, A.D. 1499. [*Cat.* S.54–56].
Trinity Coll., 53. Biblia. s.xiii ex. [*Cat.* R.36].
Univ. Coll., 25. *l*Officia liturgica (pr. bk and MS.). Paris, A.D. 1522
   and s.xvi in.
Philadelphia, Rosenbach Foundation, Inc. H491 (pr. bk). *i*W. Hilton.
   Westminster, A.D. 1494.
Sion House, Duke of Northumberland. *l*Processionale. s.xvi in.
Stonor Park, Hon. S. Stonor (pr. bk). *i*F. Titelmann. Paris, A.D. 1528.
Syon Abbey, 1. *ic*Processionale.[6] s.xv ex.
         2. *lc*Horae S. Trinitatis. s.xv.
         3. *l*Breviarium.[7] s.xv.
         4. *lc*Horae. s.xv.
         6. *lc*Officia liturgica. s.xv.
Uppsala, U.L., C.159.[8] W. Hilton. s.xv in.
Worcester, Cathedral, Sel. B.50.3 (pr. bk). *i*F. de Mayronis. [*Cat.*
   D.106].
Xanten, Stiftsbibliothek, 3070 B (pr. bk). *e*J. P. Bergamensis. Brescia,
   A.D. 1485.
Untraced: London, Messrs Maggs (in 1935).[9] *l*Psalterium. s.xv/xvi.
Rejected: Cambridge, Corpus Christi Coll., 137; Emmanuel Coll., 35;
   Gonv. and Caius Coll., 127; St John's Coll., 69; Trinity Coll., 388.
   New York, Pierpont Morgan, M.162. Oxford, Merton Coll., 77.b.5
   (pr. bk).

TARRANT KEYNSTON (Tarent Kaines, Locus benedictus regine super
   Tarent), Dorset. *Abbey of B.V.M., of Cist. nuns.*

Dublin, Trinity Coll., 209. *i*Poems (in French). s.xiv.
Oxford, Bodleian, Lyell 23. *c*Psalterium, etc. s.xv.
Redlynch, Major J. R. Abbey. *i*Psalterium. s.xiii.
Stonyhurst Coll., 12. *e*Psalterium. s.xv.

TATTERSHALL, Lincolnshire. *Collegiate church of Holy Trinity.*

Note of books seen by J. Leland printed from B.M., Royal MS. App. 69,
fo. 9, in *Eng. Hist. Rev.*, liv. 95.

London, B.M., Royal 8 G.ii. *e*W. de Monte, etc. s.xiii–xiv. [*Leland*].
               8 G.vi. *e*Roger de Waltham. s.xv. [*Leland*].
               9 B.ix. *e*P. Lombardus. s.xiii in.
               11 A.xiii. *e*J. Lathbury. s.xv. [*Leland*].
               11 B.vi. *e*R. Cowton. s.xv. [*Leland*].
               12 E.xxv. *e*Augustinus. s.xiii/xiv. [*Leland*].
Oxford, Bodleian, Bodl. 419, fos 1–105. *e*W. de Monte. s.xiii–xiv.
   [*Leland*].

[6] Formerly at Sion College, London.
[7] This MS. is said to have been in the possession of the nuns of Syon since
s.xv.
[8] Written by Clement Maidstone, 'diaconus' of Syon, and given by him to
Vadstena.
[9] 166 leaves; book-plate of Lord Arundell of Wardour.

TAUNTON, Somerset. *Aug. priory of St Peter and St Paul.*

Books noted by J. Leland, *Collectanea,* iv. 153.

New York, Pierpont Morgan, 823. *e*Biblia. s.xii ex.

TAVISTOCK, Devon. *Ben. abbey of B.V.M. and St Rumonus.*

Books noted by J. Leland, *Collectanea,* iv. 152.

Cambridge, U.L., Ii.4.6.[1] Homilies (in English). s.xi.
Colchester, Museum.[2] *e*Jeronimus. s.xii. ?
London, B.M., Cotton Vit. C.v.[1] Homilies (in English). s.xi in. ?
Oxford, Bodleian, Digby 81, fos 67–88. *c*Chronica. s.xiii. ?

TEWKESBURY (Theokesburia), Gloucestershire. *Ben. abbey of B.V.M.*
(*Cf.* cell at **CARDIFF.**)

Books noted by J. Leland, *Collectanea,* iv. 160.

Cambridge, U.L., Gg.3.21. *lc*Missale. s.xiii–xiv.
      Trinity Coll., Grylls 2.179. (pr. bk).[3] *i*J. Duns Scotus.
                       Venice, A.D. 1490.
Gloucester, Cathedral (pr. bk). *i*Bartholomaeus Anglicus. Strasbourg,
   A.D. 1480.
Hereford, Cathedral, P.iv.6. *i*Jeronimus. s.xii.
London, B.M., Cotton Claudius E.i. *i*Anselmus, etc. s.xii/xiii. ?
              Cleop. A.vii, fos 7–103. *c*Annales, etc. s.xiii.
              Royal 8 C.vii, fos 5–8. *c*Kalendarium. s.xii/xiii.
Oxford, Bodleian, Lat. misc. b.2 (R). *c*Chronica. s.xv. ?
              Top. Gloucs. d.2. *c*Chronica. s.xv.
              Trinity Coll., 50. *e*R. Grosseteste. s.xiii ex.
Paris, B.N., Lat. 9376, fos 21–31. *c*Kalendarium; annales. s.xii.
Princeton, U.L., R. Garrett 34. *c*Psalterium. s.xiii. ?

THAME (de parco de Tama), Oxfordshire. *Cist. abbey of B.V.M.*

Cambridge, U.L., Ii.6.36. *e*Preces. s.xiv.
      St Catherine's Coll. (pr. bk). *i*Euclides (in Latin). Venice,
                        A.D. 1517.
London, B.M., Burney 246.[4] Sedulius. s.xii.
              285.[4] Anselmus, etc. s.xii.
              295.[4] *e*Augustinus, etc. s.xii.
              341.[4] Jul. Toletanus, etc. s.xii.
              344.[4] Prosper. s.xii.
              357.[4] *e*Misc. theologica. s.xii.
Oxford, St John's Coll., 60. *e*Hymni. s.xv.

THETFORD, Norfolk. *Cluniac priory of B.V.M.*

Books noted by J. Leland, *Collectanea,* iv. 25.

Cambridge, Corpus Christi Coll., 329. *c*Joh. Bramei historia Waldei,
   etc. s.xv in. ?

---

[1] Cambridge, U.L., Ii.4.6 and another Anglo-Saxon MS., probably Cotton
Vitellius C.v (see H. Wanley, *Catalogus Librorum Septentrionalium* (1705),
p. 208), were found at Tavistock Abbey in 1566.
[2] On loan from Professor L. S. Penrose.
[3] Trinity Coll., Grylls 2.179 was later (?) at St Albans.
[4] Burney 246, 285, 295, 341, 344 were part of Burney 357.

Oxford, Bodleian, Digby 99. *i*Statuta synodalia, etc. (partly in English).
s.xiv ex.
Rejected: Cambridge, Corpus Christi Coll., 460.

THETFORD. *Priory of St George, of Ben. nuns.*
Alnwick Castle, Duke of Northumberland, 449. *i*New Testament (in English). ?

THORNEY, Cambridgeshire. *Ben. abbey of B.V.M. and St Botolph.*
Lists of books lent from the book-closet in 1324, 1327, 1329, and 1330, in Bodleian, MS. Tanner 10* (*Sum. Cat.* 27694), printed by K. W. H[umphreys] in *Bodl. Lib. Rec.*, ii (1948), 205. Books noted by J. Leland, *Collectanea*, iv. 30; *cf.* Leland, *De Scriptoribus Britannicis*, p. 237.

Cambridge, Corpus Christi Coll., 297. *i*Statuta, etc. s.xiii/xiv.
Dublin, Trinity Coll., 448. *e*Martinus Polonus etc. s.xv.
Edinburgh, N.L., Adv. 18.6.12.[5] *e*Persius, etc. s.xi/xii.
            18.7.7.[5] Sedulius. s.x ex.
            18.7.8.[5] *e*Cicero, etc. s.xi/xii.
London, B.M., Add. 40000. *c*Evangelia, etc. s.x–xv.
            Cotton Nero C.vii, fos 80–84.[6] *c*Annales. s.xii in.
            Royal 15 A.x. *e*W. de Insulis, etc. s.xii–xiii.
Oxford, Bodleian, Auct. 2.Q.5.19 (pr. bk). *i*W. Burley. Louvain, s.a.
            Bodl. 680. *e*Libellus afforismorum Ursonis. s.xiii.
            Laud misc. 364. *e*Sulpicius Severus, etc. s.xii.
            Tanner 10. *b*Bede (in English). s.x. ?
    St John's Coll., 17.[6] *c*Beda, etc. A.D. 1109–10.
Rejected: Cambridge, Sid. Sussex Coll., 95. New York, Pierpont Morgan, 708. Oxford, Bodleian, Rawl. G.22.

THORNHOLM, Lincolnshire. *Aug. priory of B.V.M.*
Note about books seen there by J. Leland printed from London, B.M., Royal MS. App. 69, fo. 4ᵛ, *in Eng. Hist. Rev.*, liv. 91.

Oxford, Bodleian Bodl. 655. *e*Speculum juniorum, etc.
    A.D. 1302–3(?). ?
Rejected: Oxford, Bodleian, Hatton 28.

THORNTON-ON-HUMBER, Lincolnshire. *Aug. priory of B.V.M.*
Note of books seen there by J. Leland printed from London, B.M., Royal MS. App. 69, fo. 4, in *Eng. Hist. Rev.*, liv. 91: *cf. Collectanea*, iv. 34.

London, B.M., Campbell roll xxi.4. *c*Chronica. s.xiv.
            Cotton Vesp. A.xi. *e*P. de Vineis. s.xiv. [*Leland*].
            Harley 2. *e*W. Malmesburiensis, etc. s.xiii in. [*Leland*].
            Lambeth Palace, 486. *i*W. Altissiodorensis. s.xiii ex.
Oxford, Bodleian, Tanner 166. *c*Chronicon abbatie, etc. s.xvi in.

THREMHALL, Essex. *Aug. priory of St James.*
Gloucester, Cathedral, D.3.18 (pr. bk). *i*T. Cantimpratensis, etc.
    (Cologne, etc.), s.a. ?
London, Dr Williams' Libr., 4010 Q.10 (pr. bk). *i*J. Junior. Louvain, A.D. 1485. ?

---

[5] Adv. 18.6.12, 18.7.7, 18.7.8 formed one MS. in s.xvi.
[6] Cotton Nero C.vii, fos 80–84, was part of Oxford, St John's Coll. 17.

THURGARTON, Nottinghamshire. *Aug. priory of St Peter.*

Cambridge, Trinity Coll., 290. *e*J. de Atona. s.xiv/xv.
London, Royal College of Physicians, 358. *c*Astronomica, etc. s.xv in.
Rejected: Cambridge, Trinity Coll., 105.

TINTERN, Monmouthshire. *Cist. abbey of B.V.M.*

London, B.M., Royal 14 C.vi. *c*Flores historiarum. s.xiv. ?

TITCHFIELD, Hampshire. *Prem. abbey of the Assumption.*

Catalogue of A.D. 1400 printed from MS. I.A.1 of the Duke of Portland at Welbeck[7] in *Hants. Field Club and Arch. Soc. Papers and Proceedings,* VII. iii (1916), and by R. M. Wilson, 'The Medieval Libr. of Titchfield Abbey', *Proceedings of the Leeds Philos. Soc. (Lit. and Hist. Section),* v (1938–41), 150 and 252. Facsimiles of the catalogue in *New Pal. Soc.,* i, pl. 18.
The pressmark, P.X, of the second Welbeck MS. is reproduced *ibid.,* i, pl. 17, no. 7; in other MSS the commas, instead of dots, preceding the letter, between the letter and figure, and following the figure, are a distinguishing feature of the mark.

Cambridge, U.L.,Ff.4.45. Speculum juniorum, etc. s.xiv ex. [G.XV; *cat.* G.XV].
Kk.5.33. R. de Glanvilla, etc. s.xiv. [P.IIII; *cat.* P.IIII].
Cambridge (U.S.A.), Harvard Law School, 28. *e*Magna carta cum statutis. s.xiv. [P.II; *cat.* P.II].
Oxford, Bodleian, Auct. 1.Q.6.1 (pr. bk). *i*Ant. de Rampegollis, etc. Paris, A.D. 1497.
Bodl. 249. *e*Augustinus. s.xiv. [B.XXV; *cat.* B.XXV].
Digby 154. *e*Expo. misse, etc. s.xiii–xiv. [*Cat.* N.II].
Laud misc. 357. Lethbertus super psalmos, etc. s.xii ex.–xiii. [B.XXII; *cat.* B.XXII].
Welbeck Abbey,
Duke of Portland, I.A.1.[7] *c*Catalogus librorum, etc. A.D. 1400–5.
I.A.2.[8] Rememoratorium de Tychefeld. s.xiv ex.– xvi. [P.X.; *cat.* P.X].

TONBRIDGE, Kent. *Aug. priory of St Mary Magdalen.*

Oxford, Bodleian, Digby 156. *e*P. Lombardus. s.xiii. ?

TOTNES, Devon. *Ben. alien priory of B.V.M.; cell of St Serge, Angers.*

Seven service-books named in inventory of A.D. 1337 in P.R.O., printed by G. Oliver, *Monasticon Dioecesis Exon.* (1846), p. 242. Book noted by J. Leland, *Collectanea,* iv. 151.

TRENTHAM, Staffordshire. *Aug. priory of B.V.M. and All Saints.*

Oxford, Bodleian, Laud misc. 453. *e*Sermones festivales. s.xiv.

TRURO, Cornwall. *Dominican convent.*

Cambridge, Emmanuel Coll., 20. *e*Witelo. s.xiv.

[7] Deposited in the British Museum, Loans 29/56.
[8] Deposited in the British Museum, Loans 29/55.

TUPHOLME, Lincolnshire.   *Prem. abbey of B.V.M.*

Note of book seen by J. Leland printed from B.M., Royal MS. App. 69, fo. 6ᵛ, in *Eng. Hist. Rev.*, liv. 93; *cf. Collectanea*, iv. 32.

London, B.M., Royal 4 A.iv.   *e*Unum ex quatuor glo.   s.xii/xiii.
    [*Leland*].

TWINHAM.   *See* **CHRISTCHURCH.**

TYNEMOUTH, Northumberland.   *Ben. priory of B.V.M. and St Oswin; cell of St Albans.*

The *ex libris* inscription in four MSS, beginning *Hunc librum dedit*, is in the same form as in St Albans' MSS, *q.v.*

Cambridge, Christ's Coll., D.10.9–11 (pr. bks).   *i*Antoninus archiepisc.
        Florent. (3 vols).   Basel, A.D. 1502.
        Pembr. Coll., 82.   *c*Beda.   s.xii.
        Trinity Coll., 847.   *l*Psalterium.   s.xiii–xv.   ?
Durham, Cathedral, A.IV.6.   *e*Daniel et Esdras glo.   s.xii ex.
London,
    B.M., Cotton Julius A.x, fos 2–43.   *c*Vita S. Oswini.   s.xii/xiii.   ?
        Galba A.v.[9]   Psalterium.   s.xiii (?).   ?
        Vit. A.xx.   *e*Chronica.   s.xiii.
        Faust. B.ix, fos 76–244.   Chronica.   s.xv.   [*Leland,*
                                Coll., i. 173].
    Harley 3847.   *e*H. de S. Victore.   s.xii.
Oxford, Bodleian, Gough liturg. 18.   *l*Processionale.   s.xiv.
        Lat. liturg. g.8.[1]   *i*Kalendarium, etc.   s.xv.
        Laud misc.   4.   *l*Processionale.   s.xii.
             657.   *e*R. de Wallingford, etc.   s.xv.
Corpus Christi Coll., 134.   *cl*Vita S. Oswini, etc.   s.xii.
               144.   *e*Astronomica varia, etc.   s.xv.
York, Minster, xiv.K.3 (pr. bk).   *i*P. de Aquila.   Speyer, s.a.

TYWARDREATH, Cornwall.   *Ben. alien priory of St Andrew; cell of St Serge, Angers.*

St Austell, Mr P. S. Rashleigh.[2]   *c*Liber collationum, etc.   s.xv in.–xvi in.

ULVERSCROFT, Leicestershire.   *Aug. priory of B.V.M.*

Rejected: Oxford, Bodleian, Rawl. poet. 138.

VALE ROYAL, Cheshire.   *Cist. abbey of B.V.M.*

Oxford, Bodleian, Ashmole 750.   *c*Misc. theol. etc.   s.xv.   ?

VALLE CRUCIS, Denbighshire.   *Cist. abbey of B.V.M.*

Eton Coll., 37.   *e*Gregorius, etc.   s.xii/xiii.

[9] Archbishop Usher noted of this now badly damaged MS. in Bodleian MS. Add. 91, fo. 73ᵛ, 'cui præfixa fuerant hæc verba "Liber Oswini Deiorum regis".'
[1] Eighty leaves.   The remainder of this manuscript, a psalter and canticles on 226 leaves, s.xiv, has been dismembered, but photographs of the six pages with historiated initials are in the Bodleian.   When still complete the manuscript was in a Dyson Perrins sale at Sotheby's, 11 April 1961, lot 123.
[2] Deposited at the County Record Office, Truro.

London, B.M., Add. 21253. *i*N. de Aquavilla. s.xv.
Oxford, Bodleian, e Mus. 3. *e*Steph. Langton, etc. s.xii/xiii.

VAUDEY (de valle Dei), Lincolnshire. *Cist. abbey of B.V.M.*
Oxford, All Souls Coll., 21. *e*T. Aquinas. s.xiv.

WALDEN, SAFFRON, Essex. *Ben. abbey of B.V.M. and St James.*

M. R. James, 'MSS from Essex Monastic Libraries', *Trans. Essex Archaeol. Soc.*, N.S., xxi (1933), 38. Books noted by J. Leland, *Collectanea*, iv. 163, and *De Scriptoribus Britannicis*, p. 255.

London, B.M., Cotton Titus D.xx, fos 68–92. *c*Chronicon abbatie. s.xv.

WALLINGFORD, Berkshire. *Ben. priory of Holy Trinity; cell of St Albans.*

London, B.M., Royal 5 F.x. *c*Cesarius Arelatensis, etc. s.xii. ?

WALSINGHAM, Norfolk. *Aug. priory of B.V.M.*

Books noted by J. Leland, *Collectanea*, iv. 29.

Dublin, Chester Beatty Libr., W.22. *b*Biblia, pars prima. s.xii. ?
London, B.M., Sloane 1933. *e*Varia medica. s.xiii–xiv.
Oxford, Keble Coll. *i*Breviarium. s.xv ex.

WALSINGHAM. *Franciscan convent.*

Cambridge, Gonv. and Caius Coll., F.7.20–21 (pr. bks). *e*Sermones Meffreth (2 vols). Basel, A.D. 1488.
Oxford, Bodleian, Bodl. 355, fos 159–223. *e*T. Aquinas. s.xiv.
St Bonaventure, University, Friedsam Memorial Libr. 10. *e*Biblia. s.xiii ex. [H].

WALTHAM, Essex. *Aug. abbey of Holy Cross.*

M. R. James, 'MSS from Essex Monastic Libraries', *Trans. Essex Archaeol. Soc.*, N.S., xxi (1933), 38–41. N. R. Ker, 'More MSS from Essex Monastic Libraries', *ibid.*, xxiii (1945), 298–310.
Early thirteenth-century catalogue in Mr H. C. Drayton's MS. (Bible), printed in B. Quaritch's *Cat. of Illuminated and other MSS* (1931), pp. 6, 7, and by M. R. James, *loc. cit.* Books noted by J. Leland, *Collectanea*, iv. 161.
The common form of pressmark, written usually on the front paste-down or on a flyleaf, consists of a number followed by the *al. ca.*, *al. p.*, or *al. supp.*, for *almario canonicorum, almario prioris* and *almario supprioris* respectively, and is reproduced from B.M., Stowe 35 and Harley 59 in *New Pal. Soc.*, i, pl. 17, no. 9*a*, *b*, and from Rawl. C.330 by Ker, *loc. cit.*, pl. 1(*a*). In some MSS there is also the mark *pri. dor.* (Ker, *loc. cit.*, pl. 1(*b*), from Laud misc. 515) or *Su. dor.*, usually on a flyleaf and near the short title.

Cambridge,
    U.L., Ee.3.50. *e*Steph. Langton. s.xiii.
        Gg.1.11. *e*Ambrosius. s.xii ex. [lii. al ca.; *cat.* 18].
    Gonv. and Caius Coll., 116. Tabule. s.xv. ?
                            149. Augustinus, etc. s.xii ex. [xxiiii. al. ca.].
    Magdalene Coll., 22. *e*W. Tyrensis. s.xiii in.
    St John's Coll., 126. *e*Augustinus, etc. s.xii.
    Trinity Coll., 288. *e*P. Riga, etc. s.xiii. [cxxxiiii. al. ca.].

London,
  B.M., Add. 34749. Beda, etc. s.xii–xiii. [lxiii. al. ca.].
    Harley 59. Egesippus. s.xii. [xlv. al. supp.].
      3766.[3] *c*Miracula pape Gregorii. s.xiv.
      3776, fos 1–62, 94–117.[3] *c*Vita Haroldi, etc. s.xiv.
    Lansdowne 763. *e*Varia musica. s.xv ex.
    Stowe 35. *e*Baldewinus de sacramentis. s.xiii in. [pri. dor.,
        lxxxvii. al. ca].
    Lambeth Palace, 200, fos 66–113. Aldhelmus. s.x. [dor. pri., cxxx.
        al. ca.; *Leland*].
        353. *e*Anselmus, etc. s.xiii. [cxli. al. ca.].
  Dr E. G. Millar. R. Grosseteste. s.xiii. [clxxiii. al. ca.].
Oxford,
  Bodleian, Auct. D.4.22. *e*Matheus glo. s.xiii. [Su. dor., xlv. al. p.].
    Digby 211. *e*Beda. s.xii ex. [lii. al. supp.].
    Laud lat. 109. *e*Epp. Pauli, etc. s.xiii. [xliii. al. p.].
      misc. 515. *e*Innocentius III, etc. s.xiii. [pri. dor.,
        lxxxxviii. al. ca.].
    Rawl. A.433. Gregorius. s.xii/xiii. [xliiii. al. ca.; *cf.*
        cat. 22].
      C.330. *e*Scintillarium, etc. s.xii. [lxxviii. al. ca.].
      D.1228. *e*Barth. Exoniensis, etc. s.xii–xiv. [dor.
        pri., lxx. al. ca.].
      G.62. *e*Palladius, etc. s.xiii.
Princeton, U.L., R. Garrett 114. *e*Cassiodorus, etc. s.xii/xiii. [cxxix.
  al. ca.].
Whepstead, Mr H. C. Drayton. *e*Biblia. s.xii/xiii. [xxiiii. al. p.; *cat.* 1].
Untraced: Görlitz, Bibl. der Oberlausitzischen Gesellschaft der Wissen-
  schaften. *e*Biblia. s.xiii.
Rejected: Cambridge, Corpus Christi Coll., 373. Oxford, Bodleian,
  Bodl. 577.

WARDEN (de essartis, de sartis, Wardonia), Bedfordshire. *Cist. abbey*
  of B.V.M.

  Books noted by J. Leland, *Collectanea*, iv. 12, and *De Scriptoribus Britannicis*,
pp. 234, 343. The common form of *ex libris* inscription is 'Liber Sancte Marie de
Ward'.
Cambridge,
  Gonv. and Caius Coll., 316. *e*P. Pictaviensis, etc. s.xiii.
  Sid. Sussex Coll., 71. *e*Ernaldus Bonevallensis, etc. s.xii–xiii.
  Trinity Coll., 101. *e*Augustinus. s.xii.
          122. *e*Gregorius. s.xii/xiii.
          125. *e*Origenes. s.xii/xiii.
          126. *e*Gregorius. s.xiii in.
          127, 128. *e*Cassiodorus (2 vols). s.xii/xiii.
          129. *e*Augustinus. s.xii/xiii.
          130. *s*J. Chrysostomus. s.xii/xiii. ?
          131. Jeronimus. s.xii/xiii. ?
          145. *e*Ambrosius. s.xii/xiii.
          146. *e*Beda, etc. s.xii/xiii.

[3] Harley 3766 formed part of the same volume as Harley 3776, fos 1–62,
94–117.

Cambridge (contd)
Trinity Coll., 157. eJeronimus. s.xii/xiii.
362. sH. de S. Victore. s.xii. ?
1129. cRic. de S. Victore. s.xii ex. [f.xiii]. ?
Oxford, Bodleian, Bodl. 139. eAilredus. s.xii ex. ?
Laud misc. 447. eAmbrosius. s.xii.
Rejected: Cambridge, Trinity Coll., 102, 158.

WARRINGTON, Lancashire. Convent of Austin friars.

London, St Paul's Cathedral, 11. iStatuta Anglie, etc. s.xv in.
Oxford, Corpus Christi Coll., 126. iAnt. Andreas, etc. s.xv.

WARWICK. Dominican convent.

Cambridge, U.L., Inc. 3127 (pr. bk). iAugustinus. Paris, A.D. 1499.
Inc. 3391 (pr. bk). iNich. Pergamenus. Gouda,
A.D. 1480.
Durham, U.L., Cosin F.iv.30/1 (pr. bk). iDurandus de S. Porciano, etc.
Paris, A.D. 1506.
London, B.M., Royal 6 C.ix. iBernardus. s.xii ex.
Sloane 1615, fo. ult.[4] e .
IB.26227 (pr. bk).[5] iP. Venetus. Milan, A.D. 1476.
Oxford, Magdalen Coll., lat. 54. eBiblia. s.xiii.
St John's Coll., 65. iR. Fitzralph. s.xiv.

WARWICK. Collegiate church of B.V.M.

List of service-books and a few other books in an inventory of A.D. 1407 printed from the cartulary, P.R.O., Exch. K.R. Misc. bks 22, in Vict. Co. Hist. Warw., ii. 127. List of books in inventory of 1464 copied in 1691 by H. Wanley in B.M., Harley MS. 7505 from a roll in the custody of Mr Fish of Warwick.

Cambridge, Trinity Coll., 1440. cMiscellanea. s.xiv–xv. ?
Rejected: Oxford, Bodleian, Bodl. 452.

WAVERLEY, Surrey. Cist. abbey of B.V.M.

Books noted by J. Leland, Collectanea, iv. 148.

Cambridge, U.L., Add. 5368. eOrigenes. s.xii ex.
London, B.M., Cotton Vesp. A.xvi. cAnnales abbatie, etc. s.xii ex.–xiii.
Oxford, Bodleian, Bodl. 527. eJuvencus, etc. s.xiii.
Princeton, U.L., R. Garrett 71. eBeda, etc. s.xii/xiii.
Rejected: London, B.M., Cotton Vesp. E.iv, fos 104–202.

WELBECK, Nottinghamshire. Prem. abbey of St James.

Book-list of s.xii printed from Cambridge, St John's Coll., MS. 9, by M. R. James, Descriptive Cat. of the MSS in the Library of St John's College, pp. 11–13.

Cambridge, St John's Coll., 9. eAugustinus. s.xii.
Lincoln, Cathedral, 222. cVita S. Bernardi, etc. s.xii–xiii.
Manchester, J. Rylands, Lat. 179. eSermones (partly in English).
A.D. 1432.

---

[4] London, B.M., Sloane 1615, fo. ult., is a flyleaf which may have no connexion with the main MS., containing medical works of s.xiii.
[5] B.M., IB.26227 belonged also to a member of the Dominican convent at Salisbury.

WELLOW, Lincolnshire. *Aug. abbey of St Augustine and St Olave.*

Note about books by J. Leland, printed from B.M., Royal MS. App. 69, fo. 6, in *Eng. Hist. Rev.*, liv. 92.

WELLS, Somerset. *Cathedral church of St Andrew.*

C. M. Church, 'Notes on the Buildings, Books, and Benefactors of the Library of the Dean and Chapter of Wells', *Archaeologia*, LVII. ii (1901), 201–28. T. W. Williams, 'Wells Cathedral Library', *Library Assoc. Record*, viii (1906), 372–77.

Various medieval gifts enumerated by Church, *loc. cit.* Books noted by J. Leland, *Collectanea*, iv. 37, 41, 155, and *De Scriptoribus Britannicis*, pp. 204, 387, 396, 457.

Cambridge, Trinity Coll., 881. *e*Opera T. Chaundler. A.D. 1457–61. [*Leland*].

London, B.M., Add. 6059. *l*Kalendarium. A.D. 1463.

Oxford, New Coll., 288. *e*Opera T. Chaundler. s.xv. [*Leland*].

Wells, Cathedral, s.n.[6] *c*Obituarium (2 fos). s.xvi in.

        s.n.[6] *l*Breviarium (1 fo.). s.xv.

        s.n. *l*Ordinale. s.xv/xvi.

Rejected: Cambridge, Trin. Coll., 822, 1389. Wells, Cathedral, B.1. 20 (pr. bk).

WELLS. *Cathedral Church of St Andrew, Vicars Choral.*

Oxford, Trinity Coll., 43. *e*Valerius Maximus. s.xiv/xv.

WENDLING, Norfolk. *Prem. Abbey of B.V.M.*

Cambridge, Jesus Coll., 68. *c*Notule decretalium, etc. s.xiii–xiv. ?

WENLOCK, Shropshire. *Cluniac priory of St Milburga.*

Cambridge,
    Corpus Christi Coll., 433. *c*Chronica, etc. s.xiii–xiv. ?
    Trinity Coll., 6. *c*Ambrosius. s.xii/xiii. ?
London, B.M., Harley 3145. *c*P. Comestor. s.xii/xiii. ?
Oxford, D. M. Rogers (pr. bk). *i*Augustinus, De civitate Dei. Basel, A.D. 1515.

Rejected: Holkham Hall, Earl of Leicester, 39.

WESTACRE, Norfolk. *Aug. priory of B.V.M. and All Saints.*

Cambridge, St John's Coll., 96. Antiphonale. s.xiv in. ?

WESTBURY-ON-TRYM, Gloucestershire. *College of Holy Trinity.*

Oxford, Jesus Coll., 45. *e*J. Januensis, etc. s.xv.

WESTMINSTER, Middlesex. *Ben. abbey of St Peter.* (*Cf.* cells at **HURLEY, MALVERN.**)

J. W. Clark, 'The Libraries at Lincoln, Westminster and St Paul's,' *Cambr. Antiq. Soc. Proc.*, ix (1896–98), 37. J. Armitage Robinson and M. R. James, *The MSS of Westminster Abbey* (1909).

List of ninety-four books bequeathed by Archbishop Simon Langham in 1376, printed from Westminster Muniments 9225–26 by J. A. Robinson, *op. cit.*,

---

[6] Formerly in binding of sixteenth-century Communar's accounts, now detached and kept separately.

pp. 4–7. List of thirty service-books in inventory of the Vestry, A.D. 1388, printed from Canterbury, Cathedral, MS. 102, by J. Wickham Legg in *Archaeologia*, lii (1890), 233–35. List of twenty-six service-books in inventory, A.D. 1540, printed from MS. in the P.R.O., L.R. Misc. Books 111, by M. E. C. Walcott in *Trans. London and Middlesex Arch. Soc.*, iv (1874), 320, 323, 343–44; second folios given.

Books noted by J. Leland, *Collectanea*, iv. 48; J. Bale, *Index* (p. 579).

A pressmark occurs in only five MSS and is followed in each by the words 'Pe. 7 Ed. West.'

Cambridge, U.L., Ee.4.23, fos 137–144. *i*Omelie. s.xiii in. ?

        Corpus Christi Coll., 139.[7] Simeon Dunelm., etc. s.xii ex.
                        [*Bale*]. ?

        Peterhouse, 268. *i*Manipulus florum. s.xv. ?

        Trinity Coll., 213. *c*Apocalypsis, etc. s.xiv in. ?

                1365. *e*Medica. s.xi/xii–xiii.

                1405. *i*T. Aquinas. s.xv ex.

Dublin, Trinity Coll., 548. *c*Gesta abbatum, etc. s.xv.

Edinburgh, U.L., Laing II.515. *e*Gratiani decretum. s.xiii. [M.v].

Hereford, Cathedral, O.iv.6. *e*Epp. Pauli glo. s.xiii. [M.vi].

London,

    B.M., Add. 8167. *e*Summa Guidonis, etc. s.xiii.

          10106. *cs*Chronicon Anglie, etc. s.xv. ?

        Cotton Claud. A.viii, fos 13–65. *i*Misc. historica. s.xv.

                Otho C.ii.[8] Flores historiarum. s.xiv/xv.

                        C.xi. *c*Consuetudinarium. s.xv.

                Titus A.viii, fos 2–64. *c*Miscellanea. s.xiii–xv.

        Royal 2 A.xii. *l*Psalterium. s.xii ex. [*Inv. 1388*, 13; *1540*, p. 344].

             5 B.viii. *e*Jeronimus, etc. s.xii. [S.xl].

             7 D.xxi. *i*Innocentius III, etc. s.xiv in.

             7 F.ii. *e*R. Grosseteste. s.xiv.

             9 F.iv. W. Sudbury. s.xiv/xv. [*Leland*]. ?

        IA.17230 (pr. bk). *i*Cicero. Rome, A.D. 1469. ?

    Lambeth Palace, 184. Egidius Romanus, etc. A.D. 1460–61. ?

    Sion Coll., Arc.L.40.2/E.25. *i*Gospel of Nichodemus, etc. (in English).
                        s.xiv–xv.

    Westminster Abbey, 29. *cs*De fundatione ecclesie West. s.xv. ?

                  37. *i*Missale ('Litlington Missal'). A.D. 1383–84.
                    [*Inv. 1388*, 1; *1540*, p. 343].

                38. *c*Liber regalis. s.xiv ex. ?

Dr E. G. Millar. *e*Augustinus. s.xii. [S.xxx].

Manchester, Chetham, 6712. *e*Flores historiarum. s.xiii–xiv.

        J. Rylands, Lat. 165. *i*J. Islip. s.xv ex.

Oxford,

    Bodleian, Bodl. 46. *i*Distinctiones Mauricii. s.xiii.

              157. Misc. theologica. s.xiii ex. ?

        e Mus. 249.[9] G. Foliot, etc. s.xii ex. [S.x].

        Rawl. C.425. *l*Benedictionale. s.xiv. [*Inv. 1540*, p. 344].

        liturg. g.10. *l*Liber precum, etc. s.xv ex. ?

[7] Corpus Christi Coll. 139 was earlier at Sawley, *q.v.*

[8] Otho C.ii, now badly burnt, is stated to have belonged to St Peter's, Westminster, by Dr Th. Smith in a description of the MS. at the end of Bodleian, MS. Smith 140.

[9] e Mus. 249 belonged later (?) to Belvoir.

Oxford (*contd*)
   Bodleian, R.1.23 Th. Seld. (pr. bk).   *i*R. Holcot.   Lyon, A.D. 1497.
   Balliol Coll., 223.[1]   'Sermones Laurentii abbatis.'   s.xii.
            264.   *e*Forma religiosorum.   s.xv.
St John's Coll., 147.   *i*R. Rolle, etc.   s.xv.
            178.   *e*Isidorus, etc.   s.xiii/xiv.
            190.   *e*Bonaventura, etc.   s.xiii ex.
San Marino (U.S.A.), Huntington, HM 1342.   *c*Gesta Romanorum, etc.
   s.xv.   ?
Untraced: Oxford, Balliol Coll., 142.   *i*Ovidius.
Rejected: Cambridge, Gonv. and Caius Coll., 153.   Dublin, Trinity Coll.,
   172.   London, Lambeth Pal., 761.   Oxford, University Coll., 97.

WESTMINSTER.   *Collegiate church of St Stephen.*

London, B.M., Royal 8 A.xi.   *e*G. Babion, etc.   s.xiii in.   ?
            Stowe 49.   *e*Legenda aurea.   s.xiv.
New York, Public Libr., 63.   Missale.   s.xv in.

WESTWOOD.   *See* **LESSNESS.**

WETHERAL, Cumberland.   *Priory of Holy Trinity, B.V.M., and St
   Constantine; cell of St Mary's, York.*

Bridgnorth, St Leonard's Church (pr. bk).   *i*H. Schedel.   Augsburg,
   A.D. 1497.
New York, Pierpont Morgan (pr. bk).   *ib*Albertanus Brixiensis, etc.
   Antwerp, A.D. 1485, etc.

WHALLEY (Benedictus locus), Lancashire.   *Cist. abbey of B.V.M.*   (*Cf.*
   STANLOW.)

Cambridge, Trinity Coll., 1041.   *e*Clementis recognitiones, etc.   s.xiv.
Canterbury, Cathedral, 73.   *e*Duns Scotus.   s.xiii.
London, B.M., Add. 35283.   *e*Psalterium (Lat. and Fr.).   s.xiii.
            Harley 3600.   *e*Polychronicon.   s.xv.
      Lambeth Palace, 499.   *c*Collectiones.   s.xiii.
Manchester, J. Rylands, Lat. 150.   *e*Compilacio de libris Aristotelis, etc.
   s.xiii ex.
Paris, U.L., 790.   *e*Ailredus, etc.   A.D. 1374.

WHERWELL, Hampshire.   *Abbey of Holy Cross, of Ben. nuns.*

Cambridge, Fitzwilliam Mus., McClean 45.   *c*Psalterium.   s.xiii–xiv.
            St John's Coll., 68.   *c*Psalterium.   s.xii.
Leningrad, Public Libr., Q.v.I, 62.   *c*Kalendarium.   s.xii.
London, B.M., Add. 27866.   *i*Psalterium.   s.xiv.

WHITBY, Yorkshire.   *Ben. abbey of St Peter and St Hilda.*

   Catalogue of s.xii ex. printed from the cartulary belonging to Miss L. Strick-
land, fo. 138, by L. Charlton, *History of Whitby* (1799), pp. 112–14; by G. Young,
History of Whitby (1817), pp. 918–20; in *Whitby Cartulary*, i (Surtees Soc., lxix),
341; in Edwards, *Memoirs of Libraries*, pp. 109–11; and in Becker, *Catalogi*,
no. 109. Books noted by J. Leland, *Collectanea*, iv. 39.

---

   [1] A copy of these sermons, with the same defective incipit as this MS., was
noticed at Westminster by 'Boston of Bury'.

Oxford, Bodleian, Rawl. liturg. b.1. *l*Missale. s.xiv ex.
Untraced: Lt-Col. W. E. Moss sale (Sotheby, 8 March 1937), lot 1172
 to Dulau. Psalterium. s.xiii–xiv.

WIGMORE, Herefordshire. *Aug. abbey of St James.*
Cambridge,
 Corpus Christi Coll., 402. *e*Ancrene wisse (in English). s.xiii.
 St John's Coll., 214. *e*Isidorus. s.xii ex.
 Trinity Coll., 66. *e*P. Riga, etc. s.xiii.
Chicago, Univ. of Chicago, 224. *c*Chronicles (in French and Latin).
 s.xiv. ?
Hereford, Cathedral, P.vi.3. *e*Augustinus. s.xii.
Manchester, J. Rylands, Lat. 215, fos 1–8. *c*Chronicon. s.xiv ex. ?
Rejected: Cambridge, Magdalene Coll., Pepys 2981, no. 11.

WIGTOWN, Wigtownshire.
 For a printed book see Durkan and Ross, p. 126.

WILSFORD, Lincolnshire. *Ben. alien priory; cell of Bec.*
Oxford, Bodleian, Bodl. 173. *c*P. Comestor. s.xiii ex. ?

WILTON, Wiltshire. *Abbey of B.V.M. and St Edith, of Ben. nuns.*
London,
 B.M., Cotton Faust. B.iii, fos 194–280. *c*Life of St Edith, etc. (in
 English). s.xv in. ?
 Royal College of Physicians, 409. *l*Psalterium. s.xiii.
Oxford, Bodleian, Rawl. G.23. *l*Psalterium. s.xiii/xiv.
Untraced: *l*Processionale. s.xiv. A transcript now at Solesmes was
 made by Dom Jausions, *c.*1860.

WINCHCOMB, Gloucestershire. *Ben. abbey of St Kenelm.*
 Books noted by J. Leland, *Collectanea,* iv. 161.
 The *ex libris* inscription is in the form 'quod quidem volumen pertinet ad
monasterium Winchelcombense' and is written after the title of the book on a
label on the back cover.
Camarillo (Cal.), Doheny Libr., 50.[2] *b*Ambrosiaster. s.xii in.
Cambridge, U.L., Mm.3.31. *s*Beda. s.xii in.
 Clare Coll., G.1. (pr. bk). *e*Rupertus Tuitiensis. Cologne,
 A.D. 1526.
Colchester, Harsnett Libr., K.f.11 (pr. bk). *i*P. Lombardus. Basel,
 A.D. 1498.
Dublin, Trinity Coll., 53. *e*Novum testamentum, etc. s.xii in.
Glasgow, Mitchell Libr., 163434 (pr. bk). *i*R. de Sabunde. Strasbourg,
 A.D. 1496.
Göttingen, U.L., Th.4. *i*Biblia. s.xiv.
Hereford, Cathedral, P.viii.4. *s*Augustinus. s.xii in. ?
 P.ix.5. *s*Augustinus. s.xii in.
Holkham Hall, Lord Leicester (pr. bk). *e*Rupertus Tuitiensis. Cologne,
 A.D. 1528.

 [2] For evidence that the Doheny Libr. MS. and Oxford, Jesus Coll., 102, are
from Winchcomb, see N. R. Ker in *The Library,* 5th Series, x (1955), 19–20.

London,
  B.M., Cotton Tib. E.iv. *c*Chronicon, etc. s.xii in.
  Lambeth Palace, **H 1756. A 1 (pr. bk). *i*Dictionarius pauperum.
              Paris, s.a.
  Westminster Abbey, CC.4 (pr. bk). *e*Psalterium Brunonis. (Nurem-
              berg), A.D. 1494.
Orléans, Bibl. mun., 127. *l*Sacramentarium. s.x ex.
Oxford, Bodleian, Douce 368. *e*Beda, etc. s.xii.
              Inc. d.G.5.2.1494/1 (pr. bk). *i*Augustinus. Basel,
                          A.D. 1494.
              M.9.4 Th. (pr. bk). *i*Questiones Marsilii de Inghen
                          (Strasbourg, A.D. 1501).
              Rawl. Q.d.12 (pr. bk). *i*Vitas patrum. Lyon,
                          A.D. 1502.
          Jesus Coll., 98. *e*Johannes, etc., glo. s.xiii.
                  102.³ *bs*Augustinus. s.xii in.
          Mr D. M. Rogers (pr. bk). *i*Biblia, pars i. Paris, A.D. 1527.
Sudeley Castle, Mrs Dent-Brocklehurst. *e*Augustinus, etc. s.xii.
Valenciennes, Bibl. mun., 116. *l*Breviarium. s.xii.
Untraced: Cope sale (Sotheby, 4 March 1913), lot 171 to Buddicom.
  *e*Prophete minores glo. s.xiii.   ?
Rejected: Cambridge, U.L., Ff.1.23.

WINCHELSEA, Sussex. *Franciscan convent.*

Hatfield House, Marquess of Salisbury, 309. *i*Biblia. s.xiii.

WINCHESTER, Hampshire. *Ben. cathedral priory of St Peter, St Paul,
  and St Swithun.*

Cf. J. Leland, *De Scriptoribus Britannicis,* p. 55.

Cambridge,
  U.L., Ee.2.3. *m*Pontificale. s.xii.
        Gg.2.18. *e*J. de Voragine. s.xiii/xiv.
        Sel.3.28–29 (pr. bks). *e*J. Duns Scotus (2 vols). Venice,
                    A.D. 1506.
  Corpus Christi Coll., 146, pp. 63–318. *l*Pontificale. s.x/xi.
                  163. *l*Ordinale, etc. s.xi.
                  173, fos 1–56.⁴ *c*Anglo-Saxon chronicle, etc.
                  (in English). s.ix–x.
                  173, fos 57–83. *m*Sedulius. s.viii.
                  328. *e*Vite sanctorum. s.xi–xii in.
                  339, i. *c*R. Divisiensis, etc. s.xii/xiii.   ?
                  473. *l*Troparium ('Winchester Troper'). s.xi.
  Gonv. and Caius Coll., 123. *c*Summa medulle codicis, etc. s.xiii ex.   ?
  St John's Coll., S.5.24 (pr. bk). *i*Pupilla oculi. Paris, A.D. 1510.
  Trinity Coll., 338. *e*Legenda aurea. s.xiv.
Clongowes Wood Coll. *c*T. Rudborne. s.xv.   ?
Downside Abbey, 26543. *l*Officia liturgica. s.xv.

  ³ For evidence that the Doheny Libr. MS. and Oxford, Jesus Coll., 102, are
from Winchcomb, see N. R. Ker in *The Library,* 5th Series, x (1955), 19–20.
  ⁴ Cambridge, Corpus Christi Coll., 173, fos 1–56, was at Winchester in s.x,
probably at St Swithun's, but perhaps at New Minster.

Edinburgh, U.L., *E.15.24 (pr. bk). *e*N. de Tudeschis, etc. Lyon, A.D. 1516.

Havre (Le), Bibl. mun., 330. *l*Missale. s.xi ex.

Kassel, Landesbibliothek, Anhang 19.[5] *s*Pastoral care (in English). s.ix ex.

Leyden, U.L., Voss. lat. F.93. *e*Macrobius, etc. s.xiii in.

Lincoln, Cathedral, 7, fos 44–83. *c*Passionarius, etc. s.xii. ?

London,

    B.M., Add. 29436. *c*Chronicon, cartularium, etc. s.xii–xvi.

          34652, fo. 2.[6] Royal genealogy (in English). s.xi in.

          47967.[7] *s*Orosius (in English). s.x. ?

          49598. Benedictionale S. Æthelwoldi. s.x. ?

      Cotton Galba A.xviii.[8, 9] Psalterium, etc. s.ix/x.

          Tib. B.v, part i, fos 2–73, 77–88. *c*Miscellanea (partly in English). s.x/xi. ?

          B.xi.[1] Pastoral care (in English). s.ix ex. ?

          D.iv, part ii, fos 158–66.[2] Carmen Æthelwulfi. s.xi in.

        Nero C.iv. *l*Psalterium (Lat. and Fr.). s.xii.

        Otho B.x, fos 55, 58, 62.[6] Bede (in English). s.x.

          B.xi.[6, 7] *sc*Bede, etc. (in English). s.x–xi. ?

        Vit. E.xviii. *c*Psalterium (glossed in English). s.xi in.

        Domit. xiii, fos 1–87. R. Divisiensis. s.xiii. ?

      Harley 213. *e*Alcuinus. s.x.

          315, fos 46, 47.[3] *e*Versus, etc. s.xiii/xiv.

          328. *i*Injunctiones W. Wykham, etc. s.xiv–xv.

          Roll CC 21.[3] Memoranda. s.xiii/xiv.

      Royal   5 E.viii. *e*Misc. theologica. s.xii.

          12 D.xvii.[7] *s*Medical recipes (in English). s.x. ?

          15 C.vii. *c*Vite S. Swithuni. s.xi in. ?

      Sloane 418, fos 189–352. *c*Medica. s.xv.

    Lambeth Palace, 183. *c*T. Rudborne. s.xv ex. ?

    Soc. of Antiquaries, 154*.[4] Missale. s.x.

    Westminster Abbey, CC.44 (pr. bk). *i*J. Lathbury. Oxford, A.D. 1482.

Milan, Braidense, A.F.xi. *l*Psalterium. s.xii ex. ?

New York, Pierpont Morgan, 619. *s*Biblia (1 fo.). s.xii. ?

Oxford, Bodleian, Auct. D.2.4. *e*Psalterium, etc. s.xii.

              D.2.6, fos 9–155. *l*Psalterium. s.xii. ?

---

[5] The Kassel MS., a single leaf, is from the same scriptorium as Cotton Tib. B.xi and almost certainly formed part of the Cotton MS.

[6] Add. 34652, fo. 2, and Cotton Otho B.x, fos 55, 58, 62, were part of Cotton Otho B.xi.

[7] B.M., Add. 47967, Cotton Otho B.xi, Royal 12 D.xvii, and Bodleian, Junius 27 are from the same scriptorium as parts of Corpus Christi Coll. 173, fos 1–56.

[8] See Edmund Bishop, *Liturgica historica*, 1918, p. 141.

[9] Bodleian, Rawl. B.484, fo. 85, is a detached leaf of Cotton Galba A.xviii.

[1] Cotton Tib. B.xi and Bodleian, Hatton 20 were written at King Alfred's direction and so perhaps at St Swithun's: the latter was sent to Worcester, *q.v.*

[2] Cotton Tib. D.iv, part ii, fos 158–66, was part of Winchester Cathedral 1.

[3] Harley 315, fos 46, 47, and Harley Roll CC 21 are four originally blank binding leaves of a now missing manuscript to which the *ex libris* refers.

[4] Twenty-six leaves taken from the twelfth-century binding of the Winton Domesday (MS. 154).

Oxford (*contd*)
  Bodleian, Bodl. 49. *e*Aldhelmus. s.x.
          58. *e*J. Wallensis, etc. s.xiv/xv.
          535. *c*Vite sanctorum. s.xi ex.
          755.[1] *c*Haymo, Gesta Francorum. s.xii.
          767. *c*Speculum juniorum, etc. s.xiv.
          775. *l*Troparium, etc. s.xi in.–xii in.
     Digby 63. *lc*Computistica. s.ix. ?
     Douce 125. *e*Pseudo-Boethius, Geometria. s.x ex.
             [H.B.].
     Junius 27.[2] *sc*Psalterium (in Latin and O.E.). s.x in.
     Laud misc. 368, fos 8–167. *c*P. Blesensis. s.xiii.
          572. *e*Flores historiarum. s.xiv.
     Rawl. B.484, fo. 85.[3]
          C.489. *i*Proprium sanctorum. A.D. 1424.
     Seld. sup.76. *c*Varia astronomica, etc. s.xiii. ?
  All Souls Coll., 114. *c*Chronicon abbatie. A.D. 1531.
          L.R.4.a.8 (pr. bk).[4] *i*Augustinus. Paris, s.a.
  Balliol Coll., 15. *e*Gregorius. s.xiii/xiv.
  Trinity Coll., 28. *e*Beda, etc. s.xi.
  Univ. Coll., 69. *e*Quadrilogus de vita T. Becket. s.xiii. ?
Rouen, Bibl. mun., 1385, fos 28 ff. *c*Vita S. Swithuni, etc. s.xi in. ?
Winchester, Cathedral, 1.[5] *c*Beda. s.xi in.
            2. *e*Augustinus. s.xii.
            4. *e*Cassiodorus. s.xii.
            5. *s*Jeronimus. s.xii.
          14.[6] Vitas patrum. s.xii ex. ?
          15. *e*Theodolus, etc. s.xv.
          17. Biblia (4 vols, formerly 2). s.xii.
          20. *b*Egesippus. s.xii. ?
Winchester Coll., 18.[6] Vitas patrum. s.xii ex. ?
          B.32 (pr. bk). *i*Bruno Carthus. Paris, A.D. 1523.
Worcester, Cathedral, F.173. *c*Sacramentarium. s.xi in. ?
Rejected: Laon, Bibl. mun., 238. London, B.M., Arundel 60; Lambeth
    Palace, 181. Oxford, Bodleian, Auct. F.2.14, Bodl. 153, Laud misc.
    664. Paris, B.N., Lat. 987.

WINCHESTER, *New Minster.* **See HYDE.**

WINCHESTER, *Old Minster.* **See WINCHESTER,** *Ben. cathedral*
priory.

WINCHESTER. *Abbey of B.V.M., of Ben. nuns* (Nunnaminster).

Cambridge, U.L., Mm.3.13. *e*Ordo consecrationis sanctimonialium.
  s.xvi in.

[1] Bodley 755 was later at Belvoir.   [2] See p. 200, n. 7.
[3] Rawl. B.484, fo. 85, is a detached leaf of Cotton Galba A.xviii.
[4] All Souls Coll. L.R.4.a.8 belonged earlier to a monk of Rochester.
[5] Cotton Tib. D.iv, part ii, fos 158–66, was part of Winchester Cathedral 1.
[6] Winchester Cathedral 14 and Winchester Coll. 18 are companion volumes.

London,
B.M., Cotton Nero A.ii, fos 3–13.[7] Kalendarium. s.xi in. ?
  Galba A.xiv.[7] *cl*Liber precum (partly in English).
  s.xi in. ?
  Harley 2965. *c*Liber precum. s.viii.
Oxford, Bodleian, Bodl. 451. *bc*Smaragdus, etc. s.xii in. ?
Romsey, Parish Church. *c*Psalterium. s.xv in.
Rejected: London, B.M., Royal 2 B.v, 4 A.xiv. Oxford, Bodleian, Laud
  misc. 664.

WINCHESTER. *College of St Elizabeth of Hungary.*

Oxford, Univ. Coll., 129. *e*J. Januensis. s.xiii ex.

WINCHESTER. *Dominican convent.*

London, B.M., Cotton App. xiii. *e*Ambrosius, etc. s.xii ex.–xiii.

WINCHESTER. *College of B.V.M.*

W. Oakeshott, 'Winchester College Library before 1750', *The Library*, 5th
Series, ix (1954), 1.
Catalogue of s.xv in.–xv ex. printed from a Winchester Coll. register ('Liber
albus', fos 31–36) by W. H. Gunner in *Archaeological Journal*, xv (1858), 62–74;
second folios given. Catalogues of 1405, 1421–22, 1431–32 and 22 Jan. 1432/33
on rolls among college muniments (Mun. 21863, 21865–67); second folios given.

Eton Coll., 91. *e*Ovidius. s.xiii. [liber vii].
Peterborough Cathedral, M.6.6 (pr. bk).[8] *c*Missale Sarisb. Paris, A.D.
  1514.
Winchester Coll., 4. Vita S. Thome. s.xii/xiii. [*Cat.*, p. 68].
  11. Odo de Cheriton. s.xv in. [*Cat.*, p. 66].
  15. Polychronicon. s.xiv ex. [*Cat.*, p. 70].
  17.[9] Clemens Lanthon. s.xv in.
  38. Taxatio ecclesiastica. s.xiv ex. [*Cf. Cat.*,
    p. 71]. ?
Rejected: Winchester Coll., 14 B,[9] 22.[9]

WINDSOR, Berkshire. *Royal collegiate chapel of St George.*

M. R. James, 'The MSS of St George's Chapel, Windsor', *Bibliog. Soc.
Trans.*, N.S., xiii (1932), 55–76.
List of eleven books, lately Lord Scrope's, given to the choir of the college by
King Henry V, on dorse of Precentor's compotus 1415/16 (Windsor, D. and C.
Muniments, Erary xv.56.22). A bill for books, *ibid.*, xv.57.28. Book-list in
inventory of A.D. 1384–85 printed from Bodleian, MS. Ashmole 16 in Dugdale,
Monasticon, vi. 1362 (see also M. R. James, *loc. cit.*, p. 63); second folios given.
Another similar book-list in inventory of A.D. 1409–10 is in MS. Ashmole 22.
Books noted by J. Bale, *Index* (p. 579).
The pressmark consists of a pair of capital letters, often elaborately distorted,
usually on the page facing the beginning of the text and followed by a distinctive
paraph.
It is not certain that all the books in the list below belonged to Windsor before

---

[7] Cotton Nero A.ii, fos 3–13, was probably part of Galba A.xiv.
[8] Peterborough Cathedral, M.6.6 was borrowed by a minor canon, 8 November 1902, and has not been seen since.
[9] See Oakeshott, *loc. cit.*, pp. 14–16. The 'secundo folio' of MS. 14 B does
not agree with that of the Historia Scholastica given by William Stapleford.

1540. Nearly all those in the Bodleian were a present from the Dean and Chapter in 1612. Many of them belonged to monastic houses before they came to Windsor; for details see the index, pp. 374-80.

Cambridge,
   U.L., Dd.1.7, 8. Augustinus. s.xii. [AB; BB].
   Corpus Christi Coll., 346 (pr. bk). eAugustinus. Venice, A.D. 1475.
Eton Coll., 221. cKalendarium (2 fos). s.xv.
Langley Marish, Parish Church.[1] eEvangelia. s.xi.
London, Lambeth Palace, 99. Chronica. s.xiv ex. [K(?)E].
      A. Ehrman (pr. bk). eDuns Scotus. Venice, A.D. 1497.
Oxford, Bodleian, Auct. D.1.2. Matheus et Lucas glo. s.xiii.

	D.1.4.	Matheus et Marcus glo. s.xiii in.
	D.1.5.	Marcus, etc., glo. s.xiii. [AO].
	D.1.10.	Augustinus. s.xii/xiii.
	D.1.11.	Actus apost., etc., glo. s.xiii. [ay]. ?
	D.2.3.	P. Lombardus. s.xiii.
	D.2.10.	Esaias glo. s.xiii in.
	D.2.11.	Jeremias, etc., glo. s.xiii in.
	D.2.13.	XII proph. glo. s.xiii in. [AM].
	D.3.11.	Exodus glo., s.xiii. [AD].
	D.3.13.	Paralipom. glo. s.xiii in. [AF].
Bodl.	86.	Ambrosius. s.xii.
	132.	Augustinus, etc. s.xiii. [BG (?)].
	133.	Sermones, etc. s.xiii in.
	134.	Augustinus. s.xii in.
	141.	Albertus Magnus. s.xv med. [LC (?)].
	167.	P. Blesensis, etc. s.xiv.
	172.	Sermones. s.xiii.
	192.	Gregorius. s.xii.
	194.	Gregorius. s.xiv. [CN].
	208.	eP. Comestor. s.xiii.
	223.	Gregorius. s.xi ex. [CP].
	236.	Augustinus. s.xii ex.
	258.	Jeronimus. s.xiv. [CD].
	267.	Gregorius, etc. s.xii ex. [CO].
	269.	Augustinus. s.xii in. [SV].
	275.	Concordancie bibl. s.xiv/xv. ?
	295.	J. Chrysostomus. s.xii ex. [DH].
	304.	Gregorius. s.xiv. [CQ].
	321.	Gregorius, etc. s.xiv.
	371.	P. Cantor. s.xiii in. [CI].
	372.	T. Aquinas. s.xiv. [OS].
	373.	P. Cantor. s.xiii. [KQ (?)].
	378.	Augustinus. s.xii. [BO].
	384.	Omelie. s.xiii. [DV].
	386.	Vitas patrum, etc. s.xii.
	387.	Augustinus, etc. s.xii in.
	395.	Isidorus. s.xii ex. [LB (?)].
	410.	Fasciculus morum. s.xv.
	452.	Martinus Polonus, etc. s.xiv–xv. [KC].
	453.	T. Dockyng, etc. s.xv in. [CX].

[1] Deposited in the British Museum, Loans 11.

Oxford (*contd*)

Bodleian, Bodl.	459.	Ric. de S. Victore, etc. s.xii.
	468.	Herveus Natalis. A.D. 1455. [OY].
	477.	H. de S. Victore. s.xii. [OK].
	544.	Egidius Romanus. s.xv.
	551.	'Compilacio de vitis sanctorum.' s.xv.
	582.	Jeronimus, etc. s.xii.
	583.	J. Januensis. s.xv. [OA].
	605.	Compendium theol. veritatis. s.xiv. [OG].
	684.	*e*T. Aquinas. s.xiv.
	705.	Augustinus, etc. s.xiii in. [BN].
	721.	Comment. in epp. Pauli. s.xiv. [DT].
	726.	P. Lombardus. s.xiv in. [OM (?)].
	727.	Comment. in psalterium. s.xiii ex. ?
	729.	Beda, etc. s.xii.
	735.	P. Lombardus. s.xii ex.
	741–42.	Ludolphus de Saxonia. A.D. 1444. [FP].
	773.	H. de S. Victore. s.xii.
	777.	P. Comestor. s.xiii. ?
	785.	Gregorius, etc. s.xiv. [CR (?)].
	796.	Rabanus Maurus. s.xi. ?
	799.	N. de Gorran. s.xiii/xiv. [OZ].
	802.	Distinctiones Mauricii. s.xiv in.
	811.	J. Chrysostomus. s.xiv.
	812.	Sermones, etc. s.xiv in. [EI].
	818.	Origenes. s.xii. ?
	821.	Beda, etc. s.xiv ex. [D (?) P].
	822.	*e*P. Riga. s.xiii.
	838.	Bernardus. s.xiv.
	858.	P. Lombardus. s.xiii. [GL].
	866.	Ambrosius, etc. s.xi. [CI].
	867.	Compendium theol. veritatis, etc. s.xv in. [GV].

Digby 220. R. Grosseteste, etc. s.xv in. [LE].

Princeton, U.L., 89. *e*Aeneas Silvius, Historia Bohemica. s.xv ex.

Rejected: Oxford, Bodleian, Bodl. 697.

WINTNEY, Hampshire. *Priory of B.V.M., of Cist. nuns.*

London, B.M., Cotton Claud. D.iii. *c*Martyrologium etc. (partly in English). s.xiii.

WITHAM, Somerset. *Charterhouse of B.V.M.*

List, s.xv, of sixty-eight books given certainly or probably by John Blacman, printed from Bodleian, MS. Laud misc. 154 by E. Margaret Thompson, *Carthusian Order in England* (1930), pp. 316–21; the first part of this list, containing twenty-four titles of books certainly given by Blacman, printed also by M. R. James, *J. Blacman's Memoir of King Henry VI* (1919), pp. 55–59; second folios given.

Cambridge, St John's Coll., 168. *e*Misc. theologica. s.xiii. [C].

Trinity Coll., 1288. *e*Cassiodorus. s.xii ex. [C].

Durham, Cathedral, A.IV.30. *e*Biblia. s.xiii.
Eton Coll., 213. *e*Polychronicon. s.xv. [*Blacman* 4].
Leicester, Mr H. F. Smith. *e*Biblia. s.xii/xiii.
London,
    B.M., Add. 4899. *e*Sermones. s.xii.
        Harley 1032. *c*Veritas theologie. s.xv. ?
    Lambeth Palace, 436. *e*Horologium sapientie. s.xv. [*Blacman* 34].
    Mr H. Sanders. *e*P. Capuanus. s.xiii in. [F].
Oxford,
    Bodleian, Bodl. 208. *e*P. Comestor. s.xiii. ?
              801. *e*Lucerna conscientie, etc. s.xv. [*Blacman* 6].
        Digby 104, fos 21–60. *e*Alanus de Insulis. s.xiii. [*Blacman* 13].
        Laud misc. 152.[2] *e*N. de Lyra. A.D. 1463. [*Blacman* 1].
              154.[2] *e*N. de Lyra. s.xv. [*Blacman* 2].
    Magdalen Coll., lat. 191. *e*Barth. de S. Concordio. A.D. 1440.
    St John's Coll., 182. *e*Vite sanctorum. s.xv.
Untraced: Stolen in January 1962 from Philip C. Duschnes,
    New York. *e*Augustinus. A.D. 1462.

WOBURN, Bedfordshire. *Cist. abbey of B.V.M.*

Cf. J. Leland, *De Scriptoribus Britannicis*, p. 343.

Cambridge, St John's Coll., Bb.6.17 (pr. bk). *e*Boetius, s.a.
London, B.M., IB.118 (pr. bk). *e*Cicero. Mainz, A.D. 1466.
Oxford, Balliol Coll., 178 A. *e*Florus diaconus. s.xii.

WOMBRIDGE, Shropshire. *Aug. priory of B.V.M. and St Leonard.*

Shrewsbury, School, XXXIII. *e*P. Cantor. s.xiii.

WORCESTER. *Ben. cathedral priory of B.V.M.*

    J. K. Floyer, 'The Medieval Library . . . in Worcester Cathedral' in *Archaeologia*, LVIII. ii (1903), and reprinted, with modifications, as preface to J. K. Floyer and S. G. Hamilton, *Catalogue of MSS . . . of Worcester Cathedral* (Worcs. Hist. Soc., 1906). *Catalogus Librorum MSS Bibliothecæ Wigorniensis made in 1622–1623 by Patrick Young*, ed. I. Atkins and N. R. Ker, 1944. C. H. Turner, *Early Worcester MSS* (1916). See also J. A. Robinson and M. R. James, *MSS of Westminster Abbey* (1909), pp. 103–4; J. M. Wilson, 'The Library of Printed Books in Worcester Cathedral', *The Library*, 3rd Ser., ii (1911), 1–33.
    List of eleven MSS probably belonging to Worcester, printed from Cambridge, Corpus Christi Coll., MS. 367 by C. H. Turner, *op. cit.*, p. lviii. List of books possibly belonging to Worcester, *c.*1100, printed from Bodleian, MS. Tanner 3, fo. 189[v] in *Eng. Hist. Rev.*, xxxii (1917), 388–89. List written in the hand of John Lawerne of 30 books in Worcester, Cathedral, MS. Q. 27, fo. 2. List of books obtained by Prior More, drawn up in 1528, printed from Worcester, Cathedral, A.xii, fo. 3 by J. M. Wilson, *loc. cit.*, pp. 30–31. Entries relating to the purchase of books in Prior More's journal, 1518/19–1533/54 are collected in *The Journal of Prior More*, ed. E. S. Fegan (Worcs. Hist. Soc., 1914), pp. 409–415; see also J. Noake, *Monastery and Cathedral of Worcester* (1866), pp. 412–22. Books noted by J. Leland, *Collectanea*, iv. 160.
    The pressmark of B.M., Royal 5 A.xiii is reproduced in *New Pal. Soc.*, i, pl. 17, no. 11.
    The contents of each MS. were noted *c.*1500 on a label pasted to the back cover. In the following list a dagger (†) denotes that the label remains or that there are traces of it.

---

[2] Laud misc. 152 is the second part of Laud misc. 154.

†Aberystwyth, N.L., Peniarth 386. *e*P. Riga, etc. s.xiii.
Cambridge,
    U.L., Kk.3.18.³ *s*Bede (in English). s.xi ex.
          4.6.⁴ *s*Jeronimus, etc. s.xii in.
        Mm.1.19. *b*P. Comestor, etc. s.xii–xiii. ?
    Clare Coll., 30.³ *sc*Gregorius, etc. s.xi.
    Corpus Christi Coll.,   9.⁵ *cs*Passionale. s.xi.
                   12.³ Pastoral care (in English). s.x.
                  24. *e*T. Bradwardine, etc. s.xiv.
                146. *c*Pontificale. s.x/xi–xi ex.
                162, pp. 139–60.³, ⁶ Homily (in English). s.xi.
                178.³, ⁶ Homilies, etc. (mainly in English). s.xi.
                198.³ Homilies (in English). s.xi.
                217. *e*P. Cantor, etc. s.xiii.
                265. *cs*Penitentiale, etc. (partly in English).
                      s.xi–xii.
                279. Synodus Patricii, etc. s.ix/x.
                367, part ii, fos 45–52. *c*Miscellanea (partly in
                              English). s.xi. ?
                391.³ *e*Psalterium, etc. (partly in English). s.xi.
                496. *s*Vite sanctorum (pastedowns only). s.xii
                      in. ?
                557.³, ⁷ Fragments of homily (in English)
                      formerly in bindings of SP.4 and
                      SP.260. s.xi.
    Peterhouse, 71. *i*P. Lombardus. s.xiii/xiv.
    F. J. Norton (pr. bk). *i*P. Tataretus. Paris, A.D. 1514, etc.
Dublin, Trinity Coll., 503. *c*Chronicon. s.xii.
Eton Coll., 96. P. Pictaviensis. s.xiii. [*Cf. Young* 342]. ?
Glasgow, U.L., Hunterian 431.³ Gregorius. s.x/xi–xii in. [*Cf.
    Young* 37, 38].
Gloucester, Cathedral, 25. *i*Hermannus, etc. s.xiii in.
Lawrence, University of Kansas, Y.103.³, ⁷ Homily (1 fo., in English).
                                    s.xi.
                Y.104.³, ⁸ Homily (1 fo., in English).
                                  s.xi.
London,
    B.M., Add. 25031. *bc*Misc. medica, etc. s.xiii.

---

³ Cambridge, U.L., Kk.3.18; Clare Coll., 30; Corpus Christi Coll., 12; 162, pp. 139–60; 178; 198; 391; 557; Glasgow, U.L., Hunterian 431; Lawrence, Univ. of Kansas, Y.103, Y.104; London, B.M., Cotton Otho B.x, fos 29, 30; Otho C.i, part ii; Harley 55; Oxford, Bodleian, Hatton 20; 76; 113; 114; 115; 116; Junius 121; Laud misc. 482; Worcester Cath., F.174: contain annotations in a tremulous hand, probably of s.xiii in. (see C. H. Turner, *Early Worcester MSS*, p. lvi; N. R. Ker in *Leeds Studies in English*, vii (1937), 28).
⁴ Cambridge, U.L., Kk.4.6, Bodleian, Auct. F.1.9, and Corpus Christi Coll., Oxford, 157, contain writing in the same hand.
⁵ Cambridge, Corpus Christi Coll., 9 and B.M., Cotton Nero E.i, vol. 1, vol. 2 (fos 1–180, 187, 188) are companion volumes.
⁶ Corpus Christi Coll. 162, pp. 139–60, was part of Corpus Christi Coll. 178.
⁷ Corpus Christi Coll. 557 and Lawrence, Univ. of Kansas, Y.103 are fragments of one MS.
⁸ Lawrence, Univ. of Kansas, Y.104 is a detached leaf of Bodleian, Hatton 115.

London (*contd*)
B.M., Add. 37777.⁹ Biblia (1 fo.). s.vii/viii. ?
    45025.⁸ Biblia (11 fos). s.vii/viii. ?
    Cotton Tib. B.iv, fos 3–9, 19–86. *c*Anglo-Saxon chronicle (in
                English). s.xi.
      Calig. A.x, fos 65–208. *c*Chronicon. s.xiv. ?
      Claud. A.i, fos 37–40. *c*Epistole. s.xii. ?
      A.viii, fos 198–216. *c*Misc. liturgica, etc.
                s.xiii. ?
      C.ix, fos 4–17. *c*Annales. s.xii ex. ?
    Nero C.v, fos 1–161. *c*Marianus Scotus. s.xii in. ?
      E.i, vol. 1, vol. 2 (fos 1–180, 187, 188).¹
        *cs*Passionale. s.xi.
    Otho B.x, fos 29, 30.² Homily (in English). s.xi.
      C.i, part ii.² Gregory's Dialogues (in English).
        s.xi.
    Vesp. B.x, fos 31–124. Ethicus. s.x/xi. [*Leland*]. ?
      E.iv, fos 203–10.³ *c*Epistole, etc. s.xii in.
    App. 56, fos 1–4.³ Augustinus. s.xii in.
Harley   55, fos 1–4.² Laws, etc. (in English). s.xi.
    1659. *e*W. Peraldus. s.xiii.
    4967, fos 1–76. Justinianus, etc. s.xiii in. [*Cf. Young*
        167]. ?
    5228. 'Gerardinus de modo medendi', etc. s.xii–xiii.
      [*Cf. Young* 275]. ?
    5394. Barlaam et Josaphat, etc. s.xiv. [*Young* 286]. ?
Royal   2 A.xx. Liber precum, etc. s.viii. [*Young* 309]. ?
    †2 C.vii. *e*Postille. s.xiii/xiv.
    2 D.xxvi. *e*Epp. Catholice glo. s.xiii in. [*Young* 6].
    †2 E.vi. *e*Pseudo-Chrysostomus, etc. s.xiii–xiv.
    2 E.xi. *e*XII prophete glo. s.xiii ex. [*Young* 61].
    2 F.i. *e*G. Porretanus, etc. s.xiii in. [*Young* 67].
    3 A.viii. *e*Jeremias et Danial glo. s.xiii. [*Young* 59].
    4 A.ix. *c*Leviticus glo. s.xii ex.
    4 A.xiv.⁴ Comment. in Pss 109–149. s.x. [*Young* 5].
    4 B.iv. *e*Epp. Pauli glo., etc. s.xii.
    4 B.xiii. Beda, etc. s.xii. [*Young* 70].
    4 C.ii. *c*Jeronimus. s.xii. [*Young* 3].
    4 D.xii. *e*Zach. Chrysopolitanus. s.xiii in.

⁹ B.M., Add. 37777 and Add. 45025 are fragments of one volume: *cf.* above
under **JARROW** and for the evidence connecting this Bible with Worcester,
Cat. Libr. Wigorn. . . ., ed. Atkins and Ker, pp. 77–79.
¹ Cambridge, Corpus Christi Coll. 9 and B.M., Cotton Nero E.i, vol. 2
(fos 1–180, 187, 188), are companion volumes.
² Cambridge, U.L., Kk.3.18; Clare Coll., 30; Corpus Christi Coll., 12; 162,
pp. 139–60; 178; 198; 391; 557; Glasgow, U.L., Hunterian 431; Lawrence,
Univ. of Kansas, Y.103, Y.104; London, B.M., Cotton Otho B.x, fos 29, 30;
Otho C.i, part ii; Harley 55; Oxford, Bodleian, Hatton, 20; 76; 113; 114; 115;
116; Junius 121; Laud misc. 482; Worcester Cath., F.174: contain annotations
in a tremulous hand, probably of s.xiii in. (see C. H. Turner, *Early Worcester
MSS*, p. lvi; N. R. Ker in *Leeds Studies in English*, vii (1937), 28).
³ Cotton App. 56, fos 1–4 (and possibly fos 5–61 also) and Vesp. E.iv,
fos 203–210, are fragments of one volume.
⁴ Royal 2 B.v (see under **HYDE**) is a companion volume to Royal 4 A.xiv.

London (*contd*)
B.M., Royal 5 A.xiii. *e*Augustinus, etc. s.xii. [C.xiii; *Young* 21].
      †5 A.xiv. Augustinus. s.xii ex. [*Young* 25].
      5 B.iii. Fulgentius, etc. s.xii in. [*Young* 41].
      5 C.ii. Augustinus. s.xiii. [*Young* 18].
      5 C.vi. *e*Augustinus, etc. s.xiv.
      5 E.v. Isidorus. s.xii. [*Young* 35].
      5 E.xii. Gregorius. s.xiii. [*Young* 39].
      5 E.xiii. Cyprianus, etc. s.ix ex. [*Young* 333].
      5 F.iii. Aldelmus. s.ix. [*Young* 253].
      5 F.xii. Lanfrancus, etc. s.xii. [*Young* 53].
      6 A.vii. Vita S. Gregorii. s.xi in. [*Leland: Young* 36].
      6 A.xvi. Ambrosius. s.xii. [*Young* 73].
      6 C.vii. *c*Gregorius. s.xii. [*Young* 26].
      6 D.iii. Jeronimus. s.xii in. [*Cf. Young* 28].   ?
      8 D.xiii. *e*Smaragdus, etc. s.xii in.
      9 B.v. *e*W. Altissiodorensis. A.D. 1231.
      9 B.xii. *e*Decreta. s.xii in.
      10 B.x. *e*P. de Vineis, etc. s.xiv.
      11 B.ii. *e*Misc. canonica et theologica. s.xii–xiii.
      15 A.xxxiii. Comment. in Mart. Capellam. s.x in.
            [*Leland; Young* 305].
     †15 B.iv. Grammatica, etc. s.xii ex.–xiii in. [aa.xi;
            Young 218].
      15 B.xiv. *c*Priscianus. s.xii ex. [*Young* 291 *or* 292].
Lambeth Palace, 238. *c*Senatus, etc. s.xiii in.   ?
Westminster School, 1. *e*Gregorius. s.xiii. [*Young* 37 *or* 38].
Mr A. Ehrman, R.255 (pr. bk). *i*Rupertus Tuitiensis, etc. (Cologne),
                   A.D. 1527, etc. [*Young* 37 *or* 38].
Oxford,
  Bodleian, Auct. D.inf.2.4. *e*Biblia. s.xiii. [*Young* 55].
        †F.1.9.[5, 6] Rob. Herefordensis, etc. s.xii in.
        †F.5.16.[5] Hildebertus, etc. s.xiv in.
        †F.inf.1.3. *e*Palladius, etc. s.xii ex.–xiv. [C.xxxv].
    Barlow 4. *s*Homiliarium. s.xi. [*Young* 98].
    Bodl. †81. Pseudo-Grosseteste, De lingua. s.xiii/xiv–xiv.
        223. *sc*Gregorius. s.xi ex.
        442. *e*Hilarius. s.xii.
        543. *c*Expo. super reg. S. Benedicti, etc.
            s.xii ex.–xiii.   ?
      †633.[5] *c*Bernardus, etc. s.xii ex.–xiii in. [*Leland*].
        692. *i*J. Lawerne. s.xv.
        828. *bc*Oculus sacerdotum, etc. s.xiv ex.–xv.
        861. *e*R. Rolle, etc. A.D. 1411.
        862. *e*Psalterium glo. s.xii ex.
      †868. *e*W. Malmesburiensis. s.xii.
    Hatton †6. Canones apostolorum, etc. s.xiii. [*Young*
        324].

---

[5] Bodleian, Auct. F.1.9, Auct. F.5.16, and Bodl. 633 have been identified as Worcester books by the script of the parchment label of contents.
[6] Cambridge, U.L., Kk.4.6, Bodleian, Auct. F.1.9, and Corpus Christi Coll., Oxford, 157, contain writing in the same hand.

Oxford (*contd*)

Bodleian, Hatton †11. *s*Regimen animarum, etc. A.D. 1404(?).
[*Young* 240].

20.[7] *e*Pastoral care (in English). s.ix ex.

†23. *sc*J. Cassianus, etc. s.xi ex. [*Young* 222].

30.[8] *e*Pseudo-Augustinus. s.x. [*Young* 24].

40. *e*Smaragdus. s.xii. [*Young* 217].

42. *s*Collectio canonum, etc. s.ix–x. [*Young* 221].

48. *mb*Regula sancti Benedicti. s.viii. [*Young* 216].

76.[9] Gregory's Dialogues, etc. (in English). s.xi–xii.

93.[1] *c*Expo. misse, etc. s.viii/ix. [*Young* 223].

113, 114.[9, 1] *e*Homiliary (in English). s.xi. [*Young* 318, 319].

115.[9, 2] *e*Homilies (in English). s.xi. [*Young* 317].

116.[9] Homilies (in English). s.xii. [*Young* 320].

Junius 121.[9, 1] *c*Canons, etc. (in English). s.xi. [*Young* 321].

Lat. liturg. d.20.[3] Fragmenta polyphonica (14 fos). s.xiv in.

Laud misc. 482.[9] Canons (in English). s.xi.

Rawl. C.428. *e*Liber sextus decretalium, etc. s.xiv in.

Tanner 3. *c*Gregorius. s.xi in.   ?

8° M.122 Th. (flyleaves, pr. bk). *i*Erasmus, *Encomium Moriae* (2 fos). Antwerp, A.D. 1512.

All Souls Coll., L.R.4.a.8 (pr. bk). *c*P. de Alliaco. Paris, A.D. 1498.

Corpus Christi Coll., 157.[4] *c*Flor. Wigorniensis, etc. s.xii in.

[7] Cambridge, U.L., Kk.3.18; Clare Coll. 30; Corpus Christi Coll. 12; 162, pp. 139–60; 178; 198; 391; 557; Glasgow, U.L., Hunterian 431; Univ. of Kansas, Y.103, Y.104; London, B.M., Cotton Otho B.x, fos 29, 30; Otho C.i, part ii; Harley 55; Oxford, Bodleian, Hatton 20; 76; 113; 114; 115; 116; Junius 121; Laud misc. 482; Worcester, Cath., F.174: contain annotations in a tremulous hand, probably of s.xiii in. (see C. H. Turner, *Early Worcester MSS*, p. lvi; N. R. Ker in *Leeds Studies in English*, vii (1937), 28).

[8] Leaves from the same missal of s.xi in. were used in binding Hatton 30 and Hatton 93.

[9] See above, n. 7.

[1] Junius 121 is a companion volume to Hatton 113, 114.

[2] Lawrence, Univ. of Kansas, Y.104 is a detached leaf of Bodleian, Hatton 115: *cf. Speculum*, xxxvii (1962), 60–78.

[3] Lat. liturg. d.20 consists of leaves removed from the medieval bindings of Worcester Cathedral MSS in the Bodleian (fos 12–19, 22–25, 34, 35) and photographs of leaves in the binding of B.M., Add. 25031 and in a guard-book at Worcester Cathedral (MS. Add. 68). These leaves come from at least three, but perhaps not more than three, volumes of polyphonic music: (*a*) fos 1–22, used in B.M., Add. 25031; Bodleian, Auct. F.inf.1.3, Hatton 30; Worcester Cath., F.34, 125, 133, Q.31; (*b*) fos 22–35, used in Bodleian, Bodl. 862; Magd. Coll., lat. 100; Worcester Cath., Q.72; (*c*) fos 36–39, used in an unidentified binding, possibly Worcester Cath., Q.21. *Cf.* A. Hughes, *Worcester Medieval Harmony*; L. A. Dittmer, *The Worcester Fragments* (1957).

[4] Cambridge, U.L., Kk.4.6, Bodleian, Auct. F.1.9, and Corpus Christi Coll., Oxford, 157 contain writing in the same hand, probably that of John of Worcester: for this hand see *New Pal. Soc.*, ii, pl. 87 *b*.

Oxford (*contd*)
  Magdalen Coll., lat. 100. *l*Psalterium. s.xiii.
  Merton Coll., B.8.g.17 (pr. bk). *i*Antonius Andreas, etc. Venice,
A.D. 1496.
Worcester, Cathedral,
  †F.1. *e*P. Comestor. s.xiii. [*Young* 92].
  F.2. Compendium theologice veritatis, etc. s.xiv in. [*Young* 245]. ?
  †F.3. J. Duns Scotus, etc. s.xiv in. [*Young* 227].
  †F.4, fos 1–167. Aristoteles. s.xiii.
  †F.4, fos 168–234. *i*Aristoteles. s.xiii.
  †F.5. Sermones. s.xiv in. [*Young* 101].
  †F.6. J. Dumbleton. s.xiv. [*Young* 118].
  †F.7. Summa Goffredi, etc. A.D. 1251, etc. [*Young* 186].
  F.8. *i*P. Lombardus. s.xiii.
  F.9. Josephus. s.xiii ex. [*Young* 71]. ?
  F.10. *i*Sermones (partly in English). s.xv. [*Young* 107].
  †F.11. *e*Augustinus. s.xiv. [*Young* 15].
  †F.12. Hugutio. s.xiii. [*Young* 182].
  †F.13. *i*W. Brito. s.xiii–xiv. [*Young* 284].
  †F.14. Justinianus, etc. s.xiii in. [*Young* 169].
  F.15. J. de Saxonia. s.xiv in. [*Young* 201].
  F.16. *e*Everardus de Valle Scholarium. s.xiv. [*Young* 109].
  F.18. Aristoteles. s.xiv in. [K(?).xliii; *Young* 255]. ?
  †F.19. *i*Tractatus de vitiis et virtutibus, etc. s.xv in. [*Young* 241].
  F.20. *e*Papias. s.xiii ex. [*Young* 208].
  †F.21. Rabanus Maurus. s.xiii. [*Young* 72].
  F.22. Hugutio. s.xiii ex. [H.2; *Young* 283].
  †F.23. *e*J. Dumbleton, etc. s.xiv. [*Young* 254].
  †F.24. Vacarius. s.xii. [*Young* 170].
  F.25–28. *e*N. de Lyra, Postille (4 vols). s.xiv ex. [*Young* 7–10].
  †F.29. Azo. s.xiii.
  F.30. Egesippus. s.xii med. [*Young* 323]. ?
  †F.31. W. Autissiodorensis, etc. s.xiii ex. [*Young* 152].
  F.32. *s*Augustinus. s.xiii. [*Young* 29].
  F.34. *e*Interpretationes nominum habraicorum.s. xiii ex. [*Young* 95]
  †F.35. R. Swyneshed. s.xiv ex. [*Young* 264].
  F.36. G. de Tornaco. s.xiii/xiv. [E.1; *Young* 100].
  F.37. *e*P. Comestor. s.xiii/xiv. [*Young* 88, 91 *or* 93].
  †F.38. W. Peraldus. s.xiv in. [*Young* 225].
  †F.39. *e*J. Duns Scotus. s.xiv. [*Young* 163].
  F.40. Haly abbas. s.xii med. [*Young* 270]. ?
  †F.41. *e*Anselmus. s.xiv in. [*Young* 34].
  †F.42. Aristoteles. s.xiii. [*Young* 259].
  F.43. *e*R. Kilwardby. s.xiii ex. [*Young* 106].
  †F.44. W. Autissiodorensis. s.xiii. [*Young* 159].
  F.45. *e*J. de Voragine. s.xiv in. [*Young* 247].
  F.46. *e*P. Lombardus. s.xiii.
  F.47. P. Lombardus. s.xiii in. [*Young* 86]. ?
  †F.48. Vitas patrum. s.xi. [*Young* 249].
  †F.49. Gilbertus Porretanus. s.xii. [*Young* 63].
  †F.50. *c*P. Pictavensis. s.xiii. [*Young* 153].
  †F.51. *e*Excepciones xxiii auctorum. s.xiv in. [*Young* 49].

Worcester, Cathedral (*contd*)
†F.52. Comment. in Ecclesiasticum. s.xiii ex. [*Young* 63].
F.53. P. Lombardus. s.xiii ex.
†F.54. P. Pictavensis. s.xiii in. [*Young* 137].
†F.55. Comment. in Job. s.xiii ex. [*Young* 14].
†F.56. eG. de Fontibus, etc. s.xiii ex. [*Young* 151].
†F.57. eJ. Damascenus, etc. s.xiii. [*Young* 50].
F.58. bSumma Goffredi, etc. s.xiii–xiv.
F.59. Decretales Gregorii noni. s.xiii. [*Young* 187].   ?
†F.60. eJ. Duns Scotus. s.xiv. [*Young* 224].
F.61. cW. Brito, etc. s.xiv. [*Young* 96].
†F.62. eJ. de Friburgo. s.xiv in. [*Young* 195].
F.63. Aristoteles. s.xiii/xiv. [*Young* 260].
†F.64. P. Lombardus. s.xii/xiii. [*Young* 150].
†F.65. Determinaciones, etc. s.xiv/xv. [*Young* 295].
†F.66. Porphyrius, etc. s.xiii. [G.3; *Young* 234].
†F.67. Postille super Matheum. s.xiv in. [*Young* 64].
F.68. eAristoteles. s.xiv ex. [*Young* 262].
F.69. cJ. Duns Scotus. s.xiv in. [*Young* 149].
†F.71. P. Comestor, etc. s.xii–xiii. [*Young* 80].
†F.72. Tabule super logicam. s.xiv in. [*Young* 308].
†F.73. Porphyrius, etc. s.xiv. [*Young* 203].
F.74. Tractatus varii de jure civili. s.xiii–xiv. [*Young* 168].   ?
F.75. eCesarius Arelatensis, etc. s.xiii ex. [*Young* 52].
F.76. cGenesis glo. s.xii. [*Young* 11].
F.77. eG. de Tornaco. s.xiv. [*Young* 105].
†F.78. Codex Justiniani. s.xiii. [*Young* 166].
†F.79. eH. de Gandavo. s.xiii/xiv. [*Young* 157].
F.80. eGesta Romanorum, etc. s.xv. [*Young* 307].
†F.81. eJeronimus. s.xii in. [*Young* 4].
†F.82. eJeronimus. s.xii med. [*Young* 2].
†F.83. Jeronimus. s.xii ex. [*Young* 47].
F.84. R. de Thetford, etc. s.xiii. [*Young* 51].
F.85. Joannitius, etc. s.xiii. [*Leland; Young* 272].
†F.86. eW. Burley, etc. s.xv. [*Young* 256].
†F.87. R. Glanville. s.xiii ex. [F.2; *Young* 200].
†F.88. P. Lombardus. s.xiii.
F.90. cMonaldus. s.xiv. [*Young* 179].
†F.91. Omeliarium. s.xi in. [*Young* 87].
F.92. Omeliarium. s.xii in. [*Young* 97].
F.93. iOmeliarium. s.xii in. [*Young* 27].
F.94. sOmelie et sermones. s.xii in. [*Young* 77].
†F.96. eAverroes. s.xiv. [*Young* 261].
†F.97. G. de Baysio. s.xiv. [*Young* 175 (?)].
†F.98. P. Lombardus. s.xiii.
F.99. Petrus Helias. s.xiii in. [*Young* 289].
†F.100. G. de Trano, etc. s.xiv in. [*Young* 180].
†F.101. iT. Aquinas. s.xiv in. [*Young* 142].
F.102. eT. Aquinas. s.xiii ex. [*Young* 141].
F.103. T. Aquinas. s.xiii/xiv. [*Young* 143].   ?
†F.104. eT. Aquinas. s.xiii/xiv. [*Young* 140].
†F.105. iT. Aquinas. s.xiv. [*Young* 144].

Worcester, Cathedral (*contd*)

†F.106.   T. Aquinas.   s.xiv.   [*Young* 146].
F.107.   *b*T. Aquinas.   s.xiv in.   [*Young* 136].
†F.108.   T.Aquinas.   s.xiv.   [*Young* 138].
F.109.   T. Aquinas.   s.xiii/xiv.   [*Young* 139].   ?
†F.110.   Codex Justiniani.   s.xiii ex.   [*Young* 174 (?)].
†F.111.   W. Durandus, etc.   s.xiv.   [*Young* 206].
†F.112.   T. Bradwardine.   s.xiv.   [*Young* 251].
F.113.   J. de Friburgo.   s.xiii/xiv.   [*Young* 193].   ?
F.114.   Bernardus, etc.   s.xv.   [*Young* 76].   ?
†F.115.   J. de Voragine.   s.xiv.   [*Young* 236].
†F.116.   Sophismata Heytisbury, etc.   s.xiv ex.   [*Young* 232].
†F.117.   Distinctiones theol., etc.   s.xiii–xiii/xiv.   [*Young* 250].
†F.118.   Logicalia quedam, etc.   s.xiv/xv.   [*Young* 304].   ?
F.119.   Aristoteles.   s.xiii ex.   [*Young* 306].   ?
†F.120.   Gratianus.   s.xiii med.   [*Young* 204].
F.121.   P. Repington.   s.xv.   [*Young* 108].   ?
†F.122.   Compilatio prima decretalium.   s.xiii.   [*Young* 211].
†F.123.   Grammatica.   s.xiv.   [*Young* 290].
F.124.   *e*Interp. nominum hebr., etc.   s.xiii–xiv.   [*Young* 126].
†F.125.   *i*Summa Ranfredi.   s.xiv.   [*Young* 207].
F.126.   Sermones, etc.   s.xiv/xv.   [*Young* 99].   ?
†F.127.   Summa Reymundi, etc.   s.xiv.   [*Young* 194].
†F.128.   *e*Distinctiones Cestrensis, etc.   s.xiv ex.   [*Young* 62].
F.129.   W. Durandus.   s.xiv.   [*Young* 197].   ?
F.130.   *e*Distinctiones theol.   s.xiv.   [*Young* 94].
F.131.   *e*Summa summarum.   s.xiv.   [*Young* 178].
†F.132.   *e*Anselmus.   s.xiv.   [*Young* 32].
†F.133.   *b*P. Comestor.   s.xiii.   [*Young* 116].
F.134.   P. Lombardus.   s.xiii ex.   ?
†F.135.   Digestum inforciatum.   s.xiii ex.   [*Young* 173].
†F.136.   Digestum novum.   s.xiii/xiv.   [*Young* 171].
†F.137.   *e*Petrus Helias.   s.xiv in.   [*Young* 294].
†F.138.   *e*T. Aquinas.   s.xiv.   [*Young* 258].
F.139.   *e*R. de Bromwych.   s.xiv in.   [*Young* 161].
†F.140.   Lud. de Saxonia.   s.xv.   [*Young* 127].
†F.141.   *c*G. de Baysio, etc.   s.xiv.   [*Young* 184].
†F.142.   J. Chrysostomus.   s.xiii ex.   [*Young* 1].
†F.143.   Epp. Pauli glo.   s.xiii.   [*Young* 78].
F.144.   *b*Monaldus.   s.xiv.   [*Young* 185].
†F.145.   Gilbertus Anglicus.   s.xiv in.   [G.1; *Young* 268].
F.146.   Bonaguida, etc.   s.xiii ex.   [*Young* 191].   ?
F.147.   Disticha Catonis, etc.   s.xiii.   [*Young* 271].   ?
F.149.   *e*Augustinus, etc.   s.xiii ex.   [*Young* 30].
†F.151.   J. de Saxonia.   s.xiv.   [*Young* 198].
†F.152.   R. Grosseteste, etc.   s.xiv.   [*Young* 44].
†F.153.   Manipulus florum.   s.xiv.   [*Young* 48].
†F.154.   *e*Narrationes, etc.   s.xiv ex.   [*Young* 285].
†F.155.   *e*R. Holcot.   s.xiv/xv.   [*Young* 85].
F.156.   *e*Tabula juris.   s.xiv in.   [*Young* 202].
F.157.   *e*Sermones.   s.xiii ex.   [*Young* 300].
F.159.   Casus decretorum, etc.   s.xiii in.   [*Young* 181].   ?

Worcester, Cathedral (*contd*)
F.160. *c*Antiphonale, etc. s.xiii in. [*Young* 57 (?)].
†F.164. Comment. in Sententias P. Lombardi. s.xiv in. [*Young* 160].
F.165. Porphyrius, etc. s.xiii. [*Young* 233]. ?
F.167. *e*Bonaventura. s.xiii ex. [*Young* 145].
F.168. *e*Constitutiones Clementine, cum apparatu. s.xiv. [*Young* 209 (?)].
F.169. *e*Aristoteles. s.xiv in. [*Young* 267].
†F.170. Innocentius IV. s.xiii ex. [*Young* 177].
F.174.[5] *s*Ælfric's Grammar, etc. (in English). s.xiii in.
†F.175. 'Pars concordancie a littera F usque I'. s.xiv in. [*Young* 210].
F.176. P. Lombardus. s.xiii. [*Young* 154]. ?
F.177. Compilationes 2ª et 4ª decretalium. s.xiii. [*Young* 212 (?)]. ?
†Q.1. Ivo Carnotensis. s.xii. [*Young* 219].
†Q.2. P. Comestor. s.xiii in. [*Young* 83].
†Q.3. Fasciculus morum. s.xv. [*Young* 325].
Q.4. *c*N. de Biard. s.xiii/xiv. [*Young* 331].
†Q.5. *e*Beda, etc. s.x ex. [*Leland; Young* 229].
Q.6. Sermones. s.xiii in.–xiii. [*Young* 113]. ?
†Q.7. Leo papa. s.xii ex. [*Leland; Young* 42].
Q.8. Duodecim prophete glo. s.xii ex. [lvii. E; *Young* 58 *or* 60]. ?
†Q.9. Sermones. s.xiv in. [*Young* 120].
†Q.11. Sermones. s.xiii in. [*Young* 111].
Q.12. *b*Guido Ebroicensis. s.xiv. [*Young* 121].
†Q.13. *i*P. Cornubiensis, etc. s.xiii ex. [*Young* 231].
†Q.14. Dieta salutis, etc. s.xiv. [*Young* 244].
†Q.15. Rosarium theologie. s.xv. [*Young* 242].
†Q.16. Marcus, etc., glo. s.xii in.–xii ex. [*Young* 65].
†Q.17. *m*Sermones. s.xiii/xiv. [*Young* 328].
Q.18. *c*Liber collationum. s.xiii ex.–xiv. [*Young* 312 (?)].
Q.19. Sermones. s.xiii ex. [*Young* 125]. ?
Q.20. Jac. de Viterbo. s.xiii/xiv. [*Young* 156]. ?
Q.21. Gregorius. s.x. [*Young* 40]. ?
†Q.22. *i*Speculum sacerdotum. s.xiv ex. [*Young* 243].
Q.23. *e*Manipulus florum. s.xiv. [*Young* 238].
†Q.24. Tabule operum Augustini, etc. s.xiii/xiv. [*Young* 31].
Q.25. Distinctiones theol. s.xiii ex. [*Young* 190]. ?
†Q.26. *l*'Liber capitulorum et collectarum . . .'. s.xiii in. [*Young* 302].
†Q.27. J. Wallensis, etc. s.xiv. [*Young* 340].
†Q.28. Eusebius. s.x. [*Young* 89].
†Q.29. Misc. theol. s.xii ex. [*Young* 338].
†Q.30. *e*Porphyrius, etc. s.xiii. [*Young* 230].
†Q.31. Comment. in Sententias P. Lombardi. s.xiii. [*Young* 164].
Q.32. *b*Isaias glo., etc. s.xiii.
Q.33. *i*Comment. in Sententias P. Lombardi. s.xiii. [*Young* 155].
†Q.34. Averroes in Aristotelem. s.xiii/xiv. [*Young* 263].
Q.35. *b*Comment. in Sententias P. Lombardi. s.xiii ex. [*Young* 135].
†Q.37. Osbertus, Grammatica. s.xiii ex. [*Young* 288].
Q.38. 'Questiones date a dompno Waltero de Burley'. s.xiii ex. [*Young* 226]. ?

[5] See p. 206, n. 3.

Worcester, Cathedral (*contd*)

Q.39. Constantinus Africanus. s.xiii. [*Young* 281].
Q.40. Liber passionarius et simplicis medicine. s.xii. [*Young* 273]. ?
Q.41.[6] Constantinus Africanus, etc. s.xiii. [*Young* 276]. ?
Q.42. *e*Distinctiones Mauricii. s.xiii ex. [*Young* 165].
Q.43. Abbreviatio Decreti Gratiani. s.xiii in. [*Young* 214]. ?
†Q.44. *i*Glosa super Decreta, etc. s.xii ex.–xii/xiii. [*Young* 90].
Q.45. J. Felton, etc. s.xv. [*Young* 114]. ?
†Q.46. *i*Reportationes J. de Dombletone. s.xiii ex. [*Young* 334].
†Q.47. *e*P. Lombardus. s.xiii.
†Q.48. *e*H. de S. Victore, etc. s.xii ex. [*Young* 45].
Q.49. Comment. Hali super Tegni Galieni. s.xiii. [*Young* 278]. ?
†Q.50. *m*Alex. Nequam, etc. s.xiii. [*Young* 124].
†Q.51. Passio secundum Nicodemum, etc. s.xii ex.–xiii in. [*Young* 43].
Q.52. Medica quedam. s.xiii. [Young 280]. ?
†Q.53. Themata sermonum, etc. s.xiii ex. [*Young* 220].
Q.54. *e*W. Milverley, etc. s.xv. [*Young* 310].
†Q.55. Pseudo-Chrysostomus, etc. s.xiii–xiv ex. [*Young* 326].
Q.56. Sermones, etc. s.xv in. [*Young* 115]. ?
Q.57. Gilbertus de Tornaco. s.xiii ex. [*Young* 239]. ?
Q.58. 'Not*ule* super libros priorum'. s.xiii in. [bb.iij]. ?
†Q.59. Jacobus de Lausanna, etc. s.xiv in. [*Young* 332].
Q.60. Liber Almansor, etc. s.xiii in. [*Young* 279]. ?
Q.61. *b*Postille in festis sanctorum, etc. s.xiv in. [E.3; *Young* 122].
†Q.62. T. de Capua, etc. s.xiv in. [*Young* 196].
Q.63. *e*Sermones, etc. s.xiii/xiv. [*Young* 329].
†Q.64. *i*Reportationes Januensis. s.xiii/xiv. [*Young* 237].
†Q.65. Sermones. s.xiv. [*Young* 112].
†Q.66. Jeronimus, etc. s.xii. [*Young* 336].
Q.67. Sermones, etc. s.xiii in. [*Young* 123]. ?
†Q.69. *e*Bonaventura. s.xiii/xiv. [*Young* 148].
†Q.70. Comment. in Decretum Gratiani. s.xii ex. [F.1; *Young* 215].
†Q.71. R. Fitzralph. s.xiv. [*Young* 162].
†Q.72. *e*Pseudo-Grosseteste, etc. s.xiv med. [*Young* 287].
Q.74. 'Sermones Ockam'. s.xiii ex. [*Leland; Young* 335].
†Q.76. *e*J. Damascenus. s.xiv in. [*Young* 46].
Q.77. Sermones. s.xiii. [*Young* 117]. ?
Q.78. Sermones. s.xii ex. [*Young* 341]. ?
Q.81. Avicenna, etc. s.xiii in.–xiii med. [*Young* 269]. ?
†Q.82. Lucas glo. s.xii. [*Young* 66].
†Q.85. *e*R. Lull. s.xiii ex. [*Young* 246].
Q.87. Sermones Everardi de Valle Scholarium. s.xiv. [*Young* 327]. ?
Q.88. P. Lombardus, etc. s.xiii. [*Young* 134]. ?
Q.89.[7] *m*Sermones, etc. s.xiii ex. [*Young* 299].
Q.90. Questiones in Aristotelem. s.xiii/xiv. [*Young* 265]. ?
†Q.92. W. de Pagula. s.xiv. [*Young* 311].

[6] The detached leaves noted by Floyer and Hamilton, *Catalogue*, p. 158, have been restored to Q.41.
[7] Q.89 belonged also to the Franciscans of **WORCESTER**, *q.v.*

Worcester, Cathedral (*contd*)
  Q.93. *b*P. Berchorius, etc. s.xv in. [*Young* 82].
 †Q.94. Johannes glo., etc. s.xii ex.–xiii in. [*Young* 68].
  Q.96. Tractatus de medicina. s.xiii. [*Young* 274]. ?
  Q.97. Alphabetum narrationum, etc. s.xiv. [*Young* 303]. ?
  Q.98. Summa Reymundi de Peniaforte. s.xiii. [*Young* 228]. ?
  Q.99. Disputationes theol. s.xiii/xiv. [*Young* 315 (?)]. ?
  Q.100. Sermones. s.xiv in. [*Young* 314 (?)]. ?

Rejected: Cambridge, U.L., Ii.4.34; Corpus Christi Coll., 87, 201; Queens'
    Coll. 17; Trinity Coll. 138. London, B.M., Royal 15 B.ii. Oxford,
    Bodleian, Bodl. 134, 387, Digby 86, 150, Hatton 15, Rawl. G.168.
    Vercelli, Cathedral, 117.

WORCESTER. *Franciscan convent.*

Cambridge, Sid. Sussex Coll., 60. *c*Tractatus de Machumete, etc.
    s.xiii–xiv. ?
Dublin, Trinity Coll., 43. *i* or *e*Biblia. s.xiii.
London, B.M., Burney 1. *e*Biblia. s.xiii. [Biblia 13].
           Harley 3096. *e*Bernardus. s.xiii. [Bernardus. B.].
           3239. *i*T. Aquinas. s.xv.
           Royal 5 B.v. *e*Augustinus. s.xiii. [Aug'. 10].
Worcester, Cathedral, Q.89. *e*Geometrica, etc. s.xiii ex. [Postille 22].

WORCESTER. *Dominican convent.*

Edinburgh, U.L., Inc. 33 (pr. bk). *i*P. Hispanus, etc.   Cologne,
    A.D. 1498, etc.
Helmingham Hall, Lord Tollemache, 49.[8] *e*Compendium theologice
    veritatis. s.xiii/xiv.
Oxford, Bodleian, Rawl. C.780. *e*Isidorus, etc. s.xiv–xv.
Worcester, Cathedral, F.89. *e*J. de Voragine, etc. s.xv in.

WORKSOP (or **RADFORD**), Nottinghamshire. *Aug. priory of B.V.M.*
    and St Cuthbert.

    List of five MSS and a Mappa mundi given by Philip, canon of Lincoln, in
1187, printed from the Pierpont Morgan MS. by M. R. James, *Catalogue of
MSS of J. P. Morgan* (1906), p. 165.
    The *ex libris* inscription is usually in the form 'Iste liber constat monasterio
de Wyrkesopp'.

Cambridge, U.L., Ee.5.32. *e*Gregorius, etc. s.xii.
           Hh.1.5. *e*Memoriale juniorum, etc. s.xv.
London, B.M., Harley 4124. *e*Beda. s.xii.
New York, Pierpont Morgan, 81. *e*Bestiarium, etc. s.xii ex.
           Public Libr., Spencer 26. *i*Psalterium. s.xiv in.
Oxford, Bodleian, Bodl. 388. *e*Ivo Carnotensis, etc. s.xiii in.
           Lincoln Coll., lat. 63. *e*Isidorus. s.xii.

WROXTON, Oxfordshire. *Aug. priory of B.V.M.*

London, B.M., Add. 24660. *c*Misc. theologica. s.xiii–xiv. ?

---

[8] Helmingham Hall 49 was bequeathed later to Great Malvern.

WYMONDHAM, Norfolk. *Ben. abbey of B.V.M.; originally priory and cell of St Albans.*

Books noted by J. Leland, *Collectanea*, iv. 27, and *De Scriptoribus Britannicis*, p. 405.

London, B.M., Arundel 201. Carmina, etc. s.xii–xiii in. ?
Oxford, Bodleian, Lat. liturg. g.8.[9]   Kalendarium, etc. s.xv.
    Magdalen Coll., lat. 53, pp. 1–6. *c*De electione priorum.
                · s.xiii/xiv.
Rejected: Oxford, Bodleian, Bodl. 641.

YARMOUTH, Norfolk. *Ben. priory of St Nicholas; cell of Norwich.*

List of books printed from an inventory among Norwich muniments by H. C. Beeching and M. R. James, 'The Library of the Cathedral Church of Norwich', *Norfolk Archaeology*, xix (1917), 78; pressmarks given, apparently those of Norwich cathedral priory.

YORK. *Cathedral church of St Peter.*

Handlist of MSS in *General Report . . . on the Public Records* (1837), pp. 286–287.
List of thirteen service-books in an inventory of s.xvi in. belonging to the Treasury of York Minster, printed by Raine, *Historians of the Church of York* (Rolls Series), iii. 387, and by Dugdale, *Monasticon*, vi (iii). 1205. List of books bequeathed by John Newton, Treasurer of York (†1414), printed from a York register by Raine, *Testamenta Eboracensia*, i (Surtees Soc., 1836), 365–66, 368–69. Note on the library by J. Leland, *Collectanea*, iv. 37, and *De Scriptoribus Britannicis*, p. 230.

Cambridge, Sid. Sussex Coll., 33. *l*Missale. s.xv ex.
    Trinity Coll., 728. *b*W. Malmesburiensis, etc. s.xiii–xiv. ?
      728, flyleaf 4. *e*Augustinus. [*Newton*].
Lincoln, Cathedral, 101.[1] *e*Eutropius, etc. s.xii/xiii. ?
      102.[1] *m*Orosius. s.xii ex. ?
London, B.M., Harley 46. *e*Matheus et Marcus glo. s.xii ex.
      208. *e*Epp. Alcuini, etc. s.ix/x. ?
    St Paul's Cathedral, 13. *e*P. de Crescentiis. s.xv.
Oxford,
  Bodleian, Laud misc. 140. *e*Augustinus. s.xii in.
      Rawl. B.199.[2] W. Malmesburiensis. s.xiv ex.
          [*Newton*]. ?
      B.200.[2] Alfredus Beverlacensis. s.xiv ex.
          [*Newton*]. ?
      C.162.[2] Beda. s.xiv ex. [*Newton*]. ?
York, Minster, s.n. Tabulae.[3] s.xiv ex.
      s.n. *c*Evangelia. s.x/xi.
      xvi.G.23. *e*Legenda sanctorum. s.xv.
      Q.3, 4. *e*Biblia, pars ii, iii. s.xii in.
      Q.13. *e*Hugutio. s.xiv.

[9] The calendar contains the dedication of the church. See above under TYNEMOUTH.
[1] The note of contents in MS. 102 is in the same hand as a similar note in MS. 101.
[2] Rawl. B.199, 200, C.162 formed one volume.
[3] Two wooden tryptiches containing charters and historical memoranda.

YORK. *Ben. abbey of B.V.M.* (*Cf.* cells at **ST BEES** and **WETHERAL.**)

Books noted by J. Leland, *Collectanea*, iv. 14, 37.

The pressmark, consisting of a letter and number preceded by *In*, is reproduced from Dublin, Trinity Coll., 207 and 332, and Cambridge, Corpus Christi Coll., 309, in *New Pal. Soc.*, i, pl. 147, no. 1 *a-c*. The mark is written on a flyleaf or at the foot of the first leaf of text.

Arundel Castle, Duke of Norfolk. *e*Biblia. s.xiii.

Bridgnorth, St Leonard's Church (pr. bk). *i*H. Schedel. Augsburg, A.D. 1497.

Cambridge,

    U.L., Ee.6.40. Timeus Platonis. s.xii. [In L. 12].

    Corpus Christi Coll., 181. W. Gemmeticensis, etc. s.xiv in. [In 3.J].
              309. Ric. de S. Victore, etc. s.xii/xiii. [In L.24].
              451. Epp. Hildeberti, etc. s.xii ex.–xiii in. [In O.9].

    Gonv. and Caius Coll., A* 1.12 (1) (pr. bk). *i*T. Aquinas. Cologne, A.D. 1501.

    St John's Coll., 102. *e*Consuetudinarium. s.xiv–xv.

Deventer, Mr J. P. L. van der Lande (pr. bk). *i*Speculum exemplorum. Deventer, A.D. 1481.

Dublin, Trinity Coll., 207, fos 22–79. *e*Pseudo-Grosseteste, etc. s.xv in. [In viii.H].

           332. *e*Misc. theologica. s.xiii ex. [In D.3].

London, B.M., Add. 24361. *e*Miscellanea. s.xv.
           38816, fos 21–39. *c*Miscellanea. s.xii–xiii.
           40007. *e*R. de Diceto. s.xii ex. [In A.xi; *Leland*].
           Burney 220. *i*Ovidius. s.xii ex.
           Cotton Tib. A.xv, fos 181–94.[4] R. Rolle. s.xiv/xv. [*Leland*].

           Harley 56. *e*Vita S. Dunstani. s.xii. ?

Newcastle, U.L., 1. *e*Vite sanctorum. s.xiii. [In N.xv].

Oxford,

    Bodleian, Bodl. 39. *c*Chronicon abbatie, etc. s.xiv in.
           Bodl. rolls 3. *e*Genealogia regum Anglie. s.xiii.
           Digby 186, fos 1, 2. *c*Injunctiones Johannis legati. s.xiii.
           Lat. liturg. g.1. *l*Psalterium. s.xv in. ?
           Lyell 17. *e*Martinus Polonus, etc. (partly in French). s.xiv. [In ii.a].
           Rawl. G.11, 12. *e*Vetus testamentum (2 vols). s.xiv.
    Corpus Christi Coll., 193.[4] *i*R. Rolle. s.xiv/xv. [In viii.G; *Leland*].
           224. *e*Boetius, etc. s.xii–xiii. [In xiiii.A].
    Magdalen Coll., i.1.1, 2 (pr. bks). *i*Duns Scotus (2 vols). Venice, A.D. 1497.

Ripon, Mr H. L. Bradfer-Lawrence. *c*Anonimalle chron., etc. (partly in French). s.xiv ex.

San Marino (U.S.A.), Huntington, HM 903. *e*Manuel des pechez, etc. (in French). s.xiv.

Untraced: Dunn sale (Sotheby, 11 Feb. 1913), lot 511 to Leighton. *e*Epp. Jeronimi. s.xii/xiii.

Rejected: Cambridge, Trinity Coll., 730. Eton Coll., 45.

---

[4] Cotton Tib. A.xv, fos 181–94, is a detached portion of Oxford, Corpus Christi Coll. 193.

YORK.   *Ben. alien priory of Holy Trinity; cell of Marmoutier.*

Oxford, St John's Coll., 61.   *e*Bestiarium.   s.xiii in.

YORK.   *Franciscan convent.*

Arundel Castle, Duke of Norfolk.   *e*Prick of Conscience (in English).
s.xiv ex.
Cambridge, Sid. Sussex Coll., 94.   *e*Augustinus, etc.   s.xiii.   [Aug. 5].
Durham, Cathedral, B.II.36.   *e*P. Comestor.   s.xiii ex.   [Historie 5].
London, Westminster Abbey, 22.⁵   *e*Bestiarium.   s.xiii.   [Bestiarium 5].
   Mr Raymond Russell.   *e*Gregorius, etc.   s.xiii.   [Greg. 5].
Oxford, Corpus Christi Coll., 227.⁶   Duns Scotus, etc.   s.xv ex.   ?
                     228.⁶   Questiones de anima.   s.xv ex.   ?

YORK.   *Dominican convent.*

Rejected: Malvern, C. W. Dyson Perrins, 12 (sold 29 Nov. 1960, lot 110).

YORK.   *Convent of Austin friars.*

Catalogue of A.D. 1372, with additions of s.xiv–xv, printed from Dublin,
Trinity Coll., MS. D.1.17 (359) by M. R. James, 'The Catalogue of the Library
of the Augustinian Friars at York', *Fasciculus Joanni Willis Clark dicatus* (1909),
pp. 2–96; second folios given.   *Cf.* A. Gwynn, *The English Austin Friars* (1940),
pp. 130–34.
Cambridge, U.L., Add. 2823.   *e*W. de Nassington (in English).   s.xv.   ?
London,
   B.M., Cotton Vesp. B.xxiii.   *i*J. Hanvillensis, etc.   s.xiv.   [R; *cat.* 493].
   Royal 8 B.xix.   *i*Cassiodorus.   s.xiii in.   [*Cat.* 460].
   Coll. of Arms, Arundel 6.   *i*Freculphus, etc.   s.xiv ex.   [M; *Cat.* 165].
Oxford,
   Bodleian, Bodl. 842.   Theinredus Doverensis, etc.   s.xiv/xv.   [*Cf. cat.*
               645].   ?
   Corpus Christi Coll., 81.   *i*Justinus.   s.xii ex.   [*Cat.* 160].
   St John's Coll., 150.   *i*Guido, De arte musica, etc.   s.xi–xiv.   [F;
               cat. 643].
Untraced: Thomas E. Marston sale (Sotheby, 11 Dec. 1961), lot 180 to
   'Vennor'.   *e*Codex Justiniani.   s.xiii ex.   [F.pᵐ; *cf. cat.* 411].

YORK.   *Hospital of St Leonard.*

Cambridge, U.L., Ee.4.19.   *e*Manuale.   s.xv.

YORK.   *Collegiate chapel of St Mary and Holy Angels.*

Arundel Castle, Duke of Norfolk.   *e*Antiphonale.   s.xv.

---

⁵ The table of contents of Westminster Abbey, MS. 22 is bound up with MS. 23.
⁶ MSS 227, 228 were written in the Oxford convent, but it is probable that MS.
227 at least was at the York convent at the Dissolution.

APPENDIX

Books formerly owned by parish churches and chapels

ADDERBURY, Oxfordshire. Oxford, Bodleian, Don. b.5.¹ Missale. s.xiv ex.

ALBURY, Surrey. Cambridge, Corpus Christi Coll., 211. *e*Pupilla oculi. s.xv.

ARDINGTON, Berkshire. Oxford, Brasenose Coll., Latham Room, C.3.7–9.² *c*Breviarium (12 fos used in binding).

ARLINGHAM, Gloucestershire. Salisbury, Cathedral, 152. *e*Breviarium. s.xv ex.

BATHWICK, Wiltshire. Cambridge, Jesus Coll., 31.¹ Martyrologium. s.xiii. ?

BEDWYN, GREAT, Wiltshire. Bern, Statdtbibliothek, 671. *c*Evangelia. s.viii/ix. ?

BISHOP'S CLEEVE, Gloucestershire. Oxford, Merton Coll., 62.f.23 (pr. bk). *e*W. Lyndwood. Paris, A.D. 1501.

BLYTH, Nottinghamshire. Cambridge, Jesus Coll., 19. *e*Formulare. s.xv ex.

BODENHAM, Herefordshire. Oxford, St John's Coll., b.1.1 (pr. bk). *c*Missale Heref. Rouen, s.a. ?

BORLEY, Essex. Cambridge, U.L., Ee.5.13.¹ Psalterium. s.xv.

BRASTED, Kent. Deene Park, Trustees of the late Mr G. Brudenell, XIX.c.12 (pr. bk). *e*Destructorium viciorum. (Cologne, A.D. 1485).

BRECON. Oxford, Bodleian, Laud misc. 667.¹ Ordinale Sarisburiense (Pye). s.xv.

BREDGAR, Kent. Lambeth Palace, 1362. *e*Biblia. s.xiii.

BROMPTON-ON-SWALE, Yorkshire. London, B.M., Harley 2431. *e*Kalendarium, etc. s.xv.

BROMSGROVE, Worcestershire. Cambridge, U.L., Add. 6688. *e*Missale. s.xv.

BROUGHTON (near Preston), Lancashire. Mayfield, Capt. M. Butler-Bowdon. *c*Missale. ?

BUCKINGHAM. Buckingham Parish Church. *e*Biblia. s.xiii/xiv.

BUCKLAND, Berkshire. Oxford, Bodleian, Don. b.5.¹ *c*Missale. s.xiv ex.

BULLINGHOPE, UPPER, Herefordshire. London, B.M., C.35 i.4 (pr. bk).³ *e*Missale Heref. Rouen, (A.D. 1502).

BURY ST EDMUNDS, Suffolk.
    Cambridge, U.L., Ee.1.14.¹ Horae B.V.M. s.xv. ?
    Oxford, Bodleian, Rawl. liturg. e.42. *e*Martyrologium, etc. s.xiv/xv.

---

¹ Calendar contains the dedication of the church.
² Or perhaps from Yarnton, Oxon.
³ The *ex libris* may be Marian.

CALDBECK, Cumberland. St Mary's Catholic Church, Warwick Bridge, Carlisle (on deposit at Ampleforth Abbey). *e*Missale. s.xv.

CARDINGTON, Bedfordshire. Liverpool, Public Museums, Mayer collection 12016 (on deposit in Liverpool Univ. Libr.). *e*Antiphonarium. s.xv.

CHARFORD, SOUTH. Hampshire. London, B.M., Royal 2 A.xxi. *e*Manuale. s.xv in.

CHIPPING CAMPDEN, Gloucestershire. London, B.M., Add. 16170. *e*Misc. theol. s.xv.

CLOSWORTH, Somerset. Oxford, Bodleian, Don. b.6.[4] Missale. s.xv in. ?

COLCHESTER, Essex, ST PETER. Oxford, Bodleian, Rawl. D.894, fos 64–68.[4] Kalendarium. s.xv in.

COLTISHALL, Norfolk. Durham, U.L., Cosin V.i.3.[4] *e*Missale, etc. s.xv.

COLWICH, Staffordshire. London, B.M., Harley 4919.[4] Missale. s.xiv/xv. ?

CRICH, Derbyshire. London, Lambeth Palace, 222. *e*Legenda aurea. A.D. 1356.

CRICKADARN, Brecknockshire. Hereford, Cathedral, P.iii.4. *c*Manuale. s.xv. ?

CUCKNEY, Nottinghamshire. Oxford, Univ. Coll., 78B. *e*Missale. s.xv.

DENCHWORTH, Berkshire. Oxford, Bodleian, Lat. liturg. b.14. Breviarium. s.xiv ex. ?

DRAYTON, EAST. Nottinghamshire. Oxford, Bodleian, Lat. liturg. b.5 and 6. *e*Graduale, etc. s.xv.

EASTON, GREAT, Essex. Aberystwyth, N.L., 492E.[4] Missale. s.xv. ?

EASTWELL, Kent. Ushaw Coll., 18. *e*Missale. s.xiv/xv.

ESH LAUDE, co. Durham. Ushaw Coll., 5. *e*Missale. s.xv.

EXETER, CHAPEL OF ST ANNE (in parish of St Sidwell). Exeter, Cathedral, 3515. *e*Missale. s.xiii–xv.

ST MARY MAJOR. Coutances, Bibliothèque, 2. *e*Manuale. s.xiv.

FARNWORTH (near Widnes), Lancashire. Manchester, U.L., Christie 3.f.19. *e*Sermones. s.xiv.

FENNY BENTLEY, Derbyshire. Oxford, Bodleian, Rawl. C.88. *e*Augustinus. s.xv.

FLAUNDEN, Hertfordshire. Urbana, University of Illinois, s.n.[4] Missale. s.xv. ?

FRODESLEY, Shropshire. Shrewsbury, Roman Catholic Bishopric.[4] Missale. s.xiv.

GAINSBOROUGH, Lincolnshire. Oxford, Bodleian, Lyell 25.[4] Psalterium, etc. s.xv. ?

GAWSWORTH, Cheshire. Oxford, Bodleian, Barlow 1. *c*Missale.

GLOUCESTER, ST ALDATE. London, B.M., Add. 30506. *e*Manuale. s.xv.

GORLESTON, Suffolk. London, B.M., Add. 49622.[4] Psalterium, etc. s.xiv in. ?

HALSALL, Lancashire. Manchester, J. Rylands, Lat. 339. *e*Oculus sacerdotum. s.xiv ex.

[4] Calendar contains the dedication of the church.

HAMSTALL RIDWARE, Staffordshire. Oxford, Bodleian, Auct. 1.Q.5.15 (pr. bk). *e*Bartholomaeus de Chaimis. Mainz, A.D. 1478.

HANLEY CASTLE, Worcestershire. Cambridge, U.L., Kk.2.6. *e*Missale. s.xiii.

HARDWICK [*unidentified*]. Cambridge, St John's Coll., 216. *e*Augustinus. s.xii.

HAREWOOD, Yorkshire. Aberford, Sir A. D. F. Gascoigne (on deposit in York Minster library).[5] Breviarium. s.xv.

HARLASTON, Staffordshire.
Cambridge, Christ's Coll., 8. *e*Horae. s.xiii/xiv.
Oxford, Bodleian, Ashmole 1764 (pr. bk). *e*Missale. (Paris), s.a.

HARPOLE, Northamptonshire. London, B.M., C.52 g.2 (pr. bk). *e*Manuale. London, A.D. 1506.

HEREFORD, ST PETER. London, B.M., Harley 3965. *e*Graduale. s.xiv.

HITCHIN, Hertfordshire. London, B.M., Harley 1025.[5] Psalterium. s.xv.

LAMPETER VELFREY, Pembrokeshire. Oxford, New Coll., Auct. T.6.2 (pr. bk). *e*Codex Justiniani. Paris, A.D. 1515.

LAPWORTH, Warwickshire. Oxford, Corpus Christi Coll., 394. *e*Missale. A.D. 1398.

LAVINGTON, WEST, Wiltshire. Oxford, Bodleian, Lat. liturg. f.25. Manuale Sarisb. s.xiv. ?

LAXTON, Nottinghamshire (?). London, B.M., Royal 19 C.v. *e*Comment. on Psalms (in French). s.xiii in.

LEAKE, Yorkshire (?). Oxford, Bodleian, Auct. D.4.20. *e*Epp. Pauli glo. s.xiii in.

LECHLADE. Gloucestershire. Cambridge, Magdalene Coll., 9, i. *e*Psalterium. s.xv.

LLANBEBLIG, Caernarvonshire. Aberystwyth, N.L., 17520.[5] Horae B.V.M. s.xiv ex. ?

LODDON, Norfolk. Stonyhurst Coll. (pr. bk). *e*Manuale. London, A.D. 1506.

LONDON, ALL HALLOWS THE GREAT. Dublin, Trinity Coll., 194, pp. 217–332.[5] *c*Martyrologium, etc. s.xiii.

ST BOTOLPH, WITHOUT ALDERSGATE. London, Guildhall, 515.[5] Missale. s.xv in. ?

ST BOTOLPH, ALDGATE. Oxford, Christ Church, lat. 87.[5] Missale. s.xv. ?

ST LAWRENCE, JEWRY. London, B.M., Arundel 109. *e*Missale. s.xv in.

ST MARGARET, LOTHBURY. Cambridge, U.L., Dd.1.15. *c*Missale. s.xiv.

ST MARY, ALDERMANBURY. London, B.M., Royal 2 B.xii, xiii. *e*Lectionarium. A.D. 1508.

ST PETER-UPON-CORNHILL.
London, B.M., Royal 13 D.i. *e*Polychronicon, etc. s.xiv.
St Peter-upon-Cornhill, Parish Church.[6] *e*Biblia. s.xiii ex.

LUDLOW, Shropshire, ST LAWRENCE. London, B.M., Harley 273.[5] Psalter (in French), etc. s.xiii/xiv.

[5] Calendar contains the dedication of the church.
[6] On permanent deposit in the London Guildhall.

MALDON, Essex, ALL SAINTS. London, B.M., Harley 2787.[7] Missale. s.xiv. ?

MELBOURNE, Derbyshire. London, Gray's Inn, 20. eW. Peraldus. s.xiii.

MOLTON, SOUTH, Devon. London, B.M., Harley 2367.[7] Libellus precum. s.xv. ?

MORDIFORD, Herefordshire. Hereford Cathedral, s.n. Breviarium. s.xiii ex.

NEWARK, Nottinghamshire, Chantry of William Newark. Cambridge, U.L., Inc. 3799 (pr. bk). eN. Perottus. Louvain, s.a.

NEWCASTLE-UPON-TYNE, ST JOHN BAPTIST. Oxford, Bodleian, Rawl. C.258. eNew Testament (in English). s.xv in.

ST NICHOLAS. Oxford, St John's Coll., 94. eHorae, etc. s.xv.

NORTHAMPTON, ST PETER. Oxford, Bodleian, Lat. liturg. b.4.[7] Missale. s.xiv. ?

ST JOHN BAPTIST. Dublin, Archbishop Marsh's Library, Z.4.1.18 (pr. bk). eJ. Capgrave. London, A.D. 1516.

NORTON, Suffolk.
Cambridge, U.L., Ee.5.13.[8] Psalterium, etc. s.xv.
Downing Coll.[7, 8] Kalendarium (6 fos). s.xv.

NORWICH, ST MICHAEL COSLANY. Cambridge, Gonv. and Caius Coll., B.b.23 (pr. bk). eCatholicon. s.l. et a.

ONGAR, HIGH, Essex. Ushaw Coll., 8.[7] Psalterium, etc. s.xv in.

ORPINGTON, Kent. Portsmouth, Roman Catholic Bishopric, Virtue and Cahill 8433.[7] cPsalterium, etc. s.xiv.

PENWORTHAM, Lancashire.
London, B.M., Add. 52359. eBreviarium. s.xiv.
Oxford, Bodleian, Vet. E.1.c.45 (pr. bk). cMissale. Rouen, A.D. 1508.

PERTH. Edinburgh, N.L., 652.[7] Psalterium. s.xv ex.

PINCHBECK, Lincolnshire. Longleat, Marquess of Bath, 10.[7, 9] Breviarium. s.xiv. ?

POT SHRIGLEY, Cheshire. London, B.M., Add. 41175. eCommentaries on Gospels (in English). s.xiv/xv.

RANWORTH, Norfolk. Ranworth, Parish Church. cAntiphonale. s.xv.

RAVENSWORTH, Yorkshire, CHAPEL OF ST JOHN THE EVANGELIST. London, B.M., Harley 2431. eKalendarium, etc. s.xv.

RISBY, Suffolk. London, B.M., Harley 1001. eOrdinale. s.xiv.

ROSSDHU, Dumbartonshire. Auckland, Central Libr., Grey 21.[7] Horae. s.xv.

RUDBY, Yorkshire. Durham, U.L., Cosin V.i.2. eBreviarium. s.xv.

RUSHALL, Staffordshire. Nottingham, U.L., MeLM 1.[7, 1] Psalterium, etc. s.xv. ?

ST ANDREWS, Fife, HOLY TRINITY. Dundee Burgh Charter Room.[7] Kalendarium. s.xv. ?

SALTFLEETBY, Lincolnshire. Eton Coll., Em.1.7 (pr. bk). eDestructorium vitiorum. Cologne, A.D. 1480.

[7] Calendar contains the dedication of the church.
[8] The calendar at Downing Coll. is a detached fragment of Ee.5.13.
[9] Calendar contains also the dedication of the church of Spalding.
[1] Deposited by the Mellish Trustees.

SARSDEN, Oxfordshire. Cambridge (U.S.A.), P. Hofer. *e*Horae.[2] s.xiv.

SHEPTON BEAUCHAMP, Somerset. Liverpool, Cathedral.[3] Missale. s.xiv. ?

SHERE, Surrey. Helmingham Hall, Lord Tollemache, 72. *e*Missale. s.xv in.

SHERMANBURY, Sussex. Cambridge, U.L., Dd.12.69. *e*Dieta salutis, etc. (partly in English). s.xv in.

SKELMERSDALE, Lancashire. Cambridge, U.L., Dd.15.1. *e*Dictionarium. A.D. 1278.

SOMPTING, Sussex. Cambridge, Emmanuel Coll., 27.[3] Miscellanea. s.xiii, etc.

SOUTHWARK, London, ST GEORGE. London, B.M., Add. 36672. *e*Breviarium. s.xiv.

SOUTHWICK, Hampshire. London, B.M., Royal 2 B.xv. *e*Horae. s.xv/xvi.

SPOFFORTH, Yorkshire. Oxford, Bodleian, Lat. th. e.36-7. *e*Clemens Lanthon., etc. s.xiv in.

STANHOPE, co. Durham. Durham, Cathedral, B.IV.33. *c*Pupilla oculi. s.xv. ?

STAVELEY, Derbyshire. *Untraced.* Collection of R. Hall in 1705 (*cf. Derbyshire Arch. and Nat. Hist. Soc. Journal.,* xxxiii (1911), 167). *e*Missale (?).

STUSTON, Suffolk. Oxford, Bodleian, Bodl. 280. *e*Legenda. s.xv in.

TATHAM, Lancashire. Stonyhurst Coll., 6. *c*Missale. s.xiv/xv.

TIDMARSH, Berkshire. Tidmarsh, Parish Church (pr. bk). *e*Missale. Antwerp, A.D. 1527.

TOOT BALDON, Oxfordshire. Madresfield Court, Lord Beauchamp, 34.g. *c*Manuale. s.xiv ex.

TREGARE, Monmouthshire. Oxford, All Souls Coll., 11.[3] Missale. s.xv. ?

WALLINGTON, Surrey. Rugby School, Bloxham 1009. *c*Missale. s.xv.

WALMER, Kent. Garstang, Mr M. Fitzherbert-Brockholes.[3] Missale. s.xiv/xv.

WEALD, SOUTH, Essex. Belchamp Hall, Mrs Raymond.[3] Missale. s.xv. ?

WHITCHURCH, Herefordshire. Oxford, Univ. Coll., 78A.[3] Missale. s.xv. ?

WINGFIELD, SOUTH, Derbyshire. Capetown, U.L., 1. *e*Biblia. s.xiii.

WITNEY, Oxfordshire. Bodleian, Gough Missals 25 (pr. bk). *e*Missale. Paris, A.D. 1514.

WOLLATON, Nottinghamshire. Wollaton, Parish Church.[3] *e*Antiphonale. s.xv.

WORCESTER, ST HELEN. Exeter, Cathedral, 3508. Psalterium. s.xiii. ?

WRANGLE, Lincolnshire. Downside Abbey, 950 (pr. bks). *e*Biblia glo. (vols 1, 3, 4). Basel, A.D. 1498-1502. ?

WRETHAM, WEST, Norfolk. Cambridge, Sid. Sussex Coll., 79.[3] Martyrologium. s.xv. ?

[2] Given to Sarsden in 1541.   [3] Calendar contains the dedication of the church.

WRITTLE, Essex. Liverpool, Cathedral. cKalendarium (2 fos). s.xii/xiii.

WYCOMBE, WEST, Buckinghamshire. Oxford, Bodleian, Hatton 9.[4] Psalterium. s.xv. ?

YORK, ST MARTIN, CONEY STREET. York, Minster, xvi.D.13. eBiblia. s.xiii.

ALL SAINTS, PAVEMENT. York, Minster, xvi.G.5.[4] Horae. s.xv.

Rejected: Burton Latimer Parish Church (Burton Latimer, Northampton-shire); Oxford, Bodleian, Laud misc. 299 (Launton, Oxfordshire); Oxford, Bodleian, Bodl. 948 (London, St Andrew Undershaft); Cambridge, Emmanuel Coll., 67 (London, St Dunstan-in-the-East); Oxford, Bodleian, Auct. D.inf.2.6 (Milton, near Canterbury); Oxford, Bodleian, Bodl. 547 (Rochford, Worcestershire); Oxford, Bodleian, Gough Missals 33 (South Littleton, Worcestershire); Oxford, Bodleian, Rawl. C.314 (Paignton, Devon).

[4] Calendar contains the dedication of the church.

Donors, Scribes and Other Persons concerned before 1540 with the Books recorded on pages 1–224.

Names are arranged alphabetically under houses. Words printed in roman type are derived from the inscriptions in the books. Additional information known from other sources, suppositions and explanations are in italics. Only the essential parts of inscriptions are given. In reproducing them: (1) the name of the institution, if it is that which occurs in the heading to each list, is shown by the initial letter; [1](2) case-forms of the personal name and of words agreeing with it, if not already in the nominative, have been changed to the nominative; (3) dates are in modern form; (4) —, — —, or — — — stands for the personal name, but these marks have been used, as a rule, only if the personal name comes in the middle of an inscription; (5) modern English paraphrases or translations have sometimes been preferred. The abbreviation 'g.' is used to indicate a form of inscription in which a title or pressmark is followed by a personal name in the genitive case; 'name' indicates that the inscription consists merely of a personal name in the nominative case.[2] No entry follows the call number of the book if the inscription is in the common *ex dono* or *dedit* form. A personal name preceded by * will be found in A. B. Emden, *Biographical Register of the University of Oxford*, and a personal name preceded by ** in A. B. Emden, *Biographical Register of the University of Cambridge*. In the line containing the personal name a number has sometimes been included in order to refer to a particular book in the list of books under this name: for example, in the entry under St Augustine, Canterbury, 'Byholt, fr. Willelmus de, (4) quondam prior', the number shows that Byholt is referred to as 'quondam prior' in the fourth book in the list (MS. Bodl. 299). The following examples illustrate the relation between the inscriptions in the books themselves[3] and the extracts from them recorded here:

ABERDEEN, *King's College*. Boetius. Aberdeen U.L., 214. 'Collegii Aberdonen' dono magistri Hectoris Boetii primi primarii ejusdem'.

ABINGDON. Bridport *and* Johane. B.M., Add. 42555. Two inscriptions: (1) 'Iste liber est ecclesie conventualis beate Marie Abendone ex dono domini Egidii Sar' episcopi et memoriale ipsius', followed by an anathema; (2) 'Ceste livere fust apreste a tres honurable dame Dame Johane par la grace Dieu reigne Descoce par labbe et covent de Abyndone le jour del Anunciacion Nostre Dame lan le rey Edward le tierce apres la conqueste xxxvime tank a la feste seynt Mychel procheyn ensuiaunt et liveree par Thomas Chitton chantour de mesme le lieu.'

ABINGDON. Buckland. Pembr. Coll., Cambridge, 4.18.8. The first inscription is 'Willelmi Bucklandi monachi Abendoniensis libellus ego sum'.

---

[1] The initial letter is in square brackets, if the name is implicit in the form of the inscription but not actually expressed: *cf.* the Rochester example on p. 226.

[2] See p. xxvi.

[3] As recorded on the cards prepared for *Medieval Libraries* and now deposited in the Bodleian Library.

ABINGDON. Clyff. Bodleian, Digby 146. 'Liber monasterii Abendonie quem Johannes Clyff fecit ligari anno [...]'.

ANGLESEY. Bromptoun. Corpus Christi Coll., Cambridge, 136. 'Liber domus de Angleseye acomodatus Willelmo de Bromptoun rectori ecclesie de Bricham ad restituendum sub pena x s.'

CANTERBURY. T. de Bockyng. Trin. Coll., Cambridge, 85. 'Matheus et Marcus glosati Thome de Bockyng monachi ecclesie Cristi Cantuar.'

ROCHESTER. A., precentor. B.M., Royal 10 C.iv. 'Decreta abreviata de claustro Roffensi per A. precentorem'.

THORNEY. Maxsey. Oxford, Bodleian, Auct. 2.Q.5.19. 'Frater Johannes Maxsey monacus de Thorney' on the flyleaf and 'Maxsey' on sign. a3.

ABERDEEN

Godefridus, corrector rev. doctoris et mag. sacre theologie, mag. Johannis Rath (? *John Rait, bishop of A. 1351–55*):
Oxford, Bodleian, Ashmole 1474 (scripta per manum).

Kynmonde, dom. Alexander de, episcopus A. († *1380*):
Oxford, Bodleian, Ashmole 1474.

ABERDEEN, *King's College*

Boetius, Hector, primus primarius A. († *1537*):
Aberdeen, U.L., 214, 264. Cambridge, Trin. Coll., 1421. Edinburgh, N.L., Adv. 18.3.11.

Elphinstone, mag. Willelmus de (*founder, bishop of A.;* † *1514*). *See p. 2.*

Vaus, Joannes, regens grammaticorum:
Aberdeen, U.L., 263.

ABINGDON

Bledelewe, Ricardus, monachus A.:
Leyden, Vulcanius 96 (scriptum per manus — — A.D. 1390).

*Bridport, dom. Egidius *de*, Sarisburiensis episcopus († *1262*):
London, B.M., Add. 42555 (ex dono — et memoriale ipsius).

Buckland, Willelmus, (*a*) monachus A. (*1539*):
Cambridge, Pembr. Coll., 4.18.8 (*a* — — libellus ego sum; *b* Sum Gulielmi Bocklandi Henrici domini Staffordi famulus).

Chitton, Thomas, chantour A. *See Johane.*

Clyff, Johannes (*sub-prior 1512*):
Oxford, Bodleian, Digby 146 (fecit ligari).

Crystalle, Johannes, monachus A.:
Edinburgh, U.L., *0.18.17 (name *partly legible*). Oxford, Bodleian, Rawl. C.940 (pertinet ad).

Dounehed, fr. Rogerus de:
Oxford, Bodleian, Lyell 21 (adquisitus per).

Johane, dame, reigne Descoce (†14 Aug. or 7 Sept. 1362):
London, B.M., Add. 54255 ('apreste a — par labbe et covent', **25 March** to 29 Sept. 1362, 'et liveree par Thomas Chitton chantour de mesme le lieu').

Rowland, *Thomas*, monachus A.:
Oxford, Bodleian, Rawl. D.235 (Sum — libelulus ex dono dom. J. Nuton de Glovernia monachi, S.T.D., Oxon').

AMESBURY
Wygyngton, dom. Ricardus, capellanus:
London, B.M., Add. 18362 (dedit A.D. 1508).

ANGLESEY
Bromptoun, Willelmus de, rector de Bricham:
Cambridge, Corpus Christi Coll., 136 (acomodatus — — — ad restituendum sub pena x s.).

ANKERWYKE
Lego, Alicia (*nun in 1519*):
Cambridge, Gonv. and Caius Coll., 390 (Thys ys my boke — —).

ARBROATH
Guthre, Ricardus (*abbot 1450–55, 1470–72*):
Aberdeen, U.L., 105 (liber).

ARBUTHNOTT
Arbuthnott, Robertus, fundator:
Paisley, Free Libr. and Mus., Psalter (a — — traditus A.D. 1506); Missal.
See also Sybbalde.
Sybbalde, Jacobus, capellanus († *1507*):
Paisley, Free Libr. and Mus., Psalter (fecit scribi et finiri 4 die Martii 1482 per manum — — Robertus Arbuthnot de eodem); Missal (wrote A.D. 1491); Horae (wrote).

ARUNDEL
*Rede, dom. Willelmus, episcopus Cicestrensis († *1385*):
London, B.M., Royal 10 A.xi.

ASHRIDGE
Edmund, earl of Cornwall († *1300*):
London, B.M., Royal 3 D.vi (*probably made for and given by*).
Hutton, Ricardus:
London, B.M., Royal 7 F.xi (contulit A.D. 1518).
Hyll, Thomas, fr. A. (*s.xvi in.*):
Kew, B. S. Cron (pertinet ad).
Wederore, Simon de, de Trenge (*Tring*), fr. A.:
San Marino, Huntington, EL7H.8 (scripsit et contulit . . . domui predicte . . . ob memoriam Philippi de Wederore patris sui et Petronille matris sue . . . ac ipsius ejusdem fratris Simonis, A.D. 1368, reservato tamen supradicto fratri Simoni quoad vixerit de licencia sui superioris usufructu dicti libri).

AXHOLME
Chamberlayne, dom. Johannes. *See p. 5.*
*Smyth, mag. Willelmus, rector de Belton († *by June 1528*):
Lincoln, Cath., SS.2.15 (gave A.D. 1497).

BABWELL
Bukenham, fr. Walterus de. *See* Reginaldus.
Creyk, fr. [. . .] de:
Rome, Vatican, Ottob. lat. 352 (? gave; *see also* **CAMBRIDGE**, *Fran. convent*).

227

Fakynham, fr. Nicholaus, minister († *1407*):
  London, B.M., Add. 47214 (quaternus fr. Johannis Medilton de dono
  — —).
Goddard, fr. Thomas:
  Oxford, Bodleian, lat. th. d.1 (had use for life A.D. 1538; *cf.* LYNN,
  Philip).
Hepworth, fr. Nicholaus de:
  Cambridge, U.L., Ii.1.1.; Trin. Coll., 919.   London, Royal Astron. Soc.,
  QB 7/1021.
*Hylton, fr. Johannes († *1376*).   *See* Hylton, Willelmus.
Hylton, fr. Willelmus:
  Cambridge, U.L., Add. 6866 (ex dono — — pro anima fr. Johannis
  Hylton magistri).
Medilton, fr. Johannes.   *See* Fakynham.
Reginaldus, sacerdos de eadem villa (*sc. Bury*):
  London, B.M., Burney 5 (ex dono —, cujus usus debetur fr. Waltero
  de Bukenham ad vitam).

BANGOR
Anianus, dom., episcopus B. (*1267–1305*?):
  Bangor, Cath., 1 (liber pontificalis —; *cf.* Ednam).
*Ednam, fr. Ricardus, episcopus B. († *by Apr. 1494*):
  Bangor, Cath., 1 (liber pontificalis — —, quem librum predictus
  Ricardus episcopus dedit A.D. 1485; *cf.* Anianus).

BARDNEY
**Barney, Ricardus, studencium prior Universitatis Cantab. (*monk B.*):
  Oxford, Bodleian, Douce 158 (pr. bk; [pertinet] — — A.D. 1490).
Fuldon, Rogerius *de*, archidiaconus Lincoln' (*c.1285–76*):
  London, B.M., Royal 9 B.ix.
Thornton, fr. Robertus de, quondam prior [B.]:
  London, B.M., Cotton Vit. E.vii.

BARKING
Felton, domina Sibilla de, abbatissa B. (*1394–1419*):
  Beeleigh Abbey, Miss C. Foyle (constat).   Oxford, Bodleian, Bodl. 923
  (constat); Univ. Coll., 169 (concessit ad usum abbatissarum A.D. 1404).
  Paris, B.N., Fr. 1038 (achata).
Hastyngs, domina Maria, de B.:
  London, B.M., Add. 10596 (constat; *cf.* Hayle).
Hayle, Matilda, de B.:
  London, B.M., Add. 10596 (constat; *cf.* Hastyngs).
Scroope, Margareta, monacha B.:
  Beeleigh Abbey, Miss C. Foyle (Mistris Agnes Gowldewell me possidet
  ex dono — — quondam monache . . .).   *Cf.* Felton.
Veer, Elizabeth, sumtyme countes of Oxforde:
  Oxford, Magd. Coll., 41 (gave in 1477 ?).

BARLINGS
Edenham, dom. Galfridus de, canonicus Lincoln':
  Cambridge, Emm. Coll., 17.   Wentworth Woodhouse, Lord Fitzwilliam.

BASINGWERK
Guttyn Owen:
  Aberystwyth, N.L., 7006 D (wrote).

BATH

Ælfricus (*s.xi in.*):
 Cambridge, Corpus Christi Coll., 140 (scripsi in monasterio Baðþonio et dedi Brihtwoldo preposito).
Æthelstanus, rex:
 London, B.M., Cotton Claud. B.v (tradidit).
Brihtwoldus. *See* Ælfricus.
Lutton, Johannes:
 London, B.M., Arundel 86 (scripsit).
Saltford, fr. Willelmus, monachus B. (*s.xv ex.*):
 London, B.M., Arundel 86 (ex adquisito; *cf.* Lutton).

BATTLE

Bodeham, Henricus de:
 Berlin, Staatsbibl., lat. 147 (Liber).
*Henfeld, fr. Johannes, monachus B. (*professed at Canterbury in 1487; migrated to B.*):
 Hereford, Cath., H.2.7 (Liber; *cf.* Manwode). Untraced Historia Britannie (g.).
*Manwode, fr. Robertus, monachus B. (*B.Th. sup. Oxford 1506*):
 Hereford, Cath., H.2.7 (ex labore et studio — — Oxon' studentis 1505).
Nuton, dom. Johannes, abbas B. (*1463–90*):
 Chicago, U.L., 254 (possessio ex jure debetur). London, B.M., Sloane 4031 (ex provisione); The Robinson Trust (Phillipps 8517).
Ricardus, abbas († *1235*):
 Oxford, Bodleian, Lat. misc. c.16.
Russell, fr. Thomas:
 Oxford, St John's Coll., 202 (ex provisione).
*Westfield, fr. Clemens. (*monk B., pensioned 1538*) :
 Cambridge, U.L., Inc. 1982 (ex perquisito).

BEAULY

Barcham, Nicholaus, prior B.:
 Edinburgh, N.L., Adv. 3.1.12 (pertinet — — cum suis monachis A.D. 1521).

BEAUVALE

Braystones (Brestons), Christopherus, monochus B., quondam monochus S. Marie Ebor', capellanus domini Thome Spofforth Herefordensis episcopi (*1422–48*):
 Cambridge, U.L., Mm.5.37.
*Ruwe, Andreas, almanus librarius ac legum bacalarius Oxnien' († *1517*):
 Cambridge, Trin. Coll. (dedit — — ob favorem Johannis Verypt Brabantini domus prescripti monachi et professi).
Verypt, Johannes, monachus B. *See* Ruwe.

BEDFORD, *Fran. conv.*

Grene, fr. Johannes, (2) S.T.D.:
 Oxford, Bodleian, Arch. G.e.5 (1483 — — emit hunc librum Oxon' de elemosinis amicorum suorum); (2) Laud misc. 176 (de dono — — A.D. 1521).

BELVOIR
Belvero, fr. Willelmus de, prior:
Cambridge, Trin. Coll., 317. Eton Coll., 48, ii. Oxford, Bodleian,
Bodl. 755, e Mus. 249.
Dunstaple, fr. Henricus de:
Dublin, Trin. Coll., 432 (liber).

BERMONDSEY
Aylysburrey, Willelmus, monachus B.:
Oxford, Bodleian, Rawl. C.86 (constat).
[. . .], dom. Johannes, monachus B.:
Oxford, Bodleian, Ashmole 342 (libellus).

BEVERLEY, *Dom. conv.*
Eston, fr. Robertus de (*s.xiii ex.*):
Oxford, Univ. Coll., 190 (name *in genitive*).
Stanniforth, fr. Robertus, O.P., B.:
Oxford, Corpus Christi Coll., 225 (Willelmus Mayne habuit hunc librum
ex accomodatione — — A.D. 1450).

BIDDLESDEN
Brueria, fr. Willelmus de (*s.xii*):
Cambridge, U.L., Mm.4.28 (Quisquis hunc perlegeris librum, pro — — —
precem funde, qui ipsum consummationis unguem ad usque duxit).
Byssetur, dom. Johannes, (1) monachus B.:
(1) Hendred House, T. Eyston (emit). New York, Pierpont Morgan,
757 (ex donis — — et dompni Henrici Halderton).
Halderton, dom. Henricus. *See* Byssetur.

BILSINGTON
Johannes, dom., vicarius de Newecherche (*s.xiv*):
Oxford, Bodleian, Bodl. 127 (legavit).

BODMIN
Arcuarius, dom. Johannes, canonicus B.:
London, B.M., Harley 2399 (quod).

BODMIN, *Franc. conv.*
Basseytt, Gregorius, O.F.M., B., Academie Cantabrigie litterarum divin-
arum studens:
Winchester, The Presbytery (possessor).
H., dom., decanus sancti Karentoci (? *Henry de Trefenwa 1309–11*):
London, B.M., Royal 7 A.x (dedit — communitati B. per procuracionem
fr. Ricardi de Sancta Columba et fr. Galfridi Werdour, ita quod
predicti fratres haberent usum ad tempus vite).
Pole, fr. Ricardus, O.F.M. (? *of Bodmin, fl. 1374*):
Oxford, Bodleian, Ashmole 360 (constat).
Sancta Columba, fr. Ricardus de. *See* H., decanus.
Werdour, fr. Galfridus. *See* H., decanus.

BORDESLEY
Northewode, Johannes, monachus, intravit domum probacionis B.,
A.D. 1386:
London, B.M., Add. 37787 (constat).

BOSTON, *Dom. conv.*
Claxton, fr. Johannes de, O.P., B.:
   Oxford, St John's Coll., 198 (quaternus — — —; *cf.* **CHICHESTER,**
   Dom. conv., Lovent).

BOXLEY
Godfridus, Johannes, monachus B.:
   Oxford, Corpus Christi Coll., Φ A.3.4 (libellus).
Heriettsham, dom. Johannes:
   Cambridge, Corpus Christi Coll., 37 (emptus per — — — ab executoribus
   mag. Johannis Renham nuper rectoris de Holyngbourne).

BRECON
Manwode, Robertus, prior, S.T.D. (*cf.* **BATTLE**):
   Cambridge, Fitzwilliam Mus., 269 (*a* per — — 1514; *b* composuit
   — — A.D. 1521).

BRECON, *Dom. conv.*
Texerii, fr. Bartholomeus, O.P. *See p. 12.*

BRIDGWATER, *Fran. conv.*
Blo[. . .]worth, fr. Walterius de (*s.xiv*):
   Oxford, Magd. Coll., 174 (accomodavit — — — fr. Ricardo de S. Aluno
   de beneplacito et assensu conv. B.).
*Middelton, mag. J. de (*fl. 1340*):
   London, B.M., Royal 3 A.xi.
Sancto Aluno, fr. Ricardus de. *See* Blo[. . .]worth.

BRIDLINGTON
Ashby, Thomas, canonicus B. (*c.1510*):
   Durham, U.L., Cosin V.v.19 (*commonplace book of*).
Berewic, W. de:
   Ripon, Cath., xvii.D.2, 3.

BRISTOL, *St Mark*
Colman, Johannes, (1) quondam magister B.:
   (1) Oxford, Bodleian, Bodl. 618 (*a* monogram; *b* orate pro anima; *wrote
   part*); Lyell 38 (monogram; *wrote*); St John's Coll., 173 (*a* monogram;
   b qui legat emendet scriptorem non reprehendat — —).
Lya, Savericus de, presbyter:
   Oxford, St John's Coll., 165.

BRISTOL, *Fran. conv.*
Downe, fr. Thomas, O.F.M., B.:
   Cambridge, St John's Coll., 144 (per manum — — A.D. 1381 fideliter
   consummata).
Martun (?), fr. Georgius:
London, B.M., Royal 5 E.iv (comparabitt —— ex elimosina suorum
   amicorum testante patre Ricardo Terren tunc gardiano Bristolie).
Wells, dom. Jocelinus *de*, quondam episcopus Bathon' et Wellensis (*1206–
   1242*):
   Bristol, Central Public Libr., 3.

BROMFIELD
Sebrok, Thomas, prior B. (*B.D. Oxon. 1522*):
   Oxford, Brasen. Coll., UB., S.II.51 (name).

BRUISYARD, *Fran. nunnery*
Bakon, domina Margeria, O.F.M., B.:
   Oxford, Bodleian, Tanner 191 (pr. bk; pertinet — — ex dono fr. Thome
   Monger).
Felbrygge, soror Anna:
   London, B.M., Sloane 2400 (liber — — ad terminum vite post cujus
   decessum pertinebit conv. B.).

BUCKFAST
Dove, Ricardus, monachus B.:
   London, B.M., Sloane 513 (quod).

BUILDWAS
Brug', mag. Walterus de, dictus le Paumer:
   Oxford, Ball. Coll., 35A (legavit A.D. 1277).
Gnowsal, dom. Johannes, abbas B.:
   London, Lambeth Pal., 488 (per — — in custodia fr. Henrici de Valle
   monachi de Savigniaco positus ut per unam indenturam inter ipsos
   factam plenius apparet).
Valle, Henricus de. *See* Gnowsal.

BURNHAM NORTON
Dersyngham, fr. Alanus, O.C., B.:
   London, B.M., IC.29955–56 (libellus — — Cantabrigiis theologie
   studentis anno christiani salutis 1511).

BURTON-UPON-TRENT
Edys, dom. Willelmus, monachus B., (7) abbas B.:
   Cambridge, U.L., Inc. 3057 (liber); St John's Coll., A.2.1 (constat).
   London, B.M., Cotton Cleop. A.ii (ex conjunctione — — dum esset
   studens Oxonie A.D. 1517). Norwich, City Libr. (ex emptione — —
   dum esset scolasticus Oxonie A.D. 1514). Oxford, All Souls Coll.,
   i.12.15 (ex emptione — — dum esset cellararius anno partus virginei
   1517), v.2.13 (ex emptione — — A.D. 1516), (7) v.4.12 (liber — —),
   LR.4.e.10 (liber), SR.62.a.2 (ex emptione — — dum esset studens
   Oxonie anno virginei conceptus 1515).[4]
Elkyn, dom. Johannes, monachus B.:
   Oxford, All Souls Coll., SR.77.g.13 (constat).
Swepston', mag. Willelmus de:
   Cambridge, Corpus Christi Coll., 353 (liber quondam — — — quem
   contulit eccl. de B. mag. Willelmus frater ipsius pro anima ejus).

BURY ST EDMUNDS
Aylesham, fr. Petrus de, monachus B.:
   Cambridge, Pembr. Coll., 33, 34 (*both* procuravit).
B., dom. J. de, abbas (*cf.* Brinkele):
   Cambridge, Pembr. Coll., 40. Glasgow, U.L., Hunterian 209.
*Babington, Willelmus (*abbot 1446–53*):
   Oxford, Bodleian, Bodl. 426 (initials *imply that he caused the MS. to be
   made*).

---

[4] A later book belonging to Edys is Dionysius Carthusianus, Cologne, 1537,
2 vols, one now at Worcester Coll. (EE.u.3) and the other at All Souls Coll.
(SR.73.h.6). These may have belonged to Edys only after the Dissolution,
when he became first dean of Burton College.

Baldewinus, prior B.:
    Cambridge, St John's Coll., 94 (fecit feri). Oxford, Bodleian, e Mus.
    112 (fecit scribi).
Bardwell, dom. Johannes, monachus B.:
    Oxford, Bodleian, Holkham misc. 37 (liber; *cf.* W[. . .]spet).
Bartolomeus, mag.:
    Edinburgh, U.L., 163.
*Barwe, fr. Willelmus, (2) sacrista B. (*1407, 1411*):
    Cambridge, Pembr. Coll., 89 (de empcione). (2) Oxford, Bodleian,
    Bodl. 216 (usque ad litteram D per J. abbatem sancti Edmundi set
    perficiebantur usque in finem per fr. — — hujus monasterii sacristam).
Becles, fr. Robertus de. *See* Brinkele.
*Brinkele, dom. Johannes de, abbas (*1361–79*):
    London, B.M., Royal 8 E.x (emptus per — — — in quaternis et per fr.
    Robertum de Becles colligatus). *See also* B., J. de, abbas; J. abbas;
    Johannes abbas.
Bryngkeley, fr. Ricardus, O.F.M.:
    Oxford, Bodleian, Laud or. 174 (acomodatum — — A.D. 1502).
*Bury, dom. Willelmus, monachus B. (*fl. 1435*):
    Cambridge, Pembr. Coll., 105 (constat).
*Clare, dom. Thomas, monachus B.:
    Cambridge, U.L., Add. 6190 (perscripte Oxoniis per — — A.D. 1441).
*Cranewys, fr. Johannes, (1) quondam sacrista (*1427*):
    (1) Cambridge, Pembr. Coll., 31 (de empcione). Oxford, Bodleian,
    Bodl. 716 (de empcione).
Curteys, dom. Willelmus, abbas B. (*1429–45*):
    Cambridge, Trin. Coll., 623 (de procuracione). Durham, U.L., Cosin
    V.iii.20 (de procreacione [*sic*] — —, quem librum ejusdem monasterii
    librarie ab ipso fabricate assignavit et donavit).
Denham, Reginaldus de, sacrista:
    Cambridge, Pembr. Coll., 120.
*Dersham, dom. W., monachus B., (*sacrist 1503*):
    Oxford, Bodleian, Auct. 7.Q.7.24 (de empcione).
Dice, fr. Willelmus de, monachus B.:
    Cambridge, Pembr. Coll., 27 (scribi fecit). London, B.M., Royal 7 C.v
    (scribi fecit).
Feningham, dom. Johannes, monachus B.:
    London, B.M., Harley 5334.
Freknham, Willelmus, monachus B. (*s.xv ex.*):
    Cambridge, St John's Coll., 149 (liber — — scolaris et de empcione ejus).
*Gosford, dom. Johannes, quondam prior, (*almoner 1381*):
    Cambridge, Pembr. Coll., 5 (de procuracione).
*Grossetest', mag. Robertus († *1253*):
    Cambridge, Pembr. Coll., 7 (Memoriale — — pro exameron Basilii).
Guido, precentor:
    Cambridge, Pembr. Coll., 94 (fecit scribere). London, B.M., Royal 2
    E.ix (fecit scribi).
Hakeford, Adam de. *See* Waxingam.
Halliwell, fr. J., monachus B.:
    Oxford, St John's Coll., 43 (Caucio).
**Haslingfeld, mag. Stephanus de (*fl. 1300*):
    Cambridge, Pembr. Coll., 38 (legavit).

Hemlington, dom. Galfridus de, quondam prior:
  Cambridge, Pembr. Coll., 104 (de empcione).
*Henry, dom. Willelmus, monachus B., D.Th.:
  London, B.M., Royal 7 B.ix (de procuracione et dono).
Herveus, frater Taleboti prioris:
  Cambridge, Corpus Christi Coll., 2 (*almost certainly the great bible said to
  have been written by — and illuminated by mag. Hugo*).
Hesset, Thomas, monachus B.:
  Cambridge, F. J. Norton (Sum).
Hugo, magister. *See* Herveus.
Huntedon, dom. Rogerus de:
  Oxford, Bodleian, Bodl. 240 (scribi fecit sumptibus graciarum suarum
  A.D. 1376).
Hyngham, Thomas, monachus:
  Untraced Boethius (constat).
Ikelyngham, fr. Robertus, monachus B., prior:
  Cambridge, Pembr. Coll., 98 (procuravit).
J. abbas (*cf.* Brinkele, Tymworth):
  Ipswich, Central Libr., 4 (per). *See also* Barwe.
Johannes, fr., abbas:
  Cambridge, Pembr. Coll., 1 (de empcione). *See also* Thomas, vicarius
  de Gorleston.
Kyrkstede, fr. Henricus de:
  Cambridge, Corpus Christi Coll., 404 (scripsit pro majori parte);
  Pembr. Coll., 92 (*a* Memorandum quod fr. H. de K. solvit pro scrip-
  tura et aliis sumptibus istius libri xxij s.; *b* de procuracione); St John's
  Coll., 170 (scribi fecit). London, B.M., Royal 8 B.iv (de pro-
  curacione, 8 F.xiv (per fr. H. de K.), 12 C.vi (H. de K.).
Lacford, dom. W. de:
  Cambridge, Pembr. Coll., 37 (procuravit).
Langham, S.:
  Dublin, Chester Beatty Libr., W.26 (in custodia).
Neylond, fr. Thomas:
  London, The Robinson Trust (liber).
Rokeswell, dom. Robertus de:
  Durham, U.L., Cosin V.v.3.
*Ryngsted, monachus B. (? *Thomas R., prior 1528–39*):
  London, B.M., IB.40248 (Sum).
Scrouteby, fr. Thomas de:
  Cambridge, U.L., Add. 6860; Pembr. Coll., 46.
Stephanus, mag. (*s.xiii*):
  Cambridge, Pembr. Coll., 65.
Swaffham, dom. Johannes, sacrista:
  Oxford, Bodleian, Bodl. 225 (de redempcione).
Thomas, dom., vicarius de Gorleston:
  Douai, Bibl. mun., 171 (Psalterium dompni Johannis abbatis ex dono).
Tymworth, J., abbas (*1384–90*):
  London, B.M., Harley 4968 (de empcione).
Waxingam, dom. Johannes de, monachus:
  London, B.M., Royal 8 C.iv (traditus Ade de Hakeford per).
Wesingham, fr. Robertus:
  London, B.M., Harley 51 (procuravit).

Weysnham, fr. Johannes:
 London, Lambeth Pal., 120 (liber — —1464).
Wickham, Johannes, monachus B.:
 Cambridge, Corpus Christi Coll., 135 (De sorte — — actualiter scola-
 tizantis Oxon' et permansuri ibi).
Wirlingworthe, dom. Edmundus de:
 Cambridge, Pembr. Coll., 99 (de empcione).
Wlpit, mag. Johannes de, rector de Fortune:
 Cambridge, Pembr. Coll., 55.
W[. . .]spet, dom. Johannes:
 Oxford, Bodleian, Holkham misc. 37 (Edmundo sancto pertinet et — —;
 cf. Bardwell).
Ypswich, dom. Robertus, monachus:
 Cambridge, St John's Coll., 138 (pertinet).
Yxworth, Johannes (described as monk of B. in inscription written in 1573):
 London, Lambeth Pal., 90 (Biblia — —).

BUTLEY
Thetford, fr. Johannes, canonicus B. (prior 1519):
 Ipswich, Central Libr. (ex providencia).
Wodebrigge, fr. Willelmus, subprior B.:
 London, B.M., IB.55315 (pertinet ad).

BYLAND
**Colyns, mag. Martinus, thesaurarius Ebor' († 1509):
 Cambridge, U.L., Res. b.162 (his executors gave).
Ditton, fr. Robertus de, prior B. (?) (s.xiii):
 Manchester, J. Rylands, lat. 153 (circa hunc librum laboravit; cf.
 Welton).
Gillyng, fr. Johannes, monachus B.:
 Oxford, Bodleian, Bodl. 842 (liber — — emptus a quodam carpentario
 nomine Sproxton A.D. 1477).
Orwell, J., prior beate Marie Ebor'. See Welton.
Welton, fr. Thomas, scolaris B. et bachalarius in divinis:
 Manchester, J. Rylands, Lat. 153 (ex procuracione — —. Quem
 librum J. Orwell prior monasterii beate Marie juxta Eboracum habet
 ex mutuo; cf. Ditton).

CAMBRIDGE, Gilb. priory of St Edmund
**Hanworth, mag. Johannes:
 Cambridge, U.L., Ee.6.31 + Trin. Coll., 1395. London, B.M., Add.
 18899.

CAMBRIDGE, Hospital of St John
**Somer, Henricus:
 Cambridge, Corpus Christi Coll., 21.

CAMBRIDGE, Fran. conv.
**Brynkley, fr. Ricardus, (3) minister, O.F.M. (prior provincial 1518):
 Cambridge, Gonv. and Caius Coll., 348 (name). Ipswich, Central Libr.
 (name in genitive). (3) Salisbury, Cath., M.1.27 (name in genitive).
 Untraced Euclid (name and date 1487). See also Trumpyton,
 Wyndyssor.
**Dudelington, fr. Thomas de (fl. 1328). See Thomas, rector.

Kelle, fr. Ambrosius, O.F.M., custodie Cantab':
Oxford, Corpus Christi Coll., 182 (name *in genitive and date* 1525).
Morys, fr. Willelmus, (2) O.F.M. (? **W. M.*, Cambr. conv. 1407*):
Rome, Vatican, Ottob. lat. 69 (liber); (2) Ottob. lat. 2088 (liber).
**Rameseye, fr. Nicholaus de (*fl. 1367*):
Rome, Vatican, Ottob. lat. 325 (*a* liber; *b* contulit).
**Staneweye, fr. Oliverus de:
Rome, Vatican, Ottob. lat. 101 (licencia ministri ad ordinandum de libris meis infra ordinem concedo istum librum [. . . .] A.D. 1342).
Thomas, rector de Colveston:
London, B.M., Sloane 1726 (dedit fr. Thome de Dudelingtone pro anima dom. Willelmi de Rollesby usum istius biblie versificate ad terminum vite ipsius fratris Thome ita quod post mortem ejus maneat perpetuo in communitate fr. min. Cantebrigie).
**Trumpyton, fr. Thomas, S.T.D., O.F.M. (*fl. 1465*):
London, B.M., Cotton Cleop. C.ix (liber — — `quem dedit fr. Ricardo Brynkele tunc temporis studenti Cantabrigie'). Oxford, Balliol Coll., 133 (liber constat). Rome, Vatican, Ottob. lat. 352 (name *in genitive*).
Wyndele, fr. Thomas de, O.F.M., de custodia C.:
Oxford, Balliol Coll., 214 (conceditur — — — in capitulo sancti Botulphi A.D. 1390 et est liber custodialis).
Wyndyssore, Katerina, generosa:
London, Middle Temple (fr. Ricardi Bryngkelei ex dono).

CAMBRIDGE, *Dom. conv.*
*Hunton, fr. Simon de:
Rome, Vatican, Ottob. lat. 159 (in custodia); lat. 442 (concessus — — — ad vitam suam).
**Kyllynworth, Edwardus (*fl. 1490*):
Rome, Vatican, Ottob. lat. 640 (contulit).
**Picwurth, fr. Willelmus, O.P. (*provincial prior 1397–1402*):
Rome, Vatican, Ottob. lat. 758 (liber); lat. 862 (liber — — quem propria manu scripsit quando erat studens in conventu Londoniarum et vol. quod incatinetur in comuni libraria Cantebrig').
Redymer, fr. Willelmus, S.T.P. (*s.xv*):
London, B.M., Royal 10 B.vii (ligari fecit; *cf.* Willingham).
Sancto Martino, fr. W. de:
Rome, Vatican, Ottob. lat. 99 (comodatus — — — quamdiu vixerit).
Willingham, fr. Galfridus de:
London, B.M., Royal 10 B.vii (Iste fuit Fishaker — — — et est sub custodia prioris; *later at Southwark*).
**Yx[. . . .], fr. Willelmus de:
Rome, Vatican, Ottob. lat. 150, i (liber quondam — — — quem reliquit fr. pred. Canteb').

CAMBRIDGE, *Carm. conv.*
**Pole, mag. Johannes, O.Carm. (*D.Th. 1381*):
York, Minster, xvi.K.5 (constat — — quem fecerat scribi ex elemosinis amicorum suorum).

CAMBRIDGE, *Aug. conv.*
**Bellond, fr. Edmundus (*O.H.S.A., C. 1491*; *prior provincial c. 1518*):
Rome, Vatican, Ottob. lat. 746 (constat).

**Longspey, fr. Johannes, de Broklesby, O.H.S.A.:
Rome, Vatican, Vat. lat. 4954 (dedit A.D. 1357).
**Mendham, fr. Robertus (*O.H.S.A., C. in 1470-71 and 1508*):
Dublin, Trin. Coll., 115 (pertinet A.D. 1497; *cf.* Stocton, Swyllyngton).
**Stocton, fr. Adam de, lector C.:
Dublin, Trin. Coll., 115 ('scriptus a — — — A.D. 1377', at Cambridge
and, in other years, in other places).
Swyllyngton, fr. Thomas:
Dublin, Trin. Coll., 115 (pertinet A.D. 1529; *cf.* Mendham, Stocton).

CAMBRIDGE, *University*
**Crome, Walterus († *1453*):
· Cambridge, Corpus Christi Coll., 68, + King's Coll., 9 (*presumed gift of*).
**Tunstall, Cuthbert, episcopus London' († *1559*):
Cambridge, Trin. Coll., 813. Shrewsbury School, E.VI.10.

CAMBRIDGE, *Clare College*
**Aketon, mag. Willelmus († *by Febr. 1391*):
Oxford, Magd. Coll., 195.
**Yngham, mag., quondam socius (*J. de Y., fellow 1402*):
Oxford, Bodleian, Bodl. 300.

CAMBRIDGE, *Corpus Christi College*
**Markaunt, T. *See p. 25.*

CAMBRIDGE, *Gonville Hall*
*Goldewell, mag. Nicholaus, archidiaconus Suffolchie († *1505*):
Cambridge, U.L., Inc. 3856 (ex dono — — anno salutis 1505).

CAMBRIDGE, *Jesus College*
**Gunthorp, mag. Willelmus (*for Johannes*), decanus de Wels († *1498*):
Cambridge, U.L., Ff.6.20 (contulit).

CAMBRIDGE, *King's College*
Hartwell, Johannes, super socius (*1508*):
Cambridge, U.L., AB.4.54.2.
Langport, Johannes, S.T.P. (*s.xvi in.*):
Oxford, Bodleian, Jones 41.

CAMBRIDGE, *Michaelhouse*
Filey, W.:
Ampleforth Abbey. Cambridge, St John's Coll., Qq.3.15; Trin. Coll.,
C.15.2. London, Lambeth Pal., **H. 1970.

CAMBRIDGE, *Pembroke College*
**Rawson, mag. W*illelmus* († *1495*):
Colchester, Harsnett Libr., H.f.28 (name; *presumably his gift*).

CAMBRIDGE, *Peterhouse*
**Clouygth, mag. T. (*Thomas Clough, adm. 1473*):
London, Royal Coll. of Physicians, 390 (in distribucione; *cf.* Holbrok).
**Dyngley, Willelmus, fellow 1393:
London, Lambeth Pal., 32 (caucio — — A.D. 1436; *recorded in cat. as his gift*).

**Holbrok, mag. Johannes (*master 1421–37*):
  London, B.M., Egerton 889 (contulit A.D. 1426); Royal Coll. of
  Physicians, 390 (contulit A.D. 1426). Oxford, Corpus Christi Coll.,
  151 (contulit A.D. 1426).
**Marchall, Rogerus, (1, 3) nuper socius, (3) arcium medicineque doctor
  regum medicus († *1477*):
  (1) Cambridge, Magd. Coll., Pepys 2329 (do, lego et concedo). London,
  B.M., Harley 531 (*perhaps his gift*). (3) Oxford, Bodleian, Ashmole
  424 (lego 1 Jan. 1472/73). *See also* Somerseth.
**Somerseth, mag. Johannes, arcium medicineque doctor († *by 1455*):
  London, B.M., Sloane 59 (donavit . . ., cujus tamen usum habebit mag.
  Rogerus Marchall per totam vitam suam).
*Witleseye, Willelmus, archiepiscopus Cant' († *1374*):
  Cambridge, St John's Coll., 55 (liber — — relictus collegio Canteb').

CAMPSEY
Babyngton, domina Katerina, quondam subpriorissa (*1492*):
  London, B.M., Arundel 396.
Symonde, dame Catherine. *See* Wylby.
Wylby, Elizabeth, nonne of C. (*1514, 1526*):
  Cambridge, Corpus Christi Coll., 268 (I — — gyffe thys boke [. . . .]).
  Untraced pr. bk in Harleian sale (gave to dame Catherine Symonde, to
  pass from her to another sister of the house).

CANONS ASHBY
Bolt, alias Barton, dom. Johannes, canonicus C.:
  Hereford, Cath., P.iii.1 (constat).

CANONSLEIGH
Clare, dame Matilde de (*foundress 1282*):
  London, B.M., Cotton Cleop. C.vi (dat' . . . per).

CANTERBURY, *Christ Church*[6]
Adam, prior. *See* Chillenden, Adam de.
Ælfred, aldormon (*s.ix*):
  Stockholm, Kungl. bibl. (gave jointly with his wife Werburg).
Æþelstan, (1) Anglorum basyleos, (2) rex († *940*):
  (1) London, B.M., Cotton Tib. A.ii (tribuit); (2) Lambeth Pal., 1370.
*Arundell, dom. Thomas, archiepiscopus Cant' († *1414*):
  Oxford, Bodleian, Laud misc. 165.
Becket, sanctus Thomas, (1, 3) martir, (2) archiepiscopus († *1170*):
  (1) Cambridge, Corpus Christi Coll., 46 (g); (2) Trin. Coll., 391 (g.).
  (3) Oxford, Bodleian, Auct. E.inf.7 (name *in genitive*). Cambridge,
  Trin. Coll., 90 (?), 108 (?), 109 (?), 151 (?), 637; Oxford, Bodleian,
  Bodl. 345; Magd. Coll., 166: *are or may be identical with books
  entered in cat. as 'Libri sancti Thome'.*
Beket, dom. Thomas, monachus C.:
  Oxford, New Coll., 300 (liber — — A.D. 1531: *wrote* (?); *cf.* R. Holyng-
  borne).
*Benett, Rogerus, monachus C. (†*c.1523–24*):
  London, B.M., Egerton 2867 (liber).

  [6] For the monks, *cf.* W. G. Searle, *Christ Church, Canterbury* (Camb. Antiq.
Soc., 8vo publ. xxxiv), 1902.

Bereham, mag. M. de:
  Cambridge, U.L., Ff.3.28 (g.; *name erased*; *cf.* Eastry).
Birchington, Stephanus, monachus C. († *1407*):
  London, Lambeth Pal., 303 (g.).
*Blund, mag. Johannes, cancellarius Ebor' († *1248*):
  Cambridge, Trin. Coll., 163.
Bockyng, dom. Edwardus, monachus C. († *1534*):
  Ampleforth Abbey (liber dom. Thome Goldstone monachi C. ex
    dono).
Bockyng, Thomas de, monachus C.:
  Cambridge, Trin. Coll., 85 (g.).
Bonyngton, fr. *Willelmus*, monachus C. (*1468*):
  Oxford, Bodleian, Rawl. B.188 (liber — — reparatus A.D. 1483). *See
    also* Langdon.
Boolde, W., monachus C.:
  Oxford, Bodleian, Bodl. 648 (constat — — A.D. 1468).
Boseham, mag. Herebertus de (*s.xii ex.*):
  Cambridge, Trin. Coll., 150, 152–53.   Oxford, Bodleian, Auct. E.inf.6
    (*all recorded in cat. as his gifts*).
Brito (*s.xii*):
  Oxford, Bodleian, Digby 5 (name).
Broke, monachus C.:
  Cambridge, U.L., Ii.3.1 (constat).
Cantuariensis, Rogerus (*s.xii/xiii*):
  Cambridge, Trin. Coll., 90 (peraratus calamo).
Caperun, Willelmus:
  Canterbury, Cath., 45 (g.).
Cawston, dom. Thomas, monachus C. († *1504*):
  Canterbury, Cath., 26 (fecit fieri A.D. 1486).
Chartham, dom. Willelmus, monachus C. (*1403;* † *1448*):
  London, Lambeth Pal., 78 (liber compositus et perquisitus — —
    A.D. 1448 'nunc pertinens at Johannem Sarysbury A.D. 1520').
Chelmington, R., monachus C. († *1470*):
  Canterbury, Cath., 37 (name *and date* 1461).   Oxford, Bodleian, Rawl.
    C.269 (name *and date* 1454).
Chillenden, Adam *de*, prior (*1264–74*):
  Canterbury, Cath., 17 (g.).
Chyllynden, dom. Johannes, commonachus C.:
  Cambridge, Trin. Coll., 829 (libellus — — A.D. 1513: *name over erasure
    of* ? Holyngborne).
*Chyllyndene, Thomas, prior C. (*1391–1411*):
  Cambridge, Trin. Coll., 154, flyleaf (g.).   Oxford, Bodleian, Lat. misc.
    b. 12, fo. 8 (g.).
Clyve, mag. Martinus de, monachus C. († *1301*):
  Canterbury, Cath., 42 (Liber — — — qui perquisivit et eidem ecclesie
    dedit).
Covintre, Johannes, monachus (*1465*):
  Cambridge (U.S.A.), Harvard Univ., Houghton Libr. Typ. 3 (si quis
    invenerit restituat — —).
*Courtenay, Willelmus, archiepiscopus C.:
  Cambridge, Trin. Coll., 154.   Oxford, Bodleian, Bodl. 251 (*a* g.;
    b dedit).

*Cranebroke, dom. Henricus, monachus C. (*1435;* † *1466*):
London, B.M., Royal 10 B.ix (de perquisito — — quem emit de dom. J. Hynder capellano 1452). Oxford, Bodleian, Selden supra 65 (monogram). *See also* **OXFORD**, *Canterbury Coll.*

Depham, H. de († 1292):
Canterbury, Cath., 15 (g.).

Dover, W.:
Oxford, Bodleian, Rawl. C.269 (name *and date* 1464; *cf.* Chelmington).

Eastry, Henricus *de*, prior († *1331*):
Cambridge, U.L., Ff.3.28 (g.; *name over erasure; cf.* Bereham); St John's Coll., 52 (g.); Trin. Coll., 407 (g.). London, B.M., Cotton Galba E.iv (g.).

Fro, fr. J. de:
Canterbury, Cath., 65 (de perquisicione).

*Frome, J. (*fl. 1350*):
Cambridge, U.L., Ff.5.31 (g.).

Girunde, Hugo de (*1239*):
Cambridge, Corpus Christi Coll., 222 (g.).

Goleston (Goldston), dom. Thomas, prior (*1494–1517*):
Oxford, Bodleian, Tanner 15 (perfectum ex impensis — — per me Jacobum Neell Normannum ac Rothomagi natum anno verbi incarnati 1499); Pembr. Coll., pastedowns (de perquisito). *See also* E. Bockyng.

Gyllyngham (Gylingham), Willelmus (Guillelmus), (*a*) monachus C. (*1495*):
Wisbech Mus., Town Libr., C.3.8 (*a* in custodia; *b* liber).

*Hadley, dom. Willelmus, supprior (*1471;* † *1499*):
London, B.M., Arundel 155 (Psalterium dom. Johannis Waltham mon. C. Ex dono — — ; *cf.* Ingram).

Hadley, mag. Willelmus (*1502*). *See* Hartey.

Hartey, dom. Jacobus, monachus C. (*1500*):
London, Lambeth Pal., 159 (liber — — (N. Herst *substituted*). 'Modo liber Johannis Sarysbury ex dono mag. Willelmi Hadley'). *Cf.* R. Stone.

Helias:
Dublin, Trin. Coll., 124 (g.).

Herst, Nicholas (*1510*). *See* Hartey.

Herveus:
Cambridge, U.L., Gg.4.17 (g.).

Hogerus:
Cambridge, Corpus Christi Coll., 260 (g.).

Holyngborne, dom. Johannes, monachus C. (*1510*):
London, B.M., Cotton Vesp. B.xxv (liber — — (*name over erasure*) emptus a quodam fratre A.D. 1503); Lambeth Pal., 558 (g., A.D. 150[.]). Oxford, Corpus Christi Coll., 189 (de empcione). *See also* Chyllynden.

Holyngborne, Robertus:
Oxford, New Coll., 300 (libellus manebit (?) — —).

Hospreng, Alexander de:
Cambridge, St John's Coll., 30 (g.). London, Lambeth Pal., 142 (g.).

Humphrey, dom. Thomas, custos coll. Cantuar' in Oxon' (*c.1473–78*):
Canterbury, Cath., 75 (constat).

Hynder, dom. J., capellanus. *See* Cranebroke.

Ingram (Yngram), dom. Willelmus, monachus C. (*1521*), (2) peni-
tenciarius:
Canterbury, Cath., 43 (liber constat — — qui erat compositus A.D. 1478);
(2) 53 (pertinet ad; *cf.* London). London, B.M., Arundel 155 (Si quis
invenerit restituat — —); Harley 1587 (constat).

Ivyngho, Nicholaus de († *1334*):
London, Lambeth Pal., 399 (*a* g.; *b* emit pro x s.).

*Kynton, mag. Johannes, monachus C. († *1416*):
Canterbury, Cath., 1 (liber). Oxford, Bodleian, Laud misc. 444
(g.).

*Langdon, mag. Johannes (*1465;* † *1496*):
Manchester, Northern Congreg. Coll., 1 (Biblia quondam in custodia
— — . In custodia W. Bonyngton A.D. 1483).

Langton, Stephanus, archiepiscopus († *1228*):
Cambridge, Corpus Christi Coll., 76 (g.).

Ledeberi, W. de († *1328*):
Oxford, Bodleian, Bodl. 336 (g.).

Le Palmere, Jacobus:
Oxford, Bodleian, Laud misc. 165 (liber — — — quem scripsit manu sua
propria).

London, Johannes de († *1299*):
Cambridge, U.L., Ff.3.19 (g.). London, Coll. of Arms, Arundel 20
(g.; *cf.* Sudburye).

London, dom. Willelmus:
Canterbury, Cath., 53 (liber; *cf.* Ingram).

Lo[...], Johannes:
London, B.M., Egerton 2867 (vendicatus per).

Longo Campo, Nigellus de:
London, B.M., Cotton Vesp. D.xix (g.). *See also* Nigellus.

*Mepeham, mag. Simon de, (2, 3) archiepiscopus (*1328–33*):
Cambridge, Trin. Coll., 133 (liber); (2) 969 (g.); (3) London, Sion Coll.,
Arc. L.40.2/L.2 (g.).

Mere, Henricus (*cf. M. B. Parkes in Bodl. Libr. Rec., vi. 654*):
Cambridge, Trin. Coll., 377 (*wrote*). Oxford, Bodleian, Bodl. 281
(*wrote part*).

Me[....]sall, fr. Johannes:
Oxford, Bodleian, Lyell 19 (liber).

Molasche, *Willelmus*, prior (*1428–38*):
Canterbury, Cath., 14 (name). Oxford, Bodleian, Bodl. 648
(name).

Neell, Jacobus, Normannus ac Rothomagi natus. *See* Goleston.

Nigellus (? *N. de Longo Campo, q.v.*):
Cambridge, Trin. Coll., 342 (g.).

Noreys, Rogerius (*prior;* † *1223*):
Canterbury, Cath., 57, iii (g.).

Northwico, *Walterus* de († *1328*):
Canterbury, Cath., 104 (g).

Oxeney, dom. Jacobus de (*1328;* † *1361*):
Canterbury, Cath., 74 (g.).

s   241

Pyryt, Johannes de, Cantuar' jurista:
  Oxford, Merton Coll., 328 (legavit A.D. 1435).
Reding, Rogerus de:
  Cambridge, Trin. Coll., 137 (g.).
Remensis, Radulfus:
  Cambridge, Pembr. Coll., 201 (name); Trin. Coll., 74 (g.).   Douai, Bibl.
    mun., 202 (g.).
Ricardus [. . . .]ham, monachus C. (s.xiv):
  London, B.M., Royal 10 A.xiii (liber).
Rofa, Jordanus de (1239):
  Oxford, Pembr. Coll., 5 (g.).
*Rychemont, Willelmus, monachus C. (1354; † 1406):
  Paris, Bibl. Mazarine, 5 (liber ecclesie Cristi Cant', cujus custos — —).
Salomon (sub-prior 1207):
  Cambridge, Corpus Christi Coll., 51 (g.).   London, B.M., Egerton 3314
    (wrote notes in).
Sandwyco, Nicholaus de (prior 1244–58; † 1289):
  Cambridge, Corpus Christi Coll., 288 (liber).
Sarysbury, Johannes.   See Chartham, Hartey.
Sancto Elphego, Ricardus de, prior (1258–63):
  Canterbury, Cath., 67 (g.).
Simon, supprior:
  Cambridge, U.L., Kk.1.28 (g.).
Stone, fr. Johannes, monachus:
  Cambridge, Corpus Christi Coll., 417 (liber — — quem composuit
    A.D. 1467).
Stone, Ricardus, commonachus C. (1483):
  Cambridge, Corpus Christi Coll., 375 (had use of; cf. W. A. Pantin,
    Canterbury Coll., Oxford, i (Oxf. Hist. Soc., N.S., vi, 1947), 100).
  London, Lambeth Pal., 159 (scriptum per, A.D. 1507).
Stoyl, fr. Thomas (1299; † 1333):
  Cambridge, Corpus Christi Coll., 63, i–iii (g.).
Stureya, Thomas de, senior (sub-prior 1270):
    Cambridge, Trin. Coll., 98 (resembles Laud misc. 160).   Oxford,
    Bodleian, Digby 4 (g.); Laud misc. 160 (g.); Laud misc. 161 (resembles
    Laud misc. 160).
Sudbury, dom. Johannes, monachus C.:
  London, Coll. of Arms, Arundel 20 (pertinet).
Thiodricus (s.xii):
  Cambridge, Trin. Coll., 111 (scripsit).
Truncatleonem, Gulielmus (s.xii/xiii):
  Cambridge, Trin. Coll., 144 (scripsit).
T[. . . .], Stephanus:
  Oxford, Bodleian, Rawl. B.191 (name in genitive).
*Waltham, dom. Johannes, monachus (1483).   See Hadley.
*Warham, dom. Willelmus, archiepiscopus C. (1502–32):
  Oxford, Bodleian, Rawl. C.168.
Werburg.   See Ælfred.
Werken, T.:[7]
  Cambridge, Trin. Coll., 100 (wrote), 990 (name as scribe, A.D. 1477), 991
    (name as scribe, A.D. 1478).

[7] See p. 290, n. 7.

Weynchepe, Ricardus de (*prior of Dover 1268*):
  Cambridge, Corpus Christi Coll., 441 (g.).
*Wynchelse, R*obertus* de, archiepiscopus († *1313*):
  Cambridge, Trin. Coll., 386 (g.).   Oxford, Bodleian, Bodl. 214 (g.), 379
  (g.); Univ. Coll., 68 (g.).
Wyrcestre (?), Johannes (?) de, monachus C. (?):
  Cambridge, Corpus Christi Coll., 337 (g.).

CANTERBURY, *St Augustine*
Adam supprior:
  Oxford, Bodleian, Wood empt. 13 (g.).   Paris, B.N., nouv. acq. lat. 873
  (*recorded as his gift in cat.*).
Æðelstan:
  London, B.M., Royal 1 A.xviii (*inscription of gift, s.xi*).
Alulphus, supprior:
  Cambridge, Christ's Coll., 1 (sententie — et sancti Augustini Cant').
Arnold, Thomas:
  Cambridge, U.L., Ii.2.24 (me Thomam mina precor Arnoldum Kather-
  ina *on scroll*).   Oxford, Bodleian, Bodl. 521 (name).
Bello, Nicholaus de:
  New York, Mr G. M. Crawford (g.).
Bereford, dom. Johannes, vicarius de Plumstede:
  London, B.M., Stowe 378.
Bertelot, fr. Johannes:
  Brussels, Bibl. royale, 3097 (g.).
Bracher, mag., quondam monachus S. A.:
  Cambridge, Corpus Christi Coll., 189 (given to Matthew Parker by —
  'qui fuit verus possessor hujus libri').
Brancester, Thomas de:
  Canterbury, Cath., 4 (g.).
Burgham, Henricus de:
  Oxford, Bodleian, Douce 88 (*recorded as his gift in cat.*).
Byholt, fr. Willelmus de, (4) quondam prior:
  London, B.M., Arundel 310 (de adquisicione); Royal 12 E.xxiii (liber);
  Lambeth Pal., 1213 (*a* Liber; *b* — — — quantum ad se pertinuit dedit
  et assignavit istum librum fr. Petro de Wroteham).   (4) Oxford,
  Bodleian, Bodl. 299 (g.).
Cant*uaria*, fr. Ricardus de:
  New York, Mr W. S. Glazier, 53 (name).
*Cantyrbury, Clemens, monachus S. A.:
  Canterbury, Cath., 58 (name, *as librarian* ?, A.D. 1491; *cf.* Preston).
  London, B.M., Burney 11 (*a* bought from the Oxford stationer
  Thomas Hunt in 1473, when 'monachus et scolaris monasterii' and
  gave to the monastery 28 Febr. 1474; *b* g.).   Oxford, Bodleian, Bodl.
  507 (name), 679 (name; *cf.* London), Wood empt. 13 (name).
Clara, Willelmus de (*1277*):
  Cambridge, Trin. Coll., 939 (*recorded as his gift in cat.*).   London,
  B.M., Royal 8 A.vi (liber — — — quem portavit ad sanctum Augus-
  tinum); 11 B.xiv (liber).   Oxford, Bodleian, Selden supra 26 (*as* Royal
  8 A.vi); Corpus Christi Coll., 283 (*as* Royal 8 A.vi).
Cok, Edmundus:
  London, B.M., Harley 641 (ligavit; *cf.* Thomas, abbas).

Cokerynge, Henricus de:
 Cambridge, Gonv. and Caius Coll., 361 (g.).
Cyrrencestrie, Thomas:
 London, Lambeth Pal., 144, i (liber — — quem dedit S. A. pro animabns patris et matris sui et omnium fidelium defunctorum).
Dittone, fr. Thomas de:
 Wolfenbüttel, Ducal Libr., Helmst. 481 (liber).
Elham, Robertus de. *See* Helham.
Elham, Willelmus de:
 Cambridge, Corpus Christi Coll., 364 (liber).
Elmham, fr. Thomas:
 Glasgow, U.L., Hunterian 379 (quaternio — —).
Godcheap, fr. Johannes:
 Oxford, Bodleian, Bodl. 746 (de adquisicione).
Godmersham, fr. Willelmus, monachus S. A.:
 Oxford, Bodleian, 4° B.2 Art. Seld. (liber).
Grey, dom. Patricius:
 Exeter, Cath., 3529 (de adquisicione).
Hakynton, fr. Stephanus de:
 Cambridge, Corpus Christi Coll., 301 (liber).
Helham, fr. Robertus de:
 Cambridge, U.L., Kk.1.19 (de adquisicione).
Hileghe, Willelmus:
 London, B.M., Royal 1 A.vii (*recorded as his gift in cat.*).
Hunden, T*homas*, abbas († *1419*):
 Oxford, Queen's Coll., 307 (g.).
Julianus:
 Cambridge, Gonv. and Caius Coll., 238 (g.).
*Kennington, mag. Johannes, monachus (*fl. 1389*):
 London, B.M., Lansdowne 359 (liber; *cf.* Mankael).
Langele, G. de, minor:
 Cambridge, Corpus Christi Coll., 49 (g.).
Lenham, fr. Laurentius:
 Cambridge, Corpus Christi Coll., 466 (liber de reparacione — —).
Leybourn, domina Juliana de, comitissa de Huntyngdun:
 Cambridge, Corpus Christi Coll., 20.
Lond' (London', (2) Londone, (8) Londoniis), fr. ((2) mag.) Johannes de, (1, 14) monachus, (14) S.A.:
 (1) Cambridge, Corpus Christi Coll., 154 (liber); (2) St John's Coll., 97 (de adquisicione). Canterbury, Cath., 49 (liber). Dublin, Trin. Coll., 514 (*recorded as his gift in cat.*). Glasgow, U.L., Hunterian 253 (liber). London, B.M., Add. 48178 (liber), Egerton 823 and 840 (*recorded as his gift in cat.*), (8) Harley 1 (liber), Harley 13 (liber). Oxford, Bodleian, Bodl. 679 (g.), Digby 174 (liber), e Mus. 223 (name *in genitive*), Rawl. C.117 (liber); (14) Corpus Christi Coll., 41 (liber).
Londoniis, Randulphus de:
 Oxford, Bodleian, Barlow 32 (liber).
Lovente, fr. R. de:
 London, Lambeth Pal., 179 (g.).
*Lyngfeld, fr. Johannes de (*fl. 1360*):
 London, B.M., Royal 10 B.xiv (name *in genitive*; *cf.* Maydeston, Preston).

*Mankael, fr. Johannes (*fl. 1330*):
  Cambridge, Corpus Christi Coll., 38 (adquisivit); St John's Coll., 10 (*recorded as his gift in cat.*). Durham, U.L., Cosin V.ii.9 (g.). London, B.M., Lansdowne 359 (adquisivit).
Maydeston, fr. Symon:
  London, B.M., Royal 10 B.xiv (name; *cf.* Lyngfeld). Oxford, Bodleian, Bodl. 144 (liber).
Newintone, Willelmus de:
  London, B.M., Arundel 282 (*a* g.; *b* scripsit; *c* liber).
Normannus, fr. Robertus:
  London, B.M., Add. 26770 (liber).
Northgate, fr. Michael de:
  Cambridge, U.L., Ii.1.15 (liber). London, B.M., Arundel 57 (Þis boc is dan Micheles of Northgate ywrite an Englis of his oȝene hand). Oxford, Bodleian, Bodl. 464 (g.); Corpus Christi Coll., 221 (Liber Michaelis Northgate).
Penshurst, Georgius (*abbot c.1450*):
  London, B.M., Harley 5369 (*cat.*).
Pistor, fr. J.:
  Oxford, Bodleian, Douce 88 (liber).
Pocyn, dom. Thomas, abbas S. A. (*1335–43*):
  London, B.M., Royal 9 C.vi (de adquisicione).
*Preston, fr. (*or* mag.) Johannes (*prior by 1416*):
  Cambridge, St John's Coll., 230 (de adquisicione). Canterbury, Cath., 58 (de adquisicione). London, B.M., Royal 10 B.xiv (name *in genitive*; *cf.* Lyngfeld); 12 D.ix (de adquisicione). New York, Public Libr., 8 (de adquisicione). Oxford, Bodleian, Hatton 94 (de adquisicione).
Radulphus:
  London, Dr E. G. Millar (g.).
Retlyng, Simon de:
  London, B.M., Royal 9 B.i (g.). Oxford, Univ. Coll., 21 (g.).
Robertus, abbas (*1224–52*):
  London, B.M., Burney 3 (g.).
Robertus, infirmarius:
  Oxford, Bodleian, Bodl. 600 (liber).
Rogerius, abbas:
  Cambridge, Trin. Coll., 1215 (g.). London, Lambeth Pal., 185 (g.).
Ridderne, fr. Adam de:
  London, B.M., 11 A.xii (de adquisicione).
Salomon:
  London, Royal 3 A.i, 3 A.ii, 4 A.x, 4 A.xi (*all* g.). Oxford, Bodleian, Auct. F.6.3 (*recorded as his gift in cat.*).
Sancto Georgio, Walterus de:
  London, B.M., Royal 11 A.vi (g.); 12 B.ix (liber).
Sellyng, dom. Willelmus, quondam abbas S. A., obiit 1480:
  Oxford, Bodleian, Laud misc. 296 (liber).
*Sholdone, Ricardus de (*1334*):
  New York, Mr W. S. Glazier, 18 (g.).
Sprot, Thomas:
  Oxford, Corpus Christi Coll., 125 (liber).
Stureya, Johannes de, precentor:
  Leyden, U.L., Scaliger Hebr. 8 (de adquisicione).

Taneto, R. de:
 Oxford, Bodleian, Laud misc. 225 (g.).
Thomas, abbas:[8]
 Cambridge, Corpus Christi Coll., 13 (*recorded as his gift in cat.*), 14
 (liber), 271 (Decretalis fr. Martini de Totyntoun quoad quinque libros
 et T. abbatis quoad sextum librum decret. et constituciones); St John's
 Coll., 43 (liber). London, B.M., Add. 46352 (D. Th. abbatis); Harley
 641 (distinct. T. abbatis); Lambeth Pal., 116 (*a* dist. T. abbatis; *b*
 liber). Oxford, Corpus Christi Coll., 65 (*recorded as his gift in cat.*);
 Univ. Coll., 19 (*a* liber; *b* D. T. abbatis).
Thomas, prior:
 Cambridge, Corpus Christi Coll., 314 (*recorded as his gift in cat.*).
 Oxford, Laud misc. 385 (g.).
Totyntoun, fr. Martinus de. *See* Thomas, abbas.
Tylmanstone, fr. Henricus de:
 Norwich, Castle Mus., 158.926.4g(2) (de adquisicione).
T[. . . .], W.:
 Cambridge, U.L., Add. 3578.
*Welde, fr. Thomas (*fl. 1450*):
 Cambridge, St John's Coll., 142 (de acquisicione).
*Welde, Willelmus (*abbot 1387–1405*):
 London, B.M., Harley 3224 (de adquisicione).
Wellis, Willelmus:
 Cambridge, Corpus Christi Coll., 129 (*recorded as his gift in cat.*).
Wilmintone, W. de:
 Cambridge, Trin. Coll., 115 (g.).
Wroteham, fr. P. de. *See* Byholt.
Wyvelesburgh, fr. Thomas de:
 London, Lambeth Pal., 49 (liber — — — de adquisicione). Oxford,
 Corpus Christi Coll., 125 (*recorded as his gift in cat.*); St John's Coll.,
 66B (g.; written in 1316 'Radulpho de Bourne tunc abbate S. A.').

CANTERBURY, *St Gregory*
Willelmus, archiepiscopus [*sic*] Cant' (*s.xii/xiii*):
 Cambridge, Trin. Coll., 387.

CANTERBURY, *Fran. conv.*
Bruyl, fr. Johannes, O.F.M., (*b*) de custodia London' et de conventu
 Cant':
Oxford, Bodleian, Digby 153 (*a* constat; *b* per; *c* de dono).
Burcer, fr. Rogerus:
 Lincoln, Cath., 195 (name).
*Hertepol, fr. Hugo de, minister († *1302*):
 London, B.M., Cotton Galba E.xi (de procuracione [. . . .]firmacionem
 — — —).
*Maydenstane, fr. Radulfus de, quondam episcopus Heref' († *1243*):
 London, B.M., Royal 3 C.xi.
Rya, Henricus de:
 London, B.M., Royal 3 D.iv.
Rychemund, mag. Adam de:
 London, B.M., Royal 3 D.ii.

[8] For his identity *cf.* M. R. James, *Canterbury and Dover*, p. lxxii.

CARLISLE, *Dom. conv.*
Kyrby, fr. Ricardus de:
    Edinburgh, U.L., 1 (concessus — — — ad terminum vite sue).

CHERTSEY
Ocham, fr. Thomas de:
    London, B.M., Add. 24067 (de perquisitione).
Sutton, fr. Henricus, monachus C.:
    Oxford, Bodleian, D.13.5 Linc. (pertinet).

CHESTER
Clarke, dom. Thomas, hujus cenobii (*last abbot and first dean*):
    Aberystwyth, N.L., DN 4923 (custos hujus libri; *cf.* Ley).
Higden, Ranulph:
    San Marino, Huntington, HM 132 (*wrote*).
Ley, dom. Johannes, prior hujus cenobii:
    Aberystwyth, N.L., DN 4923 (custos hujus libri; *cf.* Clarke).
Ricardus, abbas C.:
    San Marino, Huntington, HM 132 (name).

CHESTER, *nunnery*
Byrkenhed, dame Margery, of Chestre:
    San Marino, Huntington, EL 34 B. 7 (longeth to).

CHESTER, *Dom. conv.*
Alexander, mag. (*s.xiii; cf.* Staneby):
    Shrewsbury School, xxxv (g.).
Knotesford, fr. Adam de:
    Shrewsbury School, xxiv (concessus — — — ad terminum vite).
Staneby, mag. Alexander de (*s.xiii; cf.* Alexander):
    Shrewsbury School, i (g.).

CHESTER, *Fran. conv.*
*Conewey, fr. Rogerus de, minister († *1360* ?):
    London, Gray's Inn, 1 (*a* liber; *b* de dono), 5 (*a* liber; *b* de dono), 12 (de
    dono). Oxford, Bodleian, Lat. misc. d.74 (liber).
Gyn, fr. W.:
    London, Gray's Inn, 7 (per).
Wyche, fr. Radulphus:
    London, Gray's Inn, 2 (*a* script. per; *b* per (?)), 11 (per).

CHICHESTER
Glympynge, Simon:
    London, B.M., Harley 6.
Hilarius, episcopus *Cicestrensis* († *1169*):
    Oxford, St John's Coll., 49 (g.).
Rufus, W.:
    Oxford, Bodleian, Auct. D.3.14 (g.).
Seffridus, episcopus *Cicestrensis* (*1125-45*):
    Cambridge, U.L., Dd.10.20; Emm. Coll., 25 (g.).
Walterus, decanus:
    Cambridge, Emm. Coll., 28 (g.).

CHICHESTER, *Dom. conv.*
Lovent, Willelmus, O.P., C.:
    Oxford, St John's Coll., 198 (Ista sunt sophismata — — quod fr. J. Claxton de Booston; *cf.* **BOSTON,** Claxton).

CHICKSANDS
Gowshille, dom. Simon de, canonicus, quondam prior (*s.xiv*):
    Cambridge, Sid. Sussex Coll., 85 (liber; *cf.* **KIRKSTALL,** Stainborn).
Lyle, Robert de:
    London, B.M., Arundel 83 (gave to his daughters A.D. 1339, with reversion 'a touz jours a les dames de Chikessaund').

CIRENCESTER
Adam, dom., canonicus:
    Hereford, Cath., O.vi.10 (abbatis primi Serlonis tempore (*1131–47*) scriptus per manum — postea abbatis), P.v.3 (abbatis primi Serlonis tempore scriptus per manus canonicorum D. Ade postea abbatis et Fulconis postremo prioris).
Alexander, cantor:
    Oxford, Jesus Coll., 52 (dom. Andree abbatis secundi tempore (*1147–76*) scriptus per manus — postmodum cantoris et Radulfi de Pulleham cujusdam scriptoris).
Aluredus, mag.:
    Hereford, Cath., O.ii.4 (liber). Oxford, All Souls Coll., 82 (liber); Jesus Coll., 26 (liber).
Cornubiensis, dom. Simon, canonicus:
    Hereford, Cath., P.ii.14 (dom. Andree abbatis secundi tempore per manum — — scriptus).
Deodatus, canonicus:
    Hereford, Cath., P.i.12 (abbatis primi Serlonis tempore scriptus per manus canonicorum — et Fulconis postea prioris).
Fulco, dom., canonicus:
    Hereford, Cath., P.iii.7 (dom. Andree abbatis secundi tempore scriptus per manum — postea prioris), P.v.4 (*as* P.iii.7). London, B.M., Royal 3 A.xii (*as* P.iii.7). Oxford, Jesus Coll., 53, 68, 70 (*all as* P.iii.7). *See also* Adam, Deodatus.
Galfredus, quondam vicarius de Avebyri:
    Oxford, Jesus Coll., 48 (gave in 1238).
Jocelinus, dom., canonicus:
    Hereford, Cath., O.i.6 (dedit . . . dom. Serlone tunc abbate primo), O.i.10 (*as* O.i.6). London, B.M., Cotton Vesp. A.xv (*as* O.i.6).
Odo, dom., canonicus:
    Hereford, Cath., O.v.14 (dom. Andree abbatis secundi tempore scriptus per manum — canonici). Oxford, Jesus Coll., 67 (dom. Andree abbatis secundi tempore scriptus per manum — 'de Wica' canonici).
Preston, mag. Nicholaus de:
    Hereford, Cath., P.v.10 (hunc librum habuimus de — — . . . in recompensacione cujusdam debiti).
'Pulleham', Radulfus 'de', scriptor:
    Oxford, Jesus Coll., 63 (dom. Andree abbatis secundi tempore scriptus per manum). *See also* Alexander.

Serlo, dom., canonicus:
  Hereford, Cath., O.v.10 (dom. Andree abbatis secundi tempore scriptus per manum).
Walterus, canonicus et diaconus:
  London, B.M., Royal 7 F.vi (dom. Andree abbatis secundi tempore scriptus per manum).

CLATTERCOTE
W[. . . .], fr. Thomas de:
  Oxford, Bodleian, Rawl. A.420.

COLCHESTER, *Aug. priory*
Depyng, dom. Johannes, canonicus C.:
  Antwerp, Plantin-Moretus, 78 (pledged, together with mag. Guy Wysham).

COLCHESTER, *Fran. conv.*
Baldwyn, Johannes, vicarius de Ardeleigh:
  Oxford, Bodleian, Lat. misc. f.37 (contulit fr. Matheo Shypman O.F.M., C., A.D. 1510).
Shypman, fr. Matheus. *See* Baldwyn.

COLDINGHAM
Dyppyng, dom. Thomas. *See* Todd.
Hedun, Adam de:
  Durham, Cath., B.II.32 (name).
Todd. dom. —, monachus:
  London, B.M., Add. 24059 (liber dom. Thome Dyppyng ex dono — quia ipse est bonus socius).

COVENTRY
Bruches (Bruges), monachus C. *See p. 54.*
Crossely, dom. Ricardus, prior C.:
  Cambridge, Trin. Coll., 1088.
Everdone, fr. Robertus:
  Oxford, Bodleian, Auct. F.5.23, fos 7–110 (concessit).
Grenborough, fr. Johannes de, infirmarius:
  London, B.M., Royal 12 G.iv (emebat . . . ad utilitatem infirmorum in ecclesia Coventre existentium et ea que in novis quaternis sunt scripta compilavit . . .).
Luffe, fr. Ricardus, monachus C.:
  Oxford, Bodleian, Digby 33.

COVENTRY, *Charterhouse*
Odyham, Robertus (*prior c.1457–68*):
  London, B.M., Royal 5 A.v.

COVENTRY, *Fran. conv.*
Duffild, dom. Willelmus, S.T.P., O.F.M., C., Ascelenensis episcopus:
  Colchester, Harsnett Libr., H.h.14 (Pontificale — — emptum per eundem Londiniis A.D. 153[.]).
Opton, fr. P. de:
  London, B.M., Harley 5116 (liber — — — post cujus decessum est de communitate fr. min. C.).

249

COVENTRY, *Carm. conv.*
Kenton, rev. mag. fr. Nicholaus de, provincialis (*1444*)
    Durham, Cath., A.iv.19.
**Poole, rev. mag. fr. Johannes, O.C. (*D.Th. 1381*):
    Berlin, Staatsbibl., Hamilton 503.
[. . . .], fr. Willelmus. *See* **NEWCASTLE,** *Carm. conv.*

COVERHAM
Gisborne, Johannes, canonicus C.:
    London, B.M., Sloane 1584 (scriptum per me — —).
Melsynby, Percival, canonicus C.:
    New York, Mr W. S. Glazier, 39 (wrote).

CREDITON
*Lyndon, Johannes (*dean of C.*;† *by Lent 1487*):
    Oxford, Bodleian, Bodl. 159, 383, 793; Christ Church, 91 (*all* 'liber'; *see*
      p. 55). *See also* Palmer.
*Palmer, 'mag.' W., 'precentor C.' (*1438*):
    Oxford, Univ. Coll., 91 (disponitur decano et pa(ro)chianis Crediton'
      per executorem dicti — — mag. Johannem Lyndon).

CROWLAND
Bardenay, fr. Willelmus, succentor C.:
    Paris, B.N., Lat. 5557 (name; *cf.* Ricardus).
Burgh, W. de:
    Princeton, U.L., R. Garrett 119.
London (?), dom. Johannes, monachus C.:
    Cambridge, Magd. Coll., 5 (constat).
Ricardus, dom., monachus C.:
    Paris, B.N., Lat. 5557 (constat).
Slefurth, Ricardus, monachus C.:
    Bristol, Baptist Coll., Z.e.38 (name).

CROXDEN
Chalner, fr. Thomas, scolaris C.:
    Dublin, Archbishop Marsh's Libr., Q.4.16 (emptus per).

CULROSS
Marchel, Ricardus, quondam abbas C.:
    Edinburgh, N.L., Adv. 18.8.11 (fecit fieri).

DALE
North, Leonard, canonicus D., decretorum doctor:
    Oxford, Bodleian, Don. e.598 (pr. bk) (Orate pro anima — —).

DARLEY
Eydone, Johannes de, canonicus de Repyndon:
    Oxford, Bodleian, Auct. D.inf.2.8 (accomodatus — — — per abbatem et
      canonicos de D. infra annum restituendus in anno ix Ric. secundi).
*Flemmyng, mag. Robertus, decanus Lincolnie:
    Oxford, Bodleian, Laud gr. 28 (accomodatus — — in vigilia Epiphanie
      A.D. 1452).
Grovis, Thomas, abbas D. (*1524–35*):
    Cambridge, Gonv. and Caius Coll., 84 (name).

DARLINGTON
**Whitton, mag. Ricardus, decanus D. (*1428*):
　Leicester, Mr H. F. Smith (legatur per — — et decanus habebit usum).

DARTFORD
Baron, William, esquier († *1485*):
　Oxford, Bodleian, Douce 322 (of the ʒifte of — — to remayne for
　　evyr to the . . . nonrye of Dertforde and specially to the use of dame
　　Pernelle Wrattisley sister of the same place by licence of her abbas).
Brauntwath (Brainthawyt), dame Alys:
　London, B.M., Harley 2254 (longyth to — — and the worschypfull
　　prioras of D.).　Taunton, Castle Mus., 2.
Caston, sister Denyse.　*See* Chaumbre.
Chaumbre, Betrice:
　Downside Abbey, 26542 (yove to — — and after hir decese to sustir
　　Emme Wynter and to 'sistir' Denyse Caston nonnes of D. and so to
　　abide in the saam hous . . . for evere).
Wrattisley, dame Pernelle, sister D. (*1512*).　*See* Baron.
Wyntyr, soror Emma, *nun D.*:
　London, Soc. of Antiquaries, 717 (Orate pro anima — — que fieri fecit
　　istum librum).　*See also* Chaumbre.

DEER
Stephanus, Robertus (*prior* A.D. *1537*):
　St Andrews, U.L., PA.3895.P.6 (name).

DENNY
Throgkmorten, domina Elisabeth, abbatissa:
　Oxford, Bodleian, Hatton 18 (est).

DEREHAM, WEST
Johannes, dom., quondam abbas:
　Cambridge, U.L., Kk.1.11 (tradatur liber iste — apud Bertone Fen).

DORE
Bathon', Johannes:
　Hereford, Cath., P.v.5 (*ex libris of D. and* per manum — —).
Grandison, J. *de, episcopus* Exon':
　London, B.M., Cotton Cleop. C.xi (*ex libris of D. and* J. Exon' *in
　　Grandison's hand*).

DOVER
Horningeseye, Walterus de, monachus D. (?):
　Cambridge, Trin. Coll., 624 (liber).
Michael, monachus D.:
　Glasgow, U.L., Hunterian 467 (In isto volumine — continentur . . .).
Ryngwolde, Johannes, quondam monachus D.:
　Cambridge, Corpus Christi Coll., 42 (liber).
Silegrave, Henricus de:
　London, B.M., Cotton Cleop. A.xii (liber).
Warren, Willelmus, quondam major Dovorrie:
　Cambridge, Corpus Christi Coll., 365.
Whytefelde, fr. Johannes, monachus D. (*compiler of the cat. of 1389*):
　Canterbury, Cath., 71 (scriptum Rome per manus — — in quatuor
　　septimanis mensis Augusti A.D. 1380).

DROITWICH
Denton, fr. Johannes, senior et junior, conventus D.:
  Oxford, Brasen. Coll., 13 (liber).

DUNFERMLINE
Botwell, Ricardus, abbas D. (*1445–70*):
  Boulogne, Bibl. mun., 92 (fieri fecit).
Farguson, dom. Robertus, monachus et prior (*c.1530*):
  Edinburgh, U.L., 72 (ad — —).
Monymelle, dom. Thomas, monachus et sacrista:
  Glasgow, U.L., BE.7.b.8 (scriptus . . . de mandato — —; *cf. p. 59*).

DUNKELD
ʒoung, Patricius, precentor:
  Edinburgh, N.L., Adv. 18.2.6.

DUNSTABLE
Cotson, dom. Willelmus, canonicus (2) de D.:
  Cambridge, U.L., Ff.6.55 (pertinet — — A.D. 1499). (2) Manchester,
    Chetham, 6709 (*a* written by the hondis of, A.D. 1490 (etc.); *b* libellus).

DUNSTABLE, *Dom. conv.*
Lynne, fr. Willelmus (*prior D.*):
  Cambridge, U.L., Add. 2770.

DUREFORD
Cicestrensis, fr. Willelmus:
  Lincoln, Cath., 179 (— — subarravit hunc librum).

DURHAM
Adington (Adigton), mag. Robertus de (*s.xii ex.*):
  Durham, Cath., A.III.2., 5, 16, 17, 19, 24; A.IV.4. York, Minster,
    xvi.Q.5 (*presumed gift of*).
Æþelstan (*king of England;* † *940*):
  Cambridge, Corpus Christi Coll., 183 (*presumed gift of*). London,
    B.M., Cotton Otho B.ix (ic — cyning selle þas boc into sancto
    Cudberhte).
*Appylby, fr. Willelmus de (*librarian 1391, 1395*):
  Durham, Cath., B.III.31, C.IV.20B (*both* ex procuracione).
Aristotil, mag. Gilbertus:
  Durham, Cath., A.II.22.
*Aukland, Johannes, prior (*1484–94*):
  The inscription in Cambridge, Jesus Coll., 13, 45, 54; Sid. Sussex Coll.,
    56; Durham, Cath., B.1.7, 28, 32, 36; B.III.18, 26; B.IV.30; C.III.18;
    C.IV.22; Inc. 4a, 13a, b, 14c, 22, 35, 62; London, B.M., Cotton Titus
    A.xviii; Oxford, Bodleian, Laud misc. 368; York, Minster, xvi.D.9
    is Assignatur novo almariolo in claustro per.   London, B.M., Cotton
    Titus D.xix (liber dom. Thome [. . .]ton monachi ex donacione).
    York, Minster, xix.C.5 (assignatur registro ecclesie ex donacione).
    See also Bell, Elwick.
Bamborgh, dom. Robertus de:
  Durham, Cath., C.III.10 (accomodatus R. Harpon' per).
Barneby, dom. Reginaldus de:
  London, Dulwich Coll., 23.

*Bell, Ricardus, (1, 4) prior (*of D. 1464–79;* † *1496*):
    (1) Cambridge, Sid. Sussex Coll., 56 (liber dom. Willelmi Law monachi
    Dunelm' ex dono; *cf.* Seton). Durham, Cath., B.III.26 (liber sancti
    Cuthberti et — —); B.IV.42 (liber sancti Cuthberti et — — et ipse
    contulit eundem librum mag. Roberto Ebchestr'). (4) Nottingham,
    U.L., MiLM 5 (liber Johannis Aukland monachi Dunelm' ex dono).
    Oxford, Bodleian, Laud misc. 368 (liber sancti Cuthberti et — —).
    See also Seton.
Bell, dom. Rogerus, monachus D. (*1519*):
    Untraced Bible (liber; *cf.* Conforth).
Bennett, mag. Willelmus, S.T.P., prior de Finchal (*canon of D. 1541–84*):
    Tollerton, St Hugh's Coll., Jerome (liber d. Wyllelmi Wylom ex dono
    — — 'nunc autem dom. Nicholai Marley ex dono ejusdem d. Willelmi
    Wylom qui obiit A.D. 1556 et 18° Septembris').
*Beverl*ey*, fr. Johannes de, monachus D. (*fl. 1340*):
    Durham, Cath., B.II.12 (ex procuracione).
Blaklaw, dom. Robertus, S.T.B., sub-prior D.:
    Durham, Cath., A.I.3 (scriptus per manum Willelmi de Stiphol ex
    precepto — —, A.D. 1386).
Blunte, dom. Christopherus, B.Th., quondam terrarius D.:
    Cambridge, U.L., Rel. b.51.3 (liber dompni Johannis Blyth ex dono).
Blyth. *See* Blunte.
*Boldon, fr. Uthredus *de*, monachus D. († 1397):
    Cambridge, Pembr. Coll., 241 (ex procuracione). Durham, Cath.,
    C.IV.17 (ex procuracione). London, B.M., Burney 310 (*a* ex pro-
    curacione; *b* scriptus per manum Guillermi dicti du Stiphel de
    Britania pro — A.D. 1381 in Fincal).
Bolton, dom. Johannes de:
    Oxford, Univ. Coll., 86 (liber).
Brakenbyri, Robertus (1–5, 7) de (*s.xiv*):
    (1) Durham, Cath., B.I.9 (liber), (2) B.IV.15 (liber), (3) C.II.3 (liber),
    (4) C.IV.12 (liber). (5) London, B.M., Harley 491 (liber). Oxford,
    Bodleian, Laud misc. 603 (liber), (7) 641 (liber — — — pro tempore
    vite sue). *See also* Lumley.
Brantyngham, dom. Willelmus (*1522*). *See* Wylley.
*Burney, mag. Johannes, prior (*1456–64*):
    London, Lambeth Pal., 483 (usus conceditur dom. Roberto Ebchester
    per).
*Byllyngham, dom. Ricardus († *after 1472*):
    Durham, Cath., A.IV.8 (liber — — per dom. Swalwell registro seu usui
    cancellarii limitatus).
*Caly, dom. Thomas (*fl. 1460*). *See* Ebchester, Willelmus.
*Castell, dom. Thomas, (1, 2, 4) quondam custos collegii Dunelm' *Oxon.*,
    (3) prior (*1494–1519*):
    (1) Cambridge, U.L., Rel. c.50.8 (liber; *cf.* Wylom). (2) Durham,
    Cath., Inc. 48 (pertinet); (3) U.L., Cosin V.ii.5 (liber dom. Thome
    Lawson ex dono). (4) Oxford, St John's Coll., P.4.46 (pertinet).
*Castell, dom. Thomas, monachus D. (*fl. 1510*):
    Cambridge, U.L., Inc. 1049 (liber). York, Minster, x.A.7 (liber).
Castro, dom. Johannes de, monachus D.:
    Durham, Cath., C.III.16 (ex procuracione). Oxford, Bodleian, Rawl.
    C.4 (ex procuracione).

Castro, dom. Thomas de:
Durham, Cath., B.I.1.
*Cawthorn, dom. Willelmus (*prior of Finchale 1506–c.1520*):
Durham, Cath., Inc. 1f (liber).
*Chirden, mag. Alanus de (*fl. 1323, fellow of Merton Coll.*):
Durham, Cath., A.I.11 (ex colacione).
Clyffe, dom. T. *See* Conforth.
Cokken, dom. Willelmus, monachus D. (*granatarius 1456*):
Oxford, Magd. Coll., 162 (quod).
Conforth, dom. Georgius (*1520*):
Untraced Bible (liber dom. T. Clyffe ex dono; *cf.* Bell, Rogerus).
Crosby, dom. Ricardus (*1517*). *See* Whythed.
Cuthbert, Willelmus. *See* Dalton, Willelmus.
Dalton, dom. Henricus, prior insule sacre:
Cambridge, Trin. Coll., 1227 (ex dono A.D. 1513; *cf.* Ebchester, Willelmus).
*Dalton, dom. Willelmus, monachus D. (*sub-prior 1455*):
Durham, Cath., B.IV.42 (liber). Untraced Cassiodorus (liber Willelmi Cuthbert ex dono). *See also* Hoveden.
*Doncastre, Willelmus, decanus de Aukelande (*1435–39*):
Durham, Cath., B.IV.3, C.I.2, C.III.12 (*post-medieval inscription*).
*Dune, dom. Thomas (*fl. 1496*). *See* Manbe.
Dunelm', Petrus de, monachus D.:
Durham, Cath., B.IV.34 (liber).
Dunelmo, mag. Willelmus de († *1279*):
Durham, Cath., A.II.7.
*Ebchester, dom. Robertus (*prior 1479–84*). *See* Bell, Ricardus; Burney; Ebchester, Willelmus; Figy.
*Ebchester, mag. Willelmus, monachus D., S.T.P., prior (1, quondam prior) (*1446–56*):
(1) Cambridge, Trin. Coll., 1227 (liber dom. W. Elwyk ex dono). Durham, Cath., A.I.6 (ex procuracione); A.III.27 (*a* liber — — ex empcione; *b* assignatur librarie monachorum D. per); B.III.12 (assignatur . . ., *as* A.III.27); B.III.19 (assignatur . . ., *as* A.III.27); B.IV.29 (assignatur . . ., *as* A.III.27); B.IV.30 (usus conceditur dom. Roberto Ebchester per; *cf.* Aukland); C.III.11 (assignatur . . ., *as* A.III.27; *cf.* Westmerland). London, B.M., Harley 3049 (fecit fieri et assignavit librarie A.D. 1458); Harley 5234 (liber dom. Thome Caly ex dono).
*Elwick, dom. Willelmus, monachus D., (3) subprior (*chancellor 1461*):
Durham, Cath., B.I.7 (liber dom. Johannis Aukland ex dono); B.I.18 (liber dom. Roberti Wardell ex dono); (3) B.IV.41 (liber dom. [. . . .] ex dono). *See also* Ebchester, Willelmus.
*Emylton, Robertus (*monk, fl. 1440*):
Cambridge, Fitzwilliam Mus., McClean 169 (quod); Jesus Coll., 70 (quod). York, Minster, xvi.I.1 (wrote).
Estby, Johannes, vicarius de Bannebury:
Durham, Cath., B.I.32 (fecit fieri A.D. 1448; *cf.* Aukland).
*Farn, mag. Thomas, vicarius ecclesie sancti Oswaldi *Dunelm.* († *by 1519*):
Durham, Cath., Inc. 32–34 (gave in 1519); 43 (gave in 1519); 47a, 53 (gave in 1519). York, Minster, xiv.B.22 (gave in 1519).

Figy, dom. W.:
  Edinburgh, N.L., Adv. 18.6.11 (usus conceditur dom. Roberto Ebchester per).
*Fishborne, Johannes de, monachus D. († *1434*):
  Durham, Cath., C.I.11 (liber).
Fossor, dom. J., prior D. (*1342–74*). *See* Hexham.
Gisburne, [. . . .] de, quondam electus in priorem:
  Durham, Cath., C.IV.24 (donatus communi armariolo per).
Gretham, W. de (*s.xiii ex.*):
  Durham, Cath., C.III.2.
*Greystanes, fr. Robertus de († *c.1336*):
  Durham, Cath., A.I.2, B.I.10, B.II.19, 20, 28 (*all* ex procuracione).
  Durham, U.L., Cosin V.I.8 (ex procuracione).
Hacfurth, dom. Willelmus, monachus D.:
  York, Minster, xii.J.22 (liber).
Halidene (Halidon), fr. Robertus de, monachus D.:
  Durham, Cath., C.I.14 (ex procuracione), C.II.10 (liber).
Hamsterley, Johannes, monachus D. (*1514*):
  Cambridge, Jesus Coll., 61 (liber; *cf.* Whytehed).
Harpon. *See* Bamborgh.
Hemmyngburgh, dom. Johannes de, quondam prior D. (*1391–1416*):
  Durham, Cath., B.II.23, 27; B.III.4, fos 1–162; C.I.16 (*all* assignatur communi armariolo, *or* com. alm. claustri, per). London, B.M., Burney 310 (*damaged inscription probably as* Durham, Cath., B.II.23; *cf.* Boldon).
Hertylpoll, dom. Willelmus, monachus D.:
  London, B.M., Arundel 332 (liber).
Hexham, fr. Robertus de, (3) hostillarius D.:
  Dublin, Trin. Coll., 349 (usus conceditur). Durham, Cath., A.II.18 (usus conceditur); (3) B.III.7 (communi armariolo assignatus per dom. J. Fossor priorem per procuracionem — — —).
Hilton, dom. Robertus de:
  Durham, Cath., A.II.12 (liberetur).
Horbertus, mag., medicus:
  Cambridge, Jesus Coll., 44.
Hoton, Johannes, monachus (*fl. 1460*). *See* Wessyngton.
Hoveden, G.:
  London, Lambeth Pal., 23.
*Hoveden, Stephanus, subprior D. (*1420–39*):
  Durham, Cath., A.IV.5 (liber dom. Willelmi Dalton ex dono).
*Howlande, Thomas, monachus D.:
  Oxford, Brasen. Coll., 4 (liber; *cf.* Ebchester, Robertus).
Hugo, episcopus. *See* Puiset.
Insula, dom. Johannes de, miles:
  Durham, Cath., A.II.9. *Cf.* Durham, Cath., C.I.4, 6, 9, *uniform vols, the first and third of which are inscribed as the property* 'trium puerorum de Insula scilicet Henrici, Ricardi ac Johannis fratrum'.
Kaugi, Adam de (*s.xiii in.*):
  Durham, Cath., C.I.7.
Kedwely, Willelmus:
  Durham, Cath., B.IV.36, fos 149–95 (scriptus a).

Kyllerby, fr. Willelmus de:
  Cambridge, U.L., Mm.3.14 (ex procuracione; *he kneels before St Cuthbert in an initial inscribed* 'confessor vere Kyllerby gaudia quere').
Kyppier, fr. Godefredus de:
  Durham, Cath., A.III.28.
*Langchester, Robertus de, cancellarius et postea feretrarius D. (*fl. 1400*):
  Durham, Cath., C.IV.25 (quondam *and* name *in genitive*).
Langley, dom. Thomas, episcopus D. († *1437*):
  Durham, Cath., A.I.5.
*Lasynby, Willelmus, monachus D. (*fl. 1415*):
  Durham, Cath., B.IV.42 (tradatur; *cf.* Bell, Dalton).
*Law, Willelmus, monachus D. (*D.Th. 1480*):
  Durham, Cath., C.IV.23, fos 67–128 (liber); Inc. 1a–d (liber); Inc. 13a, b (liber — — et a dicto sancto Cuthberto nunquam alienandus); Inc. 20b (liber). *See also* Bell, Ricardus.
Lawson, dom. Thomas, monachus D.:
  Durham, U.L., S.R.2.B.12 (liber). *See also* Castell.
Le Berwby (Borwby):
  Durham, Cath., A.I.4 (wrote part).
Lee, dom. Petrus, monachus D. (5, quondam monachus), (*warden of Durham Coll. 1523*):
  Dublin, Trin. Coll., 440 (constat). Durham, Cath., P.V.16–17 (liber). Oxford, Oriel Coll., C.e.20 (liber). (5) Ushaw Coll., XVII.F.4.5 (liber; *cf.* Marley); XVII.F.4.13 (liber); XVIII.B.5.15 (liber; *cf.* Marley); XVIII.B.4.24 (*annotations by*); XVIII.B.7.6 (liber; *cf.* Marley); XVIII.G.3.11–12 (liber; *cf.* Wylom).
Lumlei, Emericus de (*prior of Lytham, fl. 1333*):
  Durham, Cath., A.III.7 (liber Roberti de Brakenbiri ex dono; *cf.* Puiset).
*Lund, fr. Thomas de (*prior of Finchale 1333*):
  Durham, Cath., B.I.2, B.II.25, B.III.27 (*all* ex procuracione).
*Manbe, dom. Johannes (*sub-prior 1490*):[1]
  Durham, Cath., B.IV.40 (*a* liber — — emptus de dom. Roberto Sotheron; *b* ex dono — — assignatus communi armariolo D.); Inc. 1f (liber; *cf.* Cawthorn, Werdall); Inc. 11a (liber; *cf.* Werdall). Oxford, Bodleian, Douce 129 (liber dom. Thome Dune monachi D. ex dono); Lyell 16 (liber).
Marley, (1) dom., (7) dom. (*erased*) Nicholaus, (2) S.T.P. (*monk 1529, canon 1541–60*):[2]
  (1) Durham, Cath., Inc. 25 (liber — — ex dono nullius sed care emptus 1536); (2) Inc. 45 (liber; *cf.* Swalwell, Whytehed). Ushaw Coll., XVII.E.4.1 (to dean — — yn Duram abbay delyver these); XVIII.A.3.12 (liber; *cf.* Whelden); XVIII.B.3.6 (name); XVIII.B.3.9 (name); (7) XVIII.B.6.7 (liber). *See also* Bennett, Wylom.
Marley, dom. (*except in* (1), *erased in* (2)) Stephanus, (6) monachus D. (*sub-prior 1539, canon 1541–72*):[2]

---

[1] This John Manbe, presumably, deposited Liverpool, Public Museums, Mayer collection 12036 (on deposit in Liverpool Univ. Libr.), Eugippius, etc., s.xiii, as a caution in the Danvers chest at Oxford, 30 Nov. 1475.

[2] Some of the books listed here may not have belonged to the Marleys until after the Dissolution. Two printed books, a Driedo of 1543 and a Cyril of 1546, belonging to the Yealand Conyers collection deposited at Ushaw, are inscribed

(1) Ushaw Coll., XVII.E.4.10 (name); (2) XVII.E.5.4 (liber); XVIII.B.5.15 (liber; *cf.* Lee); XVIII.C.5.10–11 (liber); (6) XVIII.C.5.15 (name). *See also* Swalwell.

*Masham, Robertus (*sacrist D. 1404–5*):
 Durham, Cath., B.IV.43 (wrote). London, B.M., Harley 3858 (wrote).

*Melsaneby, mag. Alanus de (*s.xiii in.*):
 Durham, Cath., B.I.33.

Melsaneby, mag. Henricus de (*s.xiii*):
 Durham, Cath., A.II.15, A.III.15, A.III.22.

Merley (?), fr. Johannes de:
 Durham, Cath., B.I.11 (liber — — — et reddatur sibi).

Middleton, Bertramus de, prior D. (*1244–58*):
 Cambridge, Trin. Coll., 8 (ex dono, but with use for life reserved to his chaplain Roger). Durham, Cath., A.I.8, A.I.12, A.I.16, A.III.12, A.III.21, B.IV.23.

Nigellus, dom., quondam vicarius de Stichill (*s.xiii ex.*):
 Durham, Cath., B.III.17.

Norham, Radulfus de:
 Durham, Cath., A.IV.12 ('liber iste inscribitur — — —' *in hand of s.xviii*).

*Poklyngton, Willelmus, monachus D., B.Th. (*prior of Finchale 1411–23*):
 Durham, Cath., B.II.29 (assignatur communi librarie per).

Puiset, Hugo *de*, episcopus *D.*:
 Durham, Cath., A.II.1, A.II.19, A.III.7, A.IV.1, A.IV.10 (*all* liber); B.III.13 (*recorded as his gift in cat.*); C.IV.5 (liber); U.L., Cosin V.ii.1 (*presumed gift of*). Cambridge, Trin. Coll., 1194 (g.).

R., prior de Finchale:
 Durham, Cath., A.I.7.

*Radlee, Petrus (*fl. 1410*). *See* Wessyngton.

Rana, mag. Johannes de (*s.xii ex.*):
 Durham, Cath., A.III.3 (liber); A.III.23 (liber).

Reginald of Durham:
 Durham, Cath., Hunter 101 (? *author's autograph*).

Riddell, dom. Ricardus. *See* Rok.

**Ridley, Robertus († *c.1536*):
 Durham, Cath., B.V.58 (gave in 1533); D.VII.23–24 (gave in 1534). Hereford, Cath., A.ix.2–3 (gave in 1532). Lincoln, Cath., F.1.14 (gave in 1533).

Robertus, dom., prior (*R. de Walworth, prior 1374–91*):
 Durham, Cath., C.I.19, fos 234–324 (A.D. 1384 assignatus . . . communi armariolo D. per — ut nulli extra claustrum accomodetur).

Rogerus capellanus. *See* Middleton.

Rok, dom. Robertus (*monk, fl. 1491–1505*):
 Winchester, Cath., 10 (liber dom. Ricardi [Rid]dell de empcione a).

*Rome, fr. T., S.T.P. (*fl. 1420*):
 Durham, Cath., B.III.6, B.III.22 (*both* ex procuracione). Oxford, Bodleian, Laud misc. 389 (ex procuracione).

'liber Nicholai Marley', and no. 55 in E. P. Goldschmidt's *Gothic and Renaissance Bookbindings* (R. de Sancto Victore, Paris, 1510: sold at Sotheby's, 5 April 1955, lot 294) is inscribed 'liber dompni Nicholai Marley ex dono Thome Tempest anno 1560'.

*Rypon, dom. Johannes de, monachus D., medicus (*fl. 1400*):
Durham, Cath., B.IV.32, fos 50 ff. (constat —— —— ex procuracione propria).

St Carileph, William of, bishop of D. († *1096*):
Cambridge, Peterhouse, 74. Durham, Cath., A.II.4, A.III.29, B.II.2, 6, 9–11, 13, 14, 16, 17, 21, 22, 35, B.III.1, 9–11, 16, B.IV.13, 24. Oxford, Bodleian, Laud misc. 546. *All recorded as his gifts in cat.*

Segbrok, Richard de, monk (*fl. 1396*):
London, B.M., Arundel 507 (*presumed owner*).

*Seton, (2) mag., (3) dom. Willelmus, monachus D. (*sub-prior 1461*):
Cambridge, Sid. Sussex Coll., 56 (quod; *cf.* Bell, Ricardus). (2) Durham, Cath., B.II.5 (liber quondam —— assignatus communi librar' D. per Ricardum Bell priorem A.D. 1465); (3) B.III.29 (fieri fecit; writing completed 3 Sept. 1438).

*Shyrborn, Ricardus, monachus D.:
Durham, Cath., C.IV.22, art. 3–6 (descriptus est per).

Shyrburn, fr. Gilbertus de:
Durham, Cath., C.II.2.

Sotheron, dom. Robertus. *See* Manbe.

Stanlaw, dom. Robertus de:
Durham, Cath., C.III.5 (liber).

Stiphol (Stiphel), Willelmus de (4, Guillermus dictus du — de Britania):
Durham, Cath., A.I.3 (wrote in 1386; *see* Blaklaw); A.I.4 (name; *wrote part*; *cf.* Le Berwby). Cambridge, Trin. Coll., 365 (name; *wrote part*). (4) London B.M., Burney 310 (wrote in 1381; *see* Boldon).

*Strother, dom. Robertus, monachus D. (*prior of Holy Island 1517–22*):
York, Minster, vii.G.4 (liber). *Cf.* Downside Abbey, 960 (Strother *on tail*). *See also* Whytehed.

*Swalwell, dom. (4, 13–15, mag.) Thomas, monachus D. († *1539*):
Cambridge, U.L., Kk.5.10 (assignatur almariolo noviciorum per). Downside Abbey, 970 (name, price, and date 1510), 18274 (liber —— emptus die 11 Januarii 1512). (4) Durham, Cath., Inc. 3 (liber dom. Stephani Marley ex dono — die sancte Marie Magdalene A.D. 1537); Inc. 21b (liber); Inc. 45 (liber; *cf.* Marley, Whelden); Inc. 47b (liber). London, B.M., Add. 28805 (liber); Harley 4725 (liber emptus per —— 12 die Junii 1513). Ushaw Coll., XVII.E.4.2 (liber); XVII.E.4.5 (liber —— emptus die 10 Junii 1520); XVII.F.4.1 (liber); (13) XVII.G.4.3 (liber dom. Stephani Marley ex dono — 1 die Januarii 1526); (14) XVII.G.4.5 (liber dom. Stephani Marley ex dono — A.D. 1536); (15) XVIII.A.3.15 (liber dom. Stephani Marley monachi ex dono — A.D. 1534); XVIII.B.1.2 (liber); XVIII.B.3.6, 9–11 (*all* liber; *cf.* Marley, Nicholaus); XVIII.C.2.9 (liber —— 'et jam datus est dom. Stephano Marley 1534'); XVIII.C.5.2 (liber —— emptus die 3 Sept. 1517). York, Minster, xi.G.4 (liber —— A.D. 1510); xv.A.12 (liber). *See also* Byllyngham, Watson.

Swan, dom. Willelmus, monachus D. (*fl. 1515*):
Ushaw Coll., XVIII.B.4.4 (liber).

*Thew, dom. Henricus, monachus D. (*prior of Holy Island 1525–31*):
Durham, U.L., Mickleton and Spearman, 89 (liber sancti Cuthberti et ——).

Tode, dom. Willelmus (*canon 1541–67*):
London, B.M., Harley 4843.

Tutyng, Johannes, monachus D. (*1529; canon 1541–60*):[3]
    Bristol, Central Public Libr. (liber).
Uthred. *See* Boldon.
*Wakerfeud, mag. Alanus de (*fl. 1234*):
    Durham, Cath., A.III.14.
Walworth, Robertus *de*. *See* Robertus.
*Wardell, dom. Robertus, monachus D. (*prior of Finchale 1480–90*):
    York, Minster, xvi.I.1 (liber; *cf.* Emylton). *See also* Elwick.
Watson, dom. Willelmus, monachus D.:
    Cambridge, Corpus Christi Coll., EP.S.3 (liber — — . . . `set modo est
    liber dom. T. Swalwell . . . per eundem emptus die 22 Marcii A.D. 1537´).
Werdall (Weyrdal), dom. Robertus, junior (*cf.* Wardell, Robertus),
    confrater D.:
    Durham, Cath., Inc. 1f, 11a (*both* assignatus novo armariolo in
    claustro D. per — — A.D. 1513; *cf.* Cawthorn, Manbe, *for* Inc. 1f).
    Gouda, Messrs Koch and Knuttel (liber).
*Wessyngton (Wesyngton), dom. Johannes (3) de, (1, 4, 5, 7–10, 15)
    prior D. (*1416–46;* † *1451*):
    (1) Cambridge, U.L., Ff.4.41 (liber Johannis Hoton monachi ex dono);
    Trin. Coll., 8 (liber — — accomodatus Petro Radlee; *cf.* Middleton).
    (3) Durham, Cath., A.III.35 (assignatus communi armariolo per
    fr. — — —); (4) B.I.14 (per); (5) B.I.30 (assignatus communi librarie
    per); B.III.30 (per — — pro parte laborata); (7) B.IV.26 (assignatur
    librarie infra capellam prioris per); (8) B.IV.39 A + B (assignatur
    claustro per); (9) B.IV.43 (assignatus communi librarie per); (10)
    C.I.20 (ex procuracione); C.III.17 (liber). London, B.M., Cotton
    Claud. D.iv (arms); Harley 3858 (assignatum communi librarie per);
    Lansdowne 397 (liber). (15) Oxford, Bodleian, Laud misc. 262
    (assignatus communi librarie per); Laud misc. 748 (*wrote*).
*Westmerland, Robertus (2) de, monachus D. (*fl. 1430*):
    Durham, Cath., C.III.9 (liber); (2) C.III.11 (liber — — — quem emit de
    executoribus mag. Thome Hepden; *cf.* Ebchester).
Whelden (Qwelden), dom. Ricardus, monachus († *1539*):
    Ampleforth Abbey, C.v.72 (liber — — emptus 13 die Maii A.D. 1529).
    Ushaw Coll., XVIII.A.3.12 (liber — — emptus 13 die Maii A.D. 1529).
    See also Whytehed.
Wherton, Johannes, de Kirkebythore:
    London, B.M., Cotton Titus A.xviii (liber — — post obitum ejusdem
    — — liberetur priori et conventui abbathie D. precepto suo speciali).
Whytehed, mag. Hugo (*prior 1519–40, subsequently dean;* † *1551*):
    Cambridge, Jesus Coll., 61 (assignatur almariolo noviciorum per).
    Durham, Cath., Inc. 2 (liber dom. Roberti Strother ex dono); Inc. 45
    (liber dom. Ricardi Whelden ex dono). Hawkesyard Priory (liber
    dom. Christopheri Wyllye monachi ex dono — — A.D. 1521). Lon-
    don, B.M., Harley 4664 (liber erat dom. Ricardi Crosby ex dono
    — — A.D. 1521). Ushaw Coll., XVII.G.4.12 (emptus sumptibus
    — — anno salutis 1513).

[3] London, Soc. of Antiquaries, MS. 7 is inscribed 'liber Johannis Tutyng
1541', and so also is a copy of Bersuire's Dictionarium in three vols (Nuremberg,
1499) at Ushaw Coll., on deposit from Yealand Conyers. Tutyng's name is
also on a first volume of T. Walden's Doctrinale fide (Paris, 1532), also now
at Ushaw and formerly at Yealand Conyers.

Wlveston, fr. Thomas de (*s.xiii*):
    London, B.M., Harley 5234 (ex dono et labore).
Wlton, fr. Ricardus de (*s.xiv*):
    Durham, Cath., B.III.8 (ex procuracione).
Wyllye, dom. Cristopherus, monachus D., (2) camerarius († *1530*):
    Dublin, Trin. Coll., Ff.dd.4, 5 (liber). (2) Oxford, Bodleian, Auct.
    1.Q.5.1 (*a* liber; *b* liber dom. Willelmi Brantyngham ex dono).
    Ushaw Coll., XVII.F.4.4 (liber —— emptus anno 1519); XVIII.A.3.4,
    5 (*a* liber; *b* ex dono —— A.D. 1519); XVIII.C.3.13 (liber). *See also*
    Whytehed.
Whylom, dom. Willelmus, monachus (*1516; canon 1541–56*):
    Cambridge, U.L., Rel. c.50.8 (liber —— `nunc vero dom. Nicholai
    Marley ex dono ejusdem'). Durham, Cath., Inc. 44 (liber ——
    1534). London, Law Soc., 107.d (emptus sumptibus assignatis ——).
    Tollerton, St Hugh's Coll. (Lyra) (codex —— A.C. 1536). Ushaw
    Coll., XVII.F.4.3 (codex —— 1515); XVIII.G.3.11, 12 (liber; *cf.*
    Lee). *See also* Bennett.
*Wyniston, Thomas de (*s.xiv*). *See p. 60.*

EASBY

Tanfyld, Johannes, canonicus de Skyrpynbek (*J. T., capellanus de S.,
    canon of E., 1491*):
    Cambridge, Jesus Coll., 55 (constat).

EDINGTON

Duke, Henricus, confrater, obiit anno Christi 1528:
    Cambridge, Pembr. Coll., C.48.
*Newton, dom. Willelmus:
    Oxford, Bodleian Auct. D.5.14 (caucio —— A.D. 1463 *and* 1465).
*Wey, mag. Willelmus († *1476 at E.*):
    Oxford, Bodleian, Bodl. 565.

ELSTOW

Chanvill, C. de, abbatissa E.:
    London, B.M., Royal 7 F.iii (scripsit Robertus filius Radulphi disci-
    pulus et scriptor ultimus mag. Roberti Bonni de Bedeford . . . anno
    tertio coronationis regis Ricardi quem scribere fecit —— —).
Robertus, scriptor. *See* Chanvill.

ELY

Norwico, dom. Petrus de:
    Cambridge, St John's Coll., 23 (liber; *cf.* Stewarde).
Willelmus, sacerdos de Stradesete (*s.xii*):
    Cambridge, Corpus Christi Coll., 416.
Stewarde, dom. Robertus, prior E.:
    Cambridge, St John's Coll., 23 (arma —— prioris nostri Eliensis).
    London, B.M., Cotton Calig. A.viii (arma —— prioris nostri
    Eliensis 1531); Harley 3721 (arma —— prioris Eliensis); Lambeth
    Pal., 204 (arms of ——). Untraced Horae (arma —— prioris
    Eliensis 1512). *Cf.* London, Lambeth Pal., 448 (—— Eliensis 1550).

ETON

Aiscough, Willelmus, episcopus Sarum (*1438–50*):
    Eton Coll., 28–29.

Borowe, mag. Johannes, quondam socius E.:
Eton Coll., 120.
Edyngton, dom. Robertus:
Eton Coll., 24 (scripte per — — infra hospicium strenui militis Roberti
Lysle apud Wodehouse juxta Arden, A.D. 1455).
Elys, mag. Robertus:
Eton Coll., 5 (de dono A.D. 1501).
Gybbe, Willelmus, de parochia de Wisbech:
Eton Coll., 34, fos 104–99 (scriptus per).
*Hopton, mag. Ricardus, (3) quondam socius E., S.T.P. († *1497*):
Eton Coll., 39 (*presumed gift of*); 101 (*presumed gift of*); (3) 114.
*Horman, Willelmus, quondam socius E. († *1535*):
Eton Coll., 24 (*presumed gift of*); 44 (*wrote part; presumed gift of*); 48,
79, 80, 98, 119, 122 (*presumed gift of*), 126, 127, 145, Am.4.2, By.1.9,
Ee.1.6, Fc.5.12, Ga.3.11, Ge.1.5. Gloucester, Cath., 3. Winchester
Coll., 2.
**Lupton, mag. Rogerus, quondam prepositus († *1540*):
Eton Coll., 131, By.1.3, By.2.1, Ef.4.6, Eh.1.1, 2, En.1. London, B.M.,
Cotton Titus A.xxii.
*Malberthorp, mag. Johannes (*fellow E. 1447*):
Eton Coll., 47 (*wrote; presumed gift of*).
*Mower (Moyer), mag. Johannes, vicarius de Tenterden († *by Oct.
1489*):
Eton Coll., 105 (*bequeathed*); 106.
*Weston, mag. Thomas, socius E.:
Eton Coll., 42 (ex dono — — A.D. 1453; *cf.* Wey, Wodewarde).
*Wey, mag. Willelmus, socius (1, 2, quondam socius) E. († *1476*):
(1) Eton Coll., 42 (*cf.* Weston, Wodewarde); (2) 76; 99.
Wodewarde:
Eton Coll., 42 (quod).

EVESHAM

Alcetur, Johannes, monachus E.:
London, Mr Philip Robinson (constat).
Joseph, Robert, monk of E., last prior of Gloucester Hall, Oxford:
Aberystwyth, N.L., Peniarth 119D (*wrote*).
*Marlborough, Thomas de, abbot († *1236*):*
Oxford, Bodleian, Rawl. A.287 (*see p. 80*).
*More, mag. Johannes, decretorum doctor († *1502*):
Oxford, Bodleian, Gough Missals 33 (contulit capelle de le Battell
Welle).
Norton, Johannes, junior:
Manchester, J. Rylands, Lat. 122 (name).
*Penbroke, Ricardus, (1, 2) monachus E. (*fl. 1393*):
(1) London, B.M., Royal 8 G.xiv (adquisivit); (2) 10 D.vi (adquisivit).
Oxford, Jesus Coll., 103 (de provisione).
*Wykwon, dom. Johannes, abbas E. († *by Febr. 1461*):
London, B.M., Royal 4 E.ii (ex dono — — A.D. 1458).

EXETER

Bartholomeus, episcopus E. (*1162–84*):
Oxford, Bodleian, Bodl. 449 (name *in genitive; presumed gift of*).

Bobych, J.:
 Oxford, Bodleian, Wood empt. 15 (scriptus Exon' per manus; *cf.* Snetesham).
Brounst, dom. Ricardus, vicarius de choro E. (*1417*):
 Oxford, Bodleian, Bodl. 162; 865, fos 1–88.
*Buckyngham, mag. Thomas de, quondam cancellarius E. (*fl. 1350*):
 Oxford, Bodleian, Bodl. 335.
Cicestria, Henricus de, canonicus E.:
 Manchester, J. Rylands, 24 (memoriale — — — prec' lx s.).
Clerobaldus:
 Oxford, Bodleian, Bodl. 479 (*presumed gift of*).
*Fylham, Willelmus, quondam cancellarius E. († *c.1438*):
 Oxford, Bodleian, Bodl. 830 (dedit executor testamenti — —).
Grandison, Johannes de, episcopus Exon' (*1327–69*):
 Cambridge, Trin. Coll., 1475. Exeter, Cath., 3504 (gave in 1365); 3505. London, Lambeth Pal., 104, 203. Oxford, Bodleian, Bodl. 150 (*presumed gift of*); 230, 732, 738 (gave in 1365); Bodl. Or. 135. *The inscriptions of gift are in the donor's hand in varying forms of words.*
*Gybbys, mag. Walterus († *1413*):
 Exeter, Cath., 3512 (legavit). Oxford, Bodleian, Bodl. 810 (legavit).[4]
*Hereward, Robertus, quondam canonicus E. († *by 1363*):
 Oxford, Bodleian, Bodl. 287 (ex legato).
Hugo, archidiaconus Tanton' (*fl. 1230*):
 Oxford, Bodleian, Auct. D.1.7 (legavit — ut proprietas ipsius sit ecclesie usus vero pauperum scolarium); Auct. D.1.12 (*as* Auct. D.1.7); Bodl. 494 (*as* Auct. D.1.7).
*Lacy, Edmundus, nuper episcopus E. († *1455*):
 Exeter, Cath., 3513 (dederunt executores). Oxford, Bodleian, Bodl. 268 (dedit); 463, 720, 786, 829, 859 (*all* dederunt executores; 786 to be chained 'in disco de medicinis et phisica' *and* 829 'juxta Holkotte super sapientiam Salamonis').
Leofric, episcopus E. († *1072*). *See p. 81.*
*Orum, Johannes, archidiaconus Barn' († *1436*):
 Oxford, Bodleian, Bodl. 286.
*Poundestoke, mag. Willelmus, quondam canonicus E. († *1414*):
 Exeter, Cath., 3548 (legavit).
*Pyttys, mag. Johannes, canonicus E. († *1467*):
 Exeter, Cath., 3503 (legavit).
*Raw, mag. Johannes, subdecanus E. († *1463*):
 Oxford, Bodleian, Bodl. 279.
*Ryggh, mag. Robertus, cancellarius († *c.1411*):
 Oxford, Bodleian, Bodl. 749.
Sancta Brigida, mag. Adam de, cantor E. († *1232*):
 Oxford, Bodleian, Auct. D.1.9.
*Snetesham (Stnetesham), mag. Johannes, canonicus et cancellarius E. († *1448*):
 Oxford, Bodleian, Bodl. 744 (ex dono executorum); Bodl. 748, Wood empt. 15 (*both* assignatus communi librarie . . . per executores).
*Stevenys, mag. Johannes, quondam canonicus E. († *1459*):
 Oxford, Bodleian, Bodl. 315 (dedit . . . post obitum mag. Rogeri Keys).

[4] Both these books belonged to Exeter Cathedral already in the fourteenth century and probably in the twelfth century.

*Webber, mag. Henricus, decanus E. († *1477*):
    Exeter, Cath., 3516 (disposuit). Oxford, Bodleian, Bodl. 320 (liber; *presumably gave*); 333 (disposuit et dedit).

EXETER, *Hospital of St John the Baptist*
*Westcote, mag. Johannes, canonicus E., custos († *by June 1418*):
    Exeter, Cath., 3511 (dat et concedit — — ... dum tamen eorum consensu et assensu habeat usum ejusdem ad terminum vite sue, 14 Febr. A.D. 1417/*18*).

EYE
Stowe, dom. Robertus, de E. (*monk; fl. 1525*):
    Norwich, City Libr., F.c.18 (constat cum magno gaudio et honore).

EYNSHAM
Salley, Milo, abbas E. et episcopus Landavensis († *1516*):
    Bristol, All Saints' Church, 5 (liber).
Wodetun, fr. Johannes de, monachus E.:
    Oxford, Bodleian, Bodl. 435 (liber ... quem scripsit — — —).

FAVERSHAM
Wade, Ricardus, sacerdos capellæ regiæ:
    Lampeter, St David's Coll.

FERRIBY, NORTH
Styrton, Johannes:
    London, B.M., Harley 114 (Hic liber in Feriby maneat memorando Johannis./Et ymago mundy auratus omnibus annis *and to left of couplet* Styrton).

FLIXTON
Croftys, Thomas, armiger, ob. 22 Jan. 1442/*43*:
    Cambridge, U.L., Ee.3.52 (contulit simul et donavit).

FOTHERINGHAY
Curson, David, brother professyd yn the monastery of Syon:
    London, Lambeth Pal., 1500.91 (a gift at peticion of — —, for life to John Doo, fellow F., and then 'to the commune use for evermore of the company' at F.).

FOUNTAINS
Atenulfus, medicus:
    Berlin, Staatsbibl., lat. 172.
Bageby (Bagby), fr. Johannes de, commonachus F.:
    London, B.M., Add. 24203 (*a* per — — —; *b* quod —).
Cotone, mag. Robertus de, archidiaconus Dunelm':
    Princeton, U.L., R. Garrett 94.
Coutton, Willelmus de, quondam monachus F.:
    London, B.M., Cotton Faust. A.v.
Huby, Marmaduke, abbot 1494–1526:
    Oxford, Christ Church, e.8.29 (arms). *See also* Pecke, Smythe.
Knarresburc, dom. Henricus de:
    Leeds, Public Libr., VR 6106.
Kydde, fr. Thomas, monachus F.:
    Ripon, Cath., xvii.C.15 (perquisitus per). *See also* Pecke.

Kyreby, Johannes de, monachus F.:
Manchester, J. Rylands, Lat. 365 (liber).
Munkegate, Johannes de, de Eboraco clericus, procurator abbatis et conventus F. (*c. 1380*):
London, B.M., Arundel 231 (scripsit).
Pecke, dom. Willelmus, vicarius collegii Ripon:
Leeds, Public Libr., VR 6109 (ex dono — — liberatus dom. Marmaduco abbati per manus fr. Thome Kydde monachi ejusdem A.D. 1516).
Scot, fr. Gilbertus:
Oxford, Bodleian, Lyell 8.
Smythe, dom. Robertus, S.T.P., rector de Vado (*Wath*):
Cambridge, Union Soc., Fairfax Rhodes Libr. (prayers asked 'hic ante crucifixum' for — — and Abbot Marmaduke, 'quorum alter . . . presens opusculum huic monasterio legavit, alter pie consideracionis publicum procurans profectum hic catenis obseravit').
Thyrske, Willelmus (*abbot 1526–35*):
Ripon, Cath., xvii.E.16–18 (per me — — adeptus erat).
Yong, fr. Johannes, (1) quondam monachus F. (*s.xvi in.*):
(1) Cambridge, Gonv. and Caius Coll., 126 (pertinens ad).[5]   London, B.M., Arundel 217 (name).[5]

FURNESS
Dalton, fr. Willelmus de, abbas F. (*1412–23*):
Oxford, Bodleian, Jones 48 (emit).

GLASTONBURY
*Bere, Ricardus, abbas [G.] (*1493–1525*).   *See* Wych.
*Crosse, fr. Johannes, prior G. (*D.D. 1459*):
Paris, B.N., Lat. 4167A (de perquisito).
Dunstan, abbas:
Oxford, Bodleian, Hatton 30 (scribere jussit).
*Fawkes, fr. Nicholaus, monachus G.:
Oxford, Oriel Coll., 15 (scriptus de industria — — A.D. 1389).
Langley (Langleigh), fr. Henricus, monachus G.:
Oxford, Bodleian, Auct. F.4.32 (in custodia); Laud lat. 4 (in custodia; *cf*. Merylynch).
Merylynch, fr. Johannes, (4) monachus G. (*s.xv in.*):
Brinkley, Sir G. Keynes (tabula sive [kalendare] editum per — — A.D. 1411: *hand as* Queen's Coll., 304).   London, B.M., Harley 641 (de perquisito); 651 (de perquisito).   (4) Oxford, Bodleian, Laud lat. 4 (perquisitus et scriptus per); Queen's Coll., 304 (de perquisito).
Monyton, Walterus, abbas (2, 3, quondam abbas) (*1341–74*):
Cambridge, Trin. Coll., 1460.   (2) London, B.M., Add 21614 (de perquisito).   (3) Oxford, Bodleian, Wood empt. 1 (de perquisito).
Selwode, Johannes, abbas G.:
Cambridge, St John's Coll., Ii.3.39 (de perquisito).   Oxford, Bodleian, Bodl. 80 (dom. Petro Weston monacho G. dono dedit ven. pater — —).
Taunton, Johannes, m*onachus Glaston*':
Upholland Coll., 98 (name, ? *as scribe*).
*Wason, dom. Thomas, monachus G. (*prior 1493*):
Oxford, Bodleian, Ashmole 790 (name; *wrote part*); Laud misc. 128 (name; *wrote part*).

[5] Both these MSS bear twelfth-century Fountains *ex libris* inscriptions.

Weston, dom. Petrus. *See* Selwode.

Wych, Willelmus, monachus [G.]:
 Princeton, U.L., R. Garrett 153 (quem — — scribi fecit de voluntate Ricardi Bere abbatis anno iiijᵗᵒ).

Wylton, Ricardus, monachus G.:
 Cambridge, Trin. Coll., 86 (name).

GLOUCESTER

Aldeswyrth, Ricardus de:
 Cambridge, Corpus Christi Coll., 485 (fecit scribi).

*Arndell, dom. [. . . .], monachus G. (*at Oxford 1498*):
 Williamstown, Williams Coll., Chapin Libr. (constat).

Boure, dom. Willelmus, confrater G.:
 London, B.M., Royal 10 C.vi (ex adquisitione).

Bred*on*, Thomas de, abbas G. (*1224–28*):
 Hereford, Cath., O.i.2 (liber).   London, B.M., Royal 2 C.xii.

Bruton, Nicholaus:
 Oxford, Trin. Coll., 66 (name *perhaps in genitive after* ex libris of G.).

Ernulf (*s.xii*):
 Oxford, Bodleian, Laud misc. 123 (name *in genitive*; *cf.* Lasseborgh); Jesus Coll., 65 (name *in genitive*).   London, B.M., Harley 2659 (name *in genitive*).   *Presumed donor.*

Hanley, Ricardus, abbas G. (*1457–72*):
 Hereford, Cath., P.i.6 (*a* name; *b* fecit ligari et in librariam posuit, 6 Edw. IV).

Haume, dom. Reginaldus *de*, abbas G. (*1263–84*).   *See* Twenyng.

Hortone, fr. [. . . .], commonachus G.:
 Oxford, Trin. Coll., 64 (ex adquisitione).

Lasseborgh, Johannes de, monachus G. (*s.xiii*):
 Oxford, Bodleian, Laud misc. 123 (Cautio — — — exposita Willelmo de Winterborn; *cf.* Ernulf).

Le Boteus, mag. Galfridus:
 Cambridge, Trin. Coll., 166.

Malvern, dom. Willelmus, abbas (2, nuper abbas) G.:
 Belmont Abbey (liber — — deditque dom. Thome Toby monacho G., A.D. 1527).   (2) Cambridge (U.S.A.), Harvard Law School, 26 (Hunt ex dono — —).

Nuton, J., monachus G.   *See* **ABINGDON**, Rowland.

*Paunteley, Johannes (*monk G.; fl. 1400*):
 Oxford, Bodleian, Laud misc. 706 (constat).

Stowa, Ricardus de (*s.xiii*):
 London, B.M., Harley 627.

Temese, fr. Johannes:
 London, B.M., Harley 613 (recuperatus per).

Toby, dom. Thomas, monachus G.   *See* Malvern.

Twenyng, Johannes, monachus:
 Cambridge, Corpus Christi Coll., 485 (concessit michi et deliberavit dom. Reg. abbas G. quousque Johannes Orchard monachus G. michi solverit 26 s. 8 d. nomine — —. Et predicto Reg. tradidi librum scilicet Bibliam quam implegiavit michi dictus — —; *cf.* Aldeswyrth).

GODSTOW
Gyste, Johannes, armiger:
Manchester, Chetham, 6717.

GORING
Heryerd, Robertus, et Johanna, uxor ejus:
Cambridge, Trin. Coll., 244 (contulerunt).

GRANTHAM, *Fran. conv.*
*Assewell, fr. Rogerus de, custos Oxon' (*1333*):
Lincoln, Cath., 207 (per).

GREENWICH, *Fran. conv.*
Dengayn, Willelmus:
London, B.M., Sloane 1617 (ex mutuacione; *cf.* Grene, Palmer).
Grene, Thomas, fr.:
London, B.M., Sloane 1617 (*scribe of fos 70–75ᵛ wrote at end '— —*
Explicit').
Palmer, Symon, de Grenewich:
London, B.M., Sloane 1617 (name).
Tyndall, Johannes:
London, St Paul's Cath., 13.D.16 (dedit . . . die professionis sui filii fr.
Willelmi A.D. 1508).

GUISBOROUGH
Hemmyngburth, fr. Walterus de, quondam canonicus G.:
London, B.M., Royal 3 A.xiii (ex dono A.D. 1307).
Petro, dom. Ricardus de, canonicus G.:
Cambridge, Gonv. and Caius Coll., 109 (liber).
*Pykering, mag. Robertus de, quondam decanus Ebor', obiit ultimo die
Decembris, A.D. 1332:
Cambridge, St John's Coll., 74 (legavit . . . pro eo quod libri monasterii
fuerunt combusti in combustione ecclesie sue).

GUTHRIE
Guthre, dom. Alexander, de eodem miles († *1513*):
Edinburgh, N.L., Adv. 18.2.8.

HAGNABY
Well, fr. Johannes, canonicus H.:
Cambridge, Gonv. and Caius Coll., 190 (quod — — qui scripsit ista
A.D. 1440).

HAILES
Acton, fr. Philippus, monachus H. et scolaris (*D.D. 1538; provisor of St
Bernard's Coll., Oxford*):
Edinburgh, Theol. Coll., Forbes e.34 (ex emptione). Insch, C. A.
Gordon (emptus per). Wells, Cath., G. 1.3–8.
Bristow, Johannes, monachus H.:
London, B.M., Add. 5667 (name and date of profession at H., 1451).
Coscom, fr. Rogerus, monachus H. ac studens Oxon':
Manchester, Chetham, 19495 (per me — — A.D. 1528).
Crombek, Robertus, commonachus H.:
London, B.M., Royal 8 D.xvii (name).

Huddleston, Johannes:
Wells, Cath., Chrysostom (given by Sir Christopher Urswick as executor of — —).
*Neel, mag. Willelmus, olim vicarius de Blokley:
London, B.M., Royal 5 A.xii (executor gave A.D. 1533).
Ricardus, comes Cornubie, *founder* († *1272*):
London, B.M., Add. 48984 (Abbot and convent of Caerleon gave to H. ad instanciam —).
*Urswyck, dom. Christophorus, elemosynarius regis Henrici VII († *1522*):
Wells, Cath., Psalter (written at expense of (? *and given to Hailes by*) A.D. 1514). *See also* Huddleston.
Whalley, dom. Stephanus, abbas H.:
Oxford, Balliol Coll., (ex emptione — — 1538 pro domo capitulari). Untraced pr. bk (liber). *Cf.* Windsor, St George's Chapel, III.c (pr. bks) (ex emptione, 1538, *and* chapter howse *legible, but no personal name*).

HAMPOLE
Vernun, domina Isabella de:
San Marino, Huntington, EL 9 H. 17.

HARTLAND
Helyer, mag. Ricardus, quondam registrarius de canc' Bar*nstapulensi* (? *cf.* B.R.U.O., p. 904):
London, B.M., Harley 220.
Radulphus, archidiaconus Barnast*apulensis* (*s.xiii*):
Stonyhurst Coll., 9.

HATFIELD PEVEREL
Bebseth, dom. Johannes, prior H.:
Oxford, Bodleian, Rawl. B.189 (*a* scribi fecit — — *over erasure of* Willelmus de Writele; *b* ex dono — — de licencia Willelmi *Heyworth* abbatis *S. Albani 1401–20*).

HAUGHMOND
Corvesar, Thomas, abbas [H.]:
London, B.M., Harley 622 (A.D. 1537 acquisivit istum librum huic mon' qui aliquando fuit prioratus de Ronton videlicet ante suppressionem ejusdem).
Kynge, sʳ William, canon H.:
Oxford, Bodleian, Auct. 1.Q.6.9 (pertheynyht to).
Ludlowe, Johannes, canonicus [H.] (*abbot 1464–78*):
Spalding, Gentlemen's Soc., B.96 (adquisivit).

HAVERFORDWEST
Thoresby, fr. Hugo de:
Eton Coll., 90 (mutuatus — — —).

HEREFORD
*Bayly, mag. Johannes († *by Sept. 1479*):
Hereford, Cath., O.iv.14, O.vi.7, O.vii.8.
*Bosuom (Bosom), Johannes, canonicus H. († *1444*):
Hereford, Cath., O.vii.3, O.vii.6 (*both* ex dono executorum — —).

**Bothe, dom. Carolus, episcopus H. († *1535*):
   Hereford, Cath., C.viii.14, E.ii.6–10, E.iv.1, 5, 8, 9, E.vi.5–9, I.i.10,
   M.i.1, N.vii.2–6 (*all* legatus per).
Castyll, mag. Johannes (*penitentiary 1414–30*). *See p. 97.*
Feld, dom. Ricardus:
   Hereford, Cath., P.vi.9.
*Frouceter, Edmundus, quodam decanus († *1529*):
   Hereford, Cath., A.vi.5–8, H.ii.9·
Grene (? *John G., prebendary,* † *by March 1472; cf. B.R.U.O., p. 819*):
   Hereford, Cath., P.viii.1, 9, P.ix.1 (*all presumed to be gifts of*).
*Lloyd, mag. Oweynus, quondam canonicus H. († *by Oct. 1478*):
   Hereford, Cath., E.iv.3, L.viii.6, N.i.5, O.i.9, O.v.9, 13, 15, O.viii.1, 5,
   P.ii.7, P.iii.6, 10, 11, P.iv.1, 7, P.v.6, 7, 11, P.vii.2, 4, 5, P.viii.2, 8, 11,
   P.ix.2.
*Mayewe, dom. Ricardus (*bishop of Hereford*; † *1516*):
   Hereford, Cath., P.vii.7 (repertus inter libros — — et mag. Willelmi
   Webbe archidiaconi post obitum eorum et traditus bibl. eccl. cath.
   Heref').
*Pede, Ricardus, decanus (*1463–80*):
   Hereford, Cath., P.v.15 (reparatus per — — ex gracia et pro usu).
Radulphus, (1) mag., (2–10) archidiaconus:
   (1) Hereford, Cath., O.i.5 (name *in genitive*); (2–10) O.ii.2, O.iii.7,
   O.iv.4, 7, O.v.8, O.vi.1, 5, O.viii.9, O.ix.1 (*all* — me dedit inter viginti).
   P.ii.11, P.iii.8 *are perhaps the copies of Leviticus and Exodus glossed
   recorded in the donors' book as the gifts of Archdeacon Ralph.*
*Rudhale, mag. Ricardus (*archdeacon of H. 1446–76*):
   Hereford, Cath., O.viii.7, P.v.14, P.vi.7 (*presumed to be gifts of*).
*Tawre, mag. Simon (*chancellor 1472–76*):
   Hereford, Cath., O.viii.10 (tradatur).
*Webbe, mag. Willelmus, archidiaconus (*Salop 1503–11*; † *1523*). *See*
   Mayewe.

HEREFORD, *Vicars Choral*
Mybbe, Walterus:
   Dublin, N.L., 700 (dedit A.D. 1438 per dom. J. Dyny).

HEREFORD, *Diocesan Registry*
Bothe, Carolus, episcopus H. († *1535*):
   Oxford, Bodleian, Ashmole 789.

HEREFORD, *St Guthlac*
Elmeleye, Adam de († *1273*):
   Hereford, Cath., P.iv.5.
Newinton, Ricardus de:
   Hereford, Cath., P.iii.5.
Rogerus, capellanus (*s.xii*):
   Hereford, Cath., O.v.1.   Oxford, Jesus Coll., 106.   Hereford, Cath.,
   O.iv.12 *is probably the copy of Minor prophets glossed recorded under
   Roger Caple* [*sic*] *in the donors' book of Hereford Cathedral.*
Rogerus, vicedecanus Hereford' (*s.xii*):
   Oxford, Jesus Coll., 66, 105.

HEREFORD, *Fran. conv.*
Broya (?), fr. J. de:
  Cambridge, St John's Coll., 169.
Chalbenor, dom. Willelmus de, capellanus:
  Hereford, Cath. O.ii.11 (contulit — — — fr. W. de Schypton nepoti
  suo quod habeat usum usque ad terminum vite sue. Post ejus
  decessum remaneat in communitate fr. min. H.).
Cornubiensis, dom. Ricardus:
  London, B.M., Royal 7 A.iv (de testamento — —).
*Herbert, fr. Willelmus:
  London, B.M., Add. 46919 (ex collatione — — auctoritate ministri
  generalis); Royal 7 F.viii (concessus — — ad usum quem librum ipse
  pro ordine procuravit). Oxford, Bodleian, Rawl. C.308 (ex colla-
  tione — — auctoritate generalis ministri). *Herbert's hand occurs also*
  in London, B.M., Cotton Nero A.ix and Royal 7 F.vii.
Knull, fr. W. de, de partibus Herford':
  Hereford, Cath., O.viii.12, fos 1–29 (de elemosina amicorum — — —).
Landu, fr. Philippus de:
  Hereford, Cath., P.iii.12 (tradatur — — — ex parte fr. Walteri de
  Land').
Land*u*, fr. Walterus de. *See* Landu, Philippus de.
Le Banastre, dom. Stephanus:
  Hereford, Cath., O.iii.6 (conceditur fratribus min. H. pro anima
  — — —).
Ledbury, fr. Johannes, O.F.M.:
  London, B.M., Burney 325 (*a* emit — — a mag. Gilberto Hundertone de
  elemosina amicorum suorum; *b* assignatus communitati fr. min. H.
  per — —).
Lutton, fr. Thomas de, O.F.M., H.:
  Hereford, Cath., O.viii.12, fos 29–304 (Postille — — —).
Mauns, fr. Johannes:
  London, B.M., Cotton Vesp. A.xiii (wrote).
Phelippus, Johannes, de Malmishull:
  Hereford, Cath., O.v. 12 ('datus communitati fr. min. Heref' pro anima
  — —' and others of his family).
Schypton, fr. W. de. *See* Chalbenor.

HERTFORD
Johannes II, abbas S. Albani (? *J. de Hertford, abbot 1235-60*):
  London, Lambeth Pal., 420.
Nigellus, prior [H.]:
  London, Lambeth Pal., 443.
Wynsselowe, dom. W.:
  London, Lambeth Pal., 420 (sent *in s.xv* with 16 other books 'per — —
  dom. Simoni priori S. Albani'; *cf.* Johannes).

HIGHAM FERRERS
*Chichele, Henricus, archiepiscopus Cant':
  Oxford, Trin. Coll., 23 (dedit A.D. 1428).

HINTON
Clerk, Johannes, quondam monachus H. († *1472*):
  Cambridge, St John's Coll., 125 (Orate pro anima — — et scriptoris
  hujus opusculi).

Fletcher, Thomas, ordinis Carthus', H. († *at Sheen, 1559*):
Cambridge, St John's Coll., 125 (Sum — —; *cf.* Clerk).
Marshall, mag. Ricardus:
London, B.M., Royal 12 B.iv (Oretis pro anima — — qui dedit istum librum dom. Thome Wellis monacho ordinis Carthus' de H.).
Wellis, dom. Thomas, monachus H. († *1524*). *See* Marshall.

HOLME CULTRAM
Dauy*s*, Mattheus, confrater (*abbot 1531–33*):
Carlisle, Cath., F.III.10 (de expensis — — adeptus).
Ludovicus, monachus (*s.xiii*):
Oxford, Univ. Coll., 15 (— me misit in armariolo de H.).

HOLME ST BENETS
Johannes, abbas. *See* Thomas.
Skothole, dom. Thomas, monachus H., prior:
Colchester, Harsnett Libr., K.f.11 (*a* liber; *b* ex dono; *cf.* **WINCH-COMB,** Benet).
Thomas, vicarius de Gorleston:
Douai, Bibl. mun., 171 (Psalterium dom. Johannis abbatis ex dono).

HORTON
Ælfgyþ (*s.xi*):
El Escorial, e.ii.1 (—syllþ gode into H.).

HOUNSLOW
Beckwyth, fr. Radulphus. *See* Sa[. .]dys.
Sa[. .]dys, fr. Johannes, de H.:
Untraced pr. bk (constat — —; *name erased and* Radulpho Beckwyth *substituted*).

HUNTINGDON
Laurentius, archidiaconus Bedefordensis:
Cambridge, U.L., Kk.4.21 (dedicavit).

HYDE
Ælfwine, decanus, abbot, c. 1050:
London, B.M., Cotton Titus D.xxvi, xxvii (*presumed to be owner and donor*).
Charyte, dom. Johannes, monachus *H. See* Charyte, Willelmus.
*Charyte, mag. Willelmus, vicarius S. Bartholomei (*Winchester*; † 1516*):
London, B.M., Royal 8 A.xviii (libellus dom. Johannis Charyte de dono — —).
Ricardus, abbas (*R. Hall, abbot of H. c. 1488–1530*):
London, B.M., Harley 960 (constat).

ICKLETON
Trotter, dame Elizabeth, noyne I.:
Cambridge, St John's Coll., 506 (belonges unto).

ILCHESTER, *Dom. conv.*
Clovesworth, fr. Johannes de. *See* Yvelcestria.
*Yvelc*estria*, rev. pat. fr. Willelmus de, S.T.P.:
Hereford, Cath., O.iv.11 (de perquisito — — — pertinens ad conv. fr. pred. I., concessus fr. Johanni de Clovesworth ad vitam).

INCHCOLM
Fynlay, dom. Simon, capellanus altaris s. Michaelis eccl. s. Egidii de
Edinburgo:
Darnaway Castle, Earl of Moray (scribi fecit — — quem post suum
obitum reliquit canonicis I.).

INCHMAHOME
David, prior:
Insch, C. A. Gordon (gave in 15[.]6).

IPSWICH, *Fran. conv.*
Ykewrth, fr. Ricardus de:
Cambridge, Peterhouse, 49 (scripturam hujus libri procuravit — — —
ab amicis suis dum steterat de conventu Gipewic).

JERVAULX
Aldeburgh, Ricardus de:
Lincoln, Cath., 231 (*memorandum seems to imply his gift*).
*Bromton, dom. Johannes, abbas J. (*1436*):
Cambridge, Corpus Christi Coll., 96 (ex procuracione).

KENILWORTH
*Alward, mag. Johannes, quondam rector de Stoke Bruere (*1420–57*):
Oxford, Bodleian, Auct. F.3.13 (legavit — — pro quaterno sibi in
Oxonia accommodato).
Aston, Johannes:
London, B.M., Add. 35295 (scripta per manum).
Strecche, Johannes, canonicus K. (*c. 1422*):
London, B.M., Add. 35295 (name; *wrote part*); 38665 (miserere — —;
wrote part).

KEYNSHAM
Arnolld, John, chanon of K.:
Dublin, Trin. Coll., 48 (— — boke).

KING'S LANGLEY
Mylys, fr. Robertus, provincialis (*prior K. c. 1525*):
Oxford, Blackfriars (fieri fecit anno Christi 1523).
Yngworth, Ricardus, conventus K. (*prior; bishop of Dover 1537*):
London, Middle Temple (name; *cf.* **NORWICH, Dom. conv.,**
Yngworth).

KINGSTON-UPON-HULL
Maleverey, dom. Radulphus, quondam prior K.:
London, Mr C. Hohler (orate pro — — anno Henrici VIII 27).
Smyth, Radulphus, monachus K. (*prior 1529; perhaps identical with*
Maleverey, *q.v.*):
Copenhagen, Kongelike Bibl. Heythrop Coll. London, Middle Temple.
Oakham, Church. (*All* Orate pro — —).

KINGSWOOD
Ricardus, prior (*s.xiii*):
Oxford, Bodleian, e Mus. 62 (per).

KINLOSS

Reid, mag. Robertus, subdecanus Moraviensis, nunc Orchadum episcopus
  (*1541–58; abbot K. 1528–58*):
  Cambridge, U.L., Ee.4.21 (liber).
Smyth, dom. Johannes, monachus K. († *1557*):
  London, B.M., Harley 2363 (scripsit).

KIRBY BELLARS

Brokesby, Bartholomeus, armiger:
  London, Lincoln's Inn, Hale 68 (dedit A.D. 1427).
Womyndham, Willelmus, canonicus K.:
  Cambridge, Trin. Coll., 1144 (anno Christi 1473 liber iste scriptus
  erat a).

KIRKHAM

Menythorp, fr. Thomas, canonicus K.:
  Cambridge, U.L., Dd.9.6 (Caucio —— A.D. 1421).

KIRKSTALL

Driffeld, fr. Johannes de, monachus:
  Cambridge, Jesus Coll., 75 (ex dono ——— A.D. 1344 ad memoriam
  inter fratres perpetuandam et animam precibus Deo comendandam).
Heddyngley, Christopherus:
  Oxford, Corpus Christi Coll., Δ.10.4 (per —— coemptus).
Stainborn, Johannes, monachus K.:
  Cambridge, Sid. Sussex Coll., 85 (constat).

KIRKSTEAD

Wharrun, fr. Willelmus de:
  Beaumont Coll., VI (liber).

KNARESBOROUGH

Foxton, Johannes de, capellanus (*s.xv*):
  Cambridge, Trin. Coll., 943.

KYME

Streyl, dom. Robertus, canonicus K.:
  Wisbech Mus., Town Libr. A.5.15 (constat).

LANCASTER, *Dom. conv.*

*Urswyck, dom. Christopherus, quondam helemosinarius Henrici VII
  († *1522*):
  Aberdeen, U.L., Inc. 90. Bristol, Central Public Libr. Cambridge,
  Sid. Sussex Coll., 48.

LANERCOST

Langedale, Willelmus de:
  Cambridge, Peterhouse, 247 (liber fr. Nicholai de Morland ex dono
  ———).
Morland, fr. Nicholaus de. *See* Langedale.

LANTHONY

Braci, Robertus de:
  London, B.M., Royal 8 D.xviii.

Bradefeld, fr. Thomas:
  Oxford, Queen's Coll., 309 (accomodavit prior — — in die s. Laurentii
    A.D. 1381 usque festum Pasch. prox. futurum).
*Calne, fr. Ricardus, canonicus L. et scolaris:
  London, Lambeth Pal., 70 (emptus per — — A.D. 1413); 74 (emptus
    per — — A.D. 1413?); 83 (caucio — — in cista communi canonicorum
    [...], A.D. 1412); 97 (emptus per — — A.D. 1415); 111 (emptus per
    — — A.D. 1414); 141 (caucio — — in cista communi canonicorum
    Oxon', A.D. 1421); 145 (emptus per — — tempore quo fuit scolaris
    Oxonie); 370 (emptus per — — A.D. 1418); 393 and 396 (partim
    scripsit et partim scribi fecit — — tempore quo fuit scolaris Oxonie).
Glouc', R. de, canonicus L.:
  London, Lambeth Pal., 55 (liber).
Hennelawe, Gaufredus *de*, Men' episcopus (*prior L. 1178–1203; bishop
    of St David's 1203–14*):
  London, Lambeth Pal., 195.
*Kaerwent, mag. Nicholaus († *1467*):
  London, Lambeth Pal., 128 (legavit).
Kom, Thomas:
  London, Lambeth Pal., 370 (name, ? *as scribe*; *cf.* Calne).
Langeneye, dom. Walterus de, de conv. L.:
  London, Lambeth Pal., 339 (de procuracione).
*Leche, mag. Johannes († *by Sept. 1361*):
  London, Lambeth Pal., 13, 21, 37, 39, 68, 129, 150, 375 (*all* legavit;
    cf. p. 108).
Lecksford, Robertus de, canonicus L. (*s.xiii*) :
  London, Lambeth Pal., 71, fos 119–222 (name *in dative*).
Merkeley, mag. R. de:
  London, Lambeth Pal., 217, fos 86–126 (memoriale — — — pro
    [....]).
Morganus, canonicus, de Kermerden:
  London, Lambeth Pal., 148, 165, 195, 200, 208, 215, 218, 231, 360, 377,
    390, 397, 398, 409, 449, 452, 481. Oxford, Bodleian, Bodl. 839,
    Hatton 49. (*All* name.) *See also p. 108, n. 5.*
Sancto Breavel, mag. Philippus de:
  London, Lambeth Pal., 154 (liber).
Willelmus, prior:
  London, B.M., Cotton App. xxiv (de dono); Lambeth Pal., 58 (per).
Waldink, Walterus (*s.xiii ex.*):
  Oxford, Corpus Christi Coll., 59.

LAUNDE
Barkre, John, chanon of L.:
  Oxford, Bodleian, Douce 302 (the owner of thys boke . . . — — hyt ys
    . . . gyvyn to hym . . . be on Wyatt a mynstral, *of Coventry, as appears
    from another inscription*).
Burgo, fr. Johannes de, prior L. (?) (*1309–19*):
  Eton Coll., 120 (liber — — — anno gracie 1318).
Wyatt (Vyott), minstral. *See* Barkre.

LEEDS
*Brok, mag. Willelmus, decretorum doctor († *1525*):
  Oxford, Corpus Christi Coll., 251.

Eggerton, dom. Thomas, canonicus L.:
  London, B.M., Royal 5 F.xvii (Orate pro anima Patricii qui hunc
    librum contulit — —).
Feversham (*or* Shepherd), Willelmus, canonicus *L.* (*1539*):
  Dublin, Trin. Coll., Q.cc.30 (liber).
Meydistane, fr. Thomas de, canonicus L.:
  Oxford, Bodleian, Bodl. 406 (per).
Patricius. *See* Eggerton.

LEICESTER
Charyte, fr. Willelmus:
  Edinburgh, N.L., Adv. 18.5.13 (de adquisitione).
Neuton, fr. Johannes. *See* Thurkeston.
Thurk*eston*, R*adulphus* (*canon* 1345):
  Cambridge, Trin. Coll., 293 (fr. Johannes Neuton liberavit — — istum
    librum in quaternis . . .).
Wylchur, dom. Johannes, vicarius Omnium Sanctorum, L.:
  Cambridge, King's Coll., 2.

LEICESTER, *Dom. conv.*
Glen magna, Willelmus de:
  Oxford, Bodleian, Bodl. 140 (wrote part; *cf.* Par).
P*ar*, fr. J. de, O.P., L.:
  Oxford, Bodleian, Bodl. 140 (liber).

LEICESTER, *Collegiate church*
Becansaw, mag. Gilbertus, vicarius de Bradford († *1537*):
  Leicester Mus., Wyggeston Hospital 11.

LEISTON
Galfridus, dom., archidiaconus:
  Cambridge, Corpus Christi Coll., 27.
Greene, dom. Johannes, abbas L. (*resigned 1531*):
  London, B.M., IB.24866 (name *in genitive*).

LEOMINSTER
Bray, dom. Henricus, custos L.:
  Oxford, Univ. Coll., d.6 (pertinet ad).

LESSNESS
Colman, dom. Johannes, abbas L.:
  Cambridge, Corpus Christi Coll., 387 (constat).
Mere, Eudo de (*s.xii ex.*):
  Cambridge, Trin. Coll., 1236 (fecit scribi et dedit domui b. Thome
    martyris).
Sandwyco, fr. Thomas de:
  Cambridge, Gonv. and Caius Coll., 135.   Oxford, Bodleian, Bodl. 656;
    St John's Coll., 19.

LEWES
Burghersch, fr. Johannes, monachus L.:
  Edinburgh, N.L., Adv. 18.4.2 (dom. Johannes Ok' prior L. contulit
    — — sub tali condicione quod quamdiu vixerit et mansionarius vel
    scolaris dicte domus fuerit usum de eo habeat).

Horton, dom. Willelmus, monachus L.:
  Copenhagen, Royal Libr., Ny Kgl. S.172.8° (per me — —; *wrote part*).
Ok', dom. Johannes, prior L. *See* Burghersch.

LEWES, *Fran. conv.*
****Cudner, mag. Thomas (*O.F.M.;* † *before 1538*):
  Worcester, Cath., Inc. 12.
[. . . .], fr. Thomas, lector L. (*c. 1530*). *See* **SALISBURY,** *Fran. conv ,*
  Burcham.

LICHFIELD
Admondeston, mag. Willelmus, canonicus L. (*archdeacon of Stafford;*
  † *1432*):
  London, B.M., Harley 5249.
Assheborn, Alanus de, vicarius L.:
  London, B.M., Cotton Cleop. D.ix (liber).
*Chestrefeld, mag. Thomas, canonicus residentiarius, (2) prebendarius
  de Tervyn (*1425–52*):
  Lichfield, Cath., Decretales (post mortem dom. Roberti Snapp pres-
  biteri . . . de dono). (2) Oxford, Bodleian, Bodl. 956.

LICHFIELD, *Cathedral chantries*
Gully, dom. Ricardus, nuper vicarius choralis L.:
  New York, Mr and Mrs Gordan, 24.

LICHFIELD, *Fran. conv.*
Bottisham, Ricardus:
  London, B.M., Royal 3 D.i (wrote at Gonville Hall, Cambridge, in
  1452; *cf.* Collynwood).
**Collynwood, mag. Radulphus, predicator et S.T.D. (*dean of Lichfield
  1512–21*):
  London, B.M., Royal 3 D.i.

LINCOLN
**Chesney, Robert de, bishop of Lincoln* († *1166*):
  Lincoln, Cath., 4, 31, 96, 145, 157, 201 (*all in cat. as his gifts*). Oxford,
  Balliol Coll., 36 (*in cat. as his gift*).
Dadington, Willelmus, quondam vicarius de Barton super Humbre:
  Cambridge, Fitzwilliam Mus., McClean 109 (legavit . . . ut esset sub
  custodia vicecancellarii).
David, archdeacon:
  Lincoln, Cath., 18 (*in cat. as his gift*).
*Duffeld, mag. Thomas, olim (2, nuper) cancellarius L. († *1423*):
  Cambridge, U.L., Add. 3571. (2) Lincoln, Cath., 83 (*both* legavit et assig-
  navit nove librarie A.D. 1422).
*Edyrston, mag. Johannes, canonicus residentiarius L.:
  Lincoln, Cath., 183 (ex dono A.D. 1454).
*Higgons, Edwardus, canonicus L. (*prebendary 1533*):
  Cambridge, Gonv. and Caius Coll., 667 (ex dono et opere).
Nicholaus, canonicus et archidiaconus:
  Lincoln, Cath., 1 + Cambridge, Trin. Coll., 148.
*Partrich, mag. Petrus, cancellarius L. (*1424–51*):
  Lincoln, Cath., 72. London, B.M., Royal 11 B.i.

*Repyndon, Philippus de, episcopus nuper L. († *1424*):
  London, B.M., Royal 8 G.iii (Ego — — — dono . . . nove librarie . . .
  reservando usum et possessionem . . . Ric. Fryseby . . . prebendario
  prebende de Milton ad terminum vite sue . . . A.D. 1422).
Salysbury, Thomas (*archdeacon of Bedford*; † *1460*):
  Lincoln, Cath., 3, 29, 63, 198 (*all* constat; *presumed to be of his gift*).
*Sutton, mag. Thomas de, quondam canonicus residentiarius L. († *by
  June 1316*):
  Lincoln, Cath., 45 (legavit — — — ut remaneat sub custodia vice-
  cancellarii, ut et ipse . . . deliberet cuicumque tam canonico quam
  vicario ejusdem ecclesie in eodem libro ad edificacionem populi
  studere volenti).
Warsop, dom. Johannes, canonicus L. (*1361–86*):
  London, B.M., Royal 13 E.i.

LINCOLN, *Episcopal Registry*
Russell, Johannes, episcopus L. († *1494*):
  Oxford, Univ. Coll., 156 (written by — — 'in octo septimanis' and
  'manu propria', the last page signed by him at Woburn on the
  feast of Epiphany 1491/92, to remain in the registry of the bishop
  'quicumque erit pro tempore').

LINCOLN, *Fran. conv.*
*Corbrige, fr. Radulphus de (*fl. 1245*):
  London, Lambeth Pal., 57 (ex legato).
Johannes, dom., vicarius de Edligtona:
  Lincoln, Cath., 41.
Lincoln', fr. Stephanus de:
  Lincoln, Cath., 208 (*a* Memoriale pro libris Senece [. . .] — — —;
  b ex dono — — —).
*Quappelod, fr. Thomas de. *See* Tatewic.
Retford, fr. Thomas de:
  Princeton, U.L., R. Garrett 102.
Tatewic, fr. Willelmus de:
  Cambridge, Peterhouse, 89 (pertinet ad communitatem fr. min. L. post
  decessum fr. Thome de Quappelod per assignacionem — — — de
  licencia fr. Hugonis de Hertelpoll provincialis ministri A.D. 1299 quem
  dictus frater W. scribi fecit).

LINCOLN, *Dom. conv.*
Birton, Willelmus de, junior, O.P.:
  Leyden, U.L., Lipsius 41 (*a* acomodatus Johanni de Crosholm juniori
  per — — — in presencia prioris sui fr. Willelmi de Geynesborou pro
  voluntate dicti fr. Willelmi repetendus; *b* acomodatus dom. Johanni
  Beneyt monacho de Kyrkested per — — —, in the presence of two
  monks of K. and of a friar of the L. convent 'in domo magistri
  Johannis de Hely argentarii' 12 Mar. 1333/34).

LLANTHONY
Haya, fr. Walterus de, prior L. (*s.xiii*):
  London, Lambeth Pal., 431 (liber).

LLANVAES, *Fran. conv.*
Bangor, fr. Gervasius de:
  London, Dr E. G. Millar (ad usum in vita sua).

LOCHLEVEN
Willelmus filius Dunecani, quondam persona L. (*s.xiii*):
London, Lambeth Pal., 440.

LONDON, *St Paul's Cathedral*
*Baudac, Radulphus de, archidiaconus Midd*lesexie* (*bishop of L.;* † *1313*):
Oxford, Oriel Coll., 30 (ex dono ?).
Cornhell, Henricus, decanus L.:
London, St Paul's Cath., 2.
*Gascoigne, mag. Thomas († *1458*):
Aberdeen, U.L., 137 (*no name of donor, but* 'liber datus nove librarie
eccl. sancti Pauli L.' *in G.'s hand*); 241 (*as* 137). *See also p. 121.*
*Graunt, Thomas, treasurer L. († *1474*):
Aberdeen, U.L., 244.
Ricardus, episcopus (*s.xii;* ? *R. de Belmeis 1108–27*):
Aberdeen, U.L., 4 (*presumed to be his gift*).
*Somerseth, mag. Johannes, cancellarius scaccarii Anglie († *by 1455*):
London, St Paul's Cath., 3 (do, concedo et delibero A.D. 1451).

LONDON, *Aug. nunnery*
Burton, John, citizen and mercer of L. († *1460*):
Oxford, Bodleian, Douce 372 (bequeathed to Katherine his daughter
'and after hur decesse to remayne to' L. 'for evermore').

LONDON, *St Mary of Graces*
Austen, fr. Thomas, monachus L. (*s.xvi in.*):
London, B.M., Harley 4711 (emtor).
Langton, dom. Johannes, abbas [L.] (*cf.* Wroksam):
Berlin, Staatsbibl., lat. qu. 487 (ex empcione).
Wroksam, mag. Willelmus, S.T.P.:
London, Lambeth Pal., 1484.2 (ex dono A.D. 1[4]94 regente Johanne
Langton abbate).

LONDON, *Charterhouse*
Bernham, Willelmus. *See* Lucas.
Blacman, Johannes († *1485*):
London, B.M., Sloane 2515 (London' quod — —).
Burgoyn, Bartholomew. *See* Colles.
Chawncy, mag. *Mauritius* († *1581*):
Parkminster (per — quem exaravit Willelmus Exmewe).
Colles, Elizabeth:
Cambridge, Pembr. Coll., 309 ('given by — — to fader Bartholomewe
Burgoyn moonke' of L., A.D. 1537).
Exmewe, Willelmus († *1535*). *See* Chawncy.
Henricus sextus, rex Anglie († *1471*):
Cambridge, King's Coll., 4 (*presumed to be donor*). Oxford, Bodleian,
Bodl. 277 (liber quondam — — qui postea donabatur domui Carth.
L.).
Lucas, dom. Robertus, presbiter de London':
Paris, B.N., Lat. 10434 (prestitit Willelmo Bernham fratri in domo
Cart. L., to be returned on demand and no alterations to be made on
pain of a fine of four marks).

**Lumley, dom. Marmaducus, quondam Lincoln' episcopus († *1450*):
  Yale, U.L., 286 (ex dono — — memoriale ejusdem perpetuo in dicta domo permansurum).
Rowst, dom. Willelmus:
  Partridge Green, St Hugh's Charterhouse (liber iste pertinet L. quem — — attulit secum ad domum de Witham per licenciam rev. patris dom. Willelmi Tynbyth prioris *1520–29*).
Storour, Edmundus, monachus L. (*prior 1469–77; later prior of Hinton;* † *1502/3*):
  Blackburn, Public Libr., 091.21038 (per). Douai, Bibl. mun., 269 (per). Oxford, Bodleian, Bodl. 505 (per).
Whetham, Johannes, monachus L.:
  Cambridge, U.L., Ff.1.19 (scriptus per manus — — A.D. 1492). Untraced 'liber spiritualis gracie S. Matildis' (written by, A.D. 1513). *Cf.* SHEEN, Whetham.

LONDON, *Holy Trinity, Aldgate*
Pery, Johannes, canonicus L.:
  London, B.M., Add. 10053 (fieri fecit).

LONDON, *St Bartholomew*
Bolton, Willelmus, canonicus L.:
  London, B.M., Harley 631 (constat; *see also* Knytley).
Colyer, Reginaldus, prior L.:
  London, St Bartholomew's Hospital (liber).
Gray, dom. Ricardus, canonicus L.:
  Cambridge, U.L., P*.10.43 (pertinet ad).
*Knytley, mag. Walterus, cancellarius eccl. S. Pauli († *by May 1501*):
  London, B.M., Harley 631 (liber dom. Willelmi Bolton ex dono).

LONDON, *Fran. conv.*
*Bavard, fr. (1, mag.) Andreas, (2) custos librarie (*O.F.M., L.;* † *1508*):
  (1) London, Middle Temple. (2) Rome, Vatican Ottob. lat. 1565 (fecit ligari — — A.D. 1468 de communibus elemosinis prefate librarie collatis).
Kelle, fr. (1, pater) Ambrosius, (1, 2) O.F.M., cursor sacre theol. London', (2) sentenciarius:
  (1) Oxford, Bodleian, Bodl. 429 (emit fr. Thomas Man ... a — — A.D. 1514); (2) Douce 239 (libellus); Laud misc. 545 (name *in genitive;* *cf.* SIBTON, Crofftis).
Man, fr. Thomas, informator juvenum L., A.D. 1514 (*custos at Winchelsea in 1526*). *See* Kelle.
Orléans, Charles d'. See p. 123.
Umfrey, dom. Thomas, sacerdos ecclesie S. Pauli:
  London, Lambeth Pal., 33.

LONDON, *Fran. nuns*
Bassynburne, dame Anne. *See* Hasley.
Carneburgh, Beterice (*widow;* † *1501/2*):
  Wellington (N.Z.), Bible House (geven by — — unto Dame Grace Centurio ... and after her discesse to remayne unto what syster of the menres that it shall please the same Grace to gyf it).
Centurio, dame Grace. *See* Carneburgh.
French, dam An. *See* Porter.

Hasley, dame Margaret, lady and sister L. († *1462*):
  Untraced Pore Caitiff (I — — be the licence of my sovren geve this boke
    to the use of dame Anne Bassynburne sister of the same priory and
    after hir death to the use of the sisters and not to be geve nor lent
    without the place aforesaid).
Horwode, dame Elizabeth, abbas L.:
  London, B.M., Harley 2397 (bowȝt thys boke hyt to remayne to the use
    of þe systerrs).
Porter, dame Annes:
  Reigate Church, 2322 (gafe to dam An French Meneres wythe owte
    Algate of Lundun' þis boke to gyfe after hur deses wᵗ the licens of
    hur sufferen to hom þᵗ she wull).
Seint Nicolas, dame Christyne, of þe menoress of L. († *1455/56*):
  Cambridge, Trin. Coll., 301 (ȝeff þis boke aftyr hyr dysses).

LONDON, *Dom. conv.*
Beauchamp, fr. Johannes:
  London, B.M., Royal 5 C.vii (assignatus — —).
Picwurth, fr. Willelmus, O.P. *See* **CAMBRIDGE,** *Dom. conv.*, Picwurth.
Rokesle, Willelmus de, O.P., L.:
  London, B.M., Royal 3 E.vii (pledged in 1326 for the use of the convent).
*Swan, fr. Johannes, O.P.:
  London, B.M., Royal 9 B.x (concessus — — tempore sue studencie
    Oxonie).
*Tille, fr. Johannes, O.P. († *after 1428*):
  Cambridge, U.L., Add. 2991 (de perquisito — — quem dedit conventui
    London'); Corpus Christi Coll., 299 (de perquisito A.D. 1405); 306
    (mutuatus — —); Trin. Coll., 1154 (donum — — A.D. 1421). Oxford,
    Bodleian, Laud misc. 728 (de perquisito).
Wigornia, fr. Nicholaus de:
  London, B.M., Royal 12 G.vi (memoriale — — — in conventu fr. pre.
    Lond').

LONDON, *Carm. conv.*
*Bacona (Bakonesthorp), fr. Johannes de, D.Th., O.Carm. († *1348*):
  Oxford, Bodleian, Laud lat. 87 (*a* memoriale — — — quod reliquit
    conventui Londonie A.D. 1248 [*sic*]; *b* ex perquisito).
Lambert, fr. Johannes, O.Carm.:
  Cambridge, U.L., Ee.3.51 (scriptus per).
Savage, Willelmus, fr.:
  London, B.M., Royal 5 F.i.
Suttone, fr. Willelmus, cantor:
  London, B.M., Royal 7 B.v (ex assignacione).
*Walden, mag. Thomas, (3) provincialis Anglie († *1430*):
  Cambridge, St John's Coll., 221 (ex assignatione). Oxford, Bodleian,
    Bodl. 730 (ex assignatione); (3) Trin. Coll., 58 (ex assignatione).
Wicham, fr. Thomas, O.Carm.:
  London, B.M., Royal 2 D.xxxvi (liber — — conventui Londoniarum
    post decessum).
*Yvori, mag. fr. Robertus, (1, 3) provincialis (*1379–92*):
  (1) London, B.M., Harley 40; Royal 13 A.xviii, (3) 13 C.vii.

LONDON, *Aug. conv.*
Andrew, fr. Jacobus, O.H.S.A., L.:
  Glasgow, U.L., Dp.e.6 (A.D. 1521 pertinet; *cf.* Frere, Wiman).
Frere, fr. Willelmus, O.H.S.A., L.:
  Glasgow, U.L., Dp.e.6 (pertinet; *cf.* Andrew, Wiman).
*Gunwardby, mag. Henricus, O.H.S.A., L. (*s.xiv*):
  San Francisco, John Howell (liber — —).
*Lowe, fr. Johannes (*bishop of St Asaph 1433–44;* † *1467*):
  Dublin, Trin. Coll., 486 (pro nova libraria fr. Aug. Lond' per me — —
    Assaphensem episcopum 1436). London, B.M., Add. 34652 (pro
    nova libraria London' per me — —). Untraced Hugo (*as* Add.
    34652).
Tame, fr. Johannes, de ordine Aug., L. (*s.xiv ex.*):
  London, B.M., Royal 3 A.x (constat — — et impignoratur Henrico
    Ponsthorp).
Wiman (?), fr. Thomas, O.H.S.A.:
  Glasgow, U.L., Dp.e.6 (pertinet; *cf.* Andrew, Frere).

LONDON, *Crutched friars*
Gerard, mag. *See p. 125.*

LONDON, *Elsyng spital*
Dye, Johannes, reclusus, canonicus:
  Dublin, Trin. Coll., 436.   Oxford, Bodleian, e Mus. 113.

LONDON, *St Thomas of Acon*
Jacobus, comes Ormundiae (*1539–46*):
  London, B.M., Royal 13 C.xi, 14 C.xii, 15 C.xvi.
*Pyknam, mag. Willelmus, archidiaconus Norwic' [*sic*] (*archdeacon of
    Suffolk 1472–97*):
  London, B.M., Royal 3 A.ix, 3 E.x, xi, 4 C.vii, 7 D.v.

LONDON, *Whittington Coll.*
Nangle, mag., socius L.:
  Oxford, Bodleian, H.1.14 Art. Seld.

LONDON, *Guildhall*
Horn, Andreas, (2) piscenarius London' de Bryggestrete:
  (1) Cambridge, Corpus Christi Coll., 70 + 258 (*see p. 126*). (2) London,
    Corporation Records Office (restat — — quem fieri fecit A.D. 1311;
    see p. 127).
Martil, mag. Johannes:
  London, Guildhall Libr., 3042.

LOUTH PARK
Tornaco, Willelmus de, decanus Lincoln' (*resigned 1239;* † *1258*):
  Lincoln, Cath., 47.

LYNN
Palmer, Johannes, prior L.:
  Cambridge, Gonv. and Caius Coll., 136 (constat cum magno gaudeo et
    honore).

LYNN, *Fran. conv.*
Phillip, fr. Nicholaus, de custodia Cantebr' et conventus L.:
  Oxford, Bodleian, Lat. th. d.1 (liber; *cf.* **BABWELL**, Goddard).

LYNN, *Carm. conv.*
Walton, fr. Robertus, O.Carm., L.:
Oxford, Bodleian, Ashmole 1398 (constat — — ex dono et consessione fr. Rogeri Roo).

MAIDSTONE
Halle, Willelmus:
London, Wellcome Hist. Med. Mus. (constat — — et postea datus per).

MALLING
Hull, Elizabeth, abbess M.:
Blackburn, Publ. Libr., 091.21040 (bequeathed to her godchild, Margaret, baptized 1520).

MALMESBURY
Athelwerd (? *A, abbot of Malmesbury*):
Cambridge, Corpus Christi Coll., 23.
Grandison, dom. *Johannes*, Exon' episcopus:
Cambridge, Trin. Coll., 727 (recepit mutuo ab abbate M., A.D. 1332, prima die Julii et restituit eundem priori de Pyltona anno sequenti prima die Maii).
Ricardus (*s.xii in.*):
Cambridge, Trin. Coll., 1301, art. 1 (scripsit).
Salamon (*scriptor, fl. 1193: cf. Reg. Malm. (Rolls Series), i. 461*):
Oxford, Bodleian, Barlow 6 (Explicit Policraticus per Salamonem sub abbate Roberto II *at end in the hand of the text*).
Swyneshead, Roger, monk of Glastonbury. See p. 128, n. 1.
William of Malmesbury. See p. 128, n. 9.
[. . . . . . *donor's name illegible*]:
London, B.M., Cotton Cleop. B.iii, fos 2–35 (ut ejus memoria inter monachos ibidem imperpetuum habeatur).

MALVERN
Powycke, fr. Thomas, monachus M. *See* **WORCESTER,** Straynsham.

MANCHESTER
*La Warre, mag. Thomas (*founder; † *1427*):
San Marino, Huntington, HM 26560 (g.).

MARLBOROUGH
Bastabyll, Willelmus:
Untraced pr. bk (contulit A.D. 1502).

MARRICK
Radcliffe, dame Agnes:
New York, Publ. Libr., Spencer 19 (giffen . . . by).

MEAUX
Dapton, fr. Johannes, monachus M.:
Wolfenbüttel, Herzog-August-Bibl., 4447 (adquisivit monasterio M. — — de Johanne Lowdip de Daynton A.D. 1484).
Wilflete (? **William W.,** *master of Clare Hall 1446–55*):
Oxford, Bodleian, Digby 77 (wishes that this and another book, both of which he bought from a monk of M., should go to M. 'quia dubitat utrum monachus habuit potestatem vendendi').

MEDMENHAM
Brangwen, dom. Ricardus, abbas M.:
Oxford, All Souls Coll., SR.68.g.10 (emptus per, A.D. 1525).

MEREVALE
Brantyngthorp, fr. Edmundus de (*s.xiv*):
Cambridge, U.L., Add. 3097 (ex collacione). London, B.M., Add.
31826 (ex collacione); Harley 324 (per).

MERTON
*Aishedecim (*Ashcombe*), mag. Robertus:
London, B.M., Add. 45568 (ex donatione A.D. 1528).
*Gisborne, dom. Johannes, (1) canonicus M. et scolaris Oxon' († *1502*):
(1) Oxford, Bodleian, Ashmole 1522 (traditus —— per mag. Johannem
Kyngeston priorem de M., A.D. 1456); Digby 147 (name).
Hawarde, dom. Edmundus, filius et frater illustrium ducum Norfolchie:
Oxford, St John's Coll., c.3.5.
*Kyngeston, mag. Johannes, prior M. († *1485*). *See* Gisborne.
Lacy, Johannes (*prior M. 1520–30*):
Oxford, St John's Coll., K.3.9 (liber).
Londoniensis, mag. David (*s.xii/xiii*):
London, B.M., Royal 9 E.xii.
Ramsey, Johannes, canonicus M. (*prior 1530–38*):
Ampleforth Abbey, C.v.23a (possidet). Glasgow, U.L., Eg.6.a.9
(possidet). London, Lambeth Pal., **H890.B6, B7 (liber); Soc. of
Antiquaries, 47 (possidet). Oxford, Bodleian, 4º Z.33 Th. (liber b.
Marie Merton, possessor Ramsey); Seld. supra 39 (possidet); St John's
Coll., Φ.1.32 (per —— priorem M., A.D. 1537).
Saundwyche, dom. Johannes, canonicus M.:
Shrewsbury School, A.x.15 (emebat de Thomas Twhyng, anno 10
Henrici VIII).
Willelmus, dom., prior M.:
London, B.M., Royal 4 A.xiv (Excerpta ——).
Wykes (*s.xvi in.*):
London, Lambeth Pal., 118 (donatus per executores suos).

MISSENDEN
*Burnham, Alardus de, decanus London' († *1216*):
Oxford, Bodleian, Bodl. 729.
*Hamlamstede, mag. Aluredus de (*c.1200*):
Oxford, Bodleian, Auct. D.1.10.

MONK BRETTON
Multon, Thomas, confrater M.:
Oxford, Univ. Coll., 101 (acquisitus et emptus per).

MOTTENDEN
Berton, dom. Willelmus, de Whytyngton Collage, London:
Cambridge, Corpus Christi Coll., E.P.D.Par.4 (ex dono —— A.D. 1488).
Bolton, fr. Robertus. *See* Lansyng.
Bukherst, quondam fr. M.:
Oxford, Bodleian, Auct. D.2.20 (bought by John Armorer, rector of
Sutton Valence and Headcorn, from —).

Lansyng, fr. Ricardus, (2) domus de Motynden:
  Oxford, Bodleian, Bodl. 643 (emptus per, A.D. 1467). (2) Richmond
    (U.S.A.), Virginia State Libr., 1 (constat — — ex dono fr. Roberti
    Bolton mag. domus de [. . . .]).

MOTTISFONT
Vitriaco, mag. Albericus de (*s.xiii*):
  Oxford, Bodleian, Rawl. G.183–84 (contulit).

MOUNT GRACE
Awne, John, monachus († *1472/73*):
  Ripon, Mr H. L. Bradfer-Lawrence (scripsit).
Fleycher, dom. Robertus. *See* Norton.
Methley, Richard, monk of M.:
  Cambridge, Trin. Coll., 1160 (*probably autograph, A.D. 1487*).
Norton, Johannes, prior M.:
  Oxford, Bodleian, Antiq. d.F.1512.1 (datus dom. Roberto Fleycher a
    devoto ac venerabili — — qui fuit xxiii ʒere [*canc.*] annis procurator
    et tresdecim prior Montisgracie . . .).
Scasby, Thomas, one of the parsons of the College of seynte William
    within the close of Yorke:
  Oxford, Bodleian, AA.61 Th. Seld.

MUCHELNEY
*Cory, dom. Thomas, monachus M.:
  Oxford, Magd. Coll., 182 (wrote part in 1440 and 1459).
Coscumbe, dom. Ricardus, prior M.:
  Oxford, Bodleian, Ashmole 189 (possessor).

NEWARK, Surrey
Grave, Johannes, prior N. *See* Rosse.
Hugo, capellanus dom. Winter:
  Oxford, Bodleian, Auct. D.inf.2.10 (memoriale — pro uno psalterio
    glosato).
Lyght, Johannes, canonicus N.:
  Oxford, Bodleian, Laud lat. 15 (prayers asked for soul of his mother).
Rosse, dom. Johannes, canonicus N., (2) curatus de Weyld juxta
    Alresford novam:
  Oxford, Bodleian, Bodl. 602 (*a* habuit ex deliberacione confr. nostri
    dom. Willelmi Thecher canonici de N., 6 Oct., A.D. 1538, hiis
    testibus . . .; *b* pertinet); (2) Keble Coll., A.62 (*a* Ego Johannes Grave
    prior de N. dedi confr. nostro — —, 3 Oct., A.D. 1538, hiis testibus
    . . .; *b* pertinet).
Thecher, dom. Willelmus. *See* Rosse.

NEWBATTLE
Herculus, dom. Henricus et dom. Jacobus, de Linlithgow:
  Untraced MS.
Scot, dom. Alexander, monachus N.:
  Edinburgh, N.L., Adv. 18.4.1 (Expliciunt . . . per manum — — A.D. 1523).

NEWCASTLE, *Carm. conv.*
[. . .], fr. Willelmus, O.Carm., N. (*place-name canc. and* nunc vero Coven-
    trie *substituted*):
  Oxford, Merton Coll., B.8.G.17 (pertinet ad; *see also* **WORCESTER**).

NEWCASTLE, *Reclusory*
Lacy, fr. Johannes, O.P., reclusus N.:
  Oxford, Bodleian, Rawl. C.258 (constat).

NEWNHAM
**Bedeford, Willelmus, canonicus N. (*sub-prior c.1432*):
  Cambridge, Pembr. Coll., 143 (caucio).   London, B.M., Royal 5 B.xi
  (emebat de mag. Roberto Ware executore mag. Johannis Bryan
  tempore quo studebat Cantebr', A.D. 1415).
Henricus, dom., prior N.:
  Copenhagen, Royal Libr. (pertinet A.D. 1496).   Oxford, Univ. Coll.,
  181 (pertinet — ex dono dom. Johannis Renhall predesessoris sui,
  A.D. 1490).
Renhall.   *See* Henricus.

NEWSTEAD, Nottinghamshire
Gunthorpe, Thomas, de N. (*prior 1476–1504*):
  Oxford, Bodleian, Auct. D.3.6 (constat).
Lard', mag. Gaufredus de:
  Oxford, Bodleian, Laud misc. 428 (*cf. p. 134, n. 7*).

NORTHAMPTON
Forde, dom. Willelmus:
  Oxford, Oriel Coll., 53 (isti viii quaterni dantur N. ad orandum pro
  anima — —).

NORTHAMPTON, *Dom. conv.*
Coventri (?), fr. Willelmus, prior.   *See* Gunthorpe.
**Gunthorpe, Johannes, decanus eccl. Wellensis († *1498*):
  London, Sion Coll., Arc.L.40.2/L.21 (Memorandum quod ego — —
  solvi fr. Willelmo Coventri (?) priori fr. pred. de N. 28 Maii A.D. 1484
  in domo mansionis mee apud Westm'; in toto solvi xx s. pro quinque
  parvis voluminibus isto computato).

NORWICH
Aldeby, fr. Adam de, monachus:
  Norwich, Castle Mus., 99.20 (liber).
Attleborough, dom. Johannes, monachus N. (*pitancer 1491–92*):
  Durham, U.L., Cosin V.ii.12 (in custodia).
Audruynus, dom.:
  Cambridge, U.L., Ii.3.32 (quam emit — antequam esset Parisius).
Bliclinge, Rogerus de, monachus:
  Cambridge, U.L., Ii.4.12 (g.).
Botone, Rogerus de, monachus:
  Cambridge, U.L., Kk.2.13 (g.).
Bozoun, fr. Simon, prior N. (*1344–52*):
  Cambridge, Corpus Christi Coll., 264 (liber); 407 (liber).   London.
  B.M., Royal 14 C.xiii (liber).   Oxford, Bodleian, Fairfax 20 (liber),
Cantebrigge, fr. N. de:
  Cambridge, U.L., Ii.1.18 (scripsit).
Caustone, Johannes de, monachus:
  Oxford, Magd. Coll., 180 (g.).
Chaumpneys, fr. Johannes (*monk N. c.1440*):
  Cambridge, U.L., Ii.3.31.

Donewico, fr. Robertus de (*magister celarii 1335–41, chamberlain 1341–44*):
  Cambridge, U.L., Kk.2.21 (liber).
Elingham, fr. Johannes (? *J. E., sacrist 1439*):
  Oxford, Bodleian, Bodl. 787.
Elingham, Radulfus de (*cellarer 1279*):
  Untraced Bible (g.).
Elmham, fr. Simon de, monachus:
  Cambridge, U.L., Ff.5.28 (*a* emit; *b* g.).
Elsyngge, fr. Thomas de, monachus N. (*sacrist 1393–95*):
  Cambridge, U.L., Kk.3.25 (liber).
*Eston, mag. Adam de, monachus N. († *1397*):
  Avignon, Bibl. de la ville, 996 (per).   Cambridge, Corpus Christi Coll.,
    74 (per); 180 (liber).   Oxford, Bodleian, Bodl. 151 ʹper).
Felningham, mag. Ricardus de:
  Oxford, Bodleian, Auct. D.4.8 (g.).
*Folsham, fr. Johannes, monachus N. (*s.xv*) (? *J. F., fl. c.1440*):
  Cambridge, U.L., Ii.3.22.
Fretenham, Radulphus de, monachus (*magister celarii 1273–74*):
  Cambridge, U.L., Kk.4.20 (g.).   London, B.M., Add. 30079 (g.).
  Norwich, Cath., Barth. Cotton (g.; *wrote*).
**Gressenhale, mag. Reginaldus de († *by Jan. 1292*):
  Cambridge, U.L., Ii.2.14 (g.).
Hengham, Thomas, monachus N. (? *T. H., fl. 1447*):
  Cambridge, U.L., Ii.3.10 (liber).   Edinburgh, N.L., 6125 (liber).
*Hoo, dom. Johannes, monachus N. (*prior of Yarmouth 1387*):
  Cambridge, U.L., Kk.2.15 (tradatur); Mm.3.16 (libri).
Hyndringham, fr. Thomas de, monachus N. (*almoner 1417*):
  Cambridge, U.L., Kk.2.20 (liber).
Jernemuth, dom. Robertus de, monachus N.:
  London, Messrs Maggs (per).   Norwich, Cath., Boccaccio (per).
  Oxford, Bodleian, Can. misc. 110.
Lake(n)ham, Henricus de, prior N. (*1289–1309*):
  Cambridge, U.L., Ii.1.32 (g.), Ii.4.2 (g.), Ii.4.15 (g.), Ii.4.35 (g.).
**Langrak, Henricus, monachus (*s.xv ex.*):
  Cambridge, U.L., Ii.1.30 (*a* Nicholaus Porter possessor libri. ʻRecepit
    pro isto libro 3 s. 4 d. per manus mei —— hunc librum denariis
    acquirentis ecclesie cath. N.ʹ; *b* name *in genitive*).
Lok, fr. R. de:
  Cambridge, Corpus Christi Coll., 465 (g.).
*Molett, Johannes, (1) prior N. (*1453–71*):
  (1) Cambridge, U.L., Ii.3.29; Ii.4.37 (possessio fr. —— ... mediante
    peccunia).
Morton, Thomas, monachus N.:
  Oxford, Bodleian, Vet. E.1.f.134 (name).
Ormesby, fr. Robertus de, monachus N.:
  Oxford, Bodleian, Douce 366 (Psalterium ——— per eundem assig-
    natum choro ecclesie ... ad jacendum coram suppriore qui pro
    tempore fuerit).
Ormesby, dom. Willelmus de, rector s. Marie de Marisco (*s.xiv*):
  Cambridge, U.L., Kk.4.3.
Plumpstede, Thomas de, monachus:
  Oxford, Magd. Coll., 53 (g.).

Reynham, fr. Johannes de, monachus N.:
  Cambridge, Corpus Christi Coll., 252 (liber — — — quem ipse in parte scripsit et in parte scribi fecit).
Rothewell, Robertus de, monachus:
  Cambridge, U.L., Ii.1.22 (g.).
Silton, fr. Willelmus, monachus N. (*sacrist 1418*):
  Cambridge, U.L., Ii.1.31 (liber), Ii.2.27 (liber).
Smalbergh, Galfridus de, monachus:
  London, B.M., Cotton Nero C.v (g.).
*Sproustone, Alexander de, monachus (*scholar at Oxford 1309–10*):
  Cambridge, U.L., Kk.4.11 (g.).
**Spynk, fr. Willelmus, monachus N. (*prior 1488–1502*):
  Manchester, J. Rylands, R.32528 (liber).
Steward, mag. Johannes, rector de Marisco:
  Cambridge, U.L., Ii.3.24 (attulit A.D. 1495).
*Stowe, Johannes, monachus *N.* (*fl. 1447*):
  Cambridge, Emm. Coll., 142 (liber).
Stratton, Johannes de, senior:
  Cambridge, Corpus Christi Coll., 325 (g.).
*Swafham, Herveus de (*fl. 1300*):
  Cambridge, U.L., Kk.4.12 (g.).
Walsham, fr. Ricardus, monachus N. (? *R. W.*, *sacrist 1444*):
  Cambridge, U.L., Ll.5.21 (liber).
Wroxham, Galfridus de, monachus:
  Cambridge, Trin. Coll., 883 (g.).
[. . . .], fr. Thomas, monachus (*s.xv/xvi*):
  Cambridge, U.L., Gg.1.33 (in custodia).

NORWICH, *Fran. conv.*
Berewyk, fr. Herveus de. *See* Johannes.
Johannes, mag., vicarius de Elmham (*s.xiii*):
  London, B.M., Harley 1034 (contulit — sed usus concessus est fr. Herveo de Berewyk).

NORWICH, *Dom. conv.*
Doggett, fr. Johannes, conventus N., (2) O.P.:
  Cambridge, U.L., Inc. 755 (pertinet ad). (2) Oxford, Hertford Coll., a.1.27 (possessor).
Yngworth, Ricardus, conventus N.:
  London, Middle Temple (name; *cf.* **KING'S LANGLEY,** Yngworth).

NORWICH, *Carm. conv.*
Bale, Johannes, O.Carm., N. (*B.D. Cambridge, 1528–29*; † *1563*):
  Cambridge, U.L., Ff.6.28 (possidet — — studens philosophice facultatis in alma universitate Cantabrigiensis). Oxford, Bodleian, Seld. supra 41 (*wrote c. 1528 and later*).
Cake, Ricardus (*rector of Bradfield 1503–12*). *See* Waterpytte.
*Waterpytte, doctor *Thomas* (*prior c.1486–91*):
  London, B.M., Harley 211 (— dedit Ricardo Cake).

NORWICH, *Hospital of St Giles*
Pecoc, mag. Petrus:
  London, B.M., Royal 9 E.ii.

NOTLEY
Brehyll, dom. Johannes, [. . .], de N.:
  London, Lambeth Pal., 344 (constat).
Fyschere, Johannes:
  Oxford, Bodleian, Douce 383 (fecit fieri et dedit).

NOTTINGHAM, *Fran. conv.*
Ryppon, fr. Thomas, O.F.M., *N. in 1539*:
  London, Dr Williams's Libr., Anc. 1 (concedo dom. rectori de Berton pro
  termino vite sue A.D. 1539).

NUNCOTON
Hyltoft, dame Joan. *See* Wade.
Wade, dame Mald, priorys of Swyne (*resigned 1482*):
  London, B.M., Harley 2409 (— — has gyven this boke to dame Joan
  Hyltoft in N.).

NUNEATON
Scheynton, Alicia:
  Cambridge, Fitzwilliam Mus., McClean 123 (constat — — et postea
  conventu; *cf.* Sylemon).
Sylemon, domina Margareta (*prioress N. 1367–86*):
  Cambridge, Fitzwilliam Mus., McClean 123 (constat — — et discipulas
  suas, et post mortem suam coventu de N.).

OSNEY
*Abbendune, Ricardus de:
  Oxford, Magd. Coll., 123.
Bloore, Radulphus, quondam canonicus O.:
  Oxford, Bodleian, Auct. F.6.4 (liber Thomæ Corsæri presbiteri ex
  dono — —, A.D. 1543).
Hokenorton, dom. Thomas, abbas (*1430–52*):
  Cambridge, Trin. Coll., 952 (emit). Oxford, Bodleian, Rawl. C.273
  (ex procuracione).
Holbeche, fr. Johannes, quondam prior O.:
  Oxford, St John's Coll., 109 (emit).
*Langeleia, mag. Henricus de (*probably † by Aug. 1263*):
  Oxford, Bodleian, Digby 23 (ex legato).
Sancto Martino(?), Willelmus de, capellanus (*s.xiii*):
  Oxford, Magd. Coll., 130.
Water, dom., canonicus O.:
  Cambridge, U.L., Ii.6.1 (possessor; *cf.* Zurke).
Wrthe, Ricardus de, canonicus noster:
  Oxford, Bodleian, Bodl. 477.
Zurke, Hermann, de Gripiswaldis:
  Cambridge, U.L., Ii.6.1 (wrote in 1449).

OTTERY ST MARY
Exceter, John, canon of O. 1436. See p. 141.
Murus, Johannes, olim sacrista O.:
  Berlin, Staatsbibl., lat. qu. 515 (— — me possidet).
*Silke, Willelmus (*canon of O., precentor of Exeter 1499–1508*):
  Cambridge, Corpus Christi Coll., 93 (monogram; *identifiable with the
  ordinal according to Bishop Grandison's use bequeathed by Silke to
  O. by will* (P.C.C., 35 Adeane) A.D. 1508).

OXFORD, *St Frideswide*
A., fr., subdiaconus O.:
    Paris, B.N., Fr. 24766 (*a* complevi — anno 1212 anno conversionis mee septimo (fo. 151); *b* complevi conversionis mee anno nono (fo. 174); *author's autograph* ?).

OXFORD, *Fran. conv.*
Bryngkeley, fr. Ricardus, mag.:
    Cambridge, Gonv. and Caius Coll., 403 (concessus et accomodatus).
*Colman, R.:
    Cambridge, Corpus Christi Coll., 315 (fecit ligari 1419).
*Dadynton, fr. Symon, de custodia O.:
    London, Mr E. M. Dring, A.34 (contulit).
*Dedwyth, T*homas, O.F.M., O. in 1475*:
    Oxford, Bodleian, Bodl. 703 (Nota . . . quod — *in margin, fo. 39*).[6]
*Fey, fr. J., de Florentia, O.F.M.:
    Florence, Laurenziana, Plut. xvii sin. cod. x (scripta per me — — in conventu O. A.D. 1393).
*Gascoigne, Thomas († *1458*):
    Oxford, Bodleian, Bodl. 198 (a gift to — — from the Oxford conv.).
**Grosseteste, Robert,* († *1253*):
    Oxford, Bodleian, Bodl. 198; Trin. Coll., 17 (*both contain his annotations and are presumably of his gift*).
*Maidstone, fr. Radulfus *de*, quondam episcopus Hereford' († *1243*):
    London, B.M., Harley 3249.
Notingham, dom. Hugo de:
    Oxford, Merton Coll., 158, 166, 168–72 (*in 168 and, similarly, in other vols*, prayers asked 'pro anima — — — per quem quoad omnia exhibite sunt expense et eciam pro anima fr. Willelmi de eadem per cujus tediosam sollicitudinem quia dum actu Oxonie regens erat taliter erant scripte').
*Notingham, fr. Rogerus de, S.T.D., *O.F.M., O.* (*1343–58*):
    Oxford, Bodleian, Digby 93, fos 1–8 (quaternus fr. Thome Ruvel (?) per).
*Notingham, fr. Willelmus de († *1336* ?). *See* Notingham, Hugo de.
Ruvel (?), fr. Thomas. *See* Notingham, Rogerus de.
*Salfford, *Richard* (*warden 1488–89*):
    Hereford, Cath., P.i.9 (pertinet conventui fr. [. . .] Oxonie quod —).
*Teukesbury, fr. Johannes de:
    Manchester, Chetham 6681 (liber; *wrote*). Oxford, Bodleian, Digby 90 (contulit A.D. 1388; *wrote*).
*Vavysur, fr. Willelmus, O.F.M., O. (*warden c.1500*):
    Oxford, Corpus Christi Coll., 227 (scripte per manum — — anno dominice incarnacionis 1491); 228 (quod — — A.D. 1490). *Cf. p. 142, n. 4.*

OXFORD, *Dom. conv.*
*Courteys, fr. Johannes, O.P., O., regens universitatis O.:
    Cambridge, Trin. Coll., 347 (*a* finitus per manus Cornelii Oesterwic A.D. 1430 in universitate Oxon' ad mandatum — —; *b* liber).
*Oesterwic, Cornelius. *See* Courteys.

---

[6] Information from Mr R. J. A. I. Catto.

OXFORD, *Carm. conv.*
*Glowcester, fr. Thomas, O.Carm. (*fl. 1463*):
    Copenhagen, Royal Libr., G.K.S. 1653, 4° (name).
*Hunt, fr. Walterus, doctor († *1478*):
    Cambridge, U.L., Ff.4.31 (Memoriale — — conventui Carm. O.; *cf.*
      More).
More, W.:
    Cambridge, U.L., Ff.4.31 (scripte per manum; *cf.* Hunt).

OXFORD, *Aug. conv.*
*Lowe, fr. Johannes, archidiaconus Roffensis:
    Cambridge, U.L., Ii.2.30 (ex dono — — 1466); Ii.3.14.
Soppethe, fr. Eduardus, O.S.A. (*supplicated for B.D., Oxford, 21 Apr.*
    1527):
    Stonyhurst Coll., 1.22 (usum habuit — — A.D. 1528).

OXFORD, *University*
*Alwort, mag. Johannes, quondam rector de Stoke Bru*ern* (*1420–57*):
    Oxford, St John's Coll., 172.
**Humfrey, duke of Gloucester* († *1447*). *See p. 143.*
*Kymer, Gilbertus († *1463*):
    Oxford, Bodleian, Bodl. 362, Laud misc. 558; Merton Coll., 268 (*all*
      written for — — by Hermann Zurke of Greifswald *and presumably*
      given by).
Zurke, Hermannus de Gripeswaldis. *See* Kymer.

OXFORD, *All Souls Coll.*
*Andrew, Ricardus, custos coll. A. S.:
    Antwerp, Plantin-Moretus, 144. Winchester Coll., 60A.
*Bartlett, Ricardus, M.D., quondam socius († *1557*):
    Oxford, Pembr. Coll., 2.
*Bygonell, mag. Willelmus († *1448*):
    Oxford, Bodleian, Bodl. 741–42 (ex dono — — post mortem mag.
      Byr*khed* († *1468*); *see p. 144*).
*Goldwell, Jacobus, episcopus (2, nuper episcopus) Norwic' († *1499*):
    Oxford, Bodleian, Auct. 1.Q.3.1; (2) Rawl. G.47. Tokyo, U.L.,
      A.100.1300.
*Romesey, Willelmus (*fellow of Merton;* † *1501*):
    London, B.M., Sloane 280 (fecit scribi; *presumed donor*).
*Saundyr, mag. Johannes, socius († *1495*):
    Oxford, Bodleian, Digby 44.
*Warham, rev. pater dom. Willelmus, archiepiscopus Cant' († *1532*):
    Antwerp, Plantin-Moretus 107. Glasgow, U.L., Bi.4.g.20.

OXFORD, *Balliol Coll.*
*Appilby, mag. Willelmus, vicarius (*fellow 1463;* † *by Apr. 1498*):
    Antwerp, Plantin-Moretus 57.
*Cok, mag. Robertus (*cf. B.R.U.O., pp. 455, 481*):
    Oxford, Bodleian, Auct. 7.Q.2.29 (bequeathed to Master Thomas
      Cysson with reversion to Balliol after his death).
*Cysson, mag. Thomas (*master 1512–18*). *See* Cok.

*Gray, dom. Willelmus, episcopus Eliensis († *1478*):
    Antwerp, Plantin-Moretus 52, 77. Brussels, Bibl. royale, 1557.
    Cambridge, U.L., Dd.13.2, Ff.4.11, Kk.4.2 (arms; *presumed donor*).
    Douai, Bibl. mun., 750. London, B.M., Royal 7 F.xii; Lambeth
    Pal., 759. Oxford, Bodleian, Laud misc. 209.
*Neville, George, archbishop of York († *1476*):
    Oxford, Bodleian, Bodl. 753 (arms; *presumed donor*).
*Norman, mag. Robertus, quondam socius (*1452*):
    Cambridge, U.L., Ii.2.10 (legavit).
*Populton, mag. Adam, socius († *by Aug. 1403*):
    Antwerp, Plantin-Moretus 131 (legavit).
*Saxton, mag. W*illelmus* († *by May 1424*):
    Antwerp, Plantin-Moretus 106 (legavit).
*Stapulton, mag. Ricardus (*fellow 1411*):
    Oxford, Bodleian, Digby 29.
*Thwaites, mag. Robertus, quondam magister ac decanus Aukland
    († *1458*):
    Oxford, Bodleian, Bodl. 252 (ex legato et dono).
Werken, Theodericus (2) Nycolai, (2) de Abbenbroeck:[7]
    Brussels, Bibl. royale, 1557 (wrote A.D. 1453). (2) Cambridge, U.L.,
    Dd.13.2 (per manus — — A.D. 1444).

OXFORD, *Brasenose Coll.*
*Hafter, mag. Johannes († *by Apr. 1511*):
    St Albans School, Y.4.
*Smith, rev. pat. dom. Willelmus, fundator (*bishop of Lincoln 1496–1514*):
    London, B.M., Royal 7 E.ii.

OXFORD, *Canterbury Coll.*
Bockyng, Edward (*monk of Canterbury;* † *1534*):
    Cambridge, Trin. Coll., 61 (name *and* collegium Cantuariense).
*Cranebroke, Henry, scholar 1443:
    Oxford, Bodleian, Selden supra 65 (*wrote a table in*). *See also* **CANTER-
    BURY,** *Christ Church.*
*Graunt, mag. Thomas:
    London, B.M., Add. 22572.

OXFORD, *Corpus Christi Coll.*
*Claymond, dom. *Johannes*, primus preses coll. C.:
    London, B.M., IA.17393.

OXFORD, *Exeter Coll.*
*Babbe, mag. Jacobus († *1492*):
    Oxford, Bodleian, Bodl. 42 (ex legacione).
*David, *Thomas* (*fellow 1507–13*):
    Oxford, Bodleian, Auct. D.4.9 (de eleccione — A.D. 1511).
*Dygon, Johannes, presbiter et reclusus de Bethlehem de Shene (*admitted
    1435*):
    Oxford, St John's Coll., 77 (gave jointly with Joan, anchoress of St
    Botolph's without Bishopsgate, London).
*Rede, Willelmus, episcopus Cicestrensis († *1385*):
    Douai, Bibl. mun., 860.

    [7] R. A. B. Mynors, 'A fifteenth-century Scribe: T. Werken', *Trans. Cambr.
Bibl. Soc.*, i. 97–104.

OXFORD, *Gloucester Coll.*
Langley, Ricardus, scolasticus in coll. G. (*s.xvi in.*):
    Oxford, Mr D. Rogers (ex empcione).
*Whethamstede, ven. pat. Johannes, olim abbas S. Albani († *1465*):
    London, B.M., Royal 8 G.x (assignavit). Oxford, Bodleian, Auct.
    F.inf.1.1 (assignavit); Worc. Coll., LRA 6.

OXFORD, *Lincoln Coll.*
*Gascoigne, doctor Thomas (*fellow*; † *1458*):
    London, B.M., Cotton Otho A.xiv (*annotations by*); Royal 10 A.xv.
    Oxford, Bodleian, Bodl. 198.
*Kendal, mag. Johannes:
    Oxford, Bodleian, Rawl. G.14.
*Southam, mag. Johannes, archidiaconus Oxon' († *1441*):
    Cambridge, Trin. Coll., 303.

OXFORD, *Magdalen Coll.*
*Lagharun, mag. Ricardus, quondam socius († *1494 or 1495*):
    London, B.M., Royal 6 E.iii.
Stanbrig, mag. Thomas, quondam socius, qui obiit A.D. 1522:
    Oxford, Bodleian, H.3.3–7 Th.

OXFORD, *Merton Coll.*
*Abyndon, mag. Henricus, custos coll. M. († *1437*):
    Oxford, Linc. Coll., 62.
*Balsalle, mag. Thomas, quondam socius coll. M. († *by Mar. 1492*):
    Oxford, Bodleian, Bodl. 696.
*Burbache, mag. Johannes, D.Th., quondam socius († *by Dec. 1451*):
    Oxford, Bodleian, Digby 155.
*Camsel, mag. Ricardus de (*fl. 1325*):
    London, B.M., Royal 12 E.xxv (*ex* legato).
*English, mag. Thomas († *by Sept. 1488*):
    Oxford, Bodleian, Bodl. 50 (do et lego . . . post decessum meum).
*Felowys, mag. Willelmus, quondam magister gramatice *at Evesham*
    († *1483*):
    Oxford, Bodleian, Bodl. 688.
*Fitzjames, Ricardus, nuper episcopus Cicestrensis et custos coll. M.
    († *1522*):
    Oxford, Bodleian, Bodl. 700, 751.
*Flowr, *Augustine* (*fellow M.*; † *1509*):
    Oxford, Bodleian, Bodl. 52 (6 Flowr, A.D. 1504, *i.e. the sixth book of his
    'sors'*); Digby 19 (19 Flowr).
*Giddyng, mag. Ricardus, quondam socius (*fl. 1288*):
    Oxford, Corpus Christi Coll., 489.
*Harington, mag. Willelmus de († *by Aug. 1349*):
    Oxford, Bodleian, Bodl. 752 (ex dono et legato).
Hyll, *Richard* (*fellow M.*):
    Dublin, Trin. Coll., 517 (11us de sorte —). Oxford, Bodleian, Bodl. 52
    (10 de sorte —).
*Johnson, *John* (*fellow M. 1504–10*):
    Dublin, Trin. Coll., 517 (29us de sorte —).
*Malmesfeld, mag. Henricus de († *1328*):
    Oxford, Ball. Coll., 211 (ex legato).

*Marshall, mag. Johannes, T. D. († *1496*):
    Oxford, Bodleian, Bodl. 4 (*recorded as his gift*).
*Maynsforth, Johannes, quondam socius et subdecanus eccl. cath.
    Cicestrensis († *1488* ?):
    Oxford, Bodleian, Bodl. 52 (legatur per).
*Raynham (Reynham), mag. Johannes, S.T.P., quondam socius († *by
    Nov. 1376*):
    Dublin, Trin. Coll., 517 (ex legato).   Oxford, Bodleian, Digby 67 (de
    legato).
*Reed, mag. Willelmus, episcopus Cicestrensis († *1385*):
    Oxford, Bodleian, Digby 19 (*presumed gift of*), 61, 176 (liber scolarium
    de genere — — ex dono — —), 216 (*presumed gift of*); e Mus. 19.
*Sever, mag. Henricus:
    Oxford, Bodleian, Bodl. 689 (ex dono A.D. 1468), 757 (ex dono
    A.D. 1468).
*Stanton, mag. Walterus (*fellow, living 1401–2*):
    London, B.M., Royal 12 B.iii (ex legato).

OXFORD, *New Coll.*
*Andrew, Ricardus, decanus Ebor', quondam socius coll. N. († *1477*):
    Oxford, Bodleian, Bodl. 310, 809 (*both* dedi). Winchester Coll.,
    12 (dedi).
*Elyot, mag. Willelmus clericus, magister Domus Dei de Portsmouth
    († *by Oct. 1494*):
    Oxford, Exeter Coll., 29.
Jolypace, dom. Henricus, nuper camerarius eccl. Cath. S. Pauli Londonie:
    Oxford, Bodleian, Auct. F.5.29 (datus per exsecutores A.D. 1431).
Wykeham, William, bishop of Winchester, founder:
    Oxford, Bodleian, Bodl. 238 (*recorded as his gift*).

OXFORD, *Oriel Coll.*
*Cobuldik, mag. Johannes († *by May 1337*):
    Oxford, Bodleian, Auct. F.5.28, fos ii–xlii, 1–144, 226–27 (per — —
    A.D. 1337 et non accomodetur extra domum nisi consanguineis
    predicti magistri Johannis sub racionali caucione).
*Dalton, Willelmus de († *1371*):
    Oxford, St John's Coll., 112 (. . . . — — —; *recorded as his gift*).
*Daunay, mag. Rogerus (*M.A. by 1349*):
    Bern, Stadtbibl., 69 (tradatur per).
*Gascoigne, Thomas, Ebor' diocesis, S.P.D. († *1458*):
    Oxford, Linc. Coll., 33.
*Stephyn, mag. Rogerus, quondam socius coll. O. († *1484 or 1485*):
    London, B.M., Sloane 3884, fo. 70.
*Trikyngham, mag. Elias de (*fellow of O.*; † *by 1361*):
    London, Lambeth Pal., 1106 (per).   Oxford, Bodleian, Auct. F.5.28,
    fos 145–225 (per); Digby 37 (per).
Tumensis (?), Thomas (*s.xv ex.*):
    London, Sion Coll., Arc.L.40.2/L.21 (liber — — ex dono executorum
    mag. Johannis Gunthorpe (*cf.* **NORTHAMPTON,** *Dom. conv.*) quem
    dictus Thomas contulit coll. O.).

OXFORD, *Queen's Coll.*
*Fraunce, mag. Hugo (*fellow by 1461–62*):
    London, B.M., Royal 8 A.xiii.

OXFORD, *St Edmund Hall*
Henricus octavus:
   Oxford, Bodleian, Rawl. C.900 (*see p. 149*).

OXFORD, *Staple Hall*
*Fowrman (Forman), mag. Johannes, vicarius de Ruschton, Ebor' dioc.:
   Oxford, Bodleian, Ashmole 748 (contulit A.D. 1499).

PERSHORE
Anselmus, abbas (? *A., abbot of P. 1198–1203*):
   London, B.M., Royal 2 D.ix (liber).
Beerley, dom. Richard (*monk of P. in 1538*):
   London, Lambeth Pal., 761 (owyth thys booke).
Gillebertus, prior:
   Cambridge, Emm. Coll., 38 (liber). Oxford, Jesus Coll., 4 (liber);
     St John's Coll., 96 (liber).

PETERBOROUGH
Benedict, abbas († *1193*):
   London, B.M., Cotton Jul. A.xi (g.).
Bird, fr. Rogerus. *See* Kirkton.
Clyffe, fr. Willelmus, monachus P.:
   London, Middle Temple (liber; *cf.* Lecester).
Gloucester, Griffin, monachus P.:
   Edinburgh, N.L., Adv. 18.5.16 (name).
Kirkton, dom. Robertus, abbas (*c.1496–1528*):
   London, B.M., Add. 39758 (liber fr. Rogeri Bird ex dono — — A.D. 1520
     testibus . . .; *cf.* Wytelese).
Lecester, fr. Franciscus, monachus P.:
   London, Middle Temple (*a* possessor; *b* liber — — quem emit de fr.
     Willelmo Clyffe pro 3 s.).
Lindesye, Robertus de, abbas (*1214–22*):
   Cambridge, St John's Coll., 81 (g.). London, Soc. of Antiq., 59 (g.).
Natures, fr. Humfridus, monachus P.:
   Oxford, Bodleian, Gough liturg. 17 (liber).
Rouceby, Walter de, monk of P.:
   Oxford, Bodleian, Barlow 22 (*obit in calendar, so perhaps gave*).
Spyrman (?), Robertus, capellanus P.:
   Oxford, Bodleian, Bodl. 96 (liber).
Stanford, Gilbertus de:
   Cambridge, Magd. Coll., 10 (g.).
Stivecle, fr. Hugo de, prior:
   Cambridge, Corpus Christi Coll., 53 (g.).
Swafham, R. de:
   Peterborough, Cath., 1 (liber).
Wodeforde, dom. Willelmus de, abbas († *1299*):
   Cambridge, Gonv. and Caius Coll., 454 (Summa de virtutibus — — —
     quam perfecit Walterus prior a medio usque in finem).
Wodford, fr. Willelmus:
   Cambridge, Gonv. and Caius Coll., 437 (liber).
Walterus, prior. *See* Wodeforde.
Wytelese (Witteliseye), fr. Walterus de, monachus P.:
   London, B.M., Add. 39758 (liber), 47170 (g.).

[. . .]ngham, dom. Willelmus, monachus P.:
Cambridge, U.L., Inc. 1344 (liber).

PILTON
Olston, Thomas:
Oxford, Bodleian, Rawl. liturg. g.12 (A.D. 1521 . . . nomen scriptoris
— —).

PIPEWELL
Burton, dom. Thomas, abbas P.:
Untraced Psalter (per manus Johannis Tryguran archidiaconi detur
— —).
Godfrey, Johannes, monachus (*of P. at Dissolution*):
Oxford, Bodleian, Douce HH.252 (pertinet ad; *cf.* Gresley).
Gresley, mag., monachus P.:
Oxford, Bodleian, Douce HH.252 ([. . .] ad; *cf.* Godfrey).
Howghton, Thomas:
Peterborough, Cath., D.8.17 (constat — — et monasterio de P.; bought
with benefaction of John Alen and Cecily his wife).
Webster, Johannes, clericus (*monk of P. at Dissolution*):
Dublin, Chester Beatty Libr., W.34 (pertinet ad me — — ex dono
domus b. Marie de P., A.D. 1538, 5 Nov.).

PLESHEY
Thomas, dux Gloucestrie († *1397*):
Oxford, Bodleian, Bodl. 316.

RAMSEY
Brauncestre, Alanus de:
London, B.M., Royal 8 D.iii (liber).
Eye, dom. Simon *de*, abbas R. (*1316–42*):
London, B.M., Royal 5 D.x (liber).
Gotham, Robertus:
London, B.M., Harley 649 (liber Rameseye Roberti Gotham).
Grafham (? *W. de G., cellarer R. 1297*):
Lavantal, Carinthia, Abbey of St Paul, xxv/2.19 (— honoretur).
Huntingdon, Gregorius *de*, prior R. (*s.xiii*):
Cambridge, Corpus Christi Coll., 468 (g.).
Keturing, dom. Willelmus de, monachus R.:
London, B.M., Royal 7 C.i (liber).
Lyncoln, dom. Robertus, monachus R.:
Oxford, Bodleian, Gough Missals 122 (pertinet ad — — cum magno
gaudeo).
Olneya, fr. R. de:
Cambridge, U.L., Hh.6.11.
Ranulphus, abbas (? *R., abbot of R. 1234–53*):
London, B.M., Royal 8 F.x (liber).
Raveningham, Adam de:
London, B.M., Royal 5 F.xv (g.).
Rystone, fr. Ricardus de:
Cambridge, Peterhouse, 10 (liber).
Sentyvys, dane Rolande, monke of R.:
Oxford, Bodleian, Tanner 110 (pertenyth to).

Wardeboys, dom. Johannes, *B.Th.*, (2) abbas (*1473;* † *by May 1489*):
  London, B.M., Royal 14 C.iv (ex procuratione); (2) 14 C.ix (liber).
Wellis, fr. Johannes de, monachus R.:
  Oxford, Bodleian, Bodl. 851 (constat).
Weston, G. monachus R.:
  Oxford, Mr D. Rogers (constat magno gaudio et honore; *cf.* **OXFORD,**
  Gloucester Coll., Langley).

READING
Abyndone:
  London, B.M., Add. 48179 (wrote).
Alanus, prior [R.]:
  Oxford, Worc. Coll., 3.16 A.
Besforde, fr. Thomas, monachus R.:
  London, B.M., Royal 4 C.vi.
Box, Willelmus de:
  Oxford, Bodleian, Bodl. 200.
Braye, fr. Henricus de:
  London, B.M., Royal 9 F.iii (per).
Chilmark, fr. Thomas:
  London, B.M., Royal 11 C.ii (ex adquisicione).
Clifton, dom. Johannes, prior R.:
  Belvoir Castle, Duke of Rutland. Göttingen, U.L., Theol. 2 (?; *same*
  form as in Belvoir MS., but surname illegible).
Dovera, fr. Aluredus de:
  Oxford, Bodleian, Auct. F.3.8.
Dymmoc, Radulphus de, quondam prior R.:
  Oxford, Trin. Coll., 19.
*Erlye (Erle), dom. Thomas, abbas R. (*1409–29*):
  London, B.M., Royal 11 C.xi. Oxford, Bodleian, Auct. F.inf.1.2.
Harlestone, fr. Willelmus de:
  London, B.M., Royal 12 F.xix.
Hendele, fr. Willelmus, prior R.:
  Oxford, Magd. Coll., 25.
Lutton, Johannes:
  London, B.M., Royal 4 C.vi (wrote).
Nicholaus, camerarius de R. (*s.xiii*):
  Oxford, Bodleian, Bodl. 44 (name *in genitive*).
Pag', fr. (*s.xiii*):
  London, B.M., Harley 979 (libellus iste tempore Aluerdi (?) prioris fuit
  apud Cyrencestr' memoriale pro libello Alexandri Nequam qui
  dicitur laus sapiencie quem revocari fecit —).
Pichecote, fr. Nicholaus de:
  Oxford, Bodleian, Auct. D.4.18; Corpus Christi Coll., 45.
*Redyngia, Ricardus de:
  London, B.M., Royal 11 C.iii (Oxonie fecit — — — ligari).
Sar*isburiensis*, Johannes (*s.xiii ex.*):
  Oxford, Bodleian, Bodl. 397.
Serbopoulos, John, of Constantinople:
  Cambridge, Trin. Coll., 823 (wrote at R. in 1489). Oxford, Corpus Christi
  Coll., 23–24 (wrote at R. in 1499, 1500), 106 (wrote at R. in 1495);
  New Coll., 240–41 (wrote at R. in 1497), 254 (wrote at R. in 1494).

Staunton, Thomas, prior R. (*s.xv*):
  Oxford, Bodleian, Bodl. 570.
Wargrave, Willelmus, monachus R.:
  Cambridge, U.L., Inc. 3230 (gave in 1498).   London, B.M., Harley 330
  (ex dono — — A.D. 1495).   Oxford, Bodleian, Douce F.205 (— —
  procurante constat monasterio R.); Laud misc. 79 (per latrones
  ablatus circa A.D. 1490; postea vero — — cum apud Leominstriam
  moraretur hunc librum a quodam generoso pro 10 s. 9 d. redemit).
Wokyngham, fr. Johannes:
  London, B.M., Royal 3 A.xiv.
Wynchedone, fr. Robertus de, prior R.:
  Oxford, Bodleian, Auct. D.1.19.
Wint', fr. W. de (*s.xiii ex.*):
  Oxford, Bodleian, Bodl. 848.

READING, *Fran. conv.*
*Lathbury, fr. Johannes, senior:
  London, B.M., Harley 493 (per — — 'liberetur fratribus minoribus de
  R.').

REDBOURNE
La Mare, dom. Thomas de, abbas S. Albani:
  London, B.M., Cotton Tib. E.i.
Whethamstede, ven. pat. dom. Johannes, abbas S. Albani:
  London, B.M., Royal 13 D.ix (providit).

RICHMOND, *Fran. conv.*
Hardyng, ven. pat. fr. Johannes, obiit A.D. 1460:
  Oxford, Bodleian, Rawl. liturg. e.1 (pertinet conventui R. ex testimonio
  — — qui hoc affirmavit tempore mortis sue).

RIEVAULX
Elyngton, mag. Johannes de (*s.xiii/xiv*):
  Oxford, Univ. Coll., 113 (hic attulit; *later R. ex libris*).
Houingham, Johannes de:
  Oxford, Linc. Coll., lat. 15.
Spenser, dom. Willelmus, abbas R. (*resigned 1449*):
  Oxford, Corpus Christi Coll., 155 (ex procuracione).

ROBERTSBRIDGE
Grandison, Johannes *de*, episcopus Exon':
  Oxford, Bodleian, Bodl. 132 (liber s. M. de Ponte Roberti.   Qui eum
  abstulerit . . . anathema maranatha amen.   'Ego — — nescio ubi est
  domus predicta, nec hunc librum abstuli, set modo legittimo adqui-
  sivi').
Wodecherche, fr. Willelmus de, laicus quondam conversus Pontis Roberti
  (*s.xiii*):
  Oxford, Bodleian, Bodl. 132 (scripsit; *cf.* Grandison).

ROCHESTER
A., precentor [R.]:
  London, B.M., Royal 10 C.iv (per).
A., prior [R.]:
  London, B.M., Royal 3 B.i (per); 5 E.x (g.).

A. vicarius de Stoke:
  Cambridge, Corpus Christi Coll., 62, fos 1–48 (per).
Ailesburi (Eylesburi), Radulphus de, (1) monachus:
  (1) Edinburgh, N.L., Adv. 18.5.18 (name *in genitive*).   London, B.M.,
    Royal 2 F.iv (g.).
Alexander, precentor:
  London, B.M., Royal 10 A.xii (*wrote or acquired*).
Alexander, prior [R.] (*cf.* Glanvill, A. de):
  Cambridge, St John's Coll., 89 (g.).   London, B.M., Harley 261
    (*R. ex libris followed by* Alexandro priore); Royal 3 C.vii (per),
    6 C.x (per).
Alkewinus, monachus [R.] :
  Cambridge, Corpus Christi Coll., 62, fos 209–74 (per).
Andreas, monachus [R.]:
  London, B.M., Royal 6 B.vi (per).
Asketillus, monachus [R.]:
  London, B.M., Royal 5 A.vii (per), 5 B.vii (per), 6 A.xii (g.).
Aylard, Radulfus:
  London, B.M., Royal 5 A.i (per).
B., camerarius [R.]:
  London, B.M., Royal 12 C.i (g.).
*Baldwinus, archiepiscopus (*of Canterbury 1185–90*):
  London, B.M., Royal 4 C.iv (g.).
Bambrogh, mag. Johannes, vicarius de Malling:
  Cambridge, U.L., Inc. 2179.
Benedictus, episcopus [R.] (*B. de Sawston 1215–26*):
  London, B.M., Royal 4 A.xii (per), 6 D.ii (per).
Benedictus, monachus [R.]:
  London, B.M., Cotton Vesp. A.xxii (per).
Bradewelle, mag. Thomas:
  London, B.M., Royal 11 D.i (collatus per).
Bruyn, fr. Thomas, monachus R.:
  London, B.M., Royal 9 C.iv (per).
Cokham, R. de:
  London, B.M., Royal 6 A.iv (per).
Cornubia, fr. Willelmus de, monachus [R.]:
  Cambridge, Corpus Christi Coll., 318 (per).
Cranebroke, Stephanus de:
  Oxford, St John's Coll., 4 (g.).
Elyas, precentor:
  London, B.M., Royal 5 C.i (liber).
Ernulfus (Ernulphus, Arnulphus), (1) prior [R.], (2, 3) episcopus [R.]
    (1115–24):
  (1, 2) London, B.M., Royal 5 D.i, ii (g.).   (3) Rochester, Cath., Textus
    Roffensis (per).
Fynchyngfelde, Walterus:
  London, B.M., Royal 11 D.i (per; *cf.* Bradewelle).
G., archidiaconus:
  Berlin, Staatsbibl., lat. 350 (per).   London, B.M., Royal 4 A.xvi
    (g.).
G., cellerarius [R.]:
  London, B.M., Royal 12 C.iv (per).

297

G., episcopus [R.] (? *Gilbert Glanville 1185-1214*):
London, B.M., Royal 4 B.i (per).
G., subprior [R.]:
London, B.M., Royal 12 F.i (g.).
G[...], monachus [R.]:
Oxford, Bodleian, Bodl. 387 (per).
Gelham, fr. Robertus de:
London, B.M., Royal 2 C.v (per), 6 C.iv (per).
Gerardus (Ierardus), monachus [R.]:
London, B.M., Royal 12 F.viii (per), 15 C.x (per).
Gillebertus, monachus [R.]:
London, B.M., Royal 2 E.vii (per).
Glanvill, Alexander de, prior [R.] (*1242-52*; *cf.* Alexander):
London, B.M., Royal 7 C.xiii, xiv (per), 7 E.viii (g.).
Glanvill, Johannes de:
London, B.M., Royal 4 A.xii (g.).
Goda, comitissa:
London, B.M., Royal 1 D.iii (per).
Gognostus, prior [R.]:
London, B.M., Royal 6 A.i (g.).
*Gravesend, mag. Ricardus de, episcopus Lincoln' (*1258-79*):
London, B.M., Royal 2 F.xii (per), 3 B.xiii (g.).
Gundulfus, episcopus [R.] (*1077-1108*):
San Marino, Huntington, HM 62 (per).
H., cantor [R.]:
London, B.M., Royal 6 B.ii (per).
H., episcopus (*H. de Hethe, bishop of R. 1319-52*):
London, B.M., Royal 2 E.i (g.).
H., monachus [R.]:
London, B.M., Royal 6 A.xi (g.).
Hamo, mag. (*cf.* Kok):
London, B.M., Royal 4 C.x (g.).
Hoo (?), H. de, prior [R.]:
Edinburgh, N.L., Adv. 18.3.9 (g.?).
Horstede, fr. Thomas de, monachus [R.], (4) precentor:
London, B.M., Royal 4 E.v, 5 A.x, 6 D.vii, (4) 7 E.iv, 7 F.iv (*all* per).
Hubertus, archiepiscopus (*of Canterbury 1193-1205*):
London, B.M., Royal 6 D.v (g.).
Hubertus, precentor [R.]:
London, B.M., Harley 3680 (g.).
Humfridus, precentor [R.]:
London, B.M., Royal 5 B.iv (quem in eodem claustro scripsit), 5 B.xii (memoriale).
J., episcopus (? *J. de Sheppey, bishop of R. 1352-60*; *cf.* Scapeya):
London, B.M., Royal 10 C.xii (per).
J., prior [R.]:
London, B.M., Royal 7 F.x (per).
Johannes, prior [R.]:
London, B.M., Royal 1 B.iv, 12 G.ii, iii. Rochester, Cath., P. Lombardus (*all* per).
Joseph, monachus [R.]:
London, B.M., Royal 5 E.i (per).

Kok, mag. Ha*mo* (*cf.* Hamo):
 London, B.M., Royal 5 D.ix.
L., canonicus:
 London, B.M., Royal 2 E.i (per).
Laurentius, episcopus (*L. de S. Martino, bishop of R. 1250–74*):
 London, B.M., Royal 2 F.xi (per), 5 A.xv (g.), 5 B.vi (per).
Leonardus, monachus [R.]:
 London, B.M., Royal 5 E.xx (per). Oxford, Bodleian, Laud misc. 40
  (per).
London, Laurentius de:
 London, Lambeth Pal., 76 (per).
Londoniis, Ricardus de:
 London, B.M., Royal 4 A.xv (per — — — scripta; *cf.* Whytefeld).
Mallinges, fr. Johannes:
 London, B.M., Royal 12 F.xiii (reparatum per).
Maur', monachus [R.]:
 Oxford, Bodleian, Wood B.3 (g.).
Mepeham, fr. Henricus de:
 London, B.M., Royal 4 B.ii (per), 10 B.ii (per).
Noble, Johannes, monachus R.:
 London, B.M., IA.3420 (pertinet); Messrs Maggs (pertinet).
Oxon', Jacobus de:
 Rochester, Cath., Augustine (per).
Paulinus, prior [R.]:
 Cambridge, Corpus Christi Coll., 62, fos 49–208 (per).
Paulus, prior [R.]:
 London, B.M., Royal 2 F.vi (per).
Petrus, precentor [R.]:
 London, B.M., Cotton Otho A.xv (per); Royal 5 B.xvi (g.).
R., precentor [R].:
 London, B.M., Royal 3 C.iv (per), 12 F.xiii (g.).
Radulphus, archiepiscopus (? *of Canterbury 1108–14*):
 London, B.M., Royal 6 C.vi (per).
*Renham Henricus de:
 London, B.M., Royal 12 G.ii (scripsit — — — et audivit in scolis
  Oxonie et emendavit et glosavit audiendo; *cf.* Johannes, prior).
Reyersse, fr. Willelmus de:
 London, B.M., Royal 9 E.xi (per).
Reynerius, monachus [R.]:
 London, B.M., Royal 11 B.xv (per).
Ricardus, monachus [R.]:
 Cambridge, Corpus Christi Coll., 184 (per).
Ros, Radulphus de, prior [R.] (*c.1199*):
 London, B.M., Royal 3 C.ix (per).
*Scapeya, mag. Johannes de, prior [R.] (*1333–52; bishop 1352–60*):
 London, B.M., Royal 12 D.xiv (per).
Silvester, prior [R.] (*c.1177*):
 London, B.M., Royal 8 D.xvi (g.), App. 10 (g., *s.xiii*; per, *s.xv*).
Sotton, fr. Johannes de:
 London, B.M., Royal 7 A.v (g.).
Stan', W. de:
 London, B.M., Royal 3 C.viii (name).

Stoke, Radulphus de, monachus [R.] (*s.xiii*):
  London, B.M., Royal 2 C.i (per).
Stokes, N. (?) de:
  London, B.M., Royal 2 D.xxx (g.).
Stratton, G. de, (1) mag., (2) monachus [R.]:
  (1) Cambridge, Trin. Coll., 1128 (per). (2) London, B.M., Royal 2
  D.vi (per); 4 D.xiii (per).
Syward, episcopus (*1058–75*):
  Dublin, Trin. Coll., 163 (per). London, B.M., Royal 5 B.xiii (g.).
Territius, infirmarius [R.]:
  London, B.M., Royal 4 B.vii (g.).
Theodericus, monachus [R.]:
  London, B.M., Royal 10 A.xii (liber).
*Thornden, Willelmus, B.Th., monachus Cantuar' († *1483*):
  London, B.M., Royal 7 B.xiii (liber S. Andree R. expositus — — pro
  secundo sentenciarum doctoris subtilis A.D. 1469).
W., episcopus R.:
  London, B.M., Royal 15 B.xi (per).
Walterus, episcopus (*1148–82*):
  London, B.M., Royal 3 C.x (per).
Westerham, fr. Johannes de, quondam prior [R.] (*1320–21*):
  London, B.M., Royal 11 C.i (per).
*Whytefeld, Johannes, monachus R.:
  London, B.M., Royal 4 A.xv. Oxford, Bodleian, Hatton 54 (liber).
*Wybarn, Thomas, monachus R.:
  London, B.M., Royal 2 C.i (pledged in 1467 and 1468).
Zacarias, precentor [R.]:
  Cambridge, St John's Coll., 70 (per).

ROMSEY
Lengrege, Elizabeth, mynchynne of R. *See* Lepton.
Lepton, maister Raufe, parson of Alresford and of Kyngsworthy:
  London, Royal Coll. of Physicians, 409 (gave to Elizabeth Langrege
  A.D. 1523).

ST ALBANS
*Aylesberi, fr. Thomas de, monachus S. A., (2, 3) doctor decretorum
  (*fl. 1335*):
  London, B.M., Egerton 633 (emit de Thoma Colingham ad usum
  monasterii S. A.); (2) Royal 10 E.viii (de speciali provisione); (3) 11
  D.ix (de speciali provisione; *cf.* Sarisburia).
*Beaver, dom. Johannes, monachus S. A. (*fl. 1430*):
  London, B.M., Royal 2 F.vii (fieri fecit — — quem librum ex licencia
  venerabilis mag. Johannis Whethamstede . . . abbatis contulit).
*Bury, dom. Ricardus de, episcopus Dunelm' († *1345*):
  Oxford, Bodleian, Laud misc. 363; New Coll., 274. *See also* Mentmore.
Bywell, Johannes. *See* Wylum.
Chenley, dom. Edmundus:
  Cambridge, U.L., Dd.6.7 (liber).
Colingham, Thomas. *See* Aylesberi.
Dalling, fr. Johannes de (*s.xiii*):
  London, B.M., Royal 2 B.vi (dedit — — — ex licencia dom. Johannis
  abbatis ita tamen quod habeat usum tantum in vita sua).

Dunstaple, fr. Johannes de, custos S. Amphiboli (*s.xiv*):
    Oxford, Bodleian, Laud misc. 279 (procuravit —— — per licenciam
    dom. Hugonis abbatis et assignavit specialiter ad altare S. Katerine).
Everisden, Hugo *de*, abbas (*1309–27*). *See* Dunstaple.
Eyton, dom. Hugo, subprior S. A. (*s.xv*):
    Oxford, Bodleian, Bodl. 467 (liber).
Fabianus, dom., subprior S. A. (*s.xii ex.*):
    Oxford, Bodleian, Rawl. C.31, Finch e.25; Christ Church, 97.
Hertford, dom. Johannes *de*, abbas (*1235–60*). *See* Dalling.
Hugo, abbas. *See* Everisden.
Hulle, Eleanor. *See* Huswyff.
Huswyff, Rogerus:
    Cambridge, U.L., Dd.7.7–10 (given in 1456 or 1457 by —— and
    Eleanor Hulle, he to have use for life).
Johannes, abbas. *See* Hertford, Whethamstede, Wylum.
Johannes, dom., quondam episcopus Ardfert:
    London, B.M., Add. 16164.
Kyrkeby, fr. Nicholaus, de Sancto Albano:
    Durham, U.L., Cosin V.v.15 (pertinet).
La Mare, Thomas de, abbas:
    London, B.M., Royal 10 E.viii (assigned by —— — to office of arch-
    deacon in 1376; *cf.* Aylesberi).
*Legat, dom. Hugo, monachus S. A. (*s.xv*):
    London, B.M., Harley 2624 (fecit ligari).   Oxford, Bodleian, Rawl. G.99
    (ex industria — — perquisitum ad usum conventus S. A. assingnavit
    venerabilis pater dompnus Johannes Stoke abbas).
Loukyn, fr. Johannes:
    Oxford, Bodleian, Ashmole 1796 (liber subsacriste S. A. quondam — —).
Marcyal, monomachus S. A.:
    Cambridge, Trin. Coll., Grylls 2.179 (sum libellulus).
Matheus, fr., (2) prior S. A. (*s.xiii*):
    Cambridge, U.L., Dd.11.78.   (2) Eton Coll., 26.
Maynolf, fr. Robertus:
    Cambridge, U.L., Ee.1.9.
Mentmore, Michael *de*, abbas (*1335–49*):
    London, B.M., Royal 8 G.i, 13 D.iv (hunc librum venditum dom.
    Ricardo de Biry episcopo Dunelmensi emit — ab executoribus
    predicti episcopi A.D. 1346; *cf.* Symon).   *See also* Steukle.
Michael, abbas. *See* Mentmore.
Parisiensis, fr. Matheus († *probably 1259*):
    London, B.M., Royal 14 C.vii.   *See also p. 165.*
Parys, fr. Willelmus:
    London, B.M., Royal 2 F.viii.
Raymond, prior of St A. (*c.1200*):
    London, B.M., Royal 4 D.vii (*caused writing of; cf. Gesta Abbatum*
    (*Rolls Series, 1867*), i. 233, 294).
Ricardus, abbas. *See* Wallingford.
*Sarisburia, mag. Rogerus de, S.T.P. (*fellow of Merton Coll., 1312*):
    London, B.M., Royal 11 D.ix (dedit A.D. 1336; *cf.* Aylesberi).
Steukle, fr. Henricus:
    London, Lambeth Pal., 111 (*a* liber; *b* procuravit —— de licencia
    dompni Michaelis abbatis; *cf.* **LANTHONY,** Calne).

Stoke, Johannes, abbas septimus (*1440–51*):
 Oxford, Bodleian, Rawl. G.99 (ex dono, *but cf.* Legat); Corpus Christi
 Coll., 233.
Symon, abbas S. A. (*1167–83*):
 Cambridge, St John's Coll., 183 (fecit); Trin. Coll., 1341; Trin. Hall,
 2 (fecit). El Escorial, P.i.5. London, B.M., Royal 13 D.iv (fecit).
 Stonyhurst Coll., 10 (fecit).
Teerpenninc, Gerardus, curatus in Lexmende:
 Oxford, St John's Coll., 64 (scripsit et finivit A.D. 1414).
Trumpington, dom. Willelmus *de*, abbas [S. A.] (*1214–35*):
 Oxford, Bodleian, Laud misc. 409. *Cf.* London, B.M., Royal 4 D.vii
 (Titulus istius libri in dorso Scolastica hystoria W. abbatis, *but see*
 Raymond).
Waldey, fr. Nicholaus de:
 Longleat, Marquess of Bath, 27.
Walingeford, fr. Johannes de:
 London, B.M., Cotton Julius D.vii (liber).
Wallingford, Ricardus *de*, abbas (*1328–35*):
 Oxford, Bodleian, Laud misc. 264.
*Warder, dom. Johannes, monachus S. A.:
 Oxford, New Coll., 274 ('caucio — — A.D. 1455', and in other years).
Ware, dom. Robertus (*s.xv in.*):
 Cambridge, Corpus Christi Coll., 7 (post mortem dompni Willelmi
 Wyntreshyll in quaternis derelictum connecti fecit — —).
*Whethamstede, dom. Johannes, abbas (1, 3, olim abbas) (*1420–40,
 1452–65*):
 (1) Eton Coll., 103 (ad usum conventus . . . assignavit). London, B.M.,
 Royal 13 D.v (liber . . . per quorundam negligenciam . . . deperditus,
 sed per industriam . . . Johannis abbatis sexti . . . restitutus et
 assignatus librarie conventus). (3) Oxford, Bodleian, Rawl. D.358;
 Exeter Coll., 15 (ad usum conventus . . . assignavit). *See also*
 Beaver, Wylum (?), Wyntreshull, *and p.* 165.
Willelmus, abbas. *See* Trumpington.
Wylum, fr. Henricus (*s.xv in.*):
 Oxford, St John's Coll., 130 (dedit — — fr. Johanni Bywell per licenciam
 dom. Johannis abbatis monasterii S.A. qui liber post mortem predicti
 fr. Johannis remanebit in conventu ejusdem).
*Wyntreshull, dom. Willelmus, quondam monachus S. A. (*s.xv in.*):
 Cambridge, Corpus Christi Coll., 5 (non sine magnis sumptibus fecit
 conscribi quod opus in libraria conventus ad opus claustralium
 voluit remanere. Cujus donum auctorizando confirmavit . . .
 Johannes Whethamstede, S.T.P., predictumque librum . . . ad opus
 sui conventus . . . stabilivit), 6 (*probably as M.S. 5, but inscription
 erased*). *See also* Ware.

ST ANDREWS
Bernham, David de, bishop of St A. (*1240–53*):
 Paris, B.N., Lat. 1218 (arms; *presumed gift of*).

ST MICHAEL'S MOUNT
*Tailour, mag. Johannes, S.T.P., tunc cancellarius Exon' († *1492*):
 London, B.M., Cotton Julius A.vii (scribi fecit et dedit A.D. 1479).

ST OSYTH

Busshe, Nicholaus (*canon at Dissolution*):
Beeleigh Abbey, Miss C. Foyle (pertinet ad — — presbiterum ac olim canonicum A.D. 1557).
Joly, Willelmus (*canon at Dissolution*):
New York, Mr W. S. Glazier (ad — — clericum).

SALISBURY

*Andrew, mag. Ricardus, canonicus (*archdeacon of Sarum 1441–44*):
Salisbury, Cath., 32, 73–74.
*Bellaf' (*B.R.U.O., Beaufo*), Robertus de (*canon by 1184*):
Salisbury, Cath., 42.
*Cyrcetur (Cyrcetr'), mag. Thomas, canonicus residenciarius S. († *1452*):
Salisbury, Cath., 13, 36, 39, 40, 55, 81, 84, 126, 167, 170 (*presumed gift of*), 174.
Eboraco, Radulphus de, cancellarius S. (*1288–1309*):
Salisbury, Cath., 11, 44, 45, 48 (?), 50 (?), 91, 102, 107 (?), 161. See also **SALISBURY**, *Dom. conv.*, Wudeston.
Fadir, dom. Petrus, nuper (2, quondam) vicarius S.:
Oxford, Bodleian, Digby 173 (memoriale). (2) Salisbury, Cath., 68.
Fryth:
Salisbury, Cath., 181 (name *as scribe*).
Fydyon, mag. Willelmus, canonicus S.:
Salisbury, Cath., 143.
Gregorius, canonicus S. (*s.xiii*):
Salisbury, Cath., 41.
*La Wyle, mag. Henricus de, quondam cancellarius († *1329*):
Oxford, Bodleian, Bodl. 516, flyleaf (legavit). Salisbury, Cath., 2, 19–20, 54, 60, 72, 82 (*all* legavit), 62 (*recorded as his bequest*), 93 (*presumed gift of*).
Lovell, dominus Johannes (*John, fifth Lord Lovel of Titchmarsh,* † *1408*):
London, B.M., Harley 7026 (ordinavit pro speciali memoria sui et uxoris).
*Martivall, dom. Rogerus de, episcopus S. (*1315–30*):
Oxford, Bodleian, Rawl. C.400 (legavit . . . ita quod loci episcopus qui pro tempore fuerit habeat usum ejus).
*Praty, mag. Ricardus, quondam episcopus Cicestrensis (*1438–45*):
Salisbury, Cath., 85 (liber emptus ab executoribus — — . . . `Mentitur qui dixit istum librum fuisse — — nam idem Ricardus istum librum habuit ex mutuo de capitulo Sarum dum erat cancellarius ibidem . . .').
Scamel, dom. Walterus, decanus S.:
Salisbury, Cath., 153 (dedit — — A.D. 1277 . . . ad usum canonicorum et vicariorum . . . quem postea precario recepit a dicto cancellario ad usus suos dum vixerit).
Stopynton, mag. Johannes, nuper archidiaconus Dorset' († *1447*):[8]
Salisbury, Cath., 75.
Werfton, Hugo de, notarius publicus (*s.xiv ex.*):
Salisbury, Cath., 71.

---

[8] According to J. Maunde Thompson, Stopynton bequeathed Salisbury, Cath., 144 to Salisbury Cath.

SALISBURY, *Fran. conv.*
Burcham (?), Johannes, lector S. (*c.1530*):
    Colchester, Harsnett Libr., K.d.2 (fratris Thome . . . lectoris Lewes dono p*atris* — —).

SALISBURY, *Dom. conv.*
Anstye, Johannes de. *See* Coppere.
Coppere, Willelmus, de Wymbornemynstre, presbyter:
    Göttingen, U.L., Theol. 3 (gave to the order, 'deliberans priori et conventui de Fyscherton juxta Sarum . . . et dicti fratres concedunt dictam bibliotecam dom. Johanni de Anstye rectori ecclesie de Littelton ad terminum vite sue', the book to be returned to the convent after his death).
Heskynus, Dominicus, O.P., S.:
    London, B.M., IB.26227 (me possidet). *Cf.* **WARWICK,** *Dom. conv.*, Lily.
*Wudeston, fr. Henricus de, qui pro conventu stat Oxon' (*s.xiii ex.*):
    Salisbury, Cath., 142 (comodavit dominus et magister R. cancellarius Sarisburiensis — —).

SCONE
Carwor, dom. Robertus, alias Arnat, canonicus S. (*1503*):
    Edinburgh, N.L., Adv. 5.1.15 (name).

SELBY
Roucliffe, fr. Petrus de:
    Cambridge, U.L., Dd.9.52 (per).

SEMPRINGHAM
Glynton, Johannes de, canonicus S.:
    London, B.M., Royal 3 A.xv, 3 B.iii, 5 C.v, 8 G.v (*all* ex impetracione).
Awdeley, dom. Anna, monialis S.:
    Steyning, Sir Arthur Howard (pertinet — — ex dono . . . Edmundi Awdeley Sar' episcopi ac avunculi predicte domine).
Champnys, Alicia, monialis S.:
    Cambridge, Fitzwilliam Mus., 2–1957 (pertinet — — quem dicta Alicia emit . . .).
Horder, Johannes:
    London, B.M., Add. 11748 (hunc librum vocatum gracia Dei . . . habeant abbatissa et conventus S. in succursum anime — —).

SHEEN
Benet, quondam procurator in Carthusia de S. († *1517/18*):
    Cambridge, Trin. Coll., 354 (scriptus . . . per —, quod Grenehalgh . . . manu sua 1499).
Bromley, dom. Johannes, de S.:
    Colchester, Harsnett Libr., H.c.27–31 (name).   Glasgow, U.L., Bn.6.b.11 (name).   Lincoln, Cath., 64 (name).   London, B.M., Royal 7 D.xvii (name; *cf.* London).
*Bury, mag. Johannes, Augustiniensis (*Clare conv.*, *1460*), S.T.P.:
    Oxford, Bodleian, Bodl. 797.
Chaffer, Robertus, monachus S., professus A.D. 1507:
    Oxford, St John's Coll., b.3.22 (memorandum by, *implies ownership, perhaps before Dissolution*).

Darker, dom. Willelmus, monachus S. († *1512/13*):
  London, B.M., Add. 22121 (scripsit . . . in remissionem peccatorum
  suorum).
Doddzam (Dodesham), dane Stephen, (1) monke of S. (*at Witham c.1471*;
  † *1481/82*):
  (1) Glasgow, U.L., Hunterian 77 ('wrettyn be þe hand of', in 1475).
  Oxford, Trin. Coll., 46 (orate pro anima — — hujus libri scriptoris).
Feriby, dom. Johannes, monachus S., sacerdos et professus († *1444*):
  Oxford, Bodleian, lat. th. e.26 (scripsit . . . in remissionem peccatorum
  suorum).
Grenehalgh, Jacobus (*at Coventry by 1508;* † *at Sheen 1529/30*). **See**
  p. 178 and cf. Benet.
Henricus quintus, rex Anglie, fundator S.:
  Paris, Mazarine, 34.
Kyngeslow, Johannes, primus reclusus S.:
  Oxford, Bodleian, Rawl. C.57.
London, Johannes:
  Douai, Bibl. mun., 396 (quod).   London, B.M., Royal 7 D.xvii (per).
Mede, Willelmus, monachus (†*1474*):
  Dublin, Trin. Coll., 281 (quod).   London, B.M., Cotton Vesp. D.ix
  (quod).   Oxford, Bodleian, Bodl. 117 (quod); Hatton 14 (Johannes
  Yorke generosus accomodavit — — pro tempore vite sue. Post-
  modum vero Willermus ejusdem filius dedit eidem domui).
Radcliff, mag. Edmundus:
  London, B.M., Harley 4711.
Tracy, Radulphus. *See* Whetham.
Whetham, dom. Johannes, monachus, professus domus Lond':
  Chandlers Cross, Mr W. L. Wood (wrote for Ralph Tracy, prior S., 'ad
  instanciam' J. Yngylby, bishop of Llandaff and ex-prior S., in 1496).
Yngylby, Johannes. *See* Whetham.
Yorke, Willermus. *See* Mede.

SHEEN, *Reclusory*
*Dygon, Johannes, quintus reclusus de S., et Johanna, reclusa in ecclesia
  sancti Botulphi extra Bysschoppesgate, London:
  Oxford, Magd. Coll., 177 (gave jointly to the recluse of S. 'qui pro
  tempore fuerit' and, if none, then to Magd. Coll.).
*Fraunce, mag. Hugo:
  London, B.M., Harley 3820.

SHREWSBURY, *Fran. conv.*
Muddel, fr. Thomas de:
  Shrewsbury School, xxxii.
Worth, fr. Jordanus de:
  Leicester, Bernard Halliday (ad usum — — acomodatus).

SHREWSBURY, *Dom. conv.*
Tapton, fr. Johannes, clericus:
  Rome, Vatican, Ottob. lat. 191 (pledged to, for 26 s. 8 d. 'et ut putatur
  fuit liber conv. fr. pred. S.', who may have it back from the said John
  for 20 s. 'si velint redimere', 20 Febr. [. . .] Edw. IV).

SHULBREDE
Clune, Thomas:
　　Cambridge, King's Coll., 18 (name).

SIBTON
Crofftis, Thomas, de Drosthale, armiger:
　　Oxford, Bodleian, Laud misc. 545 (dedit . . . ita quod dom. Ricardus
　　　Muttforde monachus de S. . . . habeat in usum . . . tempore vite sue
　　　et tandem remancipetur monasterio de S.).
Muttford, dom. Ricardus, monachus S.　*See* Crofftis.

SOUTHAMPTON, *Fran. conv.*
Kingestone, fr. Jordan de, *O.F.M.*:
　　Paris, Ste Geneviève, 2899 (*a* fist; *b* resingna — — — a la commune de
　　　freres menurs de S. par la volonte de graunt frere Willame de Noting-
　　　ham ministre de Engleterre dunt la commune ad sa lettre lan de grace
　　　mcccxvii).

SOUTHWARK
Appiltone, Johannes:
　　Oxford, Bodleian, Bodl. 423 (quod).
B[. . . .], dom. Johannes, canonicus S.:
　　Oxford, Bodleian, Bodl. 423 (constat).
Lecchelade, dom. Johannes de, canonicus S. (*s.xiv in.*):
　　Oxford, Bodleian, Rawl. B.177 (est — — —).
Lichefelde, mag.:
　　Oxford, Bodleian, Bodl. 924.
Wendover, fr. Hugo de:
　　Oxford, Bodleian, Ashmole 1285 (liber quondam).

SOUTHWELL
Carter, mag. Edmundus, quondam vicarius et nunc canonicus hujus col-
　　legii regii[9] (? *E. C., canon of S. 1493–1505*):
　　London, B.M., Royal 4 B.iii (ex dono — — anno Christi 1503).
Couton, Helias de, canonicus S. (*s.xiv*):
　　Winchester, Cath., 9 (*presumed gift of*).
Gunthorp, dom. Willelmus de, (2) canonicus S., obiit A.D. 1400:
　　Cambridge, Gonv. and Caius Coll., 449 (legatur per); (2) St John's
　　　Coll., 4 (legatus per).

SOUTHWICK
Kateryngton, fr. Johannes, canonicus S.:
　　Cambridge, Corpus Christi Coll., 145.

SPALDING
Oldfield, Johannes (*s.xvi in.*):
　　Cambridge, Gonv. and Caius Coll., 314 (injuste et rapaciter ablatus a
　　— — ejus vero possessore nec non dicti prioratus).
Stanton, fr. Nicholaus de:
　　London, B.M., Royal 6 B.xii (g.).

STAFFORD
Merston, fr. Philippus de (*s.xiii*):
　　Oxford, Bodleian, Auct. F.5.17 (accomodatus).

　　[9] For the idea, current in s.xvi, that Southwell was founded by King Edgar
see *V.C.H., Nottinghamshire,* ii. 155.

STAINDROP
Heddon, mag. Thomas, vicarius de Gaynforde:
  Oxford, Bodleian, Rawl. A.363 (dedit hunc librum . . . deliberatus per
    me dom. Johannem Smyth de Barnardecastell A.D. 1515).

STAMFORD, *nunnery*
Stanburne, domina Margareta, priorissa S.:
  Oxford, Bodleian, Arch. A.d.15 (constat).

STAMFORD, *Hospital of William Browne*
Trus, Sir John, chapleyn to Willyam Brown sumtyme and prest S.:
  London, B.M., Harley 2372.

STAMFORD, *Fran. conv.*
Johannes, dom., rector ecclesie de Allenton:
  Cambridge, Magd. Coll., 15.

STAMFORD, *Carm. conv.*
Heulla, fr. Rolandus de, carmelita:
  Durham, Cath., C.IV.22 (scriptus . . . in conventu S. per manum — — —
    A.D. 1449; *cf.* **DURHAM,** Aukland).

STOKE-BY-CLARE
**Burton, Ricardus, S.T.P., quondam canonicus S. († *1506*):
  Cambridge, Corpus Christi Coll., EP.C.Par.2–5.

STONE
*Stone, mag. Gilbertus de, canonicus Wellensis († *by June 1417*):
  London, B.M., Burney 323.

STONELEIGH
Kynggyswod, Johannes, monachus S.:
  Cambridge, U.L., Ff.1.20 (scripsit — — A.D. 1473).

STRATFORD LANGTHORNE
Huddylstone, Willelmus, abbas S. :
  Cambridge, Emm. Coll., 94 (gave to John Meryot in 1533).
Lamborn, fr. Thomas. *See* Serle.
London, fr. Thomas. *See* Serle.
Meryot, Johannes. *See* Huddylstone.
Serle, fr. Robertus:
  Cambridge, U.L., Inc. 124 (constat S. quem fratres — — Thomas
    Lamborn et Thomas London emerunt . . . A.D. 1480).

SUDBURY, *Dom. conv.*
Stok', fr. Johannes de, rector ecclesiarum de Twyford (*Bucks.*; *fl. 1241*) et
    Hunede:
  London, Gray's Inn, 20 (contulit . . . A.D. 1256; *later at* **MELBOURNE**
    Ch.).

SWEETHEART
Baylliol, Devorgoyl de:
  Oxford, Bodleian, Fairfax 5 (*presumed gift of*).

SWINE
Wade, dame Mald. *Cf.* **NUNCOTON.**

SWINESHEAD

Ryhale, fr. Johannes de, monachus scolaris et abbas S.:
  Cambridge, St John's Coll., 100 (ex perquisito).

SYON

**Betson, Thomas (*deacon*, † *1516*):[1]
  Cambridge, St John's Coll., 109 (orate pro anima — — de Syon; *wrote*).
    London, B.M., Add. 5208 (*wrote part*); St Paul's, Cath., 5 (*wrote part*).
Billyngham, *Richard* (*brother S. in 1428*):
  Oxford, Bodleian, Auct. D.3.1 (name *on label*).
**Bonde, *William* (*brother S.*; † *1530*):
  Oxford, Merton Coll., 77.a.20 (name *on label*); St John's Coll., A.9.5–7
    (*recorded as his gifts in cat.*). *Cf. also* Copynger.
Bracebridge, *John* (*brother S. in 1428*):
  Cambridge, St John's Coll., 219 (name *on label*); Trin. Coll., 339 (name
    on label).
Buklonde, Johanna, relicta Ricardi B., civis et piscarii London':
  Oxford, Bodleian, Bodl. 630 (dedit fr. Rogero Twiforde et ceteris
    fratribus de S.).
Catysby, *William* († *1510*):
  London, B.M., Harley 42 (name *on label*).
Colvylle, suster Anne (*nun S. in 1518*):
  London, B.M., Harley 993 (thys boke is — —). Oxford, Bodleian,
    Laud misc. 416 (name).
Copynger, J. (*confessor general S. in 1537*):
  Stonor Park, Hon. S. Stonor (*a* name; *b* pray for William Bond and — —
    good daughter).
Crychley, Elisabeth, of Syon (*nun in 1539*):
  Cambridge, Magd. Coll., 13 (name, *followed by* 13 Jan. anno 1521).
Curson, David (*brother S. in 1539*):
  Durham, Mr A. I. Doyle (name *on label*).
Danvers, dame Anne, widowe, sumtyme wyffe to Sir William D., knyght:
  Manchester, J. Rylands, English 81 (hathe gevyn this present booke unto
    mastre confessor and his bratherne encloosed in S.).
Darker, dom. Willelmus, M.A., de domo Bethlehem prope Shene, ord.
    Cart. *See* Gibbis.
Dely, Awdry (*nun of S. in 1539 and 1557*). *See* Newell.
Derham (? *Robert D., deacon S.*, † *1488*):
  Oxford, Bodleian, Lat. th. f.20 (*recorded as his gift in cat.; label lost*).
Edwardes, Elizabeth (*nun in 1539*):
  London, B.M., Cotton App. xiv (praye for the sowlys of John Edwardes
    and Margaret his wyffe and for Elisabethe ther doughter professed yn
    Syon for whos use thy[s] boke was made).
*Elyot, mag. Robertus († *1498*) :
  Bury St Edmunds, Cath., 1 (ex dono A.D. 1490).
**Fewterer, Johannes (*confessor general c.1535*):
  London, Dutch Church (name *on label*); Sion Coll., A.51.2.Aq.5Be
    (name *on label*). Oxford, Bodleian, Douce N.300 (name); 8° A.11
    Th. (name); Merton Coll., 76.b.11 (name *on label*). Worcester, Cath.,
    Sel. B.50.3 (name).

----

[1] See A. I. Doyle, 'Thomas Betson of Syon Abbey', *The Library*, Fifth Series,
xi (1956), 116.

*Fraunce, mag. Hugo:
Ipswich, Central Libr.
Gibbis, Elizabeth, abbatissa S. (*1461–1518*):
Glasgow, U.L., Hunterian 136 (orate pro — — necnon pro dom.
Willelmo Darker qui pro eadem domina abbatissa hunc librum con-
scripsit anno Dominice incarnationis 1502).
Graunte, Thomas (†*1474*):
London, B.M., Harley 632 (*recorded as his gift in cat.*).
Hastyngis, Alice (*nun of S. in 1518*):
Dublin, Archbishop Marsh's Libr., Z.4.4.3 (name; *cf.* Rade).
*Jan, Thomas, archidiaconus Essexiensis:
Xanten, Stiftsbibl., 3070 B (dedit . . . sub hac condicione quod mag.
Ricardus Terynden habeat usum ejusdem quamdiu vixerit).
**Lawsby, *John* († *1490*):
Morcombelake, Mr J. S. Cox (name *on label*).
*Lupton, mag. Edwardus:
Lincoln, Cath., 60 (A.D. 1478 — — dedit hunc librum monasterio de S. ad
perpetuum usum predicatorum in eodem).
Margareta, domina, quondam ducissa Clarencie († *1439*):
London, B.M., Add. 40006 (cujus expensis devenit liber iste ad fratres
monasterii de S. ad requisicionem (?) dom. Symonis Wyntyr fratris
ejusdem monasterii).
Maydeston, fr. Clemens, diaconus S. *See p. 187, n. 8.*
Monton, syster Elisabeth (*nun of S.*)*:*
Aberdeen, U.L., 134, *and* Oxford, Bodleian, Rawl. C.941 (belongyth to;
cf. Tailour).
Morepath, Edyth (*nun of S. in 1518;* † *1536*):
Cambridge, Sid. Sussex Coll., Bb.2.14 (name; *cf.* Palmer).
Newell, Mary (*nun of S. in 1539 and 1557;* † *1558*):
Göttingen, U.L. (gave to Awdry Dely).
Ogull, suster Elysabeth (*nun of S. in 1539*):
London, B.M., Harley 487 (name).
Pachet, Rose, professyd in Syon (*nun in 1518, 1539 and 1557*):
Oxford, All Souls Coll., 25 (name).
Palmer, Katheryn (*nun of S. in 1539*):
Cambridge, Sid. Sussex Coll., Bb.2.14 (name; *cf.* Morepath).
Pensax, domina Margeria, dudum inclusa apud Bysshopisgate (*fl.
1400*):
London, B.M., Harley 2387 (legavit).
Prestins, Thomas, brother of Syon (*in 1539*):
Cambridge, U.L., Dd.2.33 (wrytten by the hand of).
Rade, Alys (*nun of S. in 1518*):
Dublin, Archbishop Marsh's Libr., Z.4.4.3 (name; *cf.* Hastyngis).
Raynolde, Richard (*brother of S.;* † *1535*):
Cambridge, U.L., Add. 4081 (name *on label*).
Selby, Johannes (*brother of S. in 1539*):
London, Lambeth Pal., 1486.4 (hunc vendicat librum).
Sewelle, dame Jhone, syster in Syon, professed the yere of our salvacion
1500:
Philadelphia, Rosenbach Foundation, Inc. H491 (belongeth to).
Slight, Dorothy (*nun of S. in 1539 and 1557*):
Oxford, Jesus Coll., 39 (name). Syon Abbey, 1 (name).

**Steyke, mag. Johannes († *1513*) :
  Cambridge, St John's Coll., 131 (ex dono — — et pro quibus tenetur);
    Trin. Coll., 792 (*as* St John's Coll., 131), 1336 (*a* name; *b* orate pro
    anima — —). Oxford, Bras. Coll., 15 (*as* St John's Coll., 131).
Stryckland, syster Elizabeth, professeyd in Syon (*nun in 1518 and 1539*):
  New York, Public Libr., Spencer, Eng. 1519 (perteynyth to).
Tailour, R.:
  Aberdèen, U.L., 134, *and* Oxford, Bodleian, Rawl. C.941 (wryter of this
    book; *cf.* Monton).
*Terynden, mag. Ricardus († *1512*). *See* Jan.
Thorn, mag. *Jacobus* († *1500*):
  Lincoln, Cath., 244 (liber; *recorded as his gift in cat.*).
Twiforde, Rogerus. *See* Buklonde.
**Westhaw, mag. Thomas (*fl. 1470*):
  Glasgow, U.L., Hunterian 509 (passed from mag. John Sperhawk to
    — —; *probably in cat., but without donor's name*).
Wyndesore, Marguerite, (1) domina de Syon (*prioress in 1518 and 1539*):
  (1) Cambridge, Trin. Coll., C.7.12 (name). New York, Pierpont Morgan,
    600 (appartient a). Oakly Park, Earl of Plymouth (name).
Wyntyr, dom. Simon, frater S. (*in 1428*). *See* Margareta.

TARRANT KEYNSTON
Corf, Editha, priorissa:
  Redlynch, Major J. R. Abbey (constat — — post decessum predicte
    Edithe revertatur ad officium cantarie de T.).
Kaynes, domina Leticia de:
  Stonyhurst Coll., 12.
Kyngeston, domina Johanna, abbatissa T.:
  Dublin, Trin. Coll., 209 (constat).

TATTERSHALL
*Gigur, Johannes (*warden*; † *1504*):
  London, B.M., Royal 8 G.ii, 9 B.ix (emit; *presumed donor; cf.* **BARD-
    NEY**, Fuldon). Oxford, Bodleian, Bodl. 419 (liber; *presumed donor*).

TEWKESBURY
Alanus, dom., abbas (*s.xii/xiii; ? A., abbot of T.*, † *1202*):
  London, B.M., Cotton Claud. E.i.
Cheltenham, dom. Ricardus, abbas T. (*1480–1509*):
  Cambridge, Trin. Coll., Grylls 2.179 (ex mutuacione; *cf.* **ST ALBANS**,
    Marcyal).
Evesham, fr. Johannes, monachus T.:
  Gloucester, Cath., (possidet). Hereford, Cath., P.iv.6 (— — per fr.
    Thomam Wynton deliberatus).
Londoniis, Thomas de, precentor T. (*s.xiii ex.*):
  Oxford, Trin. Coll., 50 (perquisivit et de labore suo scribere fecit assig-
    nando eum claustro T. ad utilitatem claustralium ibidem studentium).
*Wynton, fr. Thomas. *See* Evesham.

THAME
Forrest, Guilielmus (*monk of T., vicar of Bledlow;* † *after 1581*):
  London, B.M., Burney 357 (liber). Oxford, St John's Coll., 60 (this is
    one of the churche bookes of Thame made by me Wylliam Foorest
    prest).[2]

[2] Probably a post-Dissolution inscription.

Redyng, Henricus, monachus T.:
  Cambridge, St Cath. Coll. (emit — — a Balthazar bibliopola Oxoniis
  anno salutis 1528).

THETFORD
Stanys, fr. Johannes, canonicus T.:
  Oxford, Bodleian, Digby 99 (constat).

THETFORD, *nunnery*
Methwold, Katherina, monaca (? *K. M., nun of T., 1492 and 1514*):
  Alnwick, Castle, Duke of Northumberland, 449 (name).

THORNEY
Brito, fr. Johannes (*precentor of T., A.D. 1292*):
  Cambridge, Corpus Christi Coll., 297 (scripsit).
Maxsey, fr. Johannes, monacus T.:
  Oxford, Bodleian, Auct. 2.Q.5.19 (name).
Neutona, Radulphus de, clericus noster (*s.xiii ex.*):
  Oxford, Bodleian, Bodl. 680.
Newton, fr. Ricardus (*s.xv*):
  Dublin, Trin. Coll., 448 (constat precentori de T. ex dono — — vel ex
  dono Roberti Smyth quod Huetth).

THORNHOLM
Sa[. . .], fr. Robertus de:
  Oxford, Bodleian, Bodl. 565 (quem scripsit — — — apud Oseney
  A.D. 1302–3; *inscription, not in main hand, looks later than book*).

THORNTON
Forsett, Ricardus, canonicus T.:
  London, Lambeth Pal., 486 (*a* constat; *b* caucio — — in cista de Gotham
  A.D. 1449/50).

THREMHALL
Herbert, dom. Johannes, prior T. (*1474–89*):
  Gloucester, Cath., D.3.18 (orate pro anima — —). London, Dr
  Williams's Libr., 4010 Q.10 (orate pro anima — —).

TITCHFIELD
Oke, dom. Thomas, abbas T.:
  Oxford, Bodleian, Auct. 1.Q.6.1 (pertinet).

TRURO, *Dom. conv.*
Coulyng, fr. Stephanus, O.P.:
  Cambridge, Emm. Coll., 20 (de perquisito — — post cujus decessum
  pertinet conventui fratrum ejusdem ordinis T.).

TYNEMOUTH
Bamburgh, dom. Johannes, quondam supprior T.:
  Oxford, Corpus Christi Coll., 144 (dedit A.D. 1447).
Blakeney, Robertus, (1, 3) prior T. (*1537–39*):
  (1) Cambridge, Christ's Coll., D.10.9–11. Oxford, Bodleian, Lat.
  liturg. g.8 (pocessor). (3) York, Minster, xiv.K.3.
Dunham, fr. Radulphus de, prior (*elected 1252*):
  London, B.M., Cotton Vit. A.xx.
Goreham, fr. Henricus de (*s.xii/xiii*):
  Durham, Cath., A.IV.6.

Henricus, dom., prior:
London, B.M., Harley 3847.
Westwyk, dom. Johannes de (*s.xv in.*):
Oxford, Bodleian, Laud misc. 657.

VALLE CRUCIS
Anianus, dom., abbas V.:
London, B.M., Add. 21253 (possidet).

WALSINGHAM
Morlee, mag. Ranulphus de:
London, B.M., Sloane 1933 (ex legato).
*Vowell, dom. Ricardus, prior W. (*1514–38*):
Oxford, Keble Coll. (pertinet).

WALSINGHAM, *Fran. conv.*
Serlys, O.F.M., W., A.D. 1524:
Cambridge, Gonv. and Caius Coll., F.7.20 (name and date).
Totyngdon, fr. Thomas. *See* Wynbotisham.
Wynbotisham, fr. Thomas de:
Oxford, Bodleian, Bodl. 355 (Istos 6 quaternos contulit fr. Thomas
Totyngdon — — — qui eos contulit postea fr. Johanni de Wyn-
botisham 'ad vitam et post conventui W.'; *earlier ex libris of the
Cambridge custody*).

WALTHAM
Bartholomeus, canonicus W. (*s.xiii*):
Cambridge, Magd. Coll., 22.
Berkyng, dom. Galfridus de:
Cambridge, Gonv. and Caius Coll., 149.
Norton, dom. Walterus de, clericus (*s.xiii*):
Oxford, Bodleian, Auct. D.4.22.
Patishale, dom. Johannes, canonicus W.:
Untraced Görlitz MS.
Petrus, archidiaconus Londonie (*s.xiii*):
Oxford, Bodleian, Rawl. G.62.
Willelmus, prior:
Oxford, Bodleian, Laud lat. 109 (g.).
Wrattyng, fr. Johannes, canonicus W.:
Cambridge, Gonv. and Caius Coll., 116 (Tabula . . . scripta per).
Wylde, dom. Johannes, quondam precentor W.:
London, B.M., Lansdowne 763 (scripsit).

WARRINGTON, *Aug. conv.*
*Penketh, fr. Thomas, O.H.S.A., W. († *1487*):
Oxford, Corpus Christi Coll., 126 (*a* quod Penketh; *b* constat).
Strynger, fr. Ricardus, O.H.S.A., W.:
London, St Paul's Cath., 11 (name).

WARWICK, *Dom. conv.*
Alexander, fr. Nicholaus, O.P., W.:
Cambridge, U.L., Inc. 3391 (pertinet — — ex dono mag. Robarti Tomp-
son, doctoris). Durham, U.L., Cosin F.iv.30 (possessor).
Chestyrfyld, fr. Willelmus (*s.xv*):
Oxford, Magd. Coll., 54 (legavit).

Lily (?), fr. Robertus, O.P., W.:
London, B.M., IB.26227 (constat; *cf.* SALISBURY, *Dom conv.*, Heskynus).
Norman, Thomas, prior:
London, B.M., Sloane 1615 (name).
Savell, dom. Johannes, O.S.B. *See* Stremer.
*Stremer, fr. Nicholaus, (1) prior provincialis *1501*, (2, 3) O.P., W.:
(1) Cambridge, U.L., Inc. 3127 (liber — — quem emit). (2) London,
B.M., Royal 6 C.ix (precium hujus libri quod solvit — — apud
Evysham A.D. 1488 tunc cursor London'). (3) Oxford, St John's Coll.,
65 (liber — — quem partim emit et partim mendicavit a dom. Johanne Savell monacho, O.S.B., anno gracie 1479 tunc diaconus et
cursor Oxon').
**Tompson, mag. Robartus. *See* Alexander.

WELLS
*Bekynton, dom. Thomas de, Bathon' et Wellen' episcopus († *1465*):
Cambridge, Trin. Coll., 881 (ex dono — — et labore mag. Thome
Chaundeler hujus ecclesie cancellarii). Oxford, New Coll., 288 (*as*
Trin. Coll., 881).
*Chaundeler, mag. Thomas († *1490*). *See* Bekynton.

WENLOCK
Bruge, dom. Rolandus, prior W.:
Oxford, Mr D. M. Rogers (ad — —).
Dudley, Willelmus de:
Cambridge, Trin. Coll., 6 (name, ? *as scribe, in verses at end*).

WESTBURY
*Okeborn, mag. Willelmus, nuper decanus W. (*1451;* † *1465*):
Oxford, Jesus Coll., 45.

WESTMINSTER[3]
Barton, dom. Thomas, B.Th., monachus W. (*1498–99*):
Oxford, Bodleian, R.1.23 Th. Seld. (liber).
Champney, fr. Thomas, monachus W. (*1485–86*):
London, B.M., Royal 7 D.xxi (constat).
Crok', R. de, abbas (? *Richard de Crokesleye, abbot of W. 1246–58*):
Cambridge, U.L., Ee.4.23 (inventus fuit in armariolo — — —).
Ebesham, William:[4]
London, B.M., Add. 10106 (*wrote part*); Westm. Abbey, 29 (*wrote*).
Oxford, St John's Coll., 147 (*wrote; cf.* Lynne).
Felix, Jhone, monachus W. (*1524–25*):
London, B.M., Cotton Claud. A.viii (orate pro me — —; *wrote part; cf.*
Sporley).
Graunt, Willelmus (*monk of W. 1465–66*):
Oxford, St John's Coll., 147 (pertinet — — teste Willelmo Grove
monacho W. *See also* Lynne).

---

[3] Dates of profession, etc., are taken from E. H. Pearce, *The Monks of Westminster* (Cambridge, 1916).
[4] See A. I. Doyle, 'The Work of a late fifteenth-century English Scribe, William Ebesham', *Bulletin of the John Rylands Libr.*, xxxix (1957), 298–325.

Grove, Willelmus, monachus W. (*1484–85*). *See* Graunt.
Hasele, fr. Willelmus de (*monk of W. c. 1266*):
  London, B.M., Add. 8167 (ex procuracione —— reservato inde eidem
  W. quoad vixerit usufructu de licencia dom. abbatis et conventus).
  Oxford, St John's Coll., 190 (ex procuracione).
Holonde, fr. Johannes, monachus W. (*1468–69*):
  London, Sion Coll., Arc.L.40.2/E.25 (pertinet).
Humfrey, Robertus, monachus W. (*1468–69;* † *1509*):
  Oxford, Bodleian, Bodl. 46 (liber dom. Thome Jay monachi W. ex dono).
Islip, John, monk of W. 1479–80, abbot 1500–32:
  Manchester, J. Rylands, Lat. 165 (*his rebus in the borders*).
Jay, dom. Thomas, monachus W. (*1501–2*). *See* Humfrey.
*Lambert, Willelmus, monachus W. (*1456–57;* † *1513*):
  Edinburgh, U.L., Laing II.515 (liber ecclesie beati Petri W. et pertinet
  ——).
Lynne, Thomas, monachus W. (*1451–52;* † *1473–74*):
  Oxford, St John's Coll., 147 (constat; *cf.* Graunt).
Sporley, Ricardus, monachus W. (*1428–29*):
  London, B.M., Cotton Claud. A.viii (compilacio per, A.D. 1450).
Stanys, monachus W. (? *John S. 1462–63*):
  Cambridge, Trin. Coll., 1405 (name). Oxford, Balliol Coll., 264 (name).
Tedyngton, R., monachus [W.] (*1428–29;* † *1487*):
  Cambridge, Trin. Coll., 1365 (g.). Oxford, Balliol Coll., 142 (fuit olim
  Ric. Teddyngton monachi W., *according to Langbaine; MS. now
  missing*).

WESTMINSTER, *St Stephen*
*Chamber, Johannes (*dean 1522–47;* † *1549*):
  New York, Public Libr., 63.
Elmham, dom. Robertus de, quondam canonicus W., qui viii⁰ die Marcii
  A.D. 1365 cursum vite presentis consummavit ibidem:
  London, B.M., Stowe 49.

WETHERAL
Hartley, Radulphus (*last prior W.*):
  New York, Pierpont Morgan (owned).
Thorntone, fr. Willelmus, prior W. (*abbot of York 1530*):
  Bridgnorth, St Leonard's Church (attinet; *cf.* **YORK,** *St Mary*, Barwyk).

WHALLEY
Gregory, dom., quondam abbas W. († *1309*):
  Manchester, J. Rylands, Lat. 150 (dimissus communi armario per).
Hartford, fr. Ricardus de, monachus W.:
  Paris, U.L., 790 (perscriptus fuit A.D. 1373 a —— quem librum fecit
  scribi dom. Thomas de Mapelton sacerdos).
Lee, Tristram, armiger, † 1479:
  London, B.M., Add. 35283.
Lind*elay*, Rogerus de:
  Cambridge, Trin. Coll., 1041 (procuratus per).
Mapelton, dom. Thomas de. *See* Hartford.
Singleton, fr. Willelmus de, quondam scolaris W.:
  Canterbury, Cath., 73 (procuratus per).

WHERWELL
Stretford, domina Johanna, monasterii W.:
London, B.M., Add. 27866 (constat — — *over erasure of another name)*.

WIGMORE
Lodel*awe*, fr. Walterus de, senior, precentor W.   *See* Purcel.
Purcel, Johannes (*s.xiii ex.*):
Cambridge, Corpus Christi Coll., 402 (— — dedit ad instanciam fr.
Walteri de Lodel*awe* senioris tunc precentoris).

WINCHCOMB
Augustinus, Johannes, monachus W.:
Oxford, Mr D. M. Rogers (liber).
Benedictus, dom. Hugo, monachus W.   *See* Leye.
Benet, dom. Robertus, monachus W.:
Colchester, Harsnett Libr., K.f.11 (liber).   Oxford, Bodleian, M.9.4 Th.
(liber).
Gloucestir, John, sumtyme of Gloucestir dyar:
Oxford, Jesus Coll., 98.
*Kydermynster, dom. Ricardus, abbas (1, 2, 4, 6 olim *or* nuper abbas), W.
(† *after 1531*):
(1) Cambridge, Clare Coll., G.1.   (2) Dublin, Trin. Coll., 53.   Glasgow,
Mitchell Libr., 163434 (liber).   (4) Holkham Hall, Lord Leicester.
London, Lambeth Pal., **H 1756.A 1 (liber); (6) Westm. Abbey,
CC.4.   Oxford, Bodleian, Inc. d.G.5.2. 1494/1 (liber); Rawl. Q.d.12
(liber).
Leye, dom. Hugo:
Göttingen, U.L., Th.4 (concessit — — dom. Hugoni Benedicto monacho
W.).

WINCHELSEA
Boydin, Henricus, de Rya.   *See* Rya.
**Rya*, fr. Gaufridus *de* (*B.R.U.O., Boydin de Rya*) *s.xiii ex.*):
Hatfield House, Marquess of Salisbury, 309 (Memoriale Henrici Boydin
de Rya.   Requiescat in pace amen.   Quod filius suus fr. Gaufridus
sibimetipsi fecit fieri, set fratri Petro de Swinefeld assignavit qui tutor
suus Oxoniis fuit, postmodum Parisius specialissimus amicus, post-
remo in fratrum minorum ordine minister tocius Anglie.   Qui quasi
prescius preoperantis sui obitus quarto mense precedente hoc ipsum
memoriale resignavit et reddidit predicto fratri G. apud Winchelese).
*Swinefeld, fr. Petrus de, O.F.M., minister *provincialis* (*c.1264–72*).   *See*
Rya.

WINCHESTER
Athelstan, king of England:
London, B.M., Cotton Galba A.xviii (*traditionally his gift*).
Avyngton, Johannes, monachus W.:
Cambridge, U.L., Sel.3.28–29 (ex sumptibus dom. — — monachi ac
etiam scholaris et baccularii W.).   Edinburgh, U.L., *E.15.24 (ex
emptione et salario mag. — — doctoris sacre theologie necnon
monachi W. anno Christi 1519).   London, Westm. Abbey, CC.44 (ex
emptione dom. — — monachi necnon scholaris et baccalarii W. 'ac
nunc sacre theologie professor').
315

Basynge, Willelmus, monachus, S.T.P. (*last prior and first dean*):
    Winchester Coll., B.32 (libellus).
Coridon, Gaufridus:
    Oxford, Bodleian, Auct. D.2.4.
Cramborne, dom. Robertus:
    Cambridge, Trin. Coll., 338.
Draytone, fr. Johannes de, monachus (*s.xiii/xiv*):
    Cambridge, U.L., Gg.2.18 (Memoriale — — —).
Exceter, Johannes, monachus W.:
    Oxford, All Souls Coll., 114 (wrote A.D. 1531).
Merleberg, H. de, monachus W.:
    Leyden, U.L., Voss lat. F.93 (contulit).
Morton, Johannes, monachus W., (1) precentor:
    (1) Cambridge, St John's Coll., S.5.24 (ex provisione — — A.D. 1518).
    London, B.M., Harley 328 (possessor).
Rægenboldus sacerdos de Wentonia (*s.ix*):
    Oxford, Bodleian, Digby 63 (scripsit).
Sylksted, Thomas, supprior (*and prior;* † *1524*):
    Winchester, Cath., 15 (constat).
Tarente, fr. Nicholaus de, prior:
    London, B.M., Harley 315.
Vincent, fr. Willelmus, monachus W.:
    Oxford, Bodleian, Rawl. C.489 (ego — — hos duos libros silicet quod-
    dam portiphorium cum suo diurnale sibi simili fieri feci et manibus
    meis propriis conscripsi A.D. 1424, quos libros . . . volo ut post obitum
    meum habeat sacrista monasterii predicti vel alius ejusdem loci
    monachus quem sacrista duxerit eligendum pro usu predictorum
    librorum habendo, quamdiu ocupans vixerit in humanis, et quod
    prefati duo libri transeant de uno ad alium).

WINCHESTER, *nunnery*
*Fox, rev. pater dom. Ricardus, episcopus W. († *1528*):
    Cambridge, U.L., Mm.3.13.

WINCHESTER, *Coll. of St Elizabeth*
*Pontoyse, dom. Johannes, quondam episcopus W. († *1304*):
    Oxford, Univ. Coll., 129 (liber — — restituendus capelle sancte E.
    juxta W.).

WINCHESTER, *Coll. of B.V.M.*
**Wale, John, second master* († *1431*):
    Winchester Coll., 11 (*recorded in cat. as his gift*).
*Wykeham, William of, bishop of Winchester († *1404*):
    Winchester Coll., 4, 15, 38 (?) (*all recorded in cat. as his gifts*).

WINDSOR
Edwardus quartus, rex († *1483*):
    Oxford, Bodleian, Bodl. 192, 729.
*Marschull, rev. pat. dom. Johannes, nuper episcopus Landavensis (*1478–
    96*) et canonicus W. (*1474–78*):
    Oxford, Bodleian, Bodl. 684.
*Stokes, mag. (2) Johannes (*canon 1486;* † *by July 1503*):
    London, A. Ehrman. (2) Oxford, Bodleian, Bodl. 785 (procurator istius
    voluminis est — —).

*Urswyke, Christophorus, quondam elemosinarius Henrici septimi ac
decanus W. (*1495;* † *1521*):
Cambridge, Corpus Christi Coll., 346.   Princeton, U.L., 89.

WITHAM
*Blacman, mag. Johannes († *1485*):
Eton Coll., 213.   London, Lambeth Pal., 436 (orate pro; *recorded as his
gift*).   Oxford, Bodleian, Bodl. 801, Digby 104, Laud misc. 152, 154;
St John's Coll., 182 (liber Witham quod — —).
Dodesham, dom. Stephanus, monachus W.:
New York, Duschnes MS. (scripsit A.D. 1462).
*Holes, mag. Andreas, archidiaconus Wellensis († *1470*):
Oxford, Magd. Coll., 191 (mag. Johannes Myddelton unus executorum
testamenti — — donavit . . . ex bonis dicti mag. Andree, 1477).
*Loryng, mag. Willelmus († *1416*):
Durham, Cath., A.IV.30.
*Menbire, dom. Simon, quondam canonicus Saresburiensis († *1423*):
London, B.M., Add. 4899.
Mere, Henricus (*cf.* **CANTERBURY,** Mere):
Oxford, Bodleian, Laud misc. 152 (wrote; *cf.* Blacman), 154 (wrote; *cf.*
Blacman).
*Myddelton, mag. Johannes.   *See* Holes.
Walterus, quondam prior de Merton (*1198–1218, entered Carthusian order
1218*):
Leicester, Mr H. F. Smith.

WOBURN
Hobs, dom. Robertus, abbas:
London, B.M., IB.118 (comparatus per — — anno 1523).   *See also*
Radulphus.
Radulphus, fr., monachus W.:
Cambridge, St John's Coll., Bb.6.17 (donatus — a meritissimo patre
Roberto [*Hobs*] abbate).

WORCESTER
*Aston, fr. Johannes de (*cellarer 1295*):
Worcester, Cath., Q.13 (liber), Q.33 (name *in genitive*).
Aubin, fr. Philippus, monachus W., prior (*1287–96*):
Worcester, Cath., F.167 (fecit scribi).
*Bedmystre, mag. W.:
Worcester, Cath., Q.45 (wrote).
*Benet, *John*, monachus W.:
Oxford, Bodleian, Auct. D.inf.2.4 (cautio —, A.D. 1482).
Broctone, dom. Thomas, precentor (*W. 1410–12*):
Worcester, Cath., F.125 (tradatur).
*Broghton, Johannes, monachus W. (*admitted at Gloucester Coll.
1435–36*):
Worcester, Cath., F.86 (liber).
*Bromwico, fr. Ricardus de, monachus W. (*precentor 1317*):
Oxford, Bodleian, Bodl. 442 (exposuit — — — Philippo de Lustushulle
pro uno parvo libello distinctionum super psalterium et tabula super
originalibus sancti Augustini).   Worcester, Cath., F.62 (sold to fr.
Henry Fouke, *q.v.*), F.63 (caucio . . . A.D. 1305 et tradatur — —),

F.79 (liber; *cf.* F.101), F.101 (*a* Caucio — —; *b* Galfridus de Kelminton habet in custodia istum librum et librum magistri H. de Gandavo in quo continentur vii quodlibeta ejusdem (*F.79*) quos accepit de manibus — — —), F.139 (*a* lectura quam fecit — — — et scripsit manu sua antequam legit librum sententiarum Oxon'; *b* gave to fr. Henry Fouke, *q.v.*), F.156 (fecit scribere Wyg' antequam precentor extiterat).

*Catthorp, Ranulfus de (*monk of W. by 1301*):
Worcester, Cath., F.124 (gave to fr. Henry Fouke, *q.v.*).

Causford, Thomas de. *See* Hambory.

Clemens, quondam rector ecclesie de Chaddesleye:
Worcester, Cath., F.157 (contulit A.D. 1305).

Cliva, Johannes de, monachus *W.* (*sacrist 1423*):
Oxford, Bodleian, Hatton 11 (*name in initial; MS. written in hand known to be his*, A.D. *1404 ?*).

Crateford, Rogerus, monachus W. (*s.xv/xvi*):
Worcester, Cath., F.169 (traditus ad usum).

Dikklesdon, fr. Robertus de, monachus W.:
Cambridge, Peterhouse, 71 (Memoriale).

*Dumbleton, Johannes de (*monk of W.; sacrist 1288*):
Worcester, Cath., Q.42 (per istos xi . . ., J. de D. and ten others contributing in all 13 s. 4 d.).

*Fordham, mag. Johannes, prior W. (*1420–38*):
Worcester, Cath., F. 128 (contulit).

Fouke, fr. Henricus, monachus W. (*fl. 1338*) :
Oxford, Bodleian, Rawl. C.428 (per). Worcester, Cath., F.62 (per — — quem emit de mag. Ricardo de Bromwych quondam priorem Bergeveneie pro xx solidis), F.77 (per — — et illum habuit a dom. R. de Mortone pro quodam jocali eburneo), F.124 (per — — ex dono Ran. de Catthorp), F.131 (per — — precium 50 s.), F.139 (per — — quem dedit ei mag. Ricardus de Bromwych).

Gloucester, fr. Johannes de, monachus W. († *1314 or 1315*):
Worcester, Cath., F.75 (per; *cf.* Webley).

*Grene, fr. Johannes, D.Th. (*prior of W. 1388 and earlier fellow of Merton Coll., Oxford*):
Worcester, Cath., F.25–28 (procuravit A.D. 1386).

*Grimeley, mag. W. de (*precentor 1301*):
Worcester, Cath., Q.5 (Memorandum quod — — — recepit dimidium marcum [*sic*] super librum istum et metafisicam).

Hambory, Robertus de:
London, B.M., Royal 15 B.xiv (liber — — — quem idem composuit . . . Datus in domo nostra capitulari Wygornie anno Edwardi tertii [. . .] quod Thomas de Causford mag. teologie et arcium).

*Hambury, dom. Nicholaus, B.Th.:
Worcester, Cath., F.130 (per).

Hatfeld, fr. Johannes, monachus W. (*s.xiv/xv*):
Worcester, Cath., F.43 (liber).

*Jolyffe, mag. Thomas († *by 1479*). *See* Ledbury, Isaac.

Kelminton, Galfridus de (*fellow of Merton Coll., Oxford, fl. 1296*).
See Bromwico.

*Lawerne, mag. Johannes (*monk of W., almoner 1448, 1455*):
Oxford, Bodleian, Bodl. 692 (*wrote*). Worcester, Cath., F.13 (constat), F.19 (liber), Q.22 (liber). *See also p. 205*

*_Ledbury_, Isaac, doctor, monachus W. (_cellarer 1448–50_):
Worcester, Cath., F.39 (ex libris of W. _and_ teste mag. Thoma Jolyffe quem habuit de doctore Isack monacho).
*Ledbury, mag. Thomas (_monk W.; † 1443_):
Worcester, Cath., F.43 (liber eccl. cath. W. in custodia — —; _cf._ Hatfeld).
*Leminster, fr. Johannes de, monachus W. (_precentor 1349_):
Worcester, Cath., F.68 (script' quondam Avinion' per).[5]
Leyntall, dom. Rogerus, monachus W.:
Worcester, Cath., F.45 (constat).
Meldenham, dom. Thomas (_prior 1499–1507_):
Worcester, Cath., F.10 (constat).
Mor', fr. Thomas, monachus W.:
Gloucester, Cath., 25 (liber). Worcester, Cath., Q.54 (_a_ liber readopcionis — —; _b_ ex procuracione).
More, Willelmus, monachus W. (_prior 1518–36_):
Oxford, Merton Coll., B.8.G.17 (liber — —; _see also_ NEWCASTLE, _Carm. conv._).
Morton, dom. R. de (_pitancer 1328_). _See_ Fouke.
Oswaldus, sanctus:
Cambridge, Corpus Christi Coll., 391 (per — —; _inscription probably of s.xiv_).
Pagah_am_, Johannes de (_s.xii ex._):
Oxford, Bodleian, Bodl. 862 (g.).
Powycke, fr. Thomas, monachus majoris Malvernie. _See_ Straynsham.
*Prestone, fr. Johannes de, de Somerset, monachus W.:
Cambridge, Corpus Christi Coll., 24 (per, A.D. 1348). Worcester, Cath., F.11 (procuratus per, A.D. 1348).
*S. Germano, fr. Johannes de, monachus W. (_sub-prior 1301 or 1302_):
Worcester, Cath., F.4, fos 168–234 (caucio — — — impignoratus in cista communi pro duobus solidis A.D. 1295), F.8 (caucio — — — exposita communi ciste magistri Luce pro quadraginta solidis A.D. 1314), G.64 (_stated in hand of s.xiv to be_ manu magistri — — — theologi et monachi W.).
Seggesberwe, fr. Thomas de, (2) monachus W. (_s.xiii/xiv_):
Worcester, Cath., F.37 (per fratres — — — et Johannem de Wyke), (2) F.102 (procurata per).
Straynsham, fr. Thomas (_chamberlain 1482–83_):
Oxford, Corpus Christi Coll., 157 (memorandum quod — — deliberavit istum librum fr. Thome Powycke monacho majoris Malvernie et ipse deliberavit predicto — — librum vocatum Guido de bello Trojano, A.D. 1480).
Temedelyn (?), fr. Rogerus de:
Worcester, Cath., F.56 (tradatur).
Webley, dom. Humfridus, monachus (1) W. (_magister capellae in 1534, prebendary of the ninth stall after 1539_):
(1) London, A. Ehrman, R.255 (liber). Oxford, Bodleian, 8° M.122 Th. (liber — — Oxoniensis scolastici et monachi).
Webley, Johannes, monachus W.:
Worcester, Cath., F.75 (constat; _cf._ Gloucester).
Westbury, dom. [. . . .] de, monachus W. (? _John de W., professed 1318_):
Worcester, Cath., F.63 (Caucio [. . . .] A.D. 1325 tradatur — —).

---

[5] The scribe of Worcester, Cath., F.68 is French.

Wulfgeatus, scriptor Wigornensis:
  Oxford, Bodleian, Junius 121 (wrote *or, more probably, wrote exemplar of*).
Wygorn', Simon de, monachus:
  Worcester, Cath., F.105 (liber).
Wyke, fr. Johannes de. *See* Seggesberwe.

WORCESTER, *Fran. conv.*
Joseph, Johannes, O.F.M., W.:
  London, B.M., Harley 3239 (liber).

WORCESTER, *Dom. conv.*
Prechett, fr. Thomas, O.P., W.:
  Edinburgh, U.L., Inc. 33 (name).
Stremer (? *Nicholas S., O.P., W. in 1482; cf.* **WARWICK,** Stremer).
  Worcester, Cath., F.89 (name).
Toroldus, fr. Laurentius:
  Oxford, Bodleian, Rawl. C.780 (ligatus et coopertus ope et expensis
  — — pro conventu fr. pred. W. 1521).

WORKSOP
*Flemmyng, Carolus, prior W. (*1453–63*). *See* Flemmyng, Robertus.
*Flemmyng, mag. Robertus, decanus Lincoln' († *by Aug. 1483*):
  Oxford, Lincoln Coll., 63 (constat monasterio W. deliberatus — — ex
  comodato et precario per manus mag. Caroli Flemmyng prioris
  ejusdem A.D. 1457).
*Forster, Willelmus, mag. in gramatica, receptus in canonicum et con-
  fratrem W. qui paulisper scolatizans Oxonii mortalitate preventus
  habitum regularem se non induit:
  Cambridge, U.L., Hh.1.5 (legavit A.D. 1401).
Philippus, canonicus Lincoln':
  New York, Pierpont Morgan, 81.
Tikyll, Johannes, prior:
  New York, Public Libr. Spencer 26 (propriis manibus scripsit necnon
  deauravit).

YORK
Gretham, Johannes de. *See* Le Cras.
Le Cras, mag. Johannes, canonicus Y. (*s.xiv med.*):
  York, Minster, xvi.Q.13 (fecit scribi ex propriis expensis — — pro
  comodo et utilitate sacerdotum et clericorum chori ejusdem ecclesie
  frequentancium . . . ad ponendam in loco communi tuto et honesto
  . . . Me scripsit Johannes de Gretham).
**Neuton, mag. Johannes de, thesaurarius Y. († *1414*):
  Cambridge, Trin. Coll., 728, flyleaf. *See also p. 216.*
**Reynald, mag. Johannes, canonicus et prebendarius de Stillington
  (*1494*; † *1506*):
  London, St Paul's Cath., 13 (liberetur eccl. cath. Ebor' ex dono — —).

YORK, *St Mary*
Arrows, dom. Thomas, monachus Y.:
  Cambridge, Gonv. and Caius Coll., A* 1.12 (1) (liber). Oxford, Magd.
  Coll., i.1.1, 2 (liber).
Barwyk, fr. Thomas, monachus Y.:
  Bridgnorth, St Leonard's Church (liber).

Both, Thomas, abbas Y. (*1464–85*). *See* Hothom.

Brudford, fr. Willelmus de:
Dublin, Trin. Coll., 332 (accomodatus fr. Ricardo de Gy[. . . .]gton per
— — — A.D. 1368, qui quidem fr. Willelmus ex licencia abbatis sui
predicti libri habuit usumfructum).

Covyrdaill (Coverdale), fr. Willelmus de, monachus Y.:
London, B.M., Add. 24361 (*see* Hothom); Burney 220 (constat).

Gasgyll, fr. T., commonachus Y.:
Dublin, Trin. Coll., 207.

Gerard (*s.xii*):
Cambridge, U.L., Ee.6.40 (iste liber fuit Gerardi et est in monimentum
apud nos in vadimonio).

Graystock, Johannes, liberar':
Oxford, Bodleian, Lyell 17 (de perquisicione).

Gryffynge, Edmundus. *See* Staveley.

Gy[. . . .]gton, fr. Ricardus de. *See* Brudford.

Hanton, fr. Johannes, monachus Y.:
Oxford, Corpus Christi Coll., 193 (liber).

*Hothom, dom. Walterus, monachus Y. († *after 1495*):
Arundel Castle, Duke of Norfolk (accomodatus — — per venerabilem
patrem dom. Thomam Both abbatem Y.; *cf.* Staveley). London,
B.M., Add. 24361 (attinens fr. Willelmo Covyrdaill ex dono — —).

Lascy (Lacy), G. de:
Newcastle, U.L., 1 (g.). London, B.M., Add. 40007 (g.).

Staveley, dom. Thomas, (2) monachus Y.:
Arundel Castle, Duke of Norfolk (acquisivit me — — ex dono Edmundi
Gryffynge London). (2) Deventer, Mr J. P. L. van der Lande (owned).

Warthwyk, fr. Clemens:
San Marino (U.S.A.), Huntington, HM 903 (emptus per).

Wellys, fr. Willelmus, abbas (*1423–26*):
London, B.M., Add. 40007 (acquisitus (?) per, A.D. 1423).

YORK, *Fran. conv.*

Geytington, fr. Thomas de (*s.xiv ex.*):
Arundel Castle, Duke of Norfolk (legavit — — — dummodo fuit
secularis post vitam suam et fratris sui).

Neu*ton* (?), mag. Symon de:
London, Mr Raymond Russel.

[. . . .], *cursor* (?) Grimesb' (*Grimsby*):
Durham, Cath., B.II.36 (A.D. 1304 assignavit hunc librum [. . . .] con-
ventus fr. min. Ebor' in manus fr. Johannis de [. . . .] et dicto conventui
Ebor' post decessum predicti fratris [. . .]).

YORK, *Aug. conv.*

*Erghom, fr. Johannes de (*prior Y. 1385*):
London, B.M., Cotton Vesp. B.xxiii (liber), Royal 8 B.xix (name *in
genitive*); College of Arms, Arundel 6 (liber). Oxford, Corpus Christi
Coll., 81 (liber); St John's Coll., 150 (liber). Untraced Codex Justiniani (liber).

YORK, *Hospital of St Leonard*

Bramelay, dom. Willelmus, capellanus. *See* Castylfurth.

Castylfurth, dom. Johannes, capellanus:
Cambridge, U.L., Ee.4.19 (gave jointly with dom. William Bramelay).

APPENDIX

Donors and other persons concerned with books formerly owned by parish churches and chapels

ALBURY
**Hutton, Ricardus, quondam rector A.:
  Cambridge, Corpus Christi Coll., 211 (ex dono, A.D. 1513).

ARLINGHAM
Longney, Walterus, olim vicarius, qui mortem passus est A.D. 1502:
  Salisbury, Cath., 152.

BISHOP'S CLEEVE
*Claymund, Johannes, olim rector B. († *1537*):
  Oxford, Merton Coll., 62. f. 23 (gave to pass from rector to rector).

BLYTH
Watson, Johannes (?), de Blida, obiit 14[. .]:
  Cambridge, Jesus Coll., 19 (fieri fecit ad usum ecclesie).

BRASTED
**Stalys, mag. Robertus, quondam rector B. (*1493*):
  Deene park, Trustees of the late Mr G. Brudenell, XIX.c.12.

BREDGAR
Mone, Sir John, sumtyme wycary B., deceased 8 June 1474:
  London, Lambeth Pal., 1362.

BROMSGROVE
*More, dom. Willelmus, prior ecclesie cathedralis Wygornie:
  Cambridge, U.L., Add. 6688 (dedit A.D. 1521).

BUCKINGHAM
*Rudyng, mag. Johannes, archidiaconus Lincoln' († *1481*):
  Buckingham, Parish Church.

BURY, St Mary's
Fuller, Ricardus, capellanus:
  Oxford, Bodleian, Rawl. liturg. e.42 (gave jointly with Richard Aleyn, kerver, A.D. 1472).

CALDBECK
Cooke, dom. Robertus:
  Ampleforth Abbey (dedit A.D. 1506).

CARDINGTON
Suetbon, Thomas:
  Liverpool, U.L.

322

CHARFORD, SOUTH
Popham, Johannes, miles de comitatu Southamtonie:
London, B.M., Royal 2 A.xxi (donavit A.D. 1409).

COLWICH
Parker, Thomas:
London, B.M., Harley 4919.

CRICH
Bankes, Richard, vicar C.:
London, Lambeth Pal., 222 (doe geve and bequethe).

CUCKNEY
Sheparde, Willelmus:
Oxford, Univ. Coll., 78B.

EASTWELL
*Goldwell, dom. Jacobus, quondam episcopus Norwicensis († *1499*):
Ushaw Coll., 18 (ex dono — — A.D. 1504).

ESH LAUDE
*Rudde, mag. Johannes, quondam decanus de Lanchester (*1462–90*):
Ushaw Coll., 5.

EXETER, St Anne
Hyotte, dom. Johannes, annivellarius in ecc. cath. Exon':
Exeter, Cath., 3515 (contulit).

EXETER, St Mary Major
Lyngham, Robertus (*rector 1427*):
Coutances, Bibl., 2 (given by his executor).

FARNWORTH
Bolde, Baldwinus, vicarius Colwychiensis:
Manchester, U.L., Christie 3.f.19.

HALSALL
Faryngton, dom. Edmundus, quondam rector H.:
Manchester, J. Rylands, Lat. 339 (constat eccl. parochiali de H. post
mortem dom. Willelmi Hoghton capellani. Ex dono — —).

HARLASTON
Vernon, Henricus, miles, qui obiit A.D. 1515:
Oxford, Bodleian, Ashmole 1764 (dedit et legavit).
Vernon, Johannes, eques auratus, obiit anno a Christo nato 1545:
Cambridge, Christ's Coll., 8.

HARPOLE
Chater, Thomas:
London, B.M., C.52 g.2.

LAPWORTH
Assheby, Thomas († *1459*):
Oxford, Corpus Christi Coll., 394.

LEAKE
Holme, Germanus de, secundus vicarius:
Oxford, Bodleian, Auct. D.4.20.

LONDON, St Mary Aldermanbury
Jenyns, Stephanus, miles et aldermannus Londonie, et Margareta uxor sua:
London, B.M., Royal 2 B.xii, xiii (dederunt A.D. 1508).

MELBOURNE
Bredone, dom. Johannes, quondam vicarius de Bredone:
London, Gray's Inn, 20 (gave in 1514, to pass from vicar to vicar).

NEWARK
Yates, Simon:
Cambridge, U.L., Inc. 3799 (constat cantarie de N. ex dono — — anno 1526).

NEWCASTLE-UPON-TYNE, St Nicholas
Lacy, Johannes, O.P., N.:
Oxford, St John's Coll., 94 (gave in 1434 to pass from priest to priest of St Nicholas).

PENWORTHAM
Harwode, dom. Thomas, capellanus:
Bournemouth, A. G. Thomas (dedit et concessit unum portiferium integrum notatum (*presumably this MS.*), A.D. 1486).

POTSHRIGLEY
**Downes, mag. Galfridus (*fellow of Queens' Coll., Cambridge, 1490*):
London, B.M., Add. 41175.

SALTFLEETBY
*Smythe, Walter (*fellow of Eton;* † *1524*):
Eton Coll., Em.1.7 (*presumed gift of*).

SARSDEN
Horne, Maystris Elysabethe, of Saresden, wydow:
Cambridge (U.S.A.), P. Hofer (gave in 1541).

SHERE
Cantmell, Johannes, capellanus cantarie de S.:
Helmingham Hall, Lord Tollemache, 72 (dedit A.D. 1477).

SHERMANBURY
Hayre (?), John:
Cambridge, U.L., Dd.12.69.

SKELMERSDALE
Bawer, Petrus, Skyrmensvallensis (*s.xv*):
Cambridge, U.L., Dd.15.1.

SOUTHWARK, St George
Lyncolm, James (*s.xvi in.*):
London, B.M., Add. 36672 (I beqweytt hefter my desses).

SOUTHWICK
Froste, Willelmus et Juliana uxor ejus (*s.xvi: in.*):
London, B.M., Royal 2 B.xv (dederunt remanere imperpetuum ad orandum b. Marie in ista capella de Suthwyke).

STAVELEY
Bartram, mag. Robertus:
Untraced missal (gave for use of 'rector ecclesie ex parte boreali . . . in perpetuum').

TIDMARSH
Leyham, master Henry (*lord of the manor of T.*):
Tidmarsh Parish Church (gave in 1544).

WINGFIELD, SOUTH
Sutton, dom. Richardus, vicarius de Crannesleia:
Capetown, U.L., 1.

WITNEY
Wenman, Anne:
Oxford, Bodleian, Gough Missals 25 ('Sir John Richardes bought this missall at Oxford' in 1526 'for the aulter of seynt Mary Maudelen yn the paryshe chyrche of Wittney, of the gyft of — — ').

WOLLATON
Husse, Willelmus, quondam rector W.:
Wollaton Parish Church (bought by his executors for the church for 10 marks).

WRANGLE
**Rede, Willelmus, rector de Allwalton vicariusque de Stokton magna, natus A.D. 1479:
Downside Abbey, 950 (bequeathed).

YORK, St Martin
Rycherdson, dom. Willelmus, quondam persona in ecclesia cathedrali s. Petri (*vicar choral, s.xvi in.*):
York, Minster, xvi.D.13 (gave in 1510).

Glossary of Words Used in References to Books and Ownership Recorded on pp. 225–325[1]

accipere. WORCESTER, Bromwico.

accomodare, accomodatio. Used of loans. *Cf.* **commodare, mutuare, restituere.** For seculars receiving books from religious houses on loan, *see* ABINGDON, Johane; ANGLESEY, Bromptoun; DARLEY, Eydon; LINCOLN, *Dom. conv.*, Birton; MALMESBURY, Grandison, Swineshead; SALISBURY, Wudeston; SALISBURY, *Dom. conv.*, Coppere; WORCESTER, Bromwico; WORKSOP, Flemmyng. Reason for loan expressed: LINCOLN, *Dom. conv.*, Birton.

acquirere, acquisitio, acquisitum. Used of books obtained or provided for a religious house.

ad. DUNFERMLINE, Farguson; ST OSYTH, Joly. Presumably for *pertinet ad.*

adipisci. FOUNTAINS, Thyrske; HOLME CULTRAM, Davys.

afferre. LONDON, *Charterhouse*, Rowst (of a book taken by a monk to another house); NORWICH, Steward; RIEVAULX, Elyngton.

almariolum (armariolum). DURHAM, Aukland, Gisburne, Hemmyngburgh, Hexham, Manbe, Robertus, Swalwell, Werdall, Wessyngton, Whytehed.

amicus. *See* **elymosina.**

anima. dare pro anima (or a similar phrase): BABWELL, Hylton; KIRKSTALL, Duffeld; NORTHAMPTON, Forde; SHAFTESBURY, Horder. *See also* **orare.**

assignare, assignatio. (1) Used in inscriptions of friars: LINCOLN, *Fran. conv.*, Tatewic; LONDON, *Dom. conv.*, Beauchamp; LONDON, *Carm. conv.*, Sutton, Walden; YORK, *Fran. conv.* (2) Used of assigning a book to a particular place within a collection of books, *e.g.* to the new cloister cupboard at DURHAM and to the 'libraria' at BURY (Curteys), EXETER (Snetesham), LINCOLN (Duffeld).

attinere. CANTERBURY, Sellyng; YORK, *St Mary*, Hothom.

auctoritas, auctorizare. HEREFORD, *Fran. conv.*, Herbert; ST ALBANS, Wyntreshull. *Cf.* **licentia.**

auferre. Used of stolen books: READING, Wargrave; ROBERTS-BRIDGE, Grandison; SPALDING, Oldfield.

catena, catenare. EXETER, Lacy; FOUNTAINS, Smythe.

cautio. Used of pledges: BURY, Haliwell; EDINGTON, Newton; GLOUCESTER, Lasseborgh; KIRKHAM, Menythorp; LANTHONY, Calne; LONDON, *Dom. conv.*, Rokesle; NEWNHAM, Bedeford; ROCHESTER, Wybarn; ST ALBANS, Warder; SHREWSBURY, Tapton; THORNTON, Forsett; WORCESTER, Benet, Bromwico, S. Germano, Westbury. *Cf.* **exponere, implegiare, memoriale, supplementum, vadimonium.**

codex. DURHAM, Wylom.

[1] All occurrences of the less ordinary words have been noted.

collatio. *See* **conferre.**

colligare. BURY, Becles. *See* **ligare.**

comodare. Occasionally used instead of **accomodare.**

comparare. BRISTOL, *Dom. conv.*, Mertun; WOBURN, Hobs.

compilare, compilatio. COVENTRY, Grenborough; WESTMINSTER, Sporley.

complere. OXFORD, *St Frideswide*, A.

componere. CANTERBURY, Chartham, Stone; WORCESTER, Hambory.

concedere, concessio. Used of books given 'ad usum'.

conferre, collatio. Used often of gifts.

confirmare. ST ALBANS, Wyntreshull.

conjunctio. BURTON, Edys.

connectere. ST ALBANS, Ware.

conscribere. ST ALBANS, Wyntreshull; WENLOCK, Dudley; WINCHESTER, Vincent. *See* **scribere.**

constare. Used commonly to express possession.

consummatio. BIDDLESDEN, Brueria.

cooperire. WORCESTER, *Dom. conv.*, Toroldus.

custodia. (1) in custodia: BURY, Langham; CAMBRIDGE, *Dom. conv.*, Hunton; CANTERBURY, Bonyngton, Gyllingham, Langdon; GLASTONBURY, Langley; NORWICH, Attleborough, Thomas; WORCESTER, Kelminton, Ledbury. (2) sub custodia: CAMBRIDGE, *Dom. conv.*, Willingham; LINCOLN, Dadington (in this second, and probably also in the first, instance the reference is to permanent guardianship by an office-holder). *Cf.* **custos.**

custodialis. CAMBRIDGE, *Fran. conv.*, Wyndele. Used of a book belonging to a Fran. custody.

custos. CANTERBURY, Rychemont; CHESTER, Clarke, Ley.

dare, donum. *Passim.* For reason of gift, *see* **anima, favor, memoria, recompensatio**; *see also* COLDINGHAM, Todd; GREENWICH, Tyndall; GUISBOROUGH, Pykering; KENILWORTH, Alward; MEAUX, Wilflete; SOUTHWICK, *Ch.*, Froste. For gifts between religious, *see e.g.* CANTERBURY, Hadley, Hartey; DURHAM, Swalwell. For a gift by a religious house to a secular, *see* OXFORD, *Fran. conv.*, Gascoigne; by one religious house to another, *see* HAILES, Ricardus.

deaurare. WORKSOP, Tikyll.

dedicare. HUNTINGDON, Laurentius.

deliberare. LINCOLN, Sutton; NEWARK, Rosse; STAINDROP, Heddon; TEWKESBURY, Evesham; WORCESTER, Straynsham; WORKSOP, Flemmyng.

deperdere. ST ALBANS, Whethamstede.

derelinquere. ST ALBANS, Ware.

dimittere. WHALLEY, Gregory.

disponere. CREDITON, Palmer; EXETER, Webber.

distributio. CAMBRIDGE, *Peterhouse*, Clouygth.

donum. *See* **dare.**

electio. OXFORD, *Exeter Coll.*, David.

elymosina. (1) de communibus elymosinis: LONDON, *Fran. conv.*, Bavard. (2) ex elymosinis amicorum: BEDFORD, *Fran. conv.*, Grene; BRISTOL, *Fran. conv.*, Martun; CAMBRIDGE, *Carm. conv.*, Pole; HEREFORD, *Fran. conv.*, Knull, Ledbury.

emere, emptio. *Passim.* For books bought (1) by seculars from friars, *see* **MEAUX,** Wilflete; **NORTHAMPTON,** *Dom. conv.,* Gunthorpe; (2) by one religious from another, *see e.g.* **CANTERBURY,** J. Holyngborne; **DURHAM,** Watson; (3) at Evesham, *see* **WARWICK,** *Dom. conv.,* Stremer; (4) at Oxford, *see* **BURTON-UPON-TRENT,** Edys; **CANTERBURY,** *St Augustine,* Cantyrbury; **THAME,** Redyng; **WARWICK,** *Dom. conv.,* Stremer.

esse. sum liber (or **libellus**). **ABINGDON,** Buckland, Rowland; etc.

exarare. **LONDON,** *Charterhouse,* Chawncy.

expensum. **OXFORD,** *Fran. conv.,* Notingham; **SYON,** Margareta; **WORCESTER,** *Dom. conv.,* Toroldus; **YORK,** Le Cras. *Cf.* **impensum, ope, salarium, sumptus.**

exponere. exponere pro, to pledge in return for another book. **ROCHESTER,** Thornden; **WORCESTER,** Bromwico. *Cf.* **cautio.**

facere. Used in the phrases *fieri fecit, ligari fecit, scribi fecit.* For *fecit* meaning apparently *scribi fecit, see* **ST ALBANS,** Symon.

favor. **BEAUVALE,** Ruwe.

fieri. fieri fecit, a variant of **scribi fecit,** *q.v.*

finire. **ST ALBANS,** Teerpenninc.

gaudium. cum magno gaudio et honore: used, with slight variations, in ownership inscriptions by religious of **EYE** (Stowe), **LYNN** (Palmer), **RAMSEY** (Lincoln, Weston); after the *ex libris* of the priory of **ELY** (Oxford, Ball. Coll. 49); by an archdeacon of Ely (Cambridge, Gonv. and Caius Coll. 204) and Margaret Salis of Methwold, Norfolk (Oxford, Bodleian, Digby 99); current, therefore, in East Anglia. *See also* Cambridge, St John's Coll. 122; Oxford, Bodleian, Rawl. C.882.

gratia. (1) **ex gratia et pro usu:** **HEREFORD,** Pede. (2) **sumptibus gratiarum suarum:** **BURY,** Huntedon.

honor. *See* **gaudium.**

honorare. **RAMSEY,** Grafham.

impensum. **CANTERBURY,** Goleston. *Cf.* **expensum.**

impetratio. **SEMPRINGHAM,** Glynton.

impignorare. **LONDON,** *Aug. conv.,* Tame; **WORCESTER,** S. Germano. *Cf.* **cautio.**

industria. **GLASTONBURY,** Fawkes; **ST ALBANS,** Legat, Whethamstede.

instantia. **HAILES,** Ricardus; **SHEEN,** Yngylby; **WIGMORE,** Lodelawe.

jus. **BATTLE,** Nuton.

labor, laborare. **BYLAND,** Ditton; **DURHAM,** Wessyngton, Wlveston; **TEWKESBURY,** Londoniis; **WELLS,** Chaundeler.

legare, legatio, legatum. *Passim.*

liber (or a book-title) followed by a personal name in the genitive case. *Passim.* For inscriptions in this form coupling the name of a religious and the name of the patron saint of his house, *see* **CANTERBURY,** *St Augustine,* Alulphus; **DURHAM,** Roger Bell. *Cf.* **pertinere.**

liberare. **DURHAM,** Hilton, Wherton; **FOUNTAINS,** Huby; **LEICESTER,** Thurkeston; **READING,** Lathbury; **YORK,** Reginald.

libraria. **BURY,** Curteys; **DURHAM,** Ebchester, Poklyngton, Seton, Wessyngton; **EXETER,** Snetesham; **GLOUCESTER,** Hanley; **LINCOLN,** Duffeld; **LONDON,** Gascoigne; **LONDON,** *Fran. conv.,*

Bavard; **LONDON,** *Aug. conv.*, Lowe; **ST ALBANS,** Whethamstede, Wyntreshull.

licentia. Permission from a superior to have a book. **ASHRIDGE,** Wederore; **CAMBRIDGE,** *Fran. conv.*, Stanwey; **DARTFORD,** Wrattisley; **HATFIELD PEVEREL,** Bebseth; **LINCOLN,** *Fran. conv.*, Tatewic; **LONDON,** *Charterhouse,* Rowst; **LONDON,** *Fran. nuns,* Hasley, Porter; **ST ALBANS,** Beaver, Dalling, Dunstaple, Steukle, Wylum; **WESTMINSTER,** Hasele; **YORK,** *St Mary,* Brudford.

ligare. **CAMBRIDGE,** *Dom. conv.*, Redymer; **CANTERBURY,** *St Augustine,* Cok; **GLOUCESTER,** Hanley; **LONDON,** *Fran. conv.*, Bavard; **OXFORD,** *Fran. conv.*, Colman; **READING,** Redyngia; **WORCESTER,** *Dom. conv.*, Toroldus. *See* **colligare, cooperire.**

limitare. **DURHAM,** Byllyngham.

mandatum. **DUNFERMLINE,** Monymelle; **OXFORD,** *Dom. conv.*, Courteys.

manere. **CAMBRIDGE,** *Fran. conv.*, Thomas. **CANTERBURY,** R. Holyngborne.

manus. (1) **scriptus per manum** (or **per manus** or **propria manu**): **ABERDEEN,** Godefridus; **ABINGDON,** Bledelowe; etc. (2) **per manum:** **BRISTOL,** *Fran. conv.*, Downe; **DORE,** Bathon; **NEWBATTLE,** Scot. (3) **deliberatus per manus:** **WORKSOP,** C. Flemmyng. (4) **detur per manus:** **PIPEWELL,** Burton. (5) **liberatus per manus:** **FOUNTAINS,** Kydde. (6) **recepit per manus:** **NORWICH,** Langrak.

memoria. **ASHRIDGE,** Wederore; **KIRKSTALL,** Duffeld; **MALMESBURY,** [....]; **SALISBURY,** Lovell.

memoriale. (1) **memoriale ... pro,** used of books left as a pledge: **BURY,** Grosseteste; **LANTHONY,** Merkley; **LINCOLN,** *Fran. conv.*, Lincoln; **NEWARK,** Hugo; **READING,** Pag'; *see also* London, Lambeth Pal. 122 (*Memoriale Lanton' ... pro ...*), Oxford, Magd. Coll. 119 (*Memoriale mag. Johannis de Hamt' pro Aug. super Johannem, c.*1200). (2) **memoriale** without following *pro* is used either of books left in memory of the donors, or has the same meaning as **memoriale ... pro: ABINGDON,** Bridport; **EXETER,** Cicestria; **LONDON,** *Charterhouse,* Lumley; **LONDON,** *Dom. conv.*, Wigornia; **LONDON,** *Carm. conv.*, Bacona; **OXFORD,** *Carm. conv.*, Hunt; **SALISBURY,** Fadir; **WINCHELSEA,** Rya; **WINCHESTER,** Drayton; **WORCESTER,** Dikklesdon; *see also* Cambridge, U.L., Ee.5.11; London, Lambeth Pal. 158, 215 (*Memoriale de Lanthonia*); Cambridge, Corpus Christi Coll. 175 (*Memoriale fr. Walteri de Conventr'*). For the requirement at Eynsham that no loan should be made without a *memoriale* 'tanti aut majoris pretii', *see* the Eynsham custumal, Oxford, Bodleian, Bodl. 235, fos 98ᵛ–99,[2] and for a similar requirement at Durham, *see Catt. Vett.*, p. 121. Manuscripts of St Germain des Prés, Corbie, and the Sorbonne marked *Memoriale ... pro* are referred to by Delisle, *Cabinet des manuscrits,* ii. 43, 125, 173, 193. *Cf.* **cautio, monimentum, recipere, recompensatio, revocare, vadimonium.**

mendicare. **WARWICK,** *Dom. conv.*, Stremer.

mittere. **HOLME CULTRAM,** Ludovicus.

monimentum. **YORK,** *St Mary,* Gerard.

mutuare, mutuum, mutuacio. **BYLAND,** Welton; **GREENWICH,** *Fran. conv.*, Dengayn; **HAVERFORDWEST,** Thoresby; **MALMESBURY,**

[2] I owe this reference to Mr R. W. Hunt.

Grandison; **SALISBURY, Praty; TEWKESBURY,** Cheltenham. *Cf.* **accomodare.**

ope, ex. WORCESTER, *Dom. conv.,* Toroldus.

opus. (1) **ex opere: LINCOLN,** Higgons. (2) **ad opus: ST ALBANS,** Wyntreshull.

orare. orate pro anima . . .: attached sometimes to *ex dono* inscriptions (*e.g.* **HINTON,** Marshall), but even when not so attached suggests that the person prayed for was the donor (*e.g.* **DALE,** North; **THREMHALL,** Herbert).

ordinare. SALISBURY, Lovell.

ordo. Used of books belonging to the Fran. (**HEREFORD,** *Fran. conv.,* Herbert) and Dom. (**SALISBURY,** *Dom conv.,* Coppere) orders.

per. If an inscription consists only of the word **per** followed by a personal name in the accusative case, it may be uncertain whether the person named wrote the manuscript, procured or gave it, or merely handed it over; *cf.* **BURY,** Barwe; **CANTERBURY,** Neell; **HEREFORD,** *Vicars Choral,* Mybbe; **HERTFORD,** Wynsselowe; **MALMESBURY,** Salamon; **OXFORD,** *Oriel Coll.,* Trikyngham; **WORCESTER,** Dumbleton, Fouke.

perarare. peraratus calamo: CANTERBURY, Cantuariensis.

perficere. PETERBOROUGH, Wodeforde.

perquirere, perquisitum. Common. *Cf.* **acquirere, acquisitum.**

perscribere. BURY, Clare; **WHALLEY,** Hartford.

pertinere. Used often of books in the temporary possession of individual religious: **BURY,** W[. . .]spet (*Edmundo sancto pertinet et . . .*); **CANTERBURY,** *St Augustine,* Byholt (*quantum ad se pertinuit*); **WESTMINSTER,** Lambert (*liber b. Petri Westmon' et pertinet . . .*).

ponere. GLOUCESTER, Hanley.

portare. CANTERBURY, *St Augustine,* Clare.

possidere, possessio, possessor. *E.g.* **BODMIN,** Basseytt.

praeceptum. DURHAM, Blaklaw, Wherton.

praestare. LONDON, *Charterhouse,* Lucas.

procurare, procuratio, procurator. *E.g.* **BODMIN,** *Fran. conv.,* H. decanus; **BURY,** Aylesham. **scripturam procuravit: IPSWICH,** *Fran. conv.,* Ykewrth. **ex procuratione propria: DURHAM,** Rypon.

proprietas contrasted with **usus. EXETER,** Hugo.

providere, provisio, providentia. *E.g.* **BATTLE,** Nuton.

quaternus. ST ALBANS, Ware.

quod. When **quod** and a personal name are written at the end of a text, as often in late-medieval manuscripts, the person named is probably the scribe: *e.g.* **BODMIN,** Arcuarius.

quondam. liber quondam: *e.g.* **BURTON,** Swepston (book in new ownership); **DURHAM,** Seton (book in new place of keeping).

readopcio. WORCESTER, Mor.

recipere. SALISBURY, Scamel. **recipere . . . super: WORCESTER,** Grimeley.

recompensatio. CIRENCESTER, Preston.

recuperare. GLOUCESTER, Temese. *Cf.* **redimere.**

reddere. DURHAM, Merley; **WINCHELSEA,** *Fran. conv.,* Rya.

redimere, redemptio. READING, Wargrave; **SHREWSBURY,** *Dom. conv.,* Tapton.

330

relinquere. CAMBRIDGE, *Dom. conv.*, Yx[. . .]; **INCHCOLM,** Fynlay; **LONDON,** *Carm. conv.*, Bacona.

remancipare. SIBTON, Crofftis.

remanere (remayne). HEREFORD, *Fran. conv.*, Chalbenor; **LONDON,** *Fran. nuns*, Carneburgh, Horwode; **ST ALBANS,** Wylum, Wyntreshull; SOUTHWICK, *Ch.*

remissio peccatorum. SHEEN, Darker, Feriby.

reparare, reparatio. CANTERBURY, *St Augustine*, Lenham; **ROCHES-TER,** Mallinges.

requisitio (?). SYON, Margareta.

reservare. ASHRIDGE, Wederore; **LINCOLN,** Repyndon.

resignare. SOUTHAMPTON, *Fran. conv.*, Kingestone; **WINCHELSEA,** *Fran. conv.*, Rya.

restituere. ANGLESEY, Bromptoun; **CANTERBURY,** Covintre, Ingram; **DARLEY,** Eydon; **MALMESBURY,** Grandison; **WINCHESTER,** *St Elizabeth*, Pontoyse. *Cf.* **accomodare.**

reverti. TARRANT KEYNSTON, Corf.

revocare. READING, Pag'.

salarium. WINCHESTER, Avyngton.

scribere. *E.g.* **BATH,** Lutton. **scribi** (or **fieri**) **fecit:** *e.g.* **ELSTOW,** Chanvill; **GLASTONBURY,** Wych; **WHALLEY,** Hartford; **YORK,** Le Cras (both scribe and employer are named in these four inscriptions). **scriptus per:** **GLASTONBURY,** Merylynch. For reasons for writing, *see* **mandatum, praeceptum, remissio, voluntas.** *Cf.* **conscribere, exarare, manus, perarare, perscribere, quod, subarrare.**

sollicitudo. OXFORD, *Fran. conv.*, Notingham.

sors. BURY, Wickham; **OXFORD,** *Merton Coll.*, Hyll, Johnson.

status. DURHAM, Wessyngton.

studium. BATTLE, Manwode.

subarrare. DUREFORD, Cicestrensis. *Cf.* **scribere.**

sumptus. ST ALBANS, Wyntreshull; **WINCHESTER,** Avyngton.

testamentum. HEREFORD, *Fran. conv.*, Cornubiensis.

tradere. Used of books conveyed from one person or place to another. **tradatur** occurs nine times (*e.g.* **DEREHAM,** Johannes), **traditus** or **tradidit** six times (*e.g.* **BURY,** Waxingam).

tribuere. CANTERBURY, Æthelstan.

usque ad. Used of termination of a loan.

usus. *Passim.* That use is 'ad terminum vitae' is often stated. For use by the holder of a particular office, *see* **DARLINGTON,** Whitton; **SALISBURY,** Martivall; **WINCHESTER,** Vincent.

ususfructus. ASHRIDGE, Wederore; **YORK,** *St Mary*, Brudford.

utilitas. TEWKESBURY, Londoniis.

vadimonium. YORK, *St Mary*, Gerard.

vendicare. CANTERBURY, Lo[. . .]; **SYON,** Selby.

volumen. WINDSOR, Stokes.

voluntas. GLASTONBURY, Wych; **LINCOLN,** *Dom. conv.*, Birton; **SOUTHAMPTON,** *Fran. conv.*, Kingestone.

331

INDEX OF MANUSCRIPTS

For index of printed books see p. 396. In references to the main list a place-name without further specification refers to the first entry under each place-name in the list; thus *London* stands for St Paul's, London, *Colchester* for St John's, Colchester. A † indicates a 'rejected' ascription. References to the Appendix of books from parish churches, etc., are indicated by *Ch.* following the place-name. An asterisk after the name of the medieval owner indicates that the book has been deposited by its present owner in another library. Two asterisks in this position indicate that the book is a deposit from another library.

---

[1] Now in Tübingen U.L.
[2] Now in Marburg, Westdeutsche Bibl.

BOSTON, *Lincolnshire*
PARISH CHURCH
—   Pontefract

BOULOGNE, *France, Pas-de-*
                    Calais
BIBL. MUN.
92   Dunfermline

BRADFER-LAWRENCE, Mr
    H. L. *See* **RIPON**

BRINKLEY, *Suffolk*
SIR G. KEYNES, THE LAMMAS
                    HOUSE
—   Glastonbury

BRISTOL, *Gloucestershire*
DEAN AND CHAPTER
—   Bristol
ALL SAINTS' CHURCH
1–4   †Bristol, Gild
BAPTIST COLL.
    Z.c.23   Harrold
    d.5   Lanthony
    d.40   Syon
    e.38   Crowland

BRUDENELL, TRUSTEES OF
    THE LATE Mr G. *See*
    DEENE PARK

BRUSSELS, *Belgium*
BIBL. ROYALE
    149 (2076–78)   Fountains
    593 (9961–62)   Peterborough
    1403 (8794–99)   Rochester
    1420 (10106–13)   Bicester
    1520 (1650)   Abingdon
    1557 (5277)   Oxford, Balliol
    2530 (606–7) Sheen Anglorum
    3097 (9903) Canterbury, St Aug.

BUCKINGHAM
PARISH CHURCH
—   Buckingham, *Ch.*

BURDETT-BROWN, Mrs A. D.
    See **LACOCK**

BURTON LATIMER, *North-*
                    amptonshire
PARISH CHURCH
—   †Burton Latimer, *Ch.*

BURY ST EDMUNDS, *Suffolk*
GRAMMAR SCHOOL
—   Bury
ST JAMES'S CATHEDRAL
1   Syon
3   Bury
4   Bury

BUTE, MARQUESS OF. *See*
    MOUNT STUART

BUTLER-BOWDON, Capt. M.
    See **MAYFIELD**

CAMARILLO, *U.S.A., Calif.*
EDWARD LAURENCE DOHENY ME-
    MORIAL LIBR.
7   Abbotsbury
50   Winchcomb

CAMBRAI, *France, Nord*
BIBL. COMMUNALE
235   †Mount Grace

CAMBRIDGE
UNIV. LIBR.
Additional 850   Bury
        2770   Dunstable,
                    Dom.
        2823   York, Aug.
        2991   London, Dom.
        3097   Merevale
        3303, no. 6 Durham
        3468   Ely, Bishopric
        3571   Lincoln
        3572   Stafford
        3578   Canterbury,
                    St Aug.
        4081   Syon
        5368   Waverley
        6006   Bury
        6190   Bury
        6578   Mount Grace
        6688   Bromsgrove,
                    Ch.
        6855   Southwark
        6860   Bury
        6865   Barnwell
        6866   Babwell
        7220   Campsey
    Dd.1.4   Canterbury
    1.7, 8   Windsor
    1.15   London,
                    St Margaret's
                    Lothbury, *Ch.*

Univ. Libr. (*contd*)		Univ. Libr. (*contd*)	
Gg.3.33	Roche	Ii.3.29	Norwich
4.11	St Albans	3.31–32	Norwich
4.15	Eynsham	3.33	Canterbury
	†Norwich	4.2	Norwich
4.17	Canterbury	4.3	Ely
4.33	Durham	4.5	†Norwich
5.34	Chester	4.6	Tavistock
5.35	Canterbury,	4.8	Norwich
	St Aug.	4.12	Norwich
6.3	Norwich	4.14	†Norwich
Hh.1.5	Worksop	4.15	Norwich
1.10	†Canterbury	4.18	Norwich
3.11	Abbotsbury	4.20	Ely
	Cerne	4.22	†Norwich
6.8	Syon	4.31	†Norwich
6.11	Ramsey	4.34	Norwich
Ii.1.1	Babwell		†Worcester
1.15	Canterbury,	4.35	Norwich
	St Aug.	4.37–38	Norwich
1.18	Norwich	6.1	Osney
1.20–23	Norwich	6.5	Bury
1.30–32	Norwich	6.32	Deer
1.34	Norwich	6.36	Thame
1.41	Canterbury	Kk.1.11	Dereham, West
2.1	Canterbury	1.17	Canterbury,
2.2	Norwich		St Aug.
2.4	Exeter	1.19	Canterbury,
	†Salisbury		St Aug.
2.6–7	Norwich	1.20	Canterbury
2.10	Oxford, Balliol	1.21	Sudbury, Dom.
2.11	Exeter	1.22	Abingdon
2.14	Norwich	1.23	Canterbury
2.15	Ely	1.24	Ely
2.16	†Bury	1.24	Canterbury
2.19–20	Norwich	2.2	Launceston
2.22	Norwich	2.6	Hanley Castle, *Ch.*
2.24	Canterbury,	2.8	Norwich
	St Aug.	2.13	Norwich
2.25	Coggeshall	2.15	Norwich
2.26	†Canterbury	2.18	Maxstoke
2.27	Norwich	2.19–21	Norwich
2.30	Oxford, Aug.	3.18	Worcester
3.1	Canterbury		†Canterbury
3.6–7	Norwich	3.21	Abingdon
3.9	Biddlesden	3.25–26	Norwich
3.10–11	Norwich	4.2	Oxford, Balliol
3.12	Canterbury	4.3	Norwich
3.14	Oxford, Aug.	4.5	Norwich
3.16	Norwich	4.6	Worcester
3.22	Norwich		†Malmesbury
3.24	Norwich	4.10–13	Norwich

CORPUS CHRISTI COLL. (*contd*)

123 (Misc. 22)	†Canterbury,
129 (H.3)	Canterbury, St Aug.
130 (Sub D.2)	†Canterbury,
	St Aug.
134 (P.8)	Peterborough
135 (L.8)	Bury
136 (P.20)	Anglesey
137 (P.19)	Canterbury
	†Syon
138 (E.11)	Norwich
139 (F.5)	†Hexham
	Sawley
	Westminster
140 (S.4)	Bath
144 (S.3)	Canterbury, St Aug.
145 (R.4)	Southwick
146 (D.3)	Winchester
	Worcester
148 (D.2)	Norwich
149 (E.5)	Hexham
150 (O.17)	Swineshead
153 (N.17)	†St David's
154 (L.13)	Canterbury,
	St Aug.
158 (O.28)	Canterbury
160 (N.4)	Peterborough
161 (A.2)	†Canterbury
162 (S.5)	Worcester
163 (I.3)	Winchester
171 (F.9)	Inchcolm
173 (S.11)	Canterbury
	Winchester
178 (S.6)	Worcester
180 (L.16)	Norwich
181 (E.8)	York, St Mary
183 (Sub D.5)	Durham
184 (Sub D.3)	Rochester
187 (A.3)	Canterbury
189 (G.7)	Canterbury, St Aug.
190 (L.12)	Exeter
191 (S.12)	Exeter
192 (E.9)	Canterbury
194 (E.8)	London,
	Hosp. of St Mary
196 (D.5)	Exeter
197 M.14)	†Canterbury,
	St Aug.
198 (S.8)	Worcester
199 (N.5)	St David's
200 (V.3)	Canterbury
201 (S.18)	Exeter

CORPUS CHRISTI COLL. (*contd*)

	†Worcester
211	Albury, *Ch.*
214	†Canterbury
217	Worcester
222	Canterbury
226	Canterbury
251 (H.7)	Bury
252 (H.5)	Norwich
253 (L.17)	†Canterbury
	†Rochester
258 (O.19)	London, Guildhall
260 (N.18)	Canterbury
263 (H.8)	Canterbury
264 (A.8)	Norwich
265 (K.2)	Worcester
266 (P.11)	London, Carm.
267 (E.7)	Canterbury, St Aug.
268 (R.5)	Campsey
269 (P.23)	Pipewell
270–71 (O.22, 21)	Canterbury,
	St Aug.
272 (O.5)	Canterbury
274 (O.7)	†Canterbury
	Canterbury, St Aug.
276 (A.5)	Canterbury, St Aug.
277 (H.9)	†Sherborne
278 (O.6)	Norwich
279 (O.20)	Worcester
280 (E.10)	†Canterbury,
	St Aug.
281 (D.7)	Burton
283 (N.20)	†Norwich
284 (K.3)	Canterbury, St Aug.
286 (L.15)	Canterbury,
	St Aug.
288 (O.11)	Canterbury
290 (A.9)	St Albans
291 (A.10)	Canterbury,
	St Aug.
295 (A.11)	Canterbury
297 (A.12)	Thorney
298 (N.7)	Canterbury
299 (T.6)	London, Dom.
301 (A.7)	Canterbury, St Aug.
304 (N.22)	Canterbury
306 (T.3)	London, Dom.
309 (T.5)	York, St Mary
312 (H.10)	Canterbury,
	St Aug.
314 (D.9)	Canterbury, St Aug.
315 (N.9)	Oxford, Fran.

EMMANUEL COLL. (*contd*)	
86 (I.4.7)	Holme Cultram
91 (I.4.12)	Norwich
94 (I.4.15)	Stratford Langthorne
142 (II.2.17)	Norwich
143 (II.2.18)	†Selby
241 (III.3.8)	Sheen
252 (III.3.21)	London, Holy Trinity

GONVILLE AND CAIUS COLL.	
84 (166)	Darley
109 (178)	Guisborough
111 (180)	Babwell
113 (182)	Bury
116 (185)	Waltham
121 (190)	Lessness
123 (60)	Winchester
126 (64)	Fountains
127 (65)	†Syon
135 (75)	Lessness
136 (76)	Lynn
144 (194)	Canterbury, St Aug.
145 (195)	Bury
	†Cambridge, Pembr. Coll.
149 (199)	Waltham
151 (201)	Lessness
153 (203)	†Westminster
154 (204)	Bury
159 (209)	†Durham
161 (82)	Norwich
177 (210)	Reading
190 (223)	Hagnaby
204 (110)	Barnwell
211 (226)	Canterbury, St Aug.
225 (240)	Bury
230 (116)	St Albans
236 (122)	Ramsey St Ives
238 (124)	Canterbury, St Aug.
297 (691)	Osney
301 (515)	†Canterbury
308 (706)	†Canterbury
309 (707)	Gloucester
314 (376)	Spalding
316 (712)	Warden
348 (541)	Cambridge, Fran. †Oxford, Fran.
356 (583)	†Barnwell
361 (442)	Canterbury, St Aug.
376 (596)	†Burwell

GONVILLE AND CAIUS COLL. (*contd*)	
378 (598)	†London, Dom.
403 (412)	Cambridge, Fran. Oxford, Fran.
406 (627)	Bridlington
426 (426)	Lessness
427 (427)	†Canterbury
433 (432)	London, Carth.
435 (435)	Canterbury, St Aug.
437 (436)	Peterborough
440 (438)	Byland
449 (390)	Southwell
454 (357)	Peterborough
456 (394)	Canterbury, St Aug.
458 (396)	Bayham
464 (571)	†Babwell
467 (574)	Cambridge, Pembr. Coll.
480 (476)	Bury
481 (477)	Osney
667	Lincoln

JESUS COLL.	
Q.A.1 (1)	Durham
Q.A.6 (6)	Durham
Q.A.12 (12)	London, Carth.
Q.A.13 (13)	Durham
Q.A.14 (14)	Durham
Q.A.15 (15)	Durham
Q.B.1 (18)	Bury
Q.B.2 (19)	Blyth, *Ch.*
Q.B.3 (20)	Durham
Q.B.5–8 (22–25)	Durham
Q.B.11–12 (28–29)	Durham
Q.B.14 (31)	Bathwick, *Ch.*
Q.B.17 (34)	Rievaulx
Q.B.18 (35)	†Durham
Q.B.21 (38)	Hexham
Q.B.25 (41)	Durham
Q.D.2 (44)	Durham
Q.D.3 (45)	Durham
Q.D.7 (48)	†Durham
Q.G.1 (49)	†Bury
Q.G.2 (50)	Durham
Q.G.4 (52)	Durham
Q.G.5 (53)	Durham
Q.G.6 (54)	Durham
Q.G.7 (55)	Easby
Q.G.9 (57)	Durham
Q.G.11 (59)	Durham
Q.G.13 (61)	Durham
Q.G.16–17 (64–65)	Durham

St John's Coll. (*contd*)	
8 (A.8)	Canterbury
9 (A.9)	Welbeck
10 (A.10)	Canterbury, St Aug.
11 (A.11)	Syon
12 (A.12)	Hyde
13 (A.13)	Sudbury, Dom.
17 (A.17)	Lincoln, Fran.
22 (A.22)	Reading
23 (B.1)	Ely
27 (B.5)	Pleshey
30 (B.8) ·	Canterbury
35 (B.13)	Bury
43 (B.21)	Canterbury, St Aug.
46 (B.24)	Hexham
47 (B.25)	Lincoln, Fran.
51 (C.1)	Canterbury
52 (C.2)	Canterbury
55 (C.5)	Cambridge, Peterho.
59 (C.9)	Dover
66 (C.16)	†Bury
68 (C.18)	Wherwell
69 (C.19)	†Syon
70 (C.20)	Rochester
71 (C.21)	London, Carth.
74 (C.24)	Guisborough
77 (D.2)	Buildwas
78 (D.3)	Canterbury, St Aug.
81 (D.6)	Peterborough
86 (D.11)	Beauchief
87 (D.12)	Dover
89 (D.14)	Rochester
90 (D.15)	Hereford, Fran.
91 (D.16)	Cambridge, Peterho.
92 (D.17)	Bury
94 (D.19)	Bury
96 (D.21)	Westacre
97 (D.22)	Canterbury, St Aug.
99 (D.24)	Canterbury, St Aug.
100 (D.25)	Swineshead
102 (D.27)	York, St Mary
103**	Ely
109 (E.6)	Syon
112 (E.9)	Durham
113 (E.10)	Robertsbridge
119 (E.16)	Newnham
125 (E.22)	Hinton
126 (E.23)	Waltham
130 (E.27)	Canterbury
131 (E.28)	Syon
132 (E.29)	Mersea
134 (E.31)	†Holme Cultram

St John's Coll. (*contd*)	
135 (E.32)	Fotheringhay
137**	St Albans
138 (F.1)	Bury
139 (F.2)	Syon
140 (F.3)	Bury
142 (F.5)	Canterbury, St Aug.
144 (F.7)	Bristol, Fran.
149 (F.12)	Bury
150 (F.13)	London, Whittington Coll.
157 (F.20)	Hereford, Fran.
164 (F.27)	Canterbury, St Aug.
168 (F.31)	Witham
169 (G.1)	Hereford, Fran.
170 (G.2)	Bury
171 (G.3)	Canterbury, St Aug.
172 (G.4)	Durham
181 (G.13)	†Bury
183 (G.15)	St Albans
209 (H.6)	Ramsey
214 (H.11)	Wigmore
216 (I.1)	Chicksands Hardwick, *Ch.*
218 (I.10)	Norwich
219 (I.11)	Syon
221 (I.15)	London, Carm.
229 (K.23)	†Canterbury
230 (K.25)	Canterbury, St Aug.
256 (S.30)	†Peterborough
262	Canterbury, St Aug.
506	Ickleton
524 (N.11)	Southwark
Sidney Sussex Coll.	
30 (Δ.2.8)	†Durham
32 (Δ.2.10)	Durham
33 (Δ.2.11)	York
36 (Δ.2.14)	Kirkham
48 (Δ.3.3.)	Lancaster
49 (Δ.3.4)	Bristol, Fran.
50 (Δ.3.5)	†Durham
51 (Δ.3.6)	Durham
55 (Δ.3.10)	†Durham
56 (Δ.3.11)	Durham
60 (Δ.3.15)	Worcester, Fran.
62 (Δ.3.17)	Kirkham
71 (Δ.4.9)	Warden
73 (Δ.4.11)	Crowland
77 (Δ.4.15)	Kingswood
79 (Δ.4.17)	West Wretham, *Ch.*
85 (Δ.4.23)	Chicksands

TRINITY COLL. (*contd*)

172 (B.5.26)	Canterbury
173 (B.5.27)	†Canterbury
174 (B.5.28)	Canterbury
212 (B.10.1)	†Canterbury
213 (B.10.2)	Westminster
215 (B.10.4)	Hyde
216 (B.10.5)	Durham
222 (B.10.11)	Canterbury
241 (B.11.2)	Exeter
244 (B.11.5)	Goring
249 (B.11.10)	Ely
250 (B.11.11)	†Canterbury
255 (B.11.16)	†Exeter
	†Hereford
288 (B.14.2)	Waltham
289 (B.14.3)	Canterbury
290 (B.14.4)	Thurgarton
291 (B.14.5)	Buildwas
293 (B.14.7)	Leicester
301 (B.14.15)	London,
	Fran. nuns
303 (B.14.17)	Oxford,
	Lincoln Coll.
315 (B.14.30)	Leicester
317 (B.14.33)	Belvoir
	Cerne
	St Albans
320 (B.14.36)	†Canterbury
	†Canterbury, St Aug.
	St Albans
321 (B.14.37)	Canterbury,
	St Aug.
338 (B.15.1)	Winchester
339 (B.15.2)	Syon
342 (B.15.5)	Canterbury
346 (B.15.9, 10)	Canterbury
347 (B.15.11)	Oxford, Dom.
348 (B.15.12)	†Hereford, Fran.
354 (B.15.18)	Sheen
357 (B.15.21)	†Buildwas
362 (B.15.26)	Warden
365 (B.15.30)	Durham
	†Finchale
373 (B.15.38)	Hailes
377 (B.16.1)	Canterbury
379 (B.16.3)	†Canterbury
381 (B.16.5)	Leicester
382–85 (B.16.6–9)	Canterbury
386 (B.16.11)	Canterbury
387 (B.16.12)	Canterbury,
	St Aug.

TRINITY COLL. (*contd*)

388 (B.16.13)	†Syon
391 (B.16.17)	Canterbury
405 (B.16.44)	Canterbury
407 (B.16.46)	Canterbury
609 (R.3.29)	Holme Cultram
610 (R.3.30)	Rochester
	†Canterbury
623 (R.3.50)	Bury
624 (R.3.51)	Dover
629 (R.3.57)	†Canterbury
637 (R.4.4.)	Canterbury
644 (R.4.11)	Canterbury
711 (R.5.16)	Glastonbury
717 (R.5.22)	Salisbury
722 (R.5.27)	†Canterbury
724 (R.5.33)	Glastonbury
727 (R.5.36)	Malmesbury
	Glastonbury
	Pilton
728 (R.5.40)	York
729 (R.5.41)	Canterbury
730 (R.5.42)	†York, St Mary
740 (R.7.2)	Malmesbury
749 (R.7.11)	Hereford,
	Fran.
751 (R.7.13)	Sherborne
770 (R.7.28)	St Neots
792 (R.8.16)	Syon
813 (R.9.9)	Cambridge, Univ.
822 (R.9.21)	†Glastonbury
	†Wells
823 (R.9.22)	Reading
825 (R.9.24)	Dover
829 (R.9.28)	Canterbury
847 (R.10.5)	St Albans
	Tynemouth
881 (R.14.5)	Wells
883 (R.14.7)	Norwich
884 (R.14.9)	Horsham
904 (R.14.31)	Canterbury,
	St Aug.
906 (R.14.34)	Bury
919 (R.14.49)	Babwell
939 (R.15.14)	Canterbury,
	St Aug.
940 (R.15.16)	Coventry, Fran.
943 (R.15.21)	Knaresborough
944 (R.15.22)	Canterbury
945 (R.15.32)	Canterbury,
	St Aug.
	Hyde

FITZWILLIAM MUSEUM (*contd*)

McClean	109	Lincoln
	123	Nuneaton
	145	Lanthony
	169	Durham
2–1957		Shaftesbury

CAMBRIDGE, *U.S.A., Mass.*
HARVARD COLLEGE LIBR.

| Latin 27 | Holme Cultram |

HARVARD LAW SCHOOL

25	Letheringham
26	Gloucester
28	Titchfield
64	Reading

HARVARD UNIVERSITY, HOUGH-
TON LIBR.

| W. K. Richardson 26 | Bury |
| Typ. 3 | Canterbury |

MR PHILIP HOFER, c/o HOUGHTON
LIBR.

| — | Sarsden, *Ch.* |

CANTERBURY, *Kent*
DEAN AND CHAPTER LIBR.

B.11 (1)	Canterbury
B.6 (4)	Canterbury, St Aug.
A.2 (11)	Canterbury
B.4 (13)	Canterbury
C.12 (14)	Canterbury
B.3 (15)	Canterbury
A.4 (16)	Canterbury
D.11 (17)	Canterbury
D.12 (26)	Canterbury
D.6 (34)	Canterbury, St Aug.
B.10 (37)	Canterbury
A.12 (42)	Canterbury
E.7 and 8 (43)	Canterbury
A.5–7 (45)	Canterbury
E.42 (46)	Canterbury
D.5 (49)	Canterbury, St Aug.
D.8 (53)	Canterbury
B.7 (57, ii)	Canterbury
B.13 (57, iii)	Canterbury
D.16 (58)	Canterbury, St Aug.
E.17 (62)	Canterbury
A.1 (65)	Canterbury
D.7 (67)	Canterbury
A.8 (68)	Canterbury, St Aug.
E.3 (71)	Dover
B.1 (73)	Whalley
A.13 (74)	Canterbury
A.9 (75)	Canterbury

DEAN AND CHAPTER LIBR. (*contd*)

B.12 (100)	Canterbury
E.10 (101)	Southwark
B.9 (104)	Canterbury
Add. 6	Canterbury
16	Canterbury, St Aug.
17	Canterbury
25	Canterbury
Box ABC	Canterbury
CCC, no. 19a	Canterbury
no. 23	Canterbury
Archdeaconry Visitations,	
Detecta 1571–72	Canterbury, St Aug.
Chart. Antiq. A.42	Canterbury
Register J	Canterbury
Register P	Canterbury

CAPETOWN, *South Africa*
UNIV LIBR.

| 1 | S. Wingfield, *Ch.* |

CARDIFF, *Glamorgan*
PUBLIC LIBR.

1.381	Barking
	Dover
	†Canterbury, St Aug.
3.833	Barking

CARLISLE, *Cumberland*
ST MARY'S CATHOLIC CHURCH

| — | Caldbeck, *Ch.** |

TULLIE HOUSE MUSEUM

| — | †Conishead |

CHANDLERS CROSS, *near
Rickmansworth, Hertford-
shire*
MR W. LYON WOOD

| — | Sheen |

CHICAGO, *U.S.A., Illinois*
ART INSTITUTE OF CHICAGO

| 23.420 | Missenden |

NEWBERRY LIBR.

| 344984 | Ford |
| Ry.24 | Reading |

UNIVERSITY OF CHICAGO

224	Wigmore
254	Battle
654	Meaux

CHICHESTER, *Sussex*
CATHEDRAL

| Anc. 1 | Kenilworth |

Trinity College (*contd*)

B.4.25 (207)	York, St Mary
B.5.1 (209)	Tarrant Keynston
C.1.4 (226)	Kelso
C.2.7 (271)	Chester
C.2.16 (279)	Rievaulx
C.2.18 (281)	Sheen
C.4.6 (318)	Mount Grace
C.4.23 (332)	York, St Mary
C.5.15 (349)	Durham
D.1.25 (370)	Crowland
D.1.26 (371)	Canterbury
D.4.18 (432)	Belvoir
D.4.22 (436)	London, Elsyng Spital
D.4.26 (440)	Durham
D.4.30 (444)	St Albans
D.5.11 (448)	Thorney
E.2.1 (486)	London, Aug.
E.2.15 (490)	Dartford
E.2.23 (492)	Bury
E.6.4 (503)	Worcester
E.5.3 (514)	Canterbury, St Aug.
E.4.12 (517)	Oxford, Merton Coll.
E.2.32 (548)	Westminster
E.4.26 (602)	Canterbury, St Aug.

DULWICH COLLEGE. *See* LONDON, Dulwich

DUNDEE, *Fife*
Burgh Charter Room
— St Andrews, *Ch.*

DUNROBIN, *Sutherland*
Duke of Sutherland
— Fearn

DURHAM
Cathedral Libr.
304 MSS and 34 pr. bks
Durham (*see p. 60*)

A.II.8	Coldingham
A.IV.6	Tynemouth
A.IV.9	Coventry, Carm.
A.IV.30	Witham
B.II.32	Coldingham
B.II.36	York, Fran.
B.IV.33	Stanhope, *Ch.*
B.IV.38	Carlisle
C.IV.22	Stamford, Carm.

Cathedral Libr. (*contd*)

Hunter 57	Hexham

University Libr.

Cosin V.i.2	Rudby, *Ch.*
i.3	Cotishall, *Ch.*
i.4	Durham
i.8	Durham
ii.1	Durham
ii.2	Durham
ii.5	Durham
ii.6	Durham
ii.8	Durham
ii.9	Canterbury, St Aug.
ii.12	Norwich
iii.1	Durham
iii.20	Bury
v.3	Bury
v.6	Durham
v.15	St Albans
v.19	Bridlington
Mickleton and Spearman 89	Durham

EDINBURGH
National Libr. of Scotland

652	Perth, *Ch.*
5048	Holyrood
6121	London, Carm.
6125	Norwich
Advocates 1.1.1	Dunfermline
3.1.12	Beauly
5.1.15	Scone
18.1.2	Edinburgh
18.2.4	Rochester
18.2.6	Dunkeld, Perthshire
18.2.8	Guthrie
18.3.9	Rochester
18.3.11	Aberdeen, King's Coll.
18.4.1	Newbattle
18.4.2	Lewes
18.4.3	Durham
18.5.1	Exeter
18.5.12	Dover
18.5.13	Leicester
18.5.16	Peterborough
18.5.18	Rochester
18.6.8	Canterbury, St Aug.

CATHEDRAL LIBR. (*contd*)

3511	Exeter, Hosp.
3512–13	Exeter
3514	†Exeter
3515	Exeter, St Anne, *Ch.*
3516	Exeter
3518	Exeter
3519	†Exeter
3520	Exeter
3521	Ottery St Mary
3525–26	†Exeter
3529	Canterbury, St Aug.
3533	Exeter
3548(D)	Exeter
3549(B)	†Exeter
3625	Exeter

FITZHERBERT-BROCK-
HOLES, Mr M. *See* **GAR-
STANG**

FITZWILLIAM, EARL. *See*
**WENTWORTH WOOD-
HOUSE**

FLACKWELL HEATH, *Buck-
inghamshire*
Mr R. W. ALLISON, TWO TREES,
LINKS ROAD
— Louth Park

FLORENCE, *Italy*
BIBL. LAURENZIANA

Amiatino 1	Jarrow
Plut. xvii, sin. cod. x	Oxford, Fran.

FOYLE, Miss C. *See* **BEE-
LEIGH ABBEY**

GARSTANG, *Lancashire*
Mr M. FITZHERBERT-BROCKHOLES
CLAUGHTON HALL
— Walmer, *Ch.*

GASCOIGNE, SIR A. D. F.
See **ABERFORD**

GENEVA, *Switzerland*
Dr MARTIN BODMER
— Salisbury (*see p. 175*)

GLASGOW
UNIVERSITY LIBR.

BD.19.h.9	London, Carm.
BE.7.b.8	Dunfermline

UNIVERSITY LIBR. (*contd*)

BE.7.e.24	Reading
BE.8.y.7	Cambuskenneth

Hunterian

S.1.4 (4)	Hertford
S.1.7 (7)	Bury
S.2.10 (20)	Chichester
T.3.15 (77)	Sheen
T.4.2 (85)	Durham
T.6.18 (136)	Syon
U.1.13 (209)	Bury
U.4.11 (253)	Canterbury, St Aug.
U.7.26 (332)	Syon
V.1.16 (379	Canterbury, St Aug.
V.5.1 (431)	Worcester
V.6.17 (467)	Dover
V.8.12 (509)	Syon

GLOUCESTER
CATHEDRAL LIBR.

3	Eton
25	Worcester
34	Gloucester

GÖTTINGEN, *Germany*
UNIVERSITÄTSBIBL.

Theol. 2	Reading
3	Salisbury, Dom.
4	Winchcomb

GORDAN, Mrs and Mr. *See*
NEW YORK

GORDON, Mr C. A. *See*
INSCH

GRENOBLE, *France, Isère*
BIBL. DE LA VILLE
985 Faversham

GRIMSTHORPE CASTLE,
Bourne, Lincolnshire
EARL OF ANCASTER
— Newsham*

HARLECH, LORD.
See **OSWESTRY**

HARVARD UNIVERSITY.
See **CAMBRIDGE,** *U.S.A.,
Mass.*

HASSON, Mr J.
See **WELLINGTON**

HAVRE (LE), *France, Seine-Mar.*
BIBL. MUNICIPALE
330	Winchester

HELMINGHAM HALL,
Stowmarket, Suffolk
LORD TOLLEMACHE
2, 3	St Osyth
6	Peterborough
8	London, Aug.
49	Great Malvern
	Worcester, Dom.
72	Shere, *Ch.*

HEREFORD
CATHEDRAL LIBR.
95 MSS and 31 pr. bks	
	Hereford
O.i.1	Hereford, Fran.
O.i.2	Gloucester
O.i.3	Cirencester
O.i.4	Hereford, Fran.
O.i.6	Cirencester
O.i.10	Cirencester
O.ii.4	Cirencester
O.ii.11	Hereford, Fran.
O.iii.1	Gloucester
O.iii.3	Flaxley
O.iii.6	Hereford, Fran.
O.iii.8	†Hereford, Fran.
O.iii.9	†Hereford, Fran.
O.iii.10	Cirencester
O.iii.12	†Hereford, Fran.
O.iv.6	Westminster
O.iv.10	Hereford, Dom.
O.iv.11	Ilchester
O.iv.12	Hereford, St Guthlac
O.v.1	Hereford, St Guthlac
O.v.5	Gloucester, Fran.
O.v.10	Cirencester
O.v.12	Hereford, Fran.
O.v.14	Cirencester
O.vi.10	Cirencester
O.vi.11	Hereford, St Guthlac
O.vii.7	Hereford, Fran.
O.viii.12	Hereford, Fran.
P.i.5	Gloucester
P.i.6	Gloucester
P.i.7	†Hereford, Fran.
P.i.9	Oxford, Fran.
P.i.10	Gloucester
P.i.12	Cirencester
P.i.13	Dore

CATHEDRAL LIBR. (*contd*)
P.i.15	Hereford, Fran.
P.i.17	Cirencester
P.ii.10	†Cirencester
P.ii.14	Cirencester
P.ii.15	Cirencester
P.iii.1	Bury
	Canons Ashby
P.iii.2	Hereford, St Guthlac
P.iii.4	Crickadarn, *Ch.*
P.iii.5	Hereford, St Guthlac
P.iii.7	Cirencester
P.iii.12	Hereford, Fran.
P.iv.5	Hereford, St Guthlac
P.iv.6	Tewkesbury
P.iv.8	Cirencester
P.iv.9	Cirencester
P.v.1	Battle
	Brecon
P.v.3	Cirencester
P.v.4	Cirencester
P.v.5	Dore
P.v.8	Hereford, Fran.
P.v.9	Cirencester
P.v.10	Canterbury, Fran.
	Hereford, Fran.
P.vi.1	Hereford, St Guthlac
P.vi.3	Wigmore
P.viii.4	Winchcomb
P.viii.11	Neath
P.ix.5	Winchcomb
P.ix.6	Mordiford, *Ch.*

HILDESHEIM, *Germany*
S. GODEHARDS BIBL.
—	Markyate
	St Albans

HODSOCK PRIORY, *Blyth,*
Nottinghamshire
THE MELLISH TRUSTEES
—	Rushall, *Ch.**

HOFER, Mr PHILIP. *See*
CAMBRIDGE, *U.S.A.,*
Mass.

HOLKHAM HALL, *Wells,*
Norfolk
EARL OF LEICESTER
26	Ramsey
39	†Wenlock

HOLYROOD. *See*
EDINBURGH

HOWARD, Sir ARTHUR. *See*
STEYNING

ILLINOIS, UNIV. OF. *See*
URBANA

INSCH, Aberdeenshire
Mr C. A. GORDON, THE OLD
MANSE
— Inchmahome
— Nocton Park

IPSWICH, *Suffolk*
CENTRAL LIBR.

1–3	†Bury
4	Bury
5	†Bury
6	Bury
8	Bury
Suffolk 1	Ipswich, Fran.

KANSAS, UNIV. OF. *See*
LAWRENCE

KASSEL, *Germany*
LANDESBIBLIOTHEK
Anhang 19 Winchester

KEW, Surrey
Mr B. S. CRON, 351 SANDY-
COMBE ROAD
— St Albans

KEYNES, Sir G. *See*
BRINKLEY

LACOCK ABBEY, *Wiltshire*
Mrs A. D. BURNETT-BROWN
— Lacock

LANGLEY MARISH, *Bucking-
hamshire*
PARISH CHURCH
— Windsor*

LAON, *France, Aisne*
BIBL. MUNICIPALE
238 Bury
†Winchester

LAVANTAL, *Carinthia*
ABBEY OF ST PAUL
xxv/2.19 Ramsey

LAWRENCE, *U.S.A., Kansas*
UNIVERSITY OF KANSAS LIBR.

Y.103	Worcester
Y.104	Worcester

LEEDS, *Yorkshire*
PUBLIC LIBR.

VR 6106–9	Fountains**
VR 6120	Fountains**

LEICESTER
MUSEUM, NEW WALK
Old Town Libr. 20
†Cambridge, Fran.
Wyggeston Hospital Collection
6 †Leicester, Collegiate Ch.
11 Leicester, Collegiate Ch.
BERNARD HALLIDAY,
124 NEW WALK
— Haltemprice
— Shrewsbury, Fran.
Mr HAROLD F. SMITH,
29 KNIGHTON GRANGE ROAD
— Darlington
— Witham

LEICESTER, EARL OF. *See*
HOLKHAM HALL

LEIDEN. *See* **LEYDEN**

LENINGRAD, *U.S.S.R.*
PUBLIC LIBR.
Q.v.1.62 Wherwell

LEYDEN, *Holland*
UNIV. LIBR.
Bibl. Publ. Lat. 114B St Albans
190 †Canter-
bury, St Aug.
Lipsius 24 (458) Cambridge,
Pembr. Coll.
41 (463) Kirkstead
Lincoln, Dom.
Scaliger 69 Canterbury,
St Aug.
Hebr. 8 Cambridge,
King's Coll.
Canterbury, St Aug.
Vossius Lat. F.18 Colchester
F.93 Winchester
Vulcanius 96 Abingdon

LICHFIELD, *Staffordshire*
CATHEDRAL LIBR.
— Lichfield
— Llandaff

LIÈGE, *Belgium*
BIBL. DE L'UNIVERSITÉ
396C Kirkstall

BRITISH MUSEUM (*contd*)

Additional 26770	Canterbury, St Aug.
27866	Wherwell
28188	Exeter
	†Romsey
28805	Durham
29436	Winchester
29704–5	London, Carm.
30079	Norwich
30506	Gloucester, *Ch.*
30514	Syon
31826	Merevale
	†Rievaulx
32246	Abingdon
33241	Canterbury, St Aug.
33350	Ramsey
33381	Ely
34633	Beddgelert Croxden
34652	†London London, Aug. Southwick Winchester
34749	Waltham
34890	Hyde
34901	London, Gray's Inn
35110	Newcastle, Aug.
35168	Crowland
35180	Byland
35283	Finchale Whalley
35285	Guisborough
35289	Canterbury, St Aug.
35295	Kenilworth
36672	Southwark, *Ch.*
37472	†Bury Canterbury
37488	Faversham, Corporation
37517	Canterbury Canterbury, St Aug.
37777	Jarrow Worcester

BRITISH MUSEUM (*contd*)

Additional 37785	Haughmond
37787	Bordesley
38129	Exeter, Hosp.
38665	Kenilworth
38666	Durham Oxford, Merton Coll.
38816	Byland York, St Mary
38817	Kirkham
38819	Bourne
39675	Hereford
39676	Beverley
39758	Peterborough
40000	Thorney
40006	Syon
40007	York, St Mary
40675	Campsey
41175	Pot Shrigley, *Ch.*
42555	Abingdon
43405–6	Muchelney
44874	Evesham
44892	London, Carm.
45025	Jarrow Worcester
45103	Canterbury
45568	Merton
46352	Canterbury, St Aug.
46487	Sherborne
46919	Hereford, Fran.
47170	Peterborough
47214	Babwell
47967	Winchester
48178	Canterbury, St Aug.
48179	Reading
48984	Caerleon Hailes
49598	Winchester
49622	Gorleston, *Ch.*
Arundel 16	Canterbury

BRITISH MUSEUM (*contd*)
Cotton (*contd*)

Tiberius	A.x	Dunstable
	A.xii	Eynsham
	A.xv	York, St Mary
	B.i	Abingdon †Canterbury
	B.ii	Bury
	B.iii	Canterbury
	B.iv	Canterbury Worcester
	B.v	Battle Ely Exeter †Glastonbury Winchester
	B.vii	†Canterbury, St Aug.
	B.viii	Glasgow
	B.xi	†Canterbury Winchester
	B.xiii	Lanthony
	C.i	Peterborough Salisbury Sherborne
	C.vii	Leicester
	C.xiii	Jervaulx
	D.iv	Winchester
	E.i	Redbourn
	E.iv	Winchcomb
Caligula	A.ii	London, Carth.
	A.viii	Beauchief Ely
	A.x	Worcester
	A.xiv	Canterbury
	A.xv	Canterbury Canterbury, St Aug.
Claudius	A.i	†Canterbury Worcester
	A.iii	Canterbury
	A.v	Belvoir †Bridlington Holme Cultram Peterborough
	A.viii	Westminster †Worcester
	A.xi	Maidstone
	A.xii	Bury
	A.xiv	Cambridge, Pembr. Coll.

BRITISH MUSEUM (*contd*)
Cotton (*contd*)

Claudius	B.ii	Canterbury
	B.iv	Canterbury, St Aug.
	B.v	Bath
	B.vi	Abingdon
	B.vii	†Lichfield
	B.ix	Cambridge, King's Hall †Canterbury, St Aug.
	C.vi	Canterbury
	C.ix	Abingdon Worcester
	D.i	St Albans
	D.ii	London, Guildhall
	D.iii	Wintney
	D.iv	Durham
	D.vi	St Albans
	D.vii	Lanercost
	E.i	Tewkesbury
	E.iii	†St Albans
	E.iv	St Albans
	E.v	Canterbury
	E.viii	Norwich
Nero	A.ii	Winchester, St Mary
	A.v	Holme Cultram
	A.viii	Canterbury Canterbury, St Aug. †Rochester
	A.ix	Hereford, Fran.
	A.xv, xvi	Ely
	C.iv	Shaftesbury Winchester
	C.v	Norwich Worcester
	C.vii	Canterbury Thorney
	C.ix	Canterbury
	D.i	St Albans
	D.ii	Battle Holme St Benets Rochester
	D.iv	Durham Lindisfarne
	D.v	St Albans
	D.vii	St Albans

356

BRITISH MUSEUM (*contd*)		BRITISH MUSEUM (*contd*)	
Harley	547	Ely	Harley	1804	Durham
	550	Dover		1916	Glastonbury
	603	Canterbury,		1918	Glastonbury
		St Aug.		1924	Durham
	612	Syon			Oxford, Durham
	613	Gloucester			Coll.
	622	Haughmond		2253	†Leominster
		Ranton		2254	Dartford
	624	Canterbury		2278	†Bury
	627	Gloucester		2363	Kinloss
	631	London,		2367	Molton, South, *Ch.*
		St Barth.		2372	Stamford, Hosp.
	632	Syon		2373	Mount Grace
	636	Canterbury		2386	Norwich, Aug.
	641	Canterbury,		2387	Syon
		St Aug.		2397	London, Fran.
		Glastonbury			nuns
	647	Canterbury,		2399	Bodmin
		St Aug.		2409	Nun Coton
	649	Ramsey			Swine
	651	Glastonbury		2431	Brompton-on-
		Reading			Swale, *Ch.*
	652	Canterbury,			Ravensworth, *Ch.*
		St Aug.		2624	St Albans
	863	Exeter		2659	Gloucester
	865	St Albans		2787	Maldon, *Ch.*
	876	Reading		2791	Studley
	960	Hyde		2904	Ramsey
	978	Reading		2931	Buckland
	979	Reading		2961	Exeter
	985	Ely		2965	Winchester,
	989	†Canterbury			St Mary
	993	Syon		2977	Bury
	1001	Risby, *Ch.*		2983	Hereford
	1005	Bury		3013	Newminster
	1025	Hitchin, *Ch.*		3038	Buildwas
	1031	Ely		3049	Durham
	1032	Witham		3061	Abingdon
	1034	Norwich, Fran.		3096	Worcester, Fran.
	1132	†Bury		3097	Peterborough
		Colchester		3100	Durham
	1246	Leominster		3145	Wenlock
	1524	Canterbury,		3173	Fountains
		St Aug.		3224	Canterbury,
	1587	Canterbury			St Aug.
	1620	Jervaulx		3239	Worcester, Fran.
	1659	Worcester		3241	Sudbury, Dom.
	1712	Haughmond		3249	Oxford, Fran.
	1751	Oxford,		3600	Whalley
		Queen's Coll.		3601	Barnwell
	1770	Kirkham		3634	Norwich

BRITISH MUSEUM (*contd*)		
Royal	1 E.vii, viii	Canterbury
	2 A.x	St Albans
	2 A.xiv	Syon
	2 A.xx	Worcester
	2 A.xxi	Charford, South, *Ch.*
	2 A.xxii	Westminster
	2 B.iv	St Albans
	2 B.v	Hyde
		† Winchester, St Mary
	2 B.vi	St Albans
	2 B.xii, xiii	London, St Mary Alderman- bury, *Ch.*
	2 B.xv	Southwick, *Ch.*
	2 C.i	Rochester
	2 C.iii	Rochester
	2 C.v	Rochester
	2 C.vii	Worcester
	2 C.x	Lanthony
	2 C.xi	Ramsey
	2 C.xii	Gloucester
	2 D.v	Lanthony
	2 D.vi	Rochester
	2 D.ix	Pershore
	2 D.x	Bristol
	2 D.xxiv	Canterbury, Fran.
	2 D.xxvi	Worcester
	2 D.xxx	Rochester
	2 D.xxxii	Canterbury
	2 D.xxxiv	†Canter- bury, St Aug.
	2 D.xxxvi	London, Carm.
	2 E.i	Rochester
	2 E.vi	Worcester
	2 E.vii	Rochester
	2 E.ix	Bury
	2 E.xi	Worcester
	2 F.i	Worcester
	2 F.iii	Hinton
	2 F.iv	Rochester
	2 F.v	†Canterbury
	2 F.vi	Rochester
	2 F.vii	St Albans
	2 F.viii	St Albans
	2 F.xi	Rochester
	2 F.xii	Rochester

BRITISH MUSEUM (*contd*)		
Royal	3 A.i	Canterbury, St Aug.
	3 A.ii	Canterbury, St Aug.
	3 A.iv	Reading
	3 A.vi	Reading
	3 A.viii	Worcester
	3 A.ix	London, Hosp. of St Thomas
	3 A.x	London, Aug.
	3 A.xi	Bridgwater
		†Bridgnorth
	3 A.xii	Cirencester
	3 A.xiii	Guisborough
	3 A.xiv	Reading
	3 A.xv	Sempringham
	3 B.i	Rochester
	3 B.ii	†Lanthony
	3 B.iii	Sempringham
	3 B.viii	Spalding
	3 B.x	Gloucester
	3 B.xi	Ramsey
	3 B.xiii	Rochester
	3 B.xv	Barlings
	3 B.xvi	Bath
	3 C.iv	Rochester
	3 C.v	St Albans
	3 C.vi	Canterbury, Fran.
	3 C.vii–x	Rochester
	3 C.xi	Canterbury, Fran.
	3 D.i	Lichfield, Fran.
	3 D.ii	Canterbury, Fran.
	3 D.iv	Canterbury, Fran.
	3 D.vi	Ashridge
	3 D.viii	Canterbury, Fran.
	3 D.ix	Kirkstead
	3 E.i–v	London, Dom.
	3 E.vi	Jervaulx
	3 E.vii	London, Dom.
	3 E.viii	London, Dom.
	3 E.ix	Canterbury, Fran.
	3 E.x, xi	London, Hosp. of St Thomas
	4 A.iv	Tupholme

BRITISH MUSEUM (*contd*)			BRITISH MUSEUM (*contd*)		
Royal	5 F.ii	Oxford, Univ.	Royal	6 E.viii	St Albans
	5 F.iii	Worcester		7 A.i	Southwark
	5 F.v	Hagnaby		7 A.ii	Muchelney
	5 F.viii	Stafford		7 A.iii	Bardney
	5 F.x	Wallingford		7 A.iv	Hereford, Fran.
	5 F.xii	Worcester		7 A.v	Rochester
	5 F.xv	Ramsey		7 A.vi	Durham
	5 F.xvi	Merton		7 A.vii	Felixstowe
	5 F.xvii	Leeds		7 A.ix	Southwark
	6 A.i	Rochester		7 A.x	Bodmin, Fran.
	6 A.iv	Rochester		7 A.xi	Rochester
	6 A.v	Durham		7 B.v	London, Carm.
	6 A.vii	Worcester		7 B.ix	Bury
	6 A.xi	Rochester		7 B.xiii	Rochester
	6 A.xii	Rochester		7 C.i	Ramsey
	6 A.xvi	Worcester		7 C.ii	Bury
	6 B.i	Bath		7 C.iv	Canterbury
	6 B.ii	Rochester		7 C.v	Bury
	6 B.vi	Rochester		7 C.vii	London,
	6 B.vii	Exeter			St Bartholomew
	6 B.x	Bury		7 C.xi	Bury
	6 B.xi	Cardiff		7 C.xiii, xiv	Rochester
	6 B.xii	Spalding		7 D.ii	Canterbury,
	6 B.xiv	Battle			St Aug.
	6 C.i	Canterbury,		7 D.v	London, Hosp.
		St Aug.			of St Thomas
	6 C.ii	Bury		7 D.xv	Revesby
	6 C.iv	Rochester		7 D.xvii	Sheen
	6 C.vi	Rochester		7 D.xxi	Westminster
	6 C.vii	Worcester		7 D.xxiv	†Canterbury
	6 C.viii	Rievaulx		7 E.i	Bury
	6 C.ix	†Evesham		7 E.ii	Oxford,
		Warwick,			Brasenose Coll.
		Dom.		7 E.iv	Rochester
	6 C.x	Rochester		7 E.vi	Canterbury
	6 C.xi	Bath		7 E.viii	Rochester
	6 D.i	Chertsey		7 E.ix	Reading
	6 D.ii	Rochester		7 F.i	Cirencester
	6 D.iii	†Evesham		7 F.ii	Westminster
		Worcester		7 F.iii	Elstow
	6 D.v	Rochester		7 F.iv	Rochester
	6 D.vi	Coggeshall		7 F.v	Kirkstead
	6 D.vii	Rochester		7 F.vi	Cirencester
	6 D.viii	Spalding		7 F.vii	Hereford, Fran.
	6 D.ix	†Gloucester		7 F.viii	Hereford,
		Lincoln, Carm.			Fran.
	6 D.x	St Albans		7 F.x	Rochester
	6 E.iii	Oxford,		7 F.xi	Ashridge
		Magdalen Coll.		7 F.xii	Oxford,
	6 E.iv	Bradenstoke			Balliol Coll.
	6 E.v	Merton		8 A.v	Hailes

British Museum (*contd*)		British Museum (*contd*)	
Royal 11 A.vi	Canterbury, St Aug.	Royal 12 F.i	Rochester
11 A.x	Lanthony	12 F.ii	St Albans
11 A.xii	Canterbury, St Aug.	12 F.iv	Horsham
		12 F.vi	Sawley
11 A.xiii	Tattershall	12 F.viii	Rochester
11 A.xvii	Reading	12 F.xiii	Rochester
11 B.i	Lincoln	12 F.xv	Bury
11 B.ii	Worcester	12 F.xix	Reading
11 B.iii	Bury	12 G.ii	Rochester
11 B.iv	Pershore	12 G.iii	Rochester
11 B.v	Merton	12 G.iv	Coventry
11 B.vi	Tattershall	12 G.vi	London, Dom.
11 B.vii	Bermondsey	12 G.xiv	St Albans
11 B.xii	London, Carm.	13 A.v	Boston, Dom.
11 B.xiii	Chester	13 A.vii	Bardney
11 B.xiv	Canterbury, St Aug.	13 A.xii	London, Carm.
		13 A.xviii	London, Carm.
11 B.xv	Rochester		
11 C.i	Rochester	13 A.xxi	Hagnaby
11 C.ii	†Canterbury Reading	13 A.xxii	Canterbury, St Aug.
11 C.iii	Reading	13 A.xxiii	Canterbury, St Aug.
11 C.xi	Reading	13 B.v	St Albans
11 D.i	Rochester	13 B.vi	Lincoln, Dom.
11 D.vii	Lincoln	13 B.viii	Canterbury, St Aug.
11 D.viii	Gloucester		
11 D.ix	St Albans	13 C.iv	Lincoln, Carm.
12 B.iii	Oxford, Merton Coll.	13 C.v	Gloucester
		13 C.vii	London, Carm.
12 B.iv	Hinton		
12 B.ix	Canterbury, St Aug.	13 C.xi	London, Hosp. of St Thomas
12 B.xii	Newark	13 C.xiv	St Albans
12 B.xvi	Athelney	13 D.i	London, St Peter-upon-Cornhill, *Ch.*
12 C.i	Rochester		
12 C.iv	Rochester		
12 C.vi	Bury	13 D.ii	Margam
12 C.xxi	Cambridge, King's Hall	13 D.iii	Rochester
		13 D.iv	St Albans
12 D.iv	Canterbury	13 D.v	St Albans
12 D.ix	Canterbury, St Aug.	13 D.vi, vii	St Albans
		13 D.viii	Syon
12 D.xiv	Rochester	13 D.ix	Redbourn
12 D.xvii	Winchester	13 E.i	Lincoln
12 E.xiv	Hailes	13 E.vi	St Albans
12 E.xxiii	Canterbury, St Aug.	13 E.ix	St Albans
		13 E.x	Paisley
12 E.xxv	Oxford, Merton Coll. Tattershall	14 C.i	Norwich St Albans
		14 C.iv	Ramsey

GRAY'S INN (contd)		LAMBETH PALACE (contd)	
6	†Chester Fran.	67	Bury
7	Chester, Fran.	68	Lanthony
9	Dieulacres	70	Lanthony
11	Chester, Fran.	71	Lanthony
12	Chester, Fran.	73	Buildwas
13	Combe	74	Lanthony
14	Chester	76	Lanthony
19	Chester		Rochester
20	Melbourne, *Ch.*	77	Lanthony
	Sudbury, Dom.	78	Canterbury
GUILDHALL		80	Lanthony
244	London, Guildhall	81	Lanthony
515	London, St Botolph	83	Lanthony
	without Aldersgate, *Ch.*	85	Lanthony
—	London, St Peter-upon-	88	Lanthony
	Cornhill, *Ch.***	90	Bury
INNER TEMPLE		95	Lanthony
511.2	Rievaulx	96	Llanthony
511.10	Canterbury		†Peterborough
Barrington 83	Dunstable	97	Lanthony
LAMBETH PALACE		99	Windsor
3	Canterbury, St Aug.	101	Lanthony
5	Peterborough	102	Lanthony
8	London		St Albans
9	†Bourne	103	Lanthony
	Peterborough	104	Exeter
10–12	Durham		†Ottery St Mary
13	Lanthony	105	Bury
18	Lanthony	106	Lanthony
20	Canterbury	107	Buildwas
21	Lanthony	109	Buildwas
23	Durham	110–12	Lanthony
28–30	Lanthony	111	St Albans
32	Cambridge, Peterho.	114	Lanthony
33	London, Fran.	115	Lanthony
37	Lanthony	116	Canterbury, St Aug.
39	Lanthony	118	Merton
40	†Ely	119	Lanthony
42	Abingdon	120	Bury
44	Lanthony	122	Lanthony
45	Lanthony	128	Lanthony
49	Canterbury, St Aug.	129	Lanthony
51	London, Holy Trinity	133	Lanthony
55	Lanthony	138	Lanthony
56	Lanthony	139	Lanthony
57	Lincoln, Fran.	141	Lanthony
58	Lanthony	142	Canterbury
59	Canterbury		Lanthony
61	Lanthony	144	Canterbury, St Aug.
62	Canterbury		Lessness
63	Lanthony	145	Crowland

LAMBETH PALACE (contd)	
411	Lanthony
414	Canterbury, St Aug.
415	Canterbury
419	Canterbury, St Aug.
420	Hertford
	St Albans
425	Lanthony
	Llanthony
427	Lanthony
430	Canterbury
	Canterbury, St Aug.
431	Lanthony
	Llanthony
433	†London,
	Hosp. of St Thomas
436	Witham
437	Lanthony
440	Holyrood
	Loch Leven
442	Lanthony
443	Hertford
448	Ely
449	Lanthony
450	London, Fran.
451	Lanthony
452	Lanthony
456–57	Buildwas
473	†Bourne
	Peterborough
475	Lanthony
477	Buildwas
481	Lanthony
483	Durham
486	Thornton
488	Buildwas
489	Exeter
497	Reading
498	Canterbury, St Aug.
	Whalley
522	Canterbury, St Aug.
540	Lanthony
546	Syon
558	Canterbury
563	St Neots
759	Oxford, Balliol Coll.
761	Pershore
	†Westminster
873	Crowland
1106	Huntingdon
	London
	Oxford, Oriel Coll.

LAMBETH PALACE (contd)	
	Ramsey
1212	Canterbury
1213	Canterbury, St Aug.
1362	Bredgar, Ch.
1370	Canterbury
LINCOLN'S INN	
Hale 1 (1)	Lincoln's Inn
68 (73)	Kirby Bellars
85 (91)	Lanthony
104 (114)	Durham
Add. XLIV	Bath
PUBLIC RECORD OFFICE	
Aug. Office Misc. books 490	
	London, Carth.
Exch. K.R.	
Misc. books i.27	Canter-
	bury, St Aug.
i.28	Ramsey
Exch. T.R.	
Misc. books 196	Canterbury
ROYAL ASTRONOMICAL SOCIETY	
QB.7/1021	Babwell
ROYAL COLL. OF PHYSICIANS	
358	Thurgarton
390	Cambridge, Peterho.
409	Romsey
	Wilton
ST BARTHOLOMEW'S HOSPITAL	
—	London, St Barth.
ST PAUL'S CATHEDRAL	
1–3	London
5	Syon
11	Warrington, Aug.
13	York
ST PETER-UPON-CORNHILL	
PARISH CHURCH	
—	London, St Peter-upon-
	Cornhill, Ch.*
SION COLLEGE	
Arc. L.40.2/E.25	Westminster
L.2	Canterbury
L.9	Bury
L.21	Northamp-
	ton, Dom.
	Oxford, Oriel
	Coll.
L.31	Canterbury
L.32	Canterbury
SOCIETY OF ANTIQUARIES	
7	Durham
47	Merton

MANCHESTER, *Lancashire*
CHETHAM'S LIBR.

6681	Oxford, Fran.
6709	Dunstable
6712	St Albans
	Westminster
6717	Godstow
27907	Syon

JOHN RYLANDS LIBR.

Engl. 81	Syon
Lat. 24	Exeter
109	†Canterbury
	Rochester
122	Evesham
150	Whalley
153	Byland
155	†Canterbury, St Aug.
	London, Guildhall
165	Westminster
179	Welbeck
185	Norwich
186	Beverley
	Roche
196	Rievaulx
215	Wigmore
217	†Chester
219	Meaux
226	Norwich
339	Halsall, *Ch.*
365	Fountains
391	Stafford, Fran.

NORTHERN CONGREGATIONAL
COLL.

1	Canterbury

UNIVERSITY LIBR.

Christie 3.f.16	Farnworth, *Ch.*

MAXWELL STUART, Mr P.
See TRAQUAIR

MAYFIELD, *Sussex*
Capt. M. BUTLER-BOWDON,
DAPSLAND

—	Broughton, *Ch.*
—	Mount Grace

MELLISH TRUSTEES. *See*
HODSOCK PRIORY

MIDDLETON, LORD. *See*
BIRDSALL

MILAN, *Italy*
BIBL. NAZIONALE BRAIDENSE

A.F.xi	Ely
	Winchester

MONSON, LORD. *See*
SOUTH CARLTON

MORAY, EARL OF. *See*
DARNAWAY

MORCOMBELAKE, *Dorset*
Mr J. STEVENS COX

—	Reading
—	Syon

MOSTYN HALL, *Flintshire*
LORD MOSTYN

—	Caerleon
	Chester

MOUNT STUART, *Bute*
MARQUESS OF BUTE

—	Ramsey
	St Albans

MUNICH, *Germany*
STAATSBIBLIOTHEK

lat. 835	Gloucester

NEW HAVEN, *U.S.A., Conn.*
YALE UNIVERSITY LIBR.

—	London, Carth.
—	Southwark
—	Stamford, Carm.

Prof. NORMAN HOLMES PEARSON,
c/o YALE UNIVERSITY

—	Roche

NEW YORK, *U.S.A., N.Y.*
COLUMBIA UNIV. LIBR.

Plimpton 76	†Fineshade
269	Norwich

NEW YORK PUBLIC LIBR.

8	Canterbury, St Aug.
63	Westminster, St Stephen
Spencer 2	Preston
19	Marrick
26	Worksop

PIERPONT MORGAN LIBR.

M. 23	†Ripon
43	†Mendham
81	Worksop
99	Gloucester
103	†Lenton
	Reading

PIERPONT MORGAN LIBR. (*contd*)
162 †Syon
302 Ramsey
521 †Bury Canterbury
610 Winchester
708 †Thorney
724 †Bury Canterbury
736 Bury
766 †Bridlington
823 Taunton
890 Fountains
WILLIAM S. GLAZIER'S COL-
LECTION
18[1] Canterbury, St Aug.
19[1] Hyde
39[1] Coverham
53[1] Canterbury, St Aug.
65[1] St Osyth
Mr JOHN M. CRAWFORD, Jr,
46 EAST EIGHTY-SECOND
STREET
— Canterbury, St Aug.
PHILIP C. DUSCHNES, LEXINGTON
AVENUE
— Witham
EXECUTORS OF THE LATE Mr
WILLIAM S. GLAZIER. *See*
NEW YORK, PIERPONT
MORGAN LIBR.
Mrs P. G. and Mr J. D. GORDAN,
113 EAST SEVENTY-EIGHTH
STREET
24 Lichfield Chantries

NEWBURY, *Berkshire*
Prof. H. A. ORMEROD, COOTES,
CROOKHAM COMMON
— Newstead (Notts.)*
— Scarborough

NEWCASTLE-UPON-TYNE,
Northumberland
CATHEDRAL LIBR.
— Hexham
UNIVERSITY LIBR.
1 York, St Mary

NORFOLK, DUKE OF. *See*
ARUNDEL

NORTHUMBERLAND, DUKE
OF. *See* ALNWICK

NORWICH, *Norfolk*
CASTLE MUSEUM
99.20 Norwich
158.926.4g(2) Canterbury, St Aug.
158.926.4g(4) Bury
CATHEDRAL
— Norwich
ST PETER MANCROFT PARISH
CHURCH
— †Norwich

NOTTINGHAM
PUBLIC LIBR.
— Newstead (Notts.)**
UNIVERSITY LIBR.
MeLM 1 Rushall, *Ch.***
MiLM 5 Durham**

OAKLY PARK, near *Ludlow,*
Shropshire
EARL OF PLYMOUTH
— Syon

O'DONNELL, MRS F. E. *See*
GUILDFORD

ORLÉANS, *France, Loiret*
BIBL. MUNICIPALE
127 Winchcomb

ORMEROD, Prof. H. A. *See*
NEWBURY

OSCOTT, NEW, *Warwickshire*
COLL. OF ST MARY
1 †Norwich

OSLO, *Norway*
RIKSARKIVET
Lat. fr. 145 Crowland

OSWESTRY, *Shropshire*
LORD HARLECH, BROGYNTYN
— Bury

OXFORD
BLACKFRIARS
— King's Langley
BODLEIAN LIBR.
Add. A.42 (30149) Amesbury
C.181 (29209) Bury
C.260 (30279) Canterbury

[1] On deposit from Mr Glazier's executors.

BODLEIAN LIBR. (*contd*)
Arch. Selden

B.16 (3362)	Malmesbury
B.26 (3340)	Salisbury
B.50 (3352)	Oxford, Univ.
Ashmole 189	Muchelney
304	St Albans
341	Canterbury, St Aug.
342	Bermondsey
360	Bodmin, Fran.
424	Cambridge, Peterho.
748	Oxford, Staple Hall
750	Vale Royal
789	Hereford, Registry
790	Glastonbury
1285	Southwark
1398	Fountains Lynn, Carm.
1431	Canterbury, St Aug.
1437	Fountains
1474	Aberdeen
1516	Garendon
1518	†Lichfield
1522	Merton
1523	Bromholm
1525	Canterbury
1796	St Albans
Aubrey 31 (6543)	†Oxford, Durham Coll.

Auct.

D.1.2 (2115)	Windsor
D.1.4 (2113)	Windsor
D.1.5 (2117)	Windsor
D.1.7 (2629)	Exeter
D.1.8 (2761)	Northampton
D.1.9 (2132)	Exeter
D.1.10 (1936)	Missenden Windsor
D.1.11 (2110)	Windsor
D.1.12 (2133)	Exeter
D.1.13 (2098)	Exeter
D.1.15 (2239)	Evesham
D.1.18 (2056)	Exeter
D.1.19 (2335)	Reading
D.2.2. (4120)	Canterbury
D.2.3 (2710)	Windsor
D.2.4 (2105)	Winchester

BODLEIAN LIBR. (*contd*)
Auct.

D.2.6 (3636)	Littlemore St Albans Winchester
D.2.7 (2104)	†Exeter
D.2.8 (2337)	Exeter
D.2.10 (2116)	†Roberts-bridge Windsor
D.2.11 (2112)	Windsor
D.2.12 (2092)	Reading
D.2.13 (2109)	Windsor
D.2.16 (2719)	Exeter
D.2.20 (2238)	Mottenden
D.3.1 (2665)	Syon
D.3.6 (2703)	Newstead (Notts.)
D.3.7 (2029)	Oxford, New Coll.
D.3.10 (2134)	Exeter
D.3.11 (2111)	†Buildwas Windsor
D.3.12 (2093)	Reading
D.3.13 (2118)	Windsor
D.3.14 (4114)	†Bury Chichester
D.3.15 (2208)	Reading
D.4.6 (1879)	Reading
D.4.7 (1961)	Syon
D.4.8 (4086)	Norwich
D.4.9 (1968)	Oxford, Exeter Coll.
D.4.10 (3563)	Reading
D.4.11 (27690)	Northampton, Fran.
D.4.13 (2571)	Cerne
D.4.15 (27633)	Kyme
D.4.18 (2094)	Reading
D.4.20 (27666)	Leake, *Ch.*
D.4.22 (2387)	Waltham
D.5.14 (1849)	Edington
D.inf.2.4 (4089)	Worcester
D.inf.2.6 (2516)	Beeleigh †Milton, *Ch.*
D.inf.2.8 (3559)	Darley Repton
D.inf.2.9 (2638)	Exeter
D.inf.2.10 (2085)	Newark
E.inf.4 (2429)	Chicksands
E.inf.6 (2051)	Canterbury
E.inf.7 (2130)	Canterbury

BODLEIAN LIBR. (*contd*)

Bodley 141	(1911)	Windsor
142	(1912)	Chichester
144	(1914)	Canterbury, St Aug.
146	(1917)	Reading
147	(1918)	Exeter
148	(1920)	Exeter
149	(1922)	Exeter
150	(1924)	Exeter
151	(1929)	Norwich
153	(1950)	†Winchester
155	(1974)	Barking
157	(1992)	Westminster
159	(2009)	Crediton
160	(2014a)	Canterbury
161	(2014b)	Canterbury
162	(2015)	Exeter
163	(2016)	Peter-borough
167	(2025)	Windsor
168	(2027)	Bordesley
172	(2034)	Windsor
173	(2036)	Wilsford
182	(2082)	Maxstoke
186	(2088)	†Reading
188	(2091)	Haughmond
190	(2095)	Exeter
192	(2099)	Windsor
193	(2100)	†Canterbury Exeter
194	(2101)	Windsor
196	(1897)	Canterbury
197	(1906)	Reading
198	(1907)	Oxford, Fran. Oxford, Lincoln Coll.
200	(1921)	Reading
201	(1923)	Exeter
206	(2012)	Exeter
207	(2021)	Newark
208	(2033)	Windsor Witham
209	(2035)	Pershore
210	(2037)	Gloucester
212	(2041)	Syon
214	(2048)	Canterbury
215	(2049)	†Oxford, Univ.
216	(2052)	Bury
217	(2053)	Canterbury

BODLEIAN LIBR. (*contd*)

Bodley 223	(2106)	Windsor Worcester
225	(2114)	Bury
229	(2120)	Exeter
230	(2123*)	Exeter
236	(1934)	Hexham Windsor
237	(1939)	Exeter
238	(2050)	Oxford, New Coll.
239	(2244)	Exeter
240	(2469)	Bury
241	(1925)	Reading
249	(2738)	Titchfield
251	(2332)	Canterbury
252	(2504)	Oxford, Balliol Coll.
253	(2123**)	Exeter
256	(2447)	Exeter
257	(2047)	Reading
258	(2240)	Windsor
263	(2440)	†Reading
267	(2128)	Windsor
268	(1927)	Exeter
269	(1935)	Eynsham Windsor
271	(1938)	Canterbury
272	(1940)	Exeter
273	(1941)	Exeter
274	(1942)	Exeter
275	(2623)	Windsor
277	(2124)	London, Carth.
279	(2241)	Exeter
280	(2246)	Stuston, *Ch.*
281	(2331)	Canterbury
284	(2339)	Cirencester
285	(2430)	Ramsey
286	(2433)	Exeter
287	(2435)	Exeter
289	(2741)	Exeter
290	(2441)	Exeter
291	(2442)	Exeter
292	(2446)	St Albans
293	(2448)	Exeter
295	(2705)	Windsor
297	(2468)	Bury
299	(2473)	Canterbury, St Aug.
300	(2474)	Cambridge, Clare Coll.

BODLEIAN LIBR. (*contd*)		BODLEIAN LIBR. (*contd*)	
Bodley 301 (2739)	Exeter	Bodley 387 (2212)	†Bury
304 (2107)	Windsor		†Canterbury
310 (2121)	Oxford,		Rochester
	New Coll.		Windsor
311 (2122)	Exeter		†Worcester
312 (2123)	Oxford,	388 (2217)	Worksop
	Balliol Coll.	389 (2218)	Exeter
314 (2129)	Exeter	390 (2220)	Crediton
315 (2712)	Exeter	391 (2222)	Canterbury,
316 (2752)	Pleshey		St Aug.
	†St Albans	392 (2223)	Salisbury
317 (2708)	Canterbury	393 (2224)	Exeter
318 (2732)	Exeter	394 (2225)	Exeter
319 (2226)	Exeter	395 (2215)	Buildwas
320 (2234)	Exeter		Windsor
321 (2237)	Windsor	396 (2227)	Reading
333 (2245)	Exeter	397 (2228)	Reading
335 (2334)	Exeter	398 (2229)	Newark
336 (2336)	Canterbury	406 (2297)	Leeds
338 (2399)	Exeter	407 (2299)	Salisbury
340 (2404)	Rochester	408 (2301)	†Reading
342 (2405)	Rochester	409 (2302)	Reading
345 (2411)	Canterbury	410 (2305)	Windsor
355 (2444)	Cambridge,	412 (2308)	Bury
	Fran.	413 (2309)	Reading
	Walsingham,	415 (2313)	Ashridge
	Fran.	417 (2316)	Sheen
356 (2716)	Bury	419 (2318)	Tattershall
357 (2452)	Bridlington	423 (2322)	Southwark
362 (2463)	Oxford, Univ.	426 (2327)	Bury
365 (2475)	Oxford,		Canterbury,
	Merton Coll.		St Aug.
371 (2717)	Buildwas	429 (2599)	London,
	Windsor		Fran.
372 (2750)	Windsor	435 (2374)	Eynsham
373 (2751)	Chester	442 (2383)	Worcester
	Windsor	444 (2385)	Salisbury
374 (2484)	Chichester	449 (2396)	Exeter
377 (2745)	Exeter	450 (2398)	†Reading
378 (2748)	†Canterbury	451 (2401)	Winchester,
	Windsor		St Mary
379 (2434)	Canterbury	452 (2402)	†Warwick,
380 (2733)	Exeter		St Mary
381 (2202)	Canterbury,		Windsor
	St Aug.	453 (2403)	Windsor
382 (2203)	Exeter	454 (2409)	Norwich
383 (2206)	Crediton	459 (2415)	Windsor
384 (2209)	Windsor	462 (2454)	St Albans
385 (2210)	Canterbury	463 (2456)	Exeter
386 (2211)	Shelford	464 (2458)	Canterbury,
	Windsor		St Aug.

BODLEIAN LIBR. (*contd*)			**BODLEIAN LIBR.** (*contd*)		
Bodley	467 (2487)	St Albans	Bodley	631 (1954)	Reading
	468 (2488)	Windsor		633 (1966)	Worcester
	473 (2213)	Exeter		637 (2024)	Oxford,
	477 (2005)	Osney			Oriel Coll.
		Windsor		639 (2080)	Reading
	479 (2013)	Exeter		641 (27706)	†Wymond-
	482 (2046)	Exeter			ham
	494 (2108)	Exeter		643 (2256)	Mottenden
	505 (2676)	London,		648 (2291)	Canterbury
		Carth.		655 (2397)	Thornholm
	507 (2171)	Canterbury,		656 (27644)	Lessness
		St Aug.		672 (3005)	Chester
	514 (2184)	Jervaulx		678 (2595)	Dover
	516 (2570)	Salisbury		679 (2596)	Canterbury,
	521 (2182)	Canterbury,			St Aug.
		St Aug.		680 (2597)	Thorney
	527 (2219)	Waverley		683 (2757)	Exeter
	528 (2221)	Reading		684 (2498)	Windsor
	535 (2254)	Winchester		688 (2502)	Oxford,
	543 (2588)	Ramsey			Merton Coll.
		Worcester		689 (2530)	Oxford,
	544 (2591)	Windsor			Merton Coll.
	547 (2286)	†Rochford,		691 (2740)	Exeter
		Ch.		692 (2508)	†Oxford,
	550 (2300)	Reading			Gloucester Coll.
	551 (2303)	Windsor			Worcester
	555 (2329)	Merton		696 (2512)	Oxford,
	565 (2351)	Edington			Merton Coll.
	569 (2311)	St Albans		697 (2520)	†Windsor
	570 (2017)	Reading		698 (2521)	Salisbury
	572 (2026)	Canterbury,		700 (2528)	Eynsham
		St Aug.			Oxford,
	577 (27645)	†Waltham			Merton Coll.
	579 (2675)	Exeter		703 (2766)	Oxford,
	582 (2204)	†Bury			Fran.
		Ely		705 (2564)	Windsor
		Windsor		706 (2605)	Garendon
	583 (2214)	Windsor			†Oxford,
	585 (2357)	London,			Carm.
		Fran. nuns		707 (2608)	Exeter
	596 (2376)	Canterbury,		708 (2609)	Exeter
		St Aug.		713 (2620)	Reading
	600 (2390)	Canterbury,		715 (2622)	Bury
		St Aug.		716 (2630)	Bury
	602 (2393)	Hatfield		717 (2631)	Exeter
		Regis		718 (2632)	Exeter
		Newark		719 (2633)	Southwick
	605 (2416)	Windsor		720 (2634)	Exeter
	618 (2149)	Bristol,		721 (2647)	Windsor
		St Mark		722 (2648)	Exeter
	630 (1953)	Syon		724 (2652)	Battle

BODLEIAN LIBR. (*contd*)		
Bodley	865 (2737)	Exeter
	866 (2742)	Windsor
	867 (2746)	Windsor
	868 (2749)	Worcester
	874 (2932)	†Abingdon
	897 (27888)	Hereford, Fran.
	901 (3034)	Coventry
	918 (2910)	Bermondsey
	923 (27701)	Barking
	924 (3021)	Southwark
	948 (3032)	†London, St Andrew Undershaft, *Ch.* †St Albans
	956 (27607)	Lichfield
Bodley Oriental		
	135 (3086)	Exeter
Bodley Rolls		
	3 (2983)	York, St Mary
	21 (3113)	†Lanthony
	22 (30445)	Pipewell
Canonici græc.		
	35	Canterbury
Canonici misc. 110		Norwich
Digby	4	Canterbury
	5	Canterbury
	11	Oxford, Fran. Stanley
	13	Canterbury Dover
	19	Oxford, Merton Coll.
	23	Osney
	28	Canterbury
	29	Oxford, Balliol Coll.
	31	Oxford, New Coll.
	33	Coventry
	37	Oxford, Oriel Coll.
	39	Abingdon
	40	Oxford, Univ.
	41	Durham Oxford, Durham Coll.
	44	Oxford, All Souls Coll.
	53	Bridlington
	61	Oxford, Merton Coll.
	63	Winchester

BODLEIAN LIBR. (*contd*)		
Digby	67	Oxford, Merton Coll.
	77	Meaux Oxford, Merton Coll.
	81	Durham Tavistock
	86	†Worcester
	90	Oxford, Fran.
	92	Canterbury
	93	Oxford, Fran.
	96	Abingdon
	99	Thetford
	104	Coventry Witham
	109	Bury
	110	†Canterbury
	112	†Bury
	115	Coventry
	139	Coventry
	146	Abingdon
	147	Merton
	148	Reading
	150	†Worcester
	151	Reading
	153	Canterbury, Fran.
	154	Titchfield
	155	Oxford, Merton Coll.
	156	Tonbridge
	157	Battle
	158	Reading
	161	Oxford, Oriel Coll.
	168	Osney
	173	Salisbury
	174	Canterbury, St Aug.
	176	Oxford, Merton Coll.
	178	Cambridge, Clare Coll.
	183	Cambridge, Clare Coll.
	184	Reading
	186	York, St Mary
	190	Oxford, Merton Coll. Oxford, Oriel Coll.
	191	Oxford, Merton Coll. Oxford, Oriel Coll.
	200	Reading
	203	†Canterbury

BODLEIAN LIBR. (*contd*)

Hatton
76 (4125)	Worcester
86 (4078)	Stafford
93 (4081)	Worcester
94 (4085)	Canterbury, St Aug.
101 (4048)	Holme Cultram
102 (4051)	Hereford, Fran.
113 (5210)	Worcester
114 (5134)	Worcester
115 (5135)	Worcester
116 (5136)	Worcester

Holkham misc. 37 — Bury

Jones 9 (8916)	Faversham
41 (8949)	Cambridge, King's Coll.
46 (8954)	Norwich, St Leonard
48 (8956)	Furness
Junius 11 (5123)	Canterbury
27 (5139)	Winchester
121 (5232)	Worcester

Lat. bib.
b.2 (P) (2202*)	Canterbury, St Aug.
c.8 (P)	Salisbury (p 175., n. 3)

Lat. hist. a.2 — Glastonbury

Lat. liturg.
a.6 (30556)	Canterbury, St Aug.
b.4 (32703)	Northampton, *Ch.*
b.5 (32940)	Drayton, *Ch.*
b.6 (32941)	Drayton, *Ch.*
b.14	Denchworth,*Ch.*
d.20	Worcester
e.6 (32558)	Chertsey
e.37	Chertsey
f.5 (29744)	Durham
f.11 (32707)	†Burnham
f.19	Norwich
f.25	West Lavington, *Ch.*
g.1 (31379)	St Bees York, St Mary
g.8	Tynemouth Wymondham

Lat. misc.
b.2 (R) (30561)	Tewkesbury
b.12	Canterbury
c.16 (32708)	Battle

BODLEIAN LIBR. (*contd*)

Lat. misc.
d.13 (30572)	Canterbury
d.14 (30573)	Canterbury
d.30 (30584)	Canterbury
d.74	Chester, Fran.
d.80	London, Aug.
e.22	Winchester, St Elizabeth
f.37	Colchester, Fran.

Lat. theol.
b.2 (30588)	Canterbury, St Aug.
c.23	Hurley
c.26	Bury
d.1 (29746)	Babwell Lynn, Fran.
d.17	†Bridlington
e.8 (32566)	Southwark
e.9 (32710)	Flanesford
e.26	Sheen
e.36–37	Spofforth, *Ch.*
e.39	Salisbury, Fran.
f.3 (31096)	Jervaulx
f.8 (34476)	†Bisham
f.20	Syon

Laud græc. 28	Darley
35	†Jarrow
Laud lat. 4	Glastonbury
5	Guisborough
12	Durham Oxford, Durham Coll.
15	Newark
17	Cirencester
18	†Canterbury, St Aug.
19	Barking
31	†Evesham Eynsham
34	Newstead(Notts.)
36	Durham
65	Canterbury, St Aug.
67	St Albans
69	Kirkstall
87	London, Carm.
95	Chichester Ely
109	Waltham
114	Lacock †Aconbury

Bodleian Libr. (*contd*)

Laud misc.	619	Fountains
	636	Peterborough
	641	Durham
	647	Ely
	657	Tynemouth
	662	†Bridgend
	664	†Pershore
		†Winchester
		†Winchester, St Mary
	667	Brecon, *Ch.*
	675	Norwich
	698	Ely
	700	Durham
	706	Gloucester
	720	†Durham
	722	Kirkstall
	723	Merton
	725	Reading
	728	London, Dom.
	730	Canterbury
		†Fountains
	742	Bury
	746	Oxford, Fran.
	748	Durham
	750	Glastonbury
Laud or.	174	Bury

Liturg.
6 (30595)	Gracedieu
407 (29071)	Amesbury

Lyell	1	Canterbury, St Aug.
	2	Holme Cultram
	6	St Osyth
	8	Fountains
	11	Lincoln, Fran.
	16	Durham
	17	York, St Mary
	19	Canterbury
	21	Abingdon
	23	Tarrant Keynston
	25	Gainsborough, *Ch.*
	38	Bristol, St Mark

Marshall 19 (5265) Canterbury, St Aug.
Malmesbury

e Museo	2 (3491)	Salisbury
	3 (3496)	Valle Crucis
	6 (3567)	Bury
	7 (3568)	Bury
	8 (3569)	Bury

Bodleian Libr. (*contd*)

e Museo	9 (3570)	Bury
	19 (3500)	Oxford, Merton Coll.
	26 (3571)	Bury
	27 (3572)	Bury
	31 (3574)	Bury
	32 (3573)	Bury
	33 (3576)	Bury
	34 (3577)	Bury
	36 (3575)	Bury
	60 (3648)	Northampton
	62 (3650)	Kingswood
	66 (3655)	Canterbury, St Aug.
	82 (3643)	Dore
	86 (3629)	Norwich, Carm.
	93 (3632)	Battle Brecon
	112 (3578)	Bury
	113 (3584)	London, Elsyng Spital
	121 (3565)	Oxford, Oriel Coll.
	195 (3608)	Kirkstall
	222 (3592)	Darley
	223 (3538)	Canterbury, St Aug.
	249 (27835)	Belvoir Westminster

Rawlinson
A.287	Evesham
A.363	Staindrop
A.374	Lanthony
A.375	Reading
A.376	Reading
A.388	Pipewell
A.389	Lichfield
A.411	Boxgrove
A.416	Reading
A.420	Clattercote
A.433	Waltham
A.445	Leicester
B.177	Southwark
B.186	†Southwark
B.188	Canterbury
B.189	Hatfield Peverel
B.191	Canterbury

BODLEIAN LIBR. (*contd*)	
Selden supra	
24 (3412)	St Albans
25 (3413)	Canterbury, St Aug.
26 (3414)	Canterbury, St Aug.
30 (3418)	Canterbury, St Aug.
31 (3419)	Bury
39 (3427)	Merton
41 (3429)	Norwich, Carm.
65 (3453)	Oxford, Canterbury Coll.
76 (3464)	Winchester
87 (3475)	†Guisborough
90 (3478)	Canterbury, St Aug.
Tanner	
3	†Keynsham
	Worcester
10	Thorney
15	Canterbury
110	Ramsey
165	Canterbury
166	Thornton-on-Humber
169* (9995)	Chester
170	Gloucester, St Oswald
196	Launceston
Top. Gloucs. d.2	Tewkesbury
Wood	
B.3 (8574)	Rochester
empt. 1 (8589)	Glastonbury
5 (8593)	Malmesbury
13 (8601)	Canterbury, St Aug.
14 (8602)	Axholme
	Hinton
15 (8603)	Exeter
23 (8611)	†Abingdon
24 (8612)	Durham
4° C.95 Art.	Oxford, Merton Coll.
ALL SOULS COLL.	
1	Canterbury, St Aug.
6	†Amesbury
	Exeter
8	Chester
11	Tregare, *Ch.*
12	Stanley
	Stoneleigh
21	Vaudey

ALL SOULS COLL. (*contd*)	
25	Syon
33	Merevale
49	Bury
82	Cirencester
114	Winchester
BALLIOL COLL.	
13	Humberstone
15	Winchester
32	Northampton
35A	Buildwas
36	Lincoln
39, 40	Buildwas
45, 46	London
49	Ely
57	Chester
85	Newark
133	Cambridge, Fran.
142 (lost)	Westminster
150	Buildwas
152	St Osyth
173B	Buildwas
175	Bury
178A	Woburn
182	Colchester, St Botolph
211	Oxford, Merton Coll.
213	Swineshead
214	Cambridge, Fran.
223	Westminster
229	Buildwas
240	Monks Kirby
264	Westminster
300B	Norwich
307	Northampton
321	Hereford
BRASENOSE COLL.	
4	Durham
9	†Mount Grace
13	Droitwich, Aug.
15	Syon
21	St Neots
Latham Room, C.3.7–9	Ardington, *Ch.*
CHRIST CHURCH	
lat. 87	London, St Botolph Aldgate, *Ch.*
88	Buildwas
90, 91	Crediton
97	St Albans
115	St Albans
CORPUS CHRISTI COLL.	
2	St Albans

LINCOLN COLL. (*contd*)	
63	Worksop
100	Malmesbury
MAGDALEN COLL.	
lat. 22	Evesham
25	Reading
37	Oxford, Univ.
41	Barking
53	Norwich
	St Albans
	Wymondham
54	Warwick, Dom.
77	Sheen, Reclusory
100	Worcester
121–32	Osney
162	Durham
166	Canterbury
170	Eye
172	†Bury
	Malmesbury
174	Bridgwater, Fran.
180	Norwich
182	Muchelney
191	Witham
195	Cambridge, Clare Coll.
199	Barlings
226	Hereford, Dom.
MERTON COLL.	
122	†Canterbury, St Aug.
132	Oxford, Dom.
158	Oxford, Fran.
166	Oxford, Fran.
168–72	Oxford, Fran.
181	Malmesbury
189	Cerne
268	Oxford, Univ.
325	Bridlington
K.1.7	Canterbury
NEW COLL.	
98	Ely
123	Coventry
204	†Canterbury
240, 241	Reading
254	Reading
274	St Albans
285	Hereford, Fran.
288	Wells
300	Canterbury
358	St Albans
ORIEL COLL.	
15	Glastonbury
30	London

ORIEL COLL. (*contd*)	
32	Oxford, Univ.
42	Malmesbury
46	London, Guildhall
53	Northampton
60	Northampton
63	Northampton
PEMBROKE COLL.	
2	Abingdon
	Oxford, All Souls Coll.
5	Canterbury
—	Canterbury
QUEEN'S COLL.	
54	†Colchester
302	Evesham
304	Glastonbury
307	Canterbury, St Aug.
309	Lanthony
317	Reading
323	Reading
362	Malvern (Great)
367	Gloucester
ST JOHN'S COLL.	
1	Reading
4	Rochester
5	Reading
11	Reading
14	Durham
17	†Canterbury, St Aug.
	Thorney
19	Lessness
20	Northampton
21	Reading
31	Lessness
39	Northampton
43	Bury
46	Byland
49	Chichester
50	Hurley
59	Reading
60	Thame
61	York, Holy Trinity
62	Southwick
64	St Albans
65	Warwick, Dom.
66B	Canterbury, St Aug.
73	Reading
77	Oxford, Exeter Coll.
88	Chichester
89	Canterbury
94	Newcastle-upon-Tyne, *Ch.*
95	Chichester

WORCESTER COLL.
3.16A (213)	Reading
LRA 6 (233)	Oxford,
	Gloucester Coll.
(273)	Rochester

Mr N. R. KER, MAGDALEN COLL.
—	Oxford, Dom.

Mr M. B. PARKES, KEBLE COLL.
—	Canterbury, St Aug.

OXTON HALL, *Newark,*
Nottinghamshire

Rear-Admiral R. St V. SHER-
BROOKE
—	Langley

PAISLEY, *Renfrewshire*
PUBLIC LIBR.
—	Arbuthnott

PARIS, *France*
BIBL. NATIONALE
fonds français
1038	Barking
24766	Oxford,
	St Frideswide

fonds latin
770	Canterbury
943	Sherborne
987	Canterbury
	†Ramsey
	†Winchester
1218	St Andrews
1792	Abingdon
3757	London, Fran.
4167A	Glastonbury
4922	Norwich
4928	Cambridge, Univ.
5557	Crowland
7805	Oxford, Univ.
8537	Oxford, Univ.
9376	Tewkesbury
10062	Canterbury
10434	London, Carth.
15157	Rievaulx
15170	Chichester

nouv. acq. latines
873	Canterbury, St Aug.
1670	Canterbury

BIBL. MAZARINE
5	Canterbury
34	Sheen

BIBL. STE GENEVIÈVE
2899	Southampton, Fran.

BIBL. DE L'UNIVERSITÉ
153	Southwark
790	Whalley

PARTRIDGE GREEN, *Sussex*
CHARTERHOUSE OF ST HUGH
—	London, Carth.
—	Mount Grace

PEARSON, Prof. N. H. *See*
NEW HAVEN

PENROSE, Prof. L. S. *See*
LONDON

PETERBOROUGH, *Northamp-*
tonshire
CATHEDRAL LIBR.
1	Peterborough
3	Peterborough
15	Peterborough

PHILADELPHIA, *U.S.A., Pa.*
FREE LIBR.
J. F. Lewis 123	†Malmesbury

PENNSYLVANIA, UNIV. LIBR.
3	Bangor

PHILLIPPS COLLECTION.
See LONDON, THE ROB-
INSON TRUST

PLYMOUTH, EARL OF. *See*
OAKLY PARK

PORTLAND, DUKE OF. *See*
WELBECK

PORTSMOUTH, *Hampshire*
ROMAN CATHOLIC BISHOPRIC
Virtue and Cahill
8433	Orpington, *Ch.*
8451	†Reading
8473	Reading

PRINCETON, *U.S.A., N.J.*
UNIV. LIBR.
89		Windsor
Garrett	27	Sweetheart
	34	Tewkesbury
	71	Waverley
	73	St Albans
	94	Fountains
	102	Lincoln, Fran.
	114	Waltham
	119	Crowland
	153	Glastonbury

Mr ROBERT H. TAYLOR,
    511 LAKE DRIVE
—   Bolton

RANWORTH, *Norfolk*
PARISH CHURCH
—   Ranworth

RASHLEIGH, Mr F. S. *See*
  ST AUSTELL

RAYMOND, Mrs. *See* **BEL-CHAMP**

REDLYNCH, *near Salisbury*
              Wiltshire
Major J. R. ABBEY, REDLYNCH
              HOUSE
—   Canterbury, St Aug.
—   Tarrant Keynston

REIGATE, *Surrey*
PARISH CHURCH
2322   London, Fran. nuns

RICHMOND, *U.S.A., Va.*
VIRGINIA STATE LIBR.
1   Mottenden

RIPON, *Yorkshire*
CATHEDRAL LIBR.
xvii.B.29   Frieston
             Mount Grace
xvii.D.2–3   Bridlington
xvii.D.19 Newcastle, Dom.
Mr H. L. BRADFER-LAWRENCE,
            SHAROW END
—   Beverley
—   Byland
—   King's Lynn
—   Mount Grace
—   York, St Mary

ROCHESTER, *Kent*
CATHEDRAL LIBR.
—   Rochester

ROME, VATICAN CITY, *Italy*
BIBL. APOSTOLICA
Ottoboni lat.
69   Cambridge, Fran.
71   Cambridge, Fran.
96   Cambridge, Fran.
99   Cambridge, Dom.
101   Cambridge, Fran.
150   Cambridge, Dom.

BIBL. APOSTOLICA (*contd*)
Ottoboni lat. (*contd*)
159   Cambridge, Dom.
191   Shrewsbury, Dom.
277   Cambridge, Dom.
325   Cambridge, Fran.
352   Babwell
       Cambridge, Fran.
442   Cambridge, Dom.
611   Cambridge, Fran.
623   Cambridge, Fran.
640   Cambridge, Dom.
746   Cambridge, Aug.
758   Cambridge, Dom.
862   Cambridge, Dom.
       London, Dom.
1126 Cambridge, Fran.
1565 †Cambridge, Fran.
       London, Fran.
2048 Cambridge, Fran.
2055 Cambridge, Dom.
2088 Cambridge, Fran.
Pal. lat. 65   Coupar Angus
Regin. lat. 12   Bury
    147   Lewes
    694 Coupar Angus
Vatican. lat. 4951 Rochester
    4954 Cambridge,
            Aug.
   11438   London,
            Aug.

ROMSEY, *Hampshire*
PARISH CHURCH
—   †Romsey
    Winchester, St Mary

ROUEN, *France, Seine-Maritime*
BIBL. MUNICIPALE
274 (Y.6)   †Hyde
368 (A.27) St Germans
369 (Y.7)   Hyde
1385 (U.107) Winchester

RUGBY, *Northamptonshire*
SCHOOL LIBR.
Bloxam 1009 Wallington, *Ch.*

RUTLAND, DUKE OF. *See*
  BELVOIR

ST ANDREWS, *Fife*
UNIV. LIBR.
BR 65.A.9   St Andrews
PA 3895.P.6   Deer

ST AUSTELL, *Cornwall*
Mr P. S. RASHLEIGH, 100 TRURO
ROAD
— Tywardreath*

ST BONAVENTURE, *U.S.A.*
New York
ST BONAVENTURE UNIVERSITY
Friedsam Memorial Libr., 10
Walsingham, Fran.

SALISBURY, *Wiltshire*
CATHEDRAL LIBR.
176 MSS Salisbury (*see p. 172*)
127 Lincoln, Fran.
152 Arlingham, *Ch.*

SAN FRANCISCO, *U.S.A., Cal.*
JOHN HOWELL, 434 POST STREET
— London, Aug.

SAN MARINO, *U.S.A., Cal.*
HENRY E. HUNTINGTON LIBR.
EL 7 H. 8 Ashridge
EL 9 H. 3 Ashridge
EL 9 H. 9 Ashridge
EL 9 H. 11 †Bury
EL 9 H. 15 Ashridge
EL 9 H. 17 Hampole
EL 34 B. 7 Chester, St Mary
HM 62 Rochester
HM 132 Chester
HM 903 York, St Mary
HM 1342 Westminster
HM 3027 †Fountains
HM 19915 Holme Cultram
HM 26052 St Osyth
HM 26560 Manchester
HM 27186 Coggeshall
HM 27187 St Albans

SANDERS, Mr H. *See* **LON-
DON**

SHERBROOKE, Rear-Admiral
R. ST V. *See* **OXTON
HALL**

SHIRBURN CASTLE, *Oxford-
shire*
EARL OF MACCLESFIELD
— Hyde

SHREWSBURY, *Shropshire*
ROMAN CATHOLIC BISHOPRIC
— Frodesley, *Ch.*

SCHOOL
I Chester, Dom.
VII Chester
XII Buildwas
XV Hereford, Fran.
XXIV Chester, Dom.
XXVI Canterbury
XXIX Lenton
XXXII Shrewsbury, Fran.
XXXIII Wombridge
XXXV Chester, Dom.

SION HOUSE, *Isleworth,*
Middlesex
DUKE OF NORTHUMBERLAND
— Syon

SMITH, Mr H. F. *See*
LEICESTER

SOUTH CARLTON, *Lincolnshire*
Baron MONSON, MANOR HOUSE
— Bardney*

SOUTHWELL, *Nottinghamshire*
MINSTER LIBR.
5 Newcastle-upon-Tyne, Dom.

SPALDING, *Lincolnshire*
GENTLEMEN'S SOCIETY
M.J.B.13 Crowland
B.96 Haughmond

STEYNING, *Sussex*
Sir ARTHUR HOWARD, WAPPING-
THORN
— Shaftesbury

STOCKHOLM, *Sweden*
KUNGL. BIBLIOTEK
— Canterbury

STONYHURST COLLEGE,
Blackburn, Lancashire
s.n. Durham
6 Tatham, *Ch.*
9 Hartland
10 St Albans
11 Stanlow
12 Tarrant Keynston
44 Ashridge

STUART, Mr P. MAXWELL.
See **TRAQUAIR**

BIBLE HOUSE
—   London, Fran. nuns

WELLINGTON, *Somerset*
Mr J. HASSON, BINDON HOUSE
—   Shaftesbury

WELLS, *Somerset*
CATHEDRAL LIBR.
—   †Exeter
—   Glastonbury
—   †Hailes
—   Wells
VICARS CHORAL HALL
—   Garendon

WEMYSS CASTLE, *Fife*
Capt. M. J. ERSKINE-WEMYSS
—   Cambuskenneth

WENTWORTH WOODHOUSE
near Rotherham, Yorkshire
EARL FITZWILLIAM
—   Barlings

WESTMINSTER ABBEY. *See*
LONDON

WHEPSTEAD, *Suffolk*
Mr H. C. DRAYTON, PLUMTON
HALL
—   Waltham

WILLIAMSTOWN, *U.S.A.,*
Mass.
WILLIAMS COLL., CHAPIN LIBR.
—   Gloucester

WINCHESTER, *Hampshire*
CATHEDRAL LIBR.
1, 2   Winchester
4, 5   Winchester
9   Southwell
10   Durham
14, 15   Winchester
17   Winchester
20   Winchester
COLLEGE
2   Eton
4   Winchester, Coll.
6   Merevale
7   Cambridge, Queens' Coll.
11   Winchester, Coll.
12   Oxford, New Coll.
14B   †Winchester, Coll.
15   Winchester, Coll.

COLLEGE (*contd*)
17   Winchester, Coll.
18   Winchester
20   Newburgh
22   †Hyde
       †Winchester, Coll.
38   Winchester, Coll.

WINDSOR, *Berkshire*
CASTLE
—   Amesbury
ST GEORGE'S CHAPEL
5   Canterbury

WISBECH, *Cambridgeshire*
MUSEUM
1   Bury
2–4   †Bury
5   Ramsey
       †Bury
6, 7   †Bury
9   †Bury

WOLFENBÜTTEL, *Germany*
HERZOG-AUGUST-BIBLIOTHEK
Helmst. 411   St Andrews
481   Canterbury,
       St Aug.
499   Arbroath
       Perth, Fran.
538   St Andrews
628   St Andrews
927   Coupar Angus
1006   Arbroath
1029   St Andrews
1108   St Andrews
4447 (Gud. lat. 143)   Meaux

WOLLATON, *Nottinghamshire*
PARISH CHURCH   Wollaton,
       Ch.

WORCESTER
CATHEDRAL LIBR.
250 MSS   Worcester (*see*
       p. 210)
F.89   Worcester, Dom.
F.150   St Dogmells
F.173   Hyde
       Winchester
Q.75   Shrewsbury, Fran.
Q.89   Worcester, Fran.
Add. 68(5)   Evesham

INDEX OF PRINTED BOOKS

UNIVERSITY LIBR.
Bi.4.g.20	Oxford, All Souls Coll.
Bn.6.b.11	Sheen
Dp.e.6	London, Aug.
E.g.6.a.9	Merton

GLOUCESTER
CATHEDRAL LIBR.
D.3.18	Thremhall
—	Higham Ferrers
—	Tewkesbury

GÖTTINGEN, *Germany*
UNIVERSITÄTSBIBL.
| — | Syon |

GOUDA, *Holland*
Messrs KOCH and KNUTTEL
| — | Durham |

HASSOP, *Derbyshire*
CATHOLIC CHURCH
| — | Durham (2 bks)* |

HAWKESYARD PRIORY, *Rugeley, Staffordshire*
| — | Durham |

HENDRED HOUSE, *East Hendred, Berkshire*
| Mr T. EYSTON | Biddlesden |

HEREFORD
CATHEDRAL LIBR.
21 pr. bks Hereford (*see p. 96*)	
A.ix.2, 3	Durham
H.ii.7	Battle

HEXHAM, *Northumberland*
CATHOLIC CHURCH
| — | Durham* |

HEYTHROP COLLEGE, *Chipping Norton, Oxfordshire*
| — | Kingston-upon-Hull |

HOHLER, Mr C. *See*
LONDON

HOLKHAM HALL, *Norfolk*
LORD LEICESTER
| — | Winchcomb |

INSCH, *Aberdeenshire*
Mr C. A. GORDON, THE OLD MANSE
| — | Hailes |

IPSWICH, *Suffolk*
CENTRAL LIBR.
—	Butley
—	Cambridge, Fran.
—	Syon

KEW, *Surrey*
Mr B. S. CRON, 351 SANDYCOMBE ROAD
| — | Ashridge |

LAMPETER, *Cardiganshire*
ST DAVID'S COLL.
| — | Faversham |

LINCOLN
CATHEDRAL LIBR.
| F.1.14 | Durham |
| SS.2.15 | Axholme |

LONDON
BRITISH MUSEUM
IA. 3420	Rochester
17230	Westminster
17393	Oxford, Corpus Christi Coll.
IB. 118	Woburn
24866	Leiston
26227	Salisbury, Dom. Warwick, Dom.
40248	Bury
48104	Canterbury
55119	Syon
55315	Butley
IC.29955–56	Burnham Norton
C.35.i.4	Upper Bullinghope, *Ch.*
C.37.c.44	Hailes
C.52.g.2	Harpole, *Ch.*
704.h.21	Sheen Anglorum

ST PAUL'S CATHEDRAL LIBR.
| 13.D.16 | Greenwich |

DUTCH CHURCH
| — | Syon* |

INCORPORATED LAW SOCIETY
| 107.d | Durham |

LAMBETH PALACE
1483.5	Canterbury, Fran.
1484.2	London, St Mary of Graces
1486.4	Syon
1494.2	Greenwich
1500.91	Fotheringhay
**H890.B6, B7	Merton

BODLEIAN LIBR. (*contd*)

C.1.5 Linc.	Southwark
D.13.5 Linc.	Chertsey
Rawl. Q.d.12 (15456)	Winch-
	comb
H.1.14 Art. Seld.	London,
	Whittington
	Coll.
4º B.2 Art. Seld.	Canterbury,
	St Aug.
A.2.8 Th. Seld.	Oxford,
	Balliol Coll.
R.1.23 Th. Seld.	Westminster
4º W.2 Th. Seld.	Syon
AA.61 Th. Seld.	Mount
	Grace
Tanner 191	Bruisyard
H.3.3–7 Th.	Oxford,
	Magdalen Coll.
M.9.4 Th.	Winchcomb
4º Z.33 Th.	Merton
8º A.11 Th.	Syon
8º B.115 Th.	London,
	Crutched Friars
8º M.122 Th.	Worcester
Vet. E.1.c.45	Penwortham, *Ch.*

ALL SOULS COLL.

i.12.15	Burton-upon-Trent
v.2.13	Burton-upon-Trent
v.4.12	Burton-upon-Trent
LR.4.a.8	Rochester
	Winchester
LR.4.c.3	Worcester
LR.4.e.10	Burton-upon-Trent
SR.68.g.10	Medmenham
SR.77.g.13	Burton-upon-Trent
SR.99.c.18	Burton-upon-Trent

BALLIOL COLL.

—	Hailes

BRASENOSE COLL.

UB.S.II.51	Bromfield

CHRIST CHURCH

e.8.29	Fountains

CORPUS CHRISTI COLL.

Z.12.6	Hailes
Δ.10.4	Kirkstall
Δ.15.5	Mottenden
Φ.A.3.4	Boxley

EXETER COLL.

9M 15792	Abingdon

HERTFORD COLL.

a.1.27	Norwich, Dom.

KEBLE COLL.

A.62	Newark

MAGDALEN COLL.

i.1.1–2	York, St Mary
Arch. C.I.1.14	Syon

MERTON COLL.

62.f.23	Bishop's Cleeve, *Ch.*
76.b.11	Syon
77.a.20	Syon
77.b.5	†Syon
B.8.G.17	Coventry, Carm.
	Newcastle, Carm.
	Worcester

NEW COLL.

Auct. T.6.2	Lampeter Velfrey,
	Ch.

ORIEL COLL.

C.e.20	Durham

ST JOHN'S COLL.

A.9.5–7	Syon
b.1.1	Bodenham, *Ch.*
b.3.22	Sheen
c.3.5	Merton
K.3.9	Merton
P.4.46	Durham
U.2.16	Merton
Φ.1.32	Merton

UNIVERSITY COLL.

d.6	Leominster
Mr JOHN ARMSTRONG,	Hertford
	Coll.
—	Mottenden
Mr D. M. ROGERS, c/o	BODLEIAN
	LIBR.
—	Ramsey
—	Wenlock
—	Winchcomb

PETERBOROUGH, *Northamptonshire*

CATHEDRAL LIBR.

D.8.17	Pipewell
M.6.6	Winchester, Coll.

PHILADELPHIA, *U.S.A., Pa.*

THE PHILIP H. AND A. S. W.
ROSENBACH FOUNDATION,
2010 DE LANCEY PLACE

Inc. H.491	Sheen
	Syon

RIPON, *Yorkshire*

CATHEDRAL LIBR.

xvii.E.16–18	Fountains
C.15	Fountains

ROGERS, Mr D. M. *See*
    OXFORD

ST ALBANS, *Hertfordshire*
SCHOOL
    Y.4   Oxford, Brasenose Coll.

SALISBURY, *Wiltshire*
CATHEDRAL
    L.5.10   Edington
    M.1.27   Cambridge, Fran.

SHOTLEY BRIDGE, *co. Durham*
TRUSTEES OF THE SILVERTOP HEIR-
        LOOMS, MINSTERACRES
    —   Durham (2 bks)*

SHREWSBURY, *Shropshire*
SCHOOL
    A.X.15 (Inc. 31)   Merton
    E.VI.10   Cambridge, Univ.

STONOR PARK, *Oxfordshire*
HON. S. STONOR
    —   Syon

STONYHURST COLL., *Lan-
                        cashire*
    S.2.5   Combermere
    —   Loddon, *Ch.*
    1.22   Oxford, Aug.

TIDMARSH, *Berkshire*
PARISH CHURCH
    —   Tidmarsh, *Ch.*

TOLLERTON, *Nottinghamshire*
ST HUGH'S COLL.
    —   Durham (2 bks)**

USHAW COLL., *co. Durham*
    XVII.E.4.1   Durham**
        E.4.2   Durham**
        E.4.6–10   Durham**
        E.5.4   Durham**
        F.4.1   Durham**
        F.4.3   Durham**
        F.4.4   Durham**
        F.4.5   Durham**
        F.4.12   Durham**
        F.4.13   Durham**
        G.4.1–2   Durham**
        G.4.3   Durham**
        G.4.5   Durham**
    XVIII.A.3.4–5   Durham
        A.3.12   Durham

XVIII.A.3.15   Durham
    B.1.2   Durham
    B.3.5–11   Durham
    B.4.4   Durham
    B.4.24   Durham
    B.5.15   Durham
    B.6.7   Durham
    B.7.6   Durham
    C.2.9   Durham
    C.3.13   Durham
    C.4.11   Durham
    C.5.2   Durham
    C.5.10–11   Durham
    C.5.15   Durham
    F.4.18   Cambridge,
                      St John's Coll.
    G.3.11–12   Durham**

VAN DER LANDE, Mr J. P. L.
    See DEVENTER

WELLS, *Somerset*
CATHEDRAL
    B.1.20   †Wells
    G.1.3–8   Hailes

WINCHESTER, *Hampshire*
COLLEGE
    B.32   Winchester
PRESBYTERY
    —   Bodmin, Fran.

WINDSOR, *Berkshire*
ST GEORGE'S CHAPEL
    III.c   Hailes

WISBECH, *Cambridgeshire*
MUSEUM
    Town Libr., A.5.15   Kyme
            C.3.8   Canterbury

WORCESTER
CATHEDRAL
    Inc. 12   Lewes, Fran.
    Sel. B.50.3   Syon

XANTEN, *Germany*
STIFTSBIBLIOTHEK
    3070B   Syon

YEALAND CONYERS,
                    Lancashire
ST MARY'S CATHOLIC CHURCH
    —   Durham (16 vols)*

YORK		MINSTER (*contd*)	
MINSTER		xiv.B.22	Durham
vii.G.4	Durham	xiv.K.3	†Durham
x.A.7	Durham		Tynemouth
x.G.13	Durham	xv.A.12	Durham
xi.G.4	Durham	xv.P.8	Southwark
xii.J.22	Durham	xix.C.5	Durham

INDEX OF UNTRACED
MANUSCRIPTS AND PRINTED BOOKS

Rossignol, E. (bookseller, 8 Rue Bonaparte, Paris)
—— in 1961   Durham
Seller, Abednego
—— in 1697   Bordesley
Stark,—
—— in 1877   Reading
Thoresby, Ralph
—— in 1715   Byland
—— in 1715   Sweetheart
Thorp, Thomas (bookseller, London)
—— in 1838   Ely

Thorp, Thomas
—— in 1831   Nocton Park
Tregaskis, J. (bookseller, London)
—— in 1932 London, Fran. nuns
'Vennor'
—— in 1961   York, Aug.
West, James
—— in 1729   Malmesbury
White, H.
—— in 1896   Reading
Unknown owner
—— in s.xix(?)   Wilton

INDEX OF PERSONAL NAMES

All the names occur in the list on pp. 225–253, unless a specific page-reference is given. The names of scribes are in italics. Spellings of well-known names have been modernized and standardized in a common form, *e.g.* Middleton, Marshall. Spellings of little-known names have been altered to coincide with a modern name only if the change does not interfere or hardly interferes with the alphabetical sequence, *e.g.* Cawston, Gressenhall, but Awne, not Alne, and Quappelod, not Whaplode, or if the form of the name can be readily modernized, *e.g.* Woodchurch, Woolpit. The letter *i* has been generalized for *y*, if a consonant follows in the same syllable, *e.g.* Smith, not Smyth, unless the spelling with *y* is the generally recognized spelling (Lynn); also *ck* for *k*.

A., precentor	Rochester	Alfred, mag.	Cirencester
A., prior	Rochester		(and p. 51)
A., subdean	Oxford	Alkewin	Rochester
A., vicar of Stoke	Rochester	Alulph	Cant., St Aug.
Abingdon, H.	Oxf., Merton Coll.	Alward (Alwort)	Kenilworth
Abingdon, R. de	Osney		Oxford, U.L.
Abingdon	Reading	Andrew	Rochester
Acton	Hailes	Andrew, J.	London, Aug.
Adam, canon	Cirencester	Andrew, R.	Oxf., All Souls
Adam, prior	Canterbury		Coll. (and p. 144)
Adam, subprior	Cant., St Aug.		Oxf., New Coll.
Adington	Durham		Salisbury
Admondeston	Lichfield	Anian	Bangor
Ælfgyth	Horton	Anian	Valle Crucis
Ælfric	Bath	Anselm, abbot	Pershore
Ælfwine	Hyde		(and p. xviii)
Aiscough	Eton Coll.	Anstey	Salisbury, Dom.
Aketon	Cambr., Clare Coll.	Appleby, W.	Oxf., Balliol Coll.
Alan, abbot	Tewkesbury	Appleby, W. de	Durham
Alan, prior	Reading	*Appleton*	Southwark
Alcester	Evesham	Arbuthnott	Arbuthnott
Aldeburgh	Jervaulx	*Arcuarius*	Bodmin
Aldeby	Norwich	Aristotle	Durham
Aldsworth	Gloucester	Arndell	Gloucester
	(and p. 91)	Arnold, J.	Keynsham
Alexander, canon	Cirencester	Arnold, T.	Cant., St Aug.
Alexander, mag.	Chester, Dom.	Arrows	York, St Mary
Alexander, precentor	Rochester	Arundel	Canterbury
	(and p. 60)	Ashbourne	Lichfield
Alexander, prior	Rochester	*Ashby, T.*	Bridlington
Alexander, N.	Warwick, Dom.	Ashby, T.	Lapworth, *Ch.*
Aleyne	Bury, *Ch.*	Ashcombe	Merton
Alfred	Canterbury	Asketill	Rochester
Alfred, king	Winchester (p. 200)	Asplyon	Oxf., Univ. Coll. (p. 149)

Assewell	Grantham, Fran.
Aston, J.	Kenilworth
Aston, J.	Worcester
Atenulfus	Fountains
Athelstan	Bath
	Canterbury
	Cant., St Aug.
	Durham (and p. 60)
	Winchester
Athelwerd	Malmesbury
Attleborough	Norwich
Aubin	Worcester
Auckland	Durham
Audley	Shaftesbury
Audruinus	Norwich
Augustinus	Winchcomb
Austen	Lond., St Mary
	of Graces
Avington	Winchester
Awne	Mount Grace
Aylard	Rochester
Aylesbury, R. de	Rochester
Aylesbury, T. de	St Albans
Aylesbury, W.	Bermondsey
Aylsham	Bury
B., chamberlain	Rochester
B[...]	Southwark
Babbe	Oxf., Exeter Coll.
Babington, K.	Campsey
Babington, W.	Bury
Bacon	Bruisyard
Bacona, J. de	Lond., Carm.
Bagby	Fountains
Baldock	Lond., St Paul's
	(and p. 120)
Baldwin, archbishop	Rochester
Baldwin, prior	Bury
Baldwin, J.	Colchester, Fran.
Bale	Norwich, Carm.
Baliol	Sweetheart
Balsall	Oxf., Merton Coll.
Bamburgh, J.	Rochester
Bamburgh, J.	Tynemouth
Bamburgh, R. de	Durham
Banchester	Cant., St Aug.
Bangor	Llanvaes
Bankes	Crich, *Ch.*
Barcham	Beauly
Bardney	Crowland
Bardwell	Bury
Barker	Launde

Barking	Waltham
Barnby	Durham
Barney	Bardney
Barnsley	Worcester
Baron	Dartford
Bartholomew, bishop	Exeter
Bartholomew, canon	Waltham
Bartholomew	Bury
Bartlett	Oxf., All Souls Coll.
Barton, J.	Canons Ashby
Barton, T.	Westminster
Bartram	Staveley, *Ch.*
Barwe	Bury
Barwick	York, St Mary
Basing	Winchester
Bassett	Bodmin
Bassingbourn	Lond., Fran.
	Nuns
Bastable	Marlborough, Carm.
Bathon'	Dore
Bavard	Lond., Fran.
Bawer	Skelmersdale, *Ch.*
Bayly	Hereford
Beauchamp, G. de	Bordesley
	(p. 11)
Beauchamp, J.	Lond., Dom.
Beaver	St Albans
Bebseth	Hatfield Peverel
Becansaw	Leicester Coll.
Beccles	Bury
Becket, T., archbishop	Canter-bury
Becket, T., monk	Canterbury
Beckington	Wells
Beckwith	Hounslow
Bedford	Newnham
Bedmister	Worcester
Beerley	Pershore
Bell, Richard	Durham
Bell, Roger	Durham
Bellaf'	Salisbury
Bello, N. de	Cant., St Aug.
Bellond	Cambr., Aug.
Belmeis	Lond., St Paul's
Belvero, W. de	Belvoir
Benedict, abbot	Peterborough
	(and p. xviii)
Benedict, bishop	Rochester
Benedict, monk	Rochester
Benedictus, H.	Winchcomb
Benet, Robert	Canterbury
Benet, Roger	Canterbury

Brueria	Biddlesden	Caston	Dartford
Brug'	Buildwas	Castro, J. de	Durham
Bruge	Wenlock	Castro, T. de	Durham
Bruton	Gloucester	Catesby	Syon
Bruyl	Canterbury, Fran.	Catherington	Southwick
Bruyn	Rochester	Catthorp	Worcester
Buckenham	Babwell	Catton	Norwich (p. 136)
Buckhurst	Mottenden	Causford	Worcester
Buckingham	Exeter	Cawston, J. de	Norwich
Buckland, J.	Syon	Cawston, T.	Canterbury
Buckland, W.	Abingdon	Cawthorn	Durham
Burbache	Oxf., Merton Coll.	Centurio	Lond., Fran. Nuns
Burcer	Canterbury, Fran.	Chabbenor	Hereford, Fran.
Burcham	Salisbury, Fran.	Chaffer	Sheen
Burgh	Crowland	Chalner	Croxden
Burgham	Cant., St Aug.	Chamber, B.	Dartford
Burghersch	Lewes	Chamber, J.	Westminster,
Burgo, J. de	Launde		St Stephen
Burgoyn	Lond., Carth.	Chamberlain	Axholme
Burney	Durham	Champney	Westminster
Burnham	Missenden	Champneys, A.	Shaftesbury
Burton, J.	Lond., Aug. Nuns	Champneys, J.	Norwich
Burton, R.	Stoke-by-Clare	Chanvill	Elstow
Burton, T.	Pipewell	Chartham	Canterbury
Bury, J.	Sheen	Charity, J.	Hyde
Bury, R. de	St Albans	Charity, W.	Hyde
	(and p. vii)	Charity, W.	Leicester
Bury, W.	Bury	Chater	Harpole, *Ch*.
Bush	St Osyth	Chaundler	Wells
Bygonell	Oxf., All Souls Coll.	Chawncy	Lond., Carth.
Byholt	Cant., St Aug.	Chelmington	Canterbury
Bywell	St Albans	Cheltenham	Tewkesbury
		Chenley	St Albans
Caerwent	Lanthony	Chesney	Lincoln
Cake	Norwich, Carm.	Chester	Chester (p. 49)
Calne	Lanthony	Chesterfield, T.	Lichfield
Caly	Durham	Chesterfield, W.	Warwick,
Cambridge	Norwich		Dom.
Campsall	Oxf., Merton Coll.	Chichele	Higham Ferrers
Canterbury	Cant., St Aug.	Chillenden, A. de	Canterbury
Cantmell	Shere	Chillenden, J.	Canterbury
Cantuaria, Richard de	Cant.,	Chillenden, T.	Canterbury
	St Aug.		(and p. 29)
Cantuar', Roger	Canterbury	Chilmark	Reading
Caperun	Canterbury	Chinnock	Malmesbury
Carneburgh	Lond., Fran. Nuns	Chirden	Durham
Carter	Southwell	Chitton	Abingdon
Carver	Scone	Cicestrensis, W.	Dureford
Castell, T.	Durham	Cicestria, H. de	Exeter
Castell, T.	Durham	Circeter	Salisbury
Castill, J.	Hereford (and p. 97)	Cirencestrie, T.	Cant., St Aug.
Castleford	York, St Leonard	Cisson	Oxf., Balliol Coll.

408

David, archdeacon	Lincoln	Eastby	Durham
David, prior	Inchmahome	Easton, A. de	Norwich
Davis	Holme Cultram		(and p. 136)
Dedwith	Oxf., Fran.	Easton, R. de	Beverley, Dom.
Deeping	Colchester	Eastry, H. de	Canterbury
Dely	Syon		(and p. 29)
Dengayn	Greenwich, Fran.	Eastry, R.	Canterbury (p. 29)
Denham	Bury	Ebchester, R.	Durham
Denton	Droitwich	Ebchester, W.	Durham
Deodatus	Cirencester	*Ebesham*	Westminster
Depham	Canterbury	Eboraco, R. de	Salisbury
Dersham	Bury	Edenham	Barlings
Dersingham	Burnham Norton	*Edington*	Eton Coll.
Dice	Bury	Edirston	Lincoln
Dicklesdon	Worcester	Edmund, earl of	
Dingley	Cambr., Peterhouse	Cornwall	Ashridge
Dipping	Coldingham	Ednam	Bangor
Ditton, R. de	Byland	Edward IV	Windsor
Ditton, T. de	Cant., St Aug.	Edwards	Syon
Dodesham	Sheen	Edys	Burton-upon-Trent
	Witham	Eggerton	Leeds
Dodford	Ramsey (p. xviii)	Elham	Cant., St Aug.
Doggett	Norwich, Dom.	Elias	Canterbury
Doncaster	Durham	Elias, precentor	Rochester
Donewico, R. de	Norwich	Elingham, J.	Norwich
Doo	Fotheringhay	Elingham, R. de	Norwich
Dove	Buckfast	Elington	Rievaulx
Dover, A. de	Reading	Elkin	Burton-upon-Trent
Dover, W.	Canterbury	Elmham, R. de	Westminster,
Downe	Bristol, Fran.		St Stephen
Downes	Potshrigley, *Ch.*	Elmham, S. de	Norwich
Downhead	Abingdon	Elmham, W. de	Cant., St Aug.
Drayton	Winchester	Elmley	Hereford, St Guthlac
Driffield	Kirkstall	Elphinston	Aberdeen,
Dudley	Wenlock		King's Coll. (and p. 2)
Dudlington	Cambr., Fran.	Elsing	Norwich
Duffield, T.	Lincoln, Fran.	Elwick	Durham
Duffield, W.	Coventry, Fran.	Elyot, R.	Syon
Duke	Edington	Elyot, W.	Oxf., New Coll.
Dumbleton	Worcester	Elys	Eton Coll.
Dune	Durham	*Embleton*	Durham
Dunelmo, P. de	Durham	English	Oxf., Merton Coll.
Dunelmo, W. de	Durham	Erghom	York, Aug.
Dunham	Tynemouth	Erle	Reading
Dunstable, H. de	Belvoir	Ernulf	Gloucester
Dunstable, J. de	St Albans	Ernulf	Rochester
Dunstan	Glastonbury	Ethelwold	Peterborough (p.150)
Dunstone	Canterbury (p. 29)	Everdon	Coventry
Dye	Lond., Elsyng	Eversdon	St Albans
Dygon	Oxf., Exeter Coll.	Evesham	Tewkesbury
	Sheen, Reclusory	Exeter, J.	Ottery (and p. 141)
Dymock	Reading	*Exeter, J.*	Winchester

Gi[. . .]gton	York, St Mary	Gregory, abbot	Whalley
Glanvill, A. de	Rochester	Gregory, canon	Salisbury
Glanvill, J. de	Rochester	Grenborough	Coventry
Glen magna, W. de	Leicester,	Grene, J.	Bedford, Fran.
	Dom.	Grene, J.	Leiston
Glimping	Chichester	Grene, J.	Worcester
Glinton	Sempringham	*Grene, T.*	Greenwich, Fran.
Gloucester, G.	Peterborough	Grene	Hereford (and p. 99)
Gloucester, J.	Winchcomb	Grenehalgh	Sheen (and p. 178)
Gloucester, J. de	Worcester	Gresley	Pipewell
Gloucester, R. de	Lanthony	Gressenhall	Norwich
Gloucester, T.	Oxf., Carm.	Gretham, J. de	York
Gloucester, Humphrey,		Gretham, W. de	Durham
duke of	Oxf., U.L.	Griffing	York, St Mary
Gloucester, Thomas,		Grimley	Worcester
duke of	Pleshey	Grosseteste	Bury
Gnosall	Buildwas		Oxf., Fran.
Goda	Rochester	Grove	Westminster
Godard	Newenham (p. 134)	Groves	Darley
Godcheap	Cant., St Aug.	Gully	Lichfield
Goddard	Babwell	Gundulf	Rochester
Godfrey	Aberdeen	Gunthorp, J.	Cambr., Jesus Coll.
Godfrey, J.	Boxley		Northampton, Dom.
Godfrey, J.	Pipewell	Gunthorp, T.	Newstead
Godmersham	Cant., St Aug.	Gunthorp, W. de	Southwell
Gognostus	Rochester	Gunwardby	Lond., Aug.
Goldstone	Canterbury	Guthrie, A.	Guthrie
Goldwell, J.	Eastwell, *Ch.*	Guthrie, R.	Arbroath
	Oxf., All Souls Coll.		(and p. 4)
Goldwell, N.	Cambr., Gonv.	*Guttyn Owen*	Basingwerk
	and Caius Coll.	Guy, precentor	Bury
Goldwell, T.	Canterbury (p. 29)	Gyste	Godstow
Gorham	Tynemouth	G[. . .], monk	Rochester
Gosford	Bury		
Gowshill	Chicksand	H., bishop	Rochester
Graffham	Ramsey	H., chanter	Rochester
Grandison, J.	Dore	H., dean of St Cran-	
	Exeter	tock	Bodmin, Fran.
	Malmesbury	H., monk	Rochester
	Robertsbridge	Hackford	Bury
Graunt, T.	Lond., St Paul's	Hackforth	Durham
	(and p. 121)	Hackington	Cant., St Aug.
	Oxf., Cant. Coll.	Hadley, W., subprior	
	Syon		Canterbury
Graunt, W.	Westminster	Hadley, W.	Canterbury
Grave	Newark	Hafter	Oxf., Brasen. Coll.
Gravesend	Rochester	Halderton	Biddlesden
Gray, P.	Cant., St Aug.	Halidene	Durham
Gray, R.	Lond., St Barth.	Hall, R.	Hyde
Gray, W.	Oxf., Balliol Coll.	Hall, W.	Maidstone
Graystanes	Durham	Halliwell	Bury
Graystock	York, St Mary	Hamlamstede	Missenden

Leofric	Exeter (and p. 81)	Lumley, E. de	Durham
Leominster	Worcester	Lumley, M.	Lond., Carth.
Leonard	Rochester	Lund	Durham
Lepton	Romsey	Lupton, E.	Syon
Ley, H.	Winchcomb	Lupton, R.	Eton
Ley, J.	Chester	*Lutton, J.*	Bath
Leybourne	Cant., St Aug.		Reading
Leyham	Tidmarsh, *Ch.*	Lutton, T. de	Hereford, Fran.
Lichfield	Southwark	Lya, S. de	Bristol, St Mark
Light	Newark	Lyle	Chicksands
Lily	Warwick, Dom.	Lynn, T.	Westminster
Lincoln, J.	Southwark, *Ch.*	Lynn, W.	Dunstable
Lincoln, R.	Ramsey		
Lincoln, S. de	Lincoln, Fran.	Maidstone, C.	Syon (and p. 187)
Lindley	Whalley	Maidstone, R. de	Canterbury,
Lindon	Crediton		Fran.
Lindsey	Peterborough		Oxf., Fran.
Lingfield	Cant., St Aug.	Maidstone, S.	Cant., St Aug.
Lingham	Exeter, *Ch.*	Maidstone, T. de	Leeds
Lloyd	Hereford	Mainsforth	Oxf., Merton Coll.
Lok	Norwich	*Malberthorp*	Eton
London, D.	Merton	Maleverey	Kingston-upon-Hull
London, J. de	Canterbury	Malling	Rochester
London, J. de	Cant., St Aug.	*Malmesburiensis, W.*	Malmes-
London, J.	Crowland		bury (and p. 128)
London, J.	Sheen	Malmesfeld	Oxf., Merton Coll.
London, L. de	Rochester	Malvern	Gloucester
London, R. de	Cant., St Aug.	Man	Lond., Fran.
London, R. de	Rochester		(and p. xxvi)
London, T.	Stratford Lang-	Manby	Durham
	thorne	Mankael	Cant., St Aug.
London, T. de	Tewkesbury	Manwood	Battle
London, W.	Canterbury		Brecon
Longney	Arlingham, *Ch.*	Mapleton	Whalley
Longo Campo, N. de		Margaret, duchess of	
	Canterbury	Clarence	Syon
Longspey	Cambr., Aug.	Markaunt	Cambr., Corpus
Loring	Witham		Christi Coll. (p. 25)
Louis	Holme Cultram	Marlborough, H. de	Winchester
Loukin	St Albans	Marlborough, T. de	Evesham
Lovell	Salisbury		(and p. 80)
Lovent, R. de	Cant., St Aug.	Marley, J. de	Durham
Lovent, W.	Chichester, Dom.	Marley, N.	Durham
Lowe, J.	Lond., Aug.	Marley, S.	Durham
Lowe, J., archdeacon		Marshall, J.	Oxf., Merton Coll.
of Rochester	Oxf., Aug.		Windsor
Lo[...]	Canterbury	Marshall, Richard	Culross
Lucas	Lond., Carth.	Marshall, Richard	Hinton
	(and p. 122)	Marshall, Roger	Cambr.,
Ludlow, J.	Haughmond		Peterhouse
Ludlow, W. de	Wigmore	Marshall	St Albans
Luffe	Coventry	Martil	Lond., Guildhall

Northwood	Bordesley	Paulinus	Rochester
Norton, J.	Evesham	Pauntley	Gloucester
Norton, J.	Mount Grace	Peacock	Norwich, St Giles
Norton, W. de	Waltham	Pecke	Fountains
Norwico, P. de	Ely	Pede	Hereford
Nottingham,	Oxf., Fran.	Pembroke	Evesham
H., R. and W.	(and p. 142)	*Penketh*	Warrington
Nuton	Abingdon	Pensax	Syon
Nuton	Battle	Penshurst	Cant., St Aug.
		Pery	Lond., Holy Trinity
Ockham	Chertsey	Peter	Rochester
Odiham	Coventry, Carth.	Peter, vicar	Swine (p. 184)
Odo	Cirencester	Peter	Waltham
Oesterwic	Oxf., Dom.	Petro, R. de	Guisborough
Ogull	Syon	Philip, canon	Worksop
Oke, J.	Lewes	Philippes	Hereford, Fran.
Oke, T.	Titchfield	Phillip	Lynn, Fran.
Okeborn	Westbury	Pickenham	Lond., St Thomas
Oldfield	Spalding		of Acon
Olney	Ramsey	Pickering	Guisborough
Olston	Pilton	*Pickworth*	Cambr., Dom.
Opton	Coventry, Fran.	Pistor	Cant., St Aug.
Orléans, Charles d'	Lond.,	Pitchcott	Reading
	Fran.	Pitts	Exeter
Ormesby, R.	Norwich	Plumstead	Norwich
Ormesby, W. de	Norwich	Pocklington	Durham
Ormond, James,	Lond., St	Pocyn	Cant., St Aug..
earl of	Thomas of Acon	Pole, J.	Cambr., Carm.
Orum	Exeter		Coventry, Carm.
Orwell	Byland	Pole, R.	Bodmin, Fran.
Ospringe	Canterbury	Pontoyse	Winchester,
Oswald	Worcester		St Elizabeth
Oxney	Canterbury	Popham	Charford, *Ch.*
Oxon', J. de	Rochester	Poppleton	Oxf., Balliol Coll.
		Porter, A.	Lond., Fran. Nuns
Pachet	Syon	Poundstock	Exeter
Pag'	Reading	Powick	Malvern
Pagham	Worcester	Praty	Salisbury
Palmer, J.,	Lynn	Prechett	Worcester, Dom.
Palmer, J. le; *see* Le Palmer		*Prestins*	Syon
Palmer, K.	Syon	Preston, J.	Cant., St Aug.
Palmer, S.	Greenwich, Fran.	Preston, J. de	Worcester
Palmer, W.	Crediton	Preston, N. de	Cirencester
Par	Leicester	Puiset	Durham (and p. 60)
Paris, M.	St Albans	*Pulham*	Cirencester
	(and p. 165)	Purcel	Wigmore
Paris, W.	St Albans	Pyryt	Canterbury
Parker	Colwich, *Ch.*		
Partridge	Lincoln	Quappelod	Lincoln, Fran.
Patishale	Waltham		
Patrick	Leeds	R., abbot	Winchcomb
Paul	Rochester	R., precentor	Rochester

Russell, T.	Battle	Sedgebrook	Durham
Ruwe	Beauvale	Seffrid	Chichester
Rye, G. de	Winchelsea	Selling, W.	Cant., St Aug.
Rye, H. de	Cant., Fran.	Selwood	Glastonbury
Ryggh	Exeter	*Serbopoulos*	Reading (and p. 155)
Ryhall	Swineshead	Serle	Stratford Langthorne
Ryston	Ramsey	Serles	Walsingham, Fran.
		Serlo	Cirencester
St Allen	Bridgwater, Fran.	*Seton*	Durham
St Briavel	Lanthony	Sever	Oxf., Merton Coll.
St Bride	Exeter	Sewell	Syon
St Carilef	Durham (and p. 60)	Shenton	Nuneaton
St Columb	Bodmin	Shepherd	Cuckney, *Ch.*
St Elphege	Canterbury	Sheppey	Rochester
St George	Cant., St Aug.	Sherburn, G. de	Durham
St German	Worcester	*Sherburn, R.*	Durham
St Ives	Ramsey	Shipman	Colchester, Fran.
St Martin, L. de	Rochester	Shipton	Hereford, Fran.
St Martin, W. de	Cambr., Dom.	Sholden	Cant., St Aug.
St Martin, W. de	Osney	*Sibbalde*	Arbuthnott
St Nicholas	Lond., Fran. Nuns	Silegrave	Dover
Salford	Oxf., Fran.	Silke	Ottery
Salisbury, J.	Canterbury	Silkstead	Winchester
Salisbury, T.	Lincoln	Silton	Norwich
	(and p. 25)	Silvester	Rochester
see also Sarisburia		Simon, abbot	Ramsey
Salley	Eynsham	Simon, abbot	St Albans
Saltford	Bath	Simon, subprior	Canterbury
Sands (?)	Hounslow	Singleton	Whalley
Sandwich, J.	Merton	Sleaford	Crowland
Sandwich, N. de	Canterbury	Slight	Syon
Sandwich, T. de	Lessness	Smallburgh	Norwich
Sarisburia, R. de	St Albans	*Smith, J.*	Kinloss
Sarisburiensis, J.	Reading	Smith, Ralph	Kingston-upon-Hull
Saunder	Oxf., All Souls Coll.		
Savage	Lond., Carm.	Smith, Robert	Fountains
Savell	Warwick, Dom.	Smith, W.	Axholme
Sawston	Rochester	Smith, W.	Oxf., Brasen. Coll.
Saxton	Oxf., Balliol Coll.	Smith, W.	Saltfleetby, *Ch.*
Sa[...]	Thornholm	Snettisham	Exeter
Scamel	Salisbury	Solomon	Canterbury
Scasby	Mount Grace	Solomon	Cant., St Aug.
Schevez	Dunfermline	*Solomon*	Malmesbury
	(p. 59)	Somer	Cambr., Hosp. of St John
Scot, A.	Newbattle		
Scot, G.	Fountains	Somerset	Cambr., Peterhouse
Scothole	Holme St Benets		Lond., St Paul's
Scrope	Barking	Soppethe	Oxf., Aug.
Scrope	Windsor (p. 202)	Sotheron	Durham
Scroutely	Bury	Sotton	Rochester
Seabrook	Bromfield	Southam	Oxf., Linc. Coll.
Sedgeberrow	Worcester	Spearman	Peterborough

Theodoric	Rochester
Thetford	Butley
Thew	Durham
Thirsk	Fountains
Thomas, abbot	Cant., St Aug.
Thomas, prior	Cant., St Aug.
Thomas, rector of	
Colveston	Cambr., Fran.
Thomas, vicar of	Bury
Gorleston	Holme St Benets
Thomas [. . .]	Norwich
Thoresby	Haverfordwest, Dom.
Thorn	Syon
Thornden	Rochester
Thornton, R. de	Bardney
Thornton, W.	Wetheral
Throckmorton	Denny
Thurcaston	Leicester
Thwaites	Oxf., Balliol Coll.
Tickhill	Worksop
Tille	Lond., Dom.
Tilmanstone	Cant., St Aug.
Timworth	Bury
Tindale	Greenwich, Fran.
Toby	Gloucester
Todd	Coldingham
Tode	Durham
Tompson	Warwick, Dom.
Tornaco, W. de	Louth Park
Toroldus	Worcester, Dom.
Totingdon	Walsingham, Fran.
Tottington	Cant., St Aug.
Tracy	Sheen
Tregenwa	Bodmin
Trickingham	Oxf., Oriel Coll.
Trotter	Ickleton
Trumpington, T.	Cambr., Fran.
Trumpington, W. de	St Albans
Truncat Leonem	Canterbury
Trus	Stamford, Hosp.
Tunstall	Cambr., U.L.
	(and p. 25)
Tuting	Durham
Twening	Gloucester
Twyford	Syon
T[. . .], S.	Canterbury
T[. . .], W.	Cant., St Aug.
Umfrey	Lond., Fran.
Urswick	Hailes
	Lancaster, Dom.
	Windsor

Valle, H. de	Buildwas
Vaus	Aberdeen, King's Coll.
Vavasour	Oxf., Fran.
	York, Fran.
Veer	Barking
Vernon, H. and J.	Harlaxton, *Ch.*
Vernon, I. de	Hampole
Verypt	Beauvale
Vincent	Winchester
Vitriaco, A. de	Mottisfont
Vowell	Walsingham
W., bishop	Rochester
Wackerfield	Durham
Wade, M.	Nuncoton
Wade, R.	Faversham
Walden	Lond., Carm.
Waldey	St Albans
Waldink	Lanthony
Wale	Winchester Coll.
Wallingford, J. de	St Albans
Wallingford, R. de	St Albans
Walsham	Norwich
Walter, bishop	Rochester
Walter, canon	Cirencester
Walter, canon	Osney
Walter, dean	Chichester
Walter, prior	Peterborough
Walter, prior	Witham
Walter, Hubert	Rochester
Waltham	Canterbury
Walton	Lynn
Warboys	Ramsey
Wardell, R.	Durham
Wardell, R., junior	Durham
Warder	St Albans
Wargrave	Reading
Warham	Canterbury
	Oxf., All Souls Coll.
	(and p. 144)
Warren	Dover
Warsop	Lincoln
Warthwick	York, St Mary
Wason	Glastonbury
Waterpit	Norwich, Carm.
Watson, J.	Blyth
Watson, W.	Durham
Waxingham	Bury
Weasenham, J.	Bury
Webbe	Hereford
Webber	Exeter